Opening Fenway Park with Style

The World Champion 1912 Boston Red Sox

edited by Bill Nowlin

Associate editors: Maurice Bouchard, Dan Desrochers, Len Levin

The SABR Digital Library

Phoenix, AZ

Opening Fenway Park In Style

Copyright © 2012 by the Society for American Baseball Research, Inc.

All rights reserved.
Reproduction in whole or in part without permission is prohibited.

ISBN 978-1-933599-35-9
(Ebook ISBN 978-1-933599-36-6)

The Society for American Baseball Research, Inc.
4455 E. Camelback Road, Ste. D-140
Phoenix, AZ 85018
sabr.org

Editors: Bill Nowlin, with Maurice Bouchard, Dan Desrochers, and Len Levin.
Interior Design: James J. Murray, Gilly Rosenthol
Cover design: Cecilia Tan

Front cover credits:

Primary image courtesy of the George Grantham Bain Collection, Library of Congress Prints and Photographs Division.

Images in left column, top to bottom, courtesy of the following: Chautauqua Sports Hall of Fame and the Hugh Imus and Greg Patterson Collections; Hunt Auctions; Robert Edward Auctions LLC; Hunt Auctions; Guernsey's Auction House; Heritage Auctions; Heritage Auctions.

Images in left column, top to bottom: Library of Congress, Music Division; Hunt Auctions; Hunt Auctions; Robert Edward Auctions LLC; Robert Edward Auctions LLC; Robert Edward Auctions LLC.

Back cover images, top to bottom: Hunt Auctions; Boston Public Library, Print Division; Benjamin K. Edwards Collection, Library of Congress Prints and Photographs Division; Boston Public Library, Print Division; Benjamin K. Edwards Collection, Library of Congress Prints and Photographs Division.

The book is the collaborative effort of 27 members of the Society for American Baseball Research and is published on the occasion of the 100th anniversary of Fenway Park.

Contents

- 1. . . . . . . Introduction - *Bill Nowlin*
- 4. . . . . . . Getting to Fenway: How Baseball's Most Storied Ballpark Came to Be - *Saul Wisnia*
- 11. . . . . . The Land of Hot Waters: 1912 Spring Training at Hot Springs - *Michael Foster*
- 22. . . . . . Christening Fenway: The Red Sox vs. Harvard Exhibition Game - *Bill Nowlin*
- 26. . . . . . Opening Day 1912 - *Bill Nowlin*
- 32. . . . . . The First Game at Fenway Park - *Bill Nowlin*
- 35. . . . . . Fenway Park Firsts - *Bill Nowlin*
- 36. . . . . . When was the first time fans booed the Red Sox at Fenway Park?

The Team
- 37. . . . . . Neal Ball - *John McMurray*
- 42. . . . . . Hugh Bedient - *John Stahl and Michael Foster*
- 47. . . . . . Hugh Bradley - *Bill Nowlin*
- 55. . . . . . Jack Bushelman - *Craig Lammers*
- 62. . . . . . Hick Cady - *William Dowell*
- 66. . . . . . Bill Carrigan - *Mark Armour*
- 69. . . . . . Eddie Cicotte - *Jim Sandoval*
- 73. . . . . . Ray Collins - *Tom Simon*
- 82. . . . . . Clyde Engle - *David Forrester*
- 85. . . . . . Larry Gardner - *Tom Simon*
- 95. . . . . . Casey Hageman - *Craig Lammers*
- 101. . . . . Charley Hall - *John Stahl*
- 106. . . . . Olaf Henriksen - *Ron Anderson*
- 113. . . . . Harry Hooper - *Paul J. Zingg and Elizabeth A. Reed*
- 118. . . . . Marty Krug - *Tom Hawthorn*
- 123. . . . . Duffy Lewis - *Mark Armour*
- 126. . . . . Les Nunamaker - *Tony Bunting*
- 132. . . . . Buck O'Brien - *Michael Foster*
- 138. . . . . Larry Pape - *Marc Aaron*
- 142. . . . . Doug Smith - *Michael Foster*
- 149. . . . . Tris Speaker - *Don Jensen*
- 153. . . . . Jake Stahl - *John Stahl*
- 157. . . . . Pinch Thomas - *Joanne Hulbert*
- 162. . . . . Ben Van Dyke - *Maurice Bouchard*
- 167. . . . . Heinie Wagner - *Joanne Hulbert*
- 173. . . . . Smoky Joe Wood - *Michael Foster*
- 177. . . . . Steve Yerkes - *Tony Bunting*
- 183. . . . . Jimmy McAleer - *David Fleitz*
- 187. . . . . John I. Taylor - *John Stahl*
- 193. . . . . Ban Johnson - *Joe Santry and Cindy Thomson*
- 197. . . . . A Question of Ownership - *Mike Lynch*

1912 Features
- 211. . . . . 1912 Day-By-Day A Season Timeline - *Bill Nowlin*
- 242. . . . . The 1912 World Series - *Bill Nowlin*
- 271. . . . . Fenway Park: The First Renovation - *Bill Nowlin*
- 274. . . . . Keeping Up With the Red Sox: Getting the News in 1912 - *Donna Halper*
- 283. . . . . Boston's Sportswriters, 1912 - *Donna Halper*
- 290. . . . . A Brief Note on Boston's "Other Big-League Team" - *Bill Nowlin*

- 293. . . . . Contributors
- 296. . . . . Image Credits

Opening Fenway Park with Style: The World Champion 1912 Boston Red Sox

The 1912 Red Sox had new ownership and they had a brand-new ballpark. This was only the 12th year of the American League, but the team had already won two pennants (in 1903 and 1904) and had also suffered adversity thanks to finishing in last place in 1906 and next-to-last in 1907. They didn't know it in 1911, when the team finished fourth, but they were on their way to creating the American League's first brief dynasty—winning the World Series four times in a seven-year span, from 1912 to 1918.

The 1912 were blessed with playing in a new ballpark, but more so by the coming together of a number of exceptional ballplayers which were each coming into their own. What can one say about a pitcher with a 34-5 record, Smoky Joe Wood? The team itself won 105 games, the most of any Red Sox club in franchise history. There wasn't a team against which they had a losing record, and they were 19-2 against New York. There was future Hall of Famer Tris Speaker in center field, flanked by Duffy Lewis in left and Harry Hooper in right—a trio who are in any conversation about the greatest outfields of all time. The team played better at home than on the road, winning 74% of their games at Fenway Park (57-20); they were 48-27 (.640) on the road.

This book looks at every one of the men who played on the 1912 team—even Douglass Smith, Casey Hageman, Jack Bushelman, and Ben Van Dyke who combined to appear in a total of nine games, none of them in more than three. There is also a look at two co-owners of the team, new owner Jimmy McAleer and also John I. Taylor, whose family had purchased the land and built Fenway Park just in time for the season to begin. There's a wonderful piece by Mike Foster on spring training in Hot Springs—the Land of Many Waters. Foster also informs us that Douglass Smith may have been the first African American ballplayer on the Red Sox—35 years before Jackie Robinson. A full season timeline chronicles how the season unfolded—where the team was coming from, its success in 1912, and what happened in the few years which followed.

This is not a book about Fenway Park itself. There are a dozen books or more books on the subject, though only one we have seen announced focuses on the first year of Fenway. Glenn Stout's book *Fenway 1912* is highly recommended as a book looking at the construction of Fenway Park itself, and the first year of play at the new facility.

The book is the collaborative effort of 27 members of the Society for American Baseball Research and is published on the occasion of the 100th anniversary of Fenway Park and the world championship season of 1912.

Fenway Park, 1912.

Exterior of Fenway Park, 1912.

Fans cheering at the 1912 World Series.

Getting to Fenway: How Baseball's Most Storied Ballpark Came To Be

By Saul Wisnia

Today's casual fan might be under the assumption that Red Sox baseball began with the opening of Fenway Park, but of course this is far from the truth.

In fact, the first great moments in the history of Boston's American League franchise took place about a mile from Kenmore Square at Fenway's predecessor, the Huntington Avenue Grounds. It was in this humble, long-forgotten locale that the Red Sox won the first modern World Series in 1903, and then repeated as American League pennant winners a year later. It's also where they stole the hearts of Boston's raucous fan base from their inner-city National League rivals at the turn of the century, a move that would have seemed preposterous just a few summers before.

Built in the first few months of 1901, the Huntington Avenue Grounds stood literally across the railroad tracks from the South End Grounds, home of the Boston Nationals, the most celebrated team of professional baseball's early years, in an attempt by the brand-new American League to gain a foothold in the hotbed of America's Pastime. First known as the Red Stockings and Beaneaters, and later to become the Braves, the Nationals were the kingpins of the National League, with eight championships since the circuit's formation in 1876 and five in the 1890s alone. Their loyal fans would serenade their heroes with songs at the South End Grounds, and then drink with them after the games at a nearby saloon. The most dedicated devotees, the self-proclaimed "Royal Rooters," even took their pennants, pins, megaphones, and drums to road games in New York and Baltimore.

But all was not perfect in the National League, at least from a player's point of view. Boston heroes like third baseman Jimmy Collins and first baseman Buck Freeman were frustrated by a $2,400 league salary cap and the reserve clause, which bound them to the same team for their entire career, giving them no say in where they might be traded or sold. Several other leagues had previously been formed to challenge National League superiority, but their owners lacked the business acumen or the organization

The last season of the Huntington Avenue Grounds, 1911.

This 1904 image of the Huntington Avenue Grounds clearly shows just how expansive was the outfield in the first park where the Red Sox played.

to last more than a season or two.

Ban Johnson was different. President of a successful, tightly-run minor league, he had the business acumen and the guts to not only establish franchises in cities without a National League presence, but to also to form teams in locales like Chicago, Philadelphia, and even Boston where the National League was already entrenched. He enticed fans by charging them half the going National League ticket rate—a quarter rather than 50 cents—and snatched up top National League talent with promises of heftier salaries and no reserve clause.

Despite their many successes, the Boston Nationals were primed for picking by the American League teams. They had once played at a beautiful double-decked ballpark (South End Grounds II) that resembled a castle, but after this structure burned down during an 1894 game, the replacement facility (South End Grounds III) had to be built on a far stingier budget because of a lack of sufficient insurance on its predecessor. This resulted in a shoddy, single-tiered ballpark and in equally stingy player salaries as the ownership tried to make up for their financial losses. Players often grumbled about these circumstances with their fans/drinking buddies, so it was only natural that Collins, Freeman, and numerous teammates jumped to the new circuit—as did their patrons.

In addition to manning third base, Collins led the Boston Americans as their first manager. The ballpark he and his charges called home was, like many of this era, nothing special. Built entirely of wood, as was the custom, the Huntington Avenue Grounds seated about 10,000 fans (mostly in uncovered grandstands) and was built on the site of a former circus lot. As Red Sox historian Ed Walton wrote: "The lot's biggest drawback was a deep pond which was at the base of chutes used by kids as a water slide during the warmer months and for skating in the winter. This 300,000 square feet of filled, sprawling empty lot… was no more than an expansive wasteland made up of heavily weeded bumps and lumps."[1]

Fans didn't seem to mind, turning out in strength at the new venue as the Americans outdrew the Nationals across the tracks by nearly 2 to 1 in their first season. With Collins and Freeman leading the hitting attack and a pitching staff paced by Denton True "Cy" Young, the new boys in town were contenders from the start and the American League champions by 1903. That fall owners Henry Killilea of the Boston Americans and Barney Dreyfus of the National League champion Pittsburg Pirates agreed to a best-of-nine-games postseason playoff, and the Americans captured this first modern World Series in dramatic fashion. Crowds literally climbed the walls at the Huntington Avenue Grounds and crowded behind outfield ropes five deep to see the action, while the South End Grounds next door sat quiet—now home to a decimated, sixth-place team.

In 1904 the Americans engaged in a thrilling pennant race with the New York Highlanders (later the Yankees) and drew an incredible 25,000 pre-fire-law fans—well above twice normal capacity—for a single-admission doubleheader on October 8. Two days later on the last day of the season, Boston claimed the title and was declared "World's Champions by default" by *The Sporting News* because the National League-winning New York Giants, initially fearful of facing their crosstown rival Highlanders in a playoff series, stood by a midsummer pledge to skip the postseason. And while the next few years were not as kind to the Americans (who fell to a dismal 49-105, last-place finish in 1906), they seemed to be improving again by 1911 with some great young players on the roster and (as of December 1907) a great new name to fit a colorful uniform switch: *the Boston Red Sox*.

The man responsible for the name change was team president John I. Taylor, whose father, General Charles Taylor,

A bucolic vintage postcard showing the Fenway at its best. It's not as though the entire area was noxious and swampy.

owned the *Boston Globe* and purchased the ballclub to give his young playboy son something to do outside the newspaper. Neither Taylor was much of a baseball man, but they did have an eye for real estate, and with the lease on the Huntington Avenue Grounds expiring after the '11 season they began looking for a new venue. Fires had decimated many wooden ballparks over the previous two decades (including South End Grounds II), and the impressive new venues now going up like Forbes Field in Pittsburgh and Shibe Park in Philadelphia were being built of steel and concrete. The Taylors wanted a similar facility for Boston, and, with a strong fan base and great young ballplayers like outfielder Tris Speaker and pitcher Joe Wood, figured they could fill many of the 20,000-plus seats it would contain.

What happened next would change the course of Boston history. A 365,308-square-foot section of land known as the Dana Lands at the corner of Lansdowne and Ipswich streets in the city's Fenway neighborhood was put up for auction in the winter of 1910-11, and wound up in the hands of the Taylors. Such a transaction would have been folly just a few decades before. The Fenway had long been nothing more than a swampy, smelly dump, a noxious reminder of when Boston's entire Back Bay was a shallow body of salt water. In the 1880s, however, it had been built up by the famed landscape architect Frederick Law Olmsted as part of his seven-mile stretch of walkways and parkland known as Boston's Emerald Necklace. Although some still thought the land was useless, the swamps were long gone and the Taylors felt the area was capable of major growth given the right "anchor" destination.

Several stories exist of how the 8-acre Dana Lands came to be the property of the Taylor family. One possibility was the subject of a theatrical re-enactment performed at none other than Fenway Park during ceremonies kicking off the ballpark's 100th birthday in December 2011. The short play was based on facts; in late 1910 the Dana Lands were sold at auction for $120,000 to the New England Mutual Life Insurance Co., which two months later sold them to the Taylors. In the Fenway re-enactment, Charles and John I. Taylor are seen in the audience at the auction (although there is no proof they were there), and appear keenly interested in the property despite letting someone else snatch it up. Two months later, they meet with the New England Mutual executive (fictitiously named Samuel Williams in the re-enactment) who had placed the winning bid.[2]

Here, directly from the re-enactment script, is how a conversation between Charles Taylor and Williams might have gone.

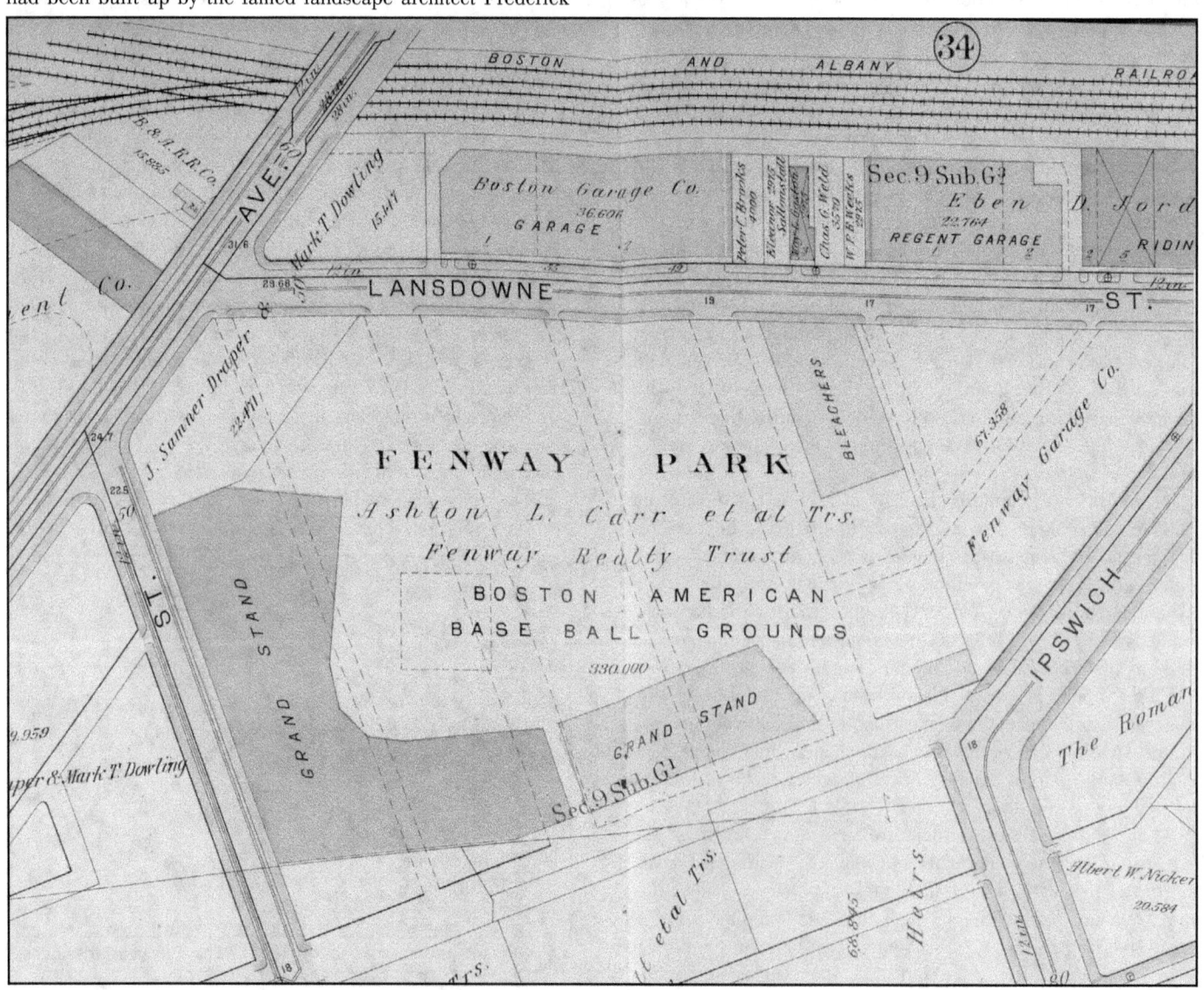

Detail of Plate 33 from the 1912 Atlas for the City of Boston.

Williams: "Before we put our signatures to the papers, Charles, I do have one question for you."

Taylor: "Of course, Sam."

Williams: "What exactly do you plan to do with this land?"

Taylor: "Well, the plot is a substantial one. I figure there are plenty of good uses."

Williams: "But what exactly? You're not planning to relocate your newspaper headquarters there, are you?"

Taylor: "Well, I don't propose so…"

Williams: "Another one of your holdings?"

Taylor: "I don't think so."

Williams (laughing): "Then what, exactly? John's baseball club?"

Taylor: "Now there's an idea!"

Williams: "You're not serious, Charles!?"

Taylor: "Why not, Sam?"

Williams: "Well, the plot, Charles. It's too misshapen! I admit there are uses for it, but a baseball diamond on that bog? Do you expect your players to field balls in a marsh?"

Taylor: "We will find a way to play ball on that plot! There is plenty of room for a diamond. Our players will not be fielding balls in a marsh!"

Williams: "They'll laugh at you, Charles! They will say you are crazy for trying to build a new ballpark there, and that I'm crazy for selling you this land."

Taylor: "Let them say we are crazy. In a year's time, they will call it the jewel of baseball!"

Williams: "And when do you plan to debut this park?"

Taylor: "April, 1912."

Williams: "Next spring? A year away!? You hope to have them build this so-called jewel of a baseball park and have it ready by next spring?"

Taylor: "We don't hope, we know! It will debut in April, and it will serve as home for generations."

Williams: "But the neighborhood, Charles. … It is not a commercial area."

Taylor: "It will be, Sam, it will be. The Fens is a growing area, and it will continue to grow around our park."

Williams: "And what of the city's leadership? Will they support this idea of a ballpark in the Fens?"

Taylor: "They certainly will. Because in 10 years' time—no, in five years' time—this area will be a bustling hub as well as any other in our fair city. After this meeting, we are meeting with the mayor—"Honey Fitz." He'll be glad to hear about this good news.

"I am telling you, Sam. I am telling you that they will be flocking to this neighborhood. Our park will rise, and it will beckon the fans. And the name of our park will be linked to the Fens, and the hearts of every New Englander."[3]

"Honey Fitz" was Boston Mayor John Fitzgerald, a Royal Rooter since the 1890s who had cheered on the Nationals in their heyday and like many Rooters had since switched his allegiance to the Red Sox. He would play an important role in the inaugural game at Fenway Park, but first it needed to be built. The Taylors, true to their interests in land over baseball, devised a plan to sell the Red Sox and use the money to build a new ballpark. Then, rather than worry about running the team, John I. could just rent out the park to the new owner on an ongoing basis.

A view from Brookline Avenue down Lansdowne Street, before Fenway Park was built. The small fence on the right side of the street has been replaced by the Green Monster of today.

A deal was struck on September 15, 1911, as the Red Sox, 65-69 at that point, were about to start their last long homestand of the year. John I. Taylor sold half of the club to the duo of James "Jimmy" McAleer and Robert McRoy, both really stand-ins for American League president and power broker Ban Johnson. (McAleer, the Washington Senators manager and a Johnson crony, used Johnson's money for his part, while McRoy was Johnson's secretary.) Sports editors not enamored of Taylor's ownership style heralded the sale as a sign of better things to come, with headlines like "McAleer Will Bolster the Sox."[4]

Under the terms of the arrangement, McAleer took over the team presidency and Taylor slid into a vice presidential role in which he would oversee development of the new ballpark. He wasted no time. "As soon as the papers are signed, work will be begun on the construction of a new steel and concrete grand stand, to cost $300,000," the *Boston Herald* reported, while the *Globe* wrote that the project would "improve the grounds so that for capacity and character, the accommodations will be second to none in the country."[5]

On March 12, 1911, Ban Johnson had been quoted in the *Globe* as saying that his intent was that within two years every American League team should have a playing venue with "mammoth fireproof stands, crowded to their capacity" and "concrete and steel structures for the accommodations of the patrons." To make this a reality in Boston, the Taylors turned to architect James McLaughlin, whose original plans called for a ballpark with an 11,500-seat covered grandstand and a total capacity of 24,400.[6]

Construction began on September 25, while the Red Sox were playing out the string at the Huntington Avenue Grounds a mile away, and although photos would surface decades later claiming to be of a Fenway Park groundbreaking, there was in fact no such official ceremony.[7] The Taylors wanted the park ready for Opening Day 1912, and that was a little over six months away. There simply wasn't time for such niceties.

General contractor Charles Logue, the man who built Fenway Park.

There was also no fanfare for the final game played at the Huntington Avenue Grounds, on October 7, 1911, in which the Red Sox defeated the Senators, 8-1, before just 846 paid fans on a cold, damp afternoon. Pitcher Charley Hall got the win, and Tris Speaker was hit by a pitch and carried away in an ambulance. An unofficial count of 4,000 youngsters (it may have been 400, with the extra "0" a typographer's error) were admitted free for "Kids Day," and although many of them likely had no recollection of the ballpark's glory years of 1903-04, all would have plenty of memories awaiting them at Lansdowne and Ipswich Streets. They would also have the "lucky" grass from the '03 World Series, as the sacred lawn from the old facility would be replanted at the new ballpark.[8]

By this point, that ballpark had a name. How this came about sounds too corny to be true, but apparently it is: Although the original architectural drawings made reference to the "Boston American Base Ball Park," John I. Taylor was quoted in the press as saying his new facility would be called Fenway Park because "it's in the Fenway section of Boston, isn't it?" This is really not so creative a quip on his part, since every other ballpark in the city's history had also been named after its residential locale. Taylor could just as easily have named the new venue Lansdowne Park, Ipswich Street Park, or Taylor Park, and any of them would sound correct today.

It could be speculated that Taylor chose Fenway Park because his father was a shareholder in the Fenway Realty Company, which helped finance the construction of the ballpark by issuing $275,000 in bonds. Putting "Fenway" on the park's entrance, he might have surmised, was as clear a case of free advertising as the names Comerica Park and U.S. Cellular Field are today. In any case, giving praise where it is due, John I. Taylor is still credited more than a century later with naming the two most important entities in New England baseball: Fenway Park and the Boston Red Sox.

Architect McLaughlin had an 8-plus-acre plot to work with, and Taylor wanted to have the field positioned in the same way with respect to the sun as the Huntington Avenue Grounds. (Boston fielders, he surmised, would thus have less difficulty adjusting to the new park's playing conditions.) This being the Deadball Era, when 300-foot fly balls were a rarity, there was plenty of room

Had an iceberg not interfered with its scheduled April 20 noon departure, the *Titanic* would have steamed out of New York Harbor as it began its return voyage to England and perhaps just had a final glimpse of the city on the horizon astern as the Highlanders were coming to bat during Fenway Park's inaugural game. *New York Times*

for a park to be built with more than ample outfield dimensions. The modern tales of Fenway being crammed into the existing city streets surrounding it simply are not true; there were not yet a slew of buildings on Lansdowne Street behind left and center field to contend with, and no other buildings bordered the plot at any point. In the earliest photos of Fenway, one can see scraggly, vacant lots surrounding the ballpark, almost as if it had been picked up and plopped down in a drought-ridden Oklahoma field.

The biggest question Taylor and McLaughlin had to decide upon was whether or not to give the new park a double deck, as had been done in Philadelphia's Shibe Park two years before. It was a considerable expense, and since Taylor was cautious about whether it would be needed, he decided upon one level of grandstands—with a contingency plan. He had McLaughlin build a strong enough foundation on the roof covering these seats so that a second deck could be added in the future.[9] In another cost-cutting measure by Taylor, the original left-field grandstand went only about halfway down the third-base line (to today's Section 27), rather than extending all the way to the tall left-field wall as it does today.

McLaughlin's influences included other baseball parks like Shibe Park as well as Harvard Stadium, the imposing Grecian-like structure just a few miles from the Fenway, where nearly 30,000 fans routinely watched the famed Crimson football team battle each fall.[10] To save time, however, he did not make all four sides of Fenway Park uniform in design. Although the main Gate A entrance on Jersey Street would feature a façade of beautiful dark red brick complemented by lighter-covered accents, most of the park was far less ornate as seen from the outside. Major design and civil-engineering work was handled by Osborn Engineering of Cleveland, which would later design Boston's next grand baseball venue—Braves Field—as well as Yankee Stadium; and many local laborers and skilled craftsmen were employed on the project.

Building went on through the winter of 1911-12 and into spring training, which the Red Sox spent in Hot Springs, Arkansas. By the time the team trained its way back north in early April, construction still was not completed; when Fenway Park housed its first game, on April 9, 1912—an exhibition contest between the Red Sox and Harvard University—fans could still spot workmen in the grandstands assembling and placing seats. Ticket prices would make today's fans drool: Private boxes cost $250 for an entire season of 77 home games, while box seats went for $1.50 and $1.25 per contest. Grandstand ducats went for $1.00, and bleachers for just 50 or 25 cents depending on your distance from the field. Some fans and sportswriters grumbled about the deepest-placed seats, with cartoonists showing men with telescopes attempting to follow the game.

The Red Sox beat the college boys, 2-0, as about 3,000 chilly fans looked on through snow flurries. Although what people observed at Fenway in 1912 was in many ways similar to a visit to the ballpark today, there were some subtle and some not-so-subtle differences. There were no video message boards or sound system, of course, and a megaphone was used to yell out the lineups for fans keeping track in their scorecards. Since players wore no uniform numbers, it was important to know who was in the game from the start, although batters were likely a bit more identifiable since none wore helmets or wrap-around sunglasses either. There were ushers, just like today, but they wore white uniforms and red caps. And while fans could find restrooms underneath the stands, they walked on dirt floors to get to them (concrete would not be added until 1914).

It's unlikely any fans at the opener thought of Fenway in John Updike terms as a "lyric little bandbox." Although it is considered "cozy" today, the ballpark's original dimensions made it one of the biggest in baseball for its day. It was well over 380 feet to the right-field fence, 300 feet to left, and nearly 550 feet to deepest center. The ballpark's most famous current feature, the 37-foot 2-inch high "Green Monster" wall, was not yet on the premises, but its smaller, more colorful predecessor was—a 25-foot-high wooden-planked fence tattooed with ads for whiskey, biscuits, and taxicabs. The barrier was designed to keep fans behind it from getting a free peek at the action from windows or roofs on Lansdowne Street, not to keep home runs from breaking windows. Nobody figured to be hitting the ball over the wall any time soon.[11]

Another quirky detail fans might have noticed was the sloping hill leading up to the base of the tall fence and extending from left field to center. This ten-foot knoll, which would be crowded with fans using it as makeshift bleachers for big games, was usually in play and presented a challenge for outfielders. Red Sox left fielder Duffy Lewis would become so adept at running up and down it in pursuit of fly balls that fans took to calling the spot Duffy's Cliff, but most defenders would just as soon it be smoothed over.

The excitement of the present and the promise of the future would extend to the surrounding streets, as the vision the Taylors had for the Fenway area came to fruition. Within a few years after the ballpark opened, an underground subway stop would bring people into the heart of Kenmore Square, where it was just a short walk to the ballpark—with restaurants and automobile showrooms to entice fans along the way. Hotels soon followed.

"Upon debut, Fenway was greeted with a range of opinions," a narrator summed up after the December 2011 re-enactment detailing the ballpark's origins. "Some writers lavished praise upon the park, calling it "splendid" and "magnificent," while others complained that it lacked intimacy and was too cavernous. But fans quickly fell for the place, making Fenway Park a Boston institution from its earliest days.

"For ten abiding decades, fans have passed through these turnstiles, entering a ballpark that has not only endured—but thrived. Closing in upon its 100th birthday, the park serves as a testament to where we've been, and a timeless compass to where we are going."

Sources

Books:

Michael Gershman. *Diamonds—The Evolution of the Ballpark* (Boston: Houghton Mifflin, 1993)

Fred Lieb. *The Boston Red Sox* (Carbondale: Southern Illinois University Press, 2003) (original printing, 1947)

Philip J. Lowry. *Green Cathedrals* (New York: Walker & Co., 2006)

Glenn Stout. *Fenway 1912* (Boston: Houghton Mifflin Harcourt, 2011)

Glenn Stout and Richard Johnson. *Red Sox Century* (Boston: Houghton Mifflin, 2000)

Saul Wisnia. *Fenway Park: The Centennial* (New York: St. Martin's Press, 2011)

Periodicals:

"Dana Lands Bought By Gen Chas. H. Taylor," *Boston Globe*, February 11, 1911

"Progress and Prestige of the National Game," *Boston Globe*, March 12, 1911

"New Grand Stand to Cost $300,000," *Boston Herald*, September 13, 1911

"McAleer Will Bolster the Sox," *Boston Evening Record*, September 13, 1911

"Fenway Park, New Home of Red Sox, Transferred to Three Trustees for Development," *Boston Globe*, September 30, 1911

"Work Started on New Red Sox Park," *Boston Post*, September 30, 1911

"Red Sox Win; Good Night!" *Boston Herald*, October 8, 1911

Online Sources:

Ballparks.com

Baseballlibrary.com

Baseball-Reference.com

ProQuest Historical Newspapers

Redsox.com

SABR.org

Video of two-act play re-enacting the sale of the Dana Lands, script by Dan Rea of the Boston Red Sox. (See note 3)

Endnotes

1. Walton is quoted in Michael Gershman's *Diamonds*.

2. Another version of events, as proclaimed by Glenn Stout and other historians, is that the Taylors were the ones who bought the land at auction. Charles Taylor was a major shareholder in the Fenway Realty Company, which owned a large amount of land in the area including that on which the park was built.

3. The two-act play can be viewed at: http://mlb.mlb.com/video/play.jsp?content_id=20030161&topic_id=8067842&tcid=fb_SOXSITE_20030161&c_id=bos&mid=552

4. *Boston Evening Record*, September 13, 1911

5. *Boston Herald*, September 13, 1911; *Boston Globe*, September 30, 1911

6. By Opening Day 1912, capacity had grown to approximately 29,000.

7. Photographs, one of which appeared in the 1975 Red Sox yearbook labeled as a Fenway groundbreaking, were in fact shots depicting the first shovels of dirt thrown at the site of the Huntington Avenue Grounds ten years before.

8. Although no piece of the Huntington Avenue Grounds remains standing, a statue of Cy Young looking in for a sign from his catcher stands at the approximate spot where the pitcher's mound was located. The land is now part of the Northeastern University campus, and most fans walking by Cy likely have no idea why he's there.

9. Although a move to a second deck was never made in the 20th century, a small second deck was added throughout Fenway Park in stages from 2002 to 2011 as a means of keeping the facility economically stable. In essence, Taylor's decision to prepare for this contingency helped save the ballpark.

10. Harvard Stadium is, like Fenway Park, still in use today—giving Boston two active outdoor sports venues that date from before World War I.

11. Actually, it took just five games before Hugh Bradley of the Red Sox accomplished the feat with a shot over the fence on April 26 against the Philadelphia Athletics

The Land of Hot Waters
by Michael Foster

During their first two trips to Hot Springs in 1909 and 1910, the Red Sox took quarters in the famed Majestic Hotel uptown on Park Avenue. However, when he came to the city to firm up training plans late the previous November, Sox executive Robert McRoy learned that the Majestic was already booked to capacity though the entire month of March. The team booked a three-week stay with the Brooklyn Dodgers at the nearby Eastman Hotel.

Internationally renowned, the mammoth "Monarch on the Glen" was one of five luxury hotels in a city that had been catering to a veritable *Who's Who* of notable Americans for over a quarter century.[1] Occupying the entire downtown along the eastern edge of Central Avenue between Spring Street and Reserve Avenue, the Eastman was just two blocks from the train depot, and a convenient walk to most of the city's 19 bathhouses and other downtown attractions. Each of the 520 elegantly furnished guestrooms was fitted with electric lights, steam or electric heat, an oversized attached closet, and a private window overlooking the surrounding Hot Springs Mountains. The grand parlor, dozens of card and writing rooms, and separate ladies and gentlemen billiards rooms, parlors and reading rooms offered round-the-clock convenience.

Morning, afternoon, and night, classical music provided by an Eastman house orchestra flowed in the 52' X 70' Grand Rotunda, where guests mingled or simply let go their worries. From cakewalks to card playing, the hotel offered an endless array of games and frivolous fun, and following a day of baths, sightseeing, horseback riding, or golf, the pampered visitor would retire to the hotel dining room for an evening meal sumptuously prepared. Then, perhaps after enjoying a sociable and a fine cigar in one of the Hotel parlors, at 9:00 sharp the Eastman Grand Ballroom came to life as guests enjoyed "rhythmic inspiration" provided by the house band at organized "hops" featuring square dancing, group dancing and waltzes.[2]

Guests from across the globe basked in the luxury of one of America's finest hotels, but to Jake Stahl and other major league managers the arrival of March meant baseball and baseball meant business.

The 1,200 foot hills surrounding Hot Springs had been providing American ballplayers with a natural gymnasium for hiking and climbing dating all the way back to 1886, when Cap Anson brought his Chicago White Stockings to town to "boil out the alcoholic microbes" in area spas. True, the advent of modern science had long since rendered obsolete many of those

The team assembled for a portrait at the Buckstaff Bathhouse. Depicted are five who failed to make the final cut: Fred Anderson, Bill Goodman, Dutch Leonard, Jack Lewis, and Jimmy Shinn.

The Eastman Hotel, spring training home of the 1912 Boston Red Sox.

old training practices, and yet, lo all these years later, these old hills stood as a vivid reminder of what was still the best way of whipping any flabby ballplayer into shape.

Stahl and Bill Carrigan were joined by Cy Young for a vigorous 10-mile hike on the morning of February 28.[3] Their workout in the Hot Springs Mountains completed, the men made their way down West Mountain and arrived at Whittington Park just southwest of downtown. The oldest of Hot Springs' three training fields, Whittington had been used mostly by Cincinnati and Pittsburgh since its opening to the public in 1894, and six years earlier it was razed to make way for a new grandstand capable of holding upward of 700 spectators. The facilities were the best Hot Springs had to offer, but after three all-star contests and a number of wet practice sessions the playing surface was a mess. Stahl no doubt expressed some measure of relief that his club would not be sharing practice at Whittington as had earlier been rumored.[4]

Red Sox president John I. Taylor had spared no expense on the construction of the new Red Sox ball grounds in the Fenway, but the same could hardly be said of the team's spring training grounds, humble Majestic Park. Built in the offseason before spring training in 1909, the bare-bone field featured a modest grandstand capable of holding a few hundred fans, with a lone screen installed behind home plate to keep passed balls from skirting off onto adjacent Carson and Belding Streets. Majestic was nothing fancy, but the playing surface was "as level as the stereotyped billiard table" and the freshly planted grass had grown in almost completely.[5] Best of all, the Red Sox would have exclusive use of Majestic through the entire run of spring training, and that was more than good enough for Jake Stahl. "This is the best playing field in the South," he commended as he walked around the untouched grounds. "Look at the infield; it couldn't be better. Let the steam roller take one trip over the sod and I wouldn't swap my field with that old one at Whittington Park."[6]

Heavy spring rains that had been sweeping across the entire South for weeks continued to fall mercilessly, and much to everyone's chagrin baseball activity was kept to a dull minimum. Old timers in Hot Springs said that the deluge was the worst in memory; roads in Garland County were transformed into veritable mud pits and rising rivers up north were a menace to rail traffic coming into and leaving Hot Springs' three train stations. To make matters worse, forecasters saw nothing but more precipitation on the horizon.[7]

A handful of Red Sox players braved the rains and, one by one, began making their way into camp. On the first of March, veteran utility infielder Clyde Engle arrived in town in the company of Nuf Ced McGreevey, king of Boston's Royal Rooters, who left the comfort of his South End saloon, *The Third Base*, to head South and work off a few pounds with the hometown team.[8]

Right-hander Charley "Sea Lion" Hall arrived unannounced two days later in the Eastman Lobby to the welcoming backslaps and jubilant howls of his teammates.

II.

The valley that the Boston Red Sox would call home for the next four weeks was known as "The Place of Hot Waters" ("Tah-Ne-Co") to the Native American tribes who settled in the region centuries before conquistador Hernando De Soto arrived in 1541.[9] Warriors wounded in battle had long recognized the seemingly miraculous healing powers of the warm waters, and in the 350 years that passed as the area evolved from outpost to settlement to resort village of nearly 15,000 year-round residents, the mystique surrounding the thermal waters only grew.

Scientists from universities across the United States had spent the better part of a generation examining the warm springs, and before the first decade of the twentieth century was out an assortment of hypotheses had emerged to explain its mysterious therapeutic effects. Most concurred with Dr. Bertram B. Boltwood of Yale University, who in 1904 found traces of radon in the springs and attributed the healing powers to the wonder of radioactivity ("the touch of God").[10] Six years later, that notion was disputed by A.H. Purdue, who conducted independent tests and concluded that the water had to be of extraterrestrial origin. Still others argued that the explanation lay in an underground cavern somewhere deep beneath the earth's surface and far outside the purview of modern science.[11]

For athletes now working out in Hot Springs, the source of water's healing power was far less intriguing than its effects—namely soothing sore muscles and helping to steam off a few extra pounds. The convenient proximately of the Majestic Bath House to the adjacent Majestic Hotel made it a popular splash point for many visiting athletes in years past, but with no fewer than 19 such facilities opened in the Valley this spring, bathing options were almost limitless.

Because of their proximity in the Eastman, this year the Red Sox were provided exclusive and unlimited access to the city's

Bathhouse Row, Hot Springs.

newest and most advanced bathing establishment, the Buckstaff Bathhouse, recently rebuilt from the ground up.[12] Located just a block from the Eastman Hotel, the Buckstaff was one of 10 bathhouses clustered along Central Avenue's famed Bathhouse Row and was "a dream come true" to its proprietors.[13] Faced with eight handsome Corinthian columns and white stone trim, the three-story brick structure was a "peerless and dignified" architectural contribution to Bathhouse Row. Fine accoutrements, such as imported marble from Italy, stained glass windows and a staff of "thermal experts" gave it, as one observer put it, "a spirit of elegance and luxury, reminiscent of old Rome at the height of its pagan glory."[14]

Entering the front door, guests were greeted by the warm smile of one of several full-time attendants (the facility prided itself as the only bathhouse in Hot Springs with an "all-white" staff), and personal items were stored in a locker behind the large marble desk. Female visitors rode an elevator to the second floor ("the latest model," stated one brochure, "large enough to permit an invalid's cot to be rolled into it"), but a gentleman needed only step through a door to the right of the front desk to enter the men's bathing facilities. On changing in the dressing room, guests would then enter the bath chamber itself, its antiseptic white tile floor and white walls glistening in ample light provided by fancy electronic lamps and the sun itself. Hot air cabinets, vapor cabinets, shower baths, and sitz baths offered any number of options to the discerning client. After enjoying a long and steamy bath, the luxurious "cooling room" awaited, where any weary bather, "tingling with the toning vitality of his bath," could stretch out on one of several divans for a leisurely afternoon snooze.[15]

When he arrived at the Eastman, Charley Hall announced that it was his intention to get in a full cycle of 21 baths before the opening of training on the 12th; Carrigan had soaked every day for over a week.[16] So far as Heinie Wagner was concerned, however, over-bathing was ill advised. "I don't intend to take the full course of baths at Hot Springs," he said en route to Arkansas. "Of course there will be plunges, but old and experienced players like Cy Young advise against too much of the hot water as being perhaps harmful."[17]

When they weren't hiking through the mountains or soaking at the Buckstaff, target practice at the recently opened gun club was a favorite recreational activity, as was golf at the world renowned Hot Springs Country Club. Lax gambling regulations made betting on the horse races at Essex Park an almost daily activity.

Town fathers had turned a blind eye to these activities for years, but this spring all that changed. Back in 1911, conservative leaders gathered to form a citizens group seeking to eliminate all gambling in city limits. Backed by local law enforcement—Hot Springs Sheriff James B. Wood—reformers conducted a series of surprise raids on underground gaming establishments, arrested proprietors, and ripped their gaming tables and roulette wheels from their fixtures and burned them on the sidewalks outside.[18] "My grandparents were founding members of the First Baptist Church," Wood's 82-year old granddaughter, Nadia Parker, defends. "That was the group behind the raids. The bets at the horse track and casinos were all illegal in Hot Springs at the time, and they were just trying to make people obey the law."[19]

Unfortunately for vacationers that spring, Wood and his reformers did not stop there. After he finished demolishing the gaming establishments and closing down the infamous Black Orchid, the stubborn Sheriff announced the prohibition of Sunday movies, billiards, and bowling. Then, in a blow directed at ball clubs training in Hot Springs, he banned all Sunday baseball practices and games as well.

Team executives, not to mention the Hot Springs Chamber of Commerce, were livid. "Indignation at the dictum that no Sunday ball is to be played pervades," observed *Boston Post* sportswriter Paul Shannon.[20] "In vain were all the arguments of Dahlen, Donovan, Stahl, and others. The players can't understand how a town that stands for back door entrances to gambling resorts and wink and fake raids can see any harm in the playing of Sunday games." The personal intervention of Father Fanahy from the local Catholic parish on behalf of the ball clubs did nothing to change the mind of the stubborn sheriff, who made it a point to pay a personal visit to each manager with the stern warning that any player caught so much as walking across the grounds in uniform on Sunday would face certain prosecution.

Thanks to Sheriff Wood, ball players would see no action on Sunday the 3rd, but the day was bright and warm and forecasters called for improved conditions for the week. Buoyed by the news, Stahl was upbeat about prospects for getting some work in before the official opening of camp. "I feel bully," he declared. "If the squad gets big enough I will start practice at Majestic Park at once."[21] When Bill Dahlen issued a challenge to American League all-stars to meet his Brooklyn Dodgers at Whittington Park for Monday afternoon, Stahl announced he would take duties at first base. Ignoring the earlier missive from Jimmy McAleer to keep his players off the field until he arrived in Hot Springs from meetings in Chicago, Stahl also granted Fred Anderson's request to pitch for the Americans.[22]

In defiance to optimistic forecasts, heavy precipitation persisted for most of the first week. The Red Sox got in two hours at Majestic Park on Tuesday, but aside from hikes and soaks, there was little for the players to do but keep warm and wait. "It's the same old story from the Southern training camp today," the *Boston Post's* Paul Shannon reported glumly on Thursday, March 8. "More rain and cold weather, more kicking and 'crabbing' among the players." That training camps across the south were all experiencing similar inclement weather was of little consolation in the Springs, and one morning after the next wisps of profanity reverberated through corridors of the Eastman as the grumbling Brooklyn Dodgers awoke to find the same sign hanging in the hotel lobby: "NOTHING DOING." [23]

Teams were not able to get in much practice time, but some unexpected excitement on Wednesday gave all the athletes in town a workout the likes of which they had never seen. It all began around 10:30, when three members of the kitchen staff at the Arlington Hotel became embroiled in a bitter dispute over a breakfast order. Without warning, one of the men pulled out a pistol and shot down his co-worker in cold blood. "Two of the disputants were colored and the third a white man," Shannon recorded the next morning. "The negro fired one shot, which went through the white man's body, killing him instantly, then struck the other colored man's right hand, carrying away three fingers."[24] As the alleged murderer made a hasty escape out a back door and down the alley, hotel employees raced out of the kitchen and into the dining room screaming for their lives.

News that a black man had killed a white man spread fast and furiously. "The temper of Hot Springs was at white heat," Shannon continued, "and the fact that a white man had been killed by a negro was given as sufficient cause for the decoration of one of the lamp posts of the man street if the victim was captured."[25] Posses of gun-toting officials and residents soon formed, and "law abiding colored citizens" made their way into town for fear of being mistaken for the perpetrator. Ball players, then just heading out for their morning hikes, also assembled into small groups to assist in the manhunt.

For two frenzied hours, mobs of men in trucks raced through the city as frustrated law enforcement officials shouted orders left and right, trying desperately to locate the accused before irate citizens got to him first. Meanwhile, some 50 major and minor leaguers—some in uniform, others wearing layers of sweaters and old overcoats—combed the hills in hot pursuit of a man believed armed and dangerous.

Later that afternoon, it was discovered that the alleged murderer had cleverly doubled back to the Arlington and spent the rest of the morning hiding in a second floor room. Unbeknownst to most of the city, at 12:30 he calmly walked down to the dining room and turned himself over to authorities. By then most of the players had dropped out of the chase. Drenched from head to toe and disgusted at not having seen so much as a footprint in the mud, they gave up the search and returned to the hotel for lunch.

The excitement of an alleged murderer at large almost overshadowed the arrival Thursday evening of two new more members of the club, catchers Chester Thomas and Forrest Cady. The two had ridden the last leg to Hot Springs aboard the very same passenger train, but it was not actually until Friday morning that Jake Stahl introduced them to each other in the Eastman lobby.[26]

The arrival of two catchers added considerably to Red Sox training activities, and on the early morning hours of Friday, March 9, the small group began to get in some practice time on the lawn in front of the Eastman. Still in their street clothes, Engle and Stahl loosened their winter-tightened arms with a game of catch, while Thomas and Cady crouched to receive throws from

Hunting a murderer: Cy Young, Jake Stahl, Bill Carrigan, and Michael "Nuf Ced" McGreevey join the hunt for the fugitive killer.

Anderson and Hall. Only 30 players had received an invitation to try out with the Red Sox this spring, and with the vast majority of them returning veterans, there were precious few openings on the bench.

The bulk of the team was due to arrive within the next 48 hours, and beginning Friday night runners were dispatched to the depots on the half-hour to look out for new arrivals. Baseball fans were pouring into the "Valley of the Vapors" in droves.

III.

"You can't bank on time tables," complained one writer, "and you can bank still less on certain railroads."[27] Late Saturday afternoon McRoy wired Stahl from Cincinnati that the team was on schedule to arrive in Hot Springs 3:55 Sunday afternoon, and in no time plans were underfoot to receive the team in grand fashion. Stahl secured a police detail and a small band to greet the express at the station house.

It was all for naught. At noon on Sunday, Stahl was notified that a freight wreck had delayed the team's arrival into Memphis, and much to everyone's disappointment all festivities had to be cancelled. The club spent the day and most of the night milling about the rail station waiting for word on their teammates. By midnight, nearly everyone had retreated back to the hotel, leaving Jake Stahl and a handful of others to welcome the Express when it pulled into town eight hours behind schedule.

The piercing wail of a train whistle off in the distance at 12:15 AM on Monday morning signaled to Stahl that the special from Little Rock was approaching. Dragging a lone Pullman and attached baggage car, Engine #1313 emerged out of the darkness and made its way up the westbound Rock Island tracks along Benton Street. It crossed over intersections at Palm, Laurel and Pleasant Streets, and then slowed to a crawl at the foot of Cottage. After exuding a healthy burst of steam, it came to a full stop at Passenger Depot.[28]

The group let out a howl when the first of the tired and travel-worn Red Sox stepped from the Pullman.[29] The depot's skeleton crew jumped into action to unload crates, suitcases, and footlockers from the baggage car onto a waiting transport, but most of the 34 members of the Red Sox party refused the invitation to ride with their bags over to the hotel. After three days on the rails, they were only too happy to stretch their legs and make the two-block walk on foot.

Back at the Eastman, McRoy and the other members of the Red Sox were greeted with warm handshakes from their teammates, which now numbered nine with the arrival of Joe Wood and veteran catcher Leslie Nunamaker late Saturday night. The contingent of players and fans from the northeast was far larger than had been expected, so Stahl had to scramble to ensure everyone got a warm bed for the evening. "Confusion prevails at the camp just now," Shannon wrote. "The hotel is crowded to the doors and people are being turned away."[30]

The bulk of the team did not turn in until the wee hours of the morning, but by 8:00 AM on Monday the corridors of the Eastman were overflowing with ballplayers and rooters.[31] Owing to the late arrival of the team and another dousing from Mother Nature, Jake Stahl cancelled all practices for the day, but the duties of settling his team into quarters kept busy. When crates containing the team's missing uniforms were brought into the lobby at noon, Jake doled out the familiar practice grays, heavy sweaters, caps, and stockings to veterans and recruits, and after lunch he led Carrigan, Engle, Hall, Anderson, Cady, and Thomas on another hike. Trainer Joe Quirk spent most of his first day in the Springs weighing in each player, and Bradley, O'Brien, Bedient, and Cicotte took their first bathing plunges over at the Buckstaff.

On Tuesday morning temperatures flirted around freezing point and a stiff breeze whipped across the valley, but after days of rain "Old Sol" at last made an appearance. Ignoring the cold and poor field conditions over at Majestic Park, Stahl called his team out for the first practice of the spring.[32]

Shortly before 9 AM, the players gathered for in the Eastman lobby for a brief meeting. The new Red Sox manager addressed the entire team for the first time. "Boys," he began, "there is no need for me to lay down any rules and regulations with you. I can see that at a glance. You've got the stuff in you. It is up to you to do your best, keep plugging all the time, be active and never let up in your work.

"I don't intend to have any drones on the team, I want men who will keep working all the time. I want you to work together. Team-work is what we want. By that you will put the team right up near the top, and I want you to keep the team up among the leaders. There is no reason why the Boston Americans shouldn't get there and stay there throughout the season. I believe you are going to deliver the goods. That's all, boys."[33]

There was neither cheering nor applause when Stahl concluded his remarks, but at least one writer sensed the team "felt just like bubbling over" as they burst out of the Eastman and headed for the clubroom at the Buckstaff.[34] They donned their practice uniforms and spikes for the first time of the season, and then the 22 players blazed their way out of the bathhouse and proceeded down Central Avenue to the south end of town. They took a moment to look things over at Majestic, and satisfied that the strong breeze would have the field sufficiently dry by early afternoon, they disappeared into the Hot Springs Mountains, Bill Carrigan leading the pace all the way. "Stahl is a great believer in road work," recorded John Hallahan for the *Herald*, "and for the first week's active training he intends sandwiching a lot of long

At the Hot Springs train station are: Henriksen, Gardner, O'Brien, Wagner, Yerkes, and Bradley.

drills in with morning and afternoon 'fungo' sessions."[35]

At 1:30, the team headed over to Majestic, and for their first time of the year the silence of winter was broken by the crack of the bat. The staff loosened as Sea Lion Hall took the mound to throw batting practice, and those who were not pitching or hitting ran sprints to the outfield or worked out with a medicine ball.

Jake was the first of the players to step into the batter's box, and on the first offering from Hall he pounced on the ball, sending it deep to right field and off the outfield fence. "Same old Jake!" Hall yelled from the mound, much to the delight of numerous onlookers.

Over the next hour, players one after the next followed him up to the plate, swinging freely and practicing laying down bunts, and each of the 11 Red Sox pitchers was given time on the mound. Jake busily stalked about the field, encouraging his players to give it their all, and at the close of batting practice he broke the infield up into two squads to commence fielding practice.

All eyes that afternoon were trained on Heinie Wagner. The former captain had joked with reporters on the train ride down that the only reason Stahl came back to Boston was to see if his former teammate "hadn't lost his arm," but there was no laughter at Majestic this afternoon as the manager carefully scrutinized the condition of his veteran second baseman.[36]

The Majestic outfield was still flooded, but the revamped infield grass was in satisfactory condition. Infielders began with a little light throwing, but not five minutes into the workout Wagner deftly scooped up an infield grounder and put pepper on a throw that nearly bowled Stahl over at first base. A number of the players watching from foul territory responded with howls of laughter, but the irate manager was not the least bit amused. "You want to go easy there," he barked. "I don't intend on having you on the injured list before we leave the Springs. That arm has got to last you all season, but it won't last a week if you start shooting that way."[37]

Back at the hotel after practice, team trainer Joe Quirk responded to endless calls for rubdowns. He did his best to apply liberal quantities of the traditional (if not vile) combination of Vaseline and Tabasco to ease the pain, but complaints of "lame whips and aching bones" nevertheless echoed through the hallways most of the evening.

Earlier in the day, an exhausted Dutch Leonard became the first of the Californians to make his way into town, declaring on arrival that seven days of isolation in a snowbound Pullman berth made him "mighty glad to see a few live people once more."[38] Flooding along the southern route that took Ray and Lillian Collins through Texas made their trip no easier, and Stahl and the other players treated the newlyweds to a warm welcome when they rolled in shortly after dinner.[39] Word also came from Duffy Lewis that it he and Stockton rookie Jimmy Shinn were bearing down on Arkansas, and shortly before midnight rookie infielder Bill Goodman arrived from distant Victoria, British Columbia.

Evidence suggested that Harry Hooper, too, was not far behind. Inexplicably, late on Tuesday evening the veteran right fielder's travel trunk appeared in the Eastman lobby. Hooper himself did not turn up at the hotel for another 12 hours.[40]

Freezing temperatures and bitter winds up in Boston called to a halt all construction on Fenway Park, and reports coming out of the city stated that concrete crews would now have to work round the clock so the work of installing the 12,000 seats in the grandstand could begin.[41]

But down in Hot Springs, Red Sox baseball was just kicking into high gear.

The team was not two days into training when, on Wednesday night, Stahl announced that on Saturday afternoon the Boston Americans would square off against Horace Fogel's Philadelphia Nationals for the first exhibition game of the spring. Fans in Hot Springs were elated by the news, and reports out of the Phillies camp indicated that the Quakers were looking forward to a date with Boston's Speed Boys.[42] But over at the Eastman there was little in the way of enthusiasm for any such contest, several players voicing complaints that it was foolhardy to schedule games so early in training.[43]

All protests fell on deaf ears. Intent on having a good look at his rookies in action, after a full double practice on Thursday and another rainout on Friday, Stahl announced his lineup for Saturday's game. Reportedly "in the best of trim" after nearly a month of training, the Phillies announced their intention to play their regular lineup.

After listening to his club bellyache about their aches and pains through most of the morning workout at Majestic, Stahl took lunch and then led his starting lineup down to Fogel Field.[44] Poor field conditions did nothing to dissuade some 700 rooters from packing the tiny grandstand far beyond capacity. A number of Brooklyn Dodgers took the afternoon off to enjoy the spectacle, and they were joined by Fred Clarke and the Pittsburgh Pirates who had arrived in the Springs earlier in the day. Fresh in from meetings in Chicago, Jimmy McAleer was in the crowd as well, and sitting with his wife and Robert McRoy, the new owner of the Boston Red Sox took his seat in the front row and proudly looked on as his club warmed up on the field.

Fred Anderson acquitted himself admirably in the early going, and through the first four frames the Nationals managed to score only twice. Things looked up for the Red Sox when they tied the game with a pair of runs in the top of the fifth (they might have scored more had Jake Stahl's blast not gotten stuck in a tree in deep center), but in the bottom of the inning Boston's fortunes unraveled. The Phillies pounced on Anderson for six runs on eight straight hits, and Dutch Leonard performed no better in relief, surrendering four more runs in the three innings of work. By game's end, the Red Sox looked at an ugly 12-2 drubbing.[45]

If nothing else, the afternoon gave Stahl a chance to give his rookies a good hard look, and over nine innings the entire reserve squad had an opportunity to bat and play the field.

Hooper's defensive work stood out in particular, and on more than one occasion play was stopped to give the modest Californian a moment to tip his cap to his appreciative fans. So far as Boston's press corps was concerned, aside from the loss the only blemish on the afternoon was the work of umpire Moore, who's calling of balls and strikes was evidently so bad that, by game's end, he had become the chief object of the fans' unbridled anger.

Both teams retreated to the spas at the close of the contest, then returned to their respective hotels. After dinner, most donned tuxedos they had brought from home, and in small groups they made their way to the Eastman ballroom. Tonight they would enjoy one the social highlights of spring training, the annual

Eastman Ball.

The Eastman Grand Ballroom was a scene of elegance and splendor. The walls were decorated with large mirrors and long tapestries, and crystal chandeliers hung majestically from the ceilings. Tables were set formally and to meticulous perfection, and the hotel orchestra set the ambience with a series of classical pieces. Some of the players danced while others mingled with other guests and talked endlessly about baseball. Buck O'Brien took the opportunity to entertain Eastman residents in the hotel music room, serenading them with a series of love ballads, and unable to resist temptation, Hugh Bradley soon joined him.

Many of these men were college educated, and in polite company they conducted themselves with respect and, in certain cases, sophisticated elegance. But they were ball players, after all, young and brazen, rugged and cocky. Looking back over half a century later, Earl Moore, a pitcher with the 1912 Philadelphia Phillies, remembered these men and their times with honesty and vivid humor. "Baseball players weren't the same kind of people they are now," he reminisced. "They did a lot of carousing and a lot of them you wouldn't want to entertain in your home."[46] Yet there they stood, the lot of them, gathered together one of the finest hotel ballrooms in the country—cursing their enemies, poking fun at the wait staff, chewing on cigars, and rocking with laughter as they unabashedly swapped yarn after backslapping yarn.

Sunday was St. Patrick's Day. As it was the Sabbath and a religious holiday, the city was even more quiet than usual that morning, and nearly all the players, Catholic and Protestant, made their way to church services. Afterwards, they spent the day relaxing at the Eastman and soaking the last of the soreness out of their muscles at the Buckstaff. Bill Carrigan was always ready to crack open a cigar and pull out his well-worn deck of playing cards for rounds of poker, and several players took advantage of the good weather to hike through the mountainside. That evening, most of the players attended a sacred concert, where Buck O'Brien enthralled the gathering with a moving rendition of *Ave Maria*.

Darkness descended upon the Eastman as evening settled in, and with a long week of work ahead of them, the players retired to their rooms. Knowing that his father back in California would be on the lookout for a letter from his 25-year-old son, Harry Hooper picked up a few sheets of Eastman stationary and penned him a note. "Dear dad," he wrote:

Well, we are down to the regular grind of the training season. We lost two days on account of rain but outside of that the weather has been good. The grounds are in good shape outside of the outfield which was soft yesterday but should be fine tomorrow. Most of the fellows are stiff and sore and I was for one day but feel fine now. We work out in the morning from 9 till 11 and in the afternoon from 2 till 4. The morning's practice consists of batting and fielding and in the afternoon, we do the same and finish up with a practice game with the Yannigans.

One rainy day last week some of us went out to attend a trap shoot. There were five of us that shot and although I was the only one that had not shot at clay pigeons I trimmed them all easily. I broke 65 out of 75. There were two or three of the best shots in the county there. They could certainly bust theirs.

We take our baths at the Buckstaff Bathhouse which is located about a block from here. We have a clubroom there where we dress and everything is fine and convenient. We have our special car to go out to the ball grounds, and have it heated on the return trip. We have three new infielders, Goodman, Shinn and Krug. They all look pretty good. We have two new pitchers, Leonard from St. Mary's and Anderson who was with us a couple of years ago. Bedient who was with us last year is also with us. Speaker and Jack Lewis the last of our bunch to report got in today. Speaker looks fine. I don't know whether he has signed or not.

With best regards to all and love to yourself, I will bid you good night.

Harry[47]

IV.

With most of the team signed and ticket sales for the Fenway opener moving forward at a brisk pace, the only real business facing Jimmy McAleer before the start of season was to secure the signatures of Speaker and Nunamaker on their annual contracts. News of an impasse with the two players had been pouring out of Boston sporting columns for the better part of two weeks now, and on the afternoon of McAleer's arrival in town, Nunamaker went on the offensive. He complained bitterly to Paul Shannon that the Red Sox offer was not close to what he felt he was worth and that he "could get more money from almost any other club in the American League."[48] The Red Sox boss feigned surprise when reporters confronted him with news of his irate catcher. "There is nothing to be fixed between Nunamaker and myself," he stated blithely. "The salary named is all that will be given."[49] Nunamaker would have none of it, and the saber rattling persisted on Sunday when the veteran catcher threatened to quit the game altogether and start a new life farming a piece of land he had recently acquired in North Dakota.

Under the rules of the hated reserve clause, short of venting his frustration to the press there was little else that Les Nunamaker or virtually any ballplayer could do "The professional baseball player, having once signed his name to the contract offered by any club, becomes the perpetual property and asset of that club until sold, released on ten days notice, traded into the bondage of another club, or drafted by a club of higher class," wrote Hugh Fullerton. "Legally, the baseball player is a slave held in bondage, but he is the best treated, most pampered slave of history." Beyond holding out, for most players the only options were signing or quitting the game.

In the absence of formal representation by agents and lawyers, it was left to players themselves to negotiate for their best interest, and here Tris Speaker was nobody's fool. "Spoke doubtless realizes that he's a handy man to have round," wrote Tim Murnane, "and he has been in the game long enough to learn the ins and outs of salary boosting."[50] The Texan knew that in this game an open assault on the front office would not get the terms he was looking for, and on arrival he quietly dismissed rumors of any contractual holdout. He stated publicly only that he had not as yet spoken with the new boss, but he believed "there would not be the slightest difficulty in the way of coming to terms."[51] No naïve businessman himself, the cagey McAleer took Speaker to the side on Saturday afternoon, then graciously announced that "things were practically agreed upon."[52]

Nunamaker's position was not quite so secure. Now going into his second season in the big leagues, the 6'2" Nebraska native had proven his mettle in 62 games with the Sox in 1911, and he enjoyed the advantage of being ace Joe Wood's favored backstop. But with promising rookies Cady and Thomas on deck to back up the veteran Carrigan, the Boston Americans were a backstop-rich club.

On Monday night the two met for the first time to hammer out their differences, had a short and productive private talk and worked out an agreement. Twenty-four hours later, Speaker followed suit. After a private meeting with McAleer, the center fielder signed for a small increase over his previous year's salary, but only a one-year deal.[53]

The club dropped a sloppy 15-12 contest to the Phillies at Majestic Park. Stahl preferred to work his team privately in the friendly confines of Majestic Park, and he announced that his club would participate in no further exhibition games. "The playing of a game with another club gives a chance of a dozen men of the outside to work out," he reasoned, "whereas in the ordinary club practice among his own men every one gets the opportunity to show."

Morning hikes. Afternoon batting and fielding practice. Baths at the Buckstaff. Inter-squad games between the veterans and Yannigans. That would be the routine from now until early April, when the team left Hot Springs to begin its barnstorming tour north through Tennessee and Ohio. Then it would be onto Boston to take on the Harvard Crimson Nine at Fenway Park.

Opening day was three weeks away.

His lineup comprised almost entirely of returning veterans, the only real question mark in Jake Stahl's starting roster lay with the middle infield. Heinie Wagner's throwing arm had yet to be tested, and Steve Yerkes' hold on the second sack was anything but secure.[54] "If that second base problem were settled," Stahl had said two days after his arrival in Hot Springs, "any worriment I might have over the chance for our team fighting it out with the Athletics would be ended. Just as soon as I know who is going to play that middle sack, we will get down to the real work."[55] Yerkes hurt his own cause by showing up so overweight he was scarcely recognized by Treasurer McRoy.[56]

The excellent early play of the new recruits, Jimmy Shinn, Marty Krug, Bill Goodman, and recent arrival Jack Lewis, made Yerkes' hold on second base that much more precarious. The speedy Krug was making "a big hit with everyone" in the early going, and McAleer and Stahl were both visibly impressed by his steady work in the field against the Phillies.

Stahl anticipated that he would have plenty of time to watch his roster develop, but almost on cue Mother Nature again vexed all plans. Rain fell for four straight days beginning on Wednesday the 20th, and on the 24th more rain and cold weather put an end to Stahl's threat to defy Sheriff Wood's prohibition against Sunday baseball. "This 'nothing to do till tomorrow' weather certainly gets on my nerves," Heinie Wagner quipped. Adding insult to injury, several members of the Red Sox party were stricken with the same mysterious fever that had swept through camp just two

Manager (and part-owner) Jake Stahl confers with owner Jimmy McAleer during a spring training game at Hot Springs.

weeks earlier, among them McRoy who was confined to his room for nearly a full week.[57]

Players did do their best to break up the monotony of the rainy week. Larry Gardner and Harry Hooper took time to rest up, and a number of the boys followed the horse races at Charleston, South Carolina, laying down bets based on tips that Dr. Quirk doled out around the hotel. There were pool games and more target shoots, and one evening Joe Wood, Charley Hall, and Duffy Lewis took time out to sit in on Andrew Carnegie's lectures on the American banking system (the steel magnate took note of the baseball men in the overflow audience, offering listeners a litany of schemes which, he insisted, would have them "batting .300 in the banking world"). Mostly, however, the team held up in their rooms dealing endless rounds of cards, doing their best to evade the staff's relentless request to pawn goods off on them at every turn.

The delay did not seem to bother Jake Stahl, who confirmed early on that the club would retain all four catchers for the summer, and Olaf Henriksen would stay on with the club to back up his veteran outfield. Clyde Engle was guaranteed his spot as a utility infielder, but so far as the rest of the middle infield was concerned anything was possible.

Pitching remained a major concern. Joe Wood, Buck O'Brien, and Eddie Cicotte were secure, and Pape, Anderson, and Bedient had all been impressive for the Yannigans. Casey Hageman had done almost no work in the offseason and was still not in the best of shape, and to complicate matters he was now complaining of a sore shoulder. However, John I. Taylor had guaranteed him $5,000 for the season, so dumping the right-hander would be no easy task. Charley Hall and Ray Collins also complained of soreness, and with McAleer showering praise on Dutch Leonard almost daily, reporters wondered if the big southpaw from Vermont wasn't "booked for emigration."[58] Endless hot baths and hikes through the countryside had left his staff in the peak of condition, but without steady throwing in the last week of camp, Stahl feared that his hurlers would leave the Springs with nothing to show but lame arms. "A good week would be a Godsend to us," he said. "We need all the sunshine we can get."[59]

Miraculously, skies cleared on Monday, and players headed back out for a final week of training. Five days of precipitation had transformed Majestic into a veritable mud bath, and when the players stepped on the field for the first time they sank ankle deep in the mud. But none of it seemed to matter. The bright sun and a steady breeze had the field dried up in a matter of hours, and by afternoon intra-squad games again commenced.

Only one day of practice was lost during the entire final week of practice, and reporters looked on with delight as Jake Stahl cracked the whip and worked his players to the limit.

After two weeks of watching the combination of Heinie Wagner and Steve Yerkes at short and second, Stahl decided at the end of the month to award Yerkes the starting job up the middle. The only injury bothering the former captain was a cut of the hand he gave himself shaving ("muffed the business end of using a razor," Wagner said)[60], and with Stahl covering necessary ground to Yerkes' weak left, the final pieces of the Red Sox infield fell into place. "Heinie Wagner's arm has regained its former strength and cunning," reported Shannon, "and there is every reason why McAleer and Stahl should feel jubilant over the outlook."[61]

By the smiling countenances of executives and players, there was little evidence in the accounts emanating from the pens of reporters of the tensions or disharmony that had already crept to the surface. Joe Wood was throwing his customary "smoke" and Buck O'Brien was pitching so well that he was mentioned as the probable starter against the Reds in Cincinnati. "When the team leaves here," enthused one reporter, "they will be pretty near right and a wonderfully different aggregation from the dejected crowd that made that slow return trip from the coast last year."[62]

The day before the scheduled end of camp, a number of players were dealt to minor league clubs. Playing professional ball was not a right, McAleer asserted, and unlike other squads that possessed an overabundance of benchwarmers, in Boston players would "work all the time for the privilege of wearing a uniform."[63] Boston would carry 21 players into 1912—four beneath the 25-player league limit—but McAleer left no doubt that additional roster cuts would come. That, however, would have to wait until after the Sox reached the Hub.

The express out of Hot Springs was scheduled to leave at noon on April 2, and on the eve of their departure the team collected their belongings and packed up their crates, and readied for departure. But Mother Nature had the last laugh. For the fifth time in less than a month, skies opened up and heavy rains descended on the Valley. Two days earlier the local papers had voiced concern that the Mississippi River was within two inches of the danger mark, and with another deluge now sweeping across the region the main artery to Memphis was now threatened. The team was forced to postpone their scheduled departure for three more days, and Stahl wired to cancel planned contests with minor leagues in Tennessee and Ohio. Worse still, the flooding Ohio River threatened the exhibitions in Cincinnati as well. Knowing he stood to lose a small fortune if these games were cancelled, on Wednesday afternoon Jimmy McAleer braved the weather and, accompanied by his wife, left Hot Springs to scout possible alternative routes north. McRoy left a few hours later, bound for Boston.

It might have been raining outside, but with spring training nearing its end the players could have cared less. Reporters wrote of a team that was trim and brimming with optimism. "I don't see how they can stop us from being one of the contenders for the American League championship," Tris Speaker said confidently. "The boys are pulling together and every one is anxious for the season to open. The pitchers will come around all right, and prospects look very bright."[64] Despite worries about lingering injuries, despite the rain, cold and mud, and despite a mysterious fever epidemic, the Boston Red Sox actually looked good.

After enjoying a farewell concert given by Buck O'Brien and Hugh Bradley on Thursday night, on the morning of Friday, April 4, the team awoke to the hustle and bustle of bellboys scouring about, offering all assistance to aid the team for its scheduled departure to Memphis. The team enjoyed a light breakfast, then proceeded directly over to Majestic Park for one final two-hour morning workout. Then it was back to the Buckstaff for one final hot bath, to the Eastman for lunch, and down to the depot.

The fireman stoked the firebox with coal, and porters stashed suitcases, trunks, and crates into the baggage car. After some brief good-byes, the 25 players and four members of the press stepped aboard and at 1:30 sharp, the team was on its way.[65]

Spring training for 1912 receded into the history books, and, as he wandered about the passenger cabins and dining car mingling with exhilarated players glad to be on their way home, it was obvious to Paul Shannon that that moment had come none too soon. "Not a man on the team but was tickled at the idea of getting away from here and heading toward the Hub," he wrote.[66] Under new ownership, a new manager, and with a fresh new ballpark waiting, a new era of Red Sox baseball was about to be ushered in.

Endnotes

1. For information on the Eastman Hotel, see Scully, Francis J. *Hot Springs, Arkansas and Hot Springs National Park; the story of a city and the Nation's health resort.* (Little Rock, Ark., Hanson Co., 1966), 165.

2. Hot Springs: *Carlsbad of America.* Courtesy of SABR member Tom Simon.

3. *Boston Post*, February 29, 1912, 13.

4. For Stahl family, see Dick Thompson, "In Name Only," *National Pastime*, January 1, 2000, 54.

5. *Boston Herald*, March 11, 1912, 10.

6. *Boston Globe*, February 28, 1912, 7.

7. *Boston Post*, March 6, 1912, 14.

8. For the arrival of Engle, see *Boston American*, March 2, 1912, 6.

9. Scully, *op. cit.*, 15.

10. John C. Paige and Laura Souliere Harrison, *Out of the vapors: a social and architectural history of bathhouse row.* Washington, DC: U.S. Department of the Interior/National Park Service, 1987, 184, 186.

11. *Ibidem.*

12. Hooper correspondence, courtesy of John Hooper.

13. For descriptions of the Buckstaff, see "Buckstaff Bathhouse" Courtesy of the Garland County Historical Society.

14. Dee Brown, *The American Spa: Hot Springs, Arkansas.* (Little Rock, Arkansas: Rose Publishing Company, 1982).

15. Scully, *op. cit.*, 206.

16. *Boston Herald*, March 4, 1912, 14.

17. *Boston American*, March 8, 1912, 7.

18. For the raids on gambling houses, see *Boston Post*, March 2, 1912, 12.

19. Author's telephone interview with Nadia Parker, January 16. 2002.

20. *Boston Post*, March 3, 1912, 14. See also *Boston Post*, March 4, 1912, 12.

21. *Boston Globe*, March 4, 1912, 6.

22. For Fred Anderson's career, see Shea files in DTP and *Boston Post*, March 10, 1912, p. 17. See also, Fred Anderson biographical file, E.H. Little Library, Davidson College, Davidson, NC.

23. *Boston Post*, March 6, 1912, 14.

24. *Boston Post*, March 7, 1912, 17.

25. *Ibidem.*

26. The author wishes to express his sincere thanks to the late Dick Thompson for his assistance in piecing together the minor-league career of Pinch Thomas. Author's e-mail correspondence with Richard Thompson, February 6, 2003. For Forrest Cady's minor-league career, see *Boston Post*, October 6, 1912, 6.

27. *Boston Post*, March 11, 1912, 10.

28. *Boston American*, March 16, 1912, 9.

29. *Boston American*, March 11, 1912, 9.

30. *Ibidem.*

31. *Boston Globe*, March 12, 1912, 9.

32. *Boston American*, March 11, 1912, 9.

33. *Boston American*, March 12, 1912, 11.

34. *Ibidem.*

35. *Boston Herald*, March 11, 1912, 10.

36. *Boston Herald*, March 9, 1912, 10.

37. *Boston Post*, March 13, 1912, 17.

38. *Boston Evening Globe*, March 12, 1912, 6.

39. *Boston Globe*, March 13, 1912, 6.

40. *Boston Herald*, March 12, 1912, 4.

41. *Boston Globe*, March 13, 1912, 7.

42. *Boston Herald*, March 15, 1912, 8.

43. *Boston Globe*, March 13, 1912, 7.

44. *Boston American*, March 16, 1912, 5.

45. *Boston Herald*, March 17, 1912, 9.

46. Clipping provided courtesy of Kathaleen Moore.

47. Hooper Family Correspondence, John Hooper Papers.

48. *Boston Post*, March 18, 1912, 9.

49. *Boston American*, March 18, 1912, 12.

50. *Boston Globe*, March 12, 1912, 6.

51. *Boston Post*, March 17, 1912, 12.

52. *Ibidem.*

53. *Boston Post*, March 20, 1912, 9.

54. *Boston Post*, April 1, 1912, 12.

55. *Boston Post*, February 29, 1912, 13.

56. *Boston Post*, March 13, 1912, 17

57. *Boston Post*, March 21, 1912, 5.

58. *Boston Post*, March 24, 1912, 19.

59. *Boston American*, March 25, 1912, 6.

60. *Boston American*, March 27 1912, 9.

61. *Boston Post*, April 12, 1912, 21.

62. *Boston Post*, April 1, 1912, 12.

63. *Boston Post*, March 30, 1912, 12

64. *Boston Herald*, April 3, 1912, 8.

65. *Boston American*, April 14, 1912, 14.

66. *Boston Post*, April 5, 1912, 8.

Christening Fenway—The Red Sox vs. Harvard Exhibition Game
By Bill Nowlin

The very first game played on Fenway's sacred ground featured Harvard University challenging the Red Sox.

The exhibition game pitted the Harvard University nine against the Boston Red Sox. This was no walkover for the Sox—and this was the 1912 edition of the BoSox, who became a world-championship team. The Red Sox entered their new home grounds following spring training in Hot Springs, Arkansas (albeit such a rainy one that they'd played only two games other than intrasquad ones), and then played two preseason games in Cincinnati.[1] Harvard had yet to play a game, and the cold weather had limited Coach Sexton's team to an inadequate amount of outside practice. In its morning edition on April 9, the *Harvard Crimson* acknowledged that the "make-up of the team is still unsettled." Despite the disparity, the game was a 2-0 squeaker, won on the strength of a one-hitter by Boston's pitcher, Casey Hageman. To top that off, Hageman drove in the only two runs of the game, one in the second inning and one in the fifth. It was Hageman's finest hour with the Red Sox.

The opening of a new ballpark is rightfully a special occasion and, despite its not being a regular-season game, and a few hundred seats on the first-base side not yet installed, some 3,000 or more hardy souls braved the elements, watching in a cold "fit to test the courage of any football crowd, with a little snow on the side for good measure of discomfort."[2] Tickets were on sale at Fenway Park itself and, for the Harvard contingent, at the Harvard Athletic Association, Leavitt & Peirce's, and at Wright and Ditson's.

Harvard's team left the university at 1:45 via "special car" and dressed for the game at the Park Riding School on Lansdowne Street. Students wishing to attend the game were advised to take the subway to Park Street, and transfer to a Chestnut Hill via Ipswich streetcar. The college team had its supporters—a "lusty-lunged following."[3]

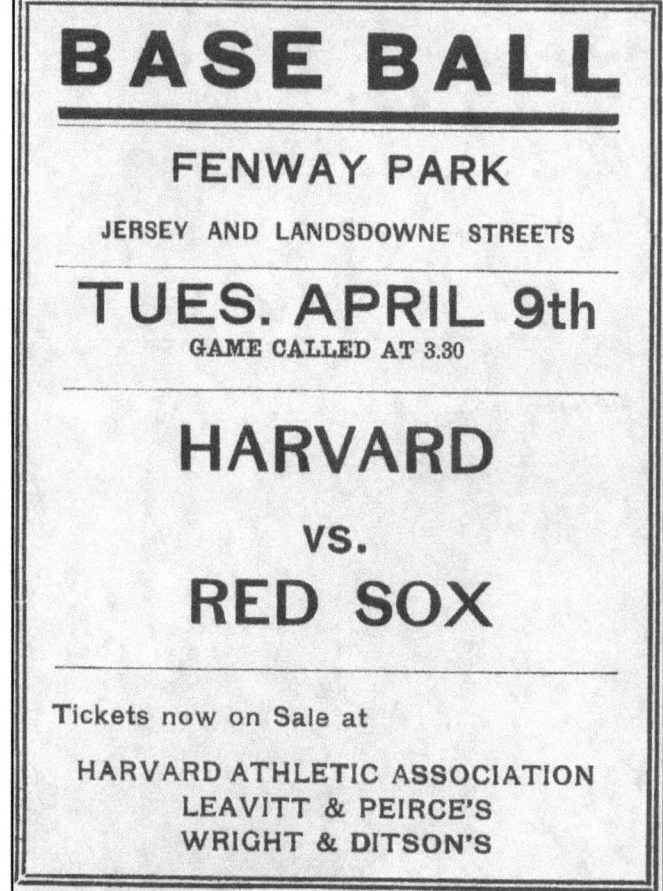

Advertisement for the first game in the new park, from the *Harvard Crimson* of April 9, 1912.

On a game day which saw snow flurries falling, the hot dog man was most welcome. *Boston Post* cartoon.

Hageman took the mound for Boston, squaring off for the 3:30 P.M. start against Harvard's third baseman Dana Joseph Paine Wingate. The first batter ever to step into the box at Fenway Park took a pitch for ball one. Wingate—that first batter—struck out.

Hageman didn't bring much experience with him. He had made his major-league debut late the previous season and had no wins against two losses for the Red Sox, though with a very good 2.12 ERA in 17 innings of work. His losses were mostly bad luck. Both were complete games, and he only yielded one earned run per game—though eight runs were scored off him. He lost the first game 4-1, and the second one 4-2. Both were home games, at the Huntington Avenue Grounds. There were only three more games ever played at the Huntington Avenue Grounds after his second loss. Debit the defense.

Hageman still had more experience than Harvard's starting pitcher, Samuel M. Felton III, who threw five innings before being relieved by Edwards Bartholf, who pitched the final inning in what proved to be a seven-inning matchup (the game was halted after seven due to cold weather). Sam Felton was pretty good, actually, when he got the ball over the plate. He gave up only

RED SOX CHRISTEN PARK WITH A WIN

Harvard Team Is Beaten 2 to 0, but Make a Fine Showing Against Major Leaguers—Both Teams Hit Weakly

WIGGLESWORTH OF HARVARD THROWN OUT AT THE PLATE ON AN ATTEMPTED DOUBLE STEAL IN THE SIXTH INNING OF YESTERDAY'S GAME BETWEEN HARVARD AND THE RED SOX AT THE NEW FENWAY PARK.

The only known action photograph from the first game played at Fenway Park. *Boston Post*, April 10, 1912.

four singles, though he didn't have much control—he walked 10 Red Sox (nine, according to some accounts). Hageman walked three batters himself, but he allowed only one single—to second baseman Robert Sturgis "Bob" Potter, the captain of the Crimson.

Harvard's student newspaper, also named the *Crimson*, noted of Felton's mound work, "Rarely does a pitcher hold his opponents to two runs when giving passes at the rate of two an inning. Felton kept the Red Sox hits well scattered and twice retired the side when the bases were full."

The Sox squad was a mixture of veterans and second-stringers. Harry Hooper, Tris Speaker, and Duffy Lewis were the outfield—as good an outfield as any team ever fielded. Not one of them had a hit, but then again, Felton was pitching around them; Speaker had only one official at-bat. Marty Krug subbed at short, so Heinie Wagner didn't have to risk his arm in the cold weather, but Larry Gardner held down the hot corner, Steve Yerkes was at second, and player-manager Jake Stahl was at first. Rookie Pinch Thomas was behind the plate.

The first hit ever made at Fenway Park was a single by Steve Yerkes in the bottom of the first inning.

It was far from the blowout it might have been. The *Boston Globe* subhead read, "Crimson None Too Easy." Herman Nickerson, covering the game for the *Boston Journal*, recognized that "to hold the Red Sox down to a 2 to 0 score was some achievement for the Crimson nine. The boys played the game with understanding, fielding splendidly, and while they failed to hit the ball, the excuse is found in the fact that they have not faced any pitching that could be called twirling this season."

Hageman made the difference offensively as well. Two of the four Sox singles were his and, as indicated, both drove in runs. Marty Krug, born in Germany, was the rookie at shortstop. He appeared in just 20 games during the season for the Red Sox, then was out of major-league ball for 10 years, before returning for one more season in 1922, with the Cubs. Krug, batting seventh, accepted one of Felton's free passes in the second inning. Thomas drew another walk. Felton fired to second, hoping to pick Krug off the base, but the ball skittered into center and both runners moved up. Hageman singled to score one, but neither Hooper, Yerkes, Speaker, nor Stahl could bring in Thomas from third.

In the fifth inning Gardner opened with a single to center. Lewis struck out and Krug walked. Thomas fouled out, but then Hageman drove in his second run of the game with a shot to center.

"Fenway Park will be a corker," commented the *Journal*. "Everyone was in praise of the new field."

In the season that followed, Hageman pitched a grand total of 1 innings despite starting in one game and appearing in another. He rang up a 27.00 ERA and that was it for his Red Sox career. 0-0. After a year off, Hageman won three and lost five in the National League, getting in 102 innings of play, but that was the end of his major-league career.

As for Harvard, they got their revenge four years later, beating the reigning world champion Red Sox at Fenway Park in 1916, the same team that would repeat as World Series winners just six months later.[4]

In an interesting aside (though not involving the 1912 baseball team), just two years after surviving the tragedy on the *Titanic*, Harvard athlete R. Norris Williams II (Harvard Class of 1916) won the US collegiate and US national singles championships. With Chuck Garland, he later won the 1920 doubles title at Wimbledon. Williams, who jumped off the sinking ship just before it capsized and then survived the night in the icy North Atlantic waters, had originally been told by doctors that his frozen legs needed to be amputated, but declared, "I'd rather die than not be able to play tennis again."—adapted from the official website of Harvard Athletics at www.GoCrimson.Com.

Dana Wingate served as captain of the Harvard baseball team in 1913 and 1914. After recurrent pneumonia contracted a year earlier, he died quite young at Saranac Lake, New York, in May of 1918. He hailed from Winchester, Massachusetts, and his father, Charles Wingate, was the Sunday editor of the *Boston Post*.

STARS OF YESTERDAY'S GAME

Felton   Hageman   Potter

Boston Post, Red Sox vs. Harvard, April 9, 1912.

Endnotes

1. The spring schedule for the Red Sox was:
    - 3/13 @ Hot Springs, Arkansas: Regulars 8, Yannigans 6 (6 innings)
    - 3/16 @ Hot Springs: Philadelphia Phillies 12, Boston 2
    - 3/18 @ Hot Springs: Philadelphia Phillies 15, Boston 12
    - 3/19 @ Hot Springs: Yannigans 8, Regulars 6
    - 3/20 @ Hot Springs: Regulars 5, Yannigans 2
    - 3/25 @ Hot Springs: Regulars 7, Yannigans 3
    - 3/26 @ Hot Springs: Regulars 6, Yannigans 6 (tie)
    - 3/27 @ Hot Springs: Regulars 3, Yannigans 2
    - 3/30 @ Hot Springs: Regulars 1, Yannigans 1
    - 4/3 @ Hot Springs: Yannigans 7, Regulars 6
    - 4/6 @ Cincinnati, Ohio: Boston 13, Cincinnati 1
    - 4/7 @ Cincinnati: Cincinnati 6, Boston 2
    - 4/9 @ Boston: Boston 2, Harvard College 0

    A very small number of games, and a great deal of rain, resulted both in a larger than usual number of games between the Regulars and Yannigans and in the number of idle days for games against other teams. This was the first season in which the Red Sox posted a losing record in exhibition play.

2. *Boston Journal*, April 10, 1912. Some accounts put attendance as high as 4,500.

3. *Boston Globe*, April 10, 1912.

4. On April 10, 1916, Harvard beat the Red Sox, 1-0. Harvard hadn't even begun to cut down its team for the spring season, but the reigning world champion Red Sox were back from spring training, ready for the season to begin, and fielded their regular lineup behind starter Vean Gregg. The weather in Greater Boston had again been bad, so much so that Harvard baseball coach Fred Mitchell (himself a Red Sox alumnus, who had played on the 1901 Boston Americans team) was said by the *Globe* to hope a snowstorm would prevent the game.

    Three Boston hurlers held the Harvards to five hits, but the lone run of the game was scored by Harvard after Larry Gardner's error, a single, and a ball hit to first baseman Dick Hoblitzell but which saw Gregg fail to cover the bag. The Red Sox made three errors; Harvard made none and executed three double plays. Harvard did well in 1916, too, with a 22-3 season. Helping hold the Sox scoreless was pitcher Eddie Mahan from Natick, relieved (like Gregg) after five innings, by W.G. Garritt for the final four. The *Harvard Crimson* termed it a "brilliant 1-0 victory from the World's Champion Red Sox," adding that the game "was not a gift from magnanimous professionals; the Crimson players simply played better ball. The offensive work of the two nines was about on a par, but in the work in the field the University was decidedly superior, playing without error and pulling off three sensational double plays, the last of which effectively nipped the Red Sox' ninth inning rally and ended the game."

Opening Fenway Park with Style: The World Champion 1912 Boston Red Sox

Harvard has played seven games in all against the Red Sox. The first two games were played at the Huntington Avenue Grounds. The April 12, 1910, match was billed in the *Harvard Crimson* as somewhat educational: "Today for the first time in 14 years the University nine will meet a professional nine on the diamond. This is one feature of a general awakening on the part of the athletic authorities, who seem to have come to realize that there is a certain satisfaction in winning, and that it is worth while to give the teams every opportunity for development. The nine will learn much from even one professional game…." The score was Red Sox 4, Harvard College 1. One wonders about the lessons learned in the 21-0 defeat in 1943, however.

4/12/1910—Red Sox 4, Harvard College 1
4/11/1911—Red Sox Colts 4, Harvard College 2
4/9/1912—Red Sox 2, Harvard 0
4/8/1913—Red Sox 5, Harvard 0
4/10/1916—Harvard 1, Red Sox 0
4/16/1943—Red Sox 21, Harvard 0
4/4/1987—Red Sox 8, Harvard 0

Interestingly, as Dan Shaughnessy pointed out in the April 5, 1987, *Boston Globe*, after Roger Clemens' start in the fated Game Six of the 1986 World Series, the very next team he faced was Harvard! The competitive Clemens mowed them down –10 K's, no hits in six innings. As Dick Thompson wrote, "Everyone knew Harvard had no right being on the same field as the Red Sox."

One of the players facing Clemens was Frank T. Caprio, former Treasurer of the State of Rhode Island. He told the *Providence Journal*'s Bill Parrillo, "I couldn't believe it. You see him on TV and you think of the MVP awards and the Cy Young and all that. And now there he is and you're trying to get a hit off him. It was hard to believe. His fastball was as fast as any pitch I had ever seen. But what made him great was his other pitches were that much better than any other curveball or slider or changeup that I had ever seen, and he had total control." Clemens wasn't the only Sox star present; Ted Williams was watching from the bench.

This early season team photograph, perhaps around the time the Red Sox played Harvard, clearly shows installed seats on the right side of the picture with the concrete base awaiting many more seats behind the team. The team appears to be enjoying the occasion.

Seated: trainer Joe Quirk (13), Charley Hall (14), Jack Bushelman (15), Olaf Henriksen (16), Jake Stahl (17), Hugh Bedient (18), Harry Hooper (19), Casey Hageman (20), Hugh Bradley (21), Duffy Lewis (22), Ray Collins (23), Steve Yerkes (24), and Larry Pape (25).

Top Row: Dutch Leonard (1), Marty Krug (2), Larry Gardner (3), Leslie Nunamaker (4), Bill Carrigan (5), Forrest Cady (6), Chester Thomas (9), Joe Wood (7), Buck O'Brien (8), Eddie Cicotte (10), Heinie Wagner (11), and Tris Speaker (12).

Opening Day 1912
By Bill Nowlin

By the time it actually occurred, Opening Day for Fenway Park was perhaps a bit anticlimactic. The opening of the new park was potentially an important enough event to be promoted in the days leading up to the scheduled opening on Thursday April 18. Even the *Boston Pilot*, the newspaper of the Archdiocese, announced in its April 13 issue that President James McAleer of the Red Sox had presented His Eminence William Cardinal O'Connell with a perpetual gold pass. The cardinal said he was "very glad to approve of any enterprise whose object was the progress of the city of Boston and the advancement of clean, manly sport." But the game was rained out.

Later that day, Red Sox first baseman Hugh Bradley came by the Boston American League headquarters and commented on the weather. Perhaps thinking of the labor unrest in Lawrence and elsewhere that year, Bradley asked team secretary Eddie Riley, "If a brass band went on a strike, would the drum stick?" Bradley's answer: "No, it would beat it."[1]

The April 18 opener was rained out. In its stead, a double bill was planned for the April 19 Patriots Day holiday. The first game was to be called at 10:30 in the morning with a second game at 3:15 in the afternoon. Tickets for the game on the 18th would be honored at any point during the season. Because the Boston Athletic Association marathon was also held on the 19th (rain or shine), Boylston Street would be roped off and all cars to the park would be routed via Huntington and Massachusetts avenues. The 3:15 start time had been pushed back a bit from the usual 3:00 PM start in order to give fans a little more time to get to the park after the Boston Marathon. But the weather still would not cooperate. Neither baseball game could be played, though not ten minutes after the second game had been called and "the big, fine-looking officers from Station 16 had been sent back to quarters the sun broke from behind the rain clouds and remained out most of the afternoon."[2] The grounds really were not in good condition; that the canvas diamond cover groundskeeper Jerome Kelley had ordered (the tarpaulin) had not yet been delivered probably didn't matter much.

On the morning of April 20, there had been three games postponed and the ballplayers were getting a little restive, but the day opened with the sun out and "so bright and blue that fans from out of town knew that they were taking no chances by coming to the city for the opening."[3] The grounds were deemed in fair shape despite the heavy rains of previous days, in large part due to the drainage system installed by Groundskeeper Kelley. Working with his crew, Kelley had the infield "in the pink of condition," said the *Boston Journal*. "Even during the heavy rain of yesterday the basepaths were remarkably hard and firm." The grass—the sod—had been brought over from the team's former home, the Huntington Avenue Grounds.

Another dark cloud of a sort hung over the opening. The sinking of the *Titanic* had shocked the nation, and Boston—being a seaport town—was perhaps affected more than many cities. More and more details of the horrific tragedy emerged as the survivors reached New York. Almost all of the Boston daily newspapers had *Titanic* coverage running many pages, and several of them had *Titanic* supplements. One enterprising outfit which specialized in postcards (Tichnor Bros. of Causeway Street) even ran a one-inch display advertisement in the April 20 *Boston Globe* soliciting street salespeople to peddle its postcards. The ad read: "S.S. TITANIC POST CARDS AND 16x22 VIEW FOR FRAMING NOW READY. BIG MONEY FOR HUSTLERS."

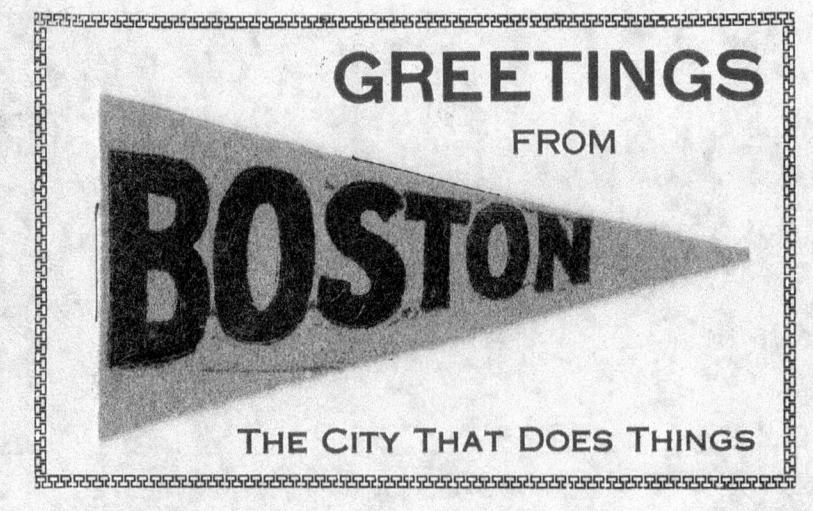

The sinking of the great ship was the most sobering of stories. On the morning of the game, the *Boston Daily Advertiser* printed a listing of 28 Massachusetts victims of the tragedy.

The Marathon was, in 1912, an exceptionally important area event and the record-breaking run of Michael J. Ryan, shaving 21 2/5 seconds off Clarence De Mar's track record time, filled up many column inches in most papers on the morning of April 20.

That the Red Sox were opening a new ballpark should have been significant news. Had Bostonians had any idea that the park would endure for more than 100 years, they would have certainly seen it as a much more meaningful event than they appeared to have at the time. But the team's prior park had only lasted 11 years, and this particular opening day was not seen as momentous an event as we might retrospectively have expected. Though the *Boston Globe* ran a game story which began on the front page of their Sunday paper, neither the *Post* nor the *Herald* did. *Titanic* news dominated the front pages. The *Journal*, the *Boston Record*, and the *Boston Traveler* did not publish on Sundays. None of them had Fenway's opening day story on the front page of their Monday editions. The *Christian Science Monitor* did not publish on Sunday, either, but had run a lengthy story on the opening in the last edition of Saturday's paper.

Opening Fenway Park with Style: The World Champion 1912 Boston Red Sox

There are two people we understand to have worked at Fenway Park in 1912 who have direct unbroken connection to two others working in 2012. Transporting team equipment back and forth between the railroad station and Fenway Park was the provenance of Pat Daley. Pat began with a horse and wagon handling equipment for Boston's National League baseball team, and assumed responsibilities with the Red Sox as well from their start as the Boston Americans in 1901. A November 1933 article in *The Sporting News* said Daley had only given up the horse and wagon for motorized transport a couple of years earlier. Pat's sons took over the business, transferring ownership to Jack Barretto and, ultimately, to Mark Tremblay, who operates the truck into Fenway's second century. And outside the park today, one finds Nick Jacobs, "the peanut man," selling a selection of nuts in front of Gate A. Nick is the third generation in his family to vend from a pushcart at Fenway Park. His grandfather Peter Davis's peanuts preceded Fenway, Davis having sold them at both the Huntington Avenue Grounds and the Braves' South End Grounds as well. Davis was succeeded by his son George Jacobs, and now George's son Nick has been selling since 1970, alongside his father from around the age of seven and now on his own. There is no real connection between Jerome Kelley and the groundskeepers of today, though one can appreciate that head groundskeeper in 2012, David Mellor, is the grandson of 1902 Baltimore Orioles first baseman Bill Mellor.

On April 20, the weather finally seemed to permit the game to be played. Despite the sunshine, however, people from out of state who may have contemplated coming to Boston to see the game were now less likely to come. Saturday was for many a day or work—at least a half-day's work. Thursday the 18th had been a state holiday in New Hampshire, and the *Boston Post* explained that "hundreds of excursionists had arranged with the railroads

Red Sox players lined up before the start of Opening Day play.

for transportation to Boston in time to be present at the opening of the Fenway park." With Fenway's first game now falling on Saturday—the Jewish Sabbath—another group of people who may have wished to attend now found religious strictures inhibiting that desire for the more orthodox among them. Opening Day at Fenway Park was Iyar 3, 5672 on the Jewish calendar.[4]

Both teams were raring to go. The Red Sox had opened on the road and brought back a record of 4-1. They were hoping to bolster their record with a win in the first game at their home park. The New York Highlanders (some newspapers referred to them as the "Yankees") were 0-5, and anxious to win their first game of the year. Reservations for tickets could be made by telephoning Fenway Park at Back Bay 5690. Tickets could be purchased at Wright and Ditson's sporting goods store on Washington Street or right at Fenway Park itself.

Both teams held a practice session in the morning to "ginger up" for the game, and another one in the early afternoon. Fans began to arrive not long after noon for the 3:00 PM game. The 1:00 PM edition of the *American* noted this early activity, and portrayed the park as the first fans filed in through the 18 gates which had been flung open: "The decorations which had been in place ever since Wednesday were a bit bedraggled by the rain, but the new park was a cheery spectacle, nevertheless." Because the construction of the clubhouses was not yet complete, the players had changed into their uniforms at the nearby Park Riding School.

Streetcars brought many to the new park at the corner of Jersey and Lansdowne Streets; the subway did not extend to Kenmore Square until 1914. For those who owned an automobile (perhaps a Decatur, the company in which team executive John I. Taylor owned a share), there was not yet a $30.00 fee for parking. As the *Boston Globe*'s John Powers pointed out in a piece written on the park's 75th anniversary, "You could park it almost anywhere you pleased near the ballpark. The only two buildings near the park were a riding school and a garage out beyond right field. The West Fens was terra nova then. Artists, students, musicians, and assorted bohemians lived there, out beyond the water and marsh. Speculators owned the land, looking to sell it to developers who would erect apartment buildings near the trolley lines. Most of the Opening Day crowd arrived by public transit, taking the Ipswich Street, Beacon Street or Commonwealth Avenue cars and walking past open lots to the park." Among the speculators, of course, were Gen. Charles Taylor and his son John I., who had acquired the land on which Fenway Park had been built.

Images of Opening Day, *Boston Post*, April 21, 1912.

Section L on the third-base grandstand (the designations have changed over time) was reserved for invited guests. Mayor John F. "Honey Fitz" Fitzgerald shared his box with Mike Ryan, the marathon winner. The right-handed Fitzgerald threw out the ceremonial first pitch. It was apparently underwhelming as ceremonies go; the *Post*'s Paul H. Shannon wrote that "Boston's modest chief executive pulled off this feat so quietly that few excepting those within closest proximity knew that this important duty had been transacted." Governor of the Commonwealth of Massachusetts Eugene Foss was unable to attend. Neither did the famed Letter Carriers Band make it to the opener. President Frank Farrell of the Highlanders was present, though not in evidence after the Red Sox tied the game in the eighth inning. The *Globe*'s Tim Murnane wrote, "The park was crowded with veteran ball players and fans, and everyone praised the new park, which is a model in every way."

The formal dedication of the park was scheduled for a later date, on May 16. Rain washed out that date, too. Dedication Day was finally held on May 17, complete with tricolor bunting outside and inside. There were "potted plants everywhere [which] lined the walks leading to the wide promenades, and there was a band which was never weary and which was augmented by a megaphone quartet which sang 'bear' songs and refused to allow ever the entre-innings to be dull."[5]

There were so many people at the park on the actual opening day—reported as between 24,000 and 27,000—that ropes were stretched across the outfield to hold back a couple of thousand paying customers who encircled the field, standing in the outer reaches of the outfield. There was to be no possibility of a home run or a triple; managers Stahl and Wolverton agreed to a ground rule that any ball hit over the ropes would count as a two-base hit. The park's official capacity at the time was 24,400. Ticket prices ranged from 25 cents in the bleachers to 50 cents in the pavilion seats, increasing to 75 cents for unreserved grandstand. Those who wished to sit in reserved seating in the first ten rows of the grandstand paid $1.25 and box seats were $1.50 apiece. Some things never change; the *Boston Traveler* predicted, "The centre field bleachers will seat the real fans."[6]

Some fans made money during the game and some lost far more than intended. Betting on games—even on individual pitches—was common. And there were at least a couple of fans who were relieved of money they hadn't wagered. The *Boston American* told the story: "When 'Steve' Yerkes, the Red Sox second baseman, scored the winning run in the eleventh inning of the baseball game at Fenway Park yesterday two pickpockets also scored. C. D. Stevens of No. 298 Boston Avenue, Everett, is an enthusiastic fan. When Yerkes crossed the plate Stevens rose up with other fans and howled. Someone—and Stevens wishes he could lay hands on him—also rose up but made no 'holler.' Instead he deftly slipped a hand into Stevens' pocket and extracted therefrom a black leather pocketbook. The pocketbook contained $65 in bills and a contract which Stevens had executed. Stevens reported the loss to the police. Hardly had Stevens reported his loss when Charles H. Cobb of No. 219 M Street, South Boston, another fan, brought in a story of having his pocket picked at the same time Stevens' was. His purse contained $40." The losses of Stevens and Cobb enriched others.

The formal opening of Fenway Park was held on May 17. In this photograph, Harry Hooper slides into third base and White Sox third baseman Harry Lord. Umpire Silk O'Loughlin makes the call.

The play on the field was well-covered in detail, but there was remarkably little coverage of the kind of atmosphere and color which would provide us today with a better understanding of what it was truly like to have been there on Opening Day 1912. The *Boston Record*'s sum comment: "And some baseball park, eh?" It's as though they were writing for others who had already experienced a game at Fenway, but the City of Boston alone had a population of 670,585 at the time of the 1910 census, not to mention the many other communities throughout Greater Boston and vicinity.

The game was a thriller, decided in the bottom of the 11th by what is now called a walkoff hit. Down 3-0 before their first time at bat, and losing 5-1 after the third inning, the Red Sox inched close in the fourth, then tied it in the sixth—only to see New York take a 6-5 lead in the eighth. But Boston scored one of their own to re-tie the score in the bottom of the eighth, and then won it, 7-6, in the 11th. Steve Yerkes had five hits, his last one high off the embankment in left which became known in time as "Duffy's Cliff."[7] One paper wrote that "the Boston team has seldom before given such an exhibition of bulldog tenacity and fight."[8]

By the time the regular season was over, Boston was in first place (105-47) and New York finished last (50-102), 55 games behind Boston in the American League standings. The Red Sox played one of the other New York teams, the Giants, in the World Series. And the final game of the World Series gave Boston a bookend to the season with another extra-inning win at Fenway Park.

The Red Sox of 1912 were the first in a series of successful teams which went on to win the World Series in 1915, 1916, and 1918 as well. It was the golden era of Red Sox baseball.

Life in Boston on Opening Day

As difficult as it is for some of us to believe, not everything centered around baseball on the date Fenway Park opened. For those who lived in the area, there were many other options as to how to spend the day. With a 3:00 PM start time, and given that only a very rare game would run as long as two hours, it would be possible to envision taking in the game, enjoying dinner in town, and then going to the theater. As it happened, the game ran about three hours and ten minutes and, the *Boston American* said, "Nearly all…went without dinner to see the finish. They went home satisfied." But of course most people in Boston didn't go to the game at all.

Some just went shopping. The Ginter Co with stores on Summer Street and Washington Street offered a dozen eggs for 24 cents, coffee for 28 cents a pound and butter for 33 cents per pound, with pork for 12 cents a pound, and a pound jar of raspberry or strawberry jam for 15 cents. The same 15 cents would also get you five pounds of flour or four bars of Ivory soap. A can of tomatoes was 11 cents and a can of corn cost 9 cents. Most wines and liquors were on sale for 89 cents—a quart of imported Jamaican rum, Scotch from England, or brandy from France. Champagne, sherry, port—they all cost 89 cents. Duffy's Pure Malt Whiskey was on sale for 75 cents a bottle; it was advertised as beneficial to health, happiness, vigor, and long life: "There can be no question of the merit of a remedy that has been tested as proven…due to its great curative qualities." A baby carriage could be bought at Osgood's furniture store for $10.95 (with free delivery), as could a refrigerator for $12.25, a porch rocker for $1.45, a three-piece parlor suite for $21.75, or a Victor Victrola hornless phonograph for $19.50 (with six Victor records of the customer's choice).

One could combine shopping and a future ballgame by purchasing a suit at American Tailors on Washington Street. One reserved grandstand seat was free with each suit ordered any day before 1:00 PM. The Union Hat Co offered flannels shirts for $2.00, khaki pants for $1.50, 50 cents for leather belts or braces or ribbed underwear. Silk neckwear or "garters, best makes" were just 25 cents each.

There were choices to be made, and some simply preferred the theater to baseball. They had a wide variety of options. The Plymouth Theatre on Eliot Street declared of its show: "Not since the Britishers' tea was dumped in Boston Harbor has anything caused such a stir and talk as H. B. Warner in *Alias Jimmy Valentine*." The Colonial Theatre had Donald Brian in "the greatest of all musical comedies," *The Siren*, which was in its "fifth whirlwind week of song, dance, and fun." The Gaiety had a two-act musical burlesque called *The Winning Widow*, complete

Numerous theatrical enterprises vied for entertainment dollars.
Boston Globe, April 20, 1912.

with "a chorus of 30 girlie girls."

The Hollis Street Theatre had a 2:00 PM matinee and an 8:00 PM evening show with Miss Billie Burke in the final two performances of *The Runaway*. Hattie Williams was at The Park, in the farce with music entitled *The Girl from Montmartre*. The Shubert had an Arabian Nights-themed production, *Sumurun*. A French vaudeville translated into English was at the Tremont Theatre: *Alma, Where Do You Live?* There was also a matinee at the Majestic featuring Lew Dockstader and His Great Minstrels. B.F. Keith's Theatre offered an all-star aggregation with the comedy *Waiting at the Church*, Eddie Leonard the famous minstrel, a number of other entertainers, and Francesca's Pony Circus.

Beginning on Sunday night was Lew Fields' All Star Company in a production of *Hanky Panky*, which promised "15 sensational scintillating stars, 1000 laughs, and 50 sirenic girlies." The show also promised patrons the opportunity to "see the university campus scene" and would present "bewildering Broadway beauties," the "Rah Rah Boys," and "the Chorus Girls." Waldron's Casino on Hanover Street featured *Taxi Girls* burlesque.

There was dancing every evening with Poole's Ballroom at Revere Beach's Nautical Ballroom. The Boston Symphony Orchestra, conducted by Max Fiedler, featured the soloist Sylvain Noach. The Boston Opera House had *Mignon*. There were motion pictures as well, though there were not that many cinemas in the city. The Tremont Temple was showing *Homer's Odyssey*.

Some citizens just settled for dinner. The Boston Tavern on Washington Street offered a 50-cent special that day. Patrons in the tavern's booths could dine on broiled live lobster and French fried potatoes served with a "stein of musty." One could go all out for 75 cents, enjoying the table d'hote at Quincy House in Brattle Square. There was "special music" on Saturday and Sunday in the afternoons and evenings. It was an elaborate meal: little neck clams, bluepoints on deep shell, consommé a la royale, chicken broth au rice, broiled Savannah shad, Saratoga potatoes, sweet mixed pickles, tomatoes, roast ribs of beef, roast turkey, cranberry sauce, Hubbard squash, string beans, boiled rice, mashed potatoes, Roman punch, lobster a la Newburg, strawberry fritters, lettuce salad, baked Indian pudding, strawberry soufflé, frozen pudding, vanilla ice cream, assorted cake, pineapple cream pie, apple pie, toasted crackers, American and Roquefort cheese, and café noir, including a small bottle of sunset sauterne, sunset claret, lager, or ginger ale.

Of course, most Bostonians just ate at home. For those who did stay closer to home, there was the usual array of neighborhood events that afternoon and evening—women's groups, whist clubs, church socials, current events discussion groups, and the like.

During the day, or after supper, one could stay home and read. The best-selling book of the week in the non-fiction category was Maria Montessori's *The Montessori Method of Teaching*. Filling out the top five were *The New Democracy*, *George the Third and Charles Fox*, *Many Celebrities and a Few Others*, and *Manual of Gardening*. Atop the fiction list was *The Bandbox* by Louis Joseph Vance. That 1911 book was in no way related to author John Updike's 1960 characterization of Fenway Park as a "lyric little bandbox"—Fenway Park was indeed one of the larger parks of the day.[9] On Fenway Park's 100th anniversary, Vance's book is still available via free ebook download, a concept no doubt inconceivable to most in 1912.[10]

Many also enjoyed reading Saturday comic strips such as the *American*'s "Us Boys," "The Dingbat Family," "Desperate Desmond," and "Sherlocko the Monk."

There was nothing on TV that afternoon and there was nothing at all on the radio; likewise, not a single person in all of Greater Boston was browsing the Internet or playing video games online—not even solitaire.

The campaign for the Presidency was already on in earnest and one in a series of rallies for President

ca. 1907 School Street, Boston, 1907-1915.

Taft was held at Faneuil Hall at noon. Front page advertisements in most of the city's newspapers promised that "The True Issues of the Campaign Will Be Discussed." The rally was presided over by former Governor John D. Long. There were "only a few empty seats" according to the Saturday evening *Globe*.

Of note just three days after the opening of Fenway Park was the launch of girls baseball at Brookline High School. It had recently been decided that girls would be allowed to play baseball "strictly among themselves and not against the boys" and 20 young women were chosen from among the candidates, under the supervision of Marion Churchill of the high school faculty. Team 1 and Team 2 were to face off in the first competition, playing with long dresses that fell just three or so inches above ankle-length.

Later in the year, there was another big opening day—for the Boston Fish Pier. On November 4, the Boston Fish Pier was opened and the ground was broken for the two identical buildings that would be built on the pier. By 1926, the seafood retailers on the Boston Fish Pier constituted the world's largest fish market. The 1920s were not good years for the Red Sox.

Endnotes

1. *Boston Globe*, April 19, 1912.

2. *Boston Globe*, April 20, 1912.

3. *Ibidem*

4. We have no way today of knowing how many Orthodox Jews may have attended Opening Day had it been on a day other than the Sabbath, but we do know that professional baseball in Boston held an appeal to a diverse spectrum of Boston society. See Roger Abrams' book *The First World Series and the Baseball Fanatics of 1903* (Boston: Northeastern University Press, 2003).

5. *Boston Globe*, May 18, 1812. Ban Johnson, Charles Comiskey, Ed Barrow, and songwriter George M. Cohan were among the notables in attendance.

6. *Boston Traveler*, April 20, 1912.

7. See the sports page cartoon by Wallace Goldsmith in the April 21 *Boston Globe*.

8. *Boston Post*, April 21, 1912.

9. The book is described thus on the site www.manybooks.net: "The tale bristles with breathless adventure, mistaken identities, detective investigations, romantic developments, and startling situations… It is a rousing story, told with a stimulating style, and culminating in love rewarded; but, before that happy end is reached, there are many thrilling revelations."

10. Interestingly, one of the characters in *The Bandbox* was Arbuthnot Ismay—not the most common surname, but coincidentally that of J. Bruce Ismay, chairman of the White Star Line, the steamship company which owned the *Titanic*. Ismay was, controversially, one of the survivors who had to bear allegations that he had used his privileged position to save his own life while those traveling in third class had been treated unfairly in the matter of filling the lifeboats. A commission appointed to interview survivors reported no wrongdoing and produced testimony from many that he had remained "aboard the stricken vessel until no women or children were visible on deck. Several women testified he had helped them." (Ismay obituary, *New York Times*, October 19, 1937)

Advertisement for the ballgame tucked in column three on page 16 of the April 20 *Boston Globe*.

The First Game at Fenway Park
By Bill Nowlin

There had been an exhibition game played against Harvard on April 9, but the first regular-season game ever played at Fenway Park took place on April 20, 1912. The Boston Red Sox hosted the New York Highlanders (sometimes already being called the Yankees). They'd already opened the season facing each other, at New York's home in the Polo Grounds, and Boston had swept the three-game series by scores of 5-3, 5-2, and 8-4. The Red Sox had traveled to Philadelphia and lost 4-1, then won 9-2. Their record was thus 4-1 when they hosted New York. The Highlanders had fared poorly, dropping those first three games to the Red Sox, then losing a close 1-0 game to the visiting Washington Nationals and a 9-1 blowout to Washington as well. The Highlanders were thus 0-5 on the season under new manager Harry Wolverton and were anxious to get into the win column.

The year before New York had been 76-76 (with one tie, too) under manager Hal Chase and finished in sixth place. The Red Sox had been in fourth place, 78-75. Clearly, there wasn't much room separating the two teams in 1911. New York had never finished in first place, though they had finished second three times in the first 11 years of the American League: in 1904 (just 1½ games behind first-place Boston), once in 1906 (three games behind the White Sox; last-place Boston finished 45½ games behind Chicago), and once in 1910 (though it was 14½ games behind the Philadelphia Athletics (Boston finished fourth, 35 games off the pace).

For the opener at Fenway Park, Red Sox manager Jake Stahl started Buck O'Brien, and Harry Wolverton countered with Ray Caldwell. The first pitch was thrown at 3:00 P.M. sharp. O'Brien was 19 days shy of his 30th birthday. He'd appeared in only six major-league games, debuting on September 9, 1911—and was 5-1 in those games with a stunning 0.38 earned-run average. Caldwell would turn 24 six days after this game; he'd been 1-0 in 1910 and 14-14 in 1911, with a 3.35 ERA.

The weather was chilly, but the *Globe* said, "The day was ideal." The 3:00 P.M. temperature was 60 degrees, dropping to 55 at 6:00 P.M. The cool conditions may have depressed the performance of both starters, and the field was "soft and slippery" (*Boston Post*) due to the rain that had caused two days of postponements. It was a little lumpy in places, not as hard a playing surface as one would have liked. There was a ground rule in effect: Because of the overflow crowd, a couple of thousand fans were standing in the outfield (all three fields, arranged in a semicircle) and held behind ropes, it was mutually agreed that any ball hit over the ropes would be a double.

The first inning

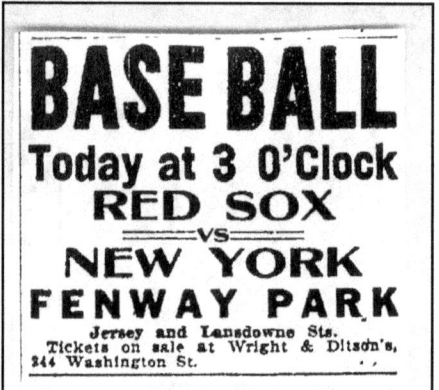

New York's leadoff batter, the left fielder Guy Zinn, had seen action in only six games before the 1912 campaign. Zinn batted left-handed. He'd batted .148 in his 27 at-bats in 1911. O'Brien walked him. Harry Wolter, playing right field, sacrificed Zinn to second and reached first base safely when both Boston first baseman (and manager) Jake Stahl and O'Brien tried to field the ball. Stahl fumbled with it while O'Brien ran to cover the bag "rather lamely" (*Post*). The *American* said it was O'Brien who fumbled the ball, and that a play could have still been made "if anybody had happened to think of first base." Hal Chase bunted to Larry Gardner, drawing him in from third base; Gardner threw Chase out at first but there were now runners on second and third with just one out. The shortstop Roy Hartzell, like first baseman Chase, had enjoyed a very good year in 1911. He singled to left field, scoring Zinn, and the Highlanders had scored the first run at Fenway Park. Wolter wisely held at third base. Bert Daniels, the center fielder, hit one right back to O'Brien, and he was out dead to rights. The pitcher could have run right at Wolter and tagged him out, but instead held the ball for a moment and then hurried his throw home. It bounced in the dirt in front of the plate and bounced into the air. Wolter scored and it was 2-0 New York. Daniels took third base and Hartzell moved up a base, too, but went a little past second and Boston catcher Les Nunamaker snapped a

quick throw to Heinie Wagner, who tagged Hartzell out before he could scramble back to the bag. O'Brien then beaned the third baseman, Cozy Dolan, at the base of his brain. New York had its own Gardner, named Earle. Gardner singled to center and drove in Daniels. Gabby Street, the catcher, then struck out. Before the Red Sox came to bat, New York held a 3-0 lead. **3-0, New York.**

Leading off for the Red Sox was Harry Hooper, who grounded one to Caldwell for an easy out. Second baseman Steve Yerkes doubled to the embankment in left field—a ball that might have gone for more than two bases had the ground rule not been in effect. Tris Speaker followed with another double, this one hit into the crowd in center field. Speaker's might even have gone for an inside-the-park home run, but the ground rule made it a two-base hit. Still, the Red Sox were on the board. Jake Stahl hit a half-hearted fly ball that shortstop Hartzell caught for the second out, and Larry Gardner hit a routine fly ball to left field. **3-1, New York.**

The second inning

O'Brien took the mound again, and faced his counterpart, Caldwell, who grounded to Yerkes at second, but Yerkes messed up and the New York pitcher reached base safely. It was back to the top of the order, and Zinn flied out to Hooper in right field. O'Brien whiffed Wolter and then got Chase to fly out to Speaker in center. **3-1, New York.**

In the bottom of the second, it was 1-2-3, with Duffy Lewis, Heinie Wagner, and Les Nunamaker all quietly retired. **3-1, New York.**

The third inning

It was not quite déjà-vu, but for the second inning in succession, New York's leadoff batter hit to Yerkes at second and Yerkes committed an error—this time a wide throw to first base. The batter, Hartzell, had to hold at first—but advanced to second a minute or two later when O'Brien dropped the ball while he was preparing to pitch. It was the first balk committed in Fenway Park. Umpire-in-chief Tom Connolly was having himself a busy day. Connolly, as it happened, had also umpired the first home game at the Huntington Avenue Grounds, back in 1901. The umpire working the bases in 1912 was Bill Hart. Daniels struck out but Dolan singled to Hooper in right. Hartzell scored, and Dolan scooted to second base on Hooper's throw to the plate. Earle Gardner's popup to short was the second out. O'Brien then threw a wild pitch and Dolan moved up another base. Street took a base on balls and then Caldwell singled, driving in Dolan. Zinn flied out to left field. Two more runs had scored. **5-1, New York.**

The Red Sox went down easily enough, despite Yerkes' two-out single and another single by Speaker. Stahl skied one to Daniels in center field. **5-1, New York.**

The fourth inning

Wolter struck out leading off the fourth. Then O'Brien hit Hal Chase on the left arm. O'Brien had him picked off first ("Hal fell flat on his face," wrote the *American*) but Stahl couldn't handle the throw and Chase got back on his feet and back on the first-base bag. Hartzell lifted a fly ball to Yerkes at second base. O'Brien walked Daniels. With men on first and second, Chase danced off second base enough to draw a throw from Nunamaker while he ran to third, taking the base. Daniels stole second and O'Brien walked Dolan to load the bases. Only sheer luck saved O'Brien from more damage. Earle Gardner was at the plate and another wildly-pitched ball sailed too close to him. Had he ducked without incident, the ball would very likely have escaped Les Nunamaker and at least one run would have scored, perhaps a pair. But when Gardner spun away to avoid getting hit, the ball struck his bat and rolled down the line to Stahl, who snapped it up and stepped on first base to retire the side. **5-1, New York.**

This game was not going well for the home team, with O'Brien struggling mightily and only the freak ending of the top of the fourth keeping any hopes alive. Larry Gardner singled to right field, Duffy Lewis walked, and Wagner's ground ball to third base handcuffed Dolan. The bases were loaded with Red Sox and nobody out. Nunamaker struck out. Buck O'Brien was due up and manager Stahl pulled him and sent up Olaf Henriksen to pinch hit. Henriksen walked, forcing in a run. New York then made a move of its own, bringing on Jack Quinn in relief of Caldwell. Hooper grounded to Gardner for a force out at second base and Lewis came in to score on the play. Then Yerkes singled, a Texas Leaguer behind third base, driving in Wagner. Speaker put the bat on the ball but it stayed in the infield and he was easily out at first base for the third out. But Boston had scored three runs and made a new game of it, and both teams had new pitchers. **5-4, New York.**

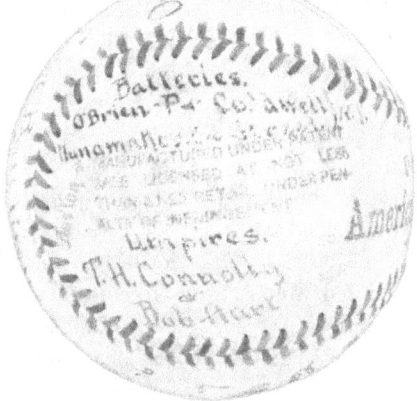

The fifth inning

Charley Hall was Boston's new man on the mound. He got Gabby Street to fly out to Lewis in left, and struck out Quinn. Zinn lifted a high fly to Larry Gardner at third base. **5-4, New York.**

After Stahl flied out to short, Larry Gardner was called out on a two-strike pitch that the *Globe* declared was "six inches inside the plate." Lewis singled and Wagner walked but Nunamaker struck out again. **5-4, New York.**

The sixth inning

After Hall retired Wolter, Chase reached first on another Red Sox error, this time Wagner's low throw to first base. After Hartzell reach first on a walk, he was cut down on a force play off Daniels' bat. But Daniels stole second, so New York had a man in scoring position. Hall induced Dolan to fly out to Speaker in center field. **5-4, New York.**

Charley Hall was up first in the bottom of the sixth and Quinn walked him. Hooper sacrificed him to second base. Yerkes singled again—his fourth hit of the game—and Hall took third base but held. An intentional walk to Tris Speaker loaded the bases. New York braced, hoping for a double play, and Stahl seemed to accommodate by hitting the ball right back to the pitcher but it was too hot to handle and glanced to Gardner at second base, who threw out Stahl but got only the one out as Hall crossed home plate with the tying run. There were runners on second and third and the Sox could have taken the lead, but Larry Gardner just hit a weaker and easier one back to Quinn, who threw him out. **5-5, tied.**

The seventh inning

It was a new ballgame. The seventh was largely uneventful. Hall retired the New Yorkers 1-2-3, and Quinn got the first two Red Sox batters, then hit Nunamaker, but got Hall to fly out to Daniels in center field. **5-5, tied.**

The eighth inning

Zinn hit a dribbler toward first base, which Stahl fielded and threw to Hall, who had covered first. Wolter walked and then stole second base as Nunamaker's peg flew into center field. Speaker always played a shallow center, and in this game had the crowd behind him, but any thought of trying to run on to third base that Wolter may have fleetingly had went by the wayside when he turned his ankle at second. Wolter had to be carried off the field and was replaced by pinch-runner Benny Kauff. After play resumed, Hall turned and threw to pick off Kauff but hit him with the ball, which skittered into center field and allowed Benny to scramble to third base. Hal Chase singled to left, giving New York a one-run lead, but tried in vain to stretch his hit to a double. Lewis threw and cut him down. Hartzell grounded out 4-3, to Yerkes. **6-5, New York.**

Daniels moved to right field in place of the injured Wolter and Kauff took over in center field. Hooper made the first out in the bottom of the eighth. Yerkes was up again, and he singled for his fourth hit of the game. Speaker flied out to Daniels, now in right. With two outs, Stahl doubled to center field and tied the game again, 6-6. Larry Gardner reached on a ball bobbled at short, and Lewis walked, which loaded the bases. Wagner hit a ball that went no farther than a bit in front of home plate, and Street took the easier play, throwing Wagner out at first. **6-6, tied.**

The ninth inning

After seeing their team down 3-0 and then 5-1, this had become quite a game for the fans, New York losing the lead twice because Boston had battled back. Defense came into play when Duffy Lewis snared a low line drive in left field. Then Hall collected consecutive assists on balls hit back to the box, by Dolan and then Gardner. **6-6, tied.**

Now it was sudden-death time, the bottom of the ninth. Nunamaker struck out for the third time. Charley Hall might then have won the game with a drive into center field over Kauff's head—but the ball landed in the crowd and therefore became a two-base hit. Harry Wolverton brought in a left-hander to take over for Quinn: Hippo Vaughn. Hooper walked, but the potential game-winner was still on first and now there was a force possibility and the double play might be easier. Yerkes was going for his fifth hit of the game, which might well have won it—but he fouled out to the catcher. Speaker drove a "fierce liner" which another "sensational" catch reeled in. Who gets credit for the catch? The *Globe* gave it to Zinn in left, while the *American* credited Daniels, now playing right field. There is just enough detail lacking in game accounts to be able to cross-foot the putouts and deduce the defender. The *Globe*'s account was generally much more detailed and more comprehensive, so Zinn might have been the man. The *New York Times* was no help at all, since that paper had someone named Carr playing right field—even though he was neither in their own box score nor on the team roster at any point in the season. **6-6, tied.**

The tenth inning

Street singled to start off the tenth but Vaughn hit into a force play. Zinn flied out to Harry Hooper in right and Kauff grounded out. **6-6, tied.**

After Stahl lifted a high fly ball to right field for the first out, Larry Gardner singled. Duffy Lewis tried to at least help him advance on the basepaths but struck out. Wagner singled, and Gardner went first to third. Rather than risk seeing Nunamaker strike out for a fourth time (the only time he'd gotten on base was when he was hit by a pitch), Stahl had Hack Engle pinch-hit. Engle hit an infield grounder and was thrown out at first. **6-6, tied.**

The 11th inning

Bill Carrigan crouched behind home plate, now catching for Boston since Nunamaker had been replaced. The skies were darkening and it was almost a foregone conclusion that the 11th would be the last inning, even if the game should end in a tie. Hal Chase singled to start. Hartzell's hit to Yerkes at second went for a fielder's choice, with Chase out and Hartzell on first base.

Daniels hit sharply to Yerkes, who misplayed the ball. Dolan hit a ball in front of the plate and Carrigan grabbed it and threw to Stahl, in time to put out Dolan. Earle Gardner walked, loading the bases. But Street hit a ball to Wagner, who stepped on second for the force out of Gardner which retired the side. At least that's what we think happened. Every newspaper had a different account, the *Globe* forgetting to mention Dolan, the *Times* having Speaker making a "great fly catch" and neither the *Herald* nor the *Post* attempted to detail the play-by-play. We're pretty much going with the *Boston American*'s telling. One thing was not in doubt. The Highlanders had failed to score. **6-6, tied.**

Charley Hall wasn't a particularly good-hitting pitcher, and it's unknown why he was allowed to bat for himself with there being little chance of a 12th inning being played. Perhaps it was because he hit left-handed; the only three batters on the bench (Bradley, Cady, and Krug) were all right-handed hitters. But pitcher Hippo Vaughn was left-handed. Maybe Stahl just figured to go with someone who was already active in the game—and Hall had struck that long double in the ninth. Hall struck out. Hooper popped up foul to the catcher. Two outs, nobody on, but here came Yerkes again. He had committed three errors on defense, but he had the hot bat. He hit a groundball to Dolan at third base. Dolan bobbled it, hurried his throw to Chase at first and threw it over his head, Yerkes racing on to claim second base. A passed ball let him move up to third base. Vaughn faced Speaker, and after him it would be Stahl. The count went to 3-and-2 and the *Globe* felt that Vaughn had decided to intentionally walk Speaker and take his chances with Stahl, but at the last moment "tried to sneak one over." Speaker was ready. He slashed the ball for a single and Yerkes scored the winning run. Where the ball was actually hit is uncertain. The *Times* said it went to center field, the *American* illogically said it was hit so hard at Dolan that Yerkes scored before Chase received the throw, while the other papers all pretty much said it was punched past the shortstop Hartzell. We'll go with that. It produced the first lead the Red Sox had in the game, and was the run that won the game. **7-6, Boston.**

Boston had committed seven errors and New York three. Six errors for the Red Sox, wrote the *Herald* and the *American*. No one disagreed on the final score.

Fenway Park Firsts

Here are a number of Fenway Park firsts, most of which occurred in 1912. All occurred in the Opening Day game, except as noted.

- First regular season game: April 20, 1912. (Boston Red Sox 7, New York Yankees 6—in 11 innings).

- Starting pitchers: Buck O'Brien (Boston) and Ray Caldwell (New York).

- Managers: Jake Stahl (Boston) and Harry Wolverton (New York).

- First pitch: thrown by Boston pitcher Buck O'Brien.

- First base on balls issued by Boston pitching: Buck O'Brien to leadoff batter Guy Zinn, in the top of the first inning.

- First Red Sox error: first baseman Jake Stahl, misplaying a bunt by New York's second batter.

- First out recorded: New York's Hal Chase hit a sacrifice bunt, 5-3, moving up two runners.

- First hit: Roy Hartzell singled in the first, driving in Zinn.

- First run scored off Boston pitching: Zinn's run, on Hartzell's single.

- First strikeout: Gabby Street, final batter in New York's first.

- First Boston batter: Harry Hooper, who grounded back to Caldwell on the mound, out 1-3.

- First Boston hit: second man up in the first inning, Steve Yerkes doubled to the incline in left field, soon known as Duffy's Cliff.

- First Red Sox run scored: Yerkes, scoring on Speaker's subsequent double.

- First Red Sox RBI: Tris Speaker doubled into the crowd, driving in Yerkes.

- First Boston sacrifice: Harry Hooper, in the sixth inning.

- First double: Yerkes (see above, Opening Day).

- First triple: April 25, a first-inning triple by Tris Speaker.

- First home run: Hugh Bradley, on April 26, 1912—a three-run homer over the Wall in left in the seventh inning off Lefty Russell. It was the only home run of the year for the .190 hitter.

- First hit by a Boston pitcher: a ninth-inning double into the crowd by Charley Hall.

- First extra-base hit by a Boston pitcher: Charley Hall's double.

- First balk by a Red Sox pitcher: O'Brien, in the third inning.

- First wild pitch by a Boston pitcher: O'Brien in the fourth.

- First Red Sox pitcher to hit an opposing batter: O'Brien (Cozy Dolan).

- First double play by Boston: third inning of April 26 game, McInnis hit a ball off Cicotte's fingers, which became a 1-4-6-3 doubleplay.

- First Boston stolen base: Tris Speaker on April 23.

- First Boston catcher to throw out a baserunner: Les Nunamaker picked Hartzell off second base in the first inning.

- First bases loaded walk earned by a Red Sox batter: Olaf Henriksen.

- First intentional walk drawn by a Red Sox batter: Tris Speaker in the bottom of the sixth.

- First relief pitcher in a game: Charley Hall.

- First win for a Red Sox pitcher: Charley Hall.

- First shutout by a Red Sox pitcher at Fenway Park: Smoky Joe Wood, on May 20, 1912.

- First ceremonial first pitch: Mayor John F. Fitzgerald.

- Umpires for the first home game: Tom Connolly and Eugene "Bob" Hart. Connolly also umpired the first game at the Huntington Avenue Grounds.

- First Sunday home game: July 3, 1932. Yankees win, 13-2.

- First night game: June 13, 1947. Red Sox 5, White Sox 3.

- First ceremonial pitch: Mayor John F. Fitzgerald, April 20, 1912.

When Was the First Time Fans Booed the Red Sox at Fenway Park?

Wait a minute! Why would you want to know that? That's not nice. You may be thinking that it probably didn't happen in Fenway's first season—1912, since the team was in the running all year long and held first place from June 10 to the end of the season, when they finished 14 games ahead of even second-place Washington. Only for one day had the Sox sunk as low as third place and that was on May 4, in Washington. In fact, it didn't take long at all—the team drew the equivalent of boos even before they got up to bat!

There were indeed public displays of dissatisfaction from almost the very beginning. The team played its first-ever game at Fenway on April 20, 1912 and there were ample opportunities for disapprobation. They were playing New York and Sox starter Buck O'Brien gave up three runs in the top of the first, and two more in the third.

There were errors—the first game the team ever played featured seven (!) Red Sox errors, a balk, a wild pitch, and O'Brien hit one of the Highlanders.

The game got off to a poor start, O'Brien walking the first batter, leadoff man Guy Zinn. The second batter up (Wolter) sacrificed Zinn to second—but first baseman (and manager) Jake Stahl fumbled the ball for error #1 and both runners were safe. This wasn't an inspiring start to the season, nor the way fans wanted to see the new ballpark broken in. Hal Chase bunted to third base and advanced both runners. A single scored Zinn. New York's fifth man up hit the ball back to O'Brien on the mound, but Buck picked up an error of his own throwing wildly toward home plate. It was 2-0, New York.

Catcher Les Nunamaker gave fans a moment to savor when he fired a strike from behind the plate and picked Wolter off second base, but then O'Brien hit the batter and gave up a single to the next batter, giving New York a 3-0 lead before the Red Sox even came up to bat.

It may not have been a "boo" but after Cozy Dolan was hit by the pitch in this ragged top of the first, the *Boston Globe*'s veteran scribe Tim Murnane offered the observation that "the 'Take him out' man grew red in the face from his exertions."

O'Brien was indeed taken out after the fourth inning, with the Sox down, 5-1. Say this for them, though: Boston battled throughout the game, and had tied it in the sixth. They lost the lead, but promptly recovered it in the eighth, and saw it go into extra innings, winning in the bottom of the 11th inning, 7-6. It wasn't the prettiest of games, but the "Take him out" man may have gone home at least mollified and perhaps a little pleased.

The *New York Times* noted that at 3:10, the game was quite a long one by the standards of the day and that everyone was ready to go home by the time it ended, "every one was in too much of a hurry to get home to cheer the victory." That's sort of sad.

But it hadn't taken long for Red Sox fans to start in on the players. Admittedly, they brought it on themselves. O'Brien bore the brunt of the early complaints for his poor work on the mound, but the *Times* added that "The local players did a great deal of muffing and fumbling, and threw wildly every time there was a chance, Capt. Stahl being repeatedly jeered by the crowd for his failures to hold thrown balls."

It went in the books as a win, though, and after the last game of the year, the Red Sox were world champions.

Neal Ball

By John McMurray

G	AB	R	H	2B	3B	HR	RBI	BB	SO	BA	OBP	SLG	SB	HBP
18	45	10	9	2	0	0	6	3	4	.200	.250	.244	5	0

After the Red Sox purchased his contract in the middle of the season, Neal Ball played in only 18 regular-season games for Boston in 1912, collecting nine hits. To the baseball world, Ball is better remembered for a defensive play he made against Boston three years earlier while playing shortstop for the Cleveland Naps: the first unassisted triple play in major-league baseball history.

In the first game of a doubleheader played at Cleveland's League Park on July 19, 1909, Boston's Heinie Wagner singled to lead off the second inning against Cleveland starting pitcher Cy Young, who was pitching in his first season for the Naps after playing for eight years with the Red Sox. Jake Stahl moved Wagner to second base with a bunt single. On a hit-and-run play, the next batter, Amby McConnell, lined a 3-2 pitch up the middle. Ball leaped to catch it, forced Wagner at second base, and then tagged Stahl to record the third out.

"I thought I could spear it and had visions of a double play," said Ball. "I reached into the air and came down with the ball. By this time, Wagner was on third and Stahl was only a few feet from second. I ran over and touched second for the second out. Stahl was slowing up and reversed his tracks toward first, but I overtook him and tagged him out to complete the triple play."[1]

Ball recounted details of his unassisted triple play more modestly during an interview in 1948 at his home in Bridgeport, Connecticut. "Nobody has asked me to tell it in thirty years, I guess," Ball said, "but you ought to know I wouldn't forget how in a hundred."[2]

After McConnell hit the ball, Ball recalled, "I didn't think there was a chance of getting it but I was on the move toward second and I gave it a try anyhow. It was dead over the bag by then so I jumped and the darned thing hit my glove and stuck. The rest was easy. Wagner was way around third base somewhere and when I came down on the bag he was out. I just stood there with my hands out and Stahl ran into them. He was halfway down when the ball was hit and couldn't stop. That's all there was to it. I can still remember how surprised I was when the ball hit in my glove."[3]

Ball's great-niece, Kathia Miller, writing in 2009 on the 100th anniversary of the unassisted triple play, said that the 11,000 people at the game gave Ball "a great ovation" and that removing all of the hats that had been thrown on the field in appreciation delayed the game by 20 minutes. She said Ball was so unassuming that after making the play he merely put his

Neal Ball in Red Sox pinstripes.

glove down and returned to the dugout, leading Cy Young to ask: "Where are you going, Neal?" To which Ball succinctly replied: "That's three outs."[4]

A little-noted postscript to Ball's feat: In the bottom half of the inning he led off for Cleveland and he hit his first major-league home run (and his only home run of the season) on the first pitch he saw from hurler Charlie Chech. The sportswriter who interviewed him in 1948 noted, "...Home runs were rare enough in those days, but this one was, in its way, as remarkable as Ball's play in the field and possibly as rare. For he hit the ball over the head of Tris Speaker in center field and ran all the way home while the great man chased it. Such a thing simply was not done. Ball is no longer the only man ever to make a triple play unassisted, but he is likely to remain forever the only one to make a triple play and a home run in the same inning. The feat was so notable that Ban Johnson, president of the league, had a medal struck and presented to Ball in commemoration."⁵ Speaker, of course, was known for playing a very shallow center field, which certainly contributed to his setting the record for unassisted double plays by an outfielder, and which probably contributed to Ball's big hit.

Batting eighth in the lineup, Ball also had a double later in the game. The next day he posed for a photograph along with McConnell, Wagner, and Stahl commemorating the historic play.

Ball is almost universally credited with having the first unassisted triple play in major-league history, as an unassisted triple play originally credited to Paul Hines with Providence in 1878 has been disputed. According to an article published in *The Sporting News* on July 29, 1909, Hines claimed that he had made a triple play unassisted, but "the files of a Providence newspaper state that one of his teammates got the third out."⁶

Largely due to the persistence of amateur historian Jules J. Bues, a close friend of Ball, the glove that Ball used to make the triple play was presented to the Baseball Hall of Fame in 1952. It was put on permanent display there on March 16, 1953. On March 7, 1955, the jersey Ball was wearing when he made the triple play was added to the display. Bues' persistence even led to Ball's feat being commemorated in photographs at the Baseball Hall of Fame in Tokyo.

Cornelius Ball, Jr. was born on April 22, 1881, in Grand Haven, Michigan. (One account lists his birthdate as September 11, 1883.)⁷ He was the second son of Cornelius Ball, an immigrant from the Netherlands, and Wilhelmina Mieras. The two had nine children. Neal was the fifth. Thinking that he would never have a son, Cornelius Ball named his third daughter Cornelia, after himself. Then the Balls went on to have four boys, including Neal.⁸

Miller, his great-niece, said all four boys were "excellent baseball players" but that Neal was the only one of the four who would play baseball on Sunday, refusing to adhere to the Dutch Reform Church's mandate not to do any work on Sundays. He learned to play baseball while growing up in Kalamazoo, Michigan. While he was initially pursued by the Detroit Tigers in 1902, Neal signed for more money with the Toledo Mud Hens of the American Association, where he was assigned the locker once used by John McGraw.⁹

Ball began his professional career as a shortstop for Toledo in 1903 before moving to Cedar Rapids of the Three-I League later in the season. During the next two seasons with Grand Rapids, he also played some at second base.

Ball almost played for Atlanta in 1906. He was in a competition there for the shortstop job with Lou Castro, and, according to one account, "Castro kidded Ball out of the Atlanta job." As manager Bill Smith tried to decide between the two players, Castro would tease Ball with comments like: "I've got this job clinched. Now watch me scoop this one. See that peg? What chance you got? Better go back to the bushes." Castro's chiding apparently got the best of Ball, who came to believe that Castro really was the better player. "Of course, Neal's playing dropped off when he got into that frame of mind, and any manager would have chosen the peppery Castro."¹⁰ Ball was back with Cedar Rapids in 1906.

In 1907 Ball moved to Montgomery of the Southern League, where there was no one else competing for the shortstop position. There, "Ball came into his own and soon was the sensation of the league, discussion being rife all over the circuit as to whether he or Nicholls, of Memphis, was the best shortstop."¹¹ According to Kathia Miller, Ball stole 55 bases in the first 50 games of that

Clyde Engle and Neal Ball, 1913.

year.[12] Near the end of the season his contract was sold to the New York Highlanders, and he made his major-league debut on September 12, 1907.

Ball, who was 5-feet-7 and weighed 145 pounds, played in only 15 games for the 1907 Highlanders. The right-handed batter hit one double and one triple while batting .205. Most often, he played behind Kid Elberfeld at shortstop, though Ball did play in five games at second base.

With Elberfeld injured for much of the 1908 season, Ball became a regular at shortstop, playing in 130 games there. Although he had a productive year at the plate, getting 110 hits, knocking in 38 runs, and stealing 32 bases, his defense was abysmal; he made 80 errors,

Elberfeld returned, and on May 18, 1909, Ball was sold to the Cleveland Indians, where he became the regular shortstop, setting the stage for his unassisted triple play two months later. Generally, though, his defense remained a sore point, as Ball committed 46 errors in 96 games in 1909. Terry Turner often took over at shortstop for Ball, leaving Ball to play as a utility infielder much of the time as he continued to struggle.

Still, Ball had his moments in Cleveland. In 1911 he enjoyed one of his best seasons at the plate, finishing with a .296 batting average and 21 stolen bases. He set a career high with 122 hits in 116 games for the Indians, who finished in third place in the American League with the help of Shoeless Joe Jackson, whose .408 batting average set a record for a rookie.

On June 25, 1912, the Naps sold Ball to the Red Sox for $2,500. Cleveland had Ray Chapman ready to take over at shortstop, and Roger Peckinpaugh also played there from time to time. With Heinie Wagner, one of the victims of his unassisted twin killing, as the regular shortstop with the Red Sox, Ball was limited to playing a utility role for the remainder of the season. In 18 games with Boston he collected 10 hits, including two doubles, while batting .200. A contemporary account said, "He has had but little work to do and has acquitted himself very creditably."[13]

Ball made one appearance in the 1912 World Series. He pinch-hit for starting pitcher Buck O'Brien in the eighth inning of the third game, and was struck out by Giants pitcher Rube Marquard. It was the only World Series appearance of his career.

Ball played in 23 games for the Red Sox in 1913, batting a career-low .172. With Wagner well established at shortstop, Ball was sold to the Baltimore Orioles of the International League, and never played in the major leagues again. He finished his seven-season major-league career with 404 hits, four home runs, 151 stolen bases, and a .250 batting average.

With the Orioles in 1914, Ball coached and became a teammate of young Babe Ruth, who had recently joined the team from St. Mary's Industrial School. Miller detailed an incident involving Ruth and Ball during spring training in 1914, when Ruth as a pitcher was learning hand signals from Ball, who was playing as a catcher. Ball apparently signaled for a "waste pitch," which Ruth delivered down the middle of the plate. The pitch was hit solidly by the batter, leading Ball to ask Ruth why he threw such a hittable pitch. "Well," said Ruth, "I threw it right by his waist."[14]

As Miller also recounted, Ball recalled that "Babe was the dumbest and the strongest player I had ever met. He had baseball sense. You'd only have to tell him something once." Ruth and Ball became friends, and Ruth came to Ball's home to get his approval to marry his first wife, Helen Woodford. Neal told Ruth: "Aw, go ahead; she seems like a nice gal."[15]

After Baltimore in 1914, Ball played with Richmond and Toronto in the International League as well as in Pittsfield, New Haven, and Springfield in the Eastern League. He managed the Bridgeport Hustlers of the Eastern League in 1916, led Augusta of the Sally League in 1922, and managed the New Haven Profs of the Eastern League in 1925.and the Pittsfield Hillies, also of the Eastern League, in 1926.[16]

In 1921 the 40-year-old Ball hit .300 as the regular second baseman for the New Haven Indians, managed by Chief Bender. In a game against the Waterbury Brasscos, the Waterbury pitcher, Jerry Kahn, had a no-hitter with two outs in the ninth inning. At that point, according to a 1951 account:

"Then, up strode Neal Ball, looking harmless enough after several discouraging experiences with Kahn's deceptive shoots. With the fans starting to file out of the park, Neal took a half-hearted swing and knocked one of those dime-a-dozen pop flies just inside the foul line that Phil Rizzuto could have caught in his hip pocket. Nine times out of ten, any Eastern League third baseman could have shut his eyes and pulled it out of the balmy June air.

"But this time, the third baseman thought it was the left fielder's or shortstop's ball and vice versa—and Jerry Kahn's no-hitter went a-glimmering in the gathering dusk. The saddest man in Mr. [George] Weiss' ball park that afternoon wasn't Jerry Kahn—a smiling kid who laughed it off and proceeded to get the next batter—but an old timer named Neal Ball who had played the game right up to the end, but, great sportsman that he was, hated to ruin a masterpiece." [17]

In somewhat of a surprise move, since many suspected that the job would go to Jack Flynn, Ball became president and manager of the Pittsfield Hillies of the Eastern League in 1926.[18] The Hillies finished in last place and Ball was fired before the end of the season. He joined the Springfield Hampdens, working as a coach and scout. A sportswriter described him as "always one of the best liked players in major league baseball." The sportswriter quoted New Haven team president George Weiss as saying, "I think Springfield is to be congratulated on obtaining a man of Ball's character as a coach and a scout."[19]

Ball retired to Bridgeport, Connecticut, after leaving baseball, with his second wife, Estelle. (His first wife, Maud, had died.) Estelle's father had moved there at around the same time that Ball was performing well in the minor leagues. Neal and Estelle had no children. [20]

In retirement Ball sold hats and also managed a bowling alley.[21] His baseball accomplishments were not forgotten, and in January 1951 he was honored by the Connecticut Sports Writers Alliance for his contributions to the sports scene in Connecticut. (Former major leaguer Red Rolfe was one of the other honorees.)[22]

More than two decades after he retired from baseball, *New York Herald Tribune* writer Al Laney described Ball's temperament: "At 64, Ball is still the same bouncy, nervous, friendly man he was in 1910. He has most of his hair and seemingly all of his old energy. He bounces out of his chair to get his scrapbooks, his old photographs and to show off the big fish he has mounted. He

Ball in 1913, his second season with the Sox.

leads the pleasantest sort of life, in which fishing seems to be the main activity. He knows all the good spots near Bridgeport and, once or twice a year, he takes long fishing trips, especially to Vermont."[23]

Ball remained interested in baseball in retirement, traveling to New York to see games from time to time. "He seems to have no complaint whatever against life," said Laney, "and the only thing he can think up is over the fact that the American League has denied him a lifetime pass. The National League, in which he never played, long ago gave him a pass, and he resents mildly the fact that he must pay his way into American League games."[24]

Ball died on October 15, 1957, at the age of 76 at his home in Bridgeport. A resident of Bridgeport for more than 40 years, he had been inactive and in failing health for some time. The official cause of death was listed as pulmonary edema. He was survived by his wife, Estelle (nee Beardslee); by his brothers John W. Ball of Pontiac, Michigan, and Jay of Kalamazoo, Michigan; and by his sisters, Mrs. William Schrier and Mrs. Minnie MacDonald, both of Kalamazoo. He is buried in Mountain Grove Cemetery, in Bridgeport.

Sources:

"Ball, Neal." No author, title, or date given. From Ball's file at the Baseball Hall of Fame.

"Ball, First to Make Unaided Triple Play in Majors, Dies: Former Infielder Was 76; Glove Used in Feat Now in Cooperstown Shrine." No publication given. October 15, 1957. From Ball's file at the Baseball Hall of Fame.

"Baseball Hall of Fame to Get Neal Ball Glove." No publication given. From Ball's file at the Baseball Hall of Fame.

Sam Cohen, "Ball's feat Hits 60th Anniversary, *Connecticut Sun Herald*, July 27, 1969.

"Connecticut Writers Honor 3," January 30, 1951. No publication given. From Ball's file at the Baseball Hall of Fame.

Walter Graham, "Neal Ball Will Coach Local Club This Year: Former Major League Player and Eastern League Manager Signed by Hampdens—Directors Vote for Most Valuable Player Award." No publication or date given. From Ball's file at the Baseball Hall of Fame.

Al Laney, "Stuck in His Glove: Cleveland Vet, at 64, Taking Life Easy at Bridgeport, Conn." *New York Herald Tribune*, February 11, 1948.

Kathia Miller e-mails to author, January 3-5, 2011.

Kathia Miller, "On the Ball for Historic Fielding Feat," *Cleveland Plain Dealer*, July 19, 2009.

Kathia Miller, "Guest Commentary: Unassisted Triple Play was One for the Record Books," *Naples* (Florida) *News*, July 20, 2009.

Neal Ball, Death Certificate.

"Neal Ball, 76, Dies in Home: Baseball Figure Made First Unassisted Triple Play in 1909." No publication or date given. From Ball's file at the Baseball Hall of Fame.

"Neal Ball Dies at 76," *New York Times*, October 15, 1957.

Dan Parker, "Neal Ball Gets Tardy Acclaim for Triple Play," No publication given, January 25, 1951. From Ball's file at the Baseball Hall of Fame.

"Player-Manager Assumes New Role," *Hartford Courant*, March 6, 1926.

"Substitute Infielder Ball," October 12, 1912, No publication given. From Ball's file at the Baseball Hall of Fame.

"Triple Play By Neal Ball: Naps' Shortstop Completes the Feature Unassisted." No publication given. July 19, 1909. From Ball's file at the Baseball Hall of Fame.

"Triple Play Hero Dies," *Bridgeport Post*, October 16, 1957.

Untitled article, October 1912. From Ball's file at the Baseball Hall of Fame.

Untitled article, *The Sporting News*, July 29, 1909. From Ball's file at the Baseball Hall of Fame.

Endnotes

1. "Ball, First to Make Unaided Triple Play in Majors, Dies: Former Infielder Was 76; Glove Used in Feat Now in Cooperstown Shrine." No publication given. October 15, 1957. From Ball's file at the Baseball Hall of Fame.

2. Al Laney, "Stuck in His Glove: Cleveland Vet, at 64, Taking Life Easy at Bridgeport, Conn." *New York Herald Tribune*, February 11, 1948.

3. *Ibid.* We recognize that Ball's two recollections of the triple play contradict each other; memories often do change over time.

   Kathia Miller observes: "Neal's two reports are contradictory: Did he overtake Stahl and tag him or did Stahl simply run into Neal's glove? The answer is probably that Neal grew more humble later on. Or perhaps his first account was told at first blush and modified on reflection. Neal always had a twinkle in his eye."

4. Kathia Miller, "Guest Commentary: Unassisted Triple Play was One for the Record Books," *Naples* (Florida) *News*, July 20, 2009.

5. Laney, *op. cit.*

6. Untitled article, *The Sporting News*, July 29, 1909. From Ball's file at the Baseball Hall of Fame.

7. "Substitute Infielder Ball," October 12, 1912. No publication given. From Ball's file at the Baseball Hall of Fame.

8. E-mail to author from Kathia Miller, January 3, 2011.

9. *Ibid.*

10. "Ball, Neal." No author, title, or date given. From Ball's file at the Baseball Hall of Fame.

11. *Ibid.*

12. E-mail to author from Kathia Miller, January 3, 2011.

13. Untitled article, October 1912. From Ball's file at the Baseball Hall of Fame.

14. Kathia Miller, *Naples News*, op. cit.

15. Kathia Miller, "On the Ball for Historic Fielding Feat," *Cleveland Plain Dealer*, July 19, 2009.

16. "Ball, First to Make Unaided Triple Play in Majors, Dies: Former Infielder Was 76; Glove Used in Feat Now in Cooperstown Shrine." No publication given. October 15, 1957. From Ball's file at the Baseball Hall of Fame.

17. Dan Parker, "Neal Ball Gets Tardy Acclaim for Triple Play," No publication given, January 25, 1951. From Ball's file at the Baseball Hall of Fame.

18. "Player-Manager Assumes New Role," *Hartford Courant*, March 6, 1926.

19. Walter Graham, "Neal Ball Will Coach Local Club This Year: Former Major League Player and Eastern League Manager Signed by Hampdens—Directors Vote for Most Valuable Player Award." No publication or date given. From Ball's file at the Baseball Hall of Fame.

20. Kathia Miller, *Naples News*, op. cit.

21. "Neal Ball Dies at 76," *New York Times*, October 15, 1957.

22. "Connecticut Writers Honor 3," January 30, 1951. No publication given. From Ball's file at the Baseball Hall of Fame.

23. Laney, *op. cit.*

24. *Ibid.*

Hugh Bedient
by Michael Foster and John Stahl

G	ERA	W	L	SV	GS	GF	CG	SHO	IP	H	R	ER	BB	SO	HR	HBP	WP	BFP
41	2.92	20	9	2	28	11	19	0	231	206	93	75	55	122	6	3	2	917

G	AB	R	H	2B	3B	HR	RBI	BB	SO	BA	OBP	SLG	SB	HBP
41	73	11	14	0	0	0	7	13	31	.192	.314	.192	0	0

"One feller I want to meet if he's still alive and can be found is that fellow Henriksen," remarked 72-year-old Hugh Bedient to *Jamestown Post-Journal* sportswriter Frank Hyde. It was March of 1962, and in four weeks' time Hugh was expected in Boston along with the other surviving members of the 1912 World Champions for the much-anticipated 50th-anniversary celebration of Boston's historic 1912 World Series victory over Christy Mathewson and the New York Giants. For Hugh, the reunion would give him the chance to pay off a debt long overdue. "Olaf is the one I remember best," he said. "I might have forgotten to thank him for that pinch-hit. So, I'll thank him when we go to Boston."[1]

Born on October 23, 1889, in Gerry, New York, Hugh Carpenter Bedient was the second child born to Orlon Bedient and Ellen Partridge Bedient.[2] According to the 1900 U.S. Census, Orlon and Ellen had two children: Emma, born in 1882, and Hugh. Ellen's mother, Ellenor Partridge, also lived with the family. Orlon worked at a nearby butter manufacturing facility.[3]

The 6-foot, 185-pound Bedient possessed a rare, somewhat contradictory personality. To the vivid recollection of his family, he was at the same time a "soft-spoken gentleman" and a "hard-nosed competitor." "Hugh was quiet, but he was just a great guy," recalled son-in-law Hermes Ames. "If he didn't like someone, he wouldn't say. He was just that kind of guy. In fact, I never heard him say anything bad about anybody—except Ty Cobb, who Hugh thought was awfully dirty."[4]

Bedient was smitten by baseball at an early age. Ellen once complained that her son was "crazy over that pesky game of baseball." In April 1905, he pitched his first game for Falconer High School, beating Jamestown Business College. During that same year, he pitched when Falconer beat archrival Jamestown for the first time in their history.

Beginning in 1905, Hugh began an annual sequence of pitching for his high school during the school year and then pitching for at least one semiprofessional team in the summer. Nearly every Saturday during the summer of 1905, he traveled to nearby Buffalo to pitch for the Buffalo Dry Docks. The 1905 Dry Docks caused a bit of a local stir by winning 26 games in a row. Hugh won 15 of these games, though he wasn't known as Hugh Bedient to the public. The *Grand Rapids Press* of November 9, 1912, said that a "pitcher from 'out of town' who became known as 'The Mysterious Murray,' would walk on the field in a Dry Dock suit, warm up, pitch—and win—his game, and slip away. None knew his identity." The following year one of the Buffalo City League teams played a game in Falconer, and the Mysterious Murray's true identity was revealed. In 1906, he won all 10 of his high-school games, striking out 160 batters. In

Hugh Bedient at White Sox Park II in 1912. The park's name changed to Comiskey Park (I) the following year.

1907, he helped the Dry Docks win Buffalo's 1907 City League Championship.

After high-school graduation in June of 1908, the right-hander pitched that summer for his local semipro team, the Falconer Independents. On July 25, his team played a club from Corry, Pennsylvania. This was a highly anticipated rematch between the two teams and drew enormous local interest. Tied at 1-1 after nine innings, the game continued on and on with Hugh piling up strikeouts along the way.

In the top of the 23rd inning, Falconer pushed across two runs on a wild throw. Likely running on adrenaline, Bedient promptly struck out all three Corry batsmen he faced in the bottom of the inning. In 23 innings, he had allowed just six hits, walked only one batter, and struck out a jaw-dropping 42 hitters.

The 42 strikeouts in one game gave Bedient national notoriety and precipitated no fewer than 19 offers from various clubs in organized ball. Bedient later called his 42-strikeout performance one of the greatest thrills in his baseball career.

In 1910, former major-league pitcher Jesse Burkett offered Bedient $180 per month to pitch for his Fall River, Massachusetts, team in the New England League. The pitcher had a successful season at Fall River, notching a 13-9 record. Subsequently reporting on his 1910 effort, *Baseball Magazine* characterized Bedient as the "mainstay" of the Fall River staff and predicted that "with the proper handling [he] should develop into a star." During the year, he came to the attention of Boston Red Sox owner John I. Taylor. Dismayed by the performance of his veteran pitchers in 1910, when Boston finished in fourth place, Taylor hoped to bring in some younger pitching talent. He invited Bedient to try out for the 1911 Red Sox during their spring training.

Unlike previous years, when the team traveled south to Hot Springs, Arkansas, for spring training, the 1911 Red Sox trained in Redondo Beach, California. The *Boston Globe* labeled the audacious plan to cross country for spring training "the great 8,000 mile $15,000 trip." Bedient saw only limited action in California. At the start of the regular season, the Red Sox sold him to the Eastern League's Providence Grays.

Obviously disappointed at not remaining in the major leagues, Hugh began his 1911 season slowly at Providence. Initially unimpressed, Providence quickly offered him back to Boston. After Boston declined the offer, Providence subsequently sold Hugh for $750 to Jersey City, another Eastern League team. Although he was now owned by Jersey City, the Jersey City team president worked out a deal with Providence that allowed Bedient to stay with the Grays until the end of 1911.[5]

Hugh's pitching finally began improving and he ended the season with an 8-11 record for the inept, last-place (54-98) club. By season's end, Bedient was once again dominating opponents, as illustrated by his late-September 7-1 victory over Newark when he struck out 11 without giving up any walks.[6] By the end of 1911, several Eastern League teams, having witnessed Bedient's significant late-season improvement, reportedly offered Jersey City $5,000 for the again-promising right-hander.

In early January 1912, Boston announced several major changes to its ownership and management structure, including a new team president, Jimmy McAleer, and a new player-manager-owner, Garland "Jake" Stahl.[7] One of the first things the new management did was review the status of all the players under contract with the Red Sox. As Boston was well-stocked with young position players and Smoky Joe Wood's 23 wins in 1911 had marked him as the ace of the 1912 Boston pitching staff, McAleer and Stahl focused their review on finding additional pitchers to augment the talented Wood. Much to their surprise, they noticed that Boston had let Bedient go. According to the *Boston Globe*, the Red Sox immediately sent Jersey City 10 players for Bedient. Calling him "high-priced," the *Globe* estimated the total value of the players sent to Jersey City at $10,000.

With a new $1,800-a-year Boston contract, Bedient began his rookie season in the major leagues as a reliever. His first appearance was on April 26 in an important early game against the defending champion Philadelphia Athletics. Relieving Eddie Cicotte in the sixth inning with the Red Sox trailing 6-3, Bedient held the Athletics scoreless the rest of the game. With the score 6-4, Boston first baseman Hugh Bradley hit a three-run homer in the seventh inning to win it, 7-6. This surprising turn of events visibly upset the Athletics. *Globe* baseball writer Tim Murnane wrote that he had "never saw and heard so much kicking by this Philadelphia team, which was simply broken up by Bradley's hit."[8]

On May 4, Bedient got his first opportunity to start a major-league game; he faced the Washington Senators. It was hardly auspicious, as Hugh lasted only two innings in an 8-7 loss.[9] Later in May, however, he pitched his first complete-game victory, leading Boston to another come-from-behind win, 4-3 over the 1911 champion Athletics. Bedient yielded just six hits, striking out three and walking three. The *Globe* characterized the Red Sox' effort as the "most brilliant game of the year."[10]

By early September, the Red Sox had all but run away with the American League pennant, and Bedient was hailed as one of the main reasons for the club's stunning success. The *Boston Post*, in a feature article about him, called Bedient "one of the most dependable" pitchers on the club, saying he had "been one of the big factors in Boston's wonderful success." The article characterized Bedient as "quiet and retiring by nature," noting that he had not even told his teammates when he married Imogene Palmer in nearby Brookline earlier in the season.[11]

Bedient finished the 1912 regular season with a 20-9 record in 231 innings, with a 2.92 ERA. He beat every AL team at least once, doing the most damage against Philadelphia (five wins) and St. Louis (four wins).[12] While there was no Rookie of the Year Award in 1912, the Society for American Baseball Research retrospectively voted him the American League Rookie of the Year for 1912.

The 1912 World Series featured the Red Sox against John McGraw's New York Giants. Bedient made his World Series debut in Game Two. As the game entered the 11th inning tied at 6-6, Stahl used him in relief. He began unfortunately, hitting the first batter he faced, right fielder Fred Snodgrass. After a strikeout, as darkness enveloped Fenway Park, the Giants went for the win. Snodgrass attempted to steal second but Boston catcher Bill Carrigan gunned him down. Larry Doyle struck out but Bedient walked the next hitter, Beals Becker. Becker attempted to steal second only to have Carrigan again throw the runner out, this time ending the inning.

Christy Mathewson quickly retired the Red Sox in order in their half of the 11th inning. As it was now too dark to continue, the umpires halted play. The game ended in a 6-6 tie. More importantly for Bedient, he had received his baptism in postseason play.[13]

Bedient started in Game Five at Boston, against Mathewson. For Bedient, facing Mathewson was a special thrill as the Giants ace was one of Hugh's boyhood baseball heroes. The game was played before a record-breaking Columbus Day crowd of 34,683.

As the game began in a misty fog, the Giants immediately decided to test the rookie's nerve by taking his first few offerings. Bedient promptly walked the first hitter, Josh Devore, on four pitches.

Showing uncommon coolness for a rookie, Bedient pulled himself together by employing a tactic he had used successfully during the regular season. He began working very deliberately to each hitter. Before each pitch, he would hitch his belt, pull down his cap, landscape the pitcher's mound, or simply do a thorough examination of the baseball.

After the second batter popped out, a double play ended the inning.

Quickly changing tactics, the Giants then attempted to rattle Bedient with a barrage of "mouth music." Bedient remained

Bedient warming up.

unfazed.[14] [15] Mixing his fastball with an occasional slow one, he allowed no Giant to reach base via a walk after the third inning. Consistently throwing first-pitch strikes, he induced the Giants to hit eight infield popouts and eight fly outs. The only Giant run came in the seventh as a result of a Boston error.

Bedient went on to a 2-1, complete-game victory, allowing only three hits. Mathewson also pitched a brilliant game, walking no one. The *Boston Globe* called the duel "one of the finest battles of the season."[16] Delirious Red Sox fans stormed the field as the game ended and Bedient had to be escorted to safety.[17]

With the Series tied, 3 games to 3, Bedient was again matched against Mathewson, who had yet to win a game in this Series. Before the game, Stahl told Bedient, "You've got to win for us, kid. Just pitch the way you did last time out, and you can take that Mathewson again."[18]

As the game began, chilly weather and a strong northwesterly wind greeted the Boston crowd of 17,034. Many fans wrapped themselves in woolen blankets to stay warm. Buoyed by their convincing victories over the Red Sox in the previous two games, the Giants appeared confident, emerging from their dressing room singing.

Again the Giants began the game attempting to disrupt Bedient's concentration. But much to their frustration, he again slowed the game down. After one lengthy interval between pitches, McGraw complained sarcastically to Silk O'Loughlin, the home-plate umpire, "Say, Silk, the young man appears to pitch at least (once) every five minutes."

Bedient ignored their antics and went to work. Years later, he recalled to Hermes Ames that the cold and dark field conditions that day could not have been more perfect for his fastball. "He said his fastball had a real pop on it that day," Ames recalled, "and he threw no more than a half-dozen curve balls the entire afternoon."

The Giants scored a run in the third inning, as Josh Devore led off with a walk and eventually scored on Red Murray's double to center. Tris Speaker barely missed making a spectacular catch as Murray's ball bounced off his fingertips.

In the fifth, Bedient was the beneficiary of one of the most spectacular catches in World Series history. Larry Doyle, the National League's Most Valuable Player that year, hit a shot deep into right-center. Off with the crack of the bat, Boston right fielder Harry Hooper turned his back and sprinted full speed toward the fence in right-center. At the last moment, as he was about to tumble over the short fence, Hooper reached over his head and caught the ball with his bare hand. His momentum carried him over the fence, off the field, and into the crowd.[19] He emerged with the ball stuck in his hand.

The attending umpires declared it a legal catch, although the Giants protested that Hooper had left the playing field when he made the play.[20] Speaker and a number of other players who were there later described the catch as the greatest they had ever seen.[21] When Bedient left for a pinch hitter in the seventh, Boston was trailing 1-0. In one of the greatest games in Red Sox history, Boston rallied to win in extra innings, 3-2.

Bedient's outstanding performance in Game Eight drew an avalanche of high praise from baseball's best, including Cy Young, Walter Johnson, Christy Mathewson, and Larry Doyle. Cy Young wrote, "To Bedient should be given the major portion of the credit for winning yesterday's game. There are others who did things, but Bedient was the man who stopped the onrush of the confident Giants. He pitched one of the most careful games I have ever seen, taking absolutely no chances with his opponents and obliging them to hit bad balls. I doubt if any other pitcher on the Boston team could have so effectively held the Giants yesterday."[22]

Despite this overwhelming praise, Bedient remained grounded. At the wild victory celebration the next day at Faneuil Hall, Boston Mayor John "Honey Fitz" Fitzgerald introduced Bedient to the madly cheering throng and asked him to speak. Hugh simply rose, bowed slightly to the crowd, and then sat down again.[23]

It was the richest World Series in baseball history up to then; each Boston player received a winner's share of $4,024.68, more than doubling Bedient's 1912 season salary of $1,800. When asked by the *Boston American* how he planned to spend the money, Bedient said he would use part of the money to buy a new home, put part of it in the bank, and use the rest for tuition at one of the law colleges.[24]

Upon returning home to Falconer, New York, Bedient received a hero's welcome. Nearly 25,000 people met his train at the local railroad station. Laudatory speeches and songs of praise were heaped upon him as a local boy who had become a national hero. At the end of one of the celebrations, an overwhelmed

Bedient rose to thank the gathering and said simply, "We have had a pleasant time since coming home and we thank you all for the interest you have shown. That is all I can say." He then sat down to a five-minute standing ovation.

Rewarded by Boston with a two-year contract with a 40 percent salary increase, Bedient began the 1913 season with high hopes. Unfortunately, the 1912 Boston success could not be extended to 1913, as the Red Sox experienced both key injuries (Wood) and internal turmoil (manager Stahl was fired in midseason). The Red Sox dropped to fourth place with a 79-71 record. Bedient went 15-14 but finished with a 2.78 ERA, his career best in the major leagues, in 259 innings. He also had five saves, which ranked third in the 1913 American League.

In 1914, the Red Sox rebounded, finishing second with a 91-62 record. Bedient, however, had his worst year in Boston, falling to 8-12 with a 3.60 ERA in 177 innings. His difficulties may have been linked to the emergence of the new rival Federal League.

The new league began operation in 1914 and put a franchise in Buffalo. Bedient had an unexpected opportunity to play the game he loved in the area he loved. It was a combination that enticed many National and American League players to move to the new league. Buffalo representatives reportedly approached Bedient during the 1914 season. At the end of the year, Boston released him and he joined Buffalo, receiving $7,000 up-front to jump leagues. The Buffalo offer nearly doubled his 1914 Boston salary of $4,000.

In 1915 at Buffalo, Bedient played with former American League players Hal Chase, Russ Ford, and Clyde Engle. He pitched a career-high 269 innings, posting a 16-18 record with a 3.17 ERA. Pitching in 53 of Buffalo's 153 games (35 percent), he led the league in saves (10) as Buffalo finished sixth with a 74-78 record. When the Federal League folded after 1915, Bedient was "despondent." Not only had he lost his team and his league, but the team he left behind, Boston, won the 1915 world championship.

Bedient joined the Toledo Mud Hens of the American Association in the spring of 1916. He posted a 16-18 record while pitching 305 innings.[25] He started again with Toledo in 1917 and went 1-2 in six games. According to the *Toledo News Bee*, he developed arm problems that season. He dropped out of baseball for nearly four years.

In the summer of 1920, testing his arm in a local game, Bedient found he could again throw pain-free. He returned to the Mud Hens in 1921, and won 20 games with 13 losses and a 4.17 ERA in 274 innings. Bedient returned to the club in 1922, going 15-18 in 271 innings with a 3.59 ERA. In 1923, his last year with Toledo, Bedient went 10-21 in 238 innings with an ERA of 5.37 as the last-place Mud Hens won only 54 games. He pitched for Portland in the Pacific Coast League in 1924, going 6-12 in 178 innings with a 5.66 ERA. In 1925, he pitched for Atlanta in the Southern Association, going 7-5 in 94 innings with a 3.06 ERA.

After baseball, Hugh returned to his beloved western New York, where he worked and continued pitching as a semipro, primarily with the Jamestown Spiders. As his speed waned, he relied more on trickery. The *Tribune* of Warren, Pennsylvania, described his 1928 pitching performance against a hard-hitting Ohio team as crafty, featuring a "bewildering" assortment of pitches.[26] Bedient pitched well into his late 40s.

He also helped Imogene raise their family. His son, also named Hugh, pitched in college for the University of Alabama. The Bedient family suffered a major blow in 1940 when young Hugh, a second lieutenant serving in the Air Reserve Corps of the United States Army, died along with 10 other young Army flyers when their two bombers locked wings and crashed during a training drill. Both planes crashed "in a ball of flame" over suburban New York City. Still a student pilot at the time of the crash, the youngster had reportedly declined an opportunity to play for the Red Sox in order to go into the Army Air Service. His father was devastated. [27]

Never straying far from his beloved home in Falconer, New York, Bedient died in nearby Jamestown, New York, of arterial sclerosis on July 21, 1965. He is buried in Falconer, in Levant Cemetery. "Hugh was my best friend for 25 years," Hermes Ames recalled with great fondness. "He was very quiet and didn't talk baseball voluntarily. He was just a very humble, down-to-earth guy."

Sources:

Timothy Gay. *Tris Speaker* (Lincoln, Nebraska: University of Nebraska Press, 2005).

Frederick G. Lieb. *The Story of the World Series* (New York: G.P. Putnam's Sons, 1965).

Bill Nowlin. *Day by Day with the Boston Red Sox* (Cambridge, Massachusetts: Rounder Books, 2006).

Glenn Stout and Richard Johnson. *Red Sox Century* (Boston: Houghton Mifflin Company, 2005).

Cecilia Tan, and Bill Nowlin. *The 50 Greatest Red Sox Games* (Hoboken, New Jersey: John Wiley & Sons, 2006).

John Thorn, Pete Palmer, Michael Gershman. *Total Baseball*, 7th edition (Kingston, New York: Total Sports Publishing, 2001).

Baseball Magazine

Boston Globe

Boston Post

Jamestown Post-Journal, Jamestown, New York.

Hugh Bedient player file at the National Baseball Hall of Fame

SABR Minor League Database

Endnotes

1. Frank Hyde, "Frankly Speaking," *Jamestown Post-Journal*, Jamestown, New York, March 1962.
2. Hugh Bedient player file, National Baseball Hall of Fame.
3. 1900 U.S. Census, New York, Chautauqua County, Elliot Township, Sheet 18, Lines 88-92.
4. Mike Foster telephone interview with Hermes Ames, May 25, 2001.
5. "Bedient Now Ranks With High Paid Boxmen." *Boston Globe*, January 24, 1912.
6. "Hugh Bedient Is a Puzzle To Redskins." *Newark Evening News*, Newark, New Jersey, September 21, 1911.
7. "Jake Stahl Has Signed Contract, Will be Manager, First Baseman, and Stockholder in Red Sox." *Boston Globe*, September 10, 1911.
8. T. H. Murnane, "Speed Boys Turn Back Athletics," *Boston Globe*, April 27, 1912. Bradley's home run was the first one ever hit at Boston's brand-new Fenway Park.
9. T. H. Murnane, "Senators On Top Again, By 8 to 7," *Boston Globe*, May 5, 1912.
10. T. H. Murnane, "Red Sox There With the Punch," *Boston Globe*, May 25, 1912.
11. "Bedient Is The Human Iceberg For the Red Sox." *Boston Post*, September 10, 1912.
12. John Thorn, Pete Palmer and Michael Gershman. *Total Baseball*, 7th Edition.(Kingston, New York: Total Sports Publishing, 2001).
13. "World Championship Baseball Extra." *Boston Globe*, October 10, 1912.
14. "Red Sox Triumph Over Giants, 2-1." *Sheboygan Evening Press*, Sheboygan, Wisconsin, October 14, 1912.
15. Billy Evans, "Tales of the Baseball Diamond." *Salt Lake City Times*, April 13, 1913.
16. James C. O'Leary, "World Championship Baseball Extra," *Boston Globe*, October 13, 1912.
17. Cecilia Tan and Bill Nowlin, *The 50 Greatest Red Sox Games in History* (Hoboken , New Jersey: John Wiley & Sons, Inc., 2006), 28-35.
18. Frederick G. Lieb, *The Story of the World Series.* (New York: G.P. Putnam's Sons, 1965), 92.
19. James C. O'Leary, "World Championship Baseball Extra." Evening Edition, *Boston Globe*, October 17, 1912.
20. Glenn Stout and Richard A. Johnson, *Red Sox Century.* (Boston: Houghton Mifflin Company, 2005), 90.
21. Timothy M. Gay, *Tris Speaker.* (Lincoln, Nebraska: University of Nebraska Press, 2005), 121.
22. "What the Experts of the Boston Papers Say of It." *Boston Globe*, October 17, 1912.
23. "Great Throng Greet Sox." *Boston Globe*, October 17, 1912.
24. "Red Sox Champions Tell How They Plan To Invest Their $4024 Winnings in the World Series." *Boston American*, October 17, 1912, Sporting Section, 2.
25. SABR Minor League Database, Hugh Bedient, Pitching, 1913-1925.
26. "Jamestown Webs Trim Akron Nine." *Warren Tribune*, Warren, Pennsylvania, June 4, 1928, 6.
27. Lieut. Palmer Bedient, Necrology, *Sporting News*, June 27, 1940, 14. Also "11 KILLED IN CRASH OF 2 BOMBERS HERE, Army Planes From Mitchel Field Lock Wings, Plunge In Flames in Queens, Both Crews Wiped Out, Two Homes Are Set Afire, Women in One of Them Being Critically Burned," June 18, 1940 newspaper article in Hugh Bedient file at the Hall of Fame.

Promotional item depicting Bedient.

Hugh Bradley
by Bill Nowlin

G	AB	R	H	2B	3B	HR	RBI	BB	SO	BA	OBP	SLG	SB	HBP
40	137	16	26	11	1	1	19	15	23	.190	.275	.307	3	1

The man who hit the first home run at Fenway Park was a native of North Grafton, Massachusetts: Hugh Frederick Bradley. Bradley's parents were Joseph A. Bradley and Sarah Nutting Bradley and they celebrated his birth on May 23, 1885. Hugh had one brother, John E. Bradley, 11 years his junior. Bradley captained the football and baseball teams at Grafton High School, and graduated in 1903.

The first time we can find Hugh Bradley mentioned in print, it was in the account of a 1904 football game between Grafton High School and Upton High. "Hugh F. Bradley, the baseball player, was referee."[1] He'd played baseball for the Spencers, the semipro town team for Spencer, Massachusetts, earlier in the 1904 season. There he "made a remarkable showing, his batting average being .361, and his fielding average 1000, accepting 87 chances."[2] Bradley attended the College of the Holy Cross in Worcester, Massachusetts, but does not seem to have graduated from there.

Bradley had an abortive start to his pro baseball career. In 1905, he was one of five outfielders who tried out for the Norwich Reds team in the Connecticut State League. [*Hartford Courant*, April 21, 1905] The season opened on April 28 but Bradley wasn't in the lineup. He had made the team but left after just a couple of days to seek a tryout with South Manchester, as reported in the May 2 *Hartford Courant*. Apparently, he injured his right hand after a month—back with Norwich, though not for certain—and had to quit playing. Later in the summer, he is reported to have played some in the Maine Central League, batting .450 in limited action.[3]

1906–Worcester

Bradley's first full-season professional team was the Worcester Busters of the New England League, a Class B team that was also having its first season. The Worcester ballclub was owned and managed by Jesse Burkett, who also played in the outfield. *Sporting Life* informed readers in its February 24 issue that Bradley and Burkett had agreed to terms. Bradley signed with the team on March 13, and was described in the *Boston Globe* dispatch as "a husky chap, standing 5 feet 11 inches and weighing 170 pounds. He is very fast on the bases." The *Worcester Telegram* wrote on March 13, "Bradley has played on several strong semi-professional teams in the vicinity of Worcester. ...He is a husky player who may prove a find for the Worcesters when he gets the practice of regular playing."

Hugh Bradley, tossing the ball to stay loose in 1912.

Bradley was, wrote *Sporting Life*, "the best-known young ballplayer in Worcester County."[4] On the same day he was signed, grading was done and the ground was staked for the stands of a new ballfield, Boulevard Park, but a snowstorm prevented actual construction of the buildings for the team.

Ballplayers reported for duty on April 19 and training began in earnest. Worcester played its home games at the brand-new facility, and had a successful year, easily winning first place in the eight-team league. First place was a status that Worcester earned all four years (1906-1909) that Bradley held down first base for them.

The first game at Worcester's Boulevard Park was a spring training game on April 19, and the next day's *Worcester Daily Telegram* recounted the 3-1 victory over visiting Bridgeport, played in front of 3,500 spectators, with a nod to cleanup hitter and first baseman Bradley (1-for-4 in the game): "Bradley of Grafton was given a trial at first. Bradley had one difficultly thrown ball to handle, the ball being thrown into the runner. He acquitted himself creditably at the bag. With the stick Bradley swung well, and hit the ball on the nose. He got one safe one."

The next day Bradley made the *Telegram*'s subhead: BRADLEY CROSSES PLATE WITH VICTORY. Worcester was playing in Providence. With two outs in the top of the 11th inning of a scoreless game, Bradley grounded the ball to the second baseman (Providence's player/manager Jack Dunn), who threw wildly to first. Bradley took second on the throw, and then scored when the next batter, Ambrose Kane, lined one to left. Kane was thrown out trying to take second, but Bradley had crossed the plate before the out was recorded.

The regular season began on April 27, and a host of dignitaries were present, including the Massachusetts lieutenant governor and Boston's Mayor John F. Fitzgerald. Bradley, "the Grafton lad," figured prominently in the game story. Not only did he manage to catch a foul ball after falling over the bag, handling 11 chances without an error, but he tripled to left field in the bottom of the seventh inning, driving in the third run of the inning, an insurance run which extended the Busters' lead to 6-4. The Worcester paper said, "Bradley played a nice game at first."

Hugh went 0-for-4 on the 30th, but on May 1 had himself a 3-for-4 game with a double and a stolen base. The *Worcester Telegram* wasn't as impressed as one might have thought, explaining of his hits, "Every one was due almost entirely to good luck." Bradley typically played first base, but even filled in as catcher once late in the May 11 game, a 13-inning tie against Manchester. Four days later, he started in right field against Lynn, then swapped positions with Kane and moved to first base.

On June 1, Bradley had a pair of hits, one of them a triple, and scored two runs. Bradley played first base throughout, but batted at several slots up and down the lineup—fourth place, fifth place, seventh. He had a three-hit game batting cleanup on August 7, hit a couple of doubles on August 30. It was a good first season. Burkett had had to choose between Kane and Bradley as his regular first baseman. "Although Bradley was pretty green then," the *Telegram* opined near the end of the season, "Burkett saw the possibilities and kept Bradley."

The Busters finished the season as New England League champions. In the postseason, the Worcesters played the Connecticut State League leaders, the Norwich Reds, but Worcester was "off-stride" and went down to defeat in the Inter-League Series. Bradley did little to help his team. All in all, he seems to have played serviceable ball in 1906, collecting 106 base hits for a .243 average in 113 games, but he rarely stood out in any way whatsoever.

After the season was over, Bradley took a position as a clerk in a Thompsonville, Connecticut hotel. He planned to do some coaching of high-school teams on the side as he waited for the 1907 season to begin.

1907–Worcester

The first home game of the season was May 1, but Bradley had already made headlines in the *Worcester Telegram*. BRADLEY'S CATCH SAVES THE GAME headlined the April 22 game story, which featured the great stop he made in extra innings during the first game of the year, a 5-4 win in 11 frames at Norwich.

Bradley had three hits and a stolen base on May 10 and another three-hit game on June 11. On July 1, Bradley was the leadoff batter, after hitting third most of the season to this point.

Later in July, Burkett held a meeting with the Boston Doves, the National League club owned by George K. Dovey. The *Washington Post* reported that it was "practically settled" that Bradley and two other players were to be sold to Boston. Two of the four players mentioned in the article served with Boston in September, but neither Bradley nor one of the pitchers were sold, for reasons that remain unknown.

Bradley played out the year with Worcester—a quite good one–finishing the year hitting .285 with 112 hits (30 for extra bases, but without a home run) in 393 at-bats. One of his better days came on August 12, when he hit third in the order and produced two doubles and a single. Worcester once more won the New England League pennant.

In November, a couple of publications reported that Bradley and teammate Eddie Russell were both sold to the Providence club for $600 apiece. Come 1908, though, Bradley was once again at first base for the Busters.

1908–Worcester

Bradley played a third season with Worcester, but it was the worst season of his 12 years in the minors, finishing the year hitting .238 with one homer in 466 at-bats.

One astonishing game near the end of preseason play didn't require any hits to win. On April 30, Worcester played Woonsocket and managed to score nine runs in the combined second and third innings without the benefit of even one base hit. There was a six-run bottom of the second produced by four bases on balls, four errors, a stolen base, and a passed ball. In the third, another walk and three more errors by Woonsocket's shortstop, Maloney, and the Worcesters held a 9-0 lead. The 117 fans at Boulevard Park were thrilled for a moment with Bradley's long drive to left field but it was hauled in "near the stone heap" in the outfield. "Brad" was 0-for-4 for the day, but with two outs in the bottom of the eighth was robbed of a clean single when the baserunner ahead of him "loafed on his way to second and was thrown out by the centerfielder."[5]

Bradley kicked off the regular season with a 2-for-4 game against the New Bedford Whalers, and hit the first home run of his professional career in the first inning of the May 13 game against the Brockton Tigers, in Brockton. He hit only one other homer in 1908, but that one doesn't show in the record books. It was another first-inning blow, over the right-field fence in a 13-0 exhibition-game victory at Clinton Oval in Woonsocket against the Machine & Press team of the mill league there.

There was a little comedy early in the season, during a 13-1 shellacking Worcester administered to the Lawrence Colts. A throw from the third baseman pulled Bradley off the base, and "Brad" failed to touch the runner as he crossed the first-base bag—but the runner missed the bag. Bradley could have just stepped on the sack to record the out, but instead took off after McLane, the Lawrence baserunner. "The latter continued to run out toward the right-field fence as if he intended to go to Bloomingdale Road if Bradley would give chase." Instead of chasing him all the way, or returning to step on first, Bradley waited until McLane came back in and then tagged him before he could dodge Bradley's touch.[6]

For the third year in a row, Burkett's Busters led the New England League. After the season, Bradley picked up a little more cash playing some semipro ball and took part as the right fielder in a game for the Spencer team, going 1-for-3 in helping beat Marlboro, 9-1, during a September 23 game at the Spencer Fair.

1909–Worcester

After being part of three championship seasons in a row, and despite an offyear with the Worcesters, Bradley, come springtime, decided to hold out for more money. Burkett said he wouldn't pay any more than he'd offered. After several weeks, Burkett gave in, though perhaps just enough that Bradley could save a little face. *The Sporting News* reported in its April 29 issue, "It is pretty much all settled now, that Bradley will get a raise, but the amount of the monthly raise would not pay his board for a week in anything better than a third-class hotel."

The additional funds may have encouraged him, however. He jumped his average dramatically to .312, hitting safely twice on July 24 to pass the century mark in hits. He was particularly praised for his fielding, with *Sporting Life* commenting on July 3 that "Hugh Bradley is the big boy of the first sack of this league. For three seasons this young man has been the best at that position in the New England League." By the end of August, the publication, called him "undoubtedly the premier fielding first sacker of the league." Manager Roger Bresnahan of the St. Louis Cardinals was reportedly interested in Bradley.

He finished the year with seven home runs and tied Brockton's Simeon Murch for the league lead in hits at 144, Bradley batting cleanup much of the year. His two standout days were May 11, when he singled, doubled, and tripled, scoring twice in a 7-5 win over Fall River, and on July 13, when he hit four singles in a losing effort against Haverhill.

On September 1, the Red Sox drafted Bradley, pitcher Fred Anderson, and shortstop Steve Yerkes.

1910–Boston Red Sox

The February 3, 1910, *Boston Globe* headlined a story "BRADLEY JOINS RED SOX TEAM—Crack First Baseman Signs Contract." Bradley had come by the team offices to sign his 1910 contract. Tim Murnane, the baseball editor of the *Globe*, revealed that Bradley was nephew to one of the earliest professional ballplayers in Boston, George H. "Foghorn" Bradley, who had pitched for the 1876 Boston Red Caps (9-10, with a 2.49 ERA) and played four games in the outfield. Foghorn, brother to Hugh's father, Joseph, played just the one season but umpired for seven seasons.

Jake Stahl was expected to play first base, with Bradley prepared to back him up. This is how it played out, with Bradley appearing in 21 games at first. Manager Patsy Donovan knew Stahl would be the stalwart at first, so he had Bradley try to develop skills as a catcher, and near the end of the year he

appeared in three games behind the plate and "handled himself like a veteran," said sportswriter A.H.C. Mitchell. He played right field in one game. The Atlanta Crackers tried to pry Bradley away from Boston in May, making an offer to the Red Sox. Boston declined, and the reference to Hugh as "Tom Bradley" in the May 19 *Atlanta Constitution* leaves one wondering if the Crackers knew which first baseman were they bidding for.

Hugh's first major-league appearance came on April 25, 1910, when he was sent up to pinch-hit for Smoky Joe Wood in the bottom of the eighth. The Athletics were ahead, 4-2, but Boston had two men on base with only one out. Bradley flied out to center field. Bradley came through in his next appearance, however. It was May 7, in a game at the newly expanded Huntington Avenue Grounds against the visiting New Yorkers. The game was tied after nine, but New York took a 4-1 lead in the top of the 10th thanks to a rally that began with a hit batsman and two errors. With one out in the bottom of the 10th, Bradley batted for pitcher Eddie Cicotte and singled to right. He was stranded on first, though, and the game was a loss.

The Red Sox Quartet / Spring training 1911: Larry Gardner, Hugh Bradley, Marty McHale, and Buck O'Brien.

On May 30, with three runs already in, Bradley's pinch-hit single to left field tied the game in the bottom of the ninth; the Sox beat the Athletics in the 10th. Three days later, in St. Louis, he doubled to the right-field fence in the top of the 11th (his second two-bagger of the game) and scored the winning run on Heinie Wagner's single. Manager Patsy Donovan called Bradley "a grand young player" who could play several positions and "a corking good man with the stick." On June 7, he had an 0-for-5 day, but in the top of the 13th he drew a walk, stole second, reached third on a passed ball, and scored the eventual winning run on Tris Speaker's single to center.

That brief cluster of activity was the best part of his year, and Brad finished with a .169 average in 83 at-bats, though steady in the field with only one error in 189 chances. Bradley was already noted as a singer and spent the winter months on the vaudeville circuit in New England. He was offered a Red Sox contract for 1911 and signed it at the beginning of January. Stahl said he was retiring and manager Donovan initially penciled in Brad as the everyday first baseman.

1911–Boston Red Sox

For spring training, President John I. Taylor had his men train at Redondo Beach in Southern California, breaking into two teams to get in more games, then playing a series of games as they traveled back east across the country. Red Sox teams engaged in an astonishing 64 preseason contests, winning 41 of them, playing games in Utah, Nevada, Nebraska, and even in the Arizona Territory.[7] To while away the time in travel to the West Coast, it was Bradley who took the lead in forming a barbershop quartet with teammates Buck O'Brien, Marty McHale, and Larry Gardner.

Bradley suffered a "serious injury" near the end of the spring training trip, and lost his shot at a starting role.[8] At first, it was reported that he had suffered a sprained ankle and then developed water on the knee. *Sporting Life*, though, reported in its season wrapup that it was a fracture of his leg; the publication termed it a broken ankle in another story a year later. Whatever the injury, it was indeed serious and he wore a plaster cast until after the midpoint of May. This left Hack Engle taking over for the departed Jake Stahl at first base. Bradley had less than half the playing time he had in his rookie year, batting only 41 times all season long. He took advantage of his moments, though, hitting for a .317 average and scoring nine runs to 1910's eight. The highlight of his year was, without a doubt, his first home run. Near the end of the season, on September 25 and playing in one of the last games held at the Huntington Avenue Grounds, Brad faced Lefty George of the St. Louis Browns in the bottom of the sixth inning and hit what the *Globe* called "a fine home run." It was the next to last homer hit at the Grounds; Joe Riggert hit one in the last inning of the final game played on Huntington Avenue, on October 7.

After the season, the Red Sox Quartet really got to work. Bradley was joined by Buck O'Brien, Marty McHale, and a new pitcher named Bill Lyons, who took Gardner's place when the third baseman had to return home to help his ailing father. They performed several shows at Keith's Theatre in Boston, and headed from there to Philadelphia. "They can sing, and sing well," noted the *Globe*. "They compare favorably with any quartet in vaudeville." Of Bradley, the newspaper—stat book not at hand—gushed, "While Hugh Bradley was hitting the ball to the music of .340 or thereabouts, he can sing rag time at an average of .598."9 John I. Taylor was pleased with the addition of Lyons, saying, "Lyons, if you can pitch as well as you can sing, we might well hoist the pennant for next year right now." Vocalizing was presumably his greater strength; Lyons never appeared in a major-league game.

It looked as if 1912 would be the year that Bradley might finally get to play major-league ball on a regular basis. Stahl was still retired in Chicago, active as a banker. Hack Engle had done very well in 1911, but— writing in October 1911—A.H.C. Mitchell saw Bradley as the man for 1912: "After a long absence caused by breaking his ankle on the spring trip, Hugh Bradley is back in the game again, and the way he is covering first and hitting the ball makes the fans forget about Jake Stahl. There is no doubt Bradley can make good and the club need look no further for a first baseman for next year."10

New club president Jimmy McAleer had other objectives. Just a month later, as it happens, the new owners of the team determined to lure Stahl back and did so successfully, hiring him as field manager on November 10 and even granting him a small ownership stake in the team. He would become the only player/manager/owner in Red Sox history.

Fortunately, Brad had his singing to look forward to. The December 2, 1911, issue of *Sporting Life* saw the songster as irrepressible: "Bradley just cannot keep from singing. It is morning, noon and night with him on the training trips, and those who do not care for music have a hard time of it with Brad around."

1912–Boston Red Sox

Bradley's vaudeville work with the Quartet continued into the new year, and the January 21 *Globe* remarked, "The second time you hear them you like them better than the first." The newspaper praised Bradley's standout number, "Oh, You Beautiful Doll." They'd performed in at least seven cities, and often stopped the show when audiences clamored for an encore before the next act came on. The January 12 *Globe* said they'd never received less than six encores per performance. Lyons may have lost his chance to play ball due to the incessant bowing: "Hold on there, I'm bowing so much now that my neck's lame."

Jake Stahl returned to the Red Sox in 1912, to manage and play first base. Hack Engle joined Bradley as a backup infielder. Even so, Bradley had his busiest season yet, with 137 at-bats in 40 games. He was well-regarded, with the *Boston Post*'s Paul Shannon writing of him on January 17, "Bradley is one of the most earnest players in the game and his heart and soul is always in his work." Most importantly, Bradley made his mark in history by hitting the first homer ever hit at Boston's new Fenway Park. The date was April 26. It was only the fifth game played at Fenway.

Hugh Bradley's 1912 T207 Brown Background cigarette baseball card.

The dominating feature of the brand new ballpark was the high left-field wall, just 310 feet or so from home plate, but with an imposing height of 31 feet. The original rendition of the wall was a 25-foot wooden barrier set atop the six-foot berm or earthen incline which took on the name Duffy's Cliff for the Red Sox left fielder who learned how to play this original version of the warning track in front of the fence—and when roped off could also serve as overflow seating.

This was baseball's Deadball Era, when home runs were few and far between, and many of them were of the inside-the-park variety. The Red Sox as a team hit 29 homers all season long, Tris Speaker's 10 roundtrippers leading both the pack and the league. He was only the third Sox player to ever reach double digits. Jake Stahl had hit 10 in 1910, and Buck Freeman had done it three times, 1901 (12), 1902 (11), and 1903 (13). Some analysts, scoping out the new park, wondered if anyone would ever hit one over the wall. It didn't take that long, and came off the bat of the unlikely Hugh Bradley, he of the one career home run to date. It was, as it played out, the last homer he ever hit in major-league ball.

Bradley was facing another pitcher known as Lefty, Lefty Russell of the 1911 world champion Philadelphia Athletics (he had hit his first home run off Lefty George). It was the bottom of the seventh inning, with two outs and two runners on base. Back in the first inning, Bradley had hammered a double off the fence. It was, wrote Paul Shannon in the *Boston Post*, a "screaming drive to left field, a swat that struck that high board fence wall well up toward the top and sent his two teammates across the plate." An accompanying note said it hit about 10 feet below the top of the fence. Gardner then singled in Bradley. But the Red Sox frittered away their 3-0 lead and now were down, 6-4. The outfield played deep, mindful of his earlier drive off the wall. After the crack of the bat, Philadelphia left fielder Amos Strunk "flattened himself against the signboard after climbing the bank. He couldn't get any farther, but the ball knew no such obstacle. It sailed over, seven feet from [the] upper rim."

The moment the bat struck the ball, reported the *Boston Globe*: "The scene that followed was indescribable. Players came bolting from the dugout to take a look at the mighty blast. They could not believe their eyes." Neither could many of the fans, apparently. The *Post*'s game notes declared, "Few of the fans who have been out to Fenway Park believed it possible to knock a ball over the left field fence, but Hugh Bradley hit one that not only cleared the barrier but also the building on the opposite side of the street." Brad had five RBIs for the game, and had scored twice. His homer, wrote Shannon, was "a feat that may never be duplicated."

It was. On May 24, Rube Oldring of the Athletics hit one that the *Globe* described as clearing the wall "at almost the same spot that Bradley sent it to beat the Athletics four weeks ago today." Duffy Lewis hit one out on July 2 and Jake Stahl hit one out on July 20. Though none at all cleared the fence in 1913, four homers had been banged out in the first three months of Fenway Park. Bradley's will forever be the first.

Bradley had his chance to become a regular. Stahl had suffered his own leg injury, which gave Brad his best chance, but he'd proven unable to lay claim to the position.

Bradley hit only .190 for the year, primarily filling in during a stretch when Stahl was hurt, and by July the Sox were looking to move him. Mid-July reports had Brad on his way to the International League's Jersey City Skeeters as soon as he cleared waivers. This proved more difficult than expected, though, and he remained with Boston throughout the season.

The *Los Angeles Times* summarized his 1912 season on September 29, saying that he had "started in like a race horse and bade fair to supplant Manager Stahl at first base, but he fell off woefully in his hitting and lost a great opportunity." Agreed, wrote the *Boston Globe*, terming Brad "a free hitter [who] could not seem to get them safe and fell off badly in his stickwork." Still young, the newspaper expected to see him back in the major leagues after another year or two of seasoning. The Boston paper announced on November 25 that he'd been sold to Jersey City.

The Red Sox might have disposed of Bradley earlier. Tim Murnane reported in the December 5 *Sporting News* that Pittsburgh had offered Boston $8,000 for Bradley back in 1911, but they couldn't get him past waivers in order to effect the sale. After his disappointing season, the Jersey City offer was the best on the table.

Brad saw no action in the World Series against the New York Giants, which the Sox won in eight games, though he collected a share which he planned to spend on real estate in the Worcester area and for some new stage clothing as the Quartette (now comprised of Bradley, Buck O'Brien, Bill Carrigan, and Heinie Wagner) planned on a two-month tour attracting what Bradley himself described as "the highest salaries ever paid for an act of this kind."[11]

1913–Jersey City and Toronto

The Quartette toured, even though Brad was a Skeeter now and not a member of the Red Sox. An early February report indicated dissatisfaction with one aspect of the demotion: "Bradley says he is not satisfied with the terms of the contract sent to him by the Jersey City club."[12] Presumably, it was not for one of the highest salaries ever paid.

One of the benefits, however, was spring training in Bermuda, and by March 1, Brad had come to terms, "counted on to shine at first base for the Pests."[13] Bradley played for both Jersey City and the Toronto Maple Leafs in 1913, starting off with the Skeeters. His old friends hadn't forgotten him and during the April 27 offday for the Red Sox, Buck O'Brien took a group of players to see Bradley, McHale, and Bill Purtell play for Jersey City against visiting Rochester. Bradley's tenure with Jersey City was fraught with some difficulty, resulting in a case being taken to baseball's National Commission. Jersey City wasn't pleased with the level of his play, and returned him to Boston, claiming that his release to their team had been conditional on his performance and stating that they hadn't found his play satisfactory during what they argued was a trial period. The Red Sox refused to take Bradley back, and demanded payment of the $1,750 owed them. There was no record of the original transfer in Commission files, but AL president Ban Johnson's files contained notice of his outright release to Jersey City on November 25. Further, there was a telegram from Montreal in the AL files offering Boston $1,500 for his release. The idea that Boston would have declined a firm offer of $1,500 for a conditional one of just $250 more was deemed unlikely, and the Commission upheld Boston's claim and ordered Bradley back to Jersey City.[14]

The Jersey City club looked around for takers, and wired the Los Angeles Angels to offer Bradley, but the Angels owner "cast the telegram aside with the remark that any player which is not fast enough for Jersey City should not look to the Coast League for a job."[15] A deal was worked out with the Toronto Maple Leafs and Bradley headed north to Canada. Within a month, manager Joe Kelley said that Brad was "playing grand ball for his club."[16] He had a good season, hitting .290 all told and added a couple more homers to his resume. Jersey City finished last in the International League, with Toronto one rung above them in the standings. A dispatch from Toronto in the November 29 *Sporting Life* reflected the thought that Brad was not the top choice of the Leafs: "First baseman Borton has declined to play here and Hugh Bradley will again cover first."

Needless to say, there would be no touring this winter as part of the Red Sox Quartette. It's possible the theatrical life had taken a toll on Bradley's play. Teammates Joe Bush and Wally Schang talked about going into vaudeville in the offseason of 1913, but Harry T. Jordan, who ran the Philadelphia operations of the Keith theater organization, advised them that they could make good money for themselves and the Keith chain, but nonetheless sufficiently discouraged them, advising, "You are both very young and I am afraid you would be open to too many temptations. If you recall, there were four singers known as the Red Sox quartet. Two of them, Buck O'Brien and Hugh Bradley, were members of the Red Sox team. They spent a full winter on the stage, and made quite a success, but neither man is in the major leagues today, although both are young and promising. The same might happen to you."[17]

1914–Pittsburgh / Federal League

In mid-February 1914, Toronto manager Joe Kelley said that Bradley was on the market. Brad became intrigued with the idea of the nascent Federal League, hoping to mount a challenge to the established National and American Leagues as a third major. There were rumors that he was going to play for the Chicago Federals, the Whales, but he was signed by the Pittsburgh Rebels. Brad jumped from "organized baseball" to the rival upstart, "because he figured the chances slim of getting back into the big ring after a fellow has been there once and passed out."[18] He also apparently got a pretty good deal for himself, a three-year contract at the rate of $4,000 per year plus a $1,000 signing bonus.

The Rebels were initially managed by Brownie Gessler, who had played for the 1908 and 1909 Red Sox. On March 14 both Bradley and center fielder Ennis "Rebel" Oakes joined Pittsburgh's spring training camp in Lynchburg, Virginia. After the first 11 games, Oakes became manager for the two years the team (and league) lasted.

Brad got off to a terrific start, occasioning correspondent Harry H. Kramer to write from Pittsburgh early in the season, "Bradley's fielding has been phenomenal and the manner in which he is hammering the ball to all corners of the lot has shown the Federal fans that Manager Gessler made a ten-strike when he secured the former Toronto first-sacker."[19] The following week, the paper said that his infield work "could not have been improved on."

There was some sense that Bradley's ego may have been considerable, not surprising in someone used to the stage during the offseason as well. A *Boston Herald* report said that "Bradley tried to live on his reputation for being the first man to lift the ball over the left-field fence at Fenway Park" but acknowledged that he was, at the time, batting .343 for the Pittfeds.[20]

Bradley was the starting first baseman for the Rebels, playing in 118 games and batting .307 in a career-high 427 at-bats, despite missing a number of games in June to a "sprained side" and in July to a severe spiking that took fully 10 minutes to bandage on the field before he could be taken to the clubhouse. He drove in 61 runs, but not one by the home-run ball. Pittsburgh finished seventh in the eight-team league. At the end of the season, the team hosted Rebel Oakes Day to honor their manager, and it fell to Bradley to step to home plate and present Oakes with a "handsome diamond stickpin."[21]

Come November, once again, there was writing on the wall that—despite his very strong season and despite his three-year deal—Brad would be asked to become a backup once more. The Rebels had acquired veteran St. Louis Cardinals first baseman Ed Konetchy. At least one report surfaced that the Indianapolis Hoosiers were considering trading for Bradley, but he stayed put for the first part of 1915.

1915–Federal League: Pittsburgh, Brooklyn, and Newark

In 1915, Pittsburgh moved up to third place in Federal League standings, finishing just a half-game out of first, just four percentage points (.562) behind the second-place Chicago Whales (.566). But Konetchy had supplanted Bradley on first base, hitting .314 with 10 homers and 93 RBIs. Brad got into 26 games, batting .273. He drove in only 6 runs and on June 22, he and former St. Louis Cardinal Eddie Holly were both unconditionally released. They had both refused to go to New Haven of the independent Colonial League. The two ballplayers claimed they would hire a lawyer to demand full payment of their salaries. Bradley, though, signed on with the Brooklyn Tip-Tops, returning to the Federal League as a backup first baseman.

The man who hit the first home run at Fenway Park: Hugh Bradley.

He hit .246 for Brooklyn, driving in 18 runs, but on August 23, the Brookfeds gave him his second unconditional release of the season. He signed on with his third Federal League ballclub, the Newark Pepper. With Newark, his batting declined further, and he finished his major-league career hitting just five singles in 33 at-bats (.152).

1916-1923–Columbus/Omaha/ Galveston/Houston/New Orleans/ Nashville/St. Petersburg

Hugh Bradley wasn't finished with baseball yet, though, nor were his legal troubles over, either. The Toronto owner was still pursuing a claim against him in the middle of 1916, arguing that Bradley's contract still belonged to the Maple Leafs for having deserted Toronto to jump to the Federal League.

In March 1916, he signed with the Columbus Senators (American Association) to play first base. He appeared in 146 games, batting .250, and hit a pair of home runs. In June, though, Bradley was looking ahead, reported to be angling for the job of player/manager for the Worcester club, even offering to buy some stock in the team.

Brad played in 1917 for the Omaha Rourkes in the Western League, upping his average to .281 in the Class A circuit. The following year, he was out of baseball, perhaps involved in some way with the war effort or, more likely, simply unable to find work given the small number of teams operating during this wartime season. He played Class B ball in the Texas League in 1919, for both Galveston and Houston, hitting for a combined .280. In 1920, Bradley moved back up a notch to play A ball for the New Orleans Pelicans; he hit .254 in the Southern Association for the Pels, and .289 for the Nashville Volunteers in 1921, appearing in only 25 games.

Bradley's last years in professional baseball were in the Florida State League with the St. Petersburg Saints. In neither 1922 nor 1923 did he play more than 105 games, but he hit .286 and then .296. In the latter year, he managed the Saints as well, named to the skipper's slot in December 1922, attracting a salary of $3,500. The Saints finished fourth in the six-team Class C league. It was during 1923 that Brad homered for the last time.

An intriguing chapter in Bradley's life appeared to open up after the 1920 campaign, when it was announced that he was going into the movie business, granted a territory by the Pathe Studios in which his job was to place films.[22] He nonetheless remained known as a Worcester man and it appeared to be but a short-lived posting.

Bradley turned up at the winter meetings in Chicago in December 1923, hoping to land a job as manager of the Pittsfield, Massachusetts, club, but he didn't get the job and Pittsfield saw three different managers during an unsettled 1924 season.

Brad took up work as an umpire, working in the Eastern League beginning in 1927; he officiated at the season opener in New Haven. There was an incident in Waterbury on June 12 when manager William McCorry of the Albany Senators was suspended for assaulting Bradley. McCorry was fined $50 for the assault and an additional $25 for using offensive language directed at Bradley. It wasn't an easy job umpiring; on August 7, a foul ball caromed off his chest protector in the eighth inning and struck him in the Adam's apple. After first aid was administered and Bradley caught his breath, he worked the remainder of the game. He was dropped from the umpire list in 1928, but—in what seemed like an odd-year phenomenon—was back again in 1929 and again in 1931.

Life after baseball

According to the 1930 Census, Hugh was 29 when he got married in 1914. He married Worcester native Rita E. Kenney. Her given name appears to be Margarita (or possibly Marguerita), and the couple had a daughter, Doris A. Bradley (b. ~1915), who married Edward P. Salmon. They provided the Bradleys with three grandchildren. Bradley was a member of the Holy Name Society of St. Paul's Church in Worcester.

In the years after his playing days were done. Bradley held a number of jobs. He worked as playground director at Worcester's Logan Field, and worked with many boys who went on to play with high-school and semipro teams in the area. He was a member of the Worcester Retired Professional Baseball Players Club and spoke up on behalf of umpires (based on his own Eastern League experiences and perhaps aware of his uncle Foghorn's umpiring career), leading an appeal in the middle 1940s for them to be included in the National Baseball Hall of Fame at Cooperstown. "They deserve a place there," he declared. "They have played a big part in building up the game."[23]

In February 1947, three-quarters of the old Red Sox Quartet reunited at the Boston Baseball Writers Association, and Gardner, McHale, and Bradley entertained the writers with songs of days long gone.

Bradley died of a heart attack at City Hospital in Worcester on January 26, 1949. He was living at 43 Austin Street in Worcester at the time, and a front-page story on his death in the *Worcester Telegram* informed readers that after being stricken at home, he tried to walk to the police station but was unable to make it. A passing motorist saw him and took him to police headquarters, where he was rushed to the hospital and died half an hour later. He was 63 years old.

At the time of his death in 1949, Bradley was employed by the Wright Machine Company, a long-established metal machining firm based in Worcester.

Former Worcester teammate Hugh J. McCune said that Bradley "was always a great fellow to have around a ball club. He was always trying to help everyone. He had a fine personality, and a great singing voice. Many times he helped cheer up the ball players with his songs after a losing game."[24]

Another photo of the Red Sox Quartet. L to R; Marty McHale, Buck O'Brien, Hugh Bradley, and Bill Lyons.

Sources:

In addition to the sources cited, the author consulted the online SABR Encyclopedia, Retrosheet.org, and Baseball-Refefence.com.

Thanks also to Bill Ballou and Peter Kneeland.

Endnotes

1. *Boston Globe*, October 1, 1904. Grafton won, 6-0.

2. *Sporting Life*, April 21, 1906

3. *Boston Globe*, March 14, 1906, *Hartford Courant*, April 23, 1905, and *Sporting Life*, February 24 and April 21, 1906

4. *Sporting Life*, April 21, 1906

5. *Worcester Telegram*, May 1, 1908

6. *Worcester Telegram*, May 13, 1908

7. This remarkable tour is exhaustively detailed in Bill Nowlin's *The Great Red Sox Spring Training Tour of 1911* (Jefferson NC: McFarland, 2011)

8. *Los Angeles Times*, September 29, 1912

9. *Boston Globe*, November 26, 1911

10. *Sporting Life*, October 7, 1911

11. *Sporting Life*, October 26, 1912

12. *Sporting Life*, February 8, 1913

13. *Sporting Life*, March 1, 1913

14. *Boston Globe*, June 15, 1913

15. *Los Angeles Times*, June 18, 1913

16. *Boston Globe*, July 18, 1913

17. *Sporting Life*, November 15, 1913

18. *Hartford Courant*, March 6, 1914

19. *Sporting Life*, May 2, 1914

20. Quoted in *Sporting Life*, August 14, 1914

21. *Sporting Life*, October 17, 1914

22. *Atlanta Constitution*, September 16, 1920

23. *Worcester Telegram*, January 27, 1949

24. *Ibidem*

Jack Bushelman
By Craig Lammers

G	ERA	W	L	SV	GS	GF	CG	SHO	IP	H	R	ER	BB	SO	HR	HBP	WP	BFP
3	4.70	1	0	0	0	1	0	0	7 2/3	9	4	4	5	5	0	0	2	34

G	AB	R	H	2B	3B	HR	RBI	BB	SO	BA	OBP	SLG	SB	HBP
3	3	1	0	0	0	0	0	1	2	.000	.250	.000	0	0

Jack Bushelman.

Sometimes the best deals are those that aren't made. In the spring of 1908, Boston was so impressed by a pitcher they faced in an exhibition game at Toledo they offered the Mud Hens $5,000 for him. Toledo Manager Bill Armour asked a reported $7,000 for the contract of Jack Bushelman that it probably didn't happen in Fenway's first season—so he remained a member of the Mud Hens. Between that spring afternoon, and Boston's acquisition of Bushelman late in the 1911 season, the right hander pitched for nine different teams and was at least briefly the property of two others.

Henry Bushelman immigrated to the United States from the Oldenberg region of Germany. Like many German immigrants in the mid 19th century, he settled in the Cincinnati, Ohio area. Henry married Mary Hoggins, an Irish immigrant. On March 17, 1855, their first child John H. Bushelman was born in Covington, Kentucky just across the river from Cincinnati. John H. Bushelman married in 1879 and settled on the Ohio side of the river, working as a gardener, a dairy farmer, and later as a teamster. On August 29, 1885, a son, John Francis Bushelman was born.[1]

Jack Bushelman grew up in Avondale and then St. Bernard, Ohio both suburbs of Cincinnati now but separate villages a century ago. John Bushelman opened a sand company and the family appears to have been fairly well off financially. Jack graduated from high school and attended the University of Cincinnati where he majored in Civil Engineering and starred as a pitcher on the baseball team. Bushelman would be the second University of Cincinnati athlete to reach the major leagues. The first was Miller Huggins.

Jack also played semipro ball, and was already regarded as a promising but inconsistent player. Just how inconsistent was later described by one of his early managers: "Jack was certainly the best youngster I ever saw, his one weakness was wildness. After pitching a fine game against the Shamrocks, striking out seven of the first nine men who faced him, I decided he would do. I took him to Middletown with the Cincinnatus club to play Miller's Middletown club. For the first four innings, the batters could not knock the ball out of the diamond, because Jack wouldn't let them come within a mile of the ball. He gave eight bases on balls."[2]

In the fall of 1905, Jack Bushelman signed his first professional contract with Cedar Rapids, Iowa of the Class B Illinois-Indiana-Iowa (Three-I) League. Cedar Rapids was managed by former major-league third baseman Belden Hill. Bushelman reported to Cedar Rapids in mid April of 1906. His first appearance for the Rabbits was in an exhibition game with Duluth. Pitching three innings in relief of starter Otis "Doc" Crandall, he surrendered three hits, struck out five, and walked one. It wouldn't be his last appearance against the Minnesota team. A few days later he followed Russ Ford (another future major leaguer) in an exhibition win over Ottumwa. The *Cedar Rapids Republican* was impressed with his performance. "He has every ear mark of being a coming pitcher and the work he did yesterday gladdened the hearts of the fans."[3] He started the second game of the season for Cedar Rapids and was much less successful than he'd been in exhibition games. The *Republican* said: "Most of the poor work for Cedar Rapids was done by Bushelman. He should have won the game with ease but at two different times he went in the air and finally threw the game away."[4] He allowed five runs each in the second and ninth inning of the 12-11 loss. Two hits and a pair of stolen bases couldn't save his place on the Rabbits roster, and he was soon sent to Grand Forks, North Dakota of the Northern Copper Country League. Cedar Rapids retained an option on his services.

The Northern Copper Country League had been formed that spring in a merger of the Northern and Copper Country Leagues. The new Class C league included four communities from Michigan's Upper Peninsula, plus Duluth, Grand Forks, Fargo,

North Dakota, and Winnipeg, Manitoba. The Grand Forks Browns were the worst team in the league and fan support was sparse at best. On July 4, Bushelman lost to Winnipeg 9-2, allowing 15 hits, six earned runs, and throwing a pair of wild pitches. In his next start, also against Winnipeg, he was beaten 13-4, striking out six but walking seven. Despite the poor efforts, he must have impressed Winnipeg manager A.R. "Spike" Anderson. When Grand Forks disbanded on July 29, Winnipeg got the team's two best players Bushelman and first baseman Fred Luderus, another future major leaguer.

The change of scenery helped Bushelman. The *Manitoba Free Press* commented on his debut, a 6-1 win over Lake Linden. "Bush as the fans soon dubbed the tall fellow [6'2"] was a trifle nervous at the start, but he soon settled down and had the ball singing over the pan in a manner most tantalizing to the Lake Linden sluggers."[5] Bushelman lost five of his first eight starts with Winnipeg.

The Maroons closed the 1906 season with a home series against Fargo, and that series was pivotal to Bushelman's baseball future. On August 27, he shut out Fargo on four hits. Three days later he beat them 9-2, but his third start in the Labor Day doubleheader was truly memorable. The *Free Press* said of the game: "Bushelman entered the mystic circle to which all pitchers aspire when he shut Fargo out without a hit in the morning game. [He] seemed to have everything at his command, and he had the Fargo men batting as if they were handcuffed." [6] The closest thing to a hit was a ground ball deflected by Bushelman and ruled an error.

After the regular season ended, the Maroons made a barnstorming tour of Alberta, playing series against Edmonton and Calgary and several smaller communities before returning home for a three-game series with Minneapolis of the American Association. Between starts and relief appearances Jack pitched in most of the games, including five of six games at one stretch. He started two of the three games against Minneapolis. The *Free Press* considered his pitching one of the highlights in the first game of the series. "The tall young pitcher was distinctly on his mettle and threw one of the best games seen here in a long time."[7] He allowed five hits, struck out four, and walked three in a 2-1 loss. Although he later spent parts of three seasons in the American Association, it may have been the best performance of his career against an A.A. team. Bushelman finished his first professional season with an 11-8 record in 22 appearances.

Jack Bushelman began and ended his 1907 season in much the same way as he had the previous year, but his season was still far from ordinary. Jack reported to Cedar Rapids in April. Again, his stay was brief. Cedar Rapids and Winnipeg were in a dispute over the pitcher's ownership. Cedar Rapids' claim was based on the fact they had optioned him to Grand Forks and the option should remain in effect even though the team disbanded. Winnipeg argued that fact made Bushelman a free agent since he hadn't been recalled when Grand Forks dropped out.

Hill used Bushelman frequently during the Rabbits exhibition schedule, and he made a pair of starts for Cedar Rapids once the regular season began. He started and lost a 2-1 start to Clinton on May 9. Taken out after five innings, the *Republican* said Bushelman "was a bit unsteady, though he deserves the credit also for working his way out of some very tight places. [He] pitched a good game but needed a larger plate." He walked two and struck out two. Bushelman made just one more appearance for Cedar Rapids losing at Springfield largely due to his own throwing error. Then he was forced to stop pitching until National Association President Thomas Farrell determined who he would be awarded to.

Winnipeg Manager Ed Herr was optimistic Bushelman would return to Winnipeg, and he was soon proven correct. When he was awarded to Winnipeg, the *Free Press* commented on his June 20 debut. "Winnipeg fans' old friend Jack Bushelman who has been among the lost, strayed or stolen since ordered to leave Cedar Rapids and report here, finally turned up yesterday and was immediately assigned to duty in right field. He accepted his one fielding chance, but failed to do anything but remove large chunks of ozone on each visit to the batting station."

The next day he lost his first start, but losses would be few and far between for Bushelman and the rest of the Winnipeg team in 1907. The team was already 22-13 and 4 ½ games ahead of second place Duluth. The Maroons had the rare distinction of winning every series on the season and leading the Northern Copper Country League pennant race every day but one. Francis Richter of *Sporting Life* said this was the first time it had been done in the minor leagues.

Jack got into the winning spirit in his second start shutting out Houghton. The *Free Press* offered colorful comment on his effort. "Bushelman was harder to find than a million-dollar job. He held the Solbraa [the Houghton manager] Sluggers down to two little hits and made nine of them hit where the ball wasn't." His next start was a Victoria Day shutout of Calumet and the *Free Press* was impressed with his effort despite six walks. "He was the real candy. Whenever danger threatened Bush tightened up like a society dame and Calumet never had a chance."[8]

Bushelman on his 1912 Broadleaf Cigarettes baseball card.

Even when defeated in 1907, the setback for Bushelman was momentary. One of his few bad outings was a July loss to Houghton. The *Free Press* described the rematch:

"Jonathon Bushelman the prize bull pup of the northern kennels was on the mound in the matinee. Jonathon pitched against the Giants in the rain the other night and had his pet curves pushed and shoved in a most exasperating manner. He was glad of the chance to get back at the Giants again and he sure delivered the goods in neat parcels. Up to the ninth but one little single had been made off the big fellow, but he let up a little in the final round; and a couple of hits with an out gave the visitors their only run."[9]

He won that game 4-1 and beat Houghton again the next day

6-1. That wasn't his last iron man performance. Just three days later he pitched and won both games of a doubleheader against Calumet. The four-win week improved his record to 9-4.

As with any successful team in the lower minors, there was talk of sales to teams either in the major or high minor leagues. Winnipeg was no exception. On August 5, the *Free Press* reported Bushelman's sale to Toledo of the American Association. As with a majority of similar sales, Bushelman would not report to his new team until the following spring.

Meanwhile there was a pennant to be clinched, and Bushelman delivered. The *Free Press* said: "Any time the tribe of Herr can hit in a couple or three runs behind Bushelman you can generally bank on another boost in the percentage. He stacked up against a couple of healthy-looking full houses, but he always held the cards and raked in every jackpot. Eleven of the [Duluth] Sox died on the bases, creating a mad scramble among the undertakers."[10] When the 1907 season ended on Labour Day in Canada, Bushelman's record was 15-7 and the Maroons compiled one of the most dominant team performances in minor league history. None of the other three Northern Copper Country League teams posted a better than .500 winning percentage.

Jack Bushelman joined the Toledo Mud Hens at Chattanooga, Tennessee in mid-March of 1908. The *Toledo News-Bee* said of his first appearance in an intrasquad game: "[He] worked as smoothly as though it were the middle of July. [He] had all brands of smoke on the mound. [He] acted as though a nine round affair would be easy [and] had the Colts standing on their heads throughout the four periods [he] worked."[11] He wasn't quite as effective in his first outing against major league competition. Against the New York Highlanders, the *News-Bee* described him as "effective but wild."[12] His last appearance in Chattanooga was one of his best in a Toledo uniform. Pitching against the defending World Champion Chicago Cubs on March 31, "Bushelman went through his three innings like a prairie fire. This big fellow has something. He worked it coming and going."[13] The Chicago lineup included many of the team's regulars.

In early April, the Mud Hens returned to Toledo for a few more exhibitions against major league opposition. The first of those games was a turning point for Jack Bushelman. On Saturday April 4, the Boston Americans came to Toledo's Armory Park for a weekend series. Jack was the starting pitcher that afternoon and was the story of the game. The *News-Bee* thought his experience at Winnipeg might have helped him that cold Ohio afternoon.

"[He] was acclimated to the hardships and rigors of the wintry weather by reason of his season's experience in Winnipeg. Bushelman has not been afflicted with a sore whip this year but he is liable to fall heir to one if he keeps on cutting loose like he did in the snow ball atmosphere. Big Jack Bushelman pitched himself into high favor with the fans and on his way to the clubhouse after his five innings toil, was enthusiastically greeted. The lofty lad worked as smoothly as he did all spring at Chattanooga."[14]

He pitched the first five innings allowing four hits and striking out four that afternoon.

Boston owner John I. Taylor witnessed the game that afternoon and offered $5,000 for Bushelman. The Mud Hens were actually owned by Charles Somers the owner of the Cleveland Naps. Between that cold afternoon in Toledo and Bushelman's late 1911 Boston debut, the big right hander would be one of the most traveled pitchers in professional baseball.

Bushelman's decline started with an exhibition appearance against the Giants. The *Toledo Blade* said: "The big bold Bushelman stepped into the box, anxious to finish his end of the afternoon engagement and beat it for the clubhouse where there is a fire that keeps the icicles from gathering along the rim of one's hat. But alas! Poor Bushelman was given an awful bombardment. Three runs were gathered from his big frame and only one was out."[15]

The decline continued into the regular season. He made his debut on April 20; the season's fourth game. Toledo won 8-7, but Jack was shaky at best. The *Blade* said: "Bushelman's seven walks kept the entire team unsteady. Three balls were frequently called before he began to get them over the pan. The young pitcher had Abbott bobbing all over the territory behind the plate. The passed ball charged to Fred was a wonderful drop curve, which broke so suddenly it fooled even the catcher."[16]

Given another start a week later, he allowed 11 hits, walked four, and threw two wild pitches in a 14-4 loss. He pitched better in a 3-1 loss at Milwaukee, but after a giving up two first inning runs and walking the first two men in the second inning of a loss to Indianapolis, he wasn't used again by the Mud Hens. When Toledo optioned him to Springfield of the Class D Ohio State League on June 5, Armour said: "This young fellow has the speed and curves to make good with any team, but he needs more experience and should be worked every four days."

At first it looked as though his Springfield assignment to Springfield might be brief, with a return to Toledo. The *Springfield Daily News* was impressed with his home debut. "Bushelman was the whole works in the first contest. He has terrific speed and a clever slow ball, and he worked a change of pace most successfully on Mansfield."[17] He shut out Mansfield, one of the league's best offensive teams on four hits.

He beat Newark 2-1 in his next start, then shut out Mansfield again. The *Mansfield Daily Shield* said: "He…had the locals guessing at all stages of the game. He struck out twelve coming within three of beating the league record held by [Harvey] Doc Bailey. He was wild during the early stages of the game, but was invincible when the bases were occupied."[18] He gave up six hits that afternoon. That was also the last time he pitched for Springfield. The franchise moved to Portsmouth after the series in Mansfield.

Bushelman started the team's first game in their new home and was again effective. He beat Marion 3-2 allowing just five hits and striking out six. Both runs scored on wild pitches. With a 4-0 record for a poor team, Bushelman seemed on the verge of another outstanding season. He dropped two of his next three decisions, but still seemed ready for a promotion, Toledo loaning him to Lincoln of the Class A Western League.

The promotion was the worst thing that could have happened to Jack Bushelman. Whether it was inactivity or an adjustment to his pitching motion by manager Bill Fox is unclear, but he wouldn't be a consistently effective pitcher again until the second half of the 1910 season. Bushelman allowed one hit and struck out six but walked eight. He made a relief appearance five days later and was equally ineffective. Unhappy in Lincoln, he wrote Armour asking for a change of scenery. On July 24, the *Newark*

Advocate announced Bushelman's return to the Ohio State League, this time with the Newark Molders.

Newark's franchise had been purchased by Cleveland through Armour earlier in the summer and former Toledo pitcher Harry Eells was the manager. It looked like a good situation for Bushelman. In his return to Ohio, Jack pitched three hitless innings striking out three but walking five. The *Advocate* said: "He has a good head in the box and works with the air of a veteran." [19] He shut Marion out in his first start and demonstrated a good pickoff move catching three runners napping. He walked five that day and also in a loss to Lancaster, but at first it seemed like he could be considered effectively wild.

That idea vanished in an August 2 start at Mansfield. The *Shield* described how much he'd regressed since his early June starts against the team. "Bushelman's wildness in the first inning gave the Tigers an advantage which they held all through the game. The ex-Toledo and Portsmouth man gave four bases on balls in that one inning, forcing two runs over the plate by his wildness." The *Mansfield News* said: "It required exactly 27 minutes to play the inning." Soon there was talk of Jack's release by Newark.

Frank Sheridan of the *Portsmouth Times* described another August start. "Bushelman was as wild as a March hare or a February hare, for that matter---one is just as wild as the other." [20] He struck out nine and walked six that day. His next start was even worse. He walked 11 in an 8-1 loss at Lima. News of his wildness was spreading beyond the Ohio State League. The *Akron Beacon Journal* printed his stats after a rumor circulated that he'd be joining the team. Those statistics included 26 strikeouts, 25 walks, 22 hits allowed, and two hit batsmen in 34 innings.

Instead he returned to Portsmouth. Portsmouth manager Billy Doyle later one of the game's outstanding scouts was also a member of the team's pitching staff, but he couldn't help Bushelman. After walking five in six innings in an early September start, Jack Bushelman was sent home for the season. At season's end, he was 7-15 in the Ohio State League. The league released more complete pitching statistics than most and they show 108 hits, 140 strikeouts, 101 walks and a league-leading 11 wild pitches in 171 innings. His walks per nine innings led the league.

That winter, Cleveland through Toledo conditionally sold Bushelman to Savannah of the South Atlantic League for $300. Bushelman refused to report to Savannah, negating the sale. In May 1909, Toledo tried to send him to Mansfield, but he didn't report, preferring to play for the Ivorydales of Cincinnati's Saturday Afternoon League.

The caliber of semipro ball in Jack Bushelman's hometown was very high. Ernie Diehl was the best known Queen City semipro. Business and political interests kept Diehl in Cincinnati most of the year, but he frequently filled in with various major league clubs as well as Toledo. In addition to the Ivorydales, Bushelman and Diehl were both members of the Hamilton Krebs. By late July, there were rumors of Bushelman's return to organized ball. Dayton of the Central League was interested, but Toledo still held his rights and he reported to Toledo in late July after Armour received a favorable telegram from Diehl.

The *Blade* said: "The lofty right-hander has the natural ability to be as good as Addie Joss, Christy Mathewson and others. If Bushelman can control his fast ball, nobody in this league will have any right to beat him." [21] Unfortunately, in his brief second chance with Toledo, he couldn't control the fastball. He appeared in both games of an August 1 doubleheader at Milwaukee, and the *News-Bee* was not impressed. "Jack Bushelman, who worked the last two innings of [the first game] in order that that multitude might be appeased started off in the afterpiece. He looked soft in the first two periods, but went entirely to the bad in the fourth and took everybody with him." [22] In four innings he allowed ten runs on as many hits. He was quickly released and returned to independent baseball.

Despite the lack of minor league success in 1908 and 1909, Jack Bushelman made his major-league debut the last day of the 1909 season. The Cincinnati Reds hosted the soon-to-be World Champion Pittsburgh Pirates in an October 5 doubleheader, and—though he wasn't signed to a contract—it was a tryout of sorts when Reds manager Clark Griffith started Jack in the second game. As might be expected, the Pirates won the game 7-4. Just two of the runs were earned, Bushelman allowing seven hits including a home run by Dots Miller. He walked four and struck out three in the seven-inning contest.

Four days later, pitching for the Krebs at the Butler County Fair, he faced Louisville of the American Association and shut them out 2-0 allowing just one hit. He struck out seven and walked four, impressing Louisville manager Heinie Pietz enough to be signed for the 1910 season. He turned down an offer from Buffalo believing Pietz, a former catcher would make him a better pitcher.

Hopes for a successful return to the American Association were quickly dashed. He allowed four runs in three innings against the Athletics and was beaten 7-2 by the Cubs allowing nine hits and walking eight. Appearing briefly in the regular season for Louisville he was equally ineffective. On May 3, his sale to the Syracuse Stars of the New York State League was announced. The president of the team said of Bushelman: "[Manager Ed] Ashenback has had his eye on this man for some time past…. Bushelman is a big fellow with lots of ginger and his purchase will materially strengthen the pitching corps."

Jack made his Syracuse debut in the team's home opener. The *Syracuse Post Standard* was impressed with the new pitcher. "Bushelman owns to three inches over six feet and has a hand like a ham. He was altogether too lavish with his gifts of bases, two of the gifts resulting in runs, but he pitched an excellent game, nevertheless as the record attests." He allowed five walks striking out eight in a 4-3 loss to Utica. The *Post Standard* was even more impressed with his next start: "He pitched consistent ball. The [Albany] Senators found him for nine hits all save three of which were widely scattered." [23] Most importantly he walked only one batter in an 8-1 win. It seemed like he'd found a home, but after three straight ineffective starts was released in late May.

He was soon signed by Lawrence (Massachusetts) of the New England League, but was no more effective than he'd been at Louisville or Syracuse. In a late June start, he gave up six runs in just over an inning of work walking three. In mid-July, Lawrence released him. The release was another turning point in his career. First-place New Bedford (Massachusetts) quickly signed him. Sixteen of his 27 appearances were with his new team, and by season's end Bushelman showed signs of mastering his control and resurrecting his career, finishing the year with a 12-9 mark. Catcher Fred Ulrich was likely responsible for the improvement that would soon bring him to Boston.

Once the 1911 New England League season started, Bushelman was the Whalers' best pitcher. In a pair of May starts he struck out 15 batters walking just two. He was also batting .350 over his first six games. The Whalers as a team included nine men with previous or subsequent major league experience, including Tommy Griffith and Rabbit Maranville, but still lost more games than they won.

He had several other successful starts, and in July, the *Lowell Sun* wrote, "The fans were disappointed in not seeing Bushelman, the big league prospect in yesterday's game. Bushelman is generally regarded as the best pitching proposition in the league." [24] Chicago White Sox manager Hugh Duffy reportedly offered $4,000 for Bushelman but New Bedford management wanted $5,000. At the end of July, John I. Taylor paid that sum for Bushelman and outfielder Arthur McCrone.

Jack won 16 games against 14 losses for the Whalers before joining the Red Sox, but his last start for New Bedford was controversial. According to *Sporting Life* and the *Fitchburg (Massachusetts) Daily Sentinel*, Bushelman was accused of intentionally losing to Fall River on September 4. He was fined $50 by the Whalers but after an investigation no evidence was found that he'd indeed thrown the game. In fact such accusations were not uncommon in that era and he joined the Red Sox almost immediately after the game in question.

After the unpleasant exit from New Bedford, Bushelman's debut with the Red Sox came September 11 against one of the American League's best pitchers, Walter Johnson. Joe Jackson of the *Washington Post* described Bushelman's rocky start:

"Young Mr. Bushelman, hitherto domiciled in New Bedford, but who yesterday was handed a Boston uniform, shown where the pitching hill is located on a regular yard, and told to go in and do his worst did so. He made the mistake common to twirlers transported from the bush and sent into a major league game before getting their bearings, that of imagining that more speed, wider curves and a larger number of strikeouts are essential to success in the large league. He spent one inning in trying to show and get these things and in so doing blew the ball game. After that Bushelman steadied and pitched a very creditable game. He seemed to have plenty of stuff when he contented himself with pitching to the batters and relying on his support, instead of trying to fool them all the time. In six consecutive innings only two hits and one base on balls were charged against him, and one of the hits as well as the pass came with two out."

In the first inning, four walks, a hit batsman, a balk and at least three errors led to five runs without benefit of a base hit. In the second, he recovered to strike out Germany Schaefer and

Detail from Red Sox team photo at Fenway Park showing Bushelman, cap in hand.

Tommy Long. Washington added two more runs on four hits.

Despite the generally positive effort after the first inning, that game was Bushelman's only regular season start for Boston. He made a couple of relief appearances in a late September home series against the White Sox replacing Ray Collins and Larry Pape who were lifted for pinch hitters. In 12 innings he surrendered eight hits, walked 10, and struck out five. Only four of the nine runs scored against him were earned.

In the spring of 1912, Bushelman was one of 30 players (including 10 pitchers) listed on the Red Sox preseason roster. Sheridan of the *Portsmouth* (Ohio) *Daily Times* said "Here is a kid who if he could get the bean over the plate would be another Christy Mathewson." [25] Unfortunately for Jack, he didn't master his pitches in his brief opportunities for the 1912 Red Sox. In late April he pitched an uneventful inning against Philadelphia. A week later, he walked a pair of Washington batters in the eighth, one scoring on a throwing error by Bill Carrigan. Jack's best performance in a Boston uniform was a 4-2 exhibition win over Baltimore of the International League on May 5.

Jack's final regular season appearance in the major leagues was also his only big league win. On May 13, Boston scored nine runs in the second inning and Bushelman entered the game in relief of Charley Hall who'd surrendered four first-inning runs. Bushelman held the Browns scoreless until the seventh when according to game accounts "he went to pieces in the seventh" and had to be relieved by Hugh Bedient. Despite the rocky seventh, he allowed three runs, eight hits and a pair of walks in 5 1/3 innings. After that game, he remained with the Red Sox but never appeared in another regular season game. After a poor start in another exhibition against Baltimore, Boston sent Bushelman to Worcester (Massachusetts) of the New England League. Optioned at first, he was officially sold to Jesse Burkett's team in August. He won eight of 12 decisions for Worcester.

Jack Bushelman had his best season as a professional in 1913 but it was likely responsible for shortening his career. Burkett's Busters were battling Lowell (Massachusetts) for the New England League pennant. Jack won 26 games in 37 decisions season but his effectiveness declined in the season's final weeks and he was never really the same pitcher again. [26]

Bushelman was one of the first players to sign a 1914 Worcester contract. As the season started, Jack was still winning but not in the often dominant fashion of 1913. One of his better efforts was a mid-June start against Fitchburg. The *Fitchburg Daily Sentinel* said he "was practically invincible, holding Fitchburg to three hits. He pitched very effective ball in all the sessions but the fifth…"[27] He also pitched well in his next start a win over Lewiston (Maine), but by the end of the month was essentially finished for the season.

According to the *Lowell Sun* there was reason for optimism at the beginning of August. "Jack Bushelman is back again in the Worcester lineup and his arm feels much better. Jesse sent Bushelman out to see Bonesetter Reese and the latter guaranteed Burkett a speedy return of form for the big pitcher."[28] The rumor was overly optimistic, and Jack finished the year with an 8-4 record in just 18 appearances.

Worcester did not offer Bushelman a contract in 1915. Manager Bill Schwartz of the Southern Association's Nashville Vols was a fellow Ohioan familiar with Bushelman and signed him. Perhaps his most memorable game in a Nashville uniform was a 17-inning game against Atlanta on May 31. Bushelman pitched effectively for the first nine before being lifted for a pinch hitter. At midseason he was 4-5 in 14 appearances for the Vols. In late July, he was released to Memphis of the same league.

The Chicks were in second place when Bushelman made his debut for the team on July 25. The Atlanta *Constitution* said of his losing debut against the Crackers: "Bushelman kept himself continually in trouble through his wildness, but managed to pull himself out of each hole which he put himself in with the exception of the fifth." That inconsistency was typical of his stint with Memphis, though his effectiveness improved late in the season. Perhaps most satisfying were a pair of September wins over his former Nashville teammates. He finished the year with a 12-11 record and 97 walks in 203 innings.

The 1915 season was also the end of Jack Bushelman's organized baseball career, though he played for Cincinnati's top semipro teams for several more seasons. Jack settled into the lumber business which had been his offseason occupation. Jack and his wife Helen (generally referred to by her middle name of Zilla) had met when Jack was briefly the property of the Little Rock Southern Association club early in his professional career. The Bushelmans raised four daughters and two sons. Immediately after his baseball career, the family lived in Eastlake, Tennessee while Jack worked as a traveling lumber salesman. Moving back to the Cincinnati area by 1920, he was living in St. Bernard and was an inspector for a lumber company. The family lived in Ohio until 1932 when hired by the Tennessee Eastman Lumber Company of Kingsport. Initially working in the sales and purchasing department, he was promoted to lumber and box department superintendent in 1944. The Bushelmans lived in nearby Gate City, Virginia where he served as president of the Rotary Club. He retired in 1951 and died at a Roanoke, Virginia hospital on October 26, 1955 after a long illness.

Sources:

Sporting Life 1905-11

Cedar Rapids (Iowa) *Republican* 1906-07

(Winnipeg) *Manitoba Free Press* 1906-07

Winnipeg Daily News 1906-07

Toledo News-Bee 1908

Toledo Blade 1908-09

Springfield (Ohio) *Daily News* 1908

Mansfield (Ohio) *Shield* 1908

Mansfield (Ohio) *News* 1908-09

(Lincoln) *Nebraska State Journal* 1908

Newark (Ohio) *Advocate* 1908

Portsmouth (Ohio) *Times* 1908-12

Lancaster (Ohio) *Eagle* 1908

Cincinnati Enquirer 1909

Syracuse (New York) *Post Standard* 1910-11

Lowell (Massachusetts) *Sun* 1911-15

Fitchburg (Massachusetts) *Daily Sentinel* 1911-14

Boston Globe 1911-12

Washington Post 1911-12

Atlanta Constitution 1915

Kingsport (Tennessee) *News* 1955

Genealogical Information:

Kentucky Birth Records

Cincinnati, Ohio Directory 1890-91

U.S. Census 1880, 1900, 1910, 1920, 1930

World War I Draft Registration Eastlake, Tennessee

World War II Draft Registration Gate City, Virginia

Thanks to Jack V. Morris and Dave Pugh for tracking down the dates of many of the citations.

Endnotes

1. Handwritten census records are unclear, but Bushelman's mother's name could perhaps be Nettie. His birth year, 1885, is in some doubt because the 1900 census, and his draft cards at the time of both the first and second World Wars all say he was born in 1886.

2. *Portsmouth Daily Times*, November 22, 1909.

3. *Cedar Rapids Republican*, April 27, 1906.

4. *Ibid.*, May 5, 1906.

5. *Ibid.*, August 1, 1906.

6. *Manitoba Free Press*, September 4, 1906.

7. *Ibid.*, September 21, 1906.

8. *Ibid.*, June 26, 1907 and July 2, 1907.

9. *Ibid.*, July 22, 1907.

10. *Ibid.*, August 20, 1907.

11. *Toledo News-Bee*, March 23, 1908.

12. *Toledo News-Bee*, March 26, 1908.

13. *Toledo News-Bee*, April 1, 1908.

14. *Toledo News-Bee*, April 6, 1908.

15. *Toledo Blade*, April 8, 1908.

16. *Toledo Blade*, April 21, 1908.

17. *Springfield* (Ohio) *Daily News*, June 8, 1908.

18. *Mansfield* (Ohio) *Daily Shield*, June 15, 1908.

19. *Newark* (Ohio) *Advocate*, July 25, 1908.

20. *Portsmouth* (Ohio) *Times*, August 12, 1908.

21. *Toledo Blade*, July 21, 1909.

22. *Toledo News-Bee*, August 2, 1909.

23. *Syracuse Post-Standard*, May 7, 1910 and May 12, 1910.

24. *Lowell Sun*, July 7, 1911.

25. *Portsmouth Daily Times*, March 15, 1912.

26. On the afternoon of September 10, Bushelman was nearly responsible for Burkett's arrest. According to the *Lowell Sun:* "Jack Bushelman pitcher for the Worcester team was summoned to appear in the superior court in Taunton in the case of Thomas Dowd [Bushelman's former manager] vs. the New Bedford Baseball Association." Constable John McManus of Lowell, told the *Sun:* "I Went to the New American House [hotel] with the summons and the money [traveling expenses] and passed them to Mr. Bushelman. Mr. Burkett was there and he said that Bushelman couldn't go to Taunton. He snatched the summons and the money from Bushelman's hand and pushed me away. I told him to beware of the majesty of the law and warned him he was liable to arrest for interfering with an officer." Burkett didn't deny the facts when questioned by the *Sun's* reporter at the Lowell ballpark, noting "he wasn't worrying about any arrests being made."

    Though there were rumors that Burkett was headed to the Federal League as a manager for 1914, Jack Bushelman wouldn't have followed him.

27. *Fitchburg Daily Sentinel*, June 13, 1914.

28. *Lowell Sun*, August 3, 1914.

Hick Cady
By William D. Dowell

G	AB	R	H	2B	3B	HR	RBI	BB	SO	BA	OBP	SLG	SB	HBP
47	135	19	35	13	2	0	9	10	16	.259	.324	.385	0	3

"In Cady Boston has picked up a man who looks like a first-class player. He stands more than six foot high and throws overhead dead to the mark all the time," observed Tim Murnane, the Boston *Globe* sportswriter, on March 16, 1912. Murnane was commenting on a promising rookie catcher named Forrest "Hick" Cady, during the Boston Red Sox' spring training in Hot Springs, Arkansas. Six months earlier the Red Sox had purchased Cady from the Newark Indians of the Eastern League for the then-pricey sum of $6,000 and two players. During the 1912 spring-training season, Cady impressed first-year manager Jake Stahl enough that he accompanied the team north to Boston.

Cady went on to enjoy a seven-year career in the major leagues during the height of the Deadball Era. He played six seasons with the Boston Red Sox on some of their greatest teams, including three World Series champions, and ended his career on a less-than-stellar Philadelphia Phillies team in 1919. Noted for his defensive abilities, Cady was a light-hitting right-handed-batting catcher who had a knack for timely hitting and was known as the preferred catcher of Smokey Joe Wood.

Forrest Cady's family history and their introduction to the United States is an interesting tale. In 1846 a group of 1,100 Swedes set sail from Gavle, Sweden, in search of the religious freedom that America promised. Called Jansonists after their leader, Eric Janson, they were frequently at odds with Sweden's state-run Lutheran Church over doctrine. Many of them, especially Janson, had suffered fines and imprisonment. Looking for a place where they could practice their religion without persecution, the group had sent a member ahead to America to secure a parcel of land that would accommodate their growing numbers. By summer, land in western Illinois had been purchased and by October the first colonist arrived. Led by Janson, the group decided to name the village Bishop Hill, after a town of the similar name in their region of Sweden.

Among the first to Bishop Hill was seven-year-old Hans Martensson Hollander, who was born October 9, 1839, in Bollnas, Sweden. Accompanied to America by his parents, Hans was raised in a religious commune where it was customary to spend three hours a day during the week and six hours on Sunday in church. His parents were firm believers in Janson.

Janson met an untimely death on the courthouse steps in Cambridge, Illinois, when he was shot by John Root, a nonbeliever. Root had married a Janson follower named Charlotta, but Janson had refused to allow her to leave the colony with Root. Outraged by this, Root confronted Janson on the courthouse steps in Cambridge, the county seat. Heated words were exchanged and Root pulled out a revolver and shot Janson dead.

Over the years more followers immigrated to Bishop Hill, settling in the colony or in the nearby countryside and becoming farmers. Christena Backlean and her 4-year-old daughter, Christena "Minnie" Backlean, were among this second wave. Minnie had been born in 1865 in Sweden. Hans Hollander and Minnie's mother met in Bishop Hill, and by November 11, 1871, they were married.

In May 1883 Minnie was married to Johannes (John) Berglund, who had come to the US from Sweden in 1880 and worked as a farm laborer in Bishop Hill. By 1890, when they divorced, the couple had produced three children, Victor, Forrest, and Bessie. In 1892 Minnie married a widower, Frank E. Cady, a carpenter in Bishop Hill. Four-year-old Forrest quickly identified with Frank as a father figure and accepted his surname as his own. Frank had two children, Minnie had three, and she and Frank had three more. (In 1898 Forrest's father, John Berglund, returned to Sweden, where he worked as a farmhand until his death in 1931.)

As a youngster Forrest Cady was affectionately tabbed with the nickname Hollick, whose origin was unknown. Early in his minor-league career, teammates shortened it to Hick. In his youth he gained a reputation as a first-rate local ballplayer. Local news accounts credited Ben J.

Hick Cady.

Arnquist, a longtime supporter of baseball in the Bishop Hill community, with refining Cady's skills as an outfielder and hitter. From 1903 to 1907 Cady played primarily with the Bishop Hill club under the tutelage of Arnquist. In 1906, as his team won the amateur Western League pennant, Cady batted .361 and recorded a .978 fielding percentage.

On occasion Cady played for a semipro team from nearby Kewanee, the Clippers, for whom his older brother, Victor, played. After a tryout Cady had impressed Kewanee manager Ike Reno enough to earn a place on the team as a reserve outfielder, occasional first baseman, and pinch-hitter. His career-changing moment came in a doubleheader against a team from Bradford, Illinois, when the Clippers' regular catcher split his finger and was unable to continue. Even though he had never played the position, Cady donned the catching gear and set his professional career in motion.

For the next couple of years Cady bounced from team to team trying to earn his place in minor-league ball. In 1907 he tried out with the Rock Island, Illinois, club of the Three-I League, but was not offered a contract and went back to playing for Bishop Hill. Toward the end of the season he caught on with Monmouth, an independent club, which sold him at the end of the season to Indianapolis of the American Association for $300. Cady's trial with Indianapolis was disappointing as he never appeared in a game. Unhappy with his situation in Indianapolis, he asked for and was granted his release.

After Cady returned home to Bishop Hill, he briefly played with the Kewanee Boilermakers of the Central Association and finished the 1908 season with the Ottumwa, Iowa, Packers of the same league. With both teams he played in 81 games, collecting 58 hits in 251 at-bats for a .231 average. He showed some power, collecting 16 extra-base hits, and a penchant for running the bases by accumulating nine stolen bases. His play earned him a contract the following year with Evansville, Indiana, of the Central League. In December 1906 Cady married Kittie Monjar. They were married for 40 years, until Cady died in 1946.

Playing for the Evansville River Rats in 1909 and 1910, Cady became known as a fine defensive catcher with some pop in his bat. In 240 games during the two seasons, he batted .218 and hit 11 home runs. After the 1910 season he signed with the Newark Indians of the Eastern League, where in 1911 he set personal highs in every offensive category except home runs. Cady played in 136 games, batted .260, scored 42 runs, collected 114 hits, 16 doubles, and 7 triples, and stole 12 bases. In January 1912 the Red Sox purchased his contract for $6,000 and two players.

On April 20, 1912, when the Red Sox opened their brand-new Fenway Park, the 26-year-old Cady was on their roster as a backup catcher. The 6-foot-2, 178-pound backstop was to share backstop duties with Bill Carrigan and Les Nunamaker. He saw his first major-league action on April 26, against the Philadelphia Athletics. For the season Cady played in 47 games, and hit .259 in 135 at-bats. Behind the plate he recorded a .990 fielding percentage in 43 games and he played

Cady along Fenway's first-base line in late September 1912.

four games at first base without committing an error. On June 29, against New York, Cady singled, driving in Jake Stahl from third. Then home-plate umpire Silk O'Loughlin ruled that Stahl had actually been balked home and recalled Cady back to bat. This time, Cady doubled. The quirky incident led the newspaper feature "Ripley's Believe It or Not" to proclaim that Cady had recorded the impossible—two hits in one turn at bat.

Boston won the pennant by 14 games and played the New York Giants in the World Series. In what is considered to be one of the most exciting World Series in history, Boston defeated the Giants in eight games, winning four, losing three, and tying one game. Cady was the starting catcher in six of the games, batting .136 (3-for-22) with one RBI. He and his teammates pocketed the winner's share paycheck of $4,024.

In Game Three Cady came to bat with two outs, runners on first and third, and the Giants clinging to a 2-1 lead in the bottom of the ninth inning. He sent a sharply-hit line drive into deep right-center and into the late afternoon haze. Both baserunners appeared to score easily as Cady rounded first base. However, Giants right fielder Josh Devore had a good jump on the ball and raced back, caught the ball over his shoulder, and simply continued full-stride into the outfield clubhouse. The Boston spectators, whose view was impaired by the late-afternoon haze and were reading Devore's body language, were under the impression that the ball had fallen in and both runs had scored for a Red Sox victory. It wasn't until the following day when they read the morning newspaper that they realized the Giants had taken the game.

In 1913 Cady found himself as the Opening Day catcher for the defending World Champions. While he enjoyed a solid second season, the Red Sox could not find their way back to the World Series. Cady played in 40 games, batting a solid .250. He also improved upon his defense, and ended with a fielding percentage of .992. An article that year in *The Sporting News* identified Cady as one of the few catchers who could throw out Ty Cobb and the speedy Clyde Milan during the 1912 season.

The 1914 season was very similar to the 1913 season for both Cady and the Red Sox. Boston finished behind the Athletics and Cady once again put up very similar numbers to his first two years. Appearing in 61 games, he batted .260 and recorded a respectable .971 fielding percentage.

Cady was the Opening Day catcher for a 1915 Boston team that held high hopes of a productive season. He produced his best major-league season. Appearing in 78 games, he collected 57 hits in 205 at-bats for an impressive .278 batting average. (All were career highs.) He hit 12 doubles and two triples while knocking in 17 runs and scoring 25. His trademark defense was also spectacular, with a solid .980 fielding percentage. The Red Sox finished 2½ games ahead of the Detroit Tigers to claim the American League pennant, then defeated the Philadelphia Phillies, four games to one, in the World Series. Cady saw action in four Series games, collecting two hits in six at-bats. In that season Cady became one of the few men to pinch-hit for Babe Ruth, then a second-year pitcher.

The 1916 season started to signal the end for Cady. His fielding percentage of .967, in 63 games, was his lowest to date. At the plate the 30-year-old started to struggle significantly. He finished the season with only 31 hits in 162 at-bats, for a .191 batting average, and scored a meager five runs. (He did hit a career-high three triples.) The Red Sox once again won the pennant and beat the Brooklyn Robins in five games. Cady appeared in only two of the games and collected one hit in four at-bats.

The 1917 season was Cady's last as a member of the Boston Red Sox. The aging veteran saw action in only 17 games, 14 of them as catcher. He posted career lows in every imaginable offensive and defensive category. He hit a paltry .152, collected only seven hits, two of which were for extra bases, and scored four runs with two RBIs. In the field, Cady committed three errors to compile a career-low .959 fielding percentage. Boston finished in second place in the American League, nine games behind the pennant-winning Chicago White Sox.

Back home in Bishop Hill after the season, Cady and his wife, Kittie, were involved in a fatal automobile accident in October while returning home from Kewanee after a night out with friends. They were apparently traveling at a good rate and did not see a horse and buggy in the darkness. In an attempt to avoid the collision, Cady jerked his car to one side but still managed to clip the rear wheel of the buggy. Cady's Hupmobile continued through the ditch and rolled two or three times. Milford Lundberg, one of his passengers, was killed. His wife and Lundberg's wife escaped without serious injury as did those in the buggy. Cady suffered multiple breaks in his right shoulder.

The injuries did not stop Connie Mack of the Philadelphia Athletics from trading for Cady. On January 10, 1918, three months after the accident, Boston sent Cady along with outfielder Tilly Walker and third baseman Larry Gardner to Philadelphia for first baseman Stuffy McInnis. While dumping McInnis was more about purging salary than acquiring young talent or capable veterans, it is not clear why Mack would agree to accept a diminished player in Cady and now a debilitated one as well.

While he was with the Athletics, Cady never played for the team. Apparently his only duty was to warm up the pitchers. He was released in late June. Newspapers reported that manager Pat Moran of the National League Phillies was considering signing Cady, even noting that he worked out with the Phillies, but there is no indication that Cady was ever offered a contract by the Phillies.

Cady had other pressing matters to deal with. With the US now embroiled in the First World War, all able-bodied men were required to join the armed forces or find war-related work. During the summer Cady went to work for the Chester Ship Building Company in Pennsylvania, listing his occupation as ship builder. The shipyard had a team in the Delaware River Shipyards League, and Cady played for the team, mostly as a first baseman, as the team won 12 of its 14 games.

In 1919, with the war over, Cady made a brief comeback. In what was his last season as a major leaguer, he caught on with the Phillies. His skills significantly diminished, Cady played in 34 games and batted .214. Although he had only 98 at-bats, he had a career-high 19 RBIs and hit the only home run of his seven-year major-league career. But his major-league career ended on a sour note. On July 9 Cady and two Phillies pitchers, Gene Packard and Frank Woodward, were thrown out of the game. The three dressed and went into the center-field bleachers where they "harangued the bleacherites against the action of President Baker in changing managers." For sticking up for their beloved manager, Jack Coombs, pitchers Packard and Woodward were fined $200 while Cady was fined $100 and given 10 days' notice of his release

Before the end of the season, Cady caught on with the Vernon Tigers of the Pacific Coast League and eventually the Sacramento Senators of the same league. For the next six years he bounced

Cady, warming up at Fenway Park.

Hick Cady, all dressed up and ready to go.

around the minor-league circuit, with stops in Joplin, Missouri; Kansas City, Missouri; Augusta, Georgia; Danville, Illinois; and Columbus, Ohio. Cady briefly managed the Augusta Tygers of the South Atlantic League (1922) and the Danville Veterans of the Three-I League (1924). He ended his playing career in 1925 but quickly reappeared in organized baseball as an umpire in the Western, Pacific Coast, and Three-I Leagues for nearly two decades.

On March 3, 1946, at the age of 60, Cady died in a hotel fire in Cedar Rapids, Iowa. According to Cady's death records, he was employed as a desk clerk at the hotel. The fire was caused by sparks from an electric heater that ignited some papers in his room. Cady was discovered by the hotel manager after other guests reported smelling smoke coming from his room. The fire was contained to his room. Cady apparently forgot to turn off the heater when he went to bed. He was survived by his wife, Kittie.

Sources:

Baseball Hall of Fame Library. Forrest Cady file.

Bishop Hill (Illinois) State Historic Site. Correspondence with author.

Bishop Hill News, March 11 and May 16, 1890.

"Forrest Cady Dies In Blaze," Cedar *Rapids* (Iowa) *Gazette,* March 4, 1946.

"Chester Ship Building Co. vs. N.Y. Ship," *Chester* (Pennsylvania) *Times,* July 27, 1918.

Arthur Daley, "Strange Things Happen in the World Series." *New York Times,* October 2, 1945.

Paul Elmen. *Wheat Flour Messiah* (Carbondale, Illinois: Southern Illinois University Press, 1997).

"The Days of Forrest Cady Recalled By Francis Geiger." *Galvaland Magazine,* August 1961.

Galva (Illinois) *News,* May 24, 1883.

"Meets His Death In Auto Accident," *Galva* (Illinois) *News,* October 25, 1917.

"Bishop Hill Star Once in Series," *Galva* (Illinois) *News,* October 16, 1983.

Gary Gillette and Pete Palmer, eds. *ESPN Baseball Encyclopedia* (New York: Sterling, 2008).

Iowa State Department of Health, Forrest Cady Death Certificate, 1946.

"Connie Mack Makes Up List of Players," *Los Angeles Times,* March 16, 1918.

T. H. Murnane, "Stahl Will Try Out Six Recruits Against Dooin's Best Team." *Boston Globe,* March 16, 1912.

"Catcher Sold To Boston," *Naugatuck* (Connecticut) *Daily News,* May 15, 1911.

"Baker Fines 3 Players," *New York Times,* July 10, 1919.

Roy Ostrom, "Forrest 'Hick' Cady." E-mail message to Doug Dowell, April 15, 2007.

Herb Simmons. "They Pinch Hit For The Greats" *Baseball Digest,* November 1972, 71-76.

The Sporting News, January 23, 1913.

Trenton (New Jersey) *Evening News,* June 26, 1918.

Warren (Pennsylvania) *Evening Times,* August 12, 1918.

Bill Carrigan
By Mark Armour

G	AB	R	H	2B	3B	HR	RBI	BB	SO	BA	OBP	SLG	SB	HBP
87	266	34	70	7	1	0	24	38	20	.263	.359	.297	7	2

An excellent defensive catcher who provided the Boston Red Sox with above-average offense for his position, Bill "Rough" Carrigan batted .257 in 709 career games, and once finished as high as eighth in the American League in batting average. Behind the plate, the 5-foot-9 175-pounder compensated for his lack of size with sheer toughness. Confrontational by nature, Carrigan rarely backed down from a fight, and usually came out on the better end of his many scraps. From 1913 to 1916, Carrigan was one of the most successful player-managers of the Deadball Era, piloting the Red Sox to back-to-back world championships in 1915 and 1916. After the latter season, the 32-year-old Carrigan, whom Babe Ruth later called the best manager he ever played for, walked away from the game to spend time with family and his business.

Most sources indicate that William Francis Carrigan was born in Lewiston, Maine, on October 22, 1883, though the 1900 Census places his birth year at 1884. William was the youngest of three children of John and Annie Carrigan, Irish Catholic immigrants who had arrived in the United States prior to the Civil War. According to census records, John supported the family as a deputy sheriff. During his youth, William worked on local farms when not playing sports, and was a star football and baseball player at Lewiston High. After high school, he moved on to the College of the Holy Cross in Worcester, Massachusetts. He starred as a football halfback for the legendary Frank Cavanaugh, who was later the subject of a movie (*The Iron Major*, starring Pat O'Brien) and is a member of the College Football Hall of Fame. On the diamond Carrigan played for Tommy McCarthy, the baseball star of the 1890s, who converted his young charge from the infield to catcher, a position Carrigan would play the rest of his career.

In the spring of 1906 Carrigan was signed to a Red Sox contract by Charles Taylor, the father of Red Sox owner John I. Taylor. Carrigan joined the struggling Red Sox directly in the middle of the season, immediately catching the likes of Bill Dinneen and Cy Young. In this initial trial, he hit just .211 in 37 games, but impressed with his play behind the dish. Sent to Toronto of the Eastern League the next season, he batted .320, and rejoined the Red Sox in 1908. The right-handed-hitting Carrigan was not a feared batsman, hitting just six lifetime home runs, but was soon one of the more respected members of the team. In 1908 he hit .235 as the primary backup to Lou Criger, but assumed the bulk of the innings for the next six seasons after Criger's departure to the St. Louis Browns. His .296 average in 1909 was the highest of his career, and the eighth best in the league that season.

Carrigan's stern look in this 1915 photograph may have been part of the reason he was nicknamed "Rough."

The well-mannered Carrigan earned the nickname Rough for the way he played. He was a well-respected handler of pitchers, and had a fair throwing arm, but it was his plate blocking that caused Chicago White Sox manager Nixey Callahan to say, "You might as well try to move a stone wall." On May 17, 1909 he engaged in a famous brawl with the Tigers' George Moriarty after a collision at home plate, while their teammates stood and watched. He had a fight with Sam Crawford a couple of years later, and maintained a reputation as someone who would not back down from a confrontation.

Fully entrenched as a regular by 1911, Carrigan had a fine season at the plate (.289 in 72 games) before suffering a broken leg on an awkward slide at second base on September 4. He caught the majority of the innings for the 1912 pennant winners, hitting .263, but was hitless in only seven at bats in the Red Sox' World Series victory that fall.

In July 1913 the Red Sox were grappling with a series of injuries, fighting among themselves, and limping along in fifth place. Team president Jimmy McAleer fired manager Jake Stahl just months after his World Series triumph, and replaced him with his 29-year-old catcher. Carrigan liked Stahl, as did most of the team, and was reluctant to take charge of a team filled with veterans, many of whom were just as qualified for the job as he. McAleer persuaded Carrigan to take it. The Red Sox were a team fractured along religious lines, as Protestants like Tris Speaker, Joe Wood, and Harry Hooper often crossed swords with the Catholics on the team, including Carrigan.

The club's new manager commanded respect through the unique brand of toughness he brought to the job. Wilbert Robinson, who managed Brooklyn against Carrigan in the 1916 World Series, later said that Carrigan was serious when it came to his pitchers dusting a hitter off: "When Carrigan told one of his pitchers to knock a man down and the batter didn't hit the dirt, the

Carrigan managed the Red Sox to world championships in 1915, 1916, and 1918. He's shown here in 1916, in the dugout with pitcher Babe Ruth, whose 1.75 ERA led the league.

pitcher was fined." The team played better the remainder of 1913 before finishing a strong second to Connie Mack's Philadelphia Athletics in 1914.

The most important event of the 1914 season was the purchase, at Carrigan's urging, of pitchers Ernie Shore and Babe Ruth from Baltimore of the International League. Although Ruth gave his skipper a lot of credit for his development as a player, Carrigan was humble in his own assessment: "Nobody could have made Ruth the great pitcher and great hitter he was but himself. He made himself with the aid of his God-given talents."

Old Rough did allow that his protégé needed quite a bit of discipline, and Carrigan was there to provide it, even rooming with Ruth for a time. Carrigan caught Ruth in his pitching debut, on July 11.

Some might fault Carrigan for not seeing the potential of Ruth as a hitter. Given that the Red Sox were blessed with the game's best outfield in Duffy Lewis, Tris Speaker, and Harry Hooper, and that

Ruth soon developed into one of the game's best pitchers, it is understandable why Carrigan did not wish to mess with success. In 1915 Carrigan did use Ruth occasionally as a pinch-hitter, and Babe responded with a team-leading four home runs.

The next two seasons brought Carrigan and his team their back-to-back World Series triumphs. Against the Phillies in 1915, Carrigan famously did not pitch Ruth, which some took as a message to the Babe that the team did not need him to win. Carrigan always disputed this, claiming he wanted to avoid using left-handed pitchers against the heavily right-handed-hitting Philadelphia club.

In early September 1916, Carrigan announced that he would be leaving baseball at the end of the season. He had actually wanted to quit after the 1915 Series, and had so told owner Joe Lannin, but his owner talked him into the one additional campaign. Carrigan later wrote, "I had become fed up on being away from home from February to October. I was in my thirties, was married and had an infant daughter. I wanted to spend more time with my family than baseball would allow." He retired to his hometown of Lewiston and embarked on careers in real estate (as co-owner of several movie theaters in New England) and banking. A few years later he sold his theaters for a substantial profit and became a wealthy man.

When Lannin sold the club to Harry Frazee before the 1917 season, Frazee drove to Lewiston to try to talk Carrigan into staying on. After that, an offseason did not go by without offers from major-league teams to lure Carrigan back into the game. After a decade of trying, the Red Sox finally summoned Carrigan out of retirement in 1927 to manage the tail-end Sox. Offering proof that the players often make the manager, the Red Sox continued their struggles, finishing last for all three seasons (1927-29) during the second Carrigan regime, despite improving their record each year.

Carrigan was not happy with the way the players had changed in his time away. "These players didn't talk baseball. They talked golf and stocks and where they were going after the game." Players resisted practice, individual instruction, or talk of cutoff plays and other strategies. "Inside baseball had become a lost art," he felt. Interestingly, he thought baseball was too concerned with finding good citizens: "I'll take players who get arrested every night and win ball games two out of three afternoons to the best behaved second-division gang ever assembled."

Moving back to Lewiston for good, Carrigan continued a very successful banking career. He joined the city's Board of Finance in 1938, and became president of Peoples Savings Bank in 1953. Through the years, he was a frequent guest at Fenway Park for

Carrigan takes a cut. His .263 average in 1912 was a good one for catchers in this era.

Note: An earlier version of this biography originally appeared in David Jones, ed., *Deadball Stars of the American League* (Washington, D.C.: Potomac Books, Inc., 2006).

Sources:

A primary source for this work was Bill Carrigan's file at the National Baseball Hall of Fame Library. Other sources include:

Will Anderson, *Was Baseball Really Invented In Maine?* (Bath, ME: Will Anderson, 1992).

Jack Kavanagh, "Quit While You're Ahead." *The National Pastime 11.* SABR, 1993.

Kerry Keene, Raymond Sinibaldi, and David Hickey. *The Babe in Red Stockings* (Champaign IL: Sagamore, 1997).

Frederick G. Lieb, *The Boston Red Sox.* (New York: Putnam, 1947).

Tom Meany. *Baseball's Greatest Teams* (New York: Barnes, 1949).

Fred Stein. *And the Skipper Bats Cleanup* (Jefferson NC: McFarland, 2002).

Glenn Stout and Richard A. Johnson. *Red Sox Century* (Boston: Houghton Mifflin, 2000).

Paul J. Zingg. *Harry Hooper, An American Baseball Life.* (Urbana and Chicago: University of Illinois, 1993).

ceremonies and reunions. He was named to the Holy Cross Hall of Fame in 1968.

Carrigan married the former Beulah Bartlett in 1915, and they had two daughters, Beulah and Constance, and one son, William Jr. Wife Beulah died in 1958, but Old Rough hung on until July 8, 1969, when he passed away at the age of 85 in his beloved Lewiston. He was buried in Lewiston's Riverside Cemetery.

There's always a lot of down time in baseball, particularly in the early days before air travel and television. Players without iPads or other mobile devices often played cards. Apparently catcher Bill Carrigan caught a little extra coin, too. *Boston Post*

Eddie Cicotte
by Jim Sandoval

G	ERA	W	L	SV	GS	GF	CG	SHO	IP	H	R	ER	BB	SO	HR	HBP	WP	BFP
9	5.67	1	3	0	6	2	2	0	46	58	34	29	15	20	0	1	2	198

G	AB	R	H	2B	3B	HR	RBI	BB	SO	BA	OBP	SLG	SB	HBP
9	13	1	2	0	0	0	1	4	2	.154	.353	.154	0	0

Though he didn't invent the pitch, Eddie "Knuckles" Cicotte was perhaps the first major-league pitcher to master the knuckleball. According to one description, Cicotte gripped the knuckler by holding the ball "on the three fingers of a closed hand, with his thumb and forefinger to guide it, throwing it with an overhand motion, and sending it from his hand as one would snap a whip. The ball acts like a 'spitter,' but is a new-fangled thing." Cicotte once estimated that 75 percent of the pitches he threw were knuckleballs. The rest of the time the right-hander relied on a fadeaway, slider, screwball, spitter, emery ball, shine ball, and a pitch he called the "sailor," a rising fastball that "would sail much in the same manner of a flat stone thrown by a small boy." Whether he was sailing or sinking the ball, shining it or darkening it, the 5-foot-9, 175-pound Cicotte had more pitches than a traveling salesman. "Perhaps no pitcher in the world has such a varied assortment of wares in his repertory as Cicotte," *The Sporting News* observed in 1918. "He throws with effect practically every kind of ball known to pitching science." But the most famous pitch Cicotte ever threw was the one that nailed Cincinnati Reds leadoff man Morrie Rath squarely in the back to lead off the 1919 World Series, a pitch that signaled to the gamblers that the fix was on. After confessing to his role in the scandal one year later, Cicotte was banned from the game for life, a punishment that perhaps denied the 208-game-winner a spot in the Hall of Fame.

Edward Victor Cicotte (pronounced SEE-cot) was born June 19, 1884, in Springwells, Michigan, a former township in the Detroit metropolitan area, into a family of French heritage. He was the son of Ambrose and Archangel (Drouillard) Cicotte. Eddie's brother Alva was the grandfather of Al Cicotte, who pitched in the major leagues for five seasons from 1957 to 1962. By the time Eddie was 16 years old his father had died, forcing his mother to support her large family as a dressmaker. Leaving school early, Eddie took up work as a box maker to help pay the family bills.

Cicotte began his baseball career, according to some sources, as early as 1903, playing semiprofessional ball in the Upper Peninsula of Michigan. In 1904 he pitched for Calumet (Michigan) and Saulte Ste. Marie (Ontario) in the Northern Copper League, posting a record of 38-4 with 11 shutouts. Based on that dominating performance, Cicotte earned a tryout with the Detroit Tigers in the spring of 1905. The Tigers determined that he wasn't ready for the majors, and optioned him to Augusta (Georgia) of the South Atlantic League, where he compiled a record of 15 wins against 9 losses, and brawled with his young teammate, Ty Cobb, after a Cobb stunt cost Cicotte a shutout. As a joke Cobb had taken popcorn with him to his position in center field and as a result committed an error that led to a run. This incident notwithstanding, among his teammates Cicotte was known as an easygoing prankster who enjoyed a good laugh.

Near the end of the season Detroit brought Cicotte up and he made his major-league debut on September 3, 1905, allowing one run in relief and getting tagged with the loss in a 10-inning game. Two days later Cicotte earned his first major-league win, a complete-game victory over the Chicago White Sox. He finished the year 1-1 with a 3.50 ERA, but would not return to the major leagues for another three seasons.

Cicotte began 1906 with Indianapolis of the American Association, where he posted a 1-4 record in 72 innings before landing with Des Moines of the Western League. Cicotte blossomed with his new team, registering an 18-9 record. The following season he pitched for Lincoln, also of the Western League, going 21-14. Impressed by the young hurler's arsenal

Eddie Cicotte warming up during Boston's mid-June visit to Chicago, about three weeks before he was traded to the White Sox.

of pitches, the Boston Red Sox purchased Cicotte's contract for $2,500 at the end of the 1907 season.

During his five-year stint with the Red Sox, Cicotte lost nearly as many games as he won, and frequently found himself in trouble with Red Sox owner John Taylor, who accused the pitcher of underachieving. "He was suspended without pay so much of the time that it was like having no job," the *Chicago Tribune*'s Sam Weller wrote of Cicotte's Boston career. On a club that consistently failed to meet expectations, Cicotte often became the scapegoat, and in 1911 Taylor tried to secure waivers on his inconsistent pitcher, only to pull back when another team made a claim. "[Taylor] wouldn't like the way I was working, or perhaps the opposition had made one or two hits," Cicotte later charged. "Taylor never liked me; I never liked him, and it was seldom that I went through a game without having him comment upon it." After Cicotte started the 1912 season with a 1-3 record and 5.67 ERA in six starts, the Red Sox—though no longer owned by Taylor—had finally seen enough. On July 22 the team sold Cicotte's contract to the Chicago White Sox, where the 28-year-old right-hander began to mature into one of the game's best pitchers. With Boston Cicotte had won 51 games and lost 46. Over the next 8½ seasons with the White Sox, Eddie won 156 games against 102 losses.

The biggest reason for this improvement was Cicotte's gradual mastery of his expansive pitching repertoire. As his command over his knuckleball improved, Cicotte's walk rate dramatically decreased; from 1912 to 1920 he ranked among the league's 10 best in fewest walks per nine innings seven times, leading the league in 1918 and 1919, when he walked a combined 89 men in $572^{2}/_{3}$ innings. Cicotte also fully exploited the era's liberal regulations regarding the doctoring of the ball. In this area, his most infamous pitch was the shine ball, in which he rubbed one side of the ball against the pocket of his right trouser leg, which had been filled with talcum powder. As Fred Lieb later explained it, the pitch "worked like an emery ball that had been roughened, in reverse. When pitched against air currents, the natural side of the shined ball became rough in contrast, and the sphere wobbled on its way to the batsman." Flustered opponents protested to American League president Ban Johnson that the pitch should be outlawed, but Johnson ruled the pitch legal in 1917, and it would remain so until February 1920. Thanks to the knuckleball, the shine ball, the emery ball (ruled illegal by Johnson in 1914), and other trick pitches, Cicotte struck out a fair number of batters, placing in the top ten in strikeouts per nine innings three times, even though his fastball probably couldn't break a plane of glass. Asked to explain his success, Cicotte chalked it up to "head work," adding, "It involves an ability to adapt pitching to certain conditions when they arise and perhaps use altogether different methods in the very next inning."

In 1913 Cicotte enjoyed his first standout season in the major leagues, posting an 18-12 record to go along with a 1.58 ERA, second best in the American League. That offseason Pittsburgh of the newly-formed Federal League attempted to sign Cicotte, but White Sox owner Charles Comiskey was able to secure the pitcher's loyalty through a three-year contract. In the first year of his contract, Eddie managed only an 11-16 record, although his 2.04 ERA was fifth best in the league. After a mediocre 13-12 campaign in 1915, Cicotte finally hit his stride in 1916, when he split time between the starting rotation and bullpen, posted a 1.78 ERA, won 15 out of 22 decisions and registered five saves. The following year Cicotte moved back to the starting rotation and enjoyed the best season of his career, as the White Sox captured their first pennant in 11 seasons. Cicotte led the way, ranking first in the league in wins (28), ERA (1.53), and innings pitched ($346^{2}/_{3}$). Eddie also tossed seven shutouts, including a no-hitter against the St. Louis Browns on April 14, the first of six no-hitters pitched in the major leagues that season. In that year's World Series Cicotte contributed one win to Chicago's six-game triumph over the New York Giants.

Despite Cicotte's breakthrough season, Comiskey offered his star pitcher only a $5,000 contract, much less than pitchers of the same caliber earned for other teams. Perhaps bitter over his meager salary, in 1918 Cicotte failed to produce an encore suitable to his dominant 1917 campaign, as he wrenched his ankle in early May, limping his way through the season to a mediocre 2.77 ERA and 19 losses, tied for most in the league. It was not a performance to inspire Comiskey to hand out a raise, and when the 1919 season began, financial troubles were weighing heavily on Cicotte. According to the 1920 Census, Cicotte was the head of household for a family of 12, including his wife, Rose; their three children; his wife's parents; Eddie's brother and wife; and a brother-in-law and his wife and child. To make room for his large family, Cicotte took out a $4,000 mortgage on a Michigan farm. Despite his financial worries, Cicotte regained his 1917 form, pitching the White Sox to their second pennant in three years. Once again, Eddie led the American League in victories (29) and innings pitched ($306^{2}/_{3}$, tied with Jim Shaw). His 29-7 record also was good enough to lead the league in winning percentage

Cicotte in 1917 with White Sox manager Clarence "Pants" Rowland. Note the "two-wheeler" in the dugout.

(.806), and his 1.82 ERA ranked second. In August first baseman Chick Gandil approached Cicotte about throwing the World Series. After thinking it over for several weeks, Eddie agreed to the scheme, telling Gandil, "I'll do it for ten thousand dollars. Cash. Before the Series begins."

Contrary to conventional wisdom, Cicotte's abysmal performance in the 1919 World Series was not a complete surprise to informed observers. Throughout September, reports surfaced that the overworked Cicotte was suffering from a sore shoulder. Prior to the first game of the Series, Christy Mathewson noted, Cicotte "has had less than a week [actually two days] to rest up for his first start.…And that may not prove to be enough. If he blows up for a single inning it may cost the White Sox the championship, for I think the first battle is going to have a very strong bearing on the outcome, especially if the Reds win it."

With at least six of his other teammates in on the fix, Cicotte led the way in blowing the first game, surrendering seven hits and six runs in 3⅔ innings of work, and fueling Cincinnati's winning rally by throwing high to second base on what should have been an inning-ending double-play ball. The performance was so bad that it generated renewed speculation that Cicotte was suffering from a "dead arm." For his second start, in Game Four, with the White Sox trailing two games to one, Eddie pitched more effectively, holding the Reds to just five hits and two unearned runs, both coming in the fifth inning on two Cicotte errors, including one inexplicable play in which he muffed an attempt to cut off a throw from the outfield, allowing the ball to go to the backstop and letting a Cincinnati runner—who had already stopped at third—score. The miscues were enough to ensure that the White Sox lost the game, 2-0. Afterward, Chicago manager Kid Gleason declared, "They shouldn't have scored on Cicotte in 40 innings. … There wasn't any occasion for Cicotte to intercept that throw. He did it to prevent Kopf from going to second. But Kopf had no more intention of going to second than I have of jumping in the lake."

Though Eddie had received his $10,000 prior to the start of the Series, many of his fellow conspirators had not received the money promised them by the gamblers, so before Cicotte's third start, in Game Seven, the players decided to play the game to win. Accordingly, Cicotte put forth his best effort of the Series, allowing just one run on seven hits in a 4-1 Chicago victory. Lefty Williams threw the following game, however, giving Cincinnati the world championship. In the wake of Chicago's defeat, Mathewson publicly tossed aside rumors that the series had been fixed, saying, "No pitcher could guarantee to toss a game.… Even if a pitcher should let the other side get two or three runs before he was yanked, he could not guarantee that the other side wouldn't come up the next inning and make four or five. That wipes out any single pitcher and leaves the proposition of fixing on a club. This can't be done."

Despite the persistent rumors that swirled around the club that offseason, Cicotte re-signed with Chicago for 1920, and put forth another excellent season, posting a 21-10 record with a 3.26 ERA. That summer Babe Ruth electrified the sport with his 54 home runs for the New York Yankees, but Cicotte grabbed a few headlines of his own after he stymied Ruth in several encounters. Asked to explain his success, the crafty Cicotte allowed that he mixed up his pitches and relied heavily on the spitball, because the pitch was "hard to hit for a long clout." Before the season, the spitball and other doctored pitches—including Cicotte's famous shine ball—had been banned from baseball. However, established spitball pitchers were given a one-year exemption from the rule, and Cicotte was one of 10 AL pitchers allowed to throw the spitter—but not the shine ball—in 1920. After the 1920 season the grandfather clause was made permanent, but Cicotte was not on that list because by then he had been banned from baseball.

On September 27, 1920, the *Philadelphia North American* ran a story in which Billy Maharg, one of the gamblers in on the Series fix the previous fall, testified to his role in the affair, and specifically named Cicotte as the man who initiated the plot. The next day, Eddie met with Comiskey and admitted to his role in the scandal. "Yeah—we were crooked," he sobbed in the owner's office. "We were crooked…" Before Cicotte could unburden himself any further, however, Comiskey cut him off, barking, "Don't tell me! Tell it to the Grand Jury!"

That very day, Cicotte did appear before the grand jury, becoming the first player to confess. When asked why he had taken the gamblers' money, Cicotte blamed Gandil, shortstop Swede Risberg, and utility infielder Fred McMullin for hounding him about it for weeks before the Series. "They wanted me to go crooked. I don't know. I needed the money. I had the wife and kids. The wife and kids don't know about this. I don't know what they'll think."

Though he and the other seven accused players were acquitted of conspiracy charges the following year, Eddie Cicotte's major-league baseball career ended with his confession. For the next three years he played with several of his banned teammates for outlaw teams in Minnesota, Wisconsin, and Bastrop, Louisiana, where he pitched under the alias Moore. Although some of the other Black Sox continued to play outlaw ball, by 1924 Cicotte had moved on with his life. He worked as a Michigan game warden and managed a service station before finding a job with the Ford Motor Company, where he remained until his retirement in 1944.

During the last 25 years of his life, Cicotte raised strawberries on a 5½-acre farm near Farmington, Michigan. In an interview with Detroit writer Joe Falls in 1965 he said he lived his life quietly, answering letters from youngsters who sometimes asked about the scandal. He agreed that he had made mistakes, but insisted that he had tried to make up for it by living as clean a life as he could. "I admit I did wrong," he said, "but I've paid for it the past 45 years." Falls seemed to agree, noting that as he

Cicotte and some of his comrades on the "Black Sox" in a courtroom, 1921.

Cicotte's T205 Gold Border Caporal Cigarettes baseball card.

prepared to leave Cicotte's home, he looked at Eddie's socks. They were white.

Eddie Cicotte died on May 5, 1969 at Henry Ford Hospital in Detroit. His death certificate listed his occupation as baseball player, Chicago White Sox. He was buried in Park View Cemetery in Livonia, Michigan.

Note: An earlier version of this biography originally appeared in David Jones, ed., *Deadball Stars of the American League* (Washington, D.C.: Potomac Books, Inc., 2006).

Sources:

Eliot Asinof. *Eight Men Out* (Henry Holt and Company, 1987).

Joe Falls interview with Cicotte. *Detroit Free Press*, December 4, 1965.

Ring Lardner. *Chicago Examiner*. July 21, 1912.

Paul MacFarlane editor. *Daguerreotypes. The Sporting News*, 1981.

Al Stump. *Cobb.* (Algonquin Books, 1996).

www.findagrave.com.

Obituary. *The Sporting News*. May 24, 1969.

Michigan Death Certificate.

Obituary, *New York Times*. May 9, 1969.

1880 Wayne County, Michigan, Federal Census.

1920 Wayne County, Michigan, Federal Census.

1930 Wayne County, Michigan, Federal Census.

www.ancestry.com.

The Sporting News. February 23, 1933, 8.

www.retrosheet.com.

Contract card, National Baseball Library, Hall of Fame.

Washington Post. August 24, 1906; August 24, 1907; March 8, 1908; April 15, 1917.

New York Times. April 15, 1917.

Sporting Life. February 21, 1914.

Baseball Research Journal. "From a Researcher's notebook." SABR, 1994.

Chicago Daily Tribune. August 27, 1906.

www.baseball-reference.com.

Ray Collins
by Tom Simon

G	ERA	W	L	SV	GS	GF	CG	SHO	IP	H	R	ER	BB	SO	HR	HBP	WP	BFP
27	2.53	13	8	0	24	0	17	4	199 1/3	192	65	56	42	82	4	2	0	794

G	AB	R	H	2B	3B	HR	RBI	BB	SO	BA	OBP	SLG	SB	HBP
27	65	8	11	1	0	0	2	4	14	.169	.308	.185	0	1

Ray Collins might have been on his way to the Hall of Fame but for an abrupt and mysterious end to his career after only seven seasons. In 1913-14 he won a combined 39 games for the Red Sox, and his lifetime 2.51 ERA is impressive even for his low-scoring era. Collins was a good-hitting pitcher and an outstanding fielder, but the key to his success was his remarkable control. He consistently ranked among the league leaders in fewest walks allowed per nine innings, finishing third in the American League in 1912 (1.90), second in 1913 (1.35), and fourth in 1914 (1.85).

Though big for his time (6'1", 185 pounds), the Vermonter did not throw hard. "Ray Collins hasn't a thing," said Hall of Fame manager Clark Griffith at the height of the Collins's career, "yet he is one of the best pitchers in the American League—one of the two or three best left-handed pitchers in the business." Hugh Jennings, another Hall of Fame manager, concurred: "I class him as the best left-hander in the American League, with the possible exception of Eddie Plank."

When Collins's major-league career was cut short in 1915, he returned to his native Colchester, Vermont, and struggled to eke out an existence as a dairy farmer for 42 years. Though he never made it to Cooperstown, Ray Collins was an original inductee of the University of Vermont's Hall of Fame on October 10, 1969, and the Vermont Department of Historic Preservation honored his memory with the erection of a roadside historical marker at the Collins farm on July 19, 1998.

Collins wasn't kidding when he listed his nationality as "Yankee" on a *Baseball Magazine* survey he filled out in 1911. A ninth-generation descendant of William Bradford, second governor of Plymouth Colony, Collins was also the great-great-grandson of Captain John Collins, purportedly one of Ethan Allen's Revolutionary War Green Mountain Boys. One of Burlington's original settlers, Captain Collins arrived from Salisbury, Connecticut, on August 19, 1783, and built the first frame house in town. Ethan Allen stayed with the Collins family while building his own homestead.

The 375-acre Collins farm on Route 7 in Colchester, originally purchased by Charles Collins in 1835, was where Ray Williston Collins was born on February 11, 1887. His family moved around a lot when he was a youngster, renting farms in other parts of the state, but his father, Frank Collins, still owned the Colchester farm. It was small and wet so he rented it to others. Around 1894 the family returned to the Burlington area and purchased land in the Intervale, an area of rich farmland along the banks of the Winooski River. There, on one of the largest farms in Chittenden County, the Collinses raised a herd of Jersey cows. The brick farmhouse still stands, just down the embankment from the former site of Burlington's Athletic Park.

For a while Ray had an idyllic childhood. "Played ball today" is by far the most common entry in the journal he kept during childhood. He also went to University of Vermont baseball games. But when Ray was 10 his father died of scarlet fever. Ray's mother, Electa, was forced to sell the Intervale property and move into a house in Burlington at 76 Brookes Avenue.

Electa Collins not only survived but prospered, buying and improving lots and selling them at a profit. She rented out the farm in Colchester, where Ray helped with the haying when it didn't interfere with his studies. Later he worked as a conductor on the trolley that ran from Burlington through Winooski and out to Fort Ethan Allen.

Ray's best buddy growing up was Dwight Deyette. The pair once jumped off the railroad bridge over the Winooski River together. Both attended Pomeroy School and later Edmunds High School, where Ray was captain of the tennis, basketball, and baseball teams. He didn't play football in high school because his mother wouldn't let him, even though he was considerably larger than most boys his age.

Collins often recalled his time at the University of Vermont as the four greatest years of his life. Though he lived at home, Collie joined the Delta Psi fraternity and

Captain Collins - Collins was recruited by the Red Sox after the 1908 college season, but opted to finish out his four years at University of Vermont, serving as captain his senior year. He won 37 of the 50 games he started during his career at UVM, capped off by beating Penn State, striking out 19 batters in his finale. Collins returned to serve his alma mater, first as assistant and head coach of the baseball team, and later on the university's board of trustees, presiding over the school's transition from private to public university.

got involved in campus social life. Among other activities, he served as committee chairman of the Kake Walk, a midwinter minstrel show that was banished from campus in the 1960s when it fell out of step with changing racial values. Ray also put his wide-ranging athletic talents to use, playing center on the varsity basketball team as a freshman and varsity tennis as a sophomore.

Ray's greatest accomplishments, of course, came on the baseball diamond. In Vermont's home opener on April 17, 1906, the first baseball game ever played at Centennial Field, freshman Collins batted safely twice and pitched a complete game, allowing only one earned run.

The crowning achievement of Ray's freshman year came against Williams at Centennial Field on May 19. The Williams squad entered the game with just one loss, having ruined their undefeated record at Dartmouth the day before. Larry Gardner drew a leadoff walk in the first inning and scored what turned out to be the game's only run. Entering the ninth, Collins was pitching a no-hitter and had not walked a single batter. With two outs, a Williams batter singled cleanly to right field, but when the runner was thrown out stealing moments later, Ray was carried off the field on the shoulders of his schoolmates.

Gardner received many accolades for his role on a team that finished 9-8, but the real hero was Ray Collins. Drawing all of the tough pitching assignments, Collie finished with a 4-3 record and an ERA of 0.70, striking out 36 and giving up only 43 hits and 10 walks in 64 innings. He earned honorable mention on the *Springfield* (Mass.) *Republican*'s All-Eastern and All-New England teams.

During his sophomore year of 1907, the Vermont team improved its record to 11-6 and that year's class yearbook, *The Ariel*, praised Ray's performance as "second to that of no college player in the country." By that time his prowess had attracted the notice of major-league scouts. The Boston Red Sox followed him throughout the season, and toward the end a New York Highlanders scout offered Collins $3,000 to play from July through October. According to the *Burlington Free Press*, "on the advice of older men, Collins has declined the tempting offer, believing that he is yet too young to take up base ball in the fastest league in the world."

The previous summer Ray had played in the Adirondack Hotel League for a team sponsored by Paul Smith's Hotel on Lower St. Regis Lake. A brochure found among his papers boasted that "[t]he Paul Smith's Baseball nine have always been champion of the Adirondacks." During the summer of 1907 he pitched for semipro teams in Massachusetts, then joined his university teammates in playing for Newport, New Hampshire, of the Interstate League. In one game he struck out 21 batters.

That July, through some odd twists and turns, Collins and his teammates played a brief but full-fledged professional baseball stint in the Class D Vermont State League. When several of the original clubs dropped out, the university nine stepped in as replacements. "Many have felt all along that the Vermont team was the one to uphold the Burlington end on any baseball proposition, made up as it is of so many local favorites," the *Free Press* wrote. In his first minor-league start, Collins pitched a shutout against first-place Barre-Montpelier, snapping that club's eight-game winning streak. "Nothing like the pitching of Collins has been seen at Intercity Park since the days of Reulbach," wrote the *Montpelier Evening Argus*. The collegians fared well during their short stint in professional baseball, holding the second best record (4-3) when the league disbanded for good on July 27.

With still a month to play that summer, Collins joined the Bangor Cubs of the Maine State League. In his first game, on July 30, he pitched a four-hit shutout against a Portland club called Pine Tree. A Portland sportswriter wrote that Ray's windup resembled an "explosion in a leg and arm factory," while a Bangor scribe wrote:

> Collins is a tall, slim young feller from Burlington, Vermont, and is first string man on the University of Vermont team. This university is famous for the ball players it turns out, among whom may be mentioned Reulbach of the Chicago Cubs, and Collins seems to ably sustain the reputation of the university. He has all kinds of speed, curves and shoots, change of pace, good control, and a corkscrew delivery which is enough to scare a batsman away from the plate. Added to these important details, he has all kinds of confidence and a snap that keeps a game a'going.

Ray finished out the season with Bangor and led the Cubs to the 1907 Maine State League pennant. In his last appearance of the season, at the Eastern Maine State Fair on August 30, he pitched both ends of a doubleheader, defeating Portland 11-2 and 5-4 in ten innings—a harbinger of his greatest day in the majors seven years later.

Vermont finished with a disappointing 9-7 record in 1908, the last year both Collins and Gardner played for the varsity. Still, the season had its share of highlights, like the time Collins beat Holy Cross 1-0 and drove in the game's only run with a triple. Students celebrated the victory in traditional fashion by going downtown and staging a mini-riot:

> Shortly after the game the chapel bell began to ring, summoning the faithful to gather on the campus. About 200 students responded to the call, most of them provided with the night shirt prescribed for such occasions. Forming in line in front of the mill, they marched to the president's house, where continued cheering brought President Buckham out to make a short speech. The march was then taken up down Prospect Street and to Brookes avenue to the home of Collins, the successful pitcher. After giving rousing cheers, the students continued down town to the club rooms of the Eagles, where they [were] joined by the band. Pitcher Collins was captured and borne on the shoulders of the advance guard as far as the foot of Church Street. The line then marched down to the Van Ness house where the Holy Cross team was supposed to be. Upon finding that the team was being entertained by the Knights of Columbus, the boys marched up the street and gave lusty cheers in front of their club rooms. On the return march to the college, some little trouble was experienced with the police over possession of various signs that had taken a place in the line of march.

The students in their ardor crippled temporarily the trolley service of Pearl Street. The trolley pole on a car was pulled from the wire at the corner of Pearl and Church streets and in front of the Howard Relief hall an attempt was made to block an Essex car; but the motorman applied the juice and the students, deciding that they would be the worse for wear in the encounter with the moving car, cleared the track. The trolley pole on another Pearl street car coming down the hill from Winooski was pulled from the wire and in the mix-up a window was broken, the splintered glass cutting the conductor, George Rogers, although not seriously injuring him. On the march up Pearl Street, the large bill board at the corner of Prospect Street was taken down and borne in solemn procession by some 60 students to the campus. Here a number of tar barrels were added to the stock of combustibles and an old-fashioned bonfire and war dance took place. After the fire died down the students gradually dispersed.

Following the close of the season, Collins was elected captain for his senior year. Gardner decided to forgo his last season of eligibility, instead signing with the Boston Red Sox, but Ray shunned offers to turn professional. "The president of the Red Sox team of Boston worked hard to land Collins," the *Free Press* reported, "but the college boy, who has one more year at Vermont, decided to pitch college ball for the team of which he was recently elected captain."

Collins received a large increase in pay—reportedly $185 per month—to return to Bangor for a second summer in 1908. This time he brought with him his college catcher, Marcus Burrington of Pownal, Vermont. Combining with Ralph Good, a Colby College star who later pitched two games in the majors with the Boston Nationals in 1910, Ray led Bangor to its second straight Maine League pennant. In appointing him to its 1908 All-Maine team, one Maine newspaper called Collins the "premier twirler of the league this season, as he was the last."

Despite returning only five veterans, the 1909 Vermont team survived and even improved without Larry Gardner, posting a record of 13-9. Captain Collins pitched well throughout the season, but never better than in his last game for Vermont, on June 18. Going out in a "blaze of glory," according to the *Free Press* headline, Ray struck out 19 and beat a tough Penn State team, 4-1. It was a fitting end to an incredible college career in which he won 37 of the 50 games he started, surpassing Bert Abbey, Arlie Pond, and Ed Reulbach as the greatest pitcher in UVM history.

After the season Ray received offers from eight of the 16 major-league teams. He decided to follow in Gardner's footsteps and, shortly after the Penn State game, went down to Boston and came to terms with Red Sox president John Taylor. "That day I saw my first major-league game," he remembered years later. "The Red Sox were playing the Tigers and Ty Cobb stole second, third, and home."

Collins returned to Burlington for Senior Week. He served as marshal at the baccalaureate sermon, then carried the class banner at commencement on June 30, leading a procession of 73 undergraduates (including Larry Gardner) down the

At 6'1" and 185 lbs., Ray Collins was an imposing figure to Deadball Era batters.

aisle of Burlington's Strand Theatre. After handing out the various degrees (Collins received a B.S. in economics, as did childhood friend Dwight Deyette), President Buckham called on Ray to close the ceremony with a speech on behalf of the graduating class.

As part of his deal with the Red Sox, Collins received permission to remain in Burlington and pitch an exhibition game commemorating the 300th anniversary of Samuel de Champlain's 1609 discovery of Lake Champlain. The games were part of Tercentenary Week, which included Vermont's first-ever marathon (104 times around the oval track surrounding Centennial Field), featuring 1908 Olympic champion Johnny Hayes; a wrestling match involving Burlington's own Fritz Hanson, champion welterweight of the world; Colonel Francis Ferari's trained wild animal arena and exposition shows; and a re-enactment of the Battle of Lake Champlain on a man-made island in Burlington Harbor, attended by President Taft and the French and English ambassadors to the United States. In the opening game, as 50,000 visitors flooded into Burlington, Collins held an independent team from Pittsfield, Massachusetts, scoreless for nine innings, but the opposing pitcher was equally stingy. Each team scored once in the tenth, but in the 13th Collins's run-scoring single gave Burlington the 2-1 victory.

Ray Collins left Burlington on July 12, 1909. He first went to Boston, then caught up with the team on a road trip. On July 19, with the Red Sox down 4-0 to Cy Young after three innings at Cleveland, Boston manager Fred Lake figured it was as good a time as any to test out his acclaimed rookie. In five strong innings of relief, Ray yielded two unearned runs and even singled in his first big-league at-bat. This game is best remembered as the one in which Cleveland shortstop Neal Ball made the first unassisted triple play in major-league history. It may also be the only time three Vermont-born players performed for the same team in a major-league game: In addition to Collins, both Amby McConnell and Larry Gardner appeared in the Red Sox lineup.

Four days later, on the 23rd, Ray was the starting pitcher against the hard-hitting Detroit Tigers. Though he lost 4-2, he twice struck out the dangerous Ty Cobb. Collins was given a second chance to beat the Tigers on July 25, 1909. Pitching on only one day's rest, Ray tossed the first of his 19 shutouts in the majors. It was a three-hitter, and all three of the hits were made by Hall of Famer Sam Crawford. Collins pitched only sporadically during the rest of the 1909 season, going 4-3 with an ERA of 2.81, but he had proved that he was capable of competing in the majors without any minor-league apprenticeship. As if to prove the point, after the regular season Ray matched up against the great Christy Mathewson on October 13 and defeated him, 2-0, in an exhibition game against the New York Giants.

Collins became a regular in the Boston rotation in 1910. In his first full season in the majors, the 23-year-old pitched a one-hitter against the Chicago White Sox and compiled a 13-11 record, making him the second-winningest pitcher on the Red Sox. His ERA of 1.62 was sixth-best in the American League. He became a fan favorite at the Huntington Avenue Grounds, as demonstrated by the following clipping from the *Boston Evening Record*'s Baseball Chit-Chat column:

> Ray Collins is a star. He is the idol of all the lady fans, those bewitching young women, who coyly gaze from under piles of feathers and ribbons. Is it any wonder that he pitches wonderful ball when those brown and blue and gray and violet orbs are on him? Gee, it's great to be a big, fine pitcher. If I ever have a son that's him, a pitcher and of course he will be a dashing fine chap. Fond expectations.

In February 1911 Tim "The Silver King" Murnane, a jovial, white-haired ex-major leaguer of the 1870s who had become baseball editor of the *Boston Globe*, came to Burlington to visit Ray Collins in his hometown. The following is an excerpt from the column he wrote about that visit:

> In looking over the list of Boston Red Sox players still in love with their surroundings, living within a day's ride of Boston, I selected Mr. Collins as the player on whom to make a friendly call and wired the young man that I was coming up to see him. I had also intended calling on Larry Gardner, who winters at Enosburg Falls, about 50 miles farther north, but our signals became crossed and to my surprise Mr. Gardner was on hand to greet me on my arrival at Burlington, where he has many friends as the result of his student days at the University of Vermont, where he, like Collins, was a valuable member of the baseball team.
>
> I was soon tucked away in a roomy sleigh and started for Mr. Collins' home, 10 minutes ride from the business section of the city. "I would like to have you see mother" was all the comment that the ball player made as we went slipping over the snow. "This is my home," he remarked as the team drew up in front of a pretty house on a residential street with a grade just right for fine sledding. Before entering the house the camera man snapped a picture of the player and the writer, and Ray pointed to a field close by, saying: "There is where I learned to play ball as a schoolboy. About all that is left to remind me of the old place now is that elm tree."
>
> I was introduced to Mr. Collins' mother as "Mr. Murnane of the *Boston Globe*" and was informed by the lady that she always has read the *Globe* baseball news since Ray took up the game as a serious matter.
>
> "Ray always loved to play baseball," remarked Mrs. Collins. "When at the primary school he was captain of a team, later at the high school, and finally during his four years at college he kept up his enthusiasm for the

Ray Collins warming up in front of what looks to be a large Fenway Park crowd.

game, so I was not surprised to find that he was willing to take a position with the Boston Americans. I never tried to influence my boy to give up the game that he seemed to love so much and his success in which made so many friends for him.

"Ray seldom talks baseball, however, but loves to bring home the pictures of young men he has played with." This was very evident after a glance at his interesting den, where the green and gold colors of his alma mater were the principal decoration, with pictures of baseball parks and Red Sox players strewn around.

We then went for a sleigh ride around the city, with the ball player handling the ribbons. As we slipped through the main streets it was a continual "Hello, Ray." Everyone in the place seemed to know the player. Collins simply recognized the salute with a "Hello" in each case.

That evening I sat down to supper with the good Mrs. Collins and the pride of her heart. For the first time Ray mentioned baseball. We chatted about the Red Sox players and about the splendid treatment the boys received on their visit to Vermont last fall (when the Red Sox played an exhibition game at Centennial Field). Mrs. Collins said she had enjoyed a call from Tris Speaker and other players of whom she had read and had a great desire to see.

The delightful simplicity of the woman, and the good taste displayed in the home, made it quite easy to understand why Ray Collins is modest at all times and deeply considerate of every man's feelings.

It is said that in springtime a man's thoughts turn to love and baseball. So it was that during spring training in 1911, while the Red Sox were working out in Redondo Beach, California, Ray Collins became smitten. Her name was Lillian Marie Lovely, and it is said that her surname suited her well. She was the 18-year-old sister of Jack Lovely, one of Ray's fraternity brothers who later headed the Jones & Lamson Company, the largest gear factory in Springfield, Vermont. Jack's family had recently moved from St. Albans, Vermont, to Los Angeles, and Jack insisted that Ray meet them while he was out there.

Ray apparently left his heart and his concentration in California. He was 3-6 at one point in the 1911 season, prompting rumors that he was soon to be released. "Ominous rumblings agitate the atmosphere," wrote one poetic scribe. "The management holds, apparently, that a player who cannot pitch nine games and win, say, 15 or 20, is useless, dangerous and ought to be abolished." But before management did anything rash, Ray turned his season around, finishing at 11-12 with a 2.40 ERA.

During the offseason Ray married Lillian in Los Angeles. In a congratulatory note, Red Sox president James McAleer wrote, "May you live long and prosper and have a million little Collinses. …I think you are due for a great year and Mrs. Collins will be proud of her big boy when the season is over." The couple set out as though they were taking McAleer's blessing of fertility at face value—their first daughter, Marjorie, was born in December 1912. Four more followed: Ray Jr. in 1914; Janet in 1916; Warren in 1919; and Dorothy in 1923.

Though Bill James named Ray Collins the ugliest player of the 1910s in his *Historical Baseball Abstract*, a contemporary account described him as "the idol of all the lady fans."

During their first winter together Lillian may have made life too comfortable for her new husband. Ray was noticeably overweight when he reported for spring training at Hot Springs, Arkansas, and his problems were compounded when a spike wound resulted in an abscess on his knee. Collins missed the first two months of the 1912 season, during which time the Red Sox christened their new stadium, Fenway Park. Ray did not start a game until June 7, nor win one until June 22, but from that point on he was nearly invincible.

A half-century later, Ray's fondest memory of that season was pitching the first-place Red Sox to two victories in three days over the second-place Athletics at Philadelphia's Shibe Park. When he defeated the A's 7-2 on July 3, the headline in the next day's paper, over Ray's photograph, read, "SURPRISED ATHLETICS, RED SOX AND PROBABLY HIMSELF." Then on July 5 he surprised the A's again, 5-3. Collins finished fifth in the American League in shutouts in 1912, but all four of them came in the second half of the season. By October his record stood at 13-8 and his ERA at 2.53, fifth-best in the American League. The team's only left-hander, Collins was considered the second best pitcher on the staff behind Smoky Joe Wood (34-5) as the Red Sox walked away with the American League pennant.

Ray started Game Two of the World Series against New York Giants ace Christy Mathewson and led 4-2 after seven innings. Then in the eighth Collins was pulled with only one out after the Giants rallied for three runs. The game was called on account of darkness after 11 innings with the score tied 6-6 (which is why the Series went eight games). The Red Sox led the Series three games to one by the time it was Collins's turn to pitch again in Game Six, but player-manager Jake Stahl surprised everyone by starting fireballer Buck O'Brien. O'Brien was no slouch, coming off a 20-13 season, but the Giants shelled him for five runs in the first inning. Collins took over in the second and pitched shutout ball for seven innings, but the Red Sox lost 5-2. "Things might have been a little different had Collins been sent in from the first," Stahl admitted.

Game Six turned out to be Ray's last appearance in a World Series, and though he ended up with no decisions, he did not walk a single batter in 14 innings—quite possibly a World Series record. When a newspaperman pointed that out to him decades later, Ray responded, "Maybe I made them too good."

Collins had his best season yet in 1913, finishing at 19-8, his .714 winning percentage the second-highest in the AL. A highlight was his performance on July 9, when he pitched a four-hitter and hit a home run in a 9-0 drubbing of the St. Louis Browns. Another characteristic outing was July 26 against the Chicago White Sox, when Collins pitched a five-hitter and hit a bases-loaded triple to give Boston a 4-1 victory. "This was simply keeping up the remarkable work that he has been doing this season, no one in the business showing better form," was one Boston reporter's comment.

On August 29 Collins pitched scoreless ball for 11 innings to defeat Walter Johnson, who entered with a 14-game winning streak. It was one of three times that Ray went head-to-head against the Big Train in 1913; each game was decided by a score of 1-0, with the Vermonter winning two of them.

During the 1913 season Collins became involved in the Base Ball Players' Fraternity, an organization founded by Dave Fultz, a lawyer who had played seven years in the big leagues, 1898-1905, leading the AL in runs scored in 1903. A presage of his future leadership ability, Collins served as player representative for the Red Sox; later he was chosen as vice president for the American League and admitted to the BBPF's board of directors and advisory board.

Coming off a fine season in 1913, Ray Collins expected his $3,600 salary to increase substantially for the 1914 season, and was sorely disappointed when the contract the Red Sox sent out on January 16 called for only $4,500. On January 23 he returned it unsigned to new Red Sox owner Joseph Lannin, prompting this response:

> We have no intention of considering an increase in your case as the amount named in your contract is a very liberal one....We have the signed contracts of most of the regular men and there is now only yours and one or two others of any importance that have not been received. We expect them, however, within a day or two. I thought you would like to know this as our prospects are very good for the coming season, with the team intact and with the addition of some promising youngsters.

In a typical year Collins would have had no choice but to accept Lannin's terms, but 1914 was no typical year. That winter the Federal League was waging its war for baseball supremacy; players had options for the first time in years. Perhaps recognizing this, player-manager Bill Carrigan wrote the following note to Ray on February 14, enclosing another copy of the contract:

> You can rest easy that you will stick with me as long as I stay with this club so don't let anything trouble you and I will see that you get home when your wife needs you. I'll do anything in my power to make you feel right, Ray, and hope that you will feel alright about this contract.

Ray phoned Carrigan and told him $4,500 was not enough, but he would sign for $5,000. On February 16 Lannin wrote to Collins: "Enclosed please find contract calling for $5000.00 for the season of 1914, as per your understanding with Bill."

On February 17, 1914, about the time he received Lannin's letter, Collins also received a Western Union telegram from Youngstown, Ohio:

> I had [Earl] Mosely [a former Red Sox teammate] wire you in regard to Federal League don't sign or accept terms with Boston can go you more than they will pay you big money in sight three year contract money sure regardless of injury if you come here at my expense will wire you hundred before you leave answer my expense.
> - Jack McAleese

McAleese, a former major leaguer, was working as a sort of bounty hunter for the Federal League, and his telegram obviously caught Ray in a receptive mood. The Vermonter sent the $5,000 contract back to Boston and raised his demand to $5,400, causing this response from Lannin:

> I want to acknowledge receipt of your letter, and was very much surprised at the contents. Mr. Carrigan stated to Mr. John I. Taylor that you agreed to sign for the amount mentioned in the last contract we sent you, namely, $5000. I just talked with Mr. Carrigan on the phone, and he verified that statement to me.
> We have accepted your terms, and we consider that a contract, and binding, and expect you to report at Hot Springs, as per instructions.

Collins did report to Hot Springs, but when he arrived at the Eastman Hotel he found his teammates up in arms. "They seemed to be money mad and claimed that their contracts were no good and that nothing could stop seven or eight from jumping at the Federal League money," reported a Boston newspaper.

Most anxious to jump were pitcher Dutch Leonard and second baseman Steve Yerkes, but Federal League president James Gilmore sent the following telegram to McAleese, staying at the Arlington Hotel in Hot Springs under an assumed name: "Never mind the others; get Ray Collins by all means." Newspapers reported that the Federal League had offered Collins a three-year contract at $5,000 per year, with a signing bonus of $7,500, and that he was slated to pitch for the Brooklyn Tip-Tops.

Ray sought advice from his older sister Genevieve's husband, Dr. Frank Finney, a physician who lived in Burke, New York:

> Since wrote letter to you Boston accepted terms of mine they once turned down. I didn't write them

Collins employed a deceptive corkscrew delivery that caused hitters to swing at his motion.

between time. Does that constitute contract? Lannin comes Tuesday. Would you threaten to quit should Lannin refuse to give Federals' terms? Wire.

Finney wired back on March 10: "You have made no contract, make Lannin meet Federal terms or satisfy you." The next day he wired again: "No harm to Lillian, Genevieve talked with mother, all favor Feds."

That same day Lannin arrived at Hot Springs, issuing a proclamation that Collins had 24 hours to sign with Boston or leave the team. "As late as 4 o'clock this afternoon Collins was called to the long-distance telephone and talked with President Gilmore of the Federal League, who is at Shreveport, La.," one Boston paper reported. But Ray met with Lannin and Carrigan for an hour before dinner, and when they emerged they announced that Ray had signed a two-year contract.

That night, according to the *Boston American*, Ray walked around the lobby of the Eastman Hotel "as happy as a schoolboy starting a holiday." He issued the following statement:

> I am happy now that I have signed to play for the Red Sox for the next two years. I like Boston and its people and wouldn't like to play in any other city, although I would probably have joined the Federal League if I had not signed with the Red Sox.

> I will receive a much bigger salary with the Red Sox this year than I got in 1913. Just what my salary for the next two years will be I prefer to keep between Mr. Lannin and myself.

Though he refused to disclose exact terms, one Boston paper was probably correct in reporting that the contract called for $5,400 per year.

Ray's signing was a tough blow for the Federal League. "Collins is nothing if not deliberate and shrewd," reported one newspaper. "When the Sox saw him turn down a remarkably tempting offer from the Feds, involving the placing in his hand of a big bunch of advance coin, they suddenly lost confidence in the validity of the Feds."

With the illness of Smoky Joe Wood, the Red Sox expected Ray Collins to step up and become the ace of their pitching staff in 1914, and that is exactly what he did. His six shutouts ranked fourth in the American League that season, and he was one of only three AL pitchers to reach the 20-win plateau. He picked up his 19th and 20th victories on September 22, 1914, by pitching complete games in both ends of a doubleheader at Detroit's Navin Field. Collins won the first game, 5-3, and the nightcap, 5-0.

It's no surprise that Ray's incredible feat came against the Tigers; he seemed to own Ty Cobb, Detroit's temperamental superstar. He reportedly once walked a batter intentionally to pitch to Cobb, and the tactic worked when Ty grounded weakly back to the mound. The Georgia Peach once said that Collins gave him as much trouble as any pitcher he ever faced. He attributed his difficulty to Ray's peculiar windup, which caused hitters to "swing at his motion."

Nonetheless, Collins and Cobb were friendly, and during one road trip to Detroit Ray and Larry Gardner were invited to Cobb's home for dinner. "We went and had a nice time," Ray remembered. The psychopathic Southerner had a genuine affection for the two educated Vermonters, whom he considered his social equals. In a rambling letter dated September 17, 1958, he wrote the following to Gardner:

> Nothing would please me more than to have a few days with you and your friends in your home town amongst those real people up there that I know of and their history so well, you being such a true representative. I should tell you now though you must have for years known it so well that I liked you, also Ray, also your kind no matter where they lived. We were reared properly.

In 1915, because the Boston Red Sox were in the enviable position of having too many good pitchers, Collins was relegated to the bullpen. As early as June, newspapers began speculating that he would soon retire; one even printed a false rumor that he had purchased a hotel in Rutland, Vermont. When he pitched a two-hitter to beat Cleveland on July 14, the Red Sox players reportedly were pleased to see Ray return to his old form, but the performance turned out to be an aberration. Starting only nine games, the fewest since his rookie year, Ray finished at 4-7 with an abysmal 4.30 ERA.

What caused the sudden downturn in Ray Collins's career? The newspapers make no mention of injury. Perhaps it was just a matter of the Red Sox having better (and younger) pitchers: Rube Foster (20-8), Ernie Shore (19-8), Dutch Leonard (14-7), and a 22-year-old lefty named Babe Ruth (18-6) made up the best rotation in baseball. (Incidentally, as an educated man of strong morals, Collins did not care for Ruth's antics: "Ruth would drink to excess, party all night, get no sleep and arrive late for games," Ray Jr. remembered his father telling him. Still, Ray Sr. was amazed by how well Ruth could play under those circumstances.)

Collins did not pitch a single inning in the 1915 World Series as Boston defeated the Philadelphia Phillies four games to one. After the season the Red Sox expected him to take a cut in pay to $3,500. Rather than suffer that humiliation, on January 3, 1916, Collins announced his retirement from professional baseball, stating simply that he was "discouraged by his failure to show old-time form." He was only 29 years old.

After announcing his retirement Ray Collins was offered a position at a New York bank. With his college and baseball contacts, economics degree, and keen intellect, the job appeared to suit him well. Instead he chose to return to his family's Colchester farm—"the worst move he ever made," according to son Ray Jr., who became a physician.

Located, ironically, just north of Poor Farm Road, the Collins Farm was hilly with marshy meadows better suited to growing rush-like swale grass than hay or corn. Because he didn't own a tractor at first, Ray farmed in sweat-intensive, 19th-century fashion, walking behind a horse-drawn plow. For a long time the farmhouse lacked indoor plumbing; it had an outhouse and the family used the Sears catalogue as toilet paper. Lillian was not used to that sort of lifestyle, but she endured it without complaint. Nor did she raise a fuss when Ray's mother moved back to the farm to live with the family for the next 22 years.

For years the Collinses lived without an automobile, and some still remember Ray's forays into town on a horse-drawn wagon or sleigh: 95-year-old Walter Munson (grandson of Warren Munson, second-in-command of the Colchester Company that helped repel Pickett's Charge at Gettysburg) remembered playing "rounders" in Colchester Village with a sawdust-filled ball when Collins, on his way to the creamery, pulled a brand-new American League baseball from his overalls and tossed it to the boys.

Not every minute was a struggle. On hot summer nights Ray took his children to Nourses Beach to go swimming. On Sundays the family went to Colchester's United Church, then picnicked in the afternoon in upstate New York or at Lake Willoughby. They participated in community silo fillings, the men from local farms banding together to help one another fill their silos with corn, followed by a common supper in the barn-raising tradition. Sometimes Ray took his sons to University of Vermont basketball games, always arriving late after the evening milking. They stood in the back of the crowded gym until someone invariably recognized Ray and ushered them to courtside seats.

By the early 1920s the knack for pitching that had left Ray in 1915 started to come back. Larry Mayforth, a former Vermont catcher then working as athletic director at the college, used to come out to the farm a couple of nights each week. After supper Ray went out front of the farmhouse and pitched to him until dark. On weekends they drove up to the Montreal suburbs, where they received $100 per game to form a battery. Ray also pitched occasionally for local town teams and in university alumni games. Sometimes the competition was even tougher.

One such occasion was July 4, 1922, when 35-year-old Ray Collins took the mound at Centennial Field against the Brooklyn Royal Giants, an African-American team considered one of the finest of the era. Locked up in a pitchers' duel with Jesse Hubbard, Ray held the Giants scoreless for 12 innings and did not walk a single batter, but in the 13th he finally gave up three runs. "Collins showed the fans that he has not lost the pitching arm, and the head to go with it, which made him at one time one of the most famous twirlers in the major leagues," wrote the *Burlington Free Press*. After the game, several of the Royal Giants were boarding their bus when they saw Collins in the Centennial Field parking lot. Unaware that the man who had just pitched so effectively was a former major leaguer, they approached him and asked, "Man, where did you come from?"

Several local legends developed about the ex-Red Sox star. Colchester resident Harley Monta claimed that Collins would go into his barn on rainy days and pitch baseballs through a small hole in the wall. Eben Wolcott said he heard that Collins could stand at one end of Sunderland Hollow and throw a baseball to the other. Stories like that are flattering but untrue, said Ray Jr. But he did remember one true incident that occurred at the Champlain Valley Fair in 1924. In a cruel forerunner of the dunking stool, a midway booth advertised "Hit the Nigger, Win a Cigar." An African-American man with his head stuck through a hole in the wall waited for someone to throw a medium-soft ball at his head. The crowd urged the former major leaguer with the famous control to take his shot, but Ray refused. Then a man holding real, hard baseballs prepared to throw at the African-American. Collins became enraged. He grabbed the man's shirt with both hands, lifted him off the ground, looked him in the eye and said, "You leave him alone!"

After a couple of seasons as a part-time assistant, Collins took over as Vermont's head baseball coach on January 19, 1925. Following a successful Southern swing, highlighted by a meeting with Vermont-born President Calvin Coolidge at the White House, the Green and Gold enjoyed a memorable season. Road victories over Syracuse and Colgate caused a bonfire celebration on campus for the first time in years, and on Decoration Day more than 6,000 people showed up at Centennial Field for a game against Dartmouth. At the age of 38, Collins appeared to have finally found a position that suited him. But the coaching position did not pay enough to make up for his time away from the farm, so after the 1926 season he gave up the job.

The harder Ray threw himself into farming, it seemed, the more his luck turned against him. He used some of the money he had earned in baseball to plant an apple orchard, but the trees failed to take. In 1927 a half-dozen of his cows tested positive for tuberculosis in the state's mandatory testing program; only after Ray took the cows to St. Albans and had them butchered did he learn that the test results were false positives. Then on October 22, 1929, a spark from a blower blade ignited dry grass and Ray's barn burned to the ground. The barn had been equipped with state-of-the-art milking machines and its loss was estimated at $15,000. Unfortunately, the fire occurred before Ray had a chance to buy sufficient insurance. He was forced to cash in his life insurance to build its replacement.

Ray Jr. remembered his father lying down on the couch after dinner; with a long career in medicine behind him, he could only guess at the pain his father silently endured. The stress and hard work gradually wore down the man who twice pitched and won both ends of a doubleheader. During the winter of 1929-30 Ray came down with a severe strep infection. His physicians identified the germ under their microscopes but couldn't kill it because antibiotics hadn't been invented. They told Ray that either his immune system would kill the germ or it would kill him. Months of weakness and delirium later, Ray won.

For more than two decades the Collins family managed to scrape by. To make ends meet, Ray and Lillian took in travelers in a precursor of today's bed and breakfasts, serving meals and talking baseball with their guests. They also supplemented their income by operating a sugarbush, wresting sap from a stand of sugar maples a mile north of the farmhouse. Ray lugged the sap buckets, a hired man boiled the sap and Lillian made and sold a variety of maple products. Eventually the Collinses won an award from the Vermont Maple Sugar Industry.

During World War II Ray chaired the town draft board and the War Bond drive. Though he probably could have secured an agricultural exemption for one of his sons, both went into harm's way, serving with distinction and then returning to successful professional careers. Ray Sr. couldn't carry a rifle, but he could drive a tractor—barely, due to severe arthritis in his hip from years of strenuous labor, but well enough, especially since all the young men were gone—so he hayed and plowed his neighbors' fields, often until midnight. What drove him to sit his nearly-crippled body onto a tractor night after night, after the sun had set? Money and neighborliness, to some degree, but one can't help but imagine that he also felt a sense of obligation to the hundreds of young men his draft board sent into the armed forces. Ray Collins, Home Front Warrior, was quietly doing his bit, and then some.

Ray Jr. remembered his father lamenting bitterly about being "peons" and living like poor people. Almost all the clothing the family wore, like Ray himself, had seen better days. Yet neighbors had no idea that Ray Collins was struggling financially. To them he was a pillar in the community. His leadership credentials were impeccable: college-educated, well-traveled, well-connected in several levels of society, a star athlete, physically imposing. From 1922, when Winooski split off from Colchester, until the 1960s, when the IBM influx to the area occurred, an oligarchy of civic-minded Republican farmers represented Colchester in the state Legislature. Ray took his turn in the Legislature from 1943 to 1946, serving on the agriculture committee and as chairman of the highway traffic committee. Looking for better prices for his milk, he co-founded the Burlington milk cooperative creamery that later became H.P. Hood and served as chairman of the county agricultural stabilization board for many years.

In 1953 Ray was named Colchester's first zoning administrator, which required lots of measuring property. Ray and Lillian were a team; he would get out of the car and hold up one end of the tape measure, while Lillian did the walking with the other end. He also served on the school and cemetery boards. For many years he was moderator of town meetings, and he was always the foreman during his frequent jury duty. Longtime Burlington attorney Joe Wool told Ray Jr. that he loved seeing Ray Sr. as foreman because he knew everything would be done right.

Finally the arthritis got so bad that Ray could no longer operate the family farm, so around 1960 he sold it to Ray Jr. By the time of Fenway Park's 50th anniversary in 1962, Ray Collins needed two canes just to walk. But he had missed Fenway's 1912 opening due to a knee injury, and this time he was intent on attending. "My legs aren't what they used to be," he told the *Boston Globe* weeks before the big day, "so I've been out to the airport finding out how I can climb the staircase to get into the plane. I've been kind of training for my trip to Boston and getting accustomed to going up the staircase is part of it." On Saturday, April 21, 1962, Collins was one of nine members of the 1912 team to make it back for the celebration (the others were Larry Gardner, Bill Carrigan, Joe Wood, Harry Hooper, Duffy Lewis, Hugh Bedient, Steve Yerkes, and Olaf Henriksen). They saw Boston's Don Schwall defeat the Detroit Tigers, 4-3, despite home runs by Norm Cash and Al Kaline.

Collins was an active alumnus of the University of Vermont. During the 1950s he served on UVM's board of trustees, presiding over the school's transition from private to public university. Every year during reunions Ray hosted a Sunday brunch for the Class of '09, and 10 or so classmates made their way out to the farm to feast on fried eggs, ham, pancakes, and Ray's famous maple syrup. It was during one of those breakfasts in 1969 that he suffered a minor stroke. His condition gradually worsened until he died at Fanny Allen Hospital at 4 p.m. on January 9, 1970. He was buried in the Village Cemetery in Colchester.

Respect for athletic success goes only so far, and many stars squander it. Ray Collins used it as capital to serve his town, county, and *alma mater*. Maybe returning to Colchester and taking over the family farm wasn't such a bad move after all.

Sources

A version of this biography originally appeared in *Green Mountain Boys of Summer: Vermonters in the Major Leagues 1882-1993*, edited by Tom Simon (New England Press, 2000).

In researching this article, the author made use of the subject's file at the National Baseball Hall of Fame Library, the Tom Shea Collection, the archives at the University of Vermont, and several local newspapers. In addition, the author wishes to thank Guy Page for his research assistance.

Clyde "Hack" Engle
by David Forrester

G	AB	R	H	2B	3B	HR	RBI	BB	SO	BA	OBP	SLG	SB	HBP
58	171	32	40	5	3	0	18	28	20	.234	.348	.298	12	2

Every baseball player whose career has been eclipsed by a single bad play during a World Series—Bill Buckner, Mickey Owen, and Fred Snodgrass—benefits from the redeeming quality of infamy: They are remembered. They have also secured a place in baseball history, a much smaller berth, for the beneficiaries of their blunders. It was Mookie Wilson's groundball that went through Bill Buckner's legs in 1986. Tommy Henrich is the one who got a free ride on Mickey Owen's dropped third strike in the 1941 series. And it was Hack Engle's high fly ball that Fred Snodgrass let drop in right field in the deciding game of the 1912 World Series.

Born on March 19, 1884, in Dayton, Ohio, Arthur Clyde Engle was the youngest of three boys born to Isaac and Lina (Bitzer) Engle. Isaac was the chief engineer of the plant that powered the Dayton City Railway's electric trolleys. After gaining local baseball acclaim in and around his hometown, Clyde, as he was known to friends and census-takers throughout his life, entered the professional ranks in 1903 as a pitcher with the Nashville Volunteers of the two-year-old Southern Association.

In 1904, he played 15 undistinguished games in the outfield with the Dayton Veterans of the Class B Central League before signing with the Augusta (Georgia) Tourists of the South Atlantic League as a center fielder for the rest of that year. In Augusta, he joined several teammates who would go on to the major leagues and their own attachments to fame and infamy, including Eddie Cicotte of the 1919 Black Sox Scandal and the irascible Ty Cobb.

During the 1905 season, Engle moved from the Augusta outfield to second base and, with a .265 average, became one of the top batters on the team. In fact, he might have made it to the majors at the end of that year if it hadn't been for Cobb. The Tigers had been trying to choose between Cobb and Engle and they were leaning toward Engle because Tigers manager Bill Armour thought Cobb had "a screw loose." But Engle's hitting waned in the late summer heat while Cobb's soared and, on top of that, the rest of the team was, not surprisingly, not enjoying Cobb's pugnacious temperament. And so, in August 1905, Cobb was sent to the majors, and the next season Engle moved to Newark of the Eastern League.

Engle made progress in his three seasons with the Newark Sailors. He gained experience, playing 125 to 141 games each season, and lifted his batting average from .216 in 1906 to .259 in 1908. Near the end of that run, Engle caught the eye of New York Highlanders manager George Stallings and was signed for the 1909 season. Although he had spent most of 1908 in Newark at third base and shortstop, he often told reporters he didn't like the infield. He was happy when playing left and center fields during spring training in Macon, Georgia. But Stallings tried him in the infield—at second and third as well, with good results. Engle had earned the opportunity to play major-league ball.

In the Highlanders' season opener in Washington, Engle started his first official major-league game where he preferred to play: left field. According to the April 13, 1909, *New York Times*, 15,000 fans witnessed Engle in top fielding form:

> "The fielding feature of the game was a remarkable one-handed catch by Left Fielder Engle on a long fly from Street's bat in the third inning. There were three men on the bases and only one out at the time. Engle ran to the edge of the crowd in left, and, as the ball was sailing over his head, jumped and grabbed the ball in his ungloved hand. As Engle disappeared into the mixture of arms and legs he held to the ball."

Engle's inaugural performance with a fly ball was not the only foreshadowing of his later claim to fame. He appeared in 135 games, playing left and center fields, and his .278 average was third best on the Highlanders. The right-handed batter drove in 71 runs, tops on the team. At under 5-feet-10 and weighing 190 pounds, he even earned the nickname Hack for his resemblance to the stocky strongman and professional wrestler Georg Hackenschmidt. But in one of his last appearances of the

Hack Engle.

season, Engle made an error of nearly Snodgrassian proportions.

"Engle's Muff Dazes Hilltop Fandom" proclaimed the headline in the October 1, 1909, *New York Times*. There were two men out and none on base in the top of the ninth, with the Yankees leading the visiting St. Louis Browns, 4-1. Second baseman Hobe Ferris popped an easy fly ball. Engle was so sure of catching it that he added some flourishes to his performance—what the *Times* called a "Hogarthian curve." Hilarity ensued:

> "Hack's feeling of sureness was shared by his comrades and even most of his opponents. Almost all the players on the diamond and the benches began their dash for clubhouse before the ball, high in the air, quivered in its turn for the descent. Chase sped so swiftly toward his shower bath and street clothes that he was close to the clubhouse gate ere the ball came to earth. In addition, at least a tithe of the 1,000 spectators spraddled themselves across the diamond in the customary pursuit of the players. But, alas! The game was not at an end. No indeed! Down came the ball—down, down, shooting straight and true toward Engle's upraised hands and then—why down, down, down it kept going, right between those hands, until it bounced on the waiting lawn. Engle was so dazed by his misplay he didn't know what to do next."

The Browns went on to tie the game, which was then called on account of darkness.

New York sold Engle's contract to the Boston Red Sox early in 1910 season, on May 10. He was initially signed as a third baseman, but as he told one reporter, "I play wherever they put me and do the best I can." That perspective served him well; over the next 4½ years with Boston, he played every position except pitcher and catcher. The trade put him on a ballclub that would win the pennant a couple of years later.

Hack Engle was a little chunky, and sometimes had to work hard to keep down to his preferred 190-pound playing weight. *Boston Post*

Hack Engle (r) and Tris Speaker share billing on a vintage 1912 Hassan Triple Folder baseball card.

In 1910, Engle mostly split his time between third base and second base, although he also played seven games at shortstop and 18 games covering various outfield positions. He hit for a .264 average. He boosted that a bit in 1911, to .270.

The 1912 Red Sox had such a strong infield that Engle was relegated to a utility role and appeared in only 58 games, hitting .234. He was often used as a pinch-hitter and that is the role he played in the 1912 World Series against the New York Giants. In the sixth game, Engle stepped in for Buck O'Brien and hit a double off future Hall of Famer Rube Marquard, driving in the Red Sox' only runs in that loss. In the eighth and final game (there had been a tie game, and the teams were tied at three games each), Engle faced another future Hall of Fame inductee on the mound—the almost mythical Christy Mathewson. In the bottom of the 10th inning, with the Giants in the lead 2-1, Engle stepped up to home plate to bat for pitcher Joe Wood. Engle lofted a routine fly ball into the outfield and center-fielder Fred Snodgrass called for it, or, if you believe Snodgrass's later account, was asked to get it by left-fielder Red Murray. Snodgrass caught the ball, but dropped it before throwing it to Murray to get it to the infield. Engle made it to second base and the "$30,000 muff" went down in history (the difference between the payout to the losers and the winners of the series was $29,514).

The mistake didn't directly lose the game and, if Snodgrass had caught it, it would not have won the game either. In fact, Snodgrass made what all commentators considered an excellent running catch on the next batter, Harry Hooper. Engle moved to third on that play. Steve Yerkes walked. And the blame stuck, as another blunder occurred. First baseman Fred Merkle (already carrying the burden of a bad play in an important game), catcher Chief Myers, and Mathewson let a foul ball from Tris Speaker's bat fall between them. Speaker then slammed a ball into right field to send Engle home with the tying run. Two batters later, a sacrifice fly by Larry Gardner allowed Yerkes to score the winning run. The world championship belonged to the Red Sox.

One wonders if Engle might have been readying himself for the second act of his baseball career—as a coach—while he toiled for Boston throughout 1912 and 1913. During Red Sox spring training in Hot Springs, Arkansas, Engle was put in charge of the Yannigans, whipping the rookies and second-string players into shape. During the World Series, he was found coaching third base. His facility in this role did not go unnoticed. Legendary *Boston Globe* sportswriter and editor Tim Murnane wrote:

"I find that Engle is a fine student of the game. Last year he took a deep interest in the work of Harry Hooper, and convinced the great young player that a heavier bat than he was using would help his batting. In fact, Hooper's remarkable improvement at the bat was a revelation to the members of the American League."

In 1913, Engle's fielding was just above average for American League first basemen that year, at .987, and he made the third most errors, at 17. But from a batting perspective, it was Engle's best season in the majors; playing 133 games at first base, he batted .289 with 17 doubles, 12 triples, and two home runs in 143 games overall. Perhaps as a result of his success, Engle bargained hard for his 1914 contract. Throughout his career, Engle was one of the first players to sign his contract in the offseason; he was always among the first to show up at spring training. But in the winter before the 1914 season, rumors circulated that Engle might jump to the new Federal League. A bit of drama played out on February 12, 1914, in New York, according to the next day's *Boston Globe*.

"Engle reached New York this afternoon at 4:30, on his way to a conference with Pres. Gilmore of the Federal League, but was met at the depot by Pres. J.J. Lannin of the Boston Red Sox and escorted to the Biltmore Hotel and, after a short conference, Clyde signed his contract and said he was delighted to be with the Red Sox once more."

Engle was again assigned as first baseman. By late May, rumors were already circulating about the possible sale of Engle back to New York. In August, after just 59 appearances and one of the lowest batting averages of his career (.194), Engle was released by the Red Sox and joined the Buffalo team of the Federal League at third base. He raised his batting above .250 and rejoined Buffalo for the 1915 season, playing mostly in the outfield and ending the season at .261. At the end of the season, Engle considered a university coaching job, but decided to go another year with Buffalo. Unfortunately for him, the league folded before the 1916 season could begin and Engle was set adrift (although his contract was required to be paid in full).

The Cleveland Indians signed Engle, but he played just 11 games; he took advantage of the time and helped do some first-base coaching while there. This included a series of games where he was later accused of tipping off batters as to which pitch the Red Sox were throwing by reading the signals of his former teammates. After his short sojourn with Cleveland, Engle finished his season with the Topeka, Kansas, team of the Western League (Class A), taking on the team manager duties while batting .290 and playing third base. When Topeka left the Western League, Engle's career in professional baseball ended.

During World War I, Engle joined the shipbuilding effort at the Fore River Shipyard in Quincy, Massachusetts. He played for the shipyard team while there. In 1919, he took over as baseball coach at the University of Vermont for a year and then joined his old Red Sox teammate Smoky Joe Wood at Yale. For the next 18 years, Engle coached the freshman squad at Yale while Wood coached the varsity.

Throughout his Yale years, Engle kept in touch with his friends in professional baseball, attending old timers games and doing some scouting work for Toronto and other teams. He died from a heart attack on December 26, 1939, at the age of 55 at Boston's Lenox Hotel. He had been divorced from his wife, Natalie Miller, several years earlier and no children were listed in his death notices. His body was sent home to his brother in Dayton for burial.

When Snodgrass died 35 years after Engle, his obituary in the *New York Times* was headlined: "Fred Snodgrass, 86, Dead; Ball Player Muffed 1912 Fly." Although the error featured prominently in Engle's obituary, it was a gentler sub-head: "CLYDE ENGLE, 54; EX-YANKEE PLAYER; Baseball Coach of Freshmen Team at Yale Is Victim of a Heart Attack ALSO WITH THE RED SOX Gained Wide Notice in 1912 World Series for Hitting Fly Snodgrass Missed."

Sources:

In addition to the sources cited in the text, the author consulted US Census, military draft, birth, marriage, and divorce records via Ancestry.com; statistical data from Baseball-Reference.com and Baseball-Almanac.com; and contemporaneous reports from the following publications: *The Sporting News*, *Boston Journal*, *Kansas City Star*, *Hartford Courant*, *Augusta Chronicle*, *Grand Forks Herald*, and *Sporting Life*. The anecdote about Cobb's time with Engle in Augusta is from Al Stump's *Cobb: A Biography* and *The Detroit Tigers* by Frederick Lieb.

Engle in front of a nearly empty dugout before a 1912 road game.

Larry Gardner
by Tom Simon

G	AB	R	H	2B	3B	HR	RBI	BB	SO	BA	OBP	SLG	SB	HBP
143	517	88	163	24	18	3	86	56	38	.315	.383	.449	25	1

In the foothills of the northernmost Green Mountains, just 16 miles from Vermont's Canadian border, the village of Enosburg Falls proclaims itself "Dairy Center of the World." Its annual Vermont Dairy Festival attracts thousands of visitors, but its population of slightly over 2,000 is roughly the same as it was more than a century ago. Like many villages dependent on the undependable price of milk, Enosburg Falls is experiencing economic hard times. Every year the average age of its inhabitants creeps slightly upward as young people leave to escape life on the farm. The old folks hang on, recalling better times.

But Enosburg Falls fights to reclaim lost glory. Back in the 1990s an energetic village manager and board of aldermen spruced up Lincoln Park, the quintessential village square, with its bandstand and fountain dating from 1897. At a celebration in 1996 the village unveiled a Vermont historical site marker commemorating the birthplace of Larry Gardner. A Civil War hero? An innovator of farming techniques? Hardly. Long considered the greatest baseball player to come out of Vermont, Gardner was the regular third baseman on four World Series championship teams, the Boston Red Sox of 1912, 1915, and 1916 and the Cleveland Indians of 1920.

Larry Gardner at Fenway Park, 1915.

Back in Larry Gardner's day, Enosburg Falls was one of the most prosperous villages in Vermont. Dairy farming was more lucrative then, but the chief source of the village's prosperity was the world-famous Dr. B.J. Kendall Company, manufacturer of a liniment called Kendall's Spavin Cure. An alleged remedy for a disease that affects horses' ankle joints, Spavin Cure became hugely profitable in the 1870s when the horse was the keystone of transportation.

Economic opportunity is undoubtedly what attracted Delbert Murancie Gardner to Enosburg Falls in 1872. The son of an Episcopal minister, Delbert came from St. Armand in the Eastern Townships of Quebec. He sought his fortune less than 20 miles from St. Armand, establishing himself in a shop near the Enosburg Falls railroad depot as a "dealer in groceries, provisions, dry goods, Yankee notions, etc." Five years later, Delbert married a local girl, 18-year-old Nettie Lawrence, whose family claimed distant connection to George Washington and a great-grandfather who fought in the Battle of Bunker Hill. Delbert and Nettie had a son, Dwight Murancie, then a daughter, Glenna Maude. Their third and final child, William Lawrence, better known as Larry, was born on May 13, 1886.

Larry's childhood days in Enosburg Falls were among his happiest. He sang tenor in the school quartet and spent many evenings playing guitar with an Italian storekeeper who accompanied him on the mandolin, the beginnings of a lifelong love of music. During the winter he skated, snowshoed and hunted, and at an early age developed a passion for fishing that lasted his entire life.

The Missisquoi River cuts through the heart of Enosburg Falls, providing a summer playground for the children of the village. In 1904 Larry Gardner wrote an essay about it that was published in *The Echo*:

A DARING ADVENTURE

It was one of those warm, pleasant days of July when nearly every youngster of the village was down at the river, swimming. They were doing all sorts of dangerous tricks, but none so dangerous as the one I had in mind to do that afternoon if I could get one of the boys to go with me.

It was an easy matter to persuade one of the lads, even more adventurous than myself, to fall in with my plan; so after spending the early part of the afternoon at the river, we left our companions and started off.

The plan was to try to climb a steep rock just below the bridge. So far as we knew no one had ever scaled it, and a dog that had been thrown off it had been instantly killed. The rock was on the very edge of the river, and extended straight up into the air for about one hundred feet. The water below was about three feet deep, out of which protruded huge bowlders and sharp fragments of rocks.

It was difficult starting because the rock bulged out, making a shelf about six feet from its foot. I helped my companion upon this shelf and he pulled me after him. The rest of the way was straight up. There was once in a while a little crevice, which helped us along, but progress was slow. We had gone up over half way when we came to a crumbly-looking part of the rock. I put the fingers of one hand into a crevice and held myself up by the other. I then started to pull myself up, when a rock broke away and came tumbling down, landing upon my left hand. As this was the only hand with which I was hanging on, I almost let go. Had I done so, I should surely have rolled down with the rock, which, quicker than a flash of lightning, went splashing into the water beneath. But a small rock had rolled out of the way, which gave us a good foot-hold; and as the rest of the way was easy, we soon reached the top.

I have never attempted to climb the rock since; but I have often stood on its top and wondered how I ever had the nerve to attempt to scale its dark surface.

Tossing the ball on the sidelines, 1913.

In prophesying the fates of the next year's editorial staff in that same issue, a clairvoyant schoolmate wrote: "This is Mr. Lawrence Gardner, the future athletic editor of *The Echo*. Fame is sure to be his, if he isn't killed first."

But Larry's chief talent lay in team sports—or what little opportunity there was for organized athletics at tiny Enosburg Falls High School. "For lack of an organized leader, not much was done at football, although we had good material," he wrote in his column in *The Echo*, a student magazine. "Basketball has created some excitement among the girls, but as yet the boys have not formed a team." Larry captained the EFHS hockey club. But "the most popular sport with the townspeople as well as the school," he reported, was baseball. The first records of Gardner's diamond career date from 1902, his freshman year. In his junior year he pitched every inning of every game and batted an even .400. A 7-4 record prompted *The Echo* to claim that "we are the champion high school team in Franklin County." With five starters returning, expectations ran high for Larry's senior year.

In that season of 1905, Larry Gardner rose to what stardom a small town near the Canadian border could offer. The campaign opened with a disappointing 5-3 loss to Brigham Academy, but Larry brought the team back by pitching three consecutive shutouts. On May 20 he was finally scored on but struck out 13 in a 7-2 win. Two days later Larry pitched against Montpelier Seminary, and in 1943 he told a reporter that "of all the baseball I've ever been connected with, this particular game stands out most vividly in my mind." Thirty-eight years after the game he recalled its details:

> Going into the ninth inning we were leading 1 to 0. "Montpelier Sem" was at bat with bases full and one out. I really was in a tough spot then. The man at bat knocked a hard one that I fielded. I forced the man out at home. The catcher threw to get the man out at first, making a double play and ending the ball game. I can tell you, the men at the corner drug store talked over this game for weeks.

Enosburg Falls celebrated Gardner's fourth shutout of the season with a band concert, bonfire, and promenade, the Montpelier boys remaining overnight to enjoy the festivities.

Larry tossed his fifth shutout in seven games against Newport High School on May 27. More than two weeks later he closed the season with a 10-1 win over Newport, which "would have been a shutout, but for a wild throw in the first which let in Newport's only run." The team's 7-1 record, according to the *Enosburg Standard*, clinched the high school championship of Vermont. "The local team has worked hard, has played clean ball, and has made a great 1905 baseball record for Enosburg High School," it proclaimed, "and is entitled to all the honor and credit which the state championship gives them." In eight games on the mound Larry Gardner yielded only eight runs, the majority of which most likely were unearned. He was no weak hitter, either, finishing with a batting average of .432, second-highest on the team.

The summer following Larry's graduation from high school, four of the area's semipro teams banded together to form the Franklin County League. Larry's older teammates appointed him assistant captain of the Enosburg Falls team—called the Spavin

Curers or Liniment Makers by local newspapers. The team from St. Albans was known as the Railroaders because the town was the home of the Central Vermont Railway. Swanton was called either the Fish Hatchers, because it was home to a fish hatchery, or the Bullpout, after the game fish. Newspapermen dubbed the Richford team the Chinese Spies because the border town contained a US Customs detention center for illegal Chinese immigrants.

In a season marred by contract jumping, frequent protests, and a brawl that resulted in criminal charges against participating players, Larry Gardner stood out as the Franklin County League's top all-around talent. He played shortstop and pitched, and after one outing the *St. Albans Messenger* coined him a new nickname: "'Larry' Gardner, the child marvel from Enosburg Falls, pitched rings around the local baseball players yesterday at the local league grounds." From that point on Franklin County newspapers frequently referred to Gardner as the child marvel. Despite his heroics, the Spavin Curers (12-10) finished in third place, two games behind arch-rival Richford (15-9).

Though the rough-and-tumble circuit lasted only that one season, it had a lasting impact on Larry Gardner's life. Several "ringers" from the University of Vermont baseball team played in the Franklin County League, and they got him interested in attending UVM. In late September 1905, the 19-year-old Gardner became one of 82 men and 30 women, only 16 of whom were from out of state, to make up UVM's Class of 1909. In those days a year's tuition and expenses at UVM could run as high as $350, but with a loan from brother Dwight, who was working in Ohio as a traveling salesman for the Dr. B.J. Kendall Company, Larry scraped together the money. Even friends helped defray the enormous expense; the Saturday before he left for Burlington, 25 of them met at his home and presented him with a $5 gold piece as a farewell remembrance.

Larry majored in chemistry at UVM, his goal to go out west to the gold mines and work as an assayer. According to *The Ariel*, he was the "peerless songster of the chem. lab., and because he is very mischievous Nate has required him to change his seat quite often in lectures." (Nate was Professor Nathan Merrill, dean of the chemistry department, who had been teaching at UVM since the year before Gardner was born.) Larry was popular among his classmates; *The Ariel* called him the "'Sunny Jim' of the class" and stated that "[his] presence is a sure cure for the 'blues.'"

Though freshmen baseball players typically played for UVM's second team or their class team for at least a year, Larry was one of two first-year students to make the varsity—the other being fellow future major-leaguer Ray Collins. That season UVM christened a new baseball field, called Centennial Field because the purchase of the land on which it was built was announced on July 6, 1904, at the conclusion of a three-day celebration of the 100th anniversary of UVM's first graduating class. After two years of clearing and grading, Centennial was finally ready for the home opener against Maine on April 17, 1906.

Batting leadoff and making his debut at third base (he had played right field in the opener down at Harvard), Gardner made an out in his first at-bat, hence becoming the first UVM batter in Centennial Field history. Still he managed a pair of hits and his second stolen base of the season in a 10-4 victory. It was an auspicious opening for the new field, the *Free Press* reporting that "attendance was good, the cheering enthusiastic and the day ideal for base ball barring a bit too much breeze." Vermont's vaunted freshmen distinguished themselves: "Fielding features were contributed by Gardner and Collins, new men this year in the varsity line-up."

The largest crowd of the 1906 season climbed college hill on May 1 to take in the game against Holy Cross, winner of eight in a row before losing at Dartmouth on the way to Burlington. Four players from that Holy Cross team went on to the majors: Within 10 weeks catcher Bill Carrigan and left fielder Jack Hoey joined the Boston Red Sox; Jack Barry signed with the Philadelphia A's in 1908 and become the shortstop in Connie Mack's famous "$100,000 Infield"; and first baseman John Flynn, smashed six home runs as a Pittsburgh Pirates rookie in 1910. With Larry Gardner at third base and Ray Collins in right field for Vermont, the Holy Cross game featured six future major leaguers.

Centennial Field's bleachers were filled to overflowing with students shouting themselves hoarse. Under freshmen rules, all first-year students were required to attend "smokers" in the gymnasium to learn the college yells and songs. Those rules also mandated attendance at home athletic contests—hardly necessary since games were considered major social events. On this day the Holy Cross "Big Four" were held to three hits in 15 at-bats as UVM won easily, 9-3. Afterwards students thrilled to the traditional tolling of the college bell in the Old Mill belfry.

Then as now, UVM students knew how to celebrate. They marched 300-strong down College Street headed by the college drum corps. When they arrived at the train station, they gave a rousing send-off to Gardner and his teammates, who took the 8:15 train to Rutland where they spent the night en route to the next day's game against Williams College. The mob had achieved its main objective, but it was having too much fun to disband. The *Free Press* described the rest of its activities:

> On the return march from the depot, a happy thought struck the boys—they must have a bonfire to finish up with. What better fuel than the unsightly shed which was annexed to the "hash house," so long an eyesore to those who love to see the campus kept beautiful. The shack was quickly demolished, the debris was carried well out in the center of the field and the fatal torch applied. The boys gathered around the big fire and spent the remainder of the evening in singing songs, cracking jokes, and telling stories, breaking up about 10:30 o'clock well pleased with their celebration.

After batting safely in each of his first 10 games as a collegian, Larry Gardner led the UVM team with a .350 batting average. The rest of his season was a disaster. In his last seven games, he batted .148 and committed 10 of his season's total of 15 errors. On a team that combined for an .896 fielding percentage, Gardner's .769 was worst among regulars. For the season he batted .269, tied for fourth on the squad. On the positive side, he did steal a team-leading nine bases.

In Gardner's era, playing independent baseball during summers was a legal way for college players to defray school year expenses. Tom Hays, the UVM coach, was also in charge of stocking Burlington's team in the Northern League, probably the top independent circuit in the country. It was a tradition to

Vermont's Larry Gardner, ca. 1914-15.

announce the players' names at Burlington's Base Ball Carnival, an annual event to raise money for uniforms and equipment. "[T]he reading of the names at the fair last evening was heartily received," the *Free Press* reported in June 1906, but the last name read, "to be given a trial as utility man," drew a particularly hearty reception. It was Larry Gardner, "whose brilliant plays for Vermont during his first year in college have attracted much attention."

For the summer Larry boarded at 138 Colchester Avenue, sharing the house with Doc Hazelton, Burlington's veteran first baseman, and himself a former big leaguer. Other teammates who went on to the majors included catcher Bob Higgins, a former Brown University standout who played parts of three seasons with the Cleveland Naps and Brooklyn Superbas; pitcher Ray Tift, Higgins' batterymate at Brown who appeared in four games for the New York Highlanders in 1907; and Harry Pattee, who stole 24 bases in 74 games in his best season with the Brooklyn Superbas in 1908. In all, no less than 25 former or future major leaguers played in the four-team Northern League in 1906, but even in that heady company Gardner held his own. He became Burlington's regular right fielder and batted .296 as the team walked away with the Northern League's last pennant.

The following spring Larry received his first attention from a major-league scout. George Winter, a pitcher who had twice won 16 games in a season for the Boston Americans, was married to a woman from Burlington and lived at 70 Front Street during the offseason. To pass the time before spring training, Winter watched the UVM team work out in the cage and dubbed Gardner a prospect. Larry played shortstop for UVM in 1907. He was batting .400 after 11 games when an "inexcusable accident" occurred at Centennial Field in the third inning of a game against Massachusetts Agricultural College on May 17:

> O'Grady knocked a high fly into short left field and Higgins and Gardner both went after it, no coaching being evident. The men came together with terrific force, and both were stretched out almost senseless. Drs. Cloudman and Beecher took the cases in hand and it was discovered that Gardner had sustained a broken collar bone, while Higgins, though not considered dangerously hurt, was reported last night to be delirious and in a more serious condition than Gardner.

When it was announced that Larry would miss the remainder of the season, UVM's student newspaper, *The Cynic*, decried his loss: "Gardner will sorely be missed on the team. He was strong at the bat and wonderful at base running, his fielding was well nigh errorless, while his throwing was swift and sure as fate." Without Larry in the lineup, UVM lost its next three games and finished with a 10-7 record. Though he missed a good portion of the season, his teammates nevertheless elected him captain for his junior year. He was also elected president of the junior class for the coming school year.

By June 30 Gardner had recovered sufficiently to join his UVM teammates, who were playing summer ball in Newport, New Hampshire. As if to answer any question whether his collarbone was fully mended, Larry smashed two home runs to lead Newport to a 5-3 win in its Interstate League opener against Randolph. A couple of weeks later he played a brief but full-fledged stint in organized professional baseball. When the Burlington team dropped out of the Class D Vermont State League, the UVM nine stepped in as replacements. "Many have felt all along that the Vermont team was the one to uphold the Burlington end on any baseball proposition, made up as it is of so many local favorites," the *Free Press* wrote. The collegians fared well, holding the second-best record (4-3) when the league disbanded for good on July 27.

With still a month to play that summer, both Larry Gardner and Ray Collins joined the Bangor Cubs of the Maine State League. Batting cleanup, Gardner established himself as Bangor's best hitter as the Cubs captured the 1907 pennant. His average of .371 (39 for 105) led the league, and both he and Collins were unanimous selections to the All-Maine team. By this time both players' actions were followed closely by numerous scouts, especially Fred Lake of the Boston Americans, and newspapers frequently mentioned that they were considered "big league material."

By the spring of 1908, both Gardner and Collins were receiving offers from major-league clubs. In an April 11 letter, Connie Mack tried to induce Larry to sign a contract immediately for $300 per month, with one month's advance upon signing, and join the Athletics after UVM's season. To allay Gardner's fears that signing a professional contract would make him ineligible for college ball, Mack wrote that "it will not be necessary for anyone but you and I to know that you have signed." During the course of UVM's season Larry also received several offers by telegram from John Taylor, president of the Boston Americans (at that point just starting to be called the Red Sox).

Gardner rebuffed those offers and remained at UVM for his junior season. Bad weather caused a lack of outdoor practice and a poor 2-4 showing on the southern trip, but the team rebounded to finish with 15 wins, eight losses, and two ties against the toughest schedule UVM had played since the days of Bert Abbey and Arlie Pond in the 1890s. Calling them the "champion baseball team of New England," the *Free Press* wrote, "Capt. Gardner, the hardest hitting man on the team, has been batting at a .300 clip, and it would be hard to find a better shortstop." Nonetheless he was named the third baseman on the *Springfield Republican*'s All Eastern Nine, making room for Holy Cross' Jack

Barry at shortstop.

When Red Sox utility infielder Frank Laporte went down with an injury in late May, the Red Sox stepped up their efforts to sign Gardner. After UVM's season ended with a win over Manhattan College on June 4, Larry's brother, Dwight, and mother, Nettie, came to Burlington to assist Larry with his difficult decision. Signing would mean he could finally repay Dwight's generous loan, but it would also force him to give up his senior season at UVM. Finally Larry succumbed. After final examinations, he reported directly to St. Louis, where the Red Sox were in the midst of a western road trip.

Larry remembered feeling "like a lost kid from the green hills" that summer. "Before this time I'd never seen a big league game," he said. "I'd been to the city a few times and while there held on to the hand of an older person for fear of getting lost." If he was nervous, it didn't show in his initial performance. Larry saw his first action on June 22 in an exhibition game in Rochester, New York, as the team made its way back to Boston. He homered in his first at-bat and played shortstop in "whirlwind fashion," handling six chances without error. Three days later, in his first official major-league game, Larry replaced an injured Harry Lord in extra innings and ripped a game-winning double to beat the Washington Senators at Boston's Huntington Avenue Grounds.

On June 27 he appeared in the starting lineup for the first time as the Red Sox took on the New York Highlanders at Hilltop Park in the Bronx. Playing third base and batting fifth, he went 0-for-4 with an error as Boston lost, 7-6. To make things worse, Larry was "bunted to death" by Wee Willie Keeler, who had two bunt singles among his four hits. That night Cy Young, the legendary pitcher, invited Larry to join him at the hotel bar. The 41-year-old veteran consoled the 22-year-old rookie by sharing a bottle of a rare rye whiskey called Cascades. (In his next start, Young, at the time the oldest pitcher in the majors, tossed the third no-hitter of his distinguished career.)

Larry had appeared in three official games and was batting an even .300 when "Taylor, the owner of the club, made me a proposition: 'stay with the Red Sox and gain experience by watching or go to Lynn where there's a place open for a shortstop.'" Larry chose to play regularly, reporting to the New England League's Lynn Shoemakers on July 15. To make room for him, Lynn's regular shortstop, Barton, moved to second base, and 45-year-old Jimmy Connor was forced to the bench. The former regular second baseman of the 1898 Chicago Orphans took no offense; years later Larry said that Connor "probably helped him as much as anyone to make the big time." In 61 games for Lynn, Gardner batted .305 and showed "all the earmarks of another Harry Lord." In September the Red Sox invited him to rejoin the team for another western road trip, but Larry opted to return to UVM for the fall semester.

"With a little extra money in my pocket my senior year I lived the life of Reilly," he remembered. "On occasion I'd even eat at Dorn's Restaurant, a high-class restaurant in town at that time. Heretofore I had eaten at any hash house." For the second straight year Larry lived in the Delta Sigma house at 342 Pearl Street, which was built in 1800 by Horace Loomis but sold to Elbridge Adsit as an investment property in 1907. Gardner joined a long line of distinguished guests that included Henry Clay and President William Henry Harrison.

Come spring, Larry watched from the bleachers as Ray Collins led the UVM baseball team to a 13-9 record. Final exams ended in mid-June but commencement festivities did not start until June 26, so Larry went down to Boston and actually managed to get into a game. On June 23, 1909, after replacing Harry Lord at third base in a game against the Highlanders, Larry tripled and scored in his only at-bat. A couple of days later he came back to Burlington for graduation. Only 59 of the 112 students who started at UVM in the fall of 1905 managed to earn diplomas, but Larry was one of six to receive a B.S. in chemistry. Returning to Boston, he appeared in only 18 more games for the Red Sox in 1909. With Lord a fixture at third and Heinie Wagner at shortstop, Larry spent most of his time on the bench. He performed well when given the opportunity, batting .297 with a .432 slugging percentage.

In 1910 a position opened up in the Boston infield when second baseman Amby McConnell was stricken with appendicitis only 10 games into the season. Larry filled in even though he had never really played second base. His inexperience showed on one occasion when he took a throw in the baseline with Ty Cobb sliding in. The Georgia Peach could have cut Gardner to shreds, but instead he slid around him and was tagged out. Walking off the field, Cobb turned to Wagner and said, "Tell the kid I won't give him a break like that again." But for the most part Larry performed admirably, batting .283 in 113 games and winning accolades for his fielding. One sportswriter went so far as to call him "one of the best second basemen in the country." Gardner's development allowed the Red Sox to trade McConnell to the Chicago White Sox.

After spending the offseason in Enosburg Falls ice skating, taking long hikes, and hunting (21st century residents of the house at 14 School Street found several of his old Vermont hunter's licenses in the rafters), Larry reported to spring training in Redondo Beach, California, with new confidence in 1911. He entertained newspapermen and teammates alike with feats of ventriloquism. "Larry converses from his stomach and keeps the other players guessing from what direction the talk is being directed," wrote one reporter. He also sang baritone in the Red Sox barbershop quartet, which included pitchers Marty McHale (first tenor) and Buck O'Brien (second tenor) and first baseman Hugh Bradley (basso). The quartet was good enough to tour the Keith's vaudeville circuit for two winters at $500 per week, though Larry never traveled with them. "He used to sing around Boston but we used a ringer named Bill Lyons on the road," said O'Brien.

Despite the speed he showed when he first took over at second, Gardner seemed slow and unable to cover territory in 1911. Manager Patsy Donovan was searching for a third baseman to replace Harry Lord, who had been sent to Chicago the previous year in the same trade as McConnell. At midseason he shifted Gardner to third. "Can it be possible that Larry Gardner has been out of position all this time?" wrote Ring Lardner. "He was certainly a success as a second sacker, but right now it would be hard to convince the uninformed observer that he hadn't been playing third base for years." A Boston scribe wrote, "Third base has not been played so well in Boston since the days when Jimmie Collins was in his prime." After the season Washington manager Jimmy McAleer selected Gardner as the third baseman on a team of American League all-stars. They played a series of exhibitions against the Philadelphia Athletics, who were preparing for the 1911 World Series.

During the 1912 season Gardner and his best friend on the Red Sox, Harry Hooper, lived together in Winthrop on Boston's North Shore. During mornings the two players viewed the bay and took dips in the salt water before driving to brand-new Fenway Park in their four-cylinder Stutz roadster, which they co-owned. They cooked shellfish by digging a hole in the sand, throwing in hot rocks and covering the hole with seaweed. Once Larry attempted to duplicate the trick for his family in Enosburg Falls, using chicken instead of shellfish and hay instead of seaweed, but it tasted so awful they couldn't eat it.

That 1912 season was a breakthrough year for both the Red Sox and Larry Gardner. Boston ran away with the American League, besting second-place Washington by 14 games, and Gardner hit .315 with a team-leading 18 triples. But on September 21, in the eighth inning of a meaningless game in Detroit, he was injured diving for Donie Bush's grounder down the line. The ball hit the little finger of his bare right hand, snapping it at the first joint and causing the bone to protrude through the flesh. Larry went home to Enosburg Falls to recuperate. Initially it was feared that he might miss the World Series, but he returned to the lineup on October 6 for a couple of games against Philadelphia.

Playing with his fingers taped together, Larry performed poorly in the first three games of the 1912 World Series against the New York Giants. In Game Four at the Polo Grounds he finally broke out of his slump, blasting a single and a triple and scoring two runs in a 3-1 Boston victory. In the next three games his bat again fell relatively silent, though in Game Seven he hit Boston's only home run of the Series. Then came the eighth and deciding game at Fenway Park (Game Two had been a tie). It was one of the most dramatic games in baseball history, and one for which Larry Gardner will forever be remembered.

The game was tied at 1-1 after nine innings, Gardner having driven in Boston's only run on a groundout in the seventh. In the top half of the 10th the Giants grabbed a 2-1 lead. With Christy Mathewson on the mound for New York, Boston's chances appeared slim. Clyde Engle led off the inning by lifting a soft fly to center field, but Fred Snodgrass pulled his infamous muff. Hooper made the first out and then Steve Yerkes walked. With runners on first and second, Tris Speaker lifted a lazy fly in foul territory near the first base coach's box, but for some reason Fred Merkle didn't make much of an effort. He just stood watching as Chief Meyers, the Giants catcher, plowed down the line and tipped the ball with the end of his mitt. Given new life, Speaker singled to score Engle with the tying run. With runners at first and third, Mathewson walked Duffy Lewis intentionally to load the bases. Up to the plate stepped Gardner.

Realizing that Mathewson was working him to hit a low ball, Larry allowed two balls to go by before he swung and missed at the third pitch. A walk meant forcing in the winning run, so Matty couldn't afford to be cute. His next pitch was over the inside corner, well above the knee. Larry swung and a shout went up as the ball headed for deep right field. "I was disappointed at first because I thought the ball was going out," Larry remembered, "but then when I saw Yerkes tag up, then score to end it, I realized it meant $4,024.68, just about double my earnings for the year."

After a celebration the next day at Boston's Faneuil Hall, Larry returned to a hero's reception in Enosburg Falls. His train arrived bedecked with red lights from engine to rear coach, and explosions of railroad torpedoes went off every few rods as it swept into the village. Fully 500 people were on hand to greet him. After alighting, Gardner was escorted to the car of honor, which was beautifully trimmed with American flags, bunting and "red sox." Seated in the car with Larry were his father, Delbert Gardner, and the whole reception committee. Sixteen autos followed in a procession through the village. In front of the Perley block on Main Street, the Honorable Olin Merrill, chairman of the Vermont Republican Committee, made a speech lauding Gardner as a "clean type of ballplayer of whom any community might well feel proud." After Larry made a few short remarks, expressing his appreciation, the procession reformed and escorted him to his home at 14 School Street.

Gardner's presence was much in demand during the week following the World Series. At a reception in Enosburg Falls sponsored by the Philemon Club, Merrill spoke again, this time focusing on the significance of a small state contributing two members to the champion team of the world (he saw it as "evidence of the sterling qualities of Vermont stock"). Special guest Tim Murnane of the *Boston Globe* talked about how the earnings of baseball players all over the country were a great benefit to rural communities, as players generally hailed from those parts and spent their money there.

The next night Larry, Ray Collins and 1912 Olympic gold medal winner Albert Gutterson were feted at Burlington's Hotel Vermont. Among the 450 in attendance were Governor Fletcher, Mayor Burke, and some 300 UVM students. Each of the guests of honor received a silver loving cup presented by UVM President

Gardner, glove tucked in back pocket, appears to await a pregame ceremony.

Guy Potter Benton. Gardner's was inscribed as follows:

> From The City of Burlington and The University of Vermont, to "Larry" Gardner in loving appreciation of the deserved fame he has won for himself, for his city and his alma mater as third baseman for the Boston Americans, world's champions of 1912.

Larry Gardner was on top of the world that winter. He was named the first-team third baseman on *Baseball Magazine*'s All-America team, the first of four such selections he earned over the course of his career. Then he signed a three-year contract with the Red Sox. Still Larry remained his same humble self. "He has a disposition as sweet as the wild flowers that grow on the mountains of Vermont," wrote Tim Murnane. A few years later, T.C. Cheney wrote that "there is no more modest, unassuming or clean young man in [baseball] than our Green Mountain boy, who is an honor and credit to the game and his state." Larry also carried a reputation as an intellectual: "Off the ball field Gardner prefers to read an essay on Shakespeare's poems than to discuss baseball," wrote one reporter.

On July 11, 1914, Larry Gardner collected three hits to make a winner of a rookie southpaw in his first big-league pitching appearance—a young man by the name of George Herman Ruth. "One of the first times I saw Ruth, the guy was lying on the floor being screwed by a prostitute," Larry said. "He was smoking a cigar and eating peanuts, and this woman was working on him." Perhaps hoping some of Gardner's gentility might rub off on the Babe, the Red Sox assigned Larry as his roommate. "What's it like to room with Babe Ruth?" Larry was often asked. "I don't know," he replied. "He never stays with me in the room when I'm on the road. He's always living with women."

In 1916 Ruth matched up three times against Walter Johnson, whom Gardner always credited as the greatest pitcher he ever saw. The Babe triumphed in all three games by 1-0 scores, and in the last of them Gardner's single in the 13th inning won the game. "How can you figure hitting? I still can't," Larry said. "One pitcher I never could touch was Eddie Plank. I got one hit off him in my entire career—and it won a ballgame. Yet I always could hit Walter Johnson and he was off in a class by himself. I did it by just punching the ball to left field."

After hitting .259 and a career low .258 in the previous two seasons, Larry rebounded in 1916 to hit .308 despite playing with a dislocated big toe. His batting average was fifth best in the American League, behind only Tris Speaker, Ty Cobb, Shoeless Joe Jackson, and Amos Strunk. With Speaker gone to Cleveland, Gardner became the biggest bat in Boston's lineup as the Red Sox won their second consecutive AL pennant. Then he enhanced his reputation as a clutch player by smashing two home runs in the 1916 World Series against the Brooklyn Dodgers.

The first one came in Game Three at Ebbets Field. "I hadn't been hitting and I was really mad," Gardner remembered. "Jack Coombs was pitching for the Dodgers and he was a helluva pitcher. He broke off a curve on me, a lefty hitter. I started to swing and tried to stop because I thought it was a bad pitch, but I was committed too far and had to go through with it. I even had my eyes shut. When I opened them, I saw the ball going over the wall. Can you believe that—hitting a home run with your eyes closed?"

In Game Four, with two men on base and Boston down 2-0, Gardner hit a fastball from Rube Marquard for an inside-the-park homer, giving the Red Sox a 3-2 lead they never relinquished. "That one blow, delivered deep into the barren lands of center field, broke Marquard's heart, shattered Brooklyn's wavering defense, and practically closed out the series," wrote Grantland Rice. Boston went on to win in five games, and Larry Gardner was considered the hero of the Series. As Tim Murnane put it, he had "a way of rising to the occasion as a trout rises to a fly in one of his favorite Vermont streams."

Despite his heroics, Larry couldn't get a raise. The most Red Sox owner Harry Frazee offered was to bring Larry's new bride, the former Margaret Fourney of Canton, Ohio, to spring training at Hot Springs, Arkansas, as the club's guest. "I told my wife to take 40 baths a day and ride horses the rest of the time," Larry said. "We really stuck Harry on that one!" In 1917 his batting average fell from .308 to .265, giving the Red Sox an idea that he was slipping after 10 years of service.

On March 1, 1918, Boston traded Gardner, reserve outfielder Tillie Walker, and backup catcher Hick Cady to the Philadelphia Athletics for first baseman Stuffy McInnis. "While the loss of Walker and Cady might be accepted with cheerful resignation," wrote Paul Shannon in the *Boston Post*, "the going of Gardner, one of the most powerful hitters on the team for years, one of its most dependable members and a model player in every way, will be severely felt." Philadelphia writers, on the other hand, welcomed news of the trade. "The report that Gardner has passed the zenith of his career and is on the decline is all camouflage, probably designed to placate the Boston fans, with whom he was extremely popular," wrote one of them. "His moral and corrective influence upon the younger men of whom the team will mostly consist this year should be invaluable."

The A's were in the midst of an AL-record seven consecutive seasons in last place, and though they finished in the cellar again in 1918, the 32-year-old Gardner proved that he wasn't washed up by batting .285. Though the Red Sox won another World Series, they missed Larry's presence. "Gardner's absence last year almost cost the Red Sox the world's championship," wrote a Boston reporter. "The Sox tried out more than a dozen third sackers in an attempt to fill his shoes."

But Connie Mack was continuing his youth movement, so before the 1919 season he traded Gardner, pitcher Elmer Myers, and outfield prospect Charlie Jamieson to the Cleveland Indians for slugging outfielder Braggo Roth. The Indians had finished second in 1918 with a weak platoon of Joe Evans and 37-year-old Terry Turner at third, so Cleveland writers thought the deal strengthened the team considerably. Gardner-for-Roth straight up would have been fair, they thought, but this trade was a steal. Reunited with former Red Sox teammates Tris Speaker and Joe Wood, Larry played every inning of every game, hit an even .300, and led the team with 89 RBIs.

In 1920 Gardner did even better, batting .310 with a team-leading 118 RBIs to help Cleveland finish on top of the American League. It had taken 42 years; of the 11 cities with major-league franchises, Cleveland was the 10th to win a pennant. Larry's leadership proved instrumental. When shortstop Ray Chapman was killed by a pitched ball in August, 21-year-old Joe Sewell was called up from the minors in the middle of a tight pennant race. Sewell, who had played very little shortstop, was extremely nervous. "Larry Gardner helped me a lot," he remembered. "He talked to me all the time when we were in the field, trying to steady me." The rookie batted .329 down the stretch, the start of a Hall of Fame career.

Cleveland went on to win the 1920 World Series, and on a road trip to Washington during the 1921 season the Indians attended a White House reception to receive congratulations from President Warren Harding, who was from Ohio. When it was Gardner's turn to shake hands with the President, Harding said, "I know you are a good player, young man, because way back in the early '80s I knew a player by that name. He was with Cleveland in the old National League and was a mighty good man." Gardner drew a laugh when he said, "That was just about the time I was breaking in." Though 35, Larry had his best season ever in 1921. He established career highs for batting average (.319), runs (101), hits (187), doubles (32), and RBIs (120).

Hampered by nagging injuries, Gardner was not quite as good in 1922, though he still played in 137 games and batted .285. He considered retirement when the Indians bought minor-league phenom Rube Lutzke, a third baseman, but Speaker persuaded him to come back and serve as coach and occasional pinch-hitter. Over the course of his last two seasons, 1923-24, Larry appeared in a total of only 90 games, playing the field in only 33.

Larry Gardner had always been concerned with his career after baseball. In his early days with the Red Sox he had invested in a Cape Cod cranberry business, but an early frost one year ruined the harvest and destroyed the company. After that experience Larry went into the automobile business in Enosburg Falls. With his partner, Francis Smith, whose wife was a cousin, Larry owned a garage and Willys-Knight dealership. But when the time finally came to devote all of his attention to another occupation, he couldn't leave baseball behind.

In 1925 Larry managed Dallas of the Texas League, taking charge of a "mixture of indifferent and 'mean' ball players," according to one reporter. Though the team finished a respectable third (85-66), Gardner quit before the end of the season, giving his wife only one day's notice that they were leaving. The next two years Larry managed Asheville of the South Atlantic League. In 1926 the club won a league-record 15 consecutive games en route to a second-place finish, but in 1927 the team fell to fourth. Larry Jr. remembers his father's chief complaint about the South: "Those were the days before refrigeration, and he always said it was hard to find ice cream." After the 1927 season Larry returned to his garage and automobile business in Enosburg Falls. Margaret hated it there and was relieved when Larry joined the physical education department at the University of Vermont in 1929. Mr. and Mrs. Gardner and their two young sons lived in a rented house on Brookes Avenue, the street where Ray Collins grew up.

In 1932 Gardner became head baseball coach at UVM. He stressed sportsmanship ahead of winning—his overall record in two decades of coaching was a lackluster 141-166—and well-rounded students over specialized athletes. "I guess he liked the team to win, but all I remember was how warm and human he was with the players," said Larry Jr., who served as batboy. Nothing captures the essence of Gardner's coaching philosophy better than a letter he wrote to President Stanley King of Amherst College on May 13, 1938 (coincidentally Larry's 52nd birthday):

Larry Gardner took an interest in photography, just as Ted Williams did in later years with the Red Sox. *Boston Post*

Dear Sir:

I am writing you a somewhat belated letter to express to you the keen pleasure our boys experienced at Amherst on April 21st when we met your Amherst team in a baseball game. While we lost the game, we gained something much more valuable than is expressed by winning or losing.

In the ten years I have been connected with baseball at Vermont, I can honestly say that I never saw our boys more impressed by spirit, gentlemanly conduct, and treatment than was given and exemplified by your students.

In the thirty years of my experience in baseball, this was truly the highlight and it pleases me to hand this observation on to you.

The boys join me in expressing our gratitude to you and the Amherst men.

Three days later he received this reply from President King:

Dear Mr. Gardner:

I would not be honest if I did not say that I am deeply touched by your letter of the 13th. The qualities which you stress in your letter are of course the qualities you and we are trying to develop in our boys in the playing of competitive sports. They are the qualities which seem to me most important in our staff. The teams that you coach at Vermont and which Paul Eckley coaches here may win or lose in individual games but the qualities of sportsmanship which the boys learn from their coaches and their fellows are among the most important by-products of our college education.

I watched the Vermont game from the stands myself and congratulate you on the fine boys on your team. The score of two to one was as close as a score can be. Again my warm appreciation for your letter.

In addition to his coaching duties, Larry Gardner was named UVM's athletic director in 1942, and he held both positions until his retirement from the university in 1952. During the 1940s he also served as commissioner of the independent Northern League and as a part-time scout for the Boston Braves. After his 1952 "retirement," Gardner fished frequently and worked a regular schedule at The Camera Shop on the top block of Church Street in downtown Burlington.

Gardner and his family lived a comfortable life in Burlington. They spent summers at a spectacular camp on Colchester Point, surrounded by cedars and situated on a rocky bluff overlooking Lake Champlain, with stairs leading to a quarter-mile stretch of sandy beach. Puffing on a cigar or pipe, Larry spent evenings sitting on the wraparound porch, enjoying the cross-breezes and the nearly 360-degree view of Camel's Hump to the east and the Adirondacks to the west. The camp itself, which was built by the founder of the Laird-Shobert Shoe Company, was paneled with knotty pine on the inside and featured a large stone fireplace.

The Gardners loved to host big lobster bakes at the camp. Frequent guests included Burlington High School principal Dean Perreault, insurance agent Phillip Bell and Larry's best friend, UVM track coach Archie Post. The Gardner boys also remember the time Larry's old Red Sox teammate Dick Hoblitzell—and particularly his beautiful daughter—visited. From the camp the Gardners could watch fishermen netting sturgeon. When the south wind came up in early summer, Larry took his rowboat (equipped with a small motor) out to catch walleye and pike. His favorite spot for bass fishing was Hogback Reef, near the Colchester Lighthouse.

When the kids returned to school in the fall, the Gardners moved back to their comfortable brick cottage at 17 Overlake Park, in one of Burlington's nicest neighborhoods. It was rented through the second week of September to two women who came down from Canada every summer to live near the lake. The living room was adorned with no pictures or trophies—they were all upstairs or down the basement. Larry told visitors he'd left his playing days behind and only took private trips back to the Boston, Philadelphia, and Cleveland of the early part of the century.

Still, he kept in touch with several old teammates, especially Harry Hooper. Larry also maintained a steady correspondence with Ty Cobb. In their playing days, he and Cobb were intense rivals. "I don't think Ty ever bunted for a hit against me because I found out his secret early," Larry said. "Cobb used to fake a lot of bunts, but I noticed that when he was really going to bunt, he always licked his lips. When I saw that, I'd start in with the pitch. He never realized I'd caught on." In the 1950s Cobb wrote long, rambling letters to Gardner, trying to establish a fund for players whose careers had ended before Major League Baseball's pension system. In a letter dated September 17, 1958, Cobb wrote:

"Nothing would please me more than to have a few days with you and your friends in your home town amongst those *real* people up there that I know of and their history so well, you being such a true representative. I should tell you now though you must have for years known it so well that I liked you also Ray [presumably Ray Collins], also your kind no matter where they lived, we were *reared properly*."

Larry and Margaret Gardner enjoyed playing golf at Burlington Country Club. They didn't keep score, even though Larry was very good. On Sundays Larry read the *New York Times* and listened to classical musical all day long. He also liked Bing Crosby, Perry Como, Joey Browne, and opera—Puccini was a favorite composer. "My God, listen to that," he would say. "That's a great tune!" On television Larry watched *Perry Mason*, Ed Sullivan, and Leonard Bernstein conducting symphonies. He was an avid reader, especially books about World War II. During the war he kept a map on which he pinpointed the advance of the Allied forces—a practice he discontinued when his son John was drafted.

Larry Gardner received numerous accolades as the years went on. *Collegiate Baseball* named him the third baseman on its all-time All-America team, and he was an original inductee into the University of Vermont's Hall of Fame in 1969. In 1973, when SABR conducted a survey of its members to determine the greatest baseball player born in each state, Gardner was selected from Vermont. UVM's most valuable player award in baseball was named after him, as was UVM's cage (an honor he shared with Ray Collins). Still, the ultimate honor—induction into the National Baseball Hall of Fame—eluded him.

"I remember when Harry Hooper was being considered for the honor and Dad talked with me after I raised the question about *him* being eligible for it," said Larry Jr. "Generally speaking, Dad was very quiet, soft-spoken, reticent about his baseball career when talking with me, but at that one time he got very talkative—very adamant—and told me, 'If you boys *ever* get involved with the campaigning, the politics of getting me into the Hall of Fame, I'll be upset and angry.'"

William Lawrence Gardner died two months short of his 90th birthday on March 11, 1976, at Larry Jr.'s home in St. George, Vermont. He left his body to UVM's Department of Anatomy, and his ashes were spread at St. Paul's Cathedral in Burlington. Though he never was inducted into the Baseball Hall of Fame, he continued to receive honors even after his death. In 1986 the UVM baseball team wore commemorative patches on their sleeves in honor of his 100th birthday. And when a regional chapter of SABR was founded in the Green Mountains in 1993, its members elected to call it the Larry Gardner Chapter. It was another fitting tribute to a Vermont baseball legend.

Sources

A version of this biography originally appeared in *Green Mountain Boys of Summer: Vermonters in the Major Leagues 1882-1993*, edited by Tom Simon (New England Press, 2000).

In researching this article, the author made use of the subject's file at the National Baseball Hall of Fame Library, the Tom Shea Collection, the archives at the University of Vermont, and several local newspapers.

Kurt "Casey" Hageman
By Craig Lammers

G	ERA	W	L	SV	GS	GF	CG	SHO	IP	H	R	ER	BB	SO	HR	HBP	WP	BFP
2	27.00	0	0	0	1	1	0	0	1 2/3	5	5	4	3	1	0	0	0	13

G	AB	R	H	2B	3B	HR	RBI	BB	SO	BA	OBP	SLG	SB	HBP
2	0	0	0	0	0	0	0	1	0	-	1.000	-	0	0

Tragedy and controversy characterized the career of pitcher Kurt "Casey" Hageman. In the closing days of the 1909 season, he killed an opposing player with a pitched ball, the tragedy changing the path of his minor-league career. During the 1912 season, Hageman challenged a minor-league assignment. The ensuing court case was essentially an early challenge of baseball's reserve clause. These two events had a profound effect on a promising baseball career. There were also happier moments in his career. Hageman threw no-hitters on the same date in consecutive years, and won the first game played at Fenway Park.

Kurt Moritz Hageman was the youngest of 13 children of German immigrants. His mother Elizabeth Paul was born in October of 1843. In the fall of 1857, she left Hamburg on the *Rudolph* and became a naturalized U. S. citizen in 1867. Little is known of Kurt's father August Hageman, except that he died sometime before 1900. The Hageman family settled in Allegheny County, Pennsylvania near Pittsburgh. Kurt was born in Mount Olive (now part of Pittsburgh) on May 12, 1887 but grew up in the town of Beaver Falls. By 1900, Elizabeth was widowed and living in the city's first ward. Two older sisters were milliners and an older brother was a barber. Kurt was still in school.

Nicknamed "Casey," Hageman began playing baseball seriously in 1904 with an independent professional team in Wampum, Pennsylvania. He spent 1905 and the first part of 1906 with teams in Beaver Falls and Rochester, Pennsylvania.

In the spring of 1906, Eastern Ohio and Western Pennsylvania supported two minor leagues. The larger towns in the region participated in the Class C Ohio-Pennsylvania League. Pittsburgh sportswriter Richard Guy organized several of the smaller towns into the Class D Pennsylvania-Ohio-Maryland (POM) League, which had a tumultuous two-year existence. Waynesburg was noted for natural gas production in 1906, but the baseball team was struggling at midseason. One player picked up to try and improve the team was Casey Hageman.

His name was often spelled Hagerman in contemporary game accounts, but as a pitcher he was effective from the beginning. An early August account in the *Steubenville Herald-Star* described him: "A curly headed youth bearing a fantastic twist (curve ball) was on the mound for Waynesburg and he did just as he pleased with the Stubs. He applied his foolers to good advantage and for nine innings held the Stubs to six hits."

The POM League had several weaknesses, one of them statistics. A later article in the *Herald-Star* credited Hageman with a 13-4 record with two ties in 19 appearances in about six weeks with the team. Casey was reserved by Waynesburg that fall, but spent 1907 pitching for another POM team. Despite the league name, there was no Maryland team in the league, and Waynesburg failed to field a team, so Hageman began the season back in Beaver Falls. He appeared in an April exhibition game at Steubenville as a member of his hometown team, but soon received a chance with the defending champions from Uniontown, a team variously known as the Coal Barons and the Champs, and managed by former major-league pitcher Alex Pearson. Hageman and Pearson were among four 1907 Uniontown pitchers to reach the major leagues.

Hageman made his season debut on May 2 in the team's third game of a season-opening series at Steubenville. The *Herald Star* said he "was all O.K. For a few innings against the Stubs but when they found him they throwed the hooks into him…" He walked four and threw a wild pitch in an 8-3 loss.

Uniontown and Hageman recovered from the slow start to have a strong 1907 season. In early June, Casey allowed three hits in a 4-2 win at East Liverpool. The win undoubtedly impressed an East Liverpool expert who selected Hageman as one of five pitchers for an unofficial league all-star team. Later in the month, he starred on the mound and at the plate in a game

Hageman, all dressed up, 1912.

at Zanesville. The *Zanesville Courier* observed that Casey "had our men guessing. When the boys did hit his offering the fielders by good work took care of the bingles. Hagerman appears to be a hitting pitcher. Four times up yesterday he secured three hits." In July, he shut out Zanesville on two hits, striking out seven.

Uniontown and Zanesville spent most of the season challenging Steubenville. According to reports the Steubenville club's payroll was at least double the league's supposed $1,800 a month salary limit. By season's end Uniontown was 7 ½ games behind Steubenville, but a half-game ahead of third-place Zanesville. Record keeping was spotty in the circuit and official pitching records were not published. A report in the *Herald Star* credits Hageman with a 14-9 won/loss record.

There was more offseason uncertainty for Hageman the following winter. The POM league was dissolved and a general realignment of teams in the Ohio/Pennsylvania region occurred. Winter rumors had Casey headed for East Liverpool or Akron, but former major-league star Bobby Lowe, manager of Grand Rapids of the Class B Central League, signed him when it appeared that Uniontown would not field a team.

Casey's career at Grand Rapids almost ended before it began. Uniontown joined a new league late, and National Association Secretary John Farrell ruled that Hageman and several other players belonged to Uniontown, forcing Lowe to purchase his contract in late April. There may have been some doubt on Lowe's part, as Hageman was unimpressive in his first couple of starts.

Though effective, he was often the losing pitcher during the first half of the 1908 season. The *Herald* noted after a June loss to Dayton: "Hageman is showing symptoms of being the prize hard luck pitcher of the team. It is the second time he has been beaten in which opponents have gotten but five hits, while he has lost another game in which he allowed but two hits. Curt had the Vets breaking their backs reaching for some of his benders and he forced nine of them to strike out. He was steady as clock work, not granting a base on balls or hitting a batter." The *Herald* sportswriter was also impressed with Hageman's assortment of pitches. "When it comes to flinging a slow ball, Hageman has a deceptive one that gets the other fellows going, and the best of it is he can mix it with plenty of speed, and other variety of deceptives."

He opened July with a three-hit shutout win over Evansville, but did even better in his next start. A South Bend account published in the *Herald* described his July 5 gem. "The Grand Rapids man was simply invincible and mowed down the Bender swatters with telling effect. For five innings not a man reached first base. Hageman was simply 'it'. Only one man, [Leon] Foy, got anything that looked like a hit and then Ike Francis saved the laurels of Hageman by pulling down his stinging line drive." After the no-hitter, the *Herald* also commented: "around the circuit he is mentioned as the speediest pitcher in the league, and he seems to be able to hold that record."

Later in July, the Hageman and the team nearly went on strike over non-payment of salary. The crisis was averted and Hageman finished the month the same way he started it, with a

Hageman of the Boston Americans, baseball card.

shutout over Evansville. A local report read: "The class of curves that Casey Hageman dished up was altogether too much for the local ball tossers. Four bingles were secured off Hageman, but they were so well scattered that there was no possible chance for the locals to get a run."

When Hageman shut out Wheeling in August, a major-league owner saw the game. The *Herald* reported: "Casey had Barney Dreyfuss owner of the Pittsburg Pirates watching him as he struck out six of his opponents."

The rest of the season was unlucky for Hageman. Hard luck losses on the mound and then a late-season injury described as a "strain" proved more serious than expected and ended his season early. Casey Hageman finished his first season in the Central League with a 14-14 record, pitching better than his record would indicate. He allowed 6.8 hits and 3.0 walks per nine innings on the season. After the season Casey went back to Beaver Falls working as a designer for the Ingram Richardson Manufacturing Company.

Grand Rapids had a new manager, Joe Raidy, for 1909. Hageman was dissatisfied with the initial contract offered but soon came to terms. The season was one of triumph and tragedy for the young pitcher. After losing his first two starts, Hageman pitched 13 shutout innings against Evansville. Unfortunately, Grand Rapids also went scoreless.

He was even better in early June against Fort Wayne. The *Herald* said; "A rare exhibition was this pitching duel and the only possible fault that could be found was the bad second inning for Fort Wayne. Will one run win the game was the question asked. It most assuredly would, for there was nothing doing with Casey Hageman. He had speed, control and everything need to turn him into a winner, and used it." He struck out nine and walked one.

His record was just 7-6 when he faced South Bend on July 5, the first anniversary of his no-hitter. The score of the game was 1-0, and the *Herald* reported on the historic coincidence. "When Casey Hageman is sent to the mound on July 5, he's sure he's going to win with a very strong chance of a no-hit-no-run sort of a battle. There wasn't a drive counted that looked anything like a hit, not one of his teammates being called upon to make even a really sensational play to keep him from having a hit charged against him. During the first part of the game the speed that the twirler was showing was causing comment. For six innings but 18 men faced him. Eight of these were laid away on strikes." He walked four batters and hit another in the last three innings but kept South Bend off the scoreboard.

In his next start, Hageman threw his sixth shutout of the season in a 2-0 seven-inning victory over Evansville. The win ran his scoreless inning streak to 31.

During the latter part of July and the beginning of August, both Hageman and the Grand Rapids team struggled. Rumors had the team moving to various cities in Ohio before the ownership situation stabilized. Hageman regained effectiveness while the rest of the team's pitching staff was wearing down. The *Herald* commented on Hageman's September 5 pitching feat against

South Bend. "In the winning Casey Hageman worked the iron man stunt. Both contests did Casey work. The second session was cut to seven innings by mutual agreement. Therefore Hageman worked 16 innings. In this period he allowed but eight hits four to the game. There was one run counted. That was in the second inning of the second game. In other words the Benders had little or no chance."

Two days later, Hageman pitched both games of a doubleheader against Dayton, winning the first but losing the second contest. The Stags then left for their last two series of the season at South Bend and Dayton.

Charles Pinkney was a year younger than Hageman, and like Casey, began his professional career in 1906. Midway in the 1908 season, he was released by the New Castle PA team and signed by Newark, Ohio. When Newark's team ran into financial difficulties, Pinkney was sold to Dayton and soon became a fan favorite. Pinkney led off the first game of the September 14 doubleheader with his only home run of the season, off Hageman. Casey allowed four runs and was removed in the second inning of Dayton's 10-0 win. As was common in the Deadball Era, Hageman returned to start the second game. Charles Pinkney Sr. arrived at Fairview Park in the fifth inning and between innings briefly visited with his son on the field. By that time it was rapidly growing dark, and the *Dayton Journal's* Julian Behr commented the game should have been called after five. It was decided the seventh would be the last inning. Grand Rapids led 5-3. Hageman walked the first batter and retired the next, bringing Pinkney to the plate. As the *Journal* described it, "Pitcher Hageman threw three balls to Pinkney and the fourth appeared to be a ball which would entitle the batter to his base. It was a swift shoot, which approached the home plate like a swift shot from a rifle. It was growing very dark and before Pinkney could dodge, the ball had hit him square in the head just back of and above the left ear. The report was so loud it was heard by practically all present. The athlete fell to the ground like one shot."

Charles Pinkney died the next day in Dayton's St. Elizabeth Hospital. The *Herald* described the effect of the tragedy on the Grand Rapids pitcher. "Kurt Hageman is inconsolable. He locked himself in his room at the Hotel Beckel this morning refusing to see even his teammates, although everyone absolves him from all blame in the accident. From early in the morning he kept the phone to the hospital in constant use, asking particulars of Pinkney's condition. When he learned the second baseman was dead his grief knew no bounds. He had splendid control this season and this accident was the first that has ever befallen him. Next to the death of Pinkney nothing could be sadder than the grief of Hageman."

Hageman finished the season with just 2.9 walks per 9 innings, finishing with an 18-16 record. Determined to never pitch in Dayton again, Hageman refused a return to Grand Rapids and was sold to Denver of the Class A Western League.

Denver manager Jack Hendricks had managed at Fort Wayne in 1908 and 1909 and was familiar with Hageman. One report said Casey might have retired from the game if not for Hendricks. Hageman's first season with the Grizzlies was a disappointment. Inconsistency, especially with control was a problem. Overshadowed by most of the Denver pitching staff, Hageman struggled to an 11-10 record for a second-place club, walking 102 batters on the season. One source said "all season he was afraid to put a fast one near the plate." Part of the problem may have been similar to those faced by Colorado Rockies pitchers years later: the altitude. A 1912 article in *Baseball Magazine* said the "'mile high' climate at Denver has a big effect on the game. Twirlers who have plenty of 'stuff' in a lower altitude have to work harder to get the same 'break' to a ball than they do in lower altitudes." [1]

Casey Hageman's second season in Denver was much better than his first. Denver began April hosting a team on a protracted spring trip, the Boston Red Sox. According to *The Great Red Sox Spring Training Tour of 1911*, Hageman pitched very well against the Red Sox Colts (or B) team. On April 2, Casey held Boston scoreless through seven allowing just one hit over the first five innings. Boston also optioned young pitcher Buck O'Brien to Denver; the performance of the Denver team would be watched by Boston.

Later in the month, Denver team President James McGill organized an ambitious spring training trip covering an estimated 3,500 miles through Texas and Oklahoma. Casey continued to pitch well there, allowing seven hits and striking out 11 in a 6-0 shutout of Dallas on April 11.

The success continued into the regular season. Later in the month he held defending league champion Sioux City scoreless through seven in a 10-3 win. In early June, Boston purchased his contract for a reported $5,000 with the understanding that he'd finish the season in Denver. He pitched in 23 games for the Grizzlies in 1911, posting a 14-7 record. He was a better pitcher the first half of the Western League season, perhaps struggling after another errant pitch beaned Sioux City's Fred Stem.

Casey Hageman joined Boston during the second week of September, and made his major-league debut at Boston on September 18. Cleveland starter George "Krum" Kahler allowed just one run on four hits, but *Boston Globe* thought Hageman showed ability: "Hageman....made his first appearance in the box here and pitched a pretty good game. It was apparent he was over-anxious and for that reason was unable to do himself justice. He looks as if he had the goods and will probably be able to demonstrate this fact when he strikes his natural gait. In any event he will bear watching for awhile." Cleveland won, 4-1; Hageman allowed nine hits, struck out five, and walked two. Just one of the Cleveland runs was earned.

He made one more start in 1911, losing 4-2 to Chicago in one of the last games played at Boston's Huntington Avenue Grounds. Again, shaky defense hurt Hageman. Just one of the four runs was earned. In eight innings he gave up seven hits, struck out three, and walked three. He finished the season at 0-2, but with a solid 2.12 earned run average. It looked as though he'd be in Boston's plans for 1912.

Heading into 1912, it looked like Boston had pitching openings. A couple of veterans and rookies Hageman, O'Brien, Jack Bushelman, and Hugh Bedient were competing for two or three spots on the staff. O'Brien probably had an edge for one job, but Hageman's chances appeared strong. Coming north with the team, he still seemed to have a chance to be the fifth man on Boston's staff.

On April 9, the first game was played at brand new Fenway Park and Casey Hageman was the starting pitcher. It was an

Joe Wood and Casey Hageman on the field of play, 1912.

exhibition game against Harvard. According to *Red Sox Threads*, "4,500 hardy souls braved the elements watching in a cold 'fit to test the courage of any football crowd, with a little snow on the side for good measure of discomfort.' Hageman took the mound for Boston, squaring off against Harvard's third baseman Dana Wingate. The first batter ever to step into the box at Fenway Park took a pitch for ball one." After throwing that first ball, Hageman struck out Wingate for another first. Casey was the star that day both offensively and on the mound. He surrendered just one hit on the afternoon, that to Harvard second baseman Bob Potter. He walked three. At the plate, Casey drove in the first two runs in Fenway history. In the second inning after a couple of walks and an error, Hageman drove in shortstop Marty Krug with a single. In the fifth, the mighty Casey drove in Larry Gardner with a hard-hit single to center.

Hageman got a start against the Yankees (Highlanders) in the third game of a season-opening series at New York. It was a disaster. Casey struck out one batter, the only one he retired that day. He also walked three and gave up a pair of hits and four runs, all earned. He got one more chance in relief for Boston and was again unimpressive, giving up three hits and an unearned run. On May 21, Hageman was sent to Jersey City of the Eastern League on option. He was unimpressive with Jersey City, posting a 2-5 record in 11 games. He allowed 71 hits and walked 37 in 59 2/3 innings. On June 23, Jersey City sent him back to Boston and the Red Sox sold him back to Denver for $1,500. This began a controversy that would overshadow the rest of Hageman's career.

Sporting Life stated Denver offered Hageman "$1,500 for the season and he refused to report. Other clubs offered Hageman a position, agreeing to pay him $2,400 [the amount of his Boston contract], but President [Jimmy] McAleer, of Boston, would not consent. Hageman offered to buy his release, and McAleer said: 'You'll play ball with Denver or you'll quit baseball.' About this time a major-league club offered to assume Hageman's $2,400 contract, offering more money for the pitcher's release than Denver, but McAleer refused. Hageman was Boston's property; he must obey orders or get out of the business which gave him a living. Hageman reported at the Boston grounds daily, but after June 23 drew no money." [2]

Casey pitched no more in 1912, and on May 31, 1913, the Base Ball Players Fraternity sued the Red Sox on behalf of Hageman. Initial judgment was against Hageman and the union, but the Appellate Division of the State Supreme Court reversed the ruling in early 1915. The case continued in the courts until February 19, 1918 when Boston settled out of court, paying Base Ball Players Fraternity President Dave Fultz $2,385.19 on behalf of Hageman.

Meanwhile Hageman played two more seasons of professional baseball. He finally went to Denver in 1913 and had another solid season. There were rumors that he was being scouted by several major-league teams. The *Topeka Daily Capital* quoted Cubs owner Charles Webb Murphy as saying he would not acquire Hageman no matter how well he pitched. Ironically, Hageman was pitching for the Cubs a year later and Murphy was out of baseball. That fall the St. Louis Cardinals drafted Hageman from Denver, and got another chance at the major leagues.

Casey Hageman pitched well enough during the spring to secure a spot in the Cardinals rotation. During the preseason series with the cross-town rival Browns, *Sporting Life* offered comment on Hageman's potential. "Another prize shown by the Cardinals in the spring series is pitcher Hageman. Hageman gave a good exhibition in his first game Thursday until he became rattled with the continued objections of Branch Rickey. However Hageman and [Walton] Cruise are two of the choicest youngsters who have joined the Cardinals in some time." [3]

Unfortunately, once the season began strong performances were few and far between. Typical was an April 23 loss to Pittsburgh. In that game, "Hageman was wild. Aside from hitting a man and walking two more in the fourth, he had three wild pitches during the game." [4] Soon pitching his way out of the rotation, his best performance for St. Louis was his last. On July 1, He pitched a complete-game 5-1 victory over the Pirates. He allowed five hits, struck out four and walked three. "Until the ninth inning only two men reached second base." [5]

Five days later he was sold to the Chicago Cubs for the waiver price. Casey Hageman pitched almost exclusively in relief for the Cubs. His lone win for Chicago was a game he later remembered as one of his best. On the afternoon of August 18, the Cubs were hosting Brooklyn, allowing the visitors to jump out to a 5-0 lead after two innings. Entering in the third, Casey allowed one run on six hits over the last seven innings, striking out four batters. He also went 4-for-4 at the plate with a double and two runs scored.

On the season, Hageman was 2-4 with St. Louis and 1-1 for Chicago. In 28 appearances including eight starts, he compiled a 2.91 ERA in 102 innings, striking out 38 and walking 32. That winter there was another contract dispute involving Hageman and the Cubs. His 1914 contract with the Cardinals had called for a $240 bonus. In April of 1915 he was awarded the bonus by the National Commission and the Cubs were also instructed to offer a 1915 contract including the bonus. Evidently this contract was not offered, or other terms were unsatisfactory, and Casey Hageman left Organized Baseball.

He initially stayed in Chicago, briefly pitching for the Logan Squares semipro team. Later in 1915, Casey Hageman married Helen Geitzen and bought the Youngstown (Ohio) New Agency, selling and distributing newspapers and magazines. He stayed in baseball around Youngstown. He pitched for and managed the McElroys and Tellings clubs in Youngstown.

Although Youngstown's semipro teams generally competed at a lower level than rivals in Massillon and Canton, the 1918 and 1919 teams were noteworthy. In August of 1918, Hageman had one of the all time greats in his lineup for at least a few games.

According to the *Massillon Evening Independent*, "Manager Casey Hageman was the most surprised man in baseball when he was paid a visit the other day by Wagner and Honus importuned him to 'give him a chance' with the McElroys. Hageman lost no time coming to terms with the 'Flying Dutchman' and Honus expressed himself as well pleased with the arrangements. It is reported Wagner will collect $100 after every game." [6]

The 1919 McElroys started the season with a strong roster. In addition to Hageman, Earl Moseley, and Elmer Knetzer pitched for the team and Catcher Frank Mills was a former member of the Indians. Except for Mills and Hageman, none of the others remained in Youngstown for long.

By 1924, Hageman was helping to organize a club in Youngstown sponsored by General Tire. By that time, Youngstown no longer had the resources or talent to compete with the top independent teams. Casey continued to run the newsstand moving to New Bedford, Pennsylvania in 1951, but continuing to commute to Youngstown to run the News Agency until his retirement five years later. Casey and Helen had no children, and Helen was considered an invalid by the 1940's. Kurt Moritz Hageman died at his home in New Bedford of a heart ailment on the morning of April 1, 1964. He is buried at Mount Calvary Cemetery in Grand Rapids.

Continuing the tradition they'd begun on the spring training trip of 1911, and a successful offseason vaudeville career on the Keith's theater circuit, here is 75% of the Red Sox Quartet which had originally also featured Marty McHale and Larry Gardner. Another Sox vocal group from 1911 had featured Heinie Wagner, Red Kleinow, Bill Carrigan, and Eddie Cicotte.
Boston Post

Sources:

Steubenville (Ohio) *Herald Star* 1906-09.

East Liverpool (Ohio) *Tribune* 1906.

Zanesville (Ohio) *Courier* 1907.

Zanesville (Ohio) *Signal* 1907.

Fort Wayne (Indiana) *News* 1908-09.

Fort Wayne (Indiana) *Sentinel* 1908-09.

Grand Rapids (Michigan) *Herald* 1908-09.

Dayton (Ohio) *Journal* 1909.

Des Moines (Iowa) *News* 1910-11

Waterloo (Iowa) *Evening Courier* 1911.

Boston Globe 1911-12.

Washington Post 1911-12.

Sporting Life 1912-15.

Topeka (Kansas) *Daily Capital* 1913.

Massillon (Ohio) *Evening Independent* 1915-24.

Youngstown (Ohio) *Vindicator* 1964.

"Baseball Above the Clouds" *Baseball Magazine* 1912.

"The Baseball Player's Fraternity" *Baseball Magazine* April 1915.

SABR BioProject biography of Charles Pinkney.

Bill Nowlin. *The Great Red Sox Spring Training Tour of 1911* (Jefferson NC: McFarland, 2010).

Endnotes

1. Russell F. Norton, "Baseball Above the Clouds", *Baseball Magazine*, February 1912, 32

2. *Sporting Life*, November 16, 1912, 10

The ruling reported more of the particulars of the assignment in an article reprinted in *Baseball Magazine*:

"Stahl said, 'If you must sign a contract be absolutely sure that the terms are just the same as the contract you signed with us,' and thereupon and on the same day he went to Jersey City and reported to the Jersey City club for duty and was required to sign a 'regular International League contract,' of which he did not receive a copy, by which he was to receive a salary in the same amount as he was receiving from the defendant.'

"Hageman afterwards testified that he understood he was released by the defendant to the Jersey City Club under an 'optional release'; that no period was specified in the contract which he signed with the Jersey City Club. Hageman further testified that he played with the Jersey City club until the evening of June 23, 1912, when the secretary of the club delivered to him a check for his services and made a statement to him, which was not received in evidence but which evidently related to his transfer to the Denver Club, for he wired McAleer regarding his transfer to that club, and received a telegram from McAleer in reply as follows: 'Jersey City did not want you so have given Denver option on you. You will have to make your terms with Denver.' "

Offered $250 a month, he "wired the Denver Club that the terms were unreasonable and that he could not accept them, and he received a reply from the president of the club as follows: 'Best proposition I will make you is two fifty per month when you are ready to report wire me for transportation and will send same or you can furnish your own and we will refund. You are hereby notified that you are suspended until you accept terms and report to us.' " The opinion of the court went on to state that McAleer offered to let Hageman buy his release and then reneged on the offer after which "Hageman then informed McAleer that he would remain there and report for duty and hold defendant to its contract, to which McAleer replied, 'You are foolish, my boy, you won't get a cent.' Hageman reported to the club daily for duty until the close of the season, and subsequently assigned his claim for services to the plaintiff, and this action was brought." *Baseball Magazine*, April 1915

3. *Sporting Life*, April 25, 1914, 6

4. *Sporting Life*, May 2, 1914, 5

5. *Sporting Life*, July 11, 1914, 5

6. *Massillon Evening Independent*, August 5, 1918

Charley "Sea Lion" Hall
by John Stahl and ReBecca Glidewell-Hall

G	ERA	W	L	SV	GS	GF	CG	SHO	IP	H	R	ER	BB	SO	HR	HBP	WP	BFP
34	3.02	15	8	2	20	12	9	2	191	178	85	64	70	83	3	4	0	766

G	AB	R	H	2B	3B	HR	RBI	BB	SO	BA	OBP	SLG	SB	HBP
34	75	10	20	4	2	1	14	4	16	.267	.321	.413	0	2

Standing 6-feet-1 at 185 pounds with dark good looks, the young Charley Hall cut an imposing, often intimidating figure on the mound. Early in his baseball career, he combined his "swarthy" appearance with a blazing, high-voltage fast ball. Later, with diminished speed but more consistent control, he deftly packaged a wide array of pitches thrown at various speeds, alternately teasing and jamming hitters. Batters simply did not like to face either the young or old Charley Hall.[1]

Charley was born on July 27, 1885, in Ventura, California, to Arthur and Elvira (Mungari) Hall.[2] His roots were Spanish-American. Both Spanish and English were spoken in his boyhood home. Elvira's mother was Doña Concepcion Cota Mungari, a descendant of the Spanish settlers of the Presidio of Santa Barbara of 1762. Charley was christened Carlos Luis Hall at the San Buenaventura Mission in Ventura.[3] Elvira died from childbirth complications in 1888 when Charley was 3 years old.[4] Arthur's father (Rueben) and mother (Sarah) came to California from Wisconsin via a wagon train in the mid-1860s.

Charley started playing organized baseball as a boy. According to the *Oxnard Courier*, he "learned how to play ball" as a member of an Oxnard junior baseball team known as the Palm Street Nine.[5] Very thin as a youngster, Hall's prodigious baseball talent was not generally recognized until he began to mature physically.[6]

In 1904, Parke Wilson, the manager of the Seattle team in the Pacific Coast League, "discovered" and signed the 19-year-old Hall playing in Santa Barbara. Initially, Wilson used Hall in relief. As he gained experience and other veteran Seattle pitchers faltered, Charley became a starter as well.

By July 1904, Charley's record was 12-5, second best in the entire PCL. The *Seattle Times* called him "about the biggest sensation in the Pacific Coast League this season."[7] Opponents also noted his nerve. San Francisco catcher Ly Gordon told the *Seattle Times*, "I never saw a youngster with more backbone in him than this Seattle youngster." By the end of 1904, Charley had accumulated a 29-19 record, pitching a phenomenal 425 innings.[8]

Returning to Seattle again in 1905, Hall found himself on a horrible team. Burdened with the high expectations he established in 1904, he slumped—though he did no-hit Oakland on April 5. As the team improved, Hall rallied, finishing the year with a 23-27 record. He completed another marathon eight-month PCL season with 449 innings pitched. Although clearly overworked at times by the brutal schedule, Charley was rewarded for his diligence with over 870 innings of professional pitching experience in his first two years.

When the 1904 and 1905 seasons ended in early December, Charley went home and played semiprofessional baseball in Southern California. He would do this for most of his professional

Carlos Luis "Charley" Hall, in a posed studio shot wearing his Red Sox sweater.

career. Within this local, low-pressure, entertainment-oriented baseball environment, Charley also began coaching third base. His Spanish-laced baserunning instructions were high-volume exhortations that usually resulted in making him hoarse over the course of a game. An *Oxnard Courier* article described his hoarse coaching voice as "sounding something like the bark of hunting dog." Every time he batted during the game, the bleacher fans would mimic his coaching sounds mercilessly.[9] Later, when he did the same thing as a Red Sox third base coach, the Boston fans affectionately named him Sea Lion.

By 1906, Charley was married to Emma Larson and had fathered his first son, Marshall.[10] He was also an established veteran pitcher on Seattle's team. When injuries hit the team during the year, Seattle also used Charley occasionally as an infielder or outfielder.[11]

On May 13, 1906, against Oakland, Hall pitched his second no-hit game, winning 3-0. The *Seattle Times* called it "the finest exhibition of pitching seen in Recreation Park (Seattle's home field)." A walk in the second inning and an error by the shortstop in the ninth accounted for Oakland's only baserunners. Relying primarily on his fastball, Hall struck out seven.[12] During his next regular start, in a pregame ceremony, his teammates gave new "Papa" Hall a brand new "baby buggy in which to trundle his son and heir."[13]

In July 1906, Charley finally got his first chance in the major leagues, reporting to the Cincinnati Reds. For Seattle, he had a 1906 record of 8-14 in 196 innings with an ERA of 2.29.

In Cincinnati, Hall made his major-league debut against John McGraw's world champion New York Giants on July 12. According to the *Cincinnati Enquirer*, Charley relieved a beleaguered Cincinnati starting pitcher in the bottom of the first inning and was "pounded unmercifully" the rest of the game. The Reds lost 16-11, as Charley gave up 12 hits and walked seven in his nine innings.[14] Four days later, starting in place of an injured pitcher, Charley recorded his first major-league win against Brooklyn, striking out eight while walking four in a complete game 7-6 victory.[15] Hall finished his rookie year with a 4-8 record in 95 innings with a 3.32 ERA.[16]

In 1907, he started with Cincinnati and things quickly deteriorated. His pitching control remained inconsistent. He would be impressive in one appearance and then wild in another. After pitching 68 innings in 11 games with a 2.51 ERA, Hall was sent to Columbus in the American Association. He ended the year with Columbus going 8-3.

Hall began 1908 pitching for a Columbus team that finished in third place. He went 8-21, allowing 245 hits in 243 innings. It was his worst full-season record in professional baseball. Hall's slide into baseball oblivion, however, suddenly ended when he was sent to St. Paul at the end of the 1908 season.

At St. Paul in 1909, Hall was 4-13 with a 4.08 ERA in 172 innings. The highlight of his 1909 season was another no-hitter, a nine-inning effort against Louisville, which he eventually lost 1-0 in the 12th inning. He struck out every man in the lineup (six in a row) for a total of 16 batters in 12 innings. In the first nine innings, only two batters reached base, both on walks.

At St. Paul, however, Charley had the good fortune to pitch for one of the legends of minor-league baseball, manager Mike Kelley. On July 26, 1909, Kelley got Charley back into the major leagues when he traded him with infielder-outfielder Ed Karger to the Boston Red Sox for pitchers Charlie Chech and Jack Ryan, plus cash.[17]

With Boston, Hall compiled a 6-4 record that season, pitching 59 innings with a 2.56 ERA. Hall's joy in returning to the major leagues was tempered by the death of his first wife, Emma, during childbirth. His first child, Marshall, was subsequently raised by Emma's parents.[18]

In 1910, Charley pitched well as both a starter and a reliever for Boston. In his 35 appearances, he started 16 games and relieved in 19. His resulting record was 12 wins and 9 losses in 188 innings with his major-league career low 1.91 ERA, good enough for 10th best in the American League

Hall's 1911 role put more emphasis on relief pitching. His 32 pitching appearances included 22 in relief and 10 starts. He finished 1911 with an 8-7 record in 146 innings and a 3.75 ERA. His 1911 appearances included a number of highlights. In May, he relieved the Boston starters in both games of a doubleheader against Washington and won both games, besting Walter Johnson in the afternoon contest.[19]

On August 2, against the Detroit Tigers, Hall arguably had the best relief appearance in his major-league career. In the second game of a doubleheader, with Boston leading 8-2 in the top of the ninth inning, the Tigers loaded the bases with no outs. Hall was summoned with no time to warm up to replace the fading starter, Larry Pape. In succession, Hall had to face Ty Cobb, Wahoo Sam Crawford, and Jim Delahanty.

After teasing Cobb with two outside pitches, Charley busted two past him for called strikes. Cobb took a strong swing at the next one, tipping it slightly, but catcher Nunamaker held on to the ball for strike three. Charley used the same pitching sequence with Crawford—two pitches outside followed by two strikes. The all-time triples king swung at the fifth pitch. Again Nunamaker held the foul tip for the third strike. The doubleheader crowd of 27,354 erupted as Crawford dejectedly headed back to the dugout. For the final out, Charley got Delahanty to pop weakly to shortstop. As the infield pop fell into Steve Yerkes' glove, a boisterous crowd of very happy Boston fans stormed the field in

Hall was 15-8 in 1912, and hit for a .267 average with 14 RBIs.

We don't know the full story here, but it's clear there was a disagreement of sorts between two of the Red Sox pitchers. Cicotte's use of the word "chile" refers to Carlos Luis Hall's Mexican ancestry. *Boston Post*

celebration.[20] In later years, Hall often cited the incident as one of the biggest thrills in his baseball career.

On November 5, 1911, Charley married Boston native Marie Cullen at the Mission Church in Boston. The *Oxnard Courier*, announced the news, calling Charley "one of the best known young men in the country, from a baseballistic and friendship standpoint." The paper also reported that he would bring his bride with him when he returned to Ventura.[21]

Balancing this happy news was a less flattering incident. In late 1911, the *Boston Globe* reported that Charley was arrested in Ventura for refusing to help with firefighting.

After Boston's disappointing fourth-place finish in 1911, Charley showed up for 1912 spring training "lively and limber."[22] During the winter, the Red Sox had made several significant ownership, front office, and field manager changes. Jake Stahl, who had sat out the 1911 season, now managed the 1912 team. As the Boston first baseman on the 1909 and 1910 teams, he had witnessed Hall's success as both a starting and relief pitcher.

In 1912, Charley flourished, achieving major-league career bests in wins (15) and innings pitched. (191). He appeared in 34 games, 20 as the starting pitcher and 14 in relief.[23] This was a distinct departure from his 1911 usage pattern, when he started only 10 games during the entire season.

Hall made important contributions to the Red Sox' 1912 championship season. He got the win in the first game at Boston's brand new Fenway Park, replacing wobbly starter Buck O'Brien and pitching three-hit ball for seven strong innings to allow the Red Sox to rally in the 11th.[24] During the first 35 games of the season, Charley appeared nine times and pitched four complete-game victories. On September 10, he saved Smoky Joe Wood's 15th consecutive win in the ninth inning at Comiskey Park in Chicago.[25]

Hall was a consistently positive presence during the 1912 pennant drive. He voluntarily manned Boston's third-base coaching box, often yelling directions and encouragement to his teammates.[26] In the clubhouse, he was gregarious and friendly, often exchanging friendly banter with other veteran players. He often teased Boston pitcher Ed Cicotte that his name meant "punk" or "very poor" in Spanish. Cicotte jokingly insisted that Hall's real name was Carlos Cholo.[27]

The 1912 World Series afforded Charley an opportunity to play against his two longtime Southern California friends, Fred Snodgrass and Chief Meyers. He appeared twice and was probably under the weather each time. The *Boston Globe* reported before the Series opener that Charley had a severe cold and it was uncertain to what extent he could pitch in the Series. He was referred to the Boston team physician, Dr. Cliff, for treatment.[28]

Sick or not, Charley performed. He pitched in the Game Two 6-6 tie, entering in relief of Ray Collins in the eighth inning with runners on second and third, one out, and the Red Sox ahead 4-3. He retired the first hitter but allowed two unearned runs to score. Although walking the bases full, he pitched a scoreless ninth. In the 10th, he allowed a leadoff triple and the sixth Giants run.[29]

Hall also pitched in Boston's seventh-game loss (because of the tie, the Series ran to eight games). He relieved Wood in the second inning and pitched the rest of the game.[30] His World Series line showed 10⅔ innings pitched with a 3.38 ERA.

After their pennant-winning 1912 season, the Red Sox players, including Hall, suffered a letdown in 1913. Within an environment that included distracting 1912-related celebrations, injuries, management turmoil, a strong wire-to-wire pennant run by Connie Mack's Philadelphia Athletics, and Boston's erratic starting pitching, Hall's workload changed.

Appearing in 35 games, he was used as a relief pitcher 31 times and as a starting pitcher only four times. He ended the year with a 5-4 record in 105 innings with a 3.43 ERA. He failed to win any of his four starts and walked nearly as many hitters (46) as he struck out (48).

After the disappointing 1913 season, Boston released Hall. Unable to find another job in the major leagues, he returned to St. Paul, where in 1914 he went 12-17 in 258 innings for a mediocre American Association team.

In 1915, with an improved club around him, Charley re-emerged as a strong starting pitcher. Manager Kelley again created the kind of tight-knit club environment in which Charley thrived. At an early-season team fishing trip, he manned the stove as the chief cook. A picture in *the St. Paul Pioneer Press* showed him decked out in his apron. A later article commented on his outdoor cooking prowess, noting that he was the "master of the barbeque sauce."[31] In 1915, he was 24-10 in 298⅔ innings. His season's highlight was an American Association record-setting streak of 16 consecutive wins.[32]

As Hall's 1915 streak lengthened, scouts from both the National League and the new Federal League made visits to St. Paul to assess his pitching. Hall reportedly received a substantial offer from the Federal League to leave St. Paul and jump to the Federal League immediately.[33] He refused the offer, publicly citing his loyalty to Kelley.[34] Kelley rewarded Hall by negotiating a deal that gave him an immediate bonus and put him back in the major leagues with the St. Louis Cardinals the next season. The deal also allowed him to complete 1915 in St. Paul.[35]

In 1916, Hall, now in his early 30s, began the year in the major leagues with the Cardinals. He appeared 10 times: five as a starting pitcher; and five in relief. He did not win a game, going 0-4. His control problems re-emerged and he walked 14 in 42⅔ innings. Toward the end of July, the Cardinals sold him to the Los Angeles Angels of the Pacific Coast League.

Guided by future Hall of Famer Frank Chance, the Angels were fighting for first place.[36] During the first week in August, Hall started and won his first game for the Angels.[37] He finished with a 6-6 record in 128 innings as the Angels won the pennant. Returning in 1917, he spent the entire season with the Angels, going 14-19 in 313 innings.

Hall rejoined Kelley in St. Paul to start the 1918 season. One of his highlights was pitching yet another no-hit game, against Columbus in late June. Three runners reached base, as he walked two and one reached on an error.[38] Because of World War I, the American Association ended its season on July 21. Hall finished with a 15-8 record in 189 innings.

Primarily due to his 1918 success at St. Paul and the player shortage caused by the federal "work-or-fight" rule, the Detroit Tigers gave Charley another shot at the major leagues after the American Association season.[39] But was pounded, allowing 10 runs in 13 innings. He appeared in six games, starting once and relieving in five others, and was 0-1. He was released by Detroit after the season. Hall's major-league career was over. In parts of all of nine seasons, Hall finished with a 54-47 record, pitching 909 innings. He appeared in 188 games, starting in 80 and relieving in 108. His career ERA was 3.09.

Hall began 1919 again with Kelley in St. Paul. Starting in that season and running through 1923, Hall and the Saints amassed one of the greatest sets of seasons in minor-league history. In five years, Charley won 110 games, pitching 1,481 innings.

His 27-8 season in 1920 included a no-hit game, against Columbus. In the 6-0 shutout, only two runners reached base, one on a walk and one on an error.[40] Kelley later called Hall's 1920 season 27-8, 2.06 ERA) the greatest he'd ever seen for a pitcher. Three of those St. Paul teams (1920, 1922, and 1923, first place, first place, and second place, respectively) are ranked by baseball historians among the top 100 teams in minor-league history.

In 1924, when Kelley left St. Paul to become an owner of the Minneapolis team, Charley pitched for Sacramento in the PCL. For a last-place team, Charley went 16-21 in 305 innings. In 1925, after beginning the season with Birmingham, he rejoined Kelley in Minneapolis. Then 41 years old, Charley finished his professional baseball playing career by going 3-4 in 54 innings. His last pitching appearance was in relief against his old team, St. Paul. As a result of a controversial call by an umpire, Charley lost the game, 5-3.[41]

That pitching appearance was not Hall's last game. In the next game, Kelley let his longtime friend play first base.[42] Charley finished his 21-year professional baseball career with 54 major-league and 285 minor league wins, for a total of 339.

After leaving baseball, Hall returned to California, where he owned land and was an avid outdoorsman. He entered law enforcement and served as a policeman, a jailer, and the deputy sheriff. In 1920, his family suffered a devastating loss when their 6-year-old son, Charley, accidentally shot and killed their 3-year-old son, Kenneth.[43]

In 1943, Charley died of Parkinson's disease in his beloved Ventura. Noting his popularity in Boston, the sportswriter Fred Lieb observed in Hall's obituary, "Many a player who played with Charley or batted against him must have felt a passing regret that the big Sea Lion had roared his last."[44]

Sources:

Boston Globe

Cincinnati Enquirer

Oakland Tribune

Oxnard Courier

Seattle Times

The Sporting News

St. Louis Globe Democrat

St. Paul Pioneer Press

E-mail correspondence with ReBecca Glidewell-Hall

Jeff Maulhardt. *Baseball in Ventura County.* Arcadia Books 2007.

Bill Nowlin. *Day By Day With the Boston Red Sox.* (Cambridge, Massachusetts: Rounder Books, 2008)

Bill Nowlin. *Red Sox Threads: Odds and Ends from Red Sox History.* (Burlington, Massachusetts: Rounder Books 2006)

John Thorn, Peter Palmer, and Michael Gershman. *Total Baseball 7th Edition. Edition.* (Kingston, New York: Total Sports Publishing, 2001)

SABR Minor League Database

National Baseball Hall of Fame: Charley Hall Player File

Twelfth Census of the United States: 1900.

Footnotes

1. Bill Nowlin. *Red Sox Threads, Odds & Ends from Red Sox History.* (Burlington, Massachusetts: Rounder Books, 2006), 89.

2. Certificate of Death 3608, State of California, Department of Public Health, Charles L. Hall, December 7, 1943, and Twelfth Census of the United States, 1900: California, Ventura County, Ventura City, Schedule NO-1, Population, Enumeration District 171, June 9, 1900, Arthur Hall.

3. ReBecca Glidewell-Hall, e-mails dated May 17, 2008, and August 26, 2008.

4. ReBecca Glidewell-Hall, e-mail dated April 28, 2008.

5. "Oxnard Wins Championship in Delirious Final Ball Game," *Oxnard Courier*, Oxnard, California, December 9, 1910.

6. "Side Light From The County Seat," *Oxnard Courier*, December 16, 1904, Volume 6, No. 51.

7. "Records of the Pitchers," *Seattle Times*, July 18, 1904.

8. SABR Minor League Database, Charley Hall career pitching statistics.

9. "Captain Snodgrass Gets Winning Team Together Sunday," *Oxnard Courier*, November 12, 1910.

10. ReBecca Glidewell-Hall, e-mail dated April 28, 2008.

11. "Seattle Breaks Even On Day," *Seattle Times*, May 21, 1906.

12. "Hall Pitches No-Hit Game," *Seattle Times*, May 13, 1906.

13. "Charley Hall In Fine Form," *Seattle Times*, May 18, 1906.

14. Jack Ryder, "Fearful," *Cincinnati Enquirer*, July 13, 1906.

15. Jack Ryder, "Scooted," *Cincinnati Enquirer*, August 1, 1906.

16. John Thorn, Peter Palmer, and Michael Gershman. *Total Baseball* 7th Edition (Kingston, New York: Total Sports Publishing, 2001).

17. Bill Nowlin. *Day By Day With the Boston Red Sox* (Cambridge, Massachusetts, Rounder Books, 2006), 346.

18. ReBecca Glidewell-Hall, e-mail dated May 17, 2008.

19. "Red Sox Clean Up Two More," *Boston Globe*, May 31, 1911.

20. Paul Shannon, "27,354 See Red Sox Beat Detroit Twice," *Boston Globe* and T.H. Murnane, "Make Tigers Give Up Two," *Boston Globe*, August 3, 1911.

21. "Charley Hall Is Married in Boston," *Oxnard Courier*, November 3, 1911.

22. "Charley Hall Lively, Limber," *Oxnard Courier*, March 15, 1912.

23. Stahl Analysis of *Boston Post* and *Boston Globe* 1912 Red Sox Box Scores, May through July 2008.

24. Paul Shannon, "Fenway Park Is Formally Opened With Red Sox Win," *Boston Post*, April 21, 1912.

25. Paul Shannon, "Wood Wins His 15th With Assistance From Hall," *Boston Post*, September 11, 1912.

26. "Sea Lion Charley Hall Is The Red Sox Rescue Pitcher," *Boston Post*, September 5, 1912.

27. "Red Sox Are of a Retiring Disposition When Not Playing," *Boston Post*, April 14, 1912. Most standard baseball reference sources have mistakenly cited Hall's surname at birth as Clolo.

28. James C. O'Leary, "Gov. Foss Roots For the Red Sox, Hall Improves," *Boston Globe, October 8*, 1912.

29. T.H. Murnane, "World Championship Baseball Extra Red Sox 6 New York 6," *Boston Globe*, October 9, 1912.

30. James C. O'Leary, "Worlds Championship Baseball Extra Red Sox 4 Giants 11," *Boston Globe*, October 5, 1912.

31. "What The Pioneer Press Camera Caught At The Saints Picnic At Bald Eagle Lake," *St. Paul Pioneer Press*, July 18, 1915.

32. "Double Defeat Jolts Saints Out of First Place Hall Is Stopped At Last," *St. Paul Pioneer Press*, August 23, 1915.

33. "Fed Agents On Hall's Trail," *St. Paul Pioneer Press*, July 28, 1915.

34. "Hall Loyal To Kelley," *St. Paul Pioneer Press*, August 14, 1915.

35. "Hall and Boardman Are Sold to St. Louis," *St. Paul Pioneer Press*, Sports Section, August 22, 1915.

36. "Charley Hall Bought By Chance From Cards," *Los Angeles Times*, July 25, 1916.

37. Harry A. Williams, "Hall Wins First Game," *Los Angeles Times*, August 3, 1916.

38. "Hall Hangs Up No Hit, No Run Game Against Columbus," *St. Paul Pioneer Press*, June 24, 1918.

39. "Charley Hall," *Detroit Free Press*, July 31, 1918.

40. Leo P. Sullivan, "Charley Hall Pitches No-Hit, No-Run Game Against Columbus," *St. Paul Pioneer Press*, August 6, 1920.

41. Harry McKanna, "Old St. Paul Jinx Is On Job And Keds Lose Again 5 to 3," *Minneapolis Journal*, September 21, 1925.

42. "It's All Over Now," *Minneapolis Journal*, September 21, 1925.

43. Bill Nowlin. *Red Sox Threads: Odds and Ends from Red Sox History* (Burlington, MA: Rounder Books 2006).

44. Fred Lieb, "Death Fans the Old Sea Lion," *The Sporting News*, December 16, 1943.

Olaf Henriksen
by Ron Anderson

G	AB	R	H	2B	3B	HR	RBI	BB	SO	BA	OBP	SLG	SB	HBP
44	56	20	18	3	1	0	8	14	14	.321	.457	.411	0	0

"Pinch hit hero mobbed by rabid Red Sox enthusiasts" was a sub-headline of the October 17, 1912, edition of the *Boston Globe* reporting on young Olaf Henriksen's game-tying base hit in the eighth and deciding game of the 1912 World Series, against a dominant Christy Mathewson. It was a crucial blow off the great Mathewson, who pitched his heart out that day in a memorable performance, opening the door for the Boston team to win the game and World Series, Boston's second Series triumph, in extra innings.

Henriksen, a seldom-used reserve outfielder in his first full season with the Red Sox, deflated Mathewson with that hit and suddenly became a Boston hero. "The psychological kid," roared one rooter. And then, "After that the rooters never seemed to lose their confidence." Neither did the team. "The fever of victory mounted and mounted." [1]

Olaf Henriksen was born on April 26, 1888, in Kirkerup, Denmark, which is now part of the town of Roskilde. He was the third of nine children born to Jens Peter and Anna S. (Olsen) Henriksen, who emigrated from Denmark to the United States in 1888. They landed in New York, moved to Wareham, Massachusetts, near Cape Cod, where the family initially resided, and then to Canton, Massachusetts, a town south of Boston, where young Olaf and his siblings were raised.

Anna Henriksen died on December 17, 1908, at the young age of 46. Her husband, Jens Peter Henriksen, died in 1930 at 72. They are buried in the family plot in Wareham's Centre Cemetery.

Little is known about Olaf Henriksen's formative years in Wareham. It is presumed that he was schooled in the Wareham educational system in the lower grades. Family history supported by 1900 US Census information places Olaf with his family in Canton at the age of 12. The census report shows him "at school" then, but Olaf does not appear on Canton High School's baseball team, though he did play on Canton's town teams. According to current family members, Olaf most likely left school at an early age, which was common then, to help support the family. Olaf's father, Jens Peter, worked as a laborer in the Tremont Nail Factory in Wareham, which was still in operation in 2012. [2]

The only Danish-born player in major-league history.

Olaf was known by several nicknames including The Little General, The Owl, Kid Henriksen, and Little Henriksen given by friends and teammates, but the one that stood out during his major-league years was Hennie. To a lesser extent he was called Swede, frequently listed in baseball factbooks and encyclopedias as an "official" nickname for him that was not germane since Olaf was a Dane. He holds the distinction of being as of 2012 the only Danish-born athlete to play major-league baseball. [3]

Henriksen was of small stature, standing 5-feet-7½ inches tall with an average weight of 158 pounds. He threw and batted from the left side. Described as a slashing-type batsman, Henriksen was a contact hitter, spraying the ball to all fields. He had a good batting eye with a knack for getting on base, whether by base hits or bases on balls making him a specialty-type hitter, an ability that served him well when he reached the major leagues. Adding to that, he had great speed—"one of the fastest men in the country," boasted Red Sox President James McAleer in a January 7, 1912, *Boston Post* article—and thus always a threat to score once he was on base.

Henriksen, who emerged as pro baseball's consummate "pinchman," first appears in organized ball in June of 1904, when he had turned 16, playing for a local town team, the Eliot Athletic Association of Canton. The town's newspaper, the *Canton Journal*, announced the arrival of young Henriksen with much praise: "The Eliot A.A. played with new men and were fortunate in picking one in particular that will be an addition to the strength of the team if they can secure him. We mean Hendrickson, [sic] who is a star fielder and played center in last Saturday's game [June 18]." Such was his standout play that day that the local scribe issued a warning to the older players: "Certain members had better not think they are the only, only; they may find a vote or two will make a difference in whether or not they are needed."⁴ His play continued to impress that year, both at bat and in the field, as he shifted between infield—playing shortstop—and outfield positions.

In 1905 the Eliot A.A. built a state-of-the-art baseball park near the center of town known as Wentworth Field, "making it convenient to reach by electrics," reported the *Canton Journal*, and "The Association will wire the grounds for arc and incandescent lights." The Association also secured a building on the grounds that the players, including Henriksen, used as a dressing room. High-caliber baseball was played there against strong teams, some with former major leaguers and former minor-league players on their rosters, from nearby South Boston, Stoughton, Roxbury, and Hyde Park, among them, coming to play due to the convenience of the park to public transportation to and from outlying towns.⁵ Olaf was in fast company now; many of his teammates and opponents alike were older, some twice his age, and were mostly seasoned ballplayers.

Now 17, Olaf divided his time between Canton town teams and, for one game, was a walk-on player for a highly-regarded Stoughton semipro team in a July 13, 1905, contest against the Brockton Tigers, a good minor-league ballclub. Stoughton lost the game, 6-3, but Henriksen "had five putouts in centre field," wrote the *Canton Journal*.⁶ Henriksen appeared to be earning some money for the first time playing part-time semipro ball. This arrangement continued into 1906 when at the age of 18 Olaf played for the Canton Athletic Association ballclub, occasionally also appearing for other athletic clubs and semipro teams of surrounding towns.

His breakout year was 1907, when Henriksen, 19, caught on late in the season with the semipro Stoughton team—the Stoughtons—of the newly-formed Old Colony League. Olaf began the year with a local club, the Norwoods of Norwood, Massachusetts, playing with them through the first week in July. He then hooked up briefly with Hyde Park, also of the Old Colony League, and went on to play for the Stoughton team, first appearing for them on August 3 in a game against South Weymouth for the much-heralded Southeastern Massachusetts Championship. Olaf managed a base hit, but more than that convinced his manager that he was deserving of a permanent roster spot by making a perfect game-ending peg to home plate nailing the runner and securing a regional championship for Stoughton. He started the rest of the way for the Stoughtons, who eventually lost the Old Colony League championship to Taunton in the final game of the season. Henriksen was credited with a .304 batting average for "six games," according to the *Stoughton Sentinel*.⁷

Henriksen's solid performance at the end of the 1907 season earned him a starting berth with the 1908 Stoughton team, playing center field. Stoughton finished in second place (shared with two other teams, the Deweys and Randolph) with a 12-8 record, behind first-place Taunton, led by their star pitcher, Buck O'Brien, who later became a 20-game winner for the 1912 Red Sox and a teammate of Henriksen's. Olaf, meanwhile, rapped out 26 base hits in the 20 games, finishing with a .329 batting average.

John Blake, a scout for the minor-league Brocktons of the New England League, a Class B league, spotted Henriksen playing for the Stoughtons and quickly signed him to his first professional baseball contract at the conclusion of the 1908 Old Colony League season. Brockton's well-regarded manager, Steve Flanagan, anxious to lift his team from its fourth-place finish of the previous year, was willing to "try out a score or more of new men" to bolster his team of mostly "old men."⁸

Henriksen impressed from the start, both in the field and at bat. On April 12 Brockton held its first spring workout and Henriksen "did some great work" in the field, and "stung the ball on the nose every time," reported the *Brockton Times*. A sub-heading in the *Times* sports column the following day read, "Henricksen Begins to Shine in the Outfield." ⁹

In two practice games Henriksen went 2-for-4 and scored three runs. Manager Flanagan, reluctant though he was to place too much emphasis on youth, "gave Henricksen another trial," reported the *Times*, and he rose to the occasion. Playing against a strong Double-A Montreal team, he went 2-for-3 with a triple and one outfield assist; against Bridgeport of the Connecticut League, he was 2-for-5. This was convincing enough for manager Flanagan, who put Olaf in the starting lineup in right field on opening day, April 23, against a talent-laden 1908 New England League champion Worcester team.

Amid the hometown hoopla of a parade and flag-raising ceremony celebrating Worcester's prior-year championship, the new-look Brockton team began the season with a convincing 7-3 win. It began: "Henricksen, a new man to Brockton, was first man up. He waited for a base on balls," and then, as the *Brockton*

Olaf resting on his bat, 1915.

Times reported, was bunted to second, and later scored. He made four plate appearances, was 1-for-2, walked, reached base after being hit by a pitch, and scored three of Brockton's runs. Getting on base, however it was to be accomplished, would become Olaf's trademark throughout his pro baseball career.

However, after his quick start Henriksen faded. By the end of May he was batting .163, at the bottom of Brockton's starting nine. Yet manager Flanagan stayed with him, realizing his value as a leadoff hitter, his range in the field, speed on the base paths, and his uncanny ability to get on base and score runs. Overall the manager liked his gutsy style.

A sportswriter for the *Brockton Times*, noting Henriksen's low batting average, wrote favorably of Olaf by illustrating his highly productive qualities and otherwise immense value to the team: "This boy Henriksen is no world beater at the bat, but just keep watch on the run column. He has scored 29 runs and has reached first on hits only 19 times. If he doesn't get by on hits, he lands some other way."[10]

By the beginning of July, Henriksen had the lowest batting average on the team at .128, but was far and away the most productive player with 45 runs scored. Brockton was in second place. But Olaf caught fire and by mid-July, had raised his batting average to .220. Even more remarkably, he had scored 61 runs, 25 more than his nearest teammate, and he was second in the league in runs scored.

But on July 26 in a game against the first-place Lynn team, Henriksen, enjoying the momentum of playing good baseball, was suddenly hurt when he tagged up at third attempting to score on a fly to short center. "It was a chance that few men would take, but Henriksen made for home as though his life depended on it," reported the *Brockton Times*. "Henriksen had shot for the plate feet foremost in a daring slide," wrenching his ankle under him as he crossed the plate. He had to be carried from the field and his season appeared in jeopardy.[11]

Olaf shocked them all, however, when only two games later he pinch-hit, and was back in the lineup after that. "Henriksen is not in perfect shape….The youngster is so anxious to play that he returned to the game before he should," reported the *Brockton Times* on Olaf's surprised participation in spite of a lingering injury.[12]

Brockton finished the 1909 season in second place behind repeat champion Worcester. Henriksen had raised his batting average to a modest .254. He tied for the league lead in runs scored with 88.

The 1910 season was woeful for the Brockton team, which finished in last place, 29 games behind league leader New Bedford. Henriksen batted .256 and once again took team honors for runs scored with 66. He placed second on the club and third in the league with 46 stolen bases. A Brockton sportswriter, mentioning the all-important major-league draft after minor-league play, wrote, "A league team may pick up Henriksen, although the youngster's work was no improvement over that of last season."[13]

Olaf the super-sub.

An enthusiastic crowd of 2,400 fans, the largest turnout for an "opening game" in Brockton up to then, was present for the team's 1911 home opener on April 28. Olaf was a crowd favorite as he helped his club beat Haverhill, 5-2. "Henriksen pleased the crowd with that same ability to get on the bags that he showed last year," reported the *Brockton Daily Enterprise*. "He landed a single and a triple, and worked a base on balls, besides getting a sacrifice hit. He scored three times, and stole a base."

By the first week in June Henriksen was leading his team in hitting with a .343 batting average, among the league leaders. He was playing at a torrid pace on both offense and defense. On July 13 he became the first New England Leaguer to reach the esteemed level of 100 base hits, banging out a triple—his 10th—against Lynn, raising his batting average to .356, and putting him in contention for the lead in runs scored (63). "His hitting, fielding, and speed on the bases have already attracted attention of the scouts and before Aug. 15, when the drafting season starts, it would not be unlikely if the promising youngster is sold," reported the *Brockton Daily Enterprise*."[14]

"It takes fast fielding to keep this boy from getting on and twice yesterday he beat out hits to the infield," wrote the *Enterprise* on its report Henriksen's big day, July 27, against Lynn when he set a new mark for Brockton by stroking five base hits in a single game, raising his average to .359.[15] Major-league scouts were now swirling around ballparks where Henriksen played, hoping to pluck the youngster for the majors. "The Boston Red Sox management is interested in both men [Henriksen and shortstop Walter Lonergan of Brockton] and it is thought is likely to get its pick any time now," according to the *Enterprise* on July 28.

And so it was on August 10 that Olaf Henriksen was

Henriksen played his whole career for the Red Sox, 1911-17.

purchased by the Boston Red Sox in a five-player deal, Henriksen and Lonergan going to the Red Sox in exchange for Steve White, first baseman Tracy Baker, shortstop Joe Giannini, and $4,000 in cash. The *Enterprise*, in its lament of the loss of "Kid" Henriksen, hailed the young outfielder as "one of the sweetest hitters that ever played in the New England League, and his friends have little fear about his making good in fast company, even in competition with a star outfield like Speaker, Hooper and Lewis."[16] Henriksen finished his season with Brockton batting .360 with a league-leading 142 base hits, 87 runs scored (second in the league), 199 total bases, 28 doubles, 10 triples, and 3 home runs.

The Red Sox, not playing well and struggling with injuries, wasted no time calling on the recruit as a replacement for an injured Harry Hooper in a series against Connie Mack's world champion Athletics, in Philadelphia's Shibe Park. Olaf had taken a train from Boston to Philadelphia the night before, and with no time for rest was immediately pressed into action, making his major-league debut on August 11 playing both ends of a doubleheader.

His debut was a stunning success. He went 4-for-9 in the doubleheader and made a sensational catch off Jack Coombs to end the second game and save a win for the Red Sox. The *Boston Globe* praised him: "He is fast on his feet, is full of confidence at the bat, and his teammates believe that in Henriksen President Taylor has picked up a genuine find."[17] Matched against future Hall of Famer Chief Bender, the winner of 23 games in 1910, Henriksen belted out three base hits. On his first plate appearance before a crowd of 10,000 rabid A's fans, Olaf, in his typical hitting style lashed a ball to the left side of the infield too hot to handle for third baseman Frank Baker that went by him for a single. He later hit a double, and in the second game he beat out an infield grounder and worked a base on balls.

Seven days later Henriksen banged out four hits against Ty Cobb's Tigers. By August 21 he was leading the club in hitting with a .433 average (with a very small sample). But on August 27 in Chicago, Henriksen and Tris Speaker collided in the outfield chasing a fly ball, which went for a triple. Olaf fractured a rib and had an ankle injury, while Speaker had bruises. It was thought that Henriksen's injuries "might be fatal," according to the *Globe*. Harry Hooper, meanwhile, returned to the lineup. Henriksen returned to action briefly on September 5, filling in for Duffy Lewis, but the Red Sox regulars were now recovered from their injuries, and Henriksen was quickly relegated to pinch-hitting duties and backing up Speaker, Hooper, and Lewis, foreshadowing his future role with the Red Sox.

Henriksen continued to be plagued with a lame ankle and on September 14 was declared out for the balance of the season. But the imperturbable young outfielder was back in action on September 30, playing right field for Hooper in a doubleheader against Chicago; "Harry Hooper's understudy," as one paper noted, continued to play productively playing the remaining games in place of the injured Hooper. Henriksen finished his rookie year with a .366 batting average (34-for-93).

As much as he delighted in the experience of playing major-league baseball, especially for a good team like the Red Sox, Henriksen had the misfortune to be playing at the same time as the Million Dollar Outfield of Speaker, Hooper, and Lewis, arguably the finest outfield combination ever to play the game. Yet, the October 9, 1911, edition of the *Boston Globe* quite determinedly avowed "that a place will have to be found for this boy on next year's team as he looks to be a real find. He is as fast as a streak and a good hitter."

When the 1912 season started, on the road, Olaf found himself in a familiar role of sub behind the famous outfield trio. He played in his first game of the season on Opening Day, April 20, at the new Fenway Park before a packed house of 24,000 spectators against the New York Highlanders. He pinch-hit for pitcher O'Brien with the bases full, and he did so magnificently by drawing a walk, forcing in a run. The Red Sox went on to beat New York, 7-6.

Henriksen was being used sparingly, playing in just 19 games by the first week in July with a .250 batting average; a total of 28 games by the end of August, batting .239; and 41 games by September 30 at .296. On September 18 the Red Sox officially won the AL pennant. At season's end Henriksen had played in only 44 games with a respectable .321 batting average, and a .457 on-base percentage. Little did he realize at the time, however, what a significant part he would play in the 1912 World Series, about to take place between John McGraw's Giants and Jake Stahl's Red Sox.

The Series, considered one of the great baseball spectacles of all time, went to eight games (the second game having ended in a 6-6 tie, called due to darkness after 11 innings), with the Red Sox winning, four games to three. In the deciding eighth game, Christy "Big Six" Mathewson, a 23-game winner in 1912 and one of the great moundsmen known to the game, was pitching magnificently, shutting down the Red Sox without a run and only four hits through six innings. It appeared unlikely he was going to crack. The Giants managed a run in the third inning against a tough Hugh Bedient, winner of 20 for the Red Sox against nine defeats.

In the bottom of the seventh, though, with one out, player-manager Stahl got a Texas League single. Heinie Wagner walked. Catcher Hick Cady popped to short. Stahl motioned to 24-year old sub Olaf Henriksen to grab a bat. "I was certain—cocksure—that I could beat Matty," declared a confident Henriksen.[18]

"Then Matty stood for an instant, and I knew he was undecided what to feed me. None of them knew what I liked, and right then and there I decided to take a good look at the first one, no matter what it was," said a determined Olaf. He took a curveball for a strike and then another that he waved at, for strike two. Then, expecting Mathewson to waste a few, Olaf waited on two more pitches that didn't miss by much. Matty threw another curveball. Henriksen was waiting for it, reached out, and smacked it toward third base just inside the foul line. "I saw the ball strike the bag and go bounding out into the field," said Henriksen. "I knew I was safe, knew I had done what was expected of me and I was glad."[19] Stahl scored and Henriksen dashed to second with a game-tying double, keeping Red Sox hopes alive. The Giants scored a run in the 10th to regain the lead, setting the stage for one of the great finishes in World Series history, as the Red Sox came back with two runs, abetted by the famous error by outfielder Fred Snodgrass.

The great Tris Speaker, penning his comments about the Series for the *Boston Daily Globe*, praised Henriksen as one of its heroes: "This young player showed wonderful nerve in the emergency, and it was he who put the Boston club in a position to make the fight it did and gave it an opportunity to win the game, which went into extra innings."[20]

The Red Sox were a disappointment in 1913, finishing in fourth place. Once more Henriksen was used sparingly, but he was playing well in key roles assigned him by manager Stahl. Through May 29 he had played in 16 games and was batting .310. But on that day after a game in Washington, in which he started, Henriksen had a severe attack of appendicitis. Immediate surgery was recommended, but Olaf declined, saying he felt better the next day. On June 5 the scrappy little outfielder appeared back in uniform, and was lauded by the press: "One of the pleasing events of the afternoon was the appearance of Olaf Henriksen after his illness, showing that this clever player is ready when called upon."[21] He continued to play and by July 7 was batting .351. Then on July 12 Olaf was stricken again with appendicitis and was operated on in Chicago. He was out of action for nine weeks, returning gallantly on September 11 in a pinch-hit role. He played little after that, and finished the season batting .375 (15-for-40) with a .468 on-base percentage.[22]

In 1914, the year that marked the arrival in Boston of the new kid, George Herman "Babe" Ruth, Henriksen played in 63 games, batting .263, and hit his only major-league home run, on October 6, against Washington's Harry Harper. The Red Sox finished in second place. In 1915 and 1916 the Red Sox once again rose to the top, playing in the World Series each year, and winning each four games to one both times. Henriksen, who had batted only .196 in 73 games, a career high, during the '15 season, was 0-for-2 in the Series. He appeared once as a pinch-hitter, walked, and scored in the '16 Series. He batted only .202 during the 1916 season in a career-high 99 at-bats. Despite his anemic hitting in 1915-16, Henriksen still managed to get on base one-third of the time, drawing 18 walks to go with his 18 hits in 1915 and 19 walks with 20 hits in 1916.

On March 17, 1916, in a team practice game, an occasion on which Henriksen became a thorn in the Babe's side, he caught up to a certain home-run ball hit by Ruth, crashing against the fence and ripping out a couple of boards in the process. Ruth was disgruntled and "cracked him in the side with an inshoot" when Olaf later came to bat.

On July 7, 1916, in a game at Fenway Park, Henriksen established himself as one of the few men to pinch-hit for Babe Ruth, a further annoyance to the Bambino. Ruth had been pitching a fabulous game against Cleveland, but was behind 1-0. In the seventh inning the Red Sox filled the bases with one out. Ruth was the next batter. Manager Bill Carrigan gave the Babe instructions when he went to the plate, but Ruth ignored him, whereupon he was immediately pulled by the manager, who replaced him with Henriksen. Olaf worked a pass, forcing in the tying run. Boston went on to win, 2-1.[23]

Because of financial wars that occurred between players and teams after the upstart Federal League collapsed in 1915, owners were looking to cut player salaries. A Baseball Players' Fraternity—not quite a union—was soon formed, and among the original 10 or 12 members of the group who met with their president, Dave Fultz, in a meeting on January 18, 1917, were Red Sox players Larry Gardner, Hal Janvrin, Babe Ruth, and Olaf Henriksen. It did not set well with major-league ownership.

Whether the Red Sox and their owner, Harry Frazee, became disenchanted with Henriksen because of his involvement with the Fraternity, and thus the reason he was released by the team, cannot be reconciled. He had played in a scant 15 games with one base hit and a .083 batting average that year. On June 30, 1917, he was let go, sold outright to Roger Bresnahan's Toledo Mud Hens of the American Association. Olaf refused to report to Toledo and on July 5 was given his unconditional

After his baseball career, Henriksen worked as a house painter.

release by the Red Sox.

Henriksen went to work for Willard Battery, a Massachusetts-based company.[24] He also played and coached for the Fore River semipro team of the Bethlehem Steel League, in Boston's South Shore area, in 1918, along with such other former major-league notables as Eddie Plank and Dutch Leonard.[25]

In 1921 news accounts of local baseball activity found Henriksen playing for and coaching a team called Olaf Henriksen's Canton team, which played other local teams, including teams of the Cape Cod League. In 1922 Boston College hired him to coach its baseball team. In his three seasons there, through 1924, he had winning teams each year, including in 1923 a remarkable 30-3 record, an intercollegiate record of 22 victories in a row, and an intercollegiate championship.[26]

Semipro baseball was thriving in the New England area in the 1920s. Henriksen latched onto one such team, the Grow Tire Company of Boston, playing for it in 1922 at the age of 34. In one game of note, played on October 15 in Rhode Island, Grow Tire competed against a team known as "St. Louis," a Rhode Island club, with pros Carl Mays and Wally Schang in its lineup. Henriksen rapped three base hits off Mays.[27]

Henriksen became self-employed sometime in the middle to late 1920s, working as a painting contractor in and around the Canton area.[28]

On May 2, 1962, Olaf attended a reunion at Fenway Park with remaining members of the 1912 team celebrating the 50th anniversary of their World Series championship. Six months later, on October 17, Henriksen died of lung cancer at the age of 74. His wife, Mary, known as Mamie, died in 1969. They had two children. Peter Francis, born on April 24, 1910, died in June 1990, and Catherine, born in September 1916, was still living as of 2012.

Given his relatively short career, it is impressive that Henriksen's 29 pinch hits ranks him fifth all-time among Red Sox hitters, tied with Hall of Famer Joe Cronin and Jason Varitek.[29] A feature article on Henriksen written in 1916 artfully described his real importance to the team, for being "Only [a] Pinch-Hitter," and gave clarity on how he was truthfully viewed by the Boston fans and newsmen of the day:

"He is a good waiter in the business sense as well as up at the plate, and he will make his selection after looking them over to the limit....As Olaf strolls up from the dugout, when Manager Carrigan calls on him to deliver, the fans see the picture of that clean drive [off Mathewson, 1912 World Series]. 'Hennie' is but human. He doesn't always come through, but as pinch-hitters go, 'Hennie' is about the best in the game."[30]

Endnotes

I owe much gratitude to various living members of the Henriksen family, direct and indirect descendants, who assisted me with the research of this biography project; among them Marie (Henriksen) Leary, Olaf's granddaughter; Jens Peter Henriksen, his nephew; Marie (Henriksen) Landers, his niece; and Jill Griffin, his grandniece. Also, my appreciation to Jim Roche, past president and researcher of Canton Historical Society, Canton, Massachusetts; Charlie Stevenson, member of the Canton Sports Hall of Fame; Patty Ryburn and Mark Lague of the Canton Public Library; Amy Braitsch, assistant archival librarian, Burns Library, Boston College; St. John's Rectory, Canton, Massachusetts; staff of the Stoughton and Norwood Public Libraries; Richard Peterson of Plymouth, Massachusetts.

1. Frank P. Sibley, "Game of a Lifetime," *Boston Daily Globe*, October 17, 1912, 5.

2. Information received from Michelle Ruiz, administrative assistant to superintendent of Wareham School District, and Scott Pyy, vice principal of Wareham High School, shows that Olaf was not

The swimmer.

attending Wareham schools in 1900 or after; also, Jens Peter Henriksen, whose father was Arnold, brother of Olaf, stated that his father quit school in the eighth grade, and very likely Olaf, two years older than brother Arnold, did the same; Thanks to Jens Peter Henriksen, the grandson and namesake of Jens Peter. Correspondence and December 15, 2009, interview.

3. http://www.baseball-reference.com/bullpen/Olaf Henriksen; Boston University School of Theology Library Archives, E-Resources. "The Only Danish-Born Person Ever to Play in the Major Leagues," copyright 2009; Bill Nowlin and Jim Prime, *The Boston Red Sox World Series Encyclopedia*, (Burlington, Massachusetts: Rounder Books, 2008). The US Census information of 1900 and 1910 shows a family name spelling of Hendrickson. However, the inscription on the Wareham family burial monument reads Henriksen, the Danish spelling. Olaf's name listed on the 1910 Census also shows Hendrickson, but his World Wars I and II draft cards and other official documents properly read Henriksen.

4. "Baseball Notes," *Canton (Massachusetts) Journal*, June 24, 1904, 3.

5. Wentworth Field, over 105 years since its construction, remains a baseball field today. Olaf Henriksen not only played there in his youth, but also umpired there post-Red Sox years, per May 22, 2009 interview of Canton resident Charlie Stevenson, Canton High School football coach and member of Canton Sports Hall of Fame.

6. "Baseball," *Canton Journal*, July 14, 1905, 8.

7. "The Season: Summary of the Work of the Stoughton Baseball Club for Year 1907," *Stoughton (Massachusetts) Sentinel*, October 19, 1907, 1.

8. "Baseball Is Near at Hand," *Brockton (Massachusetts) Times*, March 23, 1909, 20.

9. "He Looks Like First Baseman," *Brockton Times*, April 13, 1909, 16.

10. *Brockton Times*, June 11, 1909, 16.

11. "Lynn Wins by Scant Margin," *Brockton Times*, July 27, 1909, 12.

12. "Crippled Team Rounding To," *Brockton Times*, August 9, 1909, 10.

13. "Ends Season In Last Place," *Brockton Times*, September 12, 1910, 12.

14. "Henriksen First to Make 100 Hits: Brockton Outfielder Turns the Trick—It's His Banner Season," *Brockton Daily Enterprise*, July 14, 1911, 10.

15. "Brockton and Lynn Play to a Draw, 5 to 5—Darkness: Henriksen Gathers Five Hits," *Brockton Daily Enterprise*, July 28, 1911, 10.

16. "Lonergan and Henriksen Pass to Red Sox Today," *Brockton Daily Enterprise*. August 11, 1911, 10.

17. "Henriksen Stars In Fast Company," *Brockton Times*, August 12, 1911, 6, quoting the *Boston Post* of same date.

18. Mike Vaccaro. *The First Fall Classic* (New York: Doubleday, 2010), 239.

19. Olaf Henriksen, "Waiting All Through Series For Just That Chance," *Boston Daily Globe*, October 17, 1912, 7.

20. Tris Speaker, "Final Game Hardest of the World Series," *Boston Daily Globe*. October 17, 1912, 7.

21. T.H. Murnane, "Red Sox Lose 5-0," *Boston Daily Globe*, June 6, 1913, 7.

22. "Cobb's Batting Lead in American League, 19 Points," *Boston Daily Globe*, October 6, 1913, 7.

23. T.H. Murnane, "Indians Start Fast, Red Sox Finish Faster," *Boston Daily Globe*, July 8, 1916, 4.

24. (Henriksen) Leary, interview December 20, 2009: 1920 US Census, "battery repairer."

25. "Leonard Loses in Duel With Plank," *Boston Daily Globe*, June 30, 1918, 12. Although Dutch Leonard was still on the Red Sox payroll in 1918, he was found also to be playing with Henriksen for the Fall River semipro team.

26. 1925 Boston College Yearbook, 247.

27. "Grow Tire Shut Out, Batting Against Mays," *Boston Daily Globe*, October 16, 1922, 8.

28. Marie (Henriksen) Leary, interview December 20, 2009: 1930 US Census.

29. Gary Gillette and Pete Palmer. *The Ultimate Red Sox Companion* (Hingham, Massachusetts: Maple Street Press, 2007), 285; Baseball-Reference.com/Batting Game logs.

30. Herman Nickerson, "Only 'pinch-hitter,' But Real Star Henriksen Invaluable Aid to Sox." July 22, 1916, from Boston College Archives, John J. Burns Library.

Harry Hooper
by Paul J. Zingg and Elizabeth A. Reed

G	AB	R	H	2B	3B	HR	RBI	BB	SO	BA	OBP	SLG	SB	HBP
147	590	98	143	20	12	2	53	66	49	.242	.326	.327	29	7

One of the best defensive right fielders in baseball history and one of the top leadoff hitters of the Deadball Era, Harry Hooper was also a team leader, superb practitioner of the inside game, and clutch hitter who played a key role in four Boston Red Sox world championships. As a product of rural California, but a college man who earned a degree in engineering, Hooper also symbolized baseball's transition, ongoing during the Deadball Era, from a game rooted in the eastern cities and played by professionals who were largely uneducated and illiterate, to a game that broadened its geographical horizons and expanded its social appeal through players like Hooper.

Although his play at times achieved the spectacular, Hooper eschewed flamboyance for simplicity, exaggeration for modesty. Possessing neither the crafted appeal of Christy Mathewson nor the raw excitement of Babe Ruth, Hooper practiced his profession quietly, skillfully, and confidently. More Everyman than Superman, he is a mirror of the game and its human touches in ways that his myth-encrusted contemporaries never can be. Though he never led the American League in any major statistical category, Hooper crafted a solid statistical resume that included 2,466 hits, 1,429 runs and 1,136 career walks, good for a lifetime .281 batting average and .368 on base percentage. In 92 career World Series at-bats, Hooper batted a solid .293; in the 1915 Fall Classic he batted .350 with two home runs.

Harry Bartholomew Hooper was born on August 24, 1887 in California's Santa Clara Valley, the fourth and youngest child of Joseph and Mary Katherine Keller Hooper. In 1876, Joseph had left Canada's Prince Edward Island, slowly working his way westward through a series of jobs before landing in California, where he met Mary Keller, a German immigrant working as a housekeeper, and married her in 1878. Growing up on the family ranch, Harry first honed his athletic skills by tossing fresh eggs against the side of the family's barn. This merited little reaction from his parents, and Harry spent more time throwing various objects, challenging himself in distance and accuracy.

His first formal exposure to nine-man-a-side baseball came during a trip East with his mother. While visiting her family in Central Pennsylvania, Harry watched with great interest the Lock Haven team play. He capped the trip with a visit to relatives living in New York City, and a chance to see his first Major League game. The Brooklyn Bridegrooms played the Louisville Colonels, and although the home team lost, Hooper's dedication and love of the game solidified. Just before he and his mother began the long journey back to California, he received from his uncle something he later called "the best of all" his boyhood treasures: a bat, ball, and well-worn fielder's glove.

Harry Hooper's formal baseball career began when he left the family's farm in August, 1902, for the high school attached to Saint Mary's College of California, then located in Oakland. Although Hooper originally arrived for a two-year secondary

Hooper with the Red Sox in 1915.

program, the Christian Brothers who ran the school quickly recognized his mathematical aptitude, and encouraged his parents to consider allowing him to complete the full baccalaureate program, which would stretch his time at the school from two years to five. Consistent with the emerging sense of education as a means to economic opportunity, Harry's parents agreed to the school's request. At roughly the same time, he earned a place on the secondary school's new baseball team.

Working his way up through the four teams at the school, Hooper earned a place as a starting pitcher on the junior varsity as a collegiate sophomore, but his stature—he stood slightly over five feet tall at the time—and pitching velocity limited his chance to earn a spot on the varsity squad. The top team's head coach suggested a switch to an outfield position, which Hooper accepted. It assured him the starting left-field spot on the College's varsity nine at the start of the 1907 season, a team regarded by many as one of collegiate baseball's finest in the pre-World War I era. With a roster that contained six future big leaguers, Hooper played alongside catcher Eddie Burns, third baseman Joe Hamilton, pitcher Harry Krause, plus outfielders Charlie Enwright and Mickey Thompson, on a team that completed a 27-game season with a perfect record. Among that year's victims were Stanford University, the University of California, a Pacific Coast League all-star team, and the Chicago White Sox who the Phoenix faced in an exhibition game prior to the start of the major league season.

Hitting for a .371 average during his senior season, Hooper drew the attention of several organized ball representatives, and signed his first contract—for 10 days—to play with the Alameda club of the California League, where he teamed with Duffy Lewis for the first time; the two had been schoolmates but not teammates at St. Mary's. Ironically, the short length of the contract was Hooper's idea. Focused primarily on his engineering career, he agreed to play only for the time between the end of the Phoenix's season and his graduation date. His strong play during the short stretch earned Hooper a contract with the Sacramento club, which he agreed to accept with the proviso that Sacramento's owner arrange a surveying position for him, which was done.

Late in the 1908 season, after hitting .347, scoring 39 runs, and stealing 34 bases in 68 games, Hooper earned the tag, "Ty Cobb of the State League," and an offer from his manager, Charlie Graham, who also served as a scout for the Boston Red Sox. Initially when approached about the possibility Hooper recalled saying he thought baseball "was a sideline to engineering to make enough money for a living." Graham persisted and Hooper agreed to meet with Red Sox owner John Taylor, who soon would be in the area to observe several prospects for his team. At their meeting at a Sacramento saloon, the two agreed to a contract that would pay the 21-year-old Hooper $2,800 for the 1909 season, approximately $1,000 more than he would have made combined through his California baseball play and his job with the Western Pacific Railroad.

Harry Hooper's career with the Boston Red Sox began on March 4, 1909 when he arrived in Hot Springs, Arkansas for the team's training camp. The Red Sox of 1909 represented a team in transition. Following the demise of the championship clubs of 1903 and 1904, owner Taylor aspired to build a pennant contender with young pitchers, power hitting, and speed on the bases. The rotation included Joe Wood, Eddie Cicotte, and Frank Arellanes. Other than Heinie Wagner (shortstop), no member of the squad had two complete seasons with the team.

Harry Hooper's major league debut came on April 16, in Washington, D.C., during the team's second series of the season. Called upon to start in left field and bat seventh, Hooper lined a single in his first at-bat that also notched his first RBI. That day he went 2-for-3 at the plate, with "a clever steal in the ninth," three flies caught including "a superb running back catch" that saved a triple, and one assist when he threw out Gabby Street at home. During the first month of the season, he played occasionally, always fielding well.

A natural right-handed hitter and fielder while at Saint Mary's, the 5'10" 168-pound Hooper experimented with switch hitting. Playing in an era when manufacturing runs one at a time mattered more than sheer power, Hooper decided to take advantage of his abilities and reduce one step from the batter's box to first base by making the move to full-time left-handed hitting. His hard work and dependable play, especially in the field, made personnel decisions easier for the club's management. By the season's midpoint, Hooper firmly held the fourth outfield position, and often entered games in the late innings because of his defensive skills. The squad finished the year in third place, 9½ games behind Detroit, but also 25 games over .500. Hooper recorded a .282 average in 81 games, while completing the transition from one side of the plate to the other.

The Red Sox that assembled in Hot Springs, Arkansas in March, 1910 had reason to be optimistic about the coming season. Most of the lineup returned, with Hooper virtually assured one outfield spot. With Tris Speaker secure in center, the only question was whether it would be right or left on a day-to-day basis. The arrival of another veteran of the Saint Mary's Phoenix in camp, George "Duffy" Lewis, largely settled the issue. The outfield trio of Tris Speaker, Harry Hooper in right, and Duffy Lewis in left made its debut on April 27. Through the course of that season—when they hit a combined .296—and the next five, the "Million Dollar Outfield" played more than 90 percent of Boston's games. After batting .267 in 1910, Hooper improved to an impressive .311 average in 1911, scored 93 runs, and posted a .399 on-base percentage. The club, however, failed to finish better than fourth in either season.

Despite his .242 batting average, Hooper was an integral piece of the 1912 pennant-winners, ranking second on the team with 98 runs scored, 66 walks, 29 stolen bases, and 12 triples. In that year's World Series against the New York Giants, Hooper elevated his play, batting .290 for the Series and making several crucial plays at bat and in the field. In Game One, Hooper rapped a game-tying double in the seventh inning to secure a 4-3 Boston victory. After taking a three-games-to-one lead in the Series, the Red Sox saw the Giants even things at three games each. There was one tie game.

Despite numerous baserunners for both teams, the Giants held a slim 1-0 lead in the seventh inning of the deciding Game

Harry Hooper slides safely into third, 1916.

The strong, silent type? Hooper was a serious student of the game, and held a college degree in engineering. *Boston Post*

Eight, which would have been greater if not for Hooper's catch of Larry Doyle's drive to the right-field fence, robbing him of a home run. The game was tied 1-1 after nine. In the 10th inning, after Clyde Engle reached second when Fred Snodgrass muffed a fly ball, Hooper followed with "a sure triple" that Snodgrass caught, but it advanced Engle to third. After a walk to Yerkes, Speaker singled in Engle with the tying run. Yerkes took third on the play, Speaker took second on the throw home, and Larry Gardner's sacrifice fly won the World Series for the Red Sox.

Hooper's "paralyzing catch" in the final game earned him accolades in the press, but John McGraw paid an even higher compliment when he labeled the Californian, "one of the most dangerous hitters in a pinch the game has ever known." In the next day's *Boston Globe*, Speaker called Hooper's catch "the greatest, I believe, that I ever saw."

Coming off the championship year, Hooper married Esther Henchy, a 20-year-old banker's daughter from nearby Capitola, California, but remained dedicated to his offseason training. Although the Red Sox struggled as a team in 1913 and 1914, Hooper personally improved his offensive output, hitting .288 in 1913 and scoring 100 runs, and batting .258 with 85 runs scored in 1914. On May 30, 1913, Hooper hit home runs to lead off both games of a double-header, a feat not equaled until Rickey Henderson did it 80 years later.

In 1915 the Red Sox returned to championship form and began a stretch of success where the team played the best, and most consistent, baseball in the major leagues. Between 1915 and 1917, the team won at least 90 games each season, and likely would have done so again in 1918 if World War I had not shortened the season. The successes came through the team's effective use of the strategies of the era. Rather than power hitting and home runs, the Red Sox won by manufacturing runs, playing strong defense, and, most of all, getting solid pitching. In fact, during the four-year stretch, the team never featured more than one hitter with an average of .300 or higher. As Hooper wrote,

"With the best pitching staff and the best defensive outfield…we played for one run—tried to get on the scoreboard first and then increase our lead."

In 1915, Hooper's average dipped to .235, but he compensated by collecting 89 walks, fifth best in the league, and posting a respectable .342 on-base percentage. Once again, he saved his best work for the World Series, when he helped Boston finish off Philadelphia in five games with a .350 batting average and two home runs, both of which came in the final game of the Series, making Hooper only the second player in World Series history to homer twice in the same game. (Both homers bounced into Baker Bowl's temporary stands; today they would be considered ground-rule doubles.)

After another championship in 1916, and a disappointing second-place finish nine games behind the Chicago White Sox the following year, Hooper's Red Sox entered the 1918 season in a tenuous position. Although Boston's roster suffered fewer losses to the military and war-related industries than other teams, the lineup managed a woeful team average of .249, the second-worst in the American League; Hooper posted a .289 average and a .405 slugging percentage (second on the team to Babe Ruth in both categories). He also helped the team to another pennant in a war-shortened season (126 games) that ended with a dramatic labor challenge during the World Series.

During the Fall Classic against the Chicago Cubs, Hooper demonstrated his clear thinking and effective leadership, representing his fellow players' concerns in a manner that

Hall of Famer Hooper helped the Red Sox win four World Series.

Opening Fenway Park with Style: The World Champion 1912 Boston Red Sox

Hooper, Boston, during batting practice, 1912.

preserved the integrity of baseball, while also exposing some of the inherent weaknesses of baseball's ruling system. Due to wartime travel restrictions, the teams played the Series in a 3-4 format, with the first games in Chicago (ironically at Comiskey Park). The rest of the games took place at Fenway. The Red Sox returned home enjoying a 2-1 lead, but all was not well. For several war-related reasons, attendance and gate receipts during the regular season and World Series in 1918 fell well below pre-war levels. However, at this time the players' postseason bonuses came from gate receipts and the owners would not guarantee a minimum payment. The two teams, traveling on the same train, appointed four representatives, including Hooper, to speak to the governing National Commission and press their case. Specifically, the teams sought a guarantee of $2,600 each for the winners and $1,400 for the losers, with 10% going as a donation to the Red Cross. The National Commission begrudgingly listened, and agreed to consider the matter, but made no promises.

With Boston leading three games to one, the players delayed the start of the fifth game by more than one hour in an attempt to secure concessions from the Commission. Although Hooper negotiated an end to the strike, and secured a verbal promise from Ban Johnson of no reprisals, he forever regretted not securing the guarantee in writing. After Boston won the Series 4-2, its last for 86 years, the players received the smallest financial awards in World Series history ($1,108.45 for each Red Sox player and $574.62 for each Cub). In December the Boston players all received letters from John A. Heydler, acting president of the National League and a Commission member. It informed them that, "Owing to the disgraceful conduct of the players in the strike during the Series...(the players) would be fined the World Series emblems that were traditionally awarded to the winners." Although a modest symbol, the emblems—really lapel pins—became a symbol of the lack of respect accorded the players in the years before a strong players union and free agency.

After a .312 season in 1920, Harry Hooper's career with the Boston Red Sox ended on March 4, 1921, when Boston owner Harry Frazee thwarted a holdout by trading him to the Chicago White Sox for Shano Collins and Nemo Liebold. Hooper posted some of the best offensive seasons of his career during his five years with the White Sox. In 1921 he batted .327; the following year he notched career highs in runs scored (111), home runs (11) and RBIs (80). In 1924, he posted a career-best .328 batting average and .413 on-base percentage. In 1925, his last major league season, Hooper batted .265. Playing in his final major league game on October 4, 1925, Hooper went 1-for-4 with a double.

Upon his retirement, Hooper returned to California and worked in real estate for one year before accepting a job as player-manager with Mission (San Francisco) in the Pacific Coast League. Hooper lasted one year with the club, batting .282 in 81 games and guiding the Missions to a disappointing 86-110 record. Let go after the season, Hooper returned to the real estate business for a few years while also playing minor league baseball in nearby Marysville and Santa Cruz, then became coach of the Princeton baseball team in September, 1930. Hooper stayed at the post for two years, posting a 21-30-1 record before Depression-era finances forced the college to cut back on Hooper's salary, leading to his resignation. He once again returned to the real estate business in California, survived the Depression, and became wealthy in his old age. He also served as postmaster of Capitola for over 20 years. His greatest honor came in 1971, when the Veteran's Committee elected him to the Baseball Hall of Fame. Hooper was also one of the inaugural inductees when the St. Mary's College Athletic Hall of Fame was established in 1973; his son John, a center fielder during the 1940s, was inducted four years later. Harry Hooper died at the age of 87 on December 18, 1974, following a stroke. He was laid to rest in an above-ground crypt in the center of Aptos Cemetery, in Aptos, California. He was survived by two sons and a daughter.

Sources:

This biography is drawn from Paul Zingg's book *Harry Hooper: An American Baseball Life* (Urbana: University of Illinois Press, 1993).

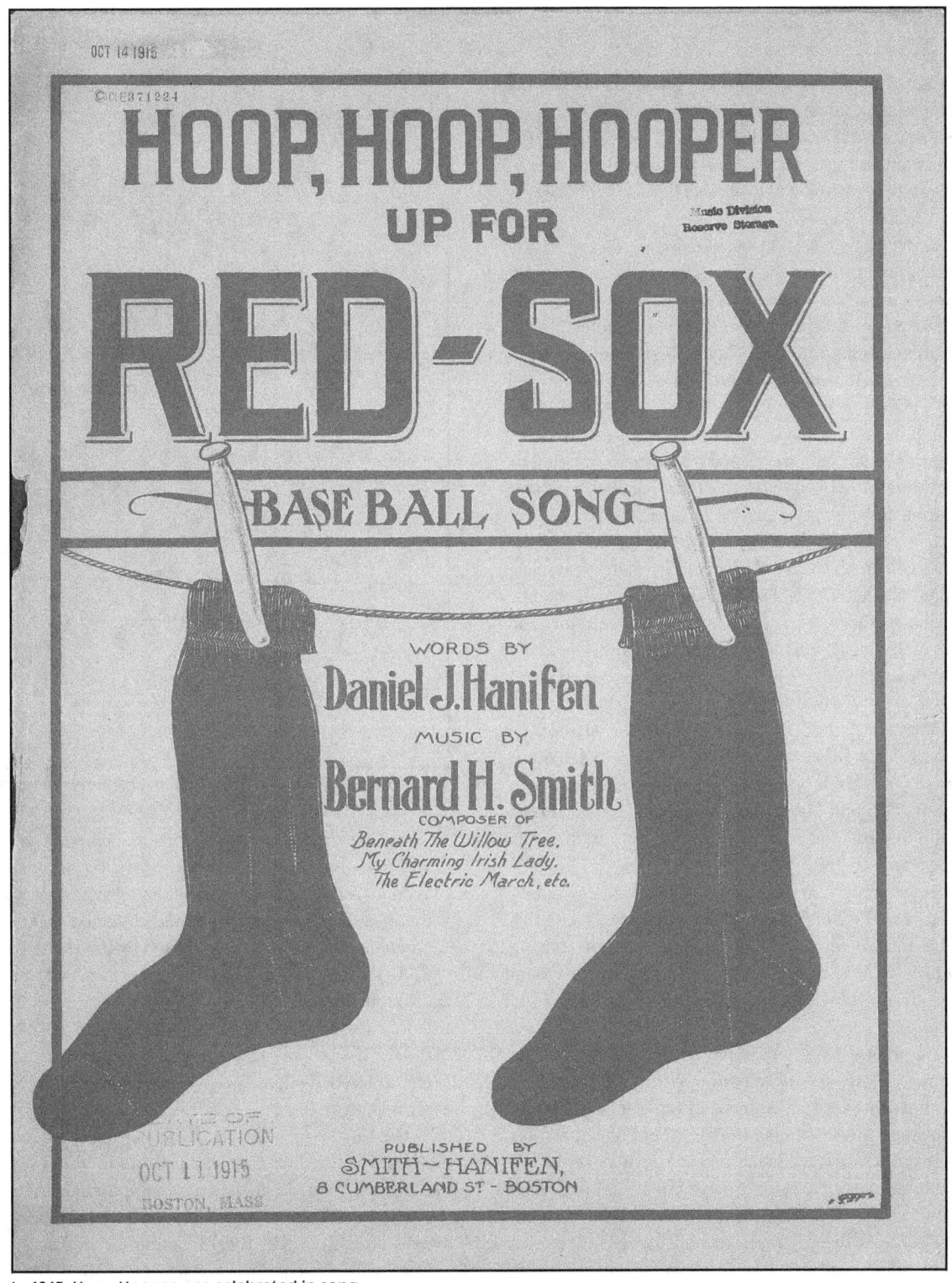

In 1915, Harry Hooper was celebrated in song.

Marty Krug
By Tom Hawthorn

G	AB	R	H	2B	3B	HR	RBI	BB	SO	BA	OBP	SLG	SB	HBP
20	39	6	12	2	1	0	7	5	6	.308	.386	.410	2	0

Marty Krug appeared in only 20 games in 1912, his rookie season, mostly as a pinch-hitter, or a late-inning replacement. He watched the World Series from the superior but disappointing vantage of the winning team's bench. He never once stepped onto the field against the New York Giants in those eight dramatic games.

The knock on Krug was that he wielded a suspect glove. After the season he returned to the minors, where he lingered for a decade before gaining employment with the Chicago Cubs. He appeared in 127 games for the Cubs and had his greatest day at the plate in a game during which all players hit with abandon, as a major-league record 49 runs were scored. (Yes, Krug committed an error, too.) His stint there also lasted just one season before he returned to the minors.

An ordinary player, Krug developed a sterling reputation as a handler of young talent. Many of those he coached credited tips learned from him for their ability to keep a major-league job. Krug won a Pacific Coast League title as manager of the Los Angeles Angels in 1926. He also served for many years as a scout, spotting raw talent in need of adjustment and refinement.

Despite those successes, Krug is remembered for one judgment that now seems ridiculously mistaken and laughably inept, though understandable under the circumstances. He was the scout who thought Ted Williams too fragile for baseball.

Martin Johannes Krieg was born on September 10, 1888, at Koblenz, in what was then the German Empire, to Johannes Krieg, a brewer, and Maria O. Krieg. Johannes immigrated to Pennsylvania in 1889 and Maria came two years later with sons Karl (Charles), August, and Martin. A fourth son, Willie, was born in Pennsylvania in 1895.[1]

They lived at first in Wilkes-Barre, Pennsylvania, before settling in Cleveland, which would later be incorrectly cited as Martin's birthplace. At least one account has him growing up as a neighbor to Rube Marquard. Young Martin Krieg's formal education ended with the sixth grade, after which he became an apprentice printer.

Krug was a promising athlete. According to family lore, he signed a contract (the team is unknown, possibly a club in New England) and headed to spring training (the place is unknown, but if the team was in New England, Krug would have been far from home). He quickly became homesick, as he had never before eaten in a restaurant, taken a train, or stayed in a hotel. He came home to play semiprofessional ball in Cleveland. When a scout for a different organization tried to sign him, he balked, saying he was already under contract. The scout suggested replacing the two vowels in the family name with a single one. Thus, Krieg became Krug.

Krug's professional career began in Kentucky with the Richmond Pioneers of the Blue Grass League, a Class D circuit. After two seasons, he moved up a notch to the South Atlantic

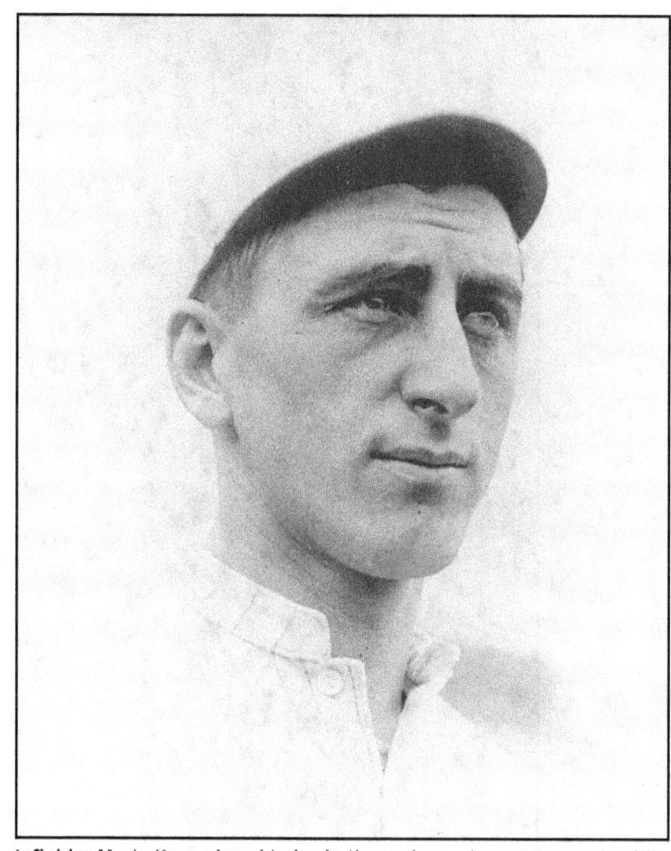

Infielder Marty Krug played twice in the majors—ten years apart, with the Red Sox in 1912 and the Cubs in 1922.

League, handling shortstop chores for Columbia, South Carolina, of the South Atlantic League (called the Gamecocks in 1910 and the Commies in 1911). In one home-game victory against rival Columbus, fans passed the hat and collected $64 to reward Krug for a home run. He was then drafted by the Boston Red Sox.

As the Red Sox arrived at Hot Springs, Arkansas, for spring training in March 1912, the *Boston Globe* noted that the rookie infielder had nearly missed the train to join his new teammates. "He is a likely-looking youngster and is already in shape," the *Globe* assured readers, "as he has been playing in Cuba since early in January."

Left unstated was that Krug's brief, 13-game stint as an outfielder with Almendares in Havana included but one double and six singles in 42 at-bats for an unpromising .167 average.

Hugh S. Fullerton, the baseball writer, wrote a preseason article predicting that the Philadelphia Athletics would face a serious challenge from the rejuvenated Red Sox in defending their American League pennant. He offered a player-by-player accounting of the Boston roster. As for Krug, "they say this fellow can slam the sphere to a fare-ye-well, but that he can't field much. He hit .297 last season, but was down among the last, both as a third baseman and shortstop, and piled up a lot of errors without much to his assist column," Fullerton wrote. Another preseason roundup merely noted that the rookie "needs seasoning."[2]

The 5-foot-9, 165-pound utility infielder, a right-hander in the field and at the plate, made his debut on May 29, 1912, in the first game of a home doubleheader against Washington. He replaced Heinie Wagner at shortstop late in a game won 21-8 by Boston.

The tyro infielder got an opportunity to showcase his talents during a weekend road trip the following month when regular second baseman Steve Yerkes became ill. On June 8 at Detroit, Krug singled in his first at-bat off Detroit's starting left-hander, Ralph Works. Batting second behind Harry Hooper and ahead of Tris Speaker, Krug went 2-for-5 with a double and a stolen base. The next day, at St. Louis, he was 3-for-4 with another double, a walk, and three runs scored. Krug also started a 4-6-3 double play as the Red Sox enjoyed two tidy victories, but he injured his ankle sliding into second base in the third inning of the Sunday game. He remained in the game even though his ankle had swelled. By evening he could barely walk. For the remainder of the season, Krug's role was to occasionally spell Wagner at short. His lone American League triple came on September 7, off Washington's Bob Groom.

On September 20 Smoky Joe Wood, invincible since July, faced Detroit, seeking his 17th consecutive victory. In the bottom of the third, with the game scoreless, Wood walked pitcher Tex Covington, then gave consecutive free passes to Donie Bush, Red Corriden, and Sam Crawford for the game's first run. "Wood continually objected to the directions of the umpire," read one account. The pitcher then induced Ty Cobb to hit a pop fly to the infield, which Krug dropped, as two more runs scored. In the fifth inning, Covington protested a call on a pitch to Krug and was tossed from the game by umpire Silk O'Loughlin. The Red Sox went up 4-3 that inning, but the Tigers answered with two of their own before eventually prevailing, 6-4. Showing no hard feelings, Wood treated the youngster to dinner that evening, a kindness Krug would never forget. He hit three singles the

Marty Krug on defense.

next day off Detroit's Ed Willett, as Boston returned to the win column.

The Red Sox finished their home schedule in dramatic fashion, overcoming a nine-run deficit against the New York Highlanders before winning 15-12 on September 26. Krug, batting second, hit a double.

The utility infielder was included on Boston's list of 22 eligible players for the World Series but he did not play. His strongest memory of the showdown was Fred Snodgrass of the Giants muffing an easy fly ball in the deciding game. The share of revenue for each player of the winning team amounted to $4,024.68. Krug said he planned to invest his stake in railroad stock.

For the season Krug batted .308 (12-for-39) with two doubles and a triple. He committed five errors (four at second, one at short) for a .900 fielding average.

Krug's new-found fame as a member of a world championship squad caused an episode in his past to catch up to him, as the Dayton (Ohio) Veterans of the Class B Central League alleged that Krug had signed for them under his birth name Krieg. It was unknown why the Ohio club waited two years to lodge a complaint, and the outcome can't be determined.

In the offseason, Krug was sold by the Red Sox to Indianapolis of the American Association, for whom he hit just .237 in 1913 while playing third base.

Krug arrived in Nebraska as an outfielder for Omaha the 1914 season, hired by team owner and manager William "Pa" Rourke, a former athlete whose playing days ended when he was struck in the eye by a pitch. Rourke stepped down before the 1915 season, asking Krug to add managerial responsibilities to his on-field duties. Krug assigned himself to the infield. The Rourkes finished in fourth place in 1915, but under their 27-year-old manager they went 92-57 to claim the Western League pennant in 1916.

The Rourkes raised the championship pennant before a July game the next year with a brass band playing "The Star-Spangled Banner" and the mayor, the league president, and the governor in attendance. Oddly, Krug resigned as manager two weeks later, though he stayed at shortstop until season's end.

In the offseason the Cleveland Indians drafted Krug, a move opposed by the Western League, which made a test case by demanding immediate payment of a $1,500 draft fee. Cleveland balked, and Krug was in limbo. He missed a season of Organized Baseball, picking up cash playing as a semipro in California. Some newspapers reported that he had written a friend suggesting he was going to enlist in the Army.

By 1919 Krug was with Salt Lake City of the Pacific Coast League, where he followed a .310 average by holding out for more money the following spring, later still threatening to jump his contract to play in an outlaw league. He skipped the team in the middle of a pennant race in late July 1920, earning a suspension and a $100 fine from the manager.

"The defection of Krug is the worst blow manager Ernie Johnson of the Bees has experienced," *Los Angeles Herald* reporter Matt Gallagher told readers of *The Sporting News*. "He has been the keystone of defense for the Salt Lake team and his hitting against Los Angeles and Vernon has been timely. Also there is a broad intimation in his desertion that all is not as harmonious under Johnson's management as outsiders have been led to believe."

The second baseman soon returned to the fold, only to be traded to the Portland (Ore.) Beavers in the offseason. His response was to threaten to retire, before holding out.

After a string of seasons batting in the .290s with one .310 campaign thrown in, Krug's hitting dipped with the Beavers, a failure the *Oakland Tribune* attributed to the team's poor fortunes. "It is no wonder that Marty Krug, last year a big star in the Coast League, is not playing up to his form," the newspaper noted on June 24, 1921. "Marty is one of those type ball players who hates to be on a losing ball club, and he seems to be very much saddled up with one this season."

But despite his difficult reputation, Krug's hitting placed him in some demand. Ty Cobb let it be known that he was interested in enlisting Marty for the Tigers. Instead, Portland traded Krug to Seattle, where he refused to sign unless paid a $100 bonus, announcing yet again his intent to retire to become a manager. Then, on March 25, 1922, Seattle sold him to the Chicago Cubs for $7,500. At the age of 33, a decade after leaving the Red Sox, Krug returned to the major leagues.

The infielder got off to a slow start in the 1922 season, hitting just .191 through the first 13 games. He improved within a fortnight to .219 and was hitting .271 by mid-June.

"When (John) Kelleher was incapacitated, Krug was placed at third and performed there with as much dexterity as he did at second, showing that the Cubs picked up a versatile infielder in the former Pacific Coast League athlete," *The Sporting News* reported. "Krug was taken off the keystone bag because he had fallen into a slump in both his fielding and hitting, but he showed the rest had done him a lot of good, for he cracked the ball vigorously as soon as he filled in at third."

In a game at the Polo Grounds on June 7, before which the Giants raised the 1921 National League pennant, the home team jumped to a quick 5-0 lead. In the third inning, with the score 5-2, Krug's triple to right scored two, narrowing the Giants lead, but the home team prevailed in the end, 9-4. Marty's first major-league home run came the next day, in the seventh inning off Giants reliever Red Causey.

One surprising game stands out—on August 25 at Cubs Park. In the second inning, Charlie Hollocher at short committed an error (his 23rd) and Krug did the same (his 25th), allowing the Phillies to score three runs. The visitors' lead was short-lived. The Cubs scored 10 in the bottom of the inning, adding another 14 runs in the fourth. The game seemed all but done, but Cubs pitchers proved characteristically generous and the Phillies managed to take a big bite out of the lead with an eight-run eighth, followed by more manic baserunning in the ninth. Six runs had scored and the bases were loaded with the Cubs desperately clinging to what had become a 26-23 lead. Philadelphia's Bevo LeBourveau stepped to the plate having gone 3-for-3 since being used as a replacement center fielder early in what had been a blowout. The terrible possibility of the home team squandering what had once been a 19-run lead ended when he struck out to end the farce. Krug went 4-for-5 with two doubles and four runs scored. He was mentioned in dispatches in a game that went into the major-league record book for the most hits (51, since bettered) and runs scored (49). The nine errors committed by both teams seemed appropriate to the occasion.

Krug's first full season on a major-league roster, coming at the age of 33, showed modest contributions at the plate. Krug wound up with a .278 average in 147 major-league games spread over two seasons a decade apart. His totals included 25 doubles, five triples, and four home runs. He had 67 runs batted in.

Millionaire chewing-gum magnate William Wrigley Jr. hired Krug to manage his Los Angeles Angels team in 1923. (Wrigley purchased the Cubs two years later.) The new skipper also covered second base at Washington Park, making his debut on April 4. The managing infielder went 0-for-4 in a 4-1 victory over the Oakland

Krug relaxing in the Red Sox dugout before a team photo, October 4, 1912.

Krug in his street clothes, 1912.

Oaks. The Angels finished in sixth place that season.

The Angels were in a tailspin early in the 1924 season, losing five of seven in a series against the Oaks and six of seven to the San Francisco Seals. In the last of those, the manager disappeared. Krug "was so disgusted with his own play and with that of his club that he left the game in the fifth inning," *The Sporting News* reported. "He went to the club house, dressed hurriedly and left the park. Seemingly he did not want anyone to know that he was connected with the Los Angeles team." But Krug brought the Angels home in second place that season, and in fourth place in 1925.

Then, a decade after winning his first pennant as a manager, Krug took another in 1926, as the Angels won 121 games against 81 losses to claim the top spot in the standings by 10½ games over the Oaks. The club was led by a stalwart pitching staff including Earl Hamilton (24-8), the veteran Doc Crandall (20-8), Elmer Jacobs (20-12), and Wayne Wright (19-7). A free-swinging offense was powered by an outfield featuring Jigger Statz, whose stats were impressive — a league-leading 291 hits, including 68 doubles and 18 triples, for a .354 average. Even the manager hit an impressive .389 in spot duty over 52 games. He platooned himself so he faced only left-handers.

After the first-place finish, the Angels tumbled to the basement in 1927, then finished in sixth place in 1928. Midway through 1929, with the team playing .500 baseball (56-54), Krug resigned to be replaced by Jack Lelivelt.

The veteran catcher Harry "Truck" Hannah, who spent nearly three decades in a crouch behind the plate including 3½ seasons with Krug and the Angels, looked back on his career to describe Krug as "the best at reading a pitcher's mind I ever saw." One example involved Harry Krause, a former Philadelphia Athletic who was a longtime Coast League nemesis with the Oaks. A spitballer, Krause held the ball to his mouth on every pitch, but it was Krug who spotted and deciphered a slight ducking of the head when phlegm was being applied to the ball.

He was also a tough boss who did not brook dissension. During one rough game, pitcher Clyde "Pea Ridge" Day made a snide comment about the proceedings from the bench. Failing to see that he may have been trying to keep the bench loose, Krug instead accused him of not having his head in the game. Soon after, the manager tried to trade him in a deal that fell though. Nonetheless, Day was sold to Wichita after season's end.

Wally Berger arrived on the Angels as a 21-year-old rookie center fielder with only 92 games of experience with the Pocatello (Idaho) Bannocks, a Class C team. He hit .327 and .335 in two full campaigns with the Angels before going on to become an All-Star with the Boston Braves in the 1930s. He credited Krug for making him good enough for the major leagues.[3]

Krug scouted for Detroit and the Philadelphia Athletics for many years. One of his finds, George "Sam" Vico, a postwar first baseman with the Tigers, was discovered playing semipro ball in the San Fernando Valley.

Krug coached the University of California, Los Angeles baseball team for three seasons beginning in 1937. During the World War II years he was on the coaching staff of the PCL's Hollywood Stars.

In 1936 Krug scouted a skinny teenager from San Diego's Herbert Hoover High, a school from which he had earlier signed its star pitcher. The scout watched a doubleheader, telling the boy's mother, "If you let this boy play baseball now, it will kill him." Young Ted Williams, just 17, stood 6-foot-3½ and weighed a scant 145 pounds. Krug's pronouncement left the mother in tears. Said Krug: "The kid is nothing but arms and legs now. He'd collapse if he tried to play regularly for a month. He needs to add at least 30 pounds to his skinny frame before he'll be ready for a pro trial."

Krug did not have to travel far to evaluate one young talent. He had married the former Emma Hartzke in 1920 and the pair had a son, Russell, in 1921. A namesake son was born at Glendale, California, two years later, toward the end of his father's first campaign as Angels manager. Marty Krug, Jr., a first baseman and sometimes outfielder, had a brief minor-league career, including a season in the British Columbia capital with the Victoria Athletics of the Western International League. His father returned to a professional dugout in 1950 as manager of the Athletics for the first time since leaving the Angels 21 years earlier.

Junior hit a respectable .278 under his father's guidance, but the team lost more than they won, finishing the season at 66-84. (The son suffered an on-field angina attack the following season while with Salt Lake City, his father's old team. He recovered, but soon became a manager. He took part in Saturday morning clinics on Salt Lake's WFYL-TV, an early televised broadcast of baseball coaching.)

In the 1950s the elder Krug made appearances as a manager in at least two old-timers' games at Wrigley Field.

He lived in retirement in Glendale, dying in a hospital

there, after a short illness, on June 26, 1966. (The cemetery offers that date, while newspaper accounts more often give the following day.) He was survived by two sons, Russell and Marty, and a brother, Willie. His remains were interred in a niche in the Iris Columbarium of the Great Mausoleum at the Forest Lawn Memorial Park in Glendale.

Sources:

Interview with Marty Krug, Jr. on March 26, 2010.

The Sporting News; *New York Times*; (Elyria, Ohio) *Evening Telegram*; *Indianapolis Star*; *Dunkirk* (New York) *Evening Observer*; *Oelwein* (Iowa) *Daily Register*; *Washington Post*; and other contemporary newspapers.

Aronoff, Jason. *Going, Going… Caught!: Baseball's Great Outfield Catches as Described By Those Who Saw Them, 1887-1964.* (Jefferson, North Carolina: McFarland. 2009).

Ned Cronin. "Stones in Their Shoes," *Baseball Digest*, May, 1957

Jorge S. Figueredo. *Cuban Baseball: A Statistical History, 1978-1961* (Jefferson, North Carolina: McFarland and Company, 2003).

Robert Long. *New York World Champions, 1933.* (Victoria, British Columbia: Trafford Publishing, 2003).

Bill Nowlin, ed. *The Kid: Ted Williams in San Diego* (Cambridge, Massachusetts: Rounder Books, 2005).

Bill O'Neal. *The Pacific Coast League, 1903-1988.* (Austin, Texas: Eakin Press, 1990).

Michael Seidel. *Ted Williams: A Baseball Life.* (Lincoln: University of Nebraska Press, 2003).

Endnotes

1. The family is listed on the 1900 US census in Cleveland, Cuyahoga County, Ohio, with the family name Kriag. Maria and the three boys came on the S.S. Karlsruhe out of Bremen, Germany, arriving in May 1891. Their place of origin is listed as Württemburg, a kingdom within the German Empire. Ancestry.com has them in the Baltimore passenger database but the ship's manifest says New York, New York. On his World War I draft card, Martin lists his place of birth as Bremen.

2. His being named to the roster caught the attention of a writer interested in ethnic heritage. "Twelve Teutons on the Red Sox team," read a headline over a two-sentence article in the *Evening Telegram* of Elyria, Ohio. "With 12 Germans on the team the Boston Red Sox are the real pretzels this season. Here's the delicatessen outfit: Stahl, Bedient, Bushelman, Pape, Hageman, Leonard, Nunamaker, Yerkes, Wagner, Gardner, Engle, and Krug."

3. A few months after resigning, Krug was the inadvertent instigator of a tragedy. On February 2, 1930, he drove to 3666 Cimarron St. in Los Angeles, the home of Gus Sandberg and his wife and two children. Sandberg was a steady if not always productive backup catcher for Krug's Angels squads. Before he came to the West Coast, he enjoyed two fine seasons with the Toronto Maple Leafs of the International League. The Cincinnati Reds called him up, penciling him in 31 games over two seasons. His batting averages in those campaigns never matched his weight of 189 pounds. If he seemed at times lethargic at bat and behind the plate, it could have been excused for his having donated blood for transfusions for his ailing infant daughter. On days when he perhaps should have rested, "he went about his work grimly, pale and underweight," one writer later noted. A weak hitter at the plate and slow on the basepaths, Sandberg was the target of boobirds even at home games. The Los Angeles critics called him Old Antelope. As Krug's visit came to an end on that winter's day, it was discovered the guest's automobile was out of gas. Sandberg siphoned fuel from his car to Krug's. "Then Gus struck a match to peer into his tank and see if he couldn't spare me a little more, leaving just enough for him to reach a gas station," Krug said. "A terrific explosion resulted." Krug suffered slight burns as he tried to quench the flames with his own coat. Sandberg died the following day from burns to his face, head, neck, and shoulders. *The Sporting News* eulogized the dead player as "an amiable and well-behaved catcher." Wrigley had his Angels and Cubs, both of which teams he owned, play a preseason exhibition game, investing the $6,500 gate on the widow's behalf.

Duffy Lewis
by Mark Armour

G	AB	R	H	2B	3B	HR	RBI	BB	SO	BA	OBP	SLG	SB	HBP
154	581	85	165	36	9	6	109	52	80	.284	.346	.408	9	3

For decades after they last played together, the Boston Red Sox' outfield of Duffy Lewis, Tris Speaker, and Harry Hooper, who toiled next to each other for six years in the Deadball Era, was often considered the greatest in baseball history. Although all three, especially Speaker, were fine hitters, their reputation was due largely to their exceptional defensive play. Lewis, the left fielder and the only one of the three not in baseball's Hall of Fame, was long remembered for the way he played the incline at the base of Fenway Park's left-field wall, a slope of grass that bore the name "Duffy's Cliff." Hooper thought Lewis was the best of the three "at making the backhand running catch at balls hit over his head." A powerful left-handed batter, the 5-foot-10, 170-pound Lewis typically batted behind Speaker in the cleanup position, and often ranked among American League leaders in home runs and runs batted in.

George Edward Lewis was born on April 18, 1888, in San Francisco to George and Mary Lewis. He was the youngest of three children, following Agnes by four years and Edward by two. Young George acquired his lifelong nickname, Duffy, from his mother's maiden name. On April 18, 1906—Duffy's 18th birthday—the infamous earthquake and fire ravaged his hometown. "I thought the whole world was coming to an end," he later said. Lewis attended and played baseball at St. Mary's College for one year, before signing with the Alameda team in the California League in 1907. In mid-1908 he joined the Oakland Oaks of the Pacific Coast League, and he continued his apprenticeship the next year, playing in 200 games and batting .279 in 1909. John I. Taylor, the Red Sox owner, first discovered Lewis playing for Yuma, Arizona, in the Imperial Valley League during the winter of 1908-09, and in September 1909 drafted his contract from the Oaks. After the 1909 season, Taylor went west and signed Lewis himself.

Lewis joined the Red Sox in spring training at Hot Springs, Arkansas, in 1910. He apparently did not take too kindly to the treatment accorded to rookies, refusing, for example, to limit his time in the batting cage or to back down from confrontations with his fellow players. Tris Speaker, in particular, did not take to Lewis's outspoken and cocky demeanor, leading to a prickly relationship that lasted throughout their many years as teammates. Lewis also irritated his new manager, Patsy Donovan, who fined and then benched the brash rookie. Duffy played in 149 games his rookie season, hitting .283 with eight home runs, only two fewer than the league-leading figure, and 29 doubles, which placed him third in the league. In 1911 Lewis's average climbed to .307, a career high, and his seven home runs tied for fourth in the circuit. After the season Lewis was to be wed to Eleanor Keane, a young baseball fan he had met at the Huntington Avenue Grounds. But at the urging of Red Sox owner Taylor, Lewis broke off the engagement two days before the wedding and headed back to California. Keane

Duffy Lewis, 1915.

was the third woman with whom Lewis had broken off an engagement, but a month later the couple reconciled and were married in San Rafael, California.

When Boston's Fenway Park was built in 1912, the ten-foot embankment in deep left field was one of its most interesting trademarks. Lewis covered this ground for six years, and became its master. "I'd go out to the ballpark mornings," he told a sportswriter, "and have somebody hit the ball again and again out to the wall. I experimented with every angle of approach up the cliff until I learned to play the slope correctly. Sometimes it would be tougher coming back down the slope than going up. With runners on base, you had to come off the cliff throwing." The slope remained until 1933, when Fenway Park was thoroughly renovated.

In 1912 Lewis's .284 batting average was solid, but it was his 109 RBIs, tied for second in the league, that contributed the most to his first championship team. In the famous duel between Walter Johnson and Smoky Joe Wood on September 6, Lewis's bloop double down the right-field line against the Big Train plated the only run of the contest. Although the Red Sox won a classic World Series over the Giants that fall, Lewis hit just .188 and made a costly error in the second game.

Lewis's frosty relationship with Speaker continued. During the summer of 1913 things deteriorated when Speaker continually knocked Lewis's cap off his head, revealing Duffy's heavily receding hairline. Finally, when Speaker persisted one time too many, Lewis threw his bat at his teammate, hitting him in the shins hard enough that Speaker had to be helped from the field. This friction did not affect their play on the field, as they helped form what may have been the best defensive outfield in baseball history. In 1913 the three accounted for an astonishing 84 assists, including 29 by Lewis.

Lewis drove in 109 runs during the 1912 season.

Lewis hit .298 with 90 RBIs in 1913 as the Red Sox dropped to fourth place, and, after resisting the advances of the Federal League to jump his team, managed just .278 the following year. A story Lewis loved telling in later years was about the time he pinch-hit for Babe Ruth. On July 11, 1914, Ruth made his major-league debut, hurling a 4-3 victory over the Cleveland Indians. Lewis hit for Ruth in the seventh inning and singled, helping to give his young teammate the victory.

Lewis hit .291 in 1915, and made up for his subpar 1912 Series performance by hitting .444 in the 1915 fall classic, driving in five of the 13 runs the Red Sox scored in their five-game triumph. He drove in the game-winner off Grover Cleveland Alexander in the bottom of the ninth of the third game and plated the winning run on a double in the fourth contest, while also making game-saving catches in both games. He also blasted a long drive that bounced into the center-field bleachers for a game-tying home run off Eppa Rixey in the finale. Of Lewis's stellar defense, the *Boston Globe*'s Tim Murnane wrote, "The all-around work of the modest Californian never has been equaled in a big Series." After this star-making performance, Lewis was in such demand that a San Francisco vaudeville production paid him $750 a week to perform that winter.

Speaker was traded to the Indians before the 1916 season, for two players and $55,000. Manager Bill Carrigan experimented briefly with Lewis in center field before Duffy moved back to his familiar cliff in left. Lewis slumped to .268 in 1916, but on his return to the World Series, he hit .353 (6-for-17). The following season Lewis hit .302 with a team-leading 167 hits.

Lewis spent the 1918 season in the US Navy, missing out on his team's 1918 World Series championship while serving as player-manager of a naval baseball team at Mare Island, California, near his hometown. Discharged from the service, in December 1918 he was traded to Yankees, along with Dutch Leonard and Ernie Shore, for $15,000 plus Frank Gilhooley, Al Walters, Slim Love, and Ray Caldwell, none of whom would contribute to the Red Sox in any way. After being dealt, Lewis initially considered quitting unless he was given a larger contract. Once he reported, he hit .272 with seven home runs (more than his previous five seasons combined, thanks to the Polo Grounds' short porch) and a team-high 89 RBIs. In 1920 he found himself fighting for playing time (.271 in 107 games) after the acquisition of Babe Ruth and the debut of rookie Bob Meusel. After the season Lewis was traded to the Washington Senators, for whom he hit .186 in just 27 games.

Early in the 1921 season Lewis joined Salt Lake City of the Pacific Coast League, where he played through the 1924 campaign. He hit a league-high .401 in 1921, and took over as manager the next three years, in which he hit .362, .358, and .392. In 1925, he was the player-manager of Portland in the PCL, hitting .294 for the Beavers. He finished his playing career with Mobile, Jersey City, and Portland (Maine) in 1926 and 1927, acting as manager at both Mobile and Portland.

His finances wiped out by the stock-market crash, Lewis was a coach for the Boston Braves from 1931 to 1935, and may have been the only man to have witnessed Babe Ruth's first home run (when he was Lewis's teammate in 1915) and last (when Ruth was playing out the string for the 1935 Braves). In 1936 he became the traveling secretary of the Braves, a post he held for 26 years, finishing in 1961 after the team had relocated to Milwaukee.

Presentation of suitcase to Boston Braves coach Duffy Lewis as Boston Braves manager Bill McKechnie and city dignitaries look on at Braves Field.

Duffy Lewis at the Polo Grounds in New York before Game Six of the 1912 World Series.

His motto was "Pay another buck and travel first class," and he became renowned around the league with bellhops and waiters as a big tipper, replete with a snap-brim fedora, diamond stickpin, and fancy vests.

In 1950 the 62-year-old Lewis played in one final professional game for the Texas League's Dallas Eagles as part of a promotional stunt. Lewis was often called upon to return to Fenway Park, and appeared in several old-timers games. He attended a celebration of the park's 50th anniversary in 1962 along with many of his 1912 teammates. In 1975 the 87-year-old Lewis threw out the first ball on Opening Day, in honor of the team's 75th season, and again before the famous sixth game of that season's World Series.

Lewis spent his later years in retirement in Salem, New Hampshire, with Eleanor. They had no children. He spent much of his time at Rockingham Park, a nearby horse track, where he had his own suite. A dapper dresser, he was said to own 72 suits. Lewis died in Salem at the age of 91 on June 17, 1979, three years after his beloved wife. At the time of his death he had no known living relatives and no money, and was buried in an unmarked grave in Holy Cross Cemetery in Londonderry, just outside of Salem. In 2001 a collection was taken up to pay for a stone, engraving, and upkeep on the plot.

Note: An earlier version of this biography originally appeared in David Jones, ed., *Deadball Stars of the American League* (Washington, D.C.: Potomac Books, Inc., 2006).

Sources

A primary source for this work was Duffy Lewis's file at the National Baseball Hall of Fame Library. Other sources include:

Ellery Clark, *Boston Red Sox 75th Anniversary History* (Hicksville, New York: Exposition Banner, 1975).

Ellery Clark. *Red Sox Fever* (Hicksville, New York: Exposition Banner, 1975).

Ellery Clark. *Red Sox Forever* (Hicksville, New York: Exposition Banner, 1977).

Frederick G. Lieb. *The Boston Red Sox* (New York: Putnam, 1947).

Glenn Stout and Richard A. Johnson. *Red Sox Century* (New York: Houghton Mifflin, 2000).

Paul J. Zingg, *Harry Hooper, An American Baseball Life* (Urbana, Illinois: University of Illinois, 1993).

Left fielder Lewis's six home runs in the regular season were second only to Tris Speaker's ten. *Boston Post*

Leslie Nunamaker
by Tony Bunting

G	AB	R	H	2B	3B	HR	RBI	BB	SO	BA	OBP	SLG	SB	HBP
35	103	15	26	5	2	0	6	6	17	.252	.313	.340	2	3

Ornery, rambunctious, and immensely talented, Leslie Nunamaker became one of baseball's stoutest hitting and best throwing catchers during the last decade of the Deadball Era—and one of the game's colorful personalities. Cut from the same temperamental cloth as contemporaries Ty Cobb and John McGraw, Nunamaker was prone to explosive on-field behavior that resulted in an assortment of ejections and punishments in his 12-year American League career. "Leslie Nunamaker wants to run amuck when he gets mad," *Washington Post* reporter J.V. Fitz Gerald remarked in 1918 after witnessing one of the catcher's outbursts. Nunamaker got mad often, and his irascible nature often attracted as much publicity as his tremendous physical gifts and feats on the diamond. Equipped with a magnificent right arm, he once threw out three baserunners in an inning, tying a major-league record. His bat could be equally formidable: Twice he led American League catchers in hitting and might have done so again had he not been seriously injured in an automobile accident while still in his prime.

Tall and long-limbed, Nunamaker didn't fit the mold of a Deadball Era receiver, but he possessed the requisite quick thinking. "Nunamaker is big and strong; he is not exactly graceful; it may be that the length of his legs gives one that impression," wrote *The Sporting News* in 1911, shortly after he joined the big leagues with the Boston Red Sox. "But for headwork he is declared to have it on a lot of the backstops who have had years the advantage in training, and he has handled the Red Sox pitchers in nice shape....Nunamaker stands six feet one, and weighs nearly 200 pounds—and is still growing. With this range and backing of beef he has a powerful whip and the base runner who can steal on the young giant has to make a good start and then hurry."

Leslie Grant Nunamaker (pronounced Noo-na-maker) was born in Malcolm, Nebraska, about 15 miles northwest of Lincoln, on August 25, 1889, the fifth of six children (four boys, two girls) of Henry Benjamin and Mary Francis (Staley) Nunamaker. A Pennsylvania native of German and English ancestry, Henry moved to Illinois, was married there, and finally settled his family in the community of Aurora in the southeastern part of Nebraska, not far from the Platte River. He owned a small farm and a dairy operation. For recreation growing up, Leslie pursued the national pastime, belonged to the Aurora Culture Club, and performed in plays at local opera houses.

Nunamaker got his semiprofessional baseball start with the Oxford (Nebraska) Indians, a collection of Native American and white players that barnstormed throughout the state. At one point in his early baseball development, he reportedly caught for future Hall of Fame pitcher and fellow Nebraskan Grover Cleveland Alexander, two years his senior, on an area town team. According to one source, Nunamaker was discovered by minor-league player-manager Billy Fox, a one-time second baseman for

Les Nunamaker throwing, 1912.

the Cincinnati Reds, while the youngster participated in an Iowa tournament.

In 1909, at the age of 20, Leslie—or Les, as he was informally called—broke into the minor leagues. He began the season catching for Lincoln of the Class A Western League, Fox's former squad, but in May was optioned to Dubuque of the Illinois-Indiana-Iowa (or Three-I) League, a Class B organization.

Despite an abundance of raw talent, the unpolished Nunamaker batted .241 for the sixth-place club and struggled behind the plate, committing 20 errors and nine passed balls in 92 games. Lincoln reclaimed him at the end of the Three-I campaign, and it appeared that he would start the 1910 season with the Western League team. But late in March, the young ballplayer received what must have been a shock. The Chicago Cubs, fresh off a 104-49 second-place National League finish and already carrying capable catchers Jimmy Archer, Pat Moran, and Tom Needham, swapped a pair of pitchers for Nunamaker. "[Manager Frank] Chance has been after Nunamaker for a long time, for the P.L. [short for Peerless Leader—Chance's nickname] has seen him in action several times and believes he can make a great catcher out of him," the *Chicago Tribune* reported. "Next to [Orval] Overall, Nunamaker will be the biggest man on the squad." [1]

The Cubs skipper planned to keep four catchers and take his time molding the Nebraska upstart, whom he kept on the bench as the season got underway. But when veteran backstop Johnny Kling completed a vaudeville tour and signed a contract with Chicago in early May after sitting out all of 1909, Chance shipped Nunamaker to Bloomington of the Three-I League. Les responded with a fine offensive campaign for the Bloomers. In 406 at-bats, he hit .264, second best on the club and 20th in the circuit. His potent throwing arm, however, alternately resembled a rifle and a shotgun. "The details of yesterday's game at Rock Island [add] another convincing argument to the growing conviction that the disarrangement of Catcher Nunamaker's optics is a permanent affliction," a sportswriter commented. "The former Dubuquer has steam and energy enough behind his pegs, but he fails to throw where he is looking or is appearing to look."[2] Les committed a league-leading 34 errors for catchers and ranked 20th out of 21 in fielding percentage. The wildness wasn't confined to his play. In August, league President Al Tierney slapped Nunamaker with a suspension for insubordination, a hint of the unruliness that would checker his career.

No one disputed his enormous ability. With a number of major-league clubs expressing interest in Nunamaker, the Cleveland Naps drafted the 21-year-old in September and dealt his rights to the Red Sox. Boston took him to spring training in California and he cinched a spot on the roster. The imposing prospect—Nunamaker eventually grew to 6-feet-2—started the 1911 season as a backup to Bill Carrigan. On April 28 at the Huntington Avenue Grounds in Boston, Les made his major-league debut against future batterymate Ray Caldwell of the New York Highlanders and went 0-for-3 in a loss. Behind the plate, he handled three chances cleanly and threw a man out stealing, but allowed one passed ball. Nunamaker caught a number of games for the Red Sox in May and June while Carrigan recovered from an injured leg (though *The Sporting News* suggested that the real reason the Red Sox kept the rookie in the lineup was to chastise Carrigan for insisting on a pay raise).

Whatever the case, Nunamaker performed solidly and gathered the bouquets of the baseball press. "The luck of Owner John I. Taylor of the Boston Red Sox in getting high-class youngsters for his team is proverbial and he apparently never made a happier strike than when he landed that husky young giant,

Nunamaker stretches to try and pull in a high throw, 1913.

Leslie Nunamaker, for backstop duty," wrote *The Sporting News*. Another observer marveled at the player's impressive physique, reservoirs of energy, and courage. "Nunamaker is built on the same plan as [former Boston catcher] Lou Criger, tall, rangy, and muscular," he wrote. "His great reach enables him to gather in wild throws and foul flies with ease, while his stamina makes it possible for him to go through the toughest kind of game without a letup. For proof of his nerve just watch him stand up unflinchingly when a base runner is trying to score and the play is at the plate."[3] Boston baseball scribe and former major-league player Tim Murnane was more circumspect. Though amazed by Les's throwing prowess, he criticized the rising star's "several weak points; he is lost on foul flies and is a rather mechanical worker."[4]

A broken finger sidelined Nunamaker early in July and limited his action the rest of the way. Nonetheless, he recorded a respectable first season: In 183 at-bats, he posted a .257 average and drove in 19 runs. Perhaps even more promising, his fielding average was .972, slightly better than the league mark for catchers, and unlike some of his colleagues, he had no trouble corralling the blazing pitches of Boston phenom Joe Wood.

His finger mended and with a major-league season under his belt, Nunamaker appeared ready to break out in 1912. After a brief contract squabble—the plaudits of the previous summer undoubtedly echoed loudly in his ears—he prepared to push Carrigan for the brunt of the catching duties. On April 20, Nunamaker caught the first major-league game ever played at Boston's Fenway Park for the Red Sox, a 7-6 victory over the New York Highlanders. But Nuny (or Nunie), as his teammates and sportswriters called him, contributed little to a club that would dramatically capture the world championship. In a game at St. Louis in June, he again fractured a finger, opening the door for Forrest "Hick" Cady, a newcomer who bunked with Nunamaker. "There's your chance to make good," Les told the rookie. "Be sure to keep up the reputation of the room." Cady good-naturedly shot back: "Just watch me, Nuny. From now on we change places." [5] Change places they did. The third-stringer shined in Nunamaker's absence, particularly on defense, and seized the backup spot. Les sat on the bench and watched Cady and Carrigan share the catching responsibilities during Boston's World Series triumph over the New York Giants. He failed to get into a single game. The year had been a rough one for Nunamaker. In a May contest with the St. Louis Browns, he had even suffered the humiliation of falling for first baseman George Stovall's hidden ball trick. Amid the disappointment, he emerged a wealthier man, collecting a $4,024.69 Series share.

Nunamaker's role on the Red Sox continued to dwindle in 1913, and he sustained yet another injury, this time hurting his knee in a collision at the plate with Detroit shortstop Donie Bush. He appeared in just 29 games. The most sensational event of Nunamaker's year occurred on May 7 at League Park in Cleveland and highlighted the Boston catcher's volatile disposition, not his baseball skills. In a contentious meeting between the Red Sox and the Naps that featured repeated collisions on the basepaths, Nunamaker's persistent badgering of Cleveland infielder Ivy Olson erupted into a 10-minute post-game brawl between members of the clubs in the runway leading to the dressing rooms. The melee furnished Les with a swollen-shut eye, courtesy of a Nap, and a $25 fine, compliments of American League President Ban Johnson. The wrangle would not be his last inside a ballpark.

His woes and wars on the diamond notwithstanding, Nunamaker warmed to life in and around Boston. An enthusiastic hunter and fisherman, he took frequent trips to Cape Cod in his touring car, before the vehicle burst into flames and had to be abandoned. He befriended another passionate sportsman, teammate Tris Speaker, and the two became lifelong shooting and fishing companions.

But his career languished in the Hub. With Carrigan, Cady, and Pinch Thomas locking up the catching chores, Boston shipped Les to the New York Yankees on May 13, 1914, for a reported $5,000. The transaction reunited Nunamaker with his first big-league manager, Frank Chance, and immediately energized the 25-year-old. A week after the consummation of the deal, he blasted his first major-league home run, prompting an excited *New York Times* to proclaim Les "the handiest acquisition the Yankees have made in some time..." He later smashed another round-tripper; the two homers were his only ones in the majors. [6]

Nunamaker's celebrated "whip" landed him in the record books on August 3, 1914, in a contest at Detroit. In the bottom of the seventh, he nabbed Hugh High straying off second base, then gunned down a pair of would-be Tigers base-stealers, fellow Nebraskan "Wahoo Sam" Crawford and Bobby Veach. The three assists in an inning marked the first by a big-league catcher since 1887 and would not be matched for another seven years, when Ray Schalk executed the trick for the Chicago White Sox. Les didn't get to revel in his accomplishment for long. Two weeks later a fan, perched in the upper deck of the Polo Grounds, fired a foul ball—perhaps intended for umpire Tommy Connolly—back onto the field and knocked Nunamaker cold. The gritty catcher regained consciousness and remained in the game. In a few days he felt sufficiently perked up to get thumbed out of New York's loss to Cleveland. If life wasn't interesting enough, Federal League agents approached the big backstop and tried to lure him to the new circuit. But Nunamaker, who was blossoming with the Yankees, declined their offer. He split the work behind the plate almost evenly with Ed Sweeney and hit a hearty .263 in 262 at-bats with 29 RBIs in 1914.

After a poor 1915, Les emerged as one of the best all-around catchers in the junior circuit in the late Teens. Taking the advice of Yankees coach Duke Farrell, he relaxed his swing in 1916 and enjoyed the greatest hitting year of his career. On April 25, he clobbered Red Sox ace Babe Ruth for a double, a triple, and two singles, then the next day followed it up with another near-cycle—a single, a double, and a triple—and four RBIs against the eventual world champions. Near the end of May, he was on a full-blown hitting spree and owned a .357 average, tops in a league that boasted Ty Cobb, Tris Speaker, and Joe Jackson. Nunamaker's contributions helped propel New York into first place in late June. But he couldn't maintain the torrid pace and soon endured a major slump. Matters worsened for Les on July 10 in a game against Cleveland when he berated umpire Silk O'Loughlin for putting a brand-new ball into play while the Indians batted under darkening skies. The arbiter ejected Nunamaker, who received a short suspension from Ban Johnson for his verbal onslaught.

The Yankees withered at the end of July and early August, dropping nine in a row and plummeting to fourth place, where they ended the season. Despite the collapse, Nunamaker sported a splendid .296 average by year's end (48 points better than the league and the highest among starting catchers in the majors) and had a slugging average of .404 in 91 games. His glove work improved, too. He committed only eight errors while wearing the mask—half his 1915 total—and posted the highest fielding percentage of his career, .983.

One aspect of Les's play inspired criticism, however: His clunky feet. "Nunamaker might be a wonderful ball player if he were possessed of a trifle more speed," opined sportswriter W.J. Macbeth. "He is a tremendously big fellow, who takes on weight readily, and so it is most difficult for him to keep in the top form of physical fitness when he is not actively engaged every day." Once, after a double-steal attempt, the *New York Times* chided him and fellow baserunner Doc Cook for moving "slower than Judge [Kenesaw Mountain] Landis's decision in the [Federal League's] anti-trust suit [against Organized Baseball]." [8]

Nevertheless, Nunamaker eased into his peak years. Although his hitting dropped off significantly in 1917, he continued to be an offensive force. In 310 at-bats, he clubbed a healthy .261 and drove in 33 runs swinging near the bottom of the Yankees order. He also fashioned a reputation as the premier pinch-hitter in baseball, coming off the bench to rap seven safeties in 13 at-bats for the season. Lifetime he went 28-for-78 in the same role for a sparkling .359 average and earned *Baseball Magazine's* title "Champion Pinch-Hitter of the Decade." His jaw perpetually operated at midseason form. In April, he engaged in a shouting match with Red Sox pitcher

Nunamaker on a cool 1912 afternoon.

George "Rube" Foster and, later in the campaign, was kicked out of a loss to Cleveland when he barked at umpire Connolly, "Why don't you give 'em the game?" [9]

The fiery Nunamaker proved to be one of the few bright spots on the team. The Yankees, expected to contend for the American League pennant in 1917, fizzled, finishing in sixth place. New York fired manager Wild Bill Donovan, and co-owner Jacob Ruppert replaced him with the man who would pilot the club to greatness, Miller Huggins. The move effectively ended Nunamaker's stint in Gotham. Huggins swapped the cantankerous catcher, along with pitchers Nick Cullop and Urban Shocker, infielders Joe Gedeon and Fritz Maisel, and $15,000, to the St. Louis Browns for star second baseman Del Pratt and aging hurler Eddie Plank.

Nunamaker, by now a seven-year veteran, joined a perennially lackluster St. Louis Browns squad in 1918, but his performance, particularly in the batter's box, didn't skip a beat. He topped American League receivers in hitting (.259) and enjoyed one of his greatest offensive afternoons when he went 5-for-5 with a walk in the second game of a doubleheader against his former Yankees at the Polo Grounds on August 27 (he had clubbed a pinch-hit single in the opener). The day also turned out to be one of his most exasperating. Filling in at first base for George Sisler, who pitched the nightcap for the Browns, he had a nightmarish time on defense, committing three errors before being shifted to right field.

The change of scenery failed to curb Les's aggressive nature. In a May contest at Washington, he blew his stack, before swatting a key double in the ninth inning to help the Browns to victory. "The St. Louis catcher got as hot under the collar as a fat man in midsummer over a decision that gave the Nationals a run in the eighth inning yesterday and when a fan chided him Leslie invited the grand-stand talker to keep a date outside the park after the game," reported the *Washington Post's* J.V. Fitz Gerald. "The backstop admitted he would change the fan's map as the kaiser is trying to alter the topographical face of Europe" [an allusion to World War I, which the United States had entered in April 1917].[10] Back at the nation's capital in July, Nunamaker unleashed a tirade—complete with a fling of the his cap—after Bill Dinneen ruled him out on a close play at second base in the ninth inning of a Browns win over the Senators. The abusive blow-up garnered Les a three-day respite imposed by the league office.

A grim reality confronted Nunamaker and other baseball players in the summer of 1918: the United States' escalating involvement in the war. Originally classified as 1-A (single male with no dependents), Les received an exemption from combat because of torn cartilage. [On July 26, Secretary of War Newton Baker, who had earlier ruled professional baseball to be nonessential industry, allowed players immunity from the "work-or-fight" order until September 1. The owners ended the regular season on September 2]. After the season, Nunamaker enlisted in the naval aviation service and, with his pal Speaker close by, began training at the Massachusetts Institute of Technology on November 8. Three days later, the Armistice was reached.

Nunamaker escaped World War I, but in a cruel bit of irony, nearly lost his life one month after the war ended. Upon returning to St. Louis, he was badly injured when a taxicab he was riding in crashed into another one. He absorbed head and facial lacerations and nearly lost an eye and an ear in the accident. Newspapers printed photos of the ballplayer's scarred and bandaged face. Nunamaker sued the cab's owner for $15,000, and the court awarded him $4,500 in damages.

While he nursed his wounds in the winter of 1919, Les was traded to the Cleveland Indians for another catcher, Josh Billings. Nunamaker wasn't the same player after the accident. In his first two years with the Indians, he appeared in a total of 60 games, 33 of them behind the plate. But when Speaker took the helm of the Indians in the middle of 1919, Nunamaker became his right-hand man for strategy. "In a crucial series, Spoke counted a good deal on Les," said former Indians outfielder Jack Graney.

Speaker likely consulted Nunamaker frequently in 1920, a year that witnessed a tight three-way race between the Indians, Yankees, and White Sox. In a dramatic stretch run that included the beaning death of Cleveland shortstop Ray Chapman and the suspension of seven White Sox for their roles in fixing the 1919 World Series, the Indians grabbed the American League championship. They met the Brooklyn Robins in the World Series and won it, five games to two. Unlike 1912, when he rode the bench for the entire Series, Nunamaker got to participate in the fall festivities. He pinch-hit twice, lined a single, and caught one inning.

Nunamaker gained national attention for a peculiar incident while the Series was underway. The night of Cleveland's Game Five victory over Brooklyn, he arrived at his room and found a roll of bills tucked beneath his pillow. Skittish over the breaking Black Sox scandal and taking no chances, he turned the money over to Ban Johnson, who counted the stash—16 Confederate dollar bills. The *New York Times* chortled over the obvious ruse: "Please Page [Confederate President] Jeff Davis!" shouted its headline.[11] Now a two-time world champion, Les shrugged off the strange episode and spent much of the offseason traveling with his sidekick Speaker. The two embarked on a hunting and fishing expedition to Rice Lake in Ontario (a favorite spot of theirs), made a similar excursion to Texas (Speaker's home state), and accompanied Rogers Hornsby at a Wild West show in Fort Worth.

Although his career was waning, Nunamaker still rode the tidal wave of offense that greeted the early '20s. Backing up catcher Steve O'Neill for the reigning world champs, he stung American League pitching for a .359 average in 131 at-bats. He would have seen even more action, but in August he broke his leg sliding into second base against Chicago. Nunamaker's big-league career came to an end in 1922, at the age of 33, when the Indians granted his release to take the manager's job for Chattanooga of the Southern Association in 1923.

Nunamaker had a brief and unsuccessful stint as skipper of the Lookouts. Playing first base, he guided the club to a seventh-place finish (63-88) in 1923. Feisty as ever, Les drew a three-day suspension in late July for squabbling with an umpire. Citing high operating costs, Chattanooga's team president, Strang Nicklin, fired Nunamaker shortly into the 1924 season and took over the club himself. Life wasn't all bad, though. In January of the same year, the 34-year-old Nunamaker married Frances Peckham, "a wealthy and socially prominent" Clevelander and baseball fan, according to one report, in a ceremony at a Chicago church. Speaker, unsurprisingly, was the best man. Les piloted Saginaw (Michigan) of the Class B Michigan-Ontario League in 1925 and for part of 1926, then the next year headed to the newly formed Class D Lone Star League, where he helped lead the Corsicana Oilers to a 48-72 record. After selling cars in Cleveland for a time, Nunamaker culminated his minor league managing—and playing—career in the place it began: Lincoln, Nebraska. In 1929, he managed part of the season for the Links of the Nebraska State League, then took over full time in 1930. At the age of 41, he played first base for the squad and hit .332 with 24 doubles and six triples. But Lincoln fared poorly, winding up 56-66, in next-to-last place. A year later, with Les at the reins once more, the club improved, capturing third place with a 55-51 record.

His sometimes turbulent, yet largely successful life in professional baseball over, Nunamaker returned to Aurora, Nebraska, the town he grew up in, and later moved to nearby Hastings to help his older brother run the Pioneer Cash (meat) Market. He pursued trap shooting, a favorite pastime, and served as director of the Nebraska Sportsmen's Association. Leslie Nunamaker developed carcinoma of the thyroid and died from complications in Hastings on November 14, 1938, at the age of 49. He is buried in Aurora.

Sources:

Jerry E. Clark. *Nebraska Diamonds: A Brief History of Baseball Major Leaguers From the Cornhusker State* (Omaha, Nebraska: Making History, 1991).

Timothy M. Gay. *Tris Speaker: The Rough-and-Tumble Life of a Baseball Legend* (Lincoln and London: University of Nebraska Press, 2005).

Steve Gietschier, ed. *Complete Baseball Record Book* (2005 edition). (St. Louis: The Sporting News, 2005).

Joe Hoppel. *The Series* (St. Louis: The Sporting News Publishing Co., 1988).

Joseph L. Reichler, ed. *The Baseball Encyclopedia* (New York: Macmillan Publishing Co., Inc., 1979).

Harold Seymour. *Baseball: The Golden Age* (New York: Oxford University Press, Inc., 1971).

Mike Sowell. *The Pitch That Killed* (New York: Macmillan, 1989).

Allan Wood. *Babe Ruth and the 1918 Red Sox* (Lincoln, Nebraska: Writers Club Press, 2000).

Articles

J. C. Kofoed. "The Live Wire of American League Catchers." *Baseball Magazine*, January 1917.

J. C. Morse. "Changes in the World of Baseball." *Baseball Magazine*, September 1911.

C. Ford Sawyer. "Baseball's Greatest Pinch-Hitter." *Baseball Magazine*, April 1919.

-----. "The Champion Pinch-Hitter of the Decade." *Baseball Magazine*, May 1922.

"Who's Who on the Diamond." *Baseball Magazine*, August 1918.

Newspapers

Altoona (Pennsylvania) *Mirror*

Augusta Chronicle

Aurora (Nebraska) *News*

Bellingham (Washington) *Herald*

Boston Globe

Chicago Tribune

Christian Science Monitor

Cleveland Plain Dealer

Dallas Morning News

Decatur (Illinois) *Review*

Detroit Free Press

Duluth (Minnesota) *News-Tribune*

Hartford Courant

Hastings (Nebraska) *Daily Tribune*

Kokomo (Indiana) *Tribune*

New York Times

Philadelphia Inquirer

Pueblo (Colorado) *Chieftain*

San Antonio Light

Sporting Life

The Sporting News

Washington Post

Web

access.newspaperarchive.com

ancestry.com

baseballlibrary.com

baseball-reference.com

chroniclingamerica.loc.gov

findagrave.com

heritagequestonline.com

hngraphical.proquest.com

infoweb.newsbank.com

la84foundation.org

marian.creighton.edu/~besser/baseball/second.html

mcpl.lib.mo.us

nebraskahistory.org/lib-arch/research/treasures/native_baseball.htm

retrosheet.org

Archives

Museum of Nebraska Major League Baseball, St. Paul, Nebraska. Leslie Nunamaker collection.

National Baseball Hall of Fame Library, Cooperstown, New York. Leslie Nunamaker file.

Correspondence

Fred Hummer (grandnephew of Leslie Nunamaker). E-mails to author, January 22, 2010; January 29, 2010; February 5, 2010; February 28, 2010.

Endnotes

1. *Chicago Tribune*, March 24, 1910

2. Unattributed article from Nunamaker's file at the Museum of Nebraska Major League Baseball

3. *Ibidem*

4. *The Sporting News*, July 13, 1911

5. *New York Times*, January 25, 1913

6. *New York Times*, May 21, 1914

7. Unidentified clipping from the National Baseball Hall of Fame Library, entitled "Nunamaker Is a Plodder, but He Gets There," August, 1917

8. *New York Times*, June 8, 1915

9. The account of the shouting match with Foster came from Edward F. Martin of the *Boston Globe*, April 13, 1917. The Connolly episode came from the *New York Times* of September 21, 1917.

10. *Washington Post*, May 23, 1918

11. *New York Times*, October 12, 1920

Buck O'Brien
by Michael Foster

G	ERA	W	L	SV	GS	GF	CG	SHO	IP	H	R	ER	BB	SO	HR	HBP	WP	BFP
37	2.58	20	13	0	34	3	25	2	275 2/3	237	107	79	90	115	3	10	5	1100

G	AB	R	H	2B	3B	HR	RBI	BB	SO	BA	OBP	SLG	SB	HBP
37	94	4	13	1	1	0	6	6	29	.138	.190	.170	0	0

Asked by a sportswriter in January 1912 which pitcher was giving him the most trouble in the American League, Ty Cobb did not mince words. "I believe I have never in my life faced a pitcher who bothered me so much as that man O'Brien," he growled. "O'Brien has everything. He has a 'spitter' the like of which I have never seen before. It breaks like a shot and is absolutely impossible to gauge it with any degree of consistency."[1]

The son of Irish immigrant John B. O'Brien and Margaret Willis, a native of nearby Braintree, Thomas Joseph O'Brien (known as Buck from an early age) was born in Brockton, Massachusetts, on May 9, 1882. The eldest of eight children (four boys and four girls), he grew up in a modest 2½-story home in the Bush, a working-class, overwhelmingly Irish Catholic neighborhood on the south side of town. Then a small but growing mill city of 27,000, Brockton fancied itself the Shoe Center of the World,[2] and like most of the city's working-class Irish, Buck's father earned a livelihood assembling footwear at the benches of the Walkover Shoe Company. At one time or another, all the O'Brien children spent time at the benches at Walkover Shoes, and at least one, Buck's younger sister, Hannah, spent a lifetime there.

As a boy, Tommy O'Brien attended St. Patrick's, a parish school opened in 1887 by the Sisters of Charity of Nazareth. He was a gifted tenor and athlete, and his life revolved around his passion for theater and sports. Throughout middle and high school, he starred in a series of operas produced at St. Patrick's, and each Sunday he was a regular soloist with the parish choir. "My father had a gorgeous voice, absolutely gorgeous," recalled Buck's daughter, Rosemarie O'Brien Moran. "He was a high tenor, and he was always singing around the house."[3] And after fulfilling his obligations at school and church, like many a young man in Brockton, his interest shifted to matters of sport.

John O'Brien made it a point to instruct all of his sons in the manly art of self-defense. Fiercely competitive and deeply athletic, Buck took to boxing even more naturally than baseball, and by his teens there wasn't a young pugilist in town who wasn't aware of his prowess in the ring. "Well, sure he was a boxer," recalls Rose Moran, "but he was never a vicious man; in fact, he was really very quiet. He was not prone to fighting, but he was big and strong, and he fought when he had to."[4]

By his 17th birthday, Buck was making a name for himself singing locally and playing ball in the Brockton city league. In the summer of 1899 he held down first base for Brockton's semipro West Enders, playing in front of wild hometown crowds against clubs in the greater Boston area. Two years later he joined Brockton's Walkover Shoe factory team. Led by a longtime friend of his, pitcher Billy Reardon, the Walkovers were enormously popular among Brockton baseball rooters, who turned out in droves at the club's Highland Park grounds.

It was during a contest against Holbrook early in 1904 that Buck's baseball career began to shift from infield to the pitching mound. During an infield play when he made a putout at first, Buck rifled a shot across the diamond and picked off a runner racing for third. According to a story reported 40 years after the events, when the inning was over, the Walkover third baseman approached Buck at the bench.

"Buck, that was a honey of a throw. Did you know it was going to jump?"

"No, I didn't," answered Buck.

"Well, it did, old top, and if you can get it under control you can become a great pitcher."[5]

Brockton, Massachusetts' Buck O'Brien, 1912.

Buck took the advice to heart, and that summer began throwing regularly. "Regarding O'Brien's early plunge into baseball, the rumor still holds water that he gained the greater part of his excellent control by chucking fast ones at an African dodger at Nantasket Beach," the *Boston Post* later reported, adding, "The mortality reports concerning the latter gentry bear out the rumor."[6]

A large measure of Buck's newfound success on the mound was tied to his quick mastery of the trick pitches that, thanks largely to Big Ed Walsh's success in Chicago, were garnering notoriety across baseball. By its very nature, the spitball was a difficult pitch to control, but Buck quickly developed a knack for it and demonstrated uncanny command. "Buck O'Brien was an enigma," the *Brockton Enterprise* said when he led local factory players to a thrilling victory over a team from the Olneyville section of Providence, Rhode Island, over the July Fourth weekend in 1906.[7] "He was as accurate as a die, not issuing a pass." Buck was also proving no slouch at the plate, elevating his batting average over 60 points (from .222 to .286) during one hot stretch in August.[8]

When the Walkovers failed to field a team for '07, O'Brien went to work elsewhere. He was hotly pursued by the Portland tam of the Maine State League but, already enjoying steady work as a solo vocalist with Brockton's Gem Theater, he indicated his desire to stay close to home. When a semipro team in Wakefield, outside Boston, made him a "financially satisfactory" offer that obligated him to play but one game a week, he jumped at it.[9] Buck's strong work finally caught scouts' eyes, and at the end of July he was tendered his first professional offer by the hometown Brockton Tigers of the New England League.

Led by the legendary Framingham brothers Mike and Marty O'Toole, the Tigers had been dogging Jesse Burkett's Worcester Busters for most of the summer, and the *Brockton Enterprise* gushed forth local pride when the team announced that it had signed a "local youngster" to its roster.[10] Buck's professional debut, on August 20, 1907, against Haverhill (Massachusetts) was well attended, but Buck was an utter wreck. After handing out six runs through the first four innings, he was benched by manager Stephen Flanagan. The Tigers rallied to win 9-7, but at least one local writer chided Buck for woeful control and "mutton" speed.[11]

O'Brien fared far better in his second start, nine days later. Facing cellar-dwelling Lawrence, he started the contest poorly, accidentally whipping the ball into the grandstand in the first inning. He settled down and, with solid speed and control, "went through nine innings in swell shape, never once faltering" and walked off the mound with a 6-2 win.[12]

Buck made one more appearance that summer, the end of his short-lived career with the New England League. With most of the Tigers lineup returning for 1908, Buck opted to accept another offer to travel to Paterson, New Jersey, to play for the outlaw Union League Intruders. A minor-league city best known for the remarkable baseball feats of its most distinguished alumnus, Honus Wagner, Paterson suffered from gross mismanagement and lax fan interest. Buck fared as poorly as his struggling franchise, limping to a 2-9 mark by late May. On May 21 he bolted from the team, which itself folded three days later.[13] Returning home, he pitched for Taunton, Massachusetts (Old Colony League), and grew stronger and more confident with each start. With the pennant on the line, on September 8 O'Brien won back-to-back complete games against Somerville, and then a 5-0 win over Rockland to help Taunton win the pennant.[14]

Buck's 12 victories that summer caught the eye of a number of big-league scouts, among them Weymouth, Massachusetts, native and Indianapolis Indians catcher Howling Dan Howley. "I had heard about Buck from the boys around Goat Valley," Howley recounted nearly 40 years later. "Brockton, not being far from Weymouth, I made a trip up there and didn't have to use my best oratory to induce him to forget to report to the Walk-Over Shoe the following season."[15]

Indianapolis had O'Brien pitch for the Evansville (Indiana) River Rats (Class B Central League) in 1909. He started slowly, but grew stronger as the season progressed, winning eight straight games and 13 of his last 15 to close out the season at 18-11.

A month later a "tickled" O'Brien traveled with the Indianapolis team to Cuba for a barnstorming trip across the island.[16] Steady rains caused the postponement of most of the games, but on October 25, Buck took the mound and whipped an aggregation of Cuban ballplayers, 4-2.[17] Two weeks later he was back in Brockton for the winter.

Unexpectedly released in February 1910, Buck joined the Connecticut State League Hartford Senators, a powerhouse of a club that had taken the flag the previous year, but as was the case with Evansville a year earlier, his new franchise was a winner turned loser. Hartford took a nose dive out of the gate, eventually finishing the summer in fifth place. And yet again, Buck O'Brien stood out as one of the top hurlers in the league, notching 20 wins (against 10 losses) for the first time in his career.

Waterbury manager Mickey Finn got in touch with the New York Giants' John McGraw in early August, but a scout McGraw sent reported, "The young feller didn't show nothing." McGraw passed.[18] Days later, on August 20, Buck's contract was scooped up by John I. Taylor and the Boston Red Sox.

After an active offseason of stage performances in and around Brockton, Buck boarded the Red Sox express bound for 1911 spring training in Redondo Beach, California, and formed the Red Sox Quartet in the course of the cross-country trip. He showed poor form for the Red Sox rookies in a 4-2 exhibition loss to the Lynn Shoemakers on April 15, and was assigned to the Denver Grizzlies of the Class A Western League. When Buck settled in, he began turning out one dazzling performance after the next. On June 5 he pitched and won both ends of a doubleheader against Des Moines (13-3 and 14-1), and facing a pack of St. Joseph's "hoodlums" three days later, he tied Marty O'Toole's Western League strikeout record by fanning 18.[19]

Buck marked Independence Day by tossing a no-hitter against Lincoln, 5-1 (Lincoln's lone run coming on an error). By early September, he led the league in strikeouts with 261 (against 77 walks), and his 26-7 record ranked him second in games won, helping lead the Grizzlies to a 111-54 mark and the pennant.

Buck's return to the Red Sox in September could not have come at a better time. Mired at .500 for most of the summer, the Sox had tanked badly, dropping seven straight games and 10 of their last 11. After three days on the rails, O'Brien met up with the team in Philadelphia on September 8. The next morning Boston manager Patsy Donovan approached Buck and asked if he was "ready for a crack at the reigning American League champs."[20] Buck had not touched a ball in five days, but he offered to loosen up and see how he felt.

The day was overcast and a light rain fell at Shibe Park. Buck took the ball, squaring off against Eddie Plank, and, given a 2-0 lead in the first inning, he never looked back. "Buck went about his business as if he were working against some bush league nine," the *Enterprise* recorded. There was no faint heart, no falter, no flurry or even indecision."[21] Philadelphia fans rocked the grandstand with the home team trailing 2-0 in the bottom of the ninth, but Buck coolly struck out Amos Strunk to secure the win and his first big-league victory.[22]

After the game manager Patsy Donovan broke into a broad smile, and remarked, "O'Brien is a corker."[23]

Winning five of six games to close out the final four weeks of the summer, Buck established himself as one of the game's

O'Brien had a 20-13 season in 1912, with a 2.58 earned run average.

hottest properties. Umpire Silk O'Loughlin remarked during the offseason that O'Brien had "all kinds of nerve and confidence," calling him "the upcoming star of the American league."[24] Detroit Tigers president Frank Navin went even further, stating, "He came in like Cy Young did, late in the season, and he made good in a way, in fact, that forecasts a career that may rival young. O'Brien is the man that will make Boston play like champions."[25]

If the accolades Buck drew from baseball circles weren't enough, there was also his budding stage career with the new Red Sox Quartet. "When he came forward to sing his solo, the crowd that filled the theater burst into applause that lasted several minutes," the *Brockton Enterprise* recorded after a performance in Biddeford, Maine.

After a brief holdout, Buck signed a $4,200 deal with new Red Sox owner Jimmy McAleer in 1912 and joined his teammates for a song-filled train ride south. Buck nailed a home run over the fence for the rookies to open camp, and despite a series of delays through the rain-filled month of March, he and his teammates slowly ground themselves into shape. "I will bank on the prediction that Joe Wood and Buck O'Brien will pitch remarkable ball this year," the *Boston Globe*'s Tim Murnane predicted as camp drew to a close.[26]

Much to the delight of the growing legion of Red Sox rooters, after launching into the regular season with a convincing sweep of the lowly New York Americans, the 1912 Red Sox quickly found a pleasing formula to keep the peace: victory. Buck opened his season in fine fashion, tossing a 5-2 victory over Russ Ford on April 12.

On April 20 Buck was far from sharp in the first game the team ever played at brand-new Fenway Park. He yielded three runs in a sloppy opening frame. He labored again in the second, then was tagged twice again in the third, thanks in large measure to his own miscue—a bizarre balk that was called when the saliva-soaked ball accidentally slipped from his hand and rolled helplessly off the mound. Jake Stahl pinch-hit for O'Brien when the pitcher's spot came up in the fourth; behind Charley "Sea Lion" Hall, the club rallied late to nail down a 7-6 victory in 11 innings.

O'Brien's rough outing in the home opener was followed by subpar performances over the next several weeks and was a major source of concern. It wasn't until Memorial Day that he finally began to find his groove. He won five of his next six through the end of June, and made several outstanding relief appearances to raise his record to 12-9 by the first week of August. As eyes across baseball grew transfixed on Joe Wood's staggering 34 victories, O'Brien quietly amassed a series of impressive outings in his own right, notching seven wins in eight starts to bring his record to 20-13 by the end of the season.

After seeing the pennant become theirs, the club returned from the road to a massive welcome and parade through the streets of downtown Boston. Hours later, Brockton treated its own hometown hero to a parade of their own.

Joe Wood opened the 1912 World Series against the New York Giants in New York's Polo Grounds with a thrilling Game One victory. Game Two a tie called at dark, and on October 10 Buck took the mound at Fenway Park against Rube Marquard. In another hotly-fought pitchers' duel, Buck threw well but was nicked for single runs in the second and fifth. Boston fought back in the ninth, but when Hick Cady lined out to deep right field leaving Heinie Wagner stranded at second, Marquard walked off the field with a 2-1 victory.

Red Sox victories in the next two games gave them a three games-to-one advantage, and most expected to see a rested Joe Wood on the mound for Boston for a decisive Game Six showdown against Rube Marquard in the Polo Grounds. Under pressure rumored to come from club president McAleer, however, shortly before game time manager Jake Stahl surprised nearly everyone by naming O'Brien as his starter. Perhaps O'Brien was simply not ready to pitch, or perhaps it was just not his day. Whatever the cause, Buck found nothing but trouble when he took the mound against Marquard for a second time. Visibly distracted by John McGraw's incessant chatter from the third-base coaching box, Buck yielded singles to Larry Doyle and Red Murray, who stood at the corners with two out. He nabbed Josh Devore on a groundout and struck out Fred Snodgrass, but against Fred Merkle he struggled. Intent on checking Murray at first, Buck wheeled away from Merkle toward Stahl, raised his arm to throw, then inexplicably held fire. "That was a balk! Balk! Balk!" howled McGraw, charging toward home plate umpire Bill Klem. Klem agreed and signaled for the baserunners to advance. "He's gone now!"[27] McGraw thundered deliriously.

Buck came completely unglued. By the close of the inning he had yielded five runs, prompting Jake Stahl to pull him in favor of Ray Collins. "Why O'Brien was not relieved...after his bad balk is up to Manager Stahl to explain," complained a bewildered Tim Murnane. "It was only too plain to the boys sitting behind the plate that the Boston moistball artist had 'nothing.' "[28] Boston battled through every frame thereafter and Collins pitched brilliantly, but in the end the five-run deficit proved too much to overcome. Boston bowed once again to Marquard, this time 5-2. For Buck it was a humiliating defeat and a major turning point in his career. "In Brockton," recalled O'Brien family friend and lifelong city resident Bob Kane, "they say Buck was never the same pitcher after committing that balk in the World Series."[29]

It seemed as though Buck disintegrated in front of the fans' very eyes. Up three games to two, the team glumly steamed back to Boston for Game Seven as the Giants whooped it up in the rear cars. As Buck sat quietly in the Pullman, teammate Joe Wood sauntered by his seat. "Well, you're a fine joke of a pitcher! Put the game on a platter and handed it to the Giants, didn't you?"[30] In a flash the two were at each other's throats, and reports of dissension in the Red Sox camp once again began leaking into the papers.

The two were pried apart the next day, with Wood wielding a baseball bat after Buck punched him in the face, but in the decisive eighth game on a cold and gray October 16, Buck looked on from the bench as Boston triumphed behind Hugh Bedient and Joe Wood in a 10-inning 3-2 thriller. The players celebrated wildly, after which Buck quietly packed his gear and headed for home.

At the Brockton station at 8:01 that evening, he was met by an estimated 3,000 cheering fans, who roared their approval to welcome him home. "What's the matter, I wonder?"[31] he said to a half-dozen friends, before realizing it was he who was the center of all the hoopla. He was paraded about town—the crowd far exceeding those who had welcomed Presidents Teddy Roosevelt and William Howard Taft a few years earlier—and landed at the Russell club for the remainder of the evening. At the reception, Buck took the stage to thank his family and all those who had supported him over the years:

> *I hardly knew what to think when I saw that great mob at the station to greet me. I know no words that can properly express my feelings. To say simply that I appreciate it all is too feeble. No one seems to care whether I won or lost my game in the world's series. My friends have done themselves proud and the magnitude of this affair is say beyond my every idea. It is something I shall never forget....*[32]

By the spring of 1913, 30-year-old Buck O'Brien was a ballplayer in his prime, and as his scuffles with Joe Wood during the World Series confirmed, his fighting spirit had diminished not a whisker. To his countless fans back in the Bush, that made all the more bitter the rapid demise of what appeared to be a promising big-league career. O'Brien once again stumbled out of the gate in 1913, but unlike years past, he seemed unable to find his rhythm and control. In all fairness, he was not helped by his slumping teammates, and open warfare between Buck and other members of the team (including owner McAleer) soon exploded. Buck struggled to a 4-9 record through June, and on July 2, over the vehement objections of manager Jake Stahl, McAleer sold him to the Chicago White Sox for $5,000.

If Boston had been a bitter experience for Buck that summer, Chicago was worse. In his debut, on July 11, he bowed to lowly

O'Brien tried to stay loose, but he struggled in 1913.

New York, giving up four runs in five innings on eight hits. "Labored is the proper word," lamented the *Chicago Tribune*, "for there wasn't a time in those five rounds when he could take it easy."[33] Five days later, against Philadelphia, he failed to make it out of the third inning. Perhaps he was hurt by a lack of control, but off-the-field battles with Comiskey and several of his new teammates—veteran outfielder Nixey Callahan in particular— did not help matters. On July 29, after just six appearances in the Chicago, Buck was sent packing to Oakland.

Over the next three years, O'Brien bounced from one minor-league club to the next. He remained in the Pacific Coast League for the remainder of 1913, making 16 appearances (111 innings) and posting a 5-5 mark. He returned to Indianapolis in the spring of 1914 and, two solid appearances aside, he struggled persistently. On July 8 manager Jack Hendricks turned him over to the Southern League's Memphis Chicks, where he fared barely better, notching five wins against six losses in

92 innings of work. Spurning rumors that he was planning to make a jump to the Federal League, in late April of 1915 O'Brien joined the International League Providence (Rhode Island) Grays. His tenure there was short and, once again, rocky. On June 24 he was turned over to the Richmond Climbers in the same league, where he appeared in 16 games and finished the season a disappointing 5-6.

Shortly after his rise to fame with the Red Sox, Buck was introduced to Miss Florence Shea, a young telephone operator from what the O'Brien family recalled as "a proper Cambridge family." Florence was nine years younger than her famous suitor, and her family was not the least bit impressed by his fearless reputation and glamorous life on the vaudeville stage. "They were not thrilled about her choice in a husband. Not at all," conceded Rose Moran. "They thought he was just too wild."[34]

Buck continued to pitch locally for the Brockton Colonials that summer, but when manager Eddie Burke relegated him to the bench in late August, he quit and headed to Syracuse in the New York State League to close the year. He appeared three times, winning his first game before being batted around mercilessly in his final two appearances. It marked the end of his professional career.

At the close of the summer O'Brien decided to hang up his professional spikes and stay close to home. He and Florence Shea were married, and within months she was pregnant—time and again. Thomas, Jr. was born in 1917 and John followed two years later. Then came Francis (1921), Killian (1922), Robert (1924), Rachel (1926), and finally Margaret (1927). All the boys, like their father, answered to the moniker Buck.

O'Brien was now a family man, but long after many of the 1912 Boston Red Sox left baseball for other careers, he continued to pitch and sing. Harnessing the notoriety he gained with the Red Sox Quartet, Buck continued performing his old stage numbers in variety shows for the better part of a decade.

And he played ball. He was a "consistent winning pitcher" for the George Dilboy VFW (Somerville, Massachusetts), the Shawmut Council Knights of Columbus, and Walkover Shoes through 1924, and at the age of 43 in 1925, he enjoyed one of the most productive summers of his career, throwing for Walkover and the towns of Amesbury and Rockland. That August he made what may well have been his final appearance, leading the Rockland (Massachusetts) all-stars to a 5-0 victory over Saxony Mills. Fans cheered wildly when it was over, and all looked on with delight as Boston Mayor James Michael Curley presented O'Brien with a gold watch and purse filled to the brim with gold coins. With tears streaming down his face, Buck was so overwhelmed by the gesture that he could barely utter a word of thanks.

When he wasn't making appearances on the mound and on the stage, through the 1920s and early '30s, Buck worked with the Boston Parks Department as a coach and director of baseball clinics. As his father had done with him, he instructed his sons in boxing and encouraged them to play ball, but the pressures of playing in the shadow of their famous father was seemingly too much for them. "It's the same with every ballplayer's son," he later lamented to a Boston sportswriter. "From the time they get on the field, they're the ones that are watched by the fans. If they happened to kick a ball … the wise guy in the stands will say, 'You'll never be as good as your old man.' Well, the result is the boy develops an inferiority complex. It was that way with my boys, and I guess that goes for the rest."[35]

In the summer of 1934 the O'Brien family suffered a major setback when Buck fell from the roof of a two-story building into a nest of barbed wire. He suffered massive injuries to his chest, neck, and face and was rushed to the hospital, where he required several bouts of surgery and hundreds of stitches. He remained in intensive care for several weeks.

To help the O'Brien family, a fundraiser was held in Randolph that September, and papers were quick to remind old-time fans of O'Brien's many contributions over the years. "He was always ready and willing to get out and do his bit for a cause," the *Brockton Enterprise* entreated. "There's scarcely a town where Buck didn't appear at one time or another, as a singer or speaker."[36]

There were doubts that Buck would ever work again and, according to his daughter, he was out of work for nearly two years. But return to work he did, in 1936, taking a job as a custodian with the Charlestown Boys Club. He remained there until the war came to the United States in 1941. Buck did his part, taking a job as a security guard with Lawley's Ship Building Company on Port Norfolk in the Neponset neighborhood of Boston, proud producer of "mighty midget" amphibious landing craft.

When the 59-year-old port closed its doors for good in 1945, Buck returned to his old job at the Charlestown Boys Club, where he remained for the next decade until chronic ulcers sidelined him for good. Never forgetting their old friend, when word spread that 73-year-old Buck was gravely ill at Boston's Carney Hospital after suffering severe hemorrhages and was in dire need of blood, no fewer than two dozen old friends turned up at the Red Cross donation center in Brockton and ponied up a pint apiece on his behalf. That was no surprise to Buck's old teammate, Howling

O'Brien with the White Sox, 1913.

Dan Howley. "I never knew a more generous fellow," he said to an interviewer. "Buck must have loaned at least five grand to his old pals, and I don't suppose he ever got a cent of it back. But that was just the kind of good-hearted guy he was."[37]

Over the next four years Buck continued to battle a variety of ailments, and on the morning of July 25, 1959, his daughter arrived at his Dorchester home to take him to a scheduled medical appointment. Buck never made it. En route to the doctor's office, Buck suffered a massive coronary occlusion and died. He was 77.

Buck O'Brien was gone, but he would not be forgotten. Three years after his death, he was again honored, this time at Fenway Park, where the surviving Speed Boys returned in April 1962 to mark the 50th anniversary of the championship summer of 1912. In acknowledgement of the first man to throw a pitch at Fenway Park, the honor of throwing out the ceremonial first pitch fell to Buck's 9-year-old grandson, Tommy O'Brien. He didn't throw a spitball as his grandfather had, but the young and able athlete did manage a perfect strike that brought cheers from the sellout crowd and an unmistakable sense of pride from O'Brien's family looking on from the grandstand.[38] In appreciation, the club presented Joe and his family with an official Red Sox team jacket, which, like the memory of Buck O'Brien himself, remains a family treasure

The author acknowledges the invaluable help of deceased SABR members Tom Shea, Dick Thompson, and Bob Kane, for their friendship and generous donation of information, insight, and encouragement in the preparation of this article.

Endnotes

1. *Sporting Life*, January 27, 1912, 14.

2. *Brockton Enterprise*, April 18, 1907.

3. Author's telephone conversation with Rosemarie Moran, January 9, 2002.

4. Author's telephone conversation with Rosemarie Moran, November 5, 2002.

5. *Brockton Enterprise*, August 14, 1944.

6. *Boston Post*, September 18, 1912, 8. The Walkovers' batboy in 1905 was Francis Joseph Spellman, a youngster out of nearby Whitman and future cardinal of the Catholic Archdiocese in New York.

7. *Brockton Enterprise*, July 5, 1906.

8. *Brockton Enterprise*, September 4, 1906.

9. *Brockton Enterprise*, April 15, 1907, 6.

10. *Brockton Enterprise*, August 12, 1907, 6.

11. *Brockton Enterprise*, August 21, 1907, 12.

12. *Brockton Enterprise*, August 30, 1907, 12.

13. *Brockton Enterprise*, May 21, 1908.

14. *Brockton Enterprise*, September 16, 1905.

15. Miscellaneous undated clipping courtesy of SABR member Dick Thompson.

16. Miscellaneous news clipping courtesy of SABR member Dick Thompson.

17. *Brockton Enterprise*. October 28, 1909.

18. *Brockton Enterprise*. December 22, 1911.

19. *Rocky Mountain News*, June 9, 1911, 8.

20. Miscellaneous news clipping courtesy of SABR member Bob Kane.

21. *Brockton Enterprise*, September 11, 1911.

22. *Boston Globe*, September 10, 1911, 16.

23. *Brockton Enterprise*, September 11, 1911.

24. *Brockton Enterprise*, September 23, 1911.

25. *Brockton Enterprise*, December 11, 1911.

26. Boston Globe article as quoted in *Brockton Enterprise*, April 1, 1912.

27. Miscellaneous news clipping courtesy of SABR member Bob Kane.

28. *Boston Globe*, October 15, 1912, 6.

29. Author's interview with Bob Kane, February 6, 2002.

30. Mathewson, Christy. "Why we lost three world's championships," *Everybody's Magazine*, October 1914, reprinted in http://www.leaptoad.com/raindelay/matty/whywelost.shtml. Accessed April 7, 2011.

31. Miscellaneous news clipping courtesy of SABR member Bob Kane.

32. *Brockton Enterprise*, October 17, 1912.

33. *Chicago Tribune*, July 12, 1913.

34. Author's telephone conversation with Rosemarie Moran, November 5, 2002.

35. *Boston Traveler*, December 4, 1946.

36. *Brockton Enterprise*, September 27, 1934.

37. Miscellaneous news clipping courtesy of SABR member Dick Thompson.

38. Author's telephone conversation with Rosemarie Moran, January 9, 2002.

Larry Pape
by Marc Z Aaron

G	ERA	W	L	SV	GS	GF	CG	SHO	IP	H	R	ER	BB	SO	HR	HBP	WP	BFP
13	4.99	1	1	1	2	8	1	0	48 2/3	74	36	27	16	17	0	2	1	220

G	AB	R	H	2B	3B	HR	RBI	BB	SO	BA	OBP	SLG	SB	HBP
13	17	1	4	1	0	0	1	2	9	.235	.316	.294	0	0

Laurence Albert Pape played his entire major-league career—three seasons—for the Boston Red Sox. He pitched in a total of 51 games in 1909, 1911, and 1912. Twenty-four of his appearances were as a starting pitcher. He appeared in 13 games with the champion Red Sox of 1912 and did not play in the World Series. The Red Sox' world championship that season was their first of four in a seven-year span. Pape never learned of the fourth, since he died on his 33rd birthday a few weeks before the 1918 World Series began.

Pape was born in Norwood, Ohio, part of the Cincinnati metropolitan area, on July 21, 1885. His mother, Fannie Kidney, was born in Cincinnati, while his father, Albert H. Pape, was an immigrant from Berlin, Germany. Both parents outlived their son. Census records for 1900 show that Albert was a railway freight agent. The couple had four children at home at the time, Larry and his three sisters. The 1910 Census lists Larry's profession as a draftsman in a machine shop.

Pape, a right-handed pitcher about 6 feet tall and weighing 170 pounds, was described by Ben Mulford Jr. of *Sporting Life* as "a clean-cut fellow, well built, of splendid habits and good common sense.…He is long on pluck and ambition, possesses the requisite brains and it is 'up to his arm.' "[1]

Pape's minor-league career started in 1908 with the Milwaukee Brewers of the Class A American Association. He was 22 years old and had taken a position in Milwaukee when the electrical department of the Allis-Chalmers plant opened shop there, and the Milwaukee organization noticed his pitching for a local semipro club. In his first year of pro ball, he recorded a 13-5 record for the Brewers, giving up just 51 runs in 172 innings. His talent was on the mound; as a batter, he was certainly substandard, hitting just .054 (three hits in 56 at-bats).

Pitching for the Brewers brought Pape to the attention of some of the Red Sox, who were looking for pitching help during the 1909 season. The June 28 *Boston Globe* reported that manager Fred Lake had signed "pitcher Herman [sic] Pape, the big right-hander of the Milwaukee club." Lake said he had observed Pape several times during a scouting trip in 1908 and had been impressed. He wanted to do a deal on the spot, but was told the St. Louis Cardinals had signed Pape. Lake learned otherwise in 1909 (and presumably learned Larry's first name in due course) and did a deal with the Brewers' owner by telegraph. Rookie pitcher Joe Wood—soon to become known as Smoky Joe—"speaks in glowing terms" of Pape's ability. The Red Sox reportedly paid $2,500 for "Herman."

Pape's first start for the Red Sox came on July 6, 1909, against Washington, a crisp 1 hour 14 minute nine-inning game, the second of a doubleheader in Boston. He set down 15 Senators in a row and struck out seven, walked one, scattered

Pape was 1-1 in 48 2/3 innings of work in 1912.

four hits, and shut out the Senators, 2-0. He singled (off right-hander Bob Groom) in three at-bats and the report in the *Globe* commented that he "handled himself like a veteran and fielded finely as well."

When Pape did well for the Red Sox, Milwaukee was asked why it had let him go so easily. Owner McCluskey said Pape had shown up that year out of shape with a lame shoulder—but glossed over the 13-5 start.

Pape started three games in 1909 and relieved in eight more, but none was stranger than the game of September 9 in Washington. In that game, Pape threw 10 innings and won the game on a hit by one of the Senators! Pape, with his "wide, sweeping curve," would have had a shutout but for his own error. As the 1-1 game went into extra innings, Doc Gessler, who had been traded to the Senators before the game began but was allowed to play for

Boston, singled in the winning run. By season's end, Pape had pitched 58 innings in his 11 games, given up 46 hits, and had a 2-0 record with a 2.01 ERA.

After the season, Pape took part in an exhibition game in Portland, Maine, playing against an all-Maine team, with the Red Sox coming out on top, 3-0.

The Red Sox trained in Hot Springs, Arkansas, before the 1910 season. Pape joined the team train as it passed through Cincinnati on March 5. He didn't make the big-league team, though; a year later, the *Washington Post* said he "wasn't seasoned enough to hold his place in fast company."[2] The Red Sox kept him close at hand, however; he pitched for the Brockton Shoemakers of the Class B New England League, winning 13 of his first 17 games by mid-July; he finished with a 19-9 record. Late in the season, the Red Sox moved him up to the Sacramento Sacts of the Pacific Coast League, with whom the Red Sox had close ties, and where the season didn't end until November.[3] Pape's team-leading ERA of 1.44 in 87 innings pitched for Sacramento was a factor in Boston's decision to bring him back to Boston for the 1911 season.

Red Sox owner John I. Taylor announced early in January that Pape would be a starter on the 1911 team. The *Globe*'s Tim Murnane wrote that Taylor had always been "sweet" on Pape, "who had a knack of pulling out of tight places and always keeping his head." Why hadn't manager Patsy Donovan been higher on Pape? The "only fault" was "an apparent lack of ambition."[4] For spring training 1911, the Red Sox were based in Redondo Beach, California, but never played a game there—crossing the country twice, playing 64 exhibition games in all, after splitting into two teams (a northern contingent and a southern one) which took separate routes back east, playing along the way in states like Nebraska and Utah where they would never play again. Pape was part of the southern team.

His "year in the tall grass" seemed to help him, wrote the *Post* as he beat Washington, 6-3, with a six-hitter on May 3. Pape was a regular part of the Red Sox rotation pitching on a staff with Joe Wood, Eddie Cicotte, Ray Collins, and Ed Karger. He pitched several strong games, acquitting himself well throughout the season, finishing 10-8 with a 2.45 ERA (10th in the league), though walking more (63) than he struck out (49). The year 1911 was his best of his three major-league seasons; he appeared in 27 games, 19 as a starter.

The Red Sox returned to Hot Springs in March 1912, and Pape once again joined the train as it passed through Cincinnati. He started the season with the Red Sox, and was on hand for the formal dedication of Fenway Park on May 17—a day he was probably glad to forget, since his ninth-inning error cost the Red Sox the game.

Pape appeared in only 13 games that season, starting just twice, and saw no action in the World Series. Red Sox manager Jake Stahl may have sensed the same thing as the sports columnist Hugh Fullerton, who wrote just before the World Series: "Charlie Hall is a good, effective pitcher and so is Pape, but I believe the Giants would hit either one of them."[5] Pape was among the world champions honored at the celebrations after the Series. For the season, Pape was 1-1 with a 4.99 ERA in 48 innings.

There were some postseason rumors that Cincinnati manager Joe Tinker was going to acquire Pape for the Reds, and the Red Sox were said to be willing, but a confusing period ensued, and Pape played no ball in 1913. On January 12, a number of newspapers reported that manager Stahl had been visiting Los Angeles and consummated a straight sale of Pape's contract to the Pacific Coast League's Vernon (California) Tigers. Two days later, the *Boston Globe* reported that Red Sox president James McAleer had sold Pape unconditionally to Buffalo of the International League for cash. Six months later, Stahl was gone—fired by McAleer. Pape probably had little to do with that, but there were indications that the Red Sox were in some form of internal disarray. A story by James O'Leary in the *Globe* said the reason Pape hadn't worked much in 1912 was that Stahl didn't have much confidence in him; the article mentioned the error he'd made in the May 17 game. Perhaps a little tension between McAleer and Stahl was reflected in McAleer's remark to O'Leary: "Many think that Pape is a good pitcher, but if the manager wouldn't work him he could be of no use to the Boston club, so I disposed of him. The boy will now have a chance to get plenty of work and show what he can do."[6]

Less than a week later, Joe S. Jackson of the *Washington Post* wrote a column headlined, "Pape Case Shows Injustice of Present Baseball Rule."[7] Jackson termed Pape's sale to Buffalo an "abuse," saying that Boston had put him on waivers and Cincinnati asked for him. The Sox then pulled him back off waivers and sold him to the Buffalo Bisons, where he would earn less than the Reds would have paid him and less than the reported $4,000 the Red Sox paid him in 1912.

Jackson wrote that Pape might have been destined for a turn in the minor leagues, "as he has shown nothing this past season." The writer apparently had a sense that there was something else at play, however, and termed it a "peculiar 1912 season," given how little Pape had been used. While all this was going on, Pape was trying to settle down and start a family. He married his childhood sweetheart, Edith M. Smith, on January 29, 1913, at the home of the bride in East Norwood.

As it happened, Pape didn't play at all in 1913. He worked out during the spring with Buffalo, but when informed in mid-May that Buffalo was going to farm him out to a Canadian team, he took a stand. He said he would not sign with any league lower than the International and asked instead for his unconditional release. When that was refused him, he announced that he was quitting baseball. He returned to his home in Pittsburgh, to which he and his wife had moved, to continue his former vocation as an electrician.

Boston Post cartoon, April 14, 1912.

At some point, he was sold to the Portland Beavers for a reported $2,000. The *Los Angeles Times'* report in its November 24, 1913, edition made the sale appear to have just occurred, but Harry A. Williams' column in the paper's May 7, 1914, edition said that the sale had occurred during the 1913 season after it was clear that he would not report to the Canadian team. Williams wrote, "Pape had trouble with [Buffalo's manager Bill] Clymer, and refused to continue with Buffalo. He was sold to Portland, but failed to show up, and declined to give any reasons for not coming." After sitting out the full season, he agreed in November to play for the Beavers in 1914—but he took his time turning up, the "high-class twirler" arriving in Palo Alto on May 8.[8]

Pape pitched 36 innings for Portland in nine games, his first win coming on July 17, a six-hitter against the Los Angeles Angels. Once again he was not getting much work, "owing to a bad arm" (according to the August 31, 1914, *Los Angeles Times*). The *Times* informed readers that Pape had been released back to Buffalo the previous day. He finished 3-2 with a 3.75 ERA for Portland.

But Buffalo was not interested and told Portland to give Pape his release. He returned to his work as an engineering draftsman for Westinghouse Electric. There was a wrangle afterward, when Pape put in a salary claim with baseball's National Commission for $660 against Portland.

The contretemps had its origin on April 20, 1914, when Pape, then living with his wife in Wilkensburg, Pennsylvania, near Pittsburgh, received a wire from Portland asking him if there was any way he could be persuaded to join the team. Pape replied that he had not played ball for a year, was not in the best of shape, had recently married, and had quit the game and taken up a good position in the industrial world. He told Portland that because of the uncertainties of the baseball business he would need some substantial guarantee in order for him and his wife to leave their life in Wilkensburg behind. Pape followed up with a wire stating that if he received a guarantee of $2,000 for the balance of the season, plus transportation for both him and his wife, he would accept a Portland offer. Pape put special emphasis in the telegram on the resulting business and domestic inconvenience he would incur in order to go to Portland. Pape assured the club it would get its money's worth. He took this guarantee as the basis for his claim for $660. However, he did not perform as expected and was therefore released and compensated only for his time on the roster, and was denied the final $660 he felt was due him. But he had not obtained any guarantee from Portland in writing, and lost his case before the National Commission.

Pape's career record as a major-league pitcher was 13-9 with an ERA of 2.80. He had three saves and pitched two shutouts. Pape surrendered only three home runs, all in 1911, and only one of those left the park on the fly. The first homer hit off him was an inside-the-park home run off the bat of Senators pitcher Walter Johnson at the Huntington Avenue Grounds on July 5. The second was a bounce home run by Bris Lord on September 2. Eleven days later, on September 13, Pape gave up his only over-the-fence home run, to the Senators' Clyde Milan at Washington's Griffith Stadium. All three home runs came with the bases empty.

Larry Pape died in Swissvale, Pennsylvania, a Pittsburgh suburb, on July 21, 1918, his 33rd birthday. The cause was reportedly complications from an earlier baseball injury suffered

Pape at Comiskey Park for a game against the White Sox in 1912.

when a batted ball hit him in the stomach. According to his death certificate, the cause of death was glandular cancer that had its onset about two years earlier.

He left behind his wife, Edith, an honors graduate of the University of Cincinnati, who taught school for 37 years and sent both of their children, Laurence and Joy, to college during the Depression. Young Laurence went on to teach at Fresno State in California. Edith lived into her 90s. Larry Pape is buried at Spring Grove Cemetery in Cincinnati.

References:

Larry Pape player file in the National Baseball Hall of Fame.

www.baseball-reference.com

Sporting Life

Baseball Magazine

Boston Globe

Chicago Daily Tribune

Christian Science Monitor

Los Angeles Times

New York Times

Washington Post

Rex Hamann and the American Association Almanac

http://sonsofsamhorn.net

http://en.wikipedia.org

http://www.sabr.org

Scott Rosner and Kenneth L. Shropshire, *The Business of Sports*, found on http://books.google.com/

Endnotes

1. *Sporting Life*, March 4, 1911

2. *Washington Post*, May 4, 1911

3. See Joe S. Jackson's column in the January 11, 1911, *Washington Post*.

4. *Boston Globe*, January 5, 1911

5. *Chicago Daily Tribune*, October 6, 1912

6. *Boston Globe*, January 15, 1913

7. *Washington Post*, January 21, 1913

8. *Los Angeles Times*, May 10, 1914

Douglass Smith
by Michael Foster

G	ERA	W	L	SV	GS	GF	CG	SHO	IP	H	R	ER	BB	SO	HR	HBP	WP	BFP
1	3.00	0	0	0	0	1	0	0	3	4	1	1	0	1	0	0	0	11

G	AB	R	H	2B	3B	HR	RBI	BB	SO	BA	OBP	SLG	SB	HBP
1	0	0	0	0	0	0	0	0	0	--	--	--	0	0

The weather in Boston had been nothing short of miserable all week. It had arrived just in time to stifle weekend Independence Day festivities, and the heat and humidity enveloped the Hub like a blanket and sent citizens by the thousands clamoring for area beaches in search of relief. At nearby Camp Bedford, cavalry horses at the 1st Squadron Army camp became so unruly that all work was suspended at noon, and that morning, July 10, the *Boston Globe* reported the week's fifth heat-related death. With nowhere else to go and no relief in sight, hundreds spent the evenings camped out on the Boston Common, or headed for rooftops in a vain attempt to secure a decent night's sleep. Morning forecasts predicted a break in temperatures and scattered thunderstorms that afternoon, but by 9:00 AM, temperatures once again surged toward 90 degrees under a blazing sun. In Boston it just didn't get any worse than this.

Two weeks had passed since 20-year-old Douglass Smith, a hard-throwing left-hander, and the pride of Turners Falls High School, boarded a Boston & Maine train and made the 85-mile trek east from his home in central Massachusetts to Boston. Blond with a winning smile, he was hardly physically imposing, standing only 5-feet-8 and weighing in at 168 pounds. Indeed, not unlike Boston Red Sox ace Joe Wood, who had arrived in the city a baby-faced rookie three years earlier, Smith looked barely more than a boy. In both cases, however, appearances were deceiving. For beneath their prep-school veneer, both men were as tough as nails and would stand toe-to-toe with anyone. Both had pitched against grown men from the time they were 14. Both had traveled widely and pitched for a variety of town and semipro clubs. And, most significantly, both possessed cannon-like arms.

When Red Sox owner Jimmy McAleer heard that Smith had arrived in town and was over at the South End Grounds watching Brooklyn whitewash the Braves, he grabbed the contract the club had prepared for Smith and raced over to the ballpark to secure a signature. Clearly amused by the sight of McAleer at a National League game, when it reported the signing the next day the *Boston Globe* mused that it was "probably the first time in league history an American League president has gone to a National League ball park to secure a player's signature to a contract."[1] After what he had gone through to bring the young firebrand to Boston, however, McAleer was not about to take any chances.

The league-leading Red Sox returned to Boston three days later, and Smith looked on from the bench as the team toyed with the New York Highlanders, scooping up five victories in six tries. On July 2 he accompanied the team to Philadelphia. He looked on as Boston dismantled baseball's world champions four times in six heavily attended contests over the holiday weekend, and after an 11-5 Red Sox rout on July 6, the team took the train back to Boston. Despite the abysmal temperatures that greeted

Smith was the only one of the two who played with the Sox, and he only saw action in one game. *Boston Globe*

them on their arrival, everyone was delighted to be back on home territory for a 17-game homestand.

St. Louis was first on tap. The hometown Red Sox were as sizzling hot as the temperatures, and with back-to-back wins over the Browns on July 8 and 9, they elevated their record to 53-24 and extended their lead over Washington to 6½ games. Sensing a sweep and his club's 11th straight victory over their hapless guests, manager Jake Stahl tabbed Hugh Bedient to take the mound in the series finale against 38-year old veteran Jack Powell.

By the time Bedient and the Red Sox took the field that Wednesday afternoon, the temperature at newly opened Fenway Park topped 97 degrees—a high mark for the week. Bedient got leadoff hitter Burt Shotton on a pop foul to catcher Bill Carrigan to open the contest, but things went downhill from there. A three-run home run by Frank LaPorte gave St. Louis the lead and brought an abrupt end to Bedient's day. Larry Pape fared no better in relief, coughing up a run in the third and a second in the fourth before turning the ball over to Ray Collins. All the while, the 16-year veteran Powell handled the mighty Red Sox lineup with apparent ease, yielding three hits and a run to open the contest but settling in and stifling Red Sox bats through the next four frames. The Red Sox got to him for a run in the sixth, but by then the Browns had already pounced on the southpaw Collins for three more tallies to bring the score to a lopsided 8-2.

- 142 -

In the seventh inning Doug Smith took the mound, facing veteran infielder Frank LaPorte. The youngster was a bundle of nerves, but he kept his cool and held his own. He cruised through the seventh and eighth, scattering three hits without yielding a run, but in the top of the ninth he was lit up for a triple by first baseman George Stovall, who scored easily when Del Pratt lofted a sacrifice fly to deep left field. Hoping to start something in the home half of the ninth, Stahl called a pinch-hitter off the bench, but in the end that move merely deprived young Smith of the opportunity to show what he could do in the batter's box. In the end, Boston bowed to St. Louis for the first time of the summer, 9-2.

It wasn't a perfect outing for Doug Smith, but eyewitnesses were impressed nonetheless and all agreed that his future looked promising. "Young Smith did very commendable work while he was on the hill-top," lauded *Boston Herald* sportswriter R.E. McMillan. "He had fine speed, a sharp breaking curve and good control. After a year or two of seasoning he will be heard from."[2] The *Globe's* Mel Webb agreed, stating that Smith's "left-hand service looked mighty good. Smith was a little nervous as well he might be in his first day in fast company, but the high school boy came over the shoulder nicely on his delivery and seemed to have a lot more on the ball than mere speed."[3]

Little did anyone looking on that sultry afternoon at Fenway Park imagine that the day would mark the beginning—and the end—of Doug Smith's big-league career.

The sixth child of Judah and Elizabeth Moore Smith, Douglass Weldon Smith was born at the family homestead on River Street in Millers Falls, a section of the town of Montague, Massachusetts, on May 25, 1892. Having immigrated to the United States from Aberdeen, Scotland, in 1879, Doug's mother was a newcomer to the country, but Judah Smith's family had been in New England for generations, the family roots grounded in the rolling hills along the section of the state that bordered Rhode Island and Connecticut.

Judah and Elizabeth were married in 1881 and soon thereafter settled in Millers Falls, just east of Greenfield. The family had a small farm on which they raised cows, horses, swine, and chickens, and Judah was a hostler by trade and a teamster for the Millers Falls Tool Company. The company had been founded after the Civil War and quickly became renowned for producing top-quality hand tools ranging from drills to miter boxes. Judah drove a delivery wagon for the company for most of his long life. By the 1890s he was a union leader, one of the most recognizable figures in town.

Judah and Elizabeth had seven children between 1881 and 1896: William, Charles, Clinton, Perry (Butch), Ida, Doug, and Alan (Abe). All the children attended the Millers Falls Grammar School, where they studied reading, arithmetic, drawing, history, geography, and physiology. In grades eight and nine, they also took non-academic subjects, such as sewing and seat-caning, and before Doug left the school in June 1910 to enter Turners Falls High School (in another section of town), his final assignment was to sand and refinish his school desk. If they weren't top-tier students, the Smith boys were strapping farm lads and gifted athletes, each imbued with speed, agility, and a natural-born passion for the national game.

Each Sunday Elizabeth herded her boys up to the village center to the First Congregational Church. Sometimes they went on foot, but more often they were delivered to services by horse-drawn wagon or sleigh, with Judah perched high up in the driver's seat. Elizabeth was a strict Scottish Calvinist, and she ruled her household full of men with an iron will, tolerating no nonsense from the six-footers in spite of her small size of barely 5-feet-1. The Sabbath was rigidly reserved for church, Bible reading in the kitchen, and a frugal meal. Any other activities she forbade— well, except for one. She had a soft spot in her heart for baseball, and her two youngest boys, Doug and Abe, both knew it. So each Sunday afternoon, beginning in early April and not ending until the snow flew, out from behind the barn the peace and quiet of the Lord's Day was punctuated by the periodic "pop, pop, pop" of a baseball smacking into a catcher's mitt, as young Doug fired one fastball after another to Abe, crouched over a plate 60 feet away.

The Smith boys played neighborhood ball at the makeshift field just up the street from home, and from there they graduated to the Millers Falls town diamond. By their teens, the boys made up nearly half of the Millers Falls starting lineup: Butch at second and Clint at third made a formidable left side of the infield, and Abe provided young Doug a steady hand behind the plate. Eldest brother Billy served as the club manager. "Any batter who tried to bunt against us was an automatic out," Doug later boasted. "Clint and I would rush in. Abe would rush out and Butch would cover first base. It was almost impossible to squeeze a bunt past us."[4]

Doug's curveball had a bedeviling dip, and, every so often he'd mix in a spitter or other trick pitch for good measure. But it was his blazing fastball that so mesmerized his growing trail of strikeout victims. "He was wild as a hawk," a Holyoke sportswriter later recounted. "He could blind the batters with his fast one, but he always had difficulty finding the plate."[5] By the age of 16, Doug was the undisputed ace of the Turners Falls nine, regularly striking out 15 or more batters in an afternoon. Under the watchful eyes of Coach French, his club squared off against foes from Holyoke to Williston to Orange to Athol. High-school baseball was big business in Franklin County, and when Doug Smith took the mound for Turners Falls, shopkeepers closed their doors and joined the thousands of baseball fans who turned out to cheer their team on. "We had tremendous crowds each time we played in Turners Falls," Doug recalled a half-century later. "The permanent grandstands were always filled with people who took special trolley excursions from Greenfield and Millers Falls."[6]

For Turners Falls there was no greater a rival than big brother Greenfield, the adjacent town; conversely, by the spring of 1910 there wasn't a schoolboy baseball fan in Greenfield who hadn't heard of Doug Smith. The competition between the two communities was beyond compare, and in a move that a century henceforth would have easily disqualified any school from competitive sports, on March 4, a representative of the Greenfield High School Athletic Association, Frank J. Manning, went so far as to extend Doug a personal invitation to leave the Turners Falls Indians and pitch for Greenfield. "Dear Smith," Manning wrote:

> *I don't know you very well, and you don't know me either. But just the same I'm going to give you a piece of advice that you can take or leave. I have heard that you*

were thinking of coming over here to school, and I would like to show you the advantages of such a school. I'm telling you, Smith, you're making a big mistake if you stick to a jerk team like [Turners Falls]. It's only going to hold you back.

Leave your studies be the last of your troubles because we can fix that here, too.[7]

Doug had no intention of pitching for any high school other than Turners Falls, and he laughed off the invitation and tossed the letter into his growing collection of clippings, box scores, photos, and other memorabilia that he kept with meticulous care.

Of course, just because he would not pitch for Greenfield it did not mean he would turn down other opportunities, particularly when money was involved. By the spring of his junior year, Doug was regularly crossing the border into New York state to pitch semipro and community ball, all the while pitching for Turners Falls High. "Team managers paid by the game, and Smith, always in demand because of his ability, pitched frequently," *Greenfield Recorder* writer Neil Perry later recorded. "In high school he often hurled two games during the week, took a train to a small town in upper New York state for a Saturday game with a touring semipro team and returned to Turners Falls Sunday at 3 a.m. and would be on deck that afternoon to pitch."[8] Occasionally those semipro contests turned rough—Doug vividly recalled having to fight his way out of Brattleboro, Vermont, more than once—but at $75 a game, it was undoubtedly worth it. "I made real money in semipro baseball," he admitted. "That was a lot more than players in Class C and D ball make today."[9]

As it happened, Doug's forays into New York state proved instrumental to his big-league future. During the summer of 1911 he accepted an invitation to pitch for semipro Cohoes (near Albany) in a series of exhibition contests against locally born New York State League all-stars. Doug was beaten once during that four-game stretch, but he mowed down the all-stars in the remaining contests, scattering nine hits and striking out an eyebrow-raising 50 batters in a three-day stretch. It easily shattered the standing record and caught the eye of several big league scouts.

Catching wind of Doug's performance in Cohoes, Pat Moran, a catcher for the Philadelphia Phillies and a Fitchburg native, was among the first big leaguers to approach him. Moran was followed by the Boston Braves, who in February of 1912 sent scout Jack Dorsher to Turners Falls to watch Doug burn over a few pitches in the high-school gym. Eldest brother William handled all negotiations, and during the spring of Doug's senior year he accepted an offer on Doug's behalf from Moran and the Phillies. William cemented the deal by signing a statement on the back of a National League contract, promising Doug's services to Philadelphia.

Elected captain of the club in his senior year, Doug was focused far more on his final season with Turners Falls than with his future in the big leagues. Behind his fastball, the Indians whipped nearly every opponent they faced that spring, jumping out to first place early in the season with a 5-0 victory over Orange in front of 1,200 raucous hometown fans and never looking back. In the fifth game of the year, against Athol, Doug tossed a no-hitter and struck out 20, and while his team was defeated four times that season, it easily outdistanced its Franklin County League opponents to earn a trip to the Connecticut Valley High School championship.

Once again Doug and the Turners Falls Indians would face Athol. After they split the first two contests of the series, there was no question who would take the mound for Turners Falls in the series finale in Athol. Doug pitched well that day, but Athol nicked him for two runs through eight innings. Behind solid pitching, Athol nursed a 2-1 lead into the top of the ninth, when suddenly Turners Falls began to rally. "There were two men out," Doug recalled in an interview in the spring of 1913. "One of our men, Morgan, was on third and I was on first. Thomas hit high a line drive that should certainly have been good for two bases and would have given us the lead, and in all probability the game."[10] But it was not meant to be. In a brilliant defensive play, Athol's shortstop lunged to his right and snagged the drive with his bare hand, giving Athol the game and the championship. The season, and Doug's high-school baseball career, came to a heartbreaking end.

A few days after the defeat, Doug received his diploma from Turners Falls High School and set his sights on the majors. Phillies president Horace Fogel rightly thought he had the talented youngster already in the bag, but in early June he learned that Doug now had other ideas in mind.

A few weeks earlier, former Red Sox manager-turned-scout Patsy Donovan arrived in Millers Falls to watch Doug pitch for the town team. Doug had a solid afternoon, striking out 18 opponents and

Wearing his letter jersey from Turners Fall, Smith is on the fence with a couple of friends.

leaving Donovan thoroughly impressed. After the game Patsy approached Doug and persuaded him to abandon Philadelphia and come to Boston. Attracted to the idea of joining a strong club nearer to home, Doug readily agreed.

Fogel wasted no time in contesting the legality of Boston's claims on Smith, and the Phillies appealed to the National Commission to nullify his contract. A week after Smith's debut against St. Louis, the commission handed down its decision, ruling in favor of the Red Sox. "[A] statement of Smith's brother and guardian, written on the back of an unsigned contract, pledging his brother's services to Philadelphia… constituted no contract," the *Globe* reported the following day.[11] The matter was closed.

Doug had barely stepped off the mound at Fenway on that hot July afternoon when he learned he was to be shipped to the Lowell (Massachusetts) Grays of the Class B New England League. It was a logical move for both parties. Boston's prolific pitching lineup already included veteran left-hander Ray Collins, and keeping a rookie left-hander on the bench in the midst of a serious run for the American League pennant made little sense. Had they won their case in front of the National Commission, perhaps the struggling Phillies might have put Doug to work on a regular basis, but in Boston there was but no question that he would be farmed out to the minors for further grooming.

The only provision Smith had inserted into his Red Sox contract stated, "Player not to be sent to any minor league club without his consent."[12] Undoubtedly believing he would be back in Boston to pitch at some point, Smith had no trouble with the move, and on July 16, six days after his debut with the Red Sox, he made his first appearance as a member of the Grays against New England League rival Lawrence. Smith gave up five hits, while striking out four and yielding two runs before being pulled in the fifth with the score tied, 2-2. He hit a batter and was charged with a balk. In October he was back at Fenway Park (though this time not in uniform) to watch the thrilling eighth and deciding game of the 1912 World Series against Christy Mathewson and the New York Giants. "I am sure," Smith later recalled, "that the greatest play I ever saw on the ball field was the catch that Harry Hooper made off Doyle…."[13]

After a long, cold winter back in Millers Falls, Smith prepared for a return to Lowell in the spring of 1913. In February he was featured as a guest columnist in the *Boston Globe*, in which he (or, more likely, a *Globe* sportswriter) relayed "unusual feats on the baseball field" for winter-weary fans.[14] Six weeks later, he headed off to spring training.

Smith made his first 1913 appearance for the Grays in the second game of the season, on May 1, allowing two hits, with three strikeouts, a walk and a hit batsman in the final three innings of a 12-4 defeat to Portland. Six days later he was nicked for two hits but no runs in one inning of relief work in an 8-7, 11-inning victory over Fall River. On May 13 he was shelled over 5 innings, giving up seven runs on nine hits, two walks and a hit batsman in a 12-5 loss to Lowell. Two weeks later, on May 30, 1913, he gave up a walk and a hit but recorded no outs in the four-run Lawrence sixth.

Suddenly, the name D Smith disappeared from the Lowell Grays roster.

Diehard New England League fans in Lowell doubtless knew

Smith honing his pitching skills away from the park.

of Doug's sudden departure from the club, but official word did not appear in the sports pages for nearly two weeks. In a brief note in its sporting briefs on June 17, the *Brockton Times* revealed that, against his doctor's advice, Doug had quit the Grays and joined the Eastern Association Springfield (Massachusetts) Ponies. "Smith…quit Lowell," the paper chided, "claiming that his physician ordered him to do so on account of a weak heart."[15]

"A weak heart." That was the official explanation. But like so much of what was passed off as fact in the local sports columns during the era—such as sportswriters' routine use of "malaria" to explain the sudden absence of players who had contracted any number of sexually transmitted diseases—the *Times's* claims that Smith quit Lowell voluntarily and that he suffered from a tragic physical ailment were pure myth. The truth behind his departure from Lowell, as it turns out, may have had nothing to do with his health and everything to do with his family.

Perhaps the enemies Smith had made as a hard-nosed, hard-throwing pitcher in Turners Falls had finally found a way to get revenge, and bring his major-league career to a screeching halt. Grandnephew Tom Gessing said Doug just felt he could make better money in "free-lance" pitching around New England rather than for a Red Sox farm team, but there's another, more sinister story rooted in small-town oral history that could still be heard almost a century later. In 1913 someone in Franklin County whom Smith later recalled as "a fellow by the name of Kufleski" penned a letter to the Red Sox alleging that Smith had no right to play in Boston, Lowell, or any other big-league city for that matter. The letter had nothing to do with baseball skills but everything to do with racial prejudice. The writer of the letter alleged that Douglass Weldon Smith had "black blood."

As Smith later told the story, shortly after receiving the information, the Red Sox dispatched someone to Franklin County to look into the matter. If the story is true, what they uncovered in Millers Falls that day was a genealogical puzzle that, a century later, remained something of a mystery.

It was quietly well-known around the village in the 1880s that Doug's father, Judah, was different. He was an imposing figure, well over 6 feet tall, and well respected in town. Family historians have determined that he descended from southern Connecticut river Indian tribes, probably a mix of Narragansett/Nehantic and/or Pequot. Judah was raised by his Indian mother, Betsy Strong, and his stepfather, Charles Scott I, a dark-skinned man of Pequot and African lineage. Tribal history shows that these tribes were clearly tri-racial (Indian/white/black). Certainly the letter writer and later the Red Sox investigator were able to locate Smith's extended family, many of whom were dark-skinned, and subsequently raised the color barrier issue. That might well have been more than enough for the Red Sox to put an end to Doug's professional career.

The mystery remains to this day, but with the rapid advances made in genealogical research, the descendants of Betsy Strong hope to uncover the truth, and share the findings in a book. Whether the Red Sox did any diligent research in Franklin County is open to question. Family members in modern times said the club never actually spoke directly to Judah Smith or to his family, and that the decision to terminate Smith's contract was based purely on second-hand information picked up in Millers Falls. "Judah was very close to his half-sister Sarah Sharpe Barnes, who lived in nearby Greenfield, and who was very dark-skinned," said David Brule, Smith's grandnephew. "When Doug separated from the Red Sox, the persistent story around town, and even now more than 90 years later was that Doug was part black, and therefore he was let go."

The family story of Smith's departure may be just that: family lore. He had struggled that spring with Lowell, and by early June more than one writer wrote that he was "uncertain" with the Class B club. "Duggy Smith has got the build and the heaving ability of a good mound artist but there seems to be something lacking in his work," the *Lowell Sun* wrote. If he shut his eyes he could come as close to the plate as he did last Friday [May 30, 1913]."[16] Perhaps indeed there was no conspiracy, and Smith was let go not because of a question of race but rather of ability.

If he was bitter over being dumped by Lowell, Smith wasted no time in moving on. After a brief stay with the Springfield Ponies during the summer of 1913, he jumped to Springfield's Eastern Association rivals, the Meriden (Connecticut) Hopes, where he went 8-8 in 18 games. He joined Eastern League New Britain (Connecticut) in 1914, dropping 20 of his 26 decisions, but his brilliant performance over Independence Day weekend against Hartford (a four-hit, 4-1 complete game) remained one of his most cherished memories of "those wonderful years" of baseball. "Why, in my day if a player got hurt he just squirted a little tobacco juice on the wound and kept on playing," he scoffed decades later. "Now a fellow will pull a muscle, get an x-ray, and get into whirlpool baths for a week and stay out of the lineup for three weeks."[17]

The following summer, Doug signed on with the Colonial League Springfield Tips, where he worked 19 games, pitched 139 innings and notched a 9-6 mark. Still filled with barrels of speed but periodic bouts of lost control, he walked 100 batters, and his woeful .058 batting average marked a low point for his career at the plate. When he wasn't obliged to throw for Springfield, he could usually be found on the mound for Millers Falls or hurling semipro ball for Billy Lubby's Twin State League team at the Park Villa Driving Park in Turners Falls.

Smith had made good money over the years throwing against a variety of Class B New York State League clubs. In the spring of 1916 he signed on with a club in the league, the Syracuse Stars. He remained with the club long enough to amass an 8-8 mark in 16 appearances, and hit .324. He had to have been pleased to see his batting eye return that summer, but without question the highlight of the season (and quite possibly, his career) came on a warm afternoon in July, when Syracuse played an exhibition contest against Smith's former teammates and baseball's reigning world champions: the Boston Red Sox.

It was not the first time a big-league club traveling through New York state had stopped to take on the Stars. Smith had been slated to take the mound in a heavily publicized exhibition contest with Mordecai "Three Finger" Brown and the Chicago Cubs earlier, on June 11, but the game was called when heavy rain swept across the region. On July 23 a second opportunity presented itself when the Red Sox, passing through en route to Cleveland, agreed to stop in Syracuse and play an exhibition contest. Syracuse tapped Smith to take the mound.

Trailing the New York Yankees by 1½ games with a 19-game Western swing looming, Red Sox manager Bill Carrigan was in no mood to play his regular lineup. Still, veterans Hooper, Janvrin, Henriksen, Gardner, and Cady got into action. Babe Ruth was rested and ready to take the mound, but Carrigan opted to sit Ruth for the meaningless contest in favor of Ernie Shore.

Syracuse fans anticipated a great game, and they weren't disappointed. Smith "twirled a magnificent game," as did Shore. The first score didn't come until Boston pushed a run across in the fifth. When Carrigan pulled Shore in favor of 23-year-old Sam Jones, it was all Syracuse from there on. The Stars pounced on Jones for four runs in the fifth, and that proved the difference. Smith ran into trouble in the sixth, allowing two men on with no one out, but he worked his way out of the jam and cruised to a 5-2 victory. "Douglass Smith twirled baffling ball throughout," the *Post-Standard* lauded the next day. "The Syracuse left-hander… fairly covered himself with glory."[18]

In the numerous interviews he gave in years to come, Smith said nothing of that memorable day in 1916 when he tamed the world champions. If nothing else, it was a rare opportunity to take some measure of revenge on a franchise that had dumped him so unceremoniously three years earlier, and in the years to come he and his brother Abe did not mince words when it came to the Red Sox. "Our grandfather, Abe, hated the Red Sox," recalled another of Doug's grandnephews, Tom Gessing. "He was a Yankee fan, which is a very unusual for people from Massachusetts." David Brule said, "Our uncle always said that both Doug and Abe didn't want anything to do with the Red Sox. There were some bad feelings."[19]

Revenge was sweet indeed, and for one day at least, Doug Smith was the king of Syracuse. That too, however, would pass. Three weeks later, the Stars released him, ironically to make room for his former Boston teammate Buck O'Brien, who himself

Smith visiting with his family, during his time in the Army.

had been dumped by the Red Sox nearly a year after they had disposed of Smith.

After a fall of local and semipro ball, in 1917 Smith signed on with Bridgeport, Connecticut, of the Eastern League. He notched a 9-10 mark in 26 appearances for the Americans, who rounded out the summer in fourth place at 44-52. Smith clearly enjoyed his work for the club that summer, and when March 1918 rolled around, he wasted no time in leaving Millers Falls for Connecticut to commence spring training.

In May, with the U.S. now in the World War, Smith was drafted into the Army. The Eastern League season was canceled, and on May 26 Smith reported to basic training at Camp Upton, New York. Most young men were hustled through training and shipped off to Europe; for Smith, however, the Army had different ideas. Shortly after he arrived at camp he was ordered to don a baseball uniform and pitch for the 152nd Depot Brigade. He quickly began receiving rave reviews. "Smith has speed, control and lots of stuff," *Stars and Stripes*, the Army newspaper, wrote, "and with a wad of slippery elm in his mouth and a little damp clay on the mound, he can make that old pill do things that no ordinary ball was ever (meant to do)."[20] Smith wound up traveling from camp to camp and entertaining soldiers in need of a diversion from the daily drudgery of preparing for war.

On June 5, 1919, just over a year after he entered the military, Private Douglass Smith received an honorable discharge. His release papers read simply: "POSITION: BASE BALL PLAYER. BATTLES: NONE."[21]

After his release Smith returned to the mound, throwing for the Union Bag and Paper Company in Hudson Falls, New York, against other company teams (International Paper Company, International Wall Company, G.P. Cement Company), as well as against town teams in the region. "Doug said he would always have a warm spot in his heart for the people of Hudson Falls," a local sportswriter noted at the close of one season. "He enjoyed his stay here more than words could express."[22] He remained with Union Bag and Paper through 1922, never hesitating to slip out of town for a quick trip back to Millers Falls to pitch for a local nine in need of his services.

Though he turned 30 years old in May 1922, leaving baseball was the last thing on his mind. But that summer he was sidelined by appendicitis. The appendectomy was successful, and Smith recovered fully. However, after the operation the stress of pitching wreaked havoc with his right side. He sat out of the game for two years until in 1924 he felt well enough to try a comeback. In a game in Erving, Mass., near Millers Falls, he pitched into the sixth inning against Chappie Johnson's Colored All Stars, but when he awoke the next morning the pain was so intense that he couldn't get out of bed.

Doug Smith realized that his playing days were over.

In 1921 Smith had married 20-year-old Gertrude Schworm, who was born and raised in Millers Falls. Gertrude's father, Jacob Schworm, was a piano case maker born in Germany, and her mother, Fannie Victoria Beltermann, was a native of New York City. The newlyweds purchased a home a short walk down the hill from the house where Doug had been born and raised.

While pitching for Union Bag and Paper in 1919, Smith took an offseason job with the Millers Falls Paper Company. After leaving baseball in 1924 he joined the firm full time. He remained with the company for the next 38 years, retiring in 1962 at the age of 70.

Smith had banked his baseball earnings during his pitching days, and he and Gertie lived in comfort even during the dark days of the Great Depression. Ever fastidious, when he wasn't at work he passed the time working in his garden, keeping his home shipshape, and manicuring his yard until it was pristine. Not a day passed that the scent of a freshly-lit cigar didn't waft through the house, and although Doug and Gertie had no children of their own, over the succeeding years his brothers married and produced an abundant crop of nieces, nephews, grandnieces, and grandnephews, all within walking distance of Doug and Gertie's home.

Smith's appendectomy knocked him out of competitive action at the age of 32, but the baseball bug never left him, and he skippered the Millers Falls town team for the next three decades. His nephew James "Rusty" Smith began catching regularly for one of Doug's local teams when he was a 15-year-old, and he remembered that Doug had a fiery fastball late into his life. One painful memory that made Rusty cringe even at the age of 90 was a game in Brattleboro in which the Smith-coached team was leading by five runs late in the game. When an opposing runner stole second, Rusty didn't try to throw him out, which brought a furious Doug Smith out to publicly chew out his nephew in front of hundreds of spectators. The young catcher remembered feeling about two feet tall with embarrassment. "Who knows," ranted Uncle Doug, "they could still get six runs and then we'll lose! Don't ever let me catch you doing that again! You throw that damn ball!"[23]

Doug also followed major-league baseball keenly, cheering on his beloved New York Yankees as they won World Series after World Series.

As it had when he was a boy, each spring the "pop, pop, pop" sound of a baseball smacking into a catcher's mitt drifted through Doug Smith's kitchen window. His reputation as a rough and tumble former ballplayer may have scared off a few neighborhood kids, who rightly feared treading across his perfectly groomed lawn, but Doug's arm remained limber well into his 70s, and he always made it a point to "burn a few over" to neighborhood boys and offer up encouragement and advice. "Keep away from the soft ball, play in the little league and never keep track of your wins and losses," he once said. "Play baseball the way Ty Cobb played it, but have fun at the same time. And finally, quit gracefully when the time comes, for while baseball is a young man's game, the memories of each game you have played will sustain you throughout the years."[24]

And so they did. In 1967 his beloved Gertie died, and though he grieved, he made it a point to send a brief note to the *Greenfield Recorder* to "express thanks to relatives, neighbors and friends for their many acts of kindness and expressions of sympathy." For the next six years Doug remained alone, until finally, in September 1973, the family determined that it was time for him to leave. Doug was taken to the Franklin Nursing Home in Greenfield. "I was the only one in the family unemployed at the time, so it was up to me and my aunt to drive him to the nursing home," David Brule remembered:

> As we wheeled him up the walk to the home, a number of the residents were out on the veranda taking the sun. Wouldn't you know, one of the old timers recognized him and called out, "Well, Doug Smith! What are you doing here?" Automatically Doug's fingers went up to touch the visor of his cap, his face brightened in the old winning smile, much as the day he walked off the Field of Dreams for the last time.
>
> Within three weeks he was gone, like a wisp of smoke. But these April days when baseball fever takes over after the long winter months, there are stirrings out in the pasture, and behind the barn, if you know what to listen for, is the unmistakable sound of a fastball burning into a catcher's mitt. Over and over[25]

On September 18, 1973, Doug Smith passed away, survived by his brother Clinton. He was laid to rest in the Highland cemetery in Millers Falls two days later. He was 81.

Endnotes

1. *Boston Globe*, June 26, 1912, 7.

2. As quoted in David Brule, "From Millers Falls to Fenway, 1912. *The Montague Reporter*, May 4, 2006, 16.

3. *Boston Globe*, July 11, 1912.

4. Miscellaneous clipping, Smith family collection.

5. Miscellaneous clipping, Smith family collection.

6. Neil L. Perry, "Baseball still 'love' for old Sox farmhand."*Greenfield Recorder*. Smith family collection.

7. Letter courtesy of David Brule, Smith family collection.

8. Perry, op. cit.

9. Perry, op. cit.

10. *Boston Globe*, February 11, 1913, 6.

11. *Boston Globe*, July 18, 1912, 7.

12. American League Baseball Contract, courtesy of David Brule.

13. *Boston Globe*, February 11, 1913, 6.

14. *Ibid.*

15. *Brockton Times*, June 17, 1913. News clipping courtesy of Dick Thompson.

16. *Lowell Sun*, "Diamond Dazzles," June 2, 1913, 8.

17. Miscellaneous clipping, Smith family collection.

18. Miscellaneous clipping, Smith family collection.

19. Author's interview with David Brule, Don Scott, and Tom Gessing, April 23, 2009.

20. Miscellaneous clipping, Smith family collection.

21. United States Army Release, Douglas W. Smith, courtesy of David Brule.

22. Miscellaneous clipping, Smith family collection.

23. Rusty Smith interview, courtesy of David Brule.

24. Perry, op. cit.

25. Miscellaneous news clipping, Smith family collection.

Tris Speaker
by Don Jensen

G	AB	R	H	2B	3B	HR	RBI	BB	SO	BA	OBP	SLG	SB	HBP
153	580	136	222	53	12	10	90	82	38	.383	.464	.567	52	6

Tris Speaker, Ty Cobb's friendly rival as the greatest center fielder of the Deadball Era, could field and throw better than the Georgia Peach even if he could not quite match him as a hitter. Legendary for his short outfield play, Speaker led the American League in putouts seven times and in double plays six times in a 22-year career with Boston, Cleveland, Washington, and Philadelphia. Speaker's career totals in both categories are still major-league records at his position. No slouch at the plate, Speaker had a lifetime batting average of .345, sixth on the all-time list, and no one has surpassed his career mark of 792 doubles. He was also one of the game's most successful player-managers. A man's man who hunted, fished, could bulldog a steer, and taught Will Rogers how to use a lariat, Speaker was involved in more than his share of umpire baiting and brawls with teammates and opposing players. But when executing a hook slide on the bases, tracking a fly ball at the crack of an opponent's bat, or slashing one of his patented extra-base hits, Speaker made everything he did look easy. "You can write him down as one of the two models of ball-playing grace," Grantland Rice wrote of the Grey Eagle. "The other was Napoleon Lajoie. Neither ever wasted a motion or gave you any sign of extra effort....They had the same elements that made a Bobby Jones or the Four Horsemen of Notre Dame—the smoothness of a summer wind."

Tristram E. Speaker was born on April 4, 1888, in Hubbard, Texas, a railroad town of 500 people 70 miles south of Dallas, to a family that had relocated from Ohio just prior to the Civil War. His father, Archie, whose two older brothers had fought for the Confederacy, was in the dry-goods business and died when Tris was 10. Tris's mother, Nancy Jane, whose brother also fought for the South, kept a boarding house. A born right-hander, young Tris taught himself to throw left-handed when he twice broke his right arm after being thrown from a bronco. Soon he began to bat left-handed as well. Tris played football in high school and was captain and pitcher on his high-school baseball team. In 1905 Speaker entered the Fort Worth Polytechnic Institute (now Texas Wesleyan University), where he pitched for the school's baseball squad, as well as for the Nicholson and Watson semipro club in Corsicana. Tris picked up extra money working as a telegraph lineman and cowpuncher.

In 1906 Speaker wrote several professional teams asking for a tryout and was signed by Cleburne of the Texas League for $65 per month. Tris bombed as a pitcher—he lost six straight games and once reportedly gave up 22 straight hits, all for extra bases—but as an outfielder he hit .268 and stole 33 bases in 84 games. When the North Texas League and South Texas League were consolidated in 1907, Speaker moved to Houston and hit a league-leading .314 with 36 steals in 118 games.

The Boston Red Sox purchased Speaker's contract at the end of the 1907 season. He appeared in seven games for the big club, but hit only .158. Unimpressed with his play, the Red Sox

Tris Speaker led the Red Sox with a .383 average in 1912 and led the American League in on-base percentage.

did not send Speaker a contract for 1908. Speaker twice begged John McGraw for a chance to play for the New York Giants, to no avail, and was also rebuffed by several other major-league clubs. Finally, Speaker paid his own way to Boston's Little Rock training camp to work out with the Red Sox. At the end of spring training, the Red Sox turned his contract over to Little Rock of the Southern Association as payment for the rent of the training field. There was one stipulation: If Speaker developed, Boston had the right to repurchase him for $500.

Speaker led the Southern Association in hitting in 1908 with a .350 average stole 28 bases, and drew raves for his outfield play. In a spring exhibition game against the Giants, sportswriter Sid Mercer recalled, Speaker "scooped up a grounder and threw out one of the fleet Giants on one of those automatic attempts to score from second on a single. It happened again the next day. That time he doubled a runner trying to score on a fly."

Despite interest from the Pittsburgh Pirates, Brooklyn Superbas, Washington Senators, and, at last, the Giants, the Travelers sold Speaker back to Boston. Speaker hit only .224 in 31 games for the Red Sox in 1909, but was flawless in the outfield. Speaker further honed his outfield skills by working with Red Sox pitcher Cy Young. "When I was a rookie," Speaker later recalled, Young "used to hit me flies to sharpen my abilities to judge in advance the direction and distance of an outfield ball."

Speaker led Boston to world championships in two of the next seven seasons, 1912 and 1915, hitting above .300 every year and perennially ranking among American League leaders in most offensive and defensive categories. With teammates Harry Hooper and Duffy Lewis, Speaker formed one of the best fielding outfields in history. During this period Speaker led AL center fielders in putouts five times and in double plays four times. Twice he had 35 assists, the American League record. In 1912 Speaker, playing in every game but one, won the Chalmers Award as the League Most Valuable Player. He batted .383, third in the league behind Cobb and Joe Jackson, and led the league in doubles, home runs (tied), and on-base percentage. ("Spoke," one of Speaker's nicknames, came, ironically, from Speaker's teammate and rival Bill Carrigan, who would yell, "Speaker spoke!" when Tris got a hit.) To cap it off, in the World Series against the New York Giants, Speaker got a key hit in the 10th inning of the decisive eighth game after his harmless foul popup fell untouched between first baseman Fred Merkle and catcher Chief Meyers. Given a second chance, Speaker singled in the tying run.

Boston fans loved him. Speaker received $50 each time he hit the Bull Durham sign, first at the Huntington Avenue Grounds and later at Fenway Park. He endorsed Boston Garters, had a $2 straw hat named in his honor, and received free mackinaws and heavy sweaters. Hassan cigarettes created popular trading cards of Speaker depicting him running the bases.

Speaker waiting for his turn at bat.

Despite the team's success on the field, tensions were often high in the clubhouse. Speaker and catcher Carrigan never got along and had several brawls. Speaker was often not on speaking terms with Duffy Lewis, who, like Carrigan, was an Irish Catholic. (Religious differences had created cliques on the club, with Speaker siding with other Protestants including Joe Wood and Larry Gardner). The atmosphere grew more complicated with the arrival of Babe Ruth in 1915. Ruth crossed Wood and Speaker never fully forgave him. In his book *Baseball As I Have Known It*, Fred Lieb wrote that Speaker once told Lieb he was a member of the Ku Klux Klan. Although the Klan kept its membership rolls secret, Speaker's alleged membership would not be surprising given that the Klan experienced a nationwide revival beginning in 1915, gaining much popularity with its anti-Catholic rhetoric. In addition, the Klan's national leader from 1922 to 1939, Imperial Wizard Hiram W. Evans, lived near Speaker in Hubbard.

Relations between the Grey Eagle and team president Joe Lannin were also far from warm. After the Red Sox World Series victory in 1915, Lannin angered Speaker by proposing that the outfielder's salary be cut from about $18,000—higher at the time than that of Ty Cobb—to $9,000, since Speaker's batting average had declined three years in a row. (Lannin had raised Speaker's salary in 1914 to keep him from jumping to the Federal League's Brooklyn Club, which had offered Speaker a three-year contract for $100,000 to be its player-manager). When Speaker held out, Lannin traded him to Cleveland for Sam Jones, Fred Thomas, and $55,000.

Speaker received a massive outpouring of affection from the fans when he returned to Boston in a Cleveland uniform on May 9, 1916, and even mistakenly headed toward the Red Sox dugout at the end of one inning. Boston pitchers, meanwhile, complained that without Spoke in center, they could no longer groove fastballs when behind in the count, certain that he would catch everything hit his way. The Red Sox won the World Series again, but Speaker became the idol of Indians fans and hit even better with his new club than he had in Boston. Overall, 1916 may have been Speaker's best season. He hit .386, to finally break Cobb's lock on the batting title, and led the American League in hits, doubles (tied), slugging, and on-base percentage. Speaker's 35 stolen bases ranked fifth in the league.

In the outfield Speaker played so shallow that he was almost a fifth infielder. "At the crack of the bat he'd be off with his back to the infield," said teammate Joe Wood, "and then he'd turn and glance over his shoulder at the last minute and catch the ball so easy it looked like there was nothing to it, nothing at all." Twice in one month, April 1918, Speaker executed unassisted double plays at second base, catching low line drives on the run and then beating the baserunner to the bag. At least once in his career Speaker was the pivot man in a routine double play. As late as 1923, after the advent of the lively ball forced Speaker to play deeper, he still had 26 assists. "I know it's easier, basically, to come in on a ball than go back," Speaker said later. "But so many more balls are hit in front of an outfielder, even now, that it it's a matter of percentage to be able to play in close enough to cut off those low ones or cheap ones in front of him. I still see more games lost by singles that drop just over the infield than a triple over the outfielder's head. I learned early that I could save more games by cutting off some of those singles than I would lose by having an occasional extra-base hit go over my head."

Almost 6 feet tall and a sturdy 193 pounds, Speaker batted from a left-handed crouch and stood deep in the batter's box. He held his bat low, moving it up and down slowly, "like the lazy twitching of a cat's tail," according to an admirer, and took a full stride. "I don't find any particular ball easy to hit," he said. "I have no rule for batting. I keep my eye on the ball and when it nears me make ready to swing." Nevertheless, "I cut my drives between the first baseman and the line and that is my favorite alley for my doubles." He was a remarkably consistent batter. In 1912, Speaker set a major-league record with three separate hitting streaks of 20 or more games, while his 11 consecutive hits in 1920 set a mark that went unsurpassed for 18 years. Speaker's major weakness as a batter was the slow, high, curve.

Speaker spent 11 seasons with the Indians, compiling a batting mark that averaged over .350. He paced the American League in doubles four straight seasons. As late as 1925, the year he married the former Mary Frances Cuddihy of Buffalo, New York, the 37-year-old outfielder hit .389 in 117 games. The following year, his final season with Cleveland, he hit .304 in 150 games.

As player-manager, Speaker piloted Cleveland to a 617-520 record (.543) between 1919 and 1926. The Indians club he took to the World Series in 1920 had been demoralized by the midseason death of shortstop Ray Chapman when he was beaned by Carl Mays. Speaker rallied the team and in the Series, Cleveland defeated Brooklyn five games to two. Speaker was one of the first skippers to platoon extensively. In the Indians' championship year, he loaded up his batting order with right-handed hitters when a left-hander pitched, and vice versa. Speaker himself

Speaker swings during the early spring, with just a few scattered fans in the stands.

Harry Hooper, Tris Speaker, and Duffy Lewis, 1939.

was the only left-handed hitter who faced left-handed pitchers. He did not believe his team should warm up in a batting cage, preferring his hitters to practice under real circumstances with a catcher behind the plate.

After the 1926 season, Hubert "Dutch" Leonard, a disgruntled former teammate, accused Speaker and Cobb of fixing a game in 1919. Commissioner Kenesaw Mountain Landis cleared both men of the charges, but by that time American League President Ban Johnson, who believed the men guilty, had persuaded Cobb and Speaker to resign in order to protect baseball's image. "Baseball in Cleveland and Tris Speaker have been synonymous for so long that a Speakerless team will seem contrary to natural law," lamented the *Cleveland Plain Dealer*. "What Mathewson was to New York, what Cobb was to Detroit, what Johnson was to Washington, Tris Speaker has been to Cleveland." In February 1927, Speaker signed with the Washington Senators, where he hit .327. (When he returned to Cleveland for a farewell tribute from Indians fans in May of that year, Speaker was touched less by the gifts he received, said someone present, than the yells from the grandstand to "Hit it against the wall, Spoke!")

Speaker finished his major-league career with Cobb on Connie Mack's Philadelphia Athletics in 1928. He spent 1929 and 1930 as the player-manager of the Newark Bears in the International League, where he hit .355 and .419 in limited play.

Although retired as a player, Speaker was far from through with baseball. With his wife he had boxes at old League Park and later Municipal Stadium, both in Cleveland. Speaker was a broadcaster for the Cubs and White Sox in 1931 and then manager and part owner of the Kansas City Blues of the American Association. He was less successful as a bench manager, however, than when he was guiding his club from center field. "Speaker was possessed of a driving personality that seemed somehow to bring mediocre players up to his own level. That was the secret of his success," wrote one observer. "As long he was in uniform playing day in and day out he was a great manager. As soon as he quit playing, he lost his inspirational force. He became just another old timer in the dugout." The Kansas City venture was not successful and Speaker eventually returned to

Not only did Tris Speaker win a Chalmers automobile as the American League's most valuable player in 1912, he drove it home to Texas after the season—no easy feat in 1912. He was fast on the basepaths, with 52 stolen bases in 1912, and covered a great deal of ground in center field. *Boston Post*

Cleveland as a broadcaster and scout. Meanwhile, newcomer Joe DiMaggio's graceful play in the Yankees outfield inevitably caused comparisons to Speaker. The proud Texan bristled at the suggestion that DiMaggio was a worthy successor. When asked about the Yankee Clipper in 1939, Speaker responded, "HIM? I could name 15 better outfielders!"

In 1947, at the request of general manager Bill Veeck, Tris returned to uniform as a special coach, to help convert Larry Doby, who had played second base in the Negro Leagues, into a center fielder. After that, Speaker frequently visited Indians training camps to work with younger players. The Grey Eagle could "still spot a batter's weakness quicker than most of us," according to Al Lopez.

The Grey Eagle also capitalized on simply being Tris Speaker. A regular on the banquet circuit, he served as president of Tris Speaker, Inc., a wholesale wine and liquor firm in Cleveland, and later as a sales representative for a Detroit steel company. In 1936 he was chairman of the Cleveland Boxing and Wrestling Commission. In 1939 Speaker was president of the National Professional Indoor Baseball League, which had a club in every major-league city except Washington, but the circuit lasted only one month. He kept busy hunting, fishing, and flying (Tris had served as a naval aviator in the fall of 1918 and was commissioned a lieutenant.) and kept in touch with old friends such as Ty Cobb, Joe Wood, and Stan Coveleski. In 1953, Speaker had lunch in the White House with President Eisenhower.

Almost immune to injury when he played, Speaker suffered a series of health problems in his later years. In 1937 he fractured his skull and broke his left arm when he fell 16 feet from a second-story porch at his home. He also had a near-fatal perforated intestine and was hospitalized for weeks after a heart ailment in 1954. Speaker suffered a fatal coronary occlusion on December 8, 1958, while he and a friend pulled their boat on a dock after an afternoon fishing in Lake Whitney, Texas. He and Mary were on an extended vacation before hoping to head on to spring training.

Tris Speaker was buried in a cedar-shaded spot in Section 1, Block 2 of Fairview Cemetery in Hubbard, where his mother and father were interred and not far from the diamond where he once played as a boy. He was elected to the Hall of Fame in 1937, one of the first eight players so honored. His plaque states that he was the "greatest centrefielder [sic] of his day."

Note: This biography originally appeared in David Jones, ed., *Deadball Stars of the American League* (Washington, D.C.: Potomac Books, Inc., 2006).

Sources:

Books

Bob Broeg. *Superstars of Baseball* (South Bend, Indiana: Diamond Communications, 1994).

Bill James. *The Bill James Historical Baseball Abstract* (New York: Villard Books, 1988).

David L. Porter, ed. *Biographical History of American Sports*. (Westport, Connecticut: Greenwood Publishing Group, 1987).

Lawrence Ritter. *The Glory of their Times*. (New York: Vintage Books, 1985).

Mike Sowell. *The Pitch that Killed* (New York: Collier Books, 1989).

Magazines

Gordon Cobbledick. "Tris Speaker—The Grey Eagle." *Sport*, July 1952.

Lee Greene. "The Grey Eagle." *Sport*, August 1960.

Tom Meany. "The Gray Eagle Was a Lion at Bat." *Baseball Digest*, February 1959.

Newspapers

Cleveland Plain Dealer

Leslie's Weekly

New York Journal-American

The Sporting News

Online

www.athomeplate.com

www.baseball-almanac.com

www.baseballlibrary.com

www.thebaseballpage.com

www.baseballhalloffame.org

www.cmgworldwide.com

Garland "Jake" Stahl
by John Stahl

G	AB	R	H	2B	3B	HR	RBI	BB	SO	BA	OBP	SLG	SB	HBP
95	326	40	98	21	6	3	60	31	53	.301	.372	.429	13	6

Big, powerful, and deceptively fast, Garland "Jake" Stahl parlayed the skills he first demonstrated as a college football and baseball star at the turn of the century into a successful major-league baseball career, primarily with the Boston Red Sox. At 6-foot-2 and 195 pounds, the right-handed Stahl was one of the most intimidating sluggers of the Deadball Era's first decade.

Jake Stahl holds a special place in Red Sox history. He remains the first and only Red Sox player who was on two different Boston World Championship teams in two different decades: 1903 and 1912.

In 1903, Jake played 40 games as a rookie catcher behind Cy Young-favorite Lou Criger. He did not play in the subsequent 1903 World Series, and his keen disappointment at missing that opportunity became one of the key forces driving him throughout the remainder of his playing career.

In 1912, Jake skillfully managed the famous "Speed Boys" to an American League pennant-winning 105-47 season record. Ninety-eight seasons later, the 1912 won-lost season record still stands as the best in Red Sox history. His Boston team subsequently won the 1912 World Series from the McGraw-led New York Giants.

Garland Stahl was born on April 13, 1879, in Elkhart, Illinois, the third son of Henry and Eliza Stahl. Henry was a front-line Union veteran of the Civil War who survived the horrors of the bloodbath at Shiloh. After the war, Henry and Eliza opened a thriving general store in Elkhart. In naming her third son, Eliza used the name of one of her brothers-in-law, Garland.

After graduating from high school (which at that time went only to the 10th grade) and working at the family store, Stahl enrolled at the University of Illinois. His fraternity brothers nicknamed him Jake. University of Illinois football coach George Huff (who briefly managed Boston in 1907) encouraged him to try out for the team.

With forward passes not allowed yet, no offensive/defensive specialization employed, and only rudimentary protective equipment used, the resulting two-way game was particularly brutal. As he matured physically, Jake became both an outstanding running back on offense and a smart, quick lineman on defense. He had his best year as a junior in 1901, when he was named to the All-Western Conference football team. He was named captain of the Illinois football team in 1902. In his first formal leadership position, Jake was required to address not only his personal needs but the needs of the entire team. It was a skill he would continue to hone throughout both his baseball and subsequent banking career.

Huff also coached baseball at the University and encouraged Jake to join his highly successful squad. As the starting catcher, Jake batted .441 his sophomore year, and in his senior campaign, led Illinois to a Western Conference Championship.

Jake Stahl, Red Sox manager, 1912.

Exhibiting an outstanding ability to organize and focus his efforts, Jake graduated with a law degree in 1903. Although his athletic and classroom activities clearly were his first priorities, Jake was no social wallflower in college. The University of Illinois yearbooks of the time contain two references to Jake's social activities, including a poem describing his carriage ride with a young woman named Clara. Jake met his future wife, Jennie Mahan, at the university.

In the spring of 1903, as Boston suffered a potentially debilitating blow to their pennant hopes with the injury of their primary backup catcher "Duke" Farrell, team owner Henry Killilea hurriedly traveled to Chicago to sign Jake to an American League contract on the playing field immediately after a late-season university ballgame. Jake got into his first game in early June and appeared in 40 games as a catcher for Boston in 1903, hitting .239. More importantly, Jake's work enabled Boston to keep Criger fresh for the postseason. As noted, Jake himself did not play in the 1903 World Series. When pinch-hitting opportunities arose in both Games One and Four, Collins twice used the still-recovering Farrell (who had played in only 17 games the entire season) and the veteran outfielder Jack O'Brien (who hit .210 in 1903.) Jake's personal disappointment

Bill Carrigan and Jake Stahl before a 1912 ballgame.

was a key factor that helped shape the rest of his professional baseball career.

With Farrell fully recovered, Boston no longer needed Jake as a backup catcher. Ban Johnson, however, grateful for Jake's role in Boston's successful 1903 season (Boston's World Series victory ensured the long-term viability of his new American League), envisioned Jake achieving long-term baseball success as a first baseman. During the winter of 1903-04, Boston shipped Jake to the floundering Washington franchise. Johnson was in charge of the team until suitable owners could be found and converted Jake into a first baseman. He appeared in 142 games and finished the year with a .262 batting average, three home runs, and 50 RBIs. Even by Deadfall Era standards, these numbers were not exceptional, yet Stahl led the woeful (38-113) Nationals in all three categories.

In 1905, Johnson promoted Jake to manager. Having just turned 26 years old the day before the season began, he became the youngest player-manager in American League history. Employing the inclusive management style he used in college, Jake quickly won the support of the team's veteran players. Coupled with a focused disciplinary approach emphasizing direct out-of-public-view communication with offenders, punctuated by demonstrations of potential physical force, Jake led the 1905 squad to 64-87 record. For a short time early in the season, Jake even had the team in first place. When the team returned from a successful road trip, Washington gave the team a rousing parade and celebratory dinner. More importantly, Johnson found new owners for the shaky Washington franchise. Stahl had become, in the words of one observer, "popular with the players, and so well liked by the club owners that it has been officially announced that he can retain his present berth until he voluntarily resigns." In the offseason, Jake married his college sweetheart, the daughter of highly-successful businessman Henry Weston Mahan.

In 1906, however, things fell apart for Jake and the Nationals. Popular shortstop Joe Cassidy unexpectedly died of typhus at the beginning of the season and the team fell into a tailspin, finishing 55-95. Upset by the death of his close friend and consumed with trying to right the fast-sinking team, Jake completely lost his personal focus, finishing with the worst batting average of his career, .222. Jake took personal blame for the team's disappointing 1907 performance, noting, "If I'd been able to hit .300 this year, as many of my friends predicted, we'd have been up in the first division, but I was a frost."

The frustrated Washington owners replaced Jake as their manager during the 1906-1907 offseason, urging him to concentrate on playing first base. Seeing the team transition that Boston was undertaking, Jake asked to be traded back to Boston. Washington management declined, trading him instead to the Chicago White Sox. Jake refused to report and spent the 1907 season working in his father-in-law's bank, managing the University of Indiana's baseball team, and playing semiprofessional baseball in Chicago.

In 1908, Chicago traded Jake to Clark Griffith's New York Highlanders. When Griffith resigned in midseason, Jake was traded back to Boston to play first base. As the future Boston stars (Wood, Speaker, Hooper, Lewis, Gardner) developed, the hard-hitting Stahl anchored the Boston lineup from 1908-1910. In 1910, Jake led the American League with 10 home runs and ranked fourth best in RBIs (77) and triples (16). He also stole 22 bases.

Despite his baseball success, Jake's off-the-field banking successes were even greater and paid more. Given the financial

A banker in Chicago, lured back to Boston for the 1912 campaign, manager Stahl knew how to dress and cut a good figure. *Boston Post*

uncertainties associated with a baseball career at the time and the fact that he had just started a family, Jake opted to retire. He served as vice president of the Washington Park National Bank on Chicago's South Side. Attempts to lure him back to baseball in 1911 were fruitless.

After a change in ownership late in the disappointing 1911 season, new Red Sox team president Jimmy McAleer convinced Jake to come out of retirement. Both he and his father-in-law became part-owners of the club, Jake becoming the player-manager-owner of a talented but uninspired Boston club. Jake signed a two-year contract. Using the same inclusive management and disciplinary styles he used earlier in Washington, he effectively focused the previously-uninspired team. Boston ran away with the 1912 American League pennant. Jake finished the year with a career-high .301 batting average. Facing the New York Giants in the 1912 World Series, Jake both outplayed the Giants' Merkle at first base, and, according to Connie Mack, consistently out-managed McGraw. Jake invested his winning World Series share in his father-in-law's Chicago banks.

In 1913, Boston started slowly and Jake suffered a serious foot injury requiring the removal of part of a bone in his right foot. Although he continued to manage the team, he could not play first base. Within a tense atmosphere of newspaper reports claiming internal dissension within the team and rumors that Jake would replace him as team president, Boston president McAleer publicly demanded that Jake return to first base.

Upset that he was being publicly portrayed in the newspapers as somehow losing control of his team, conniving for personal gain, and shirking his first-base playing duties, Jake met McAleer in Chicago during a July road trip. In the heat of the moment, the Boston president released him, paying off the remainder of his contract.

McAleer's hasty action was immediately condemned by much of the baseball community, including Ban Johnson, who called the move "hasty and ill-advised." Bill Carrigan, one of the players that Jake often consulted with, was named the new Boston manager. In October, Jake announced he was through with baseball. Later that offseason, as part of another Boston front office change, McAleer himself was released as president.

For his nine-year major league career, Jake posted a .261 batting average with 894 hits, which included 149 doubles, 87 triples, and 31 home runs. He also stole 178 bases, with his single-season high of 41 in 1906.

Jake immediately began his second career as a full-time banker. With his father-in-law serving as president, Jake became vice-president and board member of Washington Park National Bank. Jake continued as vice-president until he assumed the presidency of Washington Park in 1919.

During his years of involvement, he put in long hours at the bank, helping it more than double its deposits in three years. But the hard work came with a heavy price: in 1920, Jake suffered a nervous breakdown and was placed in a Monrovia, California, sanitarium. Though he spent two years in California, Jake's health gradually worsened and he contracted tuberculosis. With his wife and son at his bedside, Jake died on September 18, 1922. He was just 43 years old.

The Red Sox road uniform featured pinstripes in 1912, as Jake Stahl shows in this 1913 image wearing the prior year's uniform.

Sources:

David Jones, ed. *Deadball Stars of the American League* (Potomac Books, 2006)

Louis Masur. *Autumn Glory: Baseball's First World Series* (Hill & Wang, 2004)

Bill Nowlin. *Day By Day with the Boston Red Sox* (Rounder Books, 2006)

Bob Ryan. *When Boston Won the World Series* (Running Press, 2004)

John Thorn, Pete Palmer, and Michael Gershman. *Total Baseball, Seventh Edition* (Sport Classic Books, 2003)

Boston Globe, *Boston Post*, *Boston American*, *Boston Herald*, *Chicago Tribune*, *New York Times*, *The Sporting News*, *Washington Post*, *Washington Star*

U. S. Census (1880, 1900)

The ILLIO, University of Illinois Yearbook (1902-1903)

www.retrosheet.org

Hassan Cigarette baseball card, featuring Jake Stahl (r) and Eddie Cicotte. First baseman Stahl holds the bag while a New York Highlander takes a big lead.

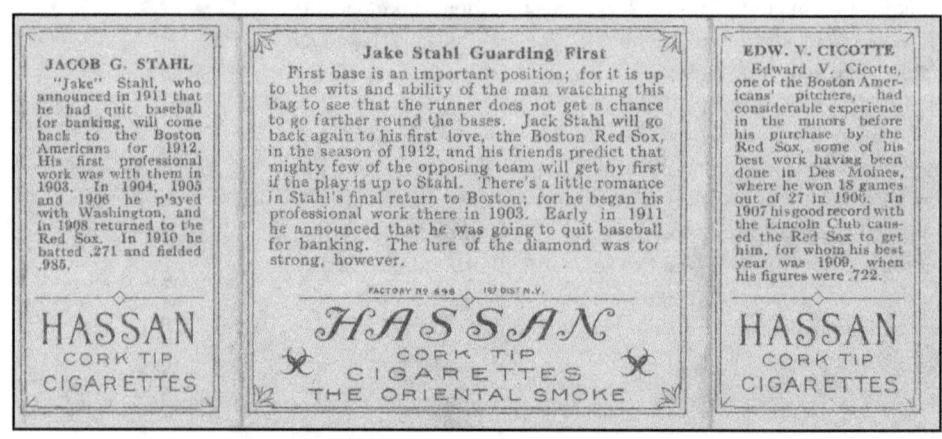

Pinch Thomas
by Joanne Hulbert

G	AB	R	H	2B	3B	HR	RBI	BB	SO	BA	OBP	SLG	SB	HBP
13	30	0	6	0	0	0	5	2	3	.200	.250	.200	1	0

The train pulled out of South Station in Boston on February 18, 1911, heading for Los Angeles and the new location for Red Sox spring training (Redondo Beach, California). Several stops were made along the way as the party picked up players from Western League teams as well as returning veteran players. Manager Patsy Donovan intended to try out at least a dozen of the prospects, hoped to keep a few and farm out other potential players to West Coast clubs for further development. The catchers and first basemen were of particular interest; those positions were where Boston's roster needed improvement. At a stopover in Chicago, several more veterans and a few Western Leaguers joined the team, and the train rolled on to Kansas City, where four recruits came aboard while a crowd of spectators waited to see Joe Wood make a brief appearance on the platform. Among the four joining the team was Chester David Thomas from Sharon, Kansas. Born on January 24, 1888, in Camp Point, Illinois, he had moved as a youngster with his family to Kansas. Known as Chet, Chess, Chubby Chester, Chatterer Chet, Tom, Thommy, the Golden West Receiver, the Kansan, the Baseball Populist, Goat, and Pinch, the sobriquet that became the enduring nickname among them. Thomas's brother said he was at a loss as to where it came from. Although Thomas was most frequently called Chet by the Boston scribes, perhaps his record as a pinch-hitter (13-for-31, .419) as a pinch hitter from 1913 to 1918 had all to do with the nickname.

Thomas started playing baseball as an infielder on local grounds in Kansas but found greater opportunities on the West Coast and took up the backstop position with the San Jose team of the California State League in 1908. In 1909 he split his time between Helena, Montana, of the Northwest League and the Oakland Oaks of the Pacific Coast League. The Chicago Cubs secured a 30-day option on Thomas, and not wanting to give him up so soon—he was merely on loan to the Helena club—the Oaks recalled him. At Oakland he was used as a pinch-hitter with great success, and was famous for getting on base by hitting weak but untouchable infield flies and for stopping basestealers.

Thomas began the 1910 season with Oakland, was purchased by the Sacramento team in June, and returned to Oakland on August 1. After a game on August 7, a disagreement erupted between Thomas and fellow Oakland catcher Carl Mitze at a local watering hole. The *Oakland Tribune* reported that they "went at it hammer and tongs" until spectators stepped in and separated them. Bad blood had existed between the two men, and when Chet started bragging about how he had landed a two-bagger that broke up a game the previous week and he wanted to know why Mitze couldn't come up with a big hit too. "Oh, I'm there with the big wallop all right," Mitze countered, as he proceeded to plant a fist on Thomas' jaw.[1] The fight would not be his last and it established his reputation as a loudmouthed scrapper.

Spring training 1911 gave the Red Sox a chance to see what their catcher prospect could do. In the first game, on February 25, Chet Thomas caught the first three innings for the Yannigans. The *Boston Globe's* Tim Murnane reported that he "looked awfully good. He shot the ball to second and nailed Wagner by a city block."[2]

On March 14, while Chet was out on the town in San Francisco for a night of sightseeing with friends, his baseball career nearly came to an abrupt end when he was beaten by a gang of street thugs. He suffered a serious head injury and doctors feared he'd lose the sight of one eye. Thomas recovered with just a black eye, his sight undamaged, and the Red Sox investment intact. He was sent back to Sacramento for the 1911 season, and his reputation improved as a smart backstop who could pull many a pitcher out of a tough spot. By September 1911 Thomas's future as a member of the Boston Red Sox was set.

In 1912 the Red Sox ended their dalliance with Redondo Beach and returned to Hot Springs, Arkansas, for spring training. Thomas arrived on March 7 along with another new catcher, Hick Cady. They joined veteran Bill Carrigan and Les Nunamaker, the 1911 rookie catcher. At first, neither Thomas nor Cady got a chance to show much behind the plate as there were few attempts at basestealing, but Thomas eventually demonstrated his skill at pegging out runners at second and showed strong at-bats, all done with banter and bluster. Paul Shannon of the *Boston Post* wrote that Thomas had an easy way of shooting the ball to the basemen with time to spare.

Although Thomas's official debut with the Red Sox took place on April 24, 1912, his first appearance at the new Fenway Park was on April 9, 1912 in the first game ever played at the

Thomas, at Fenway in 1915, served as Babe Ruth's battery mate during his stint with the Red Sox.

ballpark—against Harvard College. Thomas raised a few eyebrows when he appeared behind the plate wearing a pair of new-fangled shinguards adjustable without the use of leather straps.

Les Nunamaker appeared in 35 games, Thomas appeared in 13 (eight as a catcher), Hick Cady caught 43, and Bill Carrigan dominated in 87 games. Carrigan, the dean of Red Sox catchers, had a theory endorsed by management that catchers and pitchers worked best in set pairs. Thomas spent his time warming up pitchers, caught when Cady and Carrigan were overworked—which was not often—and filled in as a pinch-hitter. His April 24 debut was against Walter Johnson, as a pinch-hitter for Carrigan in the ninth inning, and he was thrown out at first.

Despite his infrequent appearances in 1912 (and none at all in the World Series, which Boston won over the New York Giants), Thomas earned a portion of the World Series money. He had been signed for two years and although 1912 was a year for breaking in, the *Boston Evening Record* predicted that Pinch would "make good with a vengeance" once he was allowed more work.[3] Thomas spent the offseason working on his farm in Medicine Lodge, Kansas, and arrived in Hot Springs ready for spring training on March 3, 1913. Manager Jake Stahl decided to stay with the four 1912 catchers, and appointed former Red Sox catcher Duke Farrell, an 18-year veteran of the major leagues, to find out "just who's who and what's what" with the team's pitching prospects.[4]

As the 1913 season began the sportswriters fueled the fans with predictions of a World Series repeat performance, but April was a cruel month for the Red Sox. They lost the home opener 10-9 to the Philadelphia Athletics, a loss blamed on a play by catcher Hick Cady panned as a bonehead move. They lost six of their first eight games as Hick tried to redeem himself. Thomas's first appearance in a game was on May 3, as a pinch-hitter for Hugh Bedient in the ninth inning of a losing effort against Washington. The Nationals had brought in Walter Johnson to pitch in the eight. Thomas missed three fast ones and dived head-first to the dirt after the third flew by. The invisible missile also passed the Washington catcher, Eddie Ainsmith, and hit the back wall while Pinch ran to first, but he was thrown out before he had made it halfway there. Much to the amusement of the crowd, umpire Tommy Connolly replayed Thomas's plate pratfall, spinning around as if the ball had merely touched his uniform and brought him crashing down like a ton of bricks.

By midseason the Red Sox bench was a hospital ward with every one of the regulars except Hooper and Speaker out of the lineup at one time or another. By July 16 team President Jim McAleer, frustrated with the way the team's fortunes were going, replaced manager Jake Stahl with Bill Carrigan. One result of the managerial shakeup meant less time on the bench for Pinch Thomas. By August Chet had improved his average from .189 to .267, and on September 29, the left-handed-hitting catcher hit his first major-league home run, an inside-the-park job at the Polo Grounds in New York off Yankees started Ray Fisher. By the end of the season his average was a respectable .286 in 38 games, 31 as catcher. With no return to the World Series, Thomas returned to his Kansas farm, "where drops of rain are prized like diamonds at certain times of the year."[5] The 1914 Red Sox, extending the trend, had four catchers on the roster: Carrigan, Cady, Nunamaker, and Thomas. The quartet, wrote Tim Murnane in the *Globe*, seldom got injured and were able to stay in good shape as a consequence of their rotation schedule. Although the backstops were touted as the "finest string of catchers of any club in the country," the primitive protective equipment, a pitching staff that was considered far below that needed to be competitive in the American League, and the physical impact inherent in the catching position was a constant threat.[6] Pinch started occasionally, and often picked up late innings to relieve the exhausted manager, who still preferred to monitor his pitching staff from behind the plate.

For a spell, Thomas himself was among the wounded. In a game in June, the Philadelphia Athletics' Weldon Wyckoff singled to center and Tris Speaker threw the ball to home in an attempt to stop Wally Schang at the plate, but the ball hit Pinch in the eye, causing a deep gash. He "dropped as if he had been shot, and it was several minutes before he recovered sufficiently," wrote Murnane.[7] The once "finest string of catchers" was now reduced to just Hick Cady, as Carrigan was also nursing wounds he sustained when he was spiked in a game against the Senators and Les Nunamaker was gone, sold to the Yankees on May 13.

Pinch's recovery stretched into weeks, but he eventually returned, playing an occasional relief inning until the end of the 1914 season. He posted his worst average with the Red Sox, .192, with nine runs and five runs batted in 66 games. After the season, trade rumors included one that had Boston sending Thomas and Del Gainer to St. Louis for Browns first baseman and occasional backstop Jack Leary. Browns manager Branch Rickey would have none of it. A Red Sox pitching rookie, George Herman Ruth, who appeared in only five games in 1914, looked as though he'd be a good match for the catcher, who sometimes mixed his plate

Pinch Thomas in 1913.

appearances with fisticuffs.

Bill Carrigan continued the battery joint ventures in 1915, pairing Hick Cady with Dutch Leonard and Ernie Shore, while Pinch Thomas tried his hand catching Ruth and Rube Foster. Carrigan, Cady, and Thomas all tried working with Carl Mays, with mixed results. Mays, an underhand pitcher with no previous major-league experience before arriving at Hot Springs, was a challenge. During a batting practice warm-up on April 9, Thomas stopped a Mays wild pitch, and was fortunate the ball did not hit him in the face after hitting the ground in front of him.

When the season began, Thomas became the everyday catcher while Bill Carrigan looked for ways to move the team out of fifth place. Erratic pitching was a problem and fielding needed improvement, but the catchers were doing well. In mid-June the Red Sox left fifth place behind and were tied with the Detroit Tigers for second. Chet appeared in more games than Cady and Carrigan, handled veteran Joe Wood, endured the wild pitches of Carl Mays and formed a solid partnership with Babe Ruth. Boston whittled away the Chicago White Sox' lead and on July 18 Boston was ahead in the pennant race. Smoky Joe was magnificent on the mound, wrote Tim Murnane, and praise was heaped upon Chet Thomas, not only for his handling of the pitching staff but also for his most timely and effective hitting. "Too much cannot be said for the superb all-round work of Chester Thomas in the series here," the scribe wrote from Chicago in July. "There was no department of the position in which he did not outpoint [White Sox catcher Ray] Schalk."[8]

Catcher Pinch Thomas, known for his irrepressible banter at and behind the plate, demonstrates his best batting practice pose for the cameraman.

Although Thomas had done more catching during the regular season than Cady and Carrigan, before the World Series Murnane wrote that Thomas was a fine catcher when healthy, but that an injury during a game in Cleveland had forced him to cut back, and he was out of shape and had lost his famous ability to throw out basestealers.

Chicago sportswriter Hugh Fullerton, in his pre-Series analysis, acknowledged Thomas's skill handling left-handed pitchers and his ability to prevent stolen bases—although his throwing was occasionally erratic—and considered Boston to be in a comfortable position since the Red Sox pitching staff kept runners to a minimum. The Red Sox defeated the Philadelphia Phillies, four games to one, for Boston's third World Series championship.

In 1916, despite preseason trade rumors that had Thomas going to Cleveland along with Joe Wood and Ray Collins, Chet was ready to work for Boston, and he did not want to start on the wrong foot. When assigned his room at the Copley Square Hotel, he was handed a key to Room 23. At the time, the number of 23 had a negative connotation along the lines of being forced by someone to leave quickly. Chet complained to Tillie Walker, "What do you think of that. Giving me Room 23. Gee whiz, the season hasn't opened yet and he's trying to start me with 23! Not on your life." He demanded a different room from the desk clerk.[9]

During spring training catcher Sam Agnew, acquired from the St. Louis Browns, received more attention than Chet, but by May Carrigan reconsidered partnering Agnew with Babe Ruth. During a game in May against Washington, the Babe walked nine batters, three in the eighth inning alone, and Carrigan concluded that Sam was the wrong guy to handle Babe's curves. Pinch returned to the lineup when Babe was pitching. "The wonderful form of George Ruth may be justifiably traced to Thomas," wrote a Boston sports scribe. "He has coached the Baltimorean ever since they mobilized at the ramparts in Hot Springs. Ruth has become accustomed to look to Chubby Chester for advice."[10]

Pinch continued to pull an occasional boner, causing Carrigan to reconsider catching Ruth himself. The Babe wasn't having an impressive start in 1916, either, for by mid-May he hadn't yet hit a home run. Chet caught basestealer Ty Cobb twice in one game in May. By his own count he figured that he stopped Cobb 10 times in 1916 and missed just twice, the best record of any catcher in the American League.[11] He was working harder than ever to earn back his place as the primary backstop, and his hitting was improving, too. Carrigan had also tried Thomas with Ernie Shore, the emery-ball hurler, but the relationship broke down. In June Thomas and Shore had a ninth-inning argument, Chet accusing "Emery" of crossing him up. The Shore-Thomas battery would never be the same.

The 1916 season was Chet's best year in baseball. Along with his partnership with the Babe, he also caught the frequently erratic Carl Mays, already earning a reputation for beanballs, and was credited with handling Mays as well as anyone could. When not in the lineup, he warmed up the pitchers before games, or was on the coaching lines "making as much noise as 'Sea Lion' Charlie Hall used to do."

In August Pinch's reputation as a fighter emerged again when he swapped punches with Browns third baseman Jimmy Austin, who had accused the Red Sox' Rube Foster of trying to bean him. Pinch called Jimmy yellow, told him to stand up and strike out. Austin missed the next pitch, Chet added more insults, and Jimmy took a swing at Chet's head, catching him on the side of the face. Pinch responded with three punches to Jimmy's face, and Austin's return shot hit umpire Ollie Chill instead of Chet. Thomas and Austin were both suspended indefinitely, public outrage erupted about violence on the baseball diamond, and Red Sox President James Lannin issued a statement defending Thomas's actions: "Had Thomas not gone after Austin and fought back I would have fined him for his lack of aggression."[12] A few days later Thomas was back in the lineup.

The 1916 World Series win—the Red Sox defeated the Brooklyn Robins four games to one—capped Boston's fourth championship season, and Bill Carrigan announced his retirement from baseball. A gang of players, including the Babe, Pinch, Jack Barry, Tillie Walker, and a few others celebrated Boston's fourth championship with a hunting trip to Lake Squam in New Hampshire, a gift from the Draper-Maynard Company. Besides duck hunting, the outing included a boxing match between Ruth and first baseman Doc Hoblitzel refereed by Pinch, who wisely ruled the match a draw.[13]

Chet Thomas liked playing in Chicago, and the reason became clear when he secretly wed cabaret dancer, Doxie Emmerson-Love on December 23, 1916. The *Chicago Tribune* reported the details of the romance and the wedding held at City Hall, while the *Boston Globe* printed just a brief announcement. A native of San Francisco, Doxie had caught the eye of the Boston backstop and he had returned to the Central Inn on Wabash Avenue every time he was in town over the previous two baseball seasons. With the 1916 season over, Chet had returned to his farm in Medicine Lodge, Kansas, but, finding it lonesome on the prairie in mid-December, boarded a train for Chicago and proposed to Doxie. She accepted, vowing also to abandon the Chicago café scene and move to Medicine Lodge to become a farmer's wife. "The people in this café don't know I'm going to quit dancing and go away out west and live with the cows and chickens," said Mrs. Thomas just after finishing an exhibition of her art, "but I know I'm going to like the new life."

For his part, Chet said, "The folks down in Kansas don't know anything about this, but I know it will be all right with them after they see her."[14]

Doxie was a devoted baseball wife, accompanying Chet to spring training in Hot Springs in March 1917. She went horseback riding with Helen Ruth, and after practice was over the wives joined their husbands on Ozark mountain hikes. Doxie was just beginning to learn more about her husband and his multifaceted baseball job. When Chet was on the coaching line at first base his verbal outbursts might have shocked her if she had not sat far away behind the dugout. Chet would spit on his hands and call on all the Roman gods to witness the base hit that was soon to occur, shout encouragement to the Boston baserunners, and harass the opposing first sacker. That first year of their marriage, she stayed in Boston at their apartment in the Fenway area and often attended games. On May 24, 1917, with the US having joined in the Great War, Pinch Thomas registered for the draft as the law of the land required. He was exempt from serving due to his marital status.

Jack Barry was the new manager and Harry Frazee was the new owner of the team in 1917. Although Chet had had a successful year in 1916, appearing in 99 games with 216 at-bats and hitting .264, another year brought new challenges and competition. His average in 1917 dropped to .238 in 83 games played, but he was the best catcher the Red Sox had, and he was still Babe Ruth's preferred batterymate. By the end of their partnership, Pinch Thomas had caught 68 of Babe Ruth's 144 Red Sox starts, including 10 of his 17 shutouts. Sam Agnew was next with 24 starts.

Ed Martin of the *Boston Daily Globe* called the game against the Washington Senators at Fenway Park on June 23, 1917, the best pitching seen in Boston since 1904. Ruth was the starting pitcher, Thomas was his catcher. The first Washington batter, second baseman Ray Morgan, received four balls, according to umpire Brick Owens. Ruth accused Owens of missing the call on two of them, and a verbal battle erupted between pitcher and umpire as the Babe charged home plate. Pinch Thomas placed himself between the outraged pitcher and his intended target, but Babe, swinging with both hands, caught Brick behind the left ear. Manager Barry and several policemen dragged Ruth off the field as Ernie Shore stepped up on the mound and warmed up. Agnew replaced Thomas behind home plate. Ernie Shore went on to a "no-hit, no-man-reach-first" (for Shore, at least) game. Shore confessed that he did not know he had achieved the feat until Thomas rushed up to him and shook his hand after the last out. "I was wondering what the occasion was," Shore said sheepishly. "Chet told me and then I realized the one ambition of my baseball career. I have always wanted to turn in a no-hit game but have just missed it."[15]

After the 1917 season Thomas spent the winter in California. Back in Boston, trade talks between the Red Sox and the Philadelphia Athletics brewed up a deal that brought Joe Bush, Amos Strunk, and catcher Wally Schang to Boston and gave Vean Gregg, rookie outfielder Merline "Officer" Kopp, Chet Thomas, and $60,000 to Connie Mack. The deal was considered a coup for Boston and a terrific blow to the Athletics, amid predictions

If the men weren't playing cards to while away the time, shooting dice was another option. Carrigan may have cleaned up at cards, but his fellow catcher Thomas may have cornered the market at craps. *Boston Post*

that it paved the way for Boston to win the 1918 pennant. Stuffy McInnis said he hoped Pinch would help the Athletics, "for he is very capable as far as the mechanical end of the game goes and particularly good for head work. He'll find Connie a great fellow to work for and I know he'll give his best from the start."[16]

But it didn't turn out that way. Thomas, devastated by the trade, blamed the sports reporters for deflating his worth. At spring training in March, he considered quitting baseball and said he had been working during the offseason for a movie company in California. He did not want to report to Philadelphia, and his relationship with Connie Mack deteriorated when he demanded more money than Mack considered reasonable. In Mack's opinion, Chet's reputation had been inflated by the pitchers he worked with.[17] Chet figured he could not have been such a detriment to the team as some writers said. As for the pitchers shoring him up, he claimed Babe Ruth would have been traded or released by Bill Carrigan if it had not been for him, and that he had broken in most of the other pitchers on the Red Sox team. All he wanted was to retire from baseball with everyone's goodwill.[18]

Thomas played no games with the Athletics. In June he was sold to the Cleveland Indians but spent two months in California with the movie company. He joined the team in August and appeared in 32 games, 24 of them as a catcher, and also was employed as the third-base coach. Along the sidelines his role as the "bull-throated barker" was credited with winning games for the Indians as Chet kept up streams of verbal harassment that drove opposing pitchers off the mound and knocked fielders off-kilter.[19] Indians manager Lee Fohl used Pinch as a pinch-hitter 11 times and he delivered on five occasions, finishing the season with a pinch-hitting average of .454. At the end of the season he returned to his purchasing department job with the California movie company.

Pinch returned to Cleveland in 1919 and caught 21 games, appearing in 34 overall. His legendary reputation on the third-base line followed him back to Philadelphia, where the newspapers complained about his antics, calling him a rank nuisance. In 1920 Thomas filled in as manager of the team while Tris Speaker accompanied the body of Ray Chapman home. His time presiding behind the plate decreased sharply; he caught in just nine games and spent more time on the coaching line, where his errorless judgment was said to have preserved many a baserunner and his verbal outbursts continued to be an opposing pitcher's nightmare. In 1921 he appeared in 21 games, his last on June 19. By then his attention was focused on Los Angeles and the movie business, where he had secured a job as an assistant director.

In 1928 Thomas appeared in the movie *Warming Up* with baseball players Mike Donlin and Truck Hannah. What became of his life subsequently is open to speculation. Chet and Doxie were divorced, she went back to Kansas with their son, and in 1930, Chet was living in a rooming house in Modesto, California. In 1936 the American League president received the following letter:

> Mr. William Harridge,
> On April 22 you presented lifetime passes to a number of old ball players. Among these was the name of Chet Thomas of Sharon, Kansas. I am Chet Thomas's son. My dad is in a state hospital and will never be able to use this pass. I would like to have the pass as a keepsake. Could it be possible for me to get it? Or have you sent it to Kansas. As I have already told you he is not in Kansas. Any information you could send me on the matter would be appreciated.
> Yours truly,
> Chester Frank Thomas[20]

Pinch Thomas died at the Modesto State Hospital in California on December 24, 1953. The cause of death was listed as pulmonary edema, amputation of the left leg above the knee due to arteriosclerosis, recurrent infection, gangrene, and peripheral vascular disease with the contributory, unrelated condition of psychosis. He is rarely mentioned among catchers, coaches, or other memorable characters. Chet Thomas' greatest defender and booster was himself and once gone he faded into part of the hidden history of baseball, only to appear from time to time attached to another's story. Let it be less so now.

Endnotes

1. *Oakland Tribune*, August 9, 1910

2. *Boston Globe*, February 26, 1911.

3. *Boston Evening Record*, September 26, 1912.

4. *Boston American*, March 4, 1913.

5. *Sporting Life*, May 16, 1914

6. *Boston Daily Globe*, April 12, 1914

7. *Boston Daily Globe*, June 3, 1914

8. *Boston Daily Globe*, July 21, 1915

9. *Boston Daily Globe*, April 10, 1916

10. *Boston Evening Record*, June 30, 1916

11. *Boston American*, March 11, 1917

12. *Boston American*, August 20, 1916

13. *Baseball Magazine*, 1916, p. 98

14. *Chicago Tribune*, December 24, 1916

15. *Boston Traveler*, June 25, 1917

16. *Boston Traveler*, December 15, 1917

17. *Eau Claire* (WI) *Leader*, April 4, 1918

18. Hall of Fame player file for C.D. Thomas. April 18, 1918

19. *Washington Post*, August 24, 1918

20. Hall of Fame player file for C.D. Thomas. Letter dated May 4, 1936.

Benjamin Harrison Van Dyke
by Maurice Bouchard

G	ERA	W	L	SV	GS	GF	CG	SHO	IP	H	R	ER	BB	SO	HR	HBP	WP	BFP
3	3.14	0	0	0	1	2	0	0	14 1/3	11	1	1	0	1	0	1	1	61

G	AB	R	H	2B	3B	HR	RBI	BB	SO	BA	OBP	SLG	SB	HBP
3	4	0	1	0	0	0	0	0	1	.250	.250	.250	0	0

Ben Van Dyke appeared in three games for the 1912 Red Sox.

"Van Dyke VS Keating" the *Boston Globe* article headline read on September 25, 1912. A heavyweight title fight, perhaps? No. The paper was anticipating the last regular-season contest at brand-new Fenway Park. In bookend fashion, the World Series-bound Red Sox were facing the last-place New York Highlanders, who, accommodatingly, were the losers in the inaugural game at Fenway Park the previous April 20. The ultimate game at the new ball-yard pitted two New England League pitching stars against one another, left-hander Ben Van Dyke, late of the Worcester Busters, and "moist ball" right-hander, Ray Keating, who at 18 was deemed the player most responsible for Lawrence (Massachusetts) having won its first New England League crown in the season just ended.

Although the Red Sox were on their way to winning 107 games and the New York Americans wouldn't win half that many, there was a considerable amount of hype generated, at least locally, in this otherwise meaningless game. Van Dyke and Keating were, like their teams, rivals all season, each the star of his team. In May, they had locked horns in a classic Dead Ball Era pitchers' duel with only three hits and one run made by both teams. Van Dyke, having won 20 games for Worcester, cost the Red Sox $5,000 and made his debut with them on September 15; Keating, winner of 26 games, had made his on the 12th with New York, which paid $7,000 for him. Each no doubt was ready to prove who was the better hurler, now that each was pitching in "fast company." A great pitchers' duel was anticipated as the teams took the field on September 26 before many friends and well-wishers, including each player's New England League manager. Perhaps they were overanxious, because neither pitched to his potential, with Keating pitching better but coming out on the losing end. Van Dyke was lifted for a pinch hitter in the fifth having surrendered seven runs on eight hits and three walks. The *Globe* account of the game said, "Van Dyke was hit freely from the start [and was] very wild." In addition to the eight hits, one of which was a triple, he struck out one, threw two wild pitches, hit a batter, and had a throwing error. His wildness caught the fancy of noted *Globe* cartoonist Wallace Goldsmith, who included Van Dyke in his montage of the game's events. Goldsmith drew Van Dyke's attempted throw to second sailing into left field with the caption "Mr. Van Dyke's Sense of Direction was Somewhat Faulty." It wasn't the outcome Van Dyke was looking for, not the end he had in mind. He likely thought it was merely the end of his major-league season, but it turned out to be more than that.

Benjamin Harrison Van Dyke was born, according to published baseball reference sources, on August 15, 1888, in Clintonville, Venango County, Pennsylvania, about 70 miles north of Pittsburgh. On his World War I draft registration card, Van Dyke claimed Harrisville, Pennsylvania, a small community 10 miles west of Clintonville, as his place of birth. The Van Dyke family, however, was living in Marion, in Butler County, just four miles from Harrisville, before and after Benjamin was born. Ben, named for his maternal grandfather and for the 1888 Republican nominee for president, lived on the family farm on Harrisville Road with his parents, James C. and Margaret (Nutt) Van Dyke. James and Margaret had seven children together, four daughters and three sons (Ben was the fifth child). Margaret Van Dyke died in 1897 and it was left to the eldest daughter still at home, Amanda "Jenny" Van Dyke, to tend to the younger children.

After attending grammar school and high school in the area, Van Dyke enrolled at Slippery Rock Normal School, now Slippery Rock University, which was about 10 miles from home. The mission of the Normal School was to train teachers, so presumably Van Dyke took courses in pedagogy. According to a

1912 *Boston Globe* article, Van Dyke played baseball at Slippery Rock for coach Bill Price, who took credit for his development, and was the team's leading pitcher for two years (likely 1906 and 1907). He won 24 of the 36 games in which he appeared.

After two years, Van Dyke moved on to Shamokin, Pennsylvania, in the "outlaw" Atlantic League, where he pitched for player-manager Lave Cross, veteran of 21 major-league campaigns. The 6-foot-1, 150-pound southpaw went 19-3 for Shamokin leading his team to the 1908 pennant. In one two-week period during the season, Van Dyke pitched two no-hitters. The Atlantic League folded after the season and the Philadelphia Phillies obtained Van Dyke's contract for nothing.

Van Dyke reported to the Phillies in late September but did not get into a game. He went to spring training with the Phillies in 1909 and went north with the team as the regular season opened. Van Dyke made his major-league debut on May 11, 1909, at Philadelphia's Baker Bowl against the cross-state rival Pittsburgh Pirates, who were on their way to a 110-victory pennant-winning season. Van Dyke relieved starter Bill Foxen in the fifth inning with his team on the losing end of a 6–1 score. He pitched the final five innings, yielding just one run on six hits. He walked one, struck out five, and was 0-for-2 at the plate. Van Dyke did not appear in a game again until July 14, when he was the third Phillies pitcher in what was to become an 11–2 pasting by the Cardinals in St. Louis. Again he replaced left-hander Foxen, this time in the second inning and again the score was 6–1 the wrong way. Van Dyke hurled 2 innings of two-run, one-hit ball; he walked three and struck out no one. The Phillies released the 20-year-old Van Dyke shortly after that outing to the Harrisburg (Pennsylvania) Senators of the eight-team, Class B (equivalent of today's Double-A) Tri-State League. Presumably, Philadelphia released him to get him more playing time and not because of poor performance. Van Dyke finished the season in the state capital and went 7-4 for the second-place Senators.

There was apparently some controversy about where Van Dyke would play in 1910. He went to spring training with the Phillies and was at their camp in Southern Pines, North Carolina, as late as March 20. He may have thought he was a free agent since he had the foresight at the end of July 1909 to secure his release from Harrisburg as of the end of the 1909 season. He had a letter from Harrisburg manager George W. Heckert, dated July 25, 1909, giving him his release as of September 6. In 1910, however, the Harrisburg club, with new manager Kip Selbach, was asking Van Dyke to sign. Not wanting to, Van Dyke appealed to the National Commission on March 5, 1910, to determine his status.

It is not known how National Commission president August Herrmann responded, but Van Dyke did not play for Harrisburg in 1910 or after. His contract was traded on March 18 to Syracuse in the New York State League for that of third baseman Lewis Carr but Ben never appeared there because he "failed to get into condition." Worcester, Massachusetts, native William "Kitty" Bransfield, the Phillies first baseman, came to the rescue. Bransfield befriended Van Dyke while the two were briefly teammates. Bransfield apparently recommended Van Dyke be sent to Worcester instead of Harrisburg the previous July. What didn't work then would work now as Van Dyke joined Jesse Burkett's Worcester Busters late in May 1910.

The Busters, with player-manager-owner and future Hall of Famer Burkett, were, in 1910, the four-time reigning New England League (Class B) champion. They were again a contending team, vying with New Bedford all season long for the pennant, but lately had some pitching problems. Burkett no doubt thought the "lanky portsider" would help, but it's unlikely he thought the youngster would have the impact he did.

Van Dyke made his New England League debut on June 1 at Worcester's Boulevard Park against the Haverhill Hustlers. On a very cold day (the newspaper account said, "[H]unting polar bears would have been more seasonable than playing baseball"), he led his new team to a complete-game, 4–1 victory before only 150 souls who were willing to brave the elements. The *Worcester Telegram* said, "The left-hander was a bit unsteady at the start but later got along pretty well." Pretty well indeed. Van Dyke gave up five hits and two walks while striking out five; after the first inning, only one Hustler reached second base. He was 0-for-3 at the plate.

On July 20, Van Dyke "put up a marvelous exhibition of pitching" against the Lynn (Massachusetts) Shoemakers, throwing a five-hit shutout with seven strikeouts. On July 26, he pitched another five-hitter this time defeating the Brockton (Massachusetts) Shoemakers 4–2 in 10 innings; Bennie, as he was starting to be called, struck out 11. Two days later, he pitched yet another five-hitter, this time against the first-place New Bedford (Massachusetts) Whalers; he struck out 12 in the 4–3 victory. On August 3, he pitched Worcester into first place with a 4–1 victory over the Lowell (Massachusetts) Tigers. The Busters faded after that but Van Dyke continued to win. His best effort of the season came on September 2 when he one-hit Lynn in a 5–0 Worcester triumph; he had one walk and four K's in the 110-minute contest. Overall, it was a brilliant campaign for the left-hander. He won 20 of the 24 games he started (he appeared in four games in relief) and he led the New England League in winning percentage (.883).

The Busters hoped to regain their championship form in 1911 and improve upon their third-place finish of the previous season. They would rely on Van Dyke a great deal more. He got the start in the home opener, on April 28 against Lowell. Worcester won, 8–4. Van Dyke was not at his best, giving up three runs on seven hits, including a rare home run, in seven innings. Van Dyke was "unnerved," according to the *Boston Globe*, when Lowell center fielder Cuke Barrows led off the eighth with a blast over the right-field fence, the first such hit in the five-year history of Boulevard Park. Burkett replaced Van Dyke with the Busters ahead 8–3. Van Dyke shut out New Bedford, 9–0, on May 4. On May 29, he was hit hard, giving up three runs on four hits to Brockton, and was removed after just one inning. The game was forfeited by Worcester when manager Burkett was ejected from the game in the fourth inning but refused to leave the field. In an odd arrangement, Burkett and Brockton manager Steve Flannagan conferred and decided to play immediately a game scheduled for August 10. Van Dyke started the unscheduled second game and got the win, 10–6, in a darkness-shortened, seven-inning game. He shut out Lowell, 1–0, on June 7 at Boulevard Park, though he needed the considerable help of center fielder Walter Crum, whose fielding "was of a sensational order, his timely work pulling Van Dyke out of several bad holes." On August 24, he

MADE A FINE SHOWING IN HIS DEBUT WITH RED SOX

PITCHER VAN DYKE,
Secured for the Red Sox From the Worcester Club of the New England League.

The *Boston Globe* depicted Ben Van Dyke the morning after he'd thrown 6 2/3 innings of scoreless, three-hit relief.

outdueled 17-game winner Fred Blum, giving up just one hit to the Fall River (Massachusetts) Brienies. Burkett's Pets prevailed, 2–0, in the seven-inning contest although they had only two hits themselves. Van Dyke won 21 games in 1911 against 12 losses in 42 appearances for the second-place Worcester club.

Bennie was big in 1912, arguably his most successful season. On April 30, he shut out Brockton, 9–0. He suffered a tough 1–0, 85-minute loss on May 25 to nemesis Ray Keating of the Lawrence Barristers. Van Dyke allowed only the one run on three hits, but Keating threw a no-hitter. By June 3, when he beat Haverhill on their home field, 6–1, Van Dyke claimed his 10th victory against just one loss. Considering that Worcester had only 16 victories to that point, it's safe to say Van Dyke was their most valuable player. Showing his versatility, he acted the closer on June 25, coming in the ninth inning with the bases loaded and two out. He struck out Lowell's powerful right fielder Rube DeGroff to preserve the victory. Bennie made the start the next day and was beaten again, soundly this time, by Ray Keating.

He was 14–5 when the Boston Red Sox noticed they had a prospect in their neighborhood. On July 17, Boston purchased Van Dyke's contract from Worcester with the condition he would not report until the New England League season finished September 7. The *Boston Globe* article describing the trade called Van Dyke, who was laid up at the time of the purchase with a split finger, "[Worcester's] premier pitcher" and said he "is one of the best-known and best-liked players who has ever worked for Jesse Burkett in Worcester. He is liked by fans and fellow-players alike for his extreme modesty and hard work." At that point in his career, Van Dyke had won 55 of the 76 games he started and was considered the finest pitcher ever developed in Worcester. Back on the mound again by August 1, Van Dyke suffered another heart-breaking 1–0 loss to Lawrence. He gave up only three hits in 10 innings, but lost when the winning run scored on a controversial sacrifice fly. Umpire Jack Kerin had to be rescued by police from irate Worcester fans. The Busters finished in third place, nine games behind Lawrence, but Van Dyke had another great year. He finished 20-10, winning almost a third of Worcester's 67 victories. His 1912 minor-league season was over but his major-league action was just getting started.

Van Dyke made his Red Sox debut on September 15 against the lowly St. Louis Browns at their home field, Sportsman's Park. He relieved Sox starter Charley "Sea Lion" Hall with one out in the second and five Browns runs already plated. Van Dyke pitched the remaining 6 innings, yielding no runs on three hits and four walks. He struck out seven but Boston could not complete the rally, losing 5–4. The *Globe* said Van Dyke "was displaying fine form for his first [sic] appearance in the big league company." He relieved Sea Lion Hall again four days later in Cleveland as the Red Sox worked their way home after clinching the pennant. Van Dyke entered the game with a runner on third and one out in the third inning, and six Cleveland runs already in. The next batter, Naps left-handed left-fielder Jack Graney, lined a Van Dyke offering to Steve Yerkes at short, who then doubled the runner off third. After a clean fourth inning, Bennie unraveled in the fifth, giving up three runs on two hits. The game was called due to rain with no one out in the home half of the fifth; Cleveland won 9–3. Poor pitching (and poor Red Sox fielding) notwithstanding, Van Dyke, a left-handed batter, could take some solace in his first (and only) major-league hit. He singled in the fifth off Cleveland starter and fellow Pennsylvanian Bill Steen. On the 26th, he had his first and only major-league start, the hyped affair against Ray Keating and the Highlanders. Although Boston rallied to win, 15–12, with eight runs in the eighth inning off Keating, Van Dyke pitched poorly and wildly with Jesse Burkett and other well-wishers in attendance. He likely didn't know it at the time, but it was his last appearance in a major-league game.

Van Dyke went to spring training with Red Sox in 1913 but did not last long. By March 13, he was sent back to Worcester. Jesse Burkett then sent him to St. Paul, Minnesota, on a $1,000 option that the Saints had to pay only if Van Dyke proved himself in American Association play. Bennie started the season with the Saints appearing in relief on April 15. He did not fare well there, however, leading *Sporting Life* writer J.J. Cory to opine on May 1, "Van Dyke [has] not shown anything in the slabbing line to warrant [his] retention much longer." Burkett, who needed money and pitching, demanded one or the other from the Saints. St. Paul chose to keep its money and Van Dyke was back in Worcester by May 6. In his first game in Worcester for the 1913 campaign, Van Dyke relieved "recruit" Paul in the ninth inning with the bases loaded and two out. He induced the first batter he faced to fly out, preserving Worcester's 5–4 win over Lynn. On May 21 he started in Lynn and yielded only four hits and one run (on a squeeze play), but his mates could not tally a single marker in the one hour, 20-minute contest; Van Dyke had taken another 1–0 loss for the Busters. He got his revenge, though, on May 30, again facing Lynn but now at Boulevard Park. Again he held the Shoemakers to four hits but this time they couldn't score. Worcester scored two runs and Van Dyke struck out six. He was becoming known for low-hit, low-run, fast-paced games. He needed only 72 pitches on July 16 to shut out Fall River in a nine-inning, 80-minute game in Worcester; this time he was on the plus-side of a 1–0 victory. The *Globe* thought the 72 pitches thrown to be the fewest in New England League history. He had a wild spell on September 10, uncorking four wild pitches and seven walks, yet somehow managed to win 7–1 in Lowell. For the season Van Dyke was merely ordinary at 15-15 in 39 games as his team finished third, 9½ games behind the league-leading Lowell Grays.

Bennie, who, with his family, made Worcester his home in 1914, bounced back nicely with 22 wins which led the New England League that season. Worcester moved up to second place but was still eight games behind the pennant-winning Lawrence Barristers. On May 7, Van Dyke had a 14-inning, complete-game road victory over the Portland (Maine) Duffs (managed by future Hall of Famer and Boston legend Hugh Duffy). Bennie allowed only seven hits, walked no one, and struck out five in the 3–2 victory. He pitched two scoreless innings of relief on July 20 after his team took an 11–10 lead in the top of the eighth at Lowell. He had a nice win over Lawrence on August 26 when Worcester was still in the pennant race.

The next season, 1915, was the last for the Busters in the New England League until 1933. Van Dyke was 15-10 in 31 games. He was shelled by Portland on May 24, giving up at least nine runs on nine hits in 1 innings. Again he was on the short side of a 1–0 score on July 20; Lynn made only two hits off Van Dyke in the nine-inning contest and scored only the one unearned run. On August 31, Worcester and Van Dyke were able to have a measure of revenge against their rival, Lawrence. The Busters, already eliminated from title contention, eliminated the Barristers from the pennant race, 1–0, with Van Dyke pitching a five-hitter. Worcester fell to fifth place in 1915, barely above .500 at 58-56.

The Worcester franchise was sold before the 1916 season began. Jesse Burkett was done as owner and manager. The team, now called the Boosters, moved to the 10-team, Class B Eastern League with new manager and future Cooperstown inductee Sliding Billy Hamilton. Van Dyke pitched a great game for his new manager on May 3 when he held the Hartford Senators to two hits and had the game-winning single in the third inning, plating the only run he needed that day. In the early going, good outings were the exception, though, and by May 15 the press was reporting that Van Dyke had been traded to the New York State League's Scranton Miners for second baseman Joe Murray. Bennie, not liking the deal, was threatening to pitch for a "shop team" for more money (rumored to be Remington Arms of Bridgeport, Connecticut). The deal did not go through, however, and Van Dyke was pitching for Worcester on May 18. The prospect of a trade, must have motivated him, because he started winning. On June 7, he had a one-hit, 3–0 shutout against Hartford and on June 14, he beat Portland, 2–0, at Boulevard Park, yielding only four hits. Van Dyke followed with a five-hit shutout of Lowell on June 20. He was out for about a month with diphtheria, but was strong upon his return on July 20 when he held the Springfield (Massachusetts) Ponies to six hits as the Busters won, 2–1. Four days later, Lynn and Worcester faced off at Braves Field in Boston, just the second season for the ballpark. Van Dyke won the game, a seven-inning, four-hit shutout (1–0) before no more than 1,000 spectators. For the season, his last in professional baseball, he pitched in 35 games with a record of 14-14 in 220 innings. Worcester finished fifth at 61-60. It was Hamilton's only season at the helm.

Worcester was lacking depth in the mound corps in 1917 and wanted Van Dyke to return, but he refused the team's offers and retired. He had pitched seven consecutive seasons for the central Massachusetts franchise, one of only two players in the New England/Eastern League who could boast that. He had won an impressive 127 games for Worcester against just 76 defeats, a .626 winning percentage. His major-league career was very brief. He appeared in five games over two seasons, pitching 21⅔ innings with a 3.32 ERA. He struck out 13 of the 91 batters he faced; he walked 11 and did not have a decision.

After baseball, Van Dyke, who with his wife, Margaret, had a son, Donald J. (born October 29, 1909), went to work as a machinist for the Heald Machine Company, on New Bond Street, Worcester (old friend Kitty Bransfield was a watchman at the same company). Van Dyke worked there for three years and then, along with machinist Philip H. Ramsdell, started Ramsdell and Van Dyke at 91 Exchange Street, Worcester. The new concern, which had $30,000 capital when it formed in 1920, specialized in cylinder regrinding, a process that was fairly common maintenance for the automobile engines of the day. The company continued operations into at least the 1940s, but Van Dyke left after two or three years. After 10 consecutive years, he disappeared from the Worcester City Directory in 1923. By 1930, he was enumerated on the 1930 U.S. census in Albany, New York, in the household of Elmer Van Dyke (who may have been a cousin) and was working as a salesman in an auto supply company. Van Dyke's marital status was listed as "Single" (neither his wife nor his son was living in the household). He lived in Albany for almost 30 years, working for the E.V. Holt Company and later as a salesman for Picotte Real Estate. Sometime during this period, Van Dyke met and married Esther Bradt. The couple retired to Sarasota, Florida, in 1958 and remained married until Esther died in 1970. Benjamin Van Dyke lived another three years before he, too, died on October 22, 1973, at the age of 85; he is buried at Sarasota Memorial Park.

Acknowledgements: Jon Dunkle helped show Van Dyke pitched for Harrisburg in 1909. Bob Richardson shared his New England League stats. Mike Schulz and Alice Rea McSweeny helped with Van Dyke's family history. The staff at Selby Library in Sarasota, Florida, provided his obituary. Thanks to all.

Sources:

Baseball-Reference.com. Sports Reference, LLC. http://www.baseball-reference.com: 2010.

Charlie Bevis. *The New England League* (Jefferson, North Carolina: McFarland, 2008).

Boston Globe. 1909–1916. ProQuest Historical Newspapers. Digital images. http://hngraphical.proquest.com.proxy.mcpl.lib.mo.us/hnweb/hnpl/do/search : 2010.

Boston Journal. 1909–1916. GenealogyBank Historical Newspapers. Digital images. http://www.genealogybank.com/gbnk/newspapers/ : 2010.

Charlotte (North Carolina) *Observer*. 1909–1916. GenealogyBank Historical Newspapers. Digital images. http://www.genealogybank.com/gbnk/newspapers/ : 2010.

J.J. Cory, "St. Paul Siftings." *Sporting Life*. May 10, 1913, 29. [from a story dated May 1, 1913.]

Goldsmith, Wallace. "Champions Wind Up League Season at Fenway Park With Parade to Pibroch to Hielan' Pipes." *Boston Globe*. September 27, 1912, 8.

Hartford Courant. 1909–1916. ProQuest Historical Newspapers. Digital images. http://hngraphical.proquest.com.proxy.mcpl.lib.mo.us/hnweb/hnpl/do/search : 2010.

Geo. W. Heckert. [unpublished letter releasing B.H. Van Dyke]. July 25, 1909. Original document at A. Bartlett Giamatti Research Center, National Baseball Hall of Fame, Cooperstown, New York.

Massachusetts. Worcester County. 1920 U.S. census. Digital images. *Ancestry.com*. http://www.ancestry.com : 2010. From National Archives microfilm publication T625, roll 750.

Alice Rea McSweeny. E-mail correspondence. January 7, 2010.

T.H. Murnane. "Red Sox Make Pennant Certain." *Boston Globe*. September 16, 1912, 1.

_____. "Red Sox Let Up with a Vengeance." *Boston Globe*. September 20, 1912, 1.

New York. Albany County. 1930 U.S. census. Digital images. *Ancestry.com*. http://www.ancestry.com : 2010. From National Archives microfilm publication T626, roll 1403.

New York Times. 1909–1916. ProQuest Historical Newspapers. Digital images. http://hngraphical.proquest.com.proxy.mcpl.lib.mo.us/hnweb/hnpl/do/search : 2010.

James C. O'Leary. "Sox Win Out By Eight-Run Finish." *Boston Globe*. September 27, 1912, 8.

Pennsylvania. Butler County. 1880 U.S. census, population schedule. Digital images. *Ancestry.com*. http://www.ancestry.com : 2010. From National Archives microfilm publication T9, roll 1109.

Pennsylvania. Butler County. 1900 U.S. census. Digital images. *Ancestry.com*. http://www.ancestry.com : 2010. From National Archives microfilm publication T623, roll 1387.

Pennsylvania. Mercer County. 1870 U.S. census, population schedule. Digital images. *Ancestry.com*. http://www.ancestry.com : 2010. From National Archives microfilm publication M593, roll 1373.

R.L. Polk, compiler. *Albany, New York, City Directory*. Albany: R. L. Polk Co., 1941, 1948–1949, 1957.

Retrosheet. http://www.retrosheet.org : 2010.

SABR Baseball Encyclopedia. Society for American Baseball Research. http://members.sabr.org/members.cfm?a=rtl&rtl=enc : 2010.

Sampson & Murdock Co., compiler. *Worcester, Massachusetts, City Directory*. Worcester: Sampson & Murdock Co., 1914–1922.

Michael Schulz. "Schulz Family Tree." *Ancestry.com* http://trees.ancestry.com/tree/3022889/person/-1783769682 : 2010.

Sporting Life. 1909–1916. LA84 Foundation. Digital images. http://www.la84foundation.org/5va/serials_frmst.htm : 2010.

Sporting News. 1915. PaperofRecord.com. Digital images. http://institutional.paperofrecord.com/default.asp : 2010.

United States. Social Security Administration. "Social Security Death Index." Database. *Ancestry.com* http://www.ancestry.com : 2010.

B.H. Van Dyke. [unpublished letter to Mr. Herman [sic], National Commission]. March 5, 1910; original letter at A. Bartlett Giamatti Research Center, National Baseball Hall of Fame, Cooperstown, New York.

Washington Post. 1909–1916. ProQuest Historical Newspapers. Digital images. http://hngraphical.proquest.com.proxy.mcpl.lib.mo.us/hnweb/hnpl/do/search : 2010.

Worcester (Massachusetts) *Telegram*. 1910–1917. Worcester Public Library. Microfilm publication.

"World War I Draft Registration Cards, 1917–1918." Database and images. *Ancestry.com*. http://www.ancestry.com : 2010, From National Archives microfilm publication M1509, rolls MA156, MA161.

Charles "Heinie" Wagner
by Michael Foster with Joanne Hulbert

G	AB	R	H	2B	3B	HR	RBI	BB	SO	BA	OBP	SLG	SB	HBP
144	504	75	138	25	6	2	68	62	60	.274	.358	.359	21	4

"I don't care for Rockefeller's millions and I have no desire to share Wilson's honors," Heinie Wagner once quipped to a group of players during a long, hot train ride out west. "But I would like to be as good a pitcher as Walter Johnson and always be able to pitch for a team as strong as the Athletics."[1] Although never regarded as especially fast, the longtime Red Sox shortstop and coach made a name for himself for covering wide territory from deep short and occasionally slipping his oversized feet in front of opposing base runners to trip them up as they headed for third. On and off the field, his quiet leadership, dogged loyalty and wry humor earned him the respect of teammates, adversaries, and fans in Boston for over two decades.

His nickname, "Heinie," was a lifelong reminder of his German ancestry, but Charles Francis Wagner, son of German-born John Wagner and American-born Catherine Siedle, born in New York City on September 23, 1880, was as American as they came. As a boy, Wagner mastered the inside game in gritty fashion, playing barefoot on the rough-and-tumble side streets and vacant sandlots of Harlem. His first experience on the baseball diamond took place on the streets of Manhattan, and by the age of 17 he was among the most prominent amateurs on the island. Billy Rodenbach, a player and manager of a semipro team on the upper West Side, had a game scheduled with a crack team in New Jersey when his third baseman fell ill. Dismayed, Billy searched for a substitute, and he nearly gave up the search when a friend urged him to check out a kid playing on the streets in Hell's Kitchen. "Go take a slant at him," he was told.

Heinie Wagner in 1911.

Rodenbach would not regret the trip. On a cobblestone street near 39th Street and 11th Avenue, he found the "championship of the Kitchen" in progress. He was impressed by what he saw, and between innings he approached Wagner and complimented him on his ability to scoop hot grounders off the uneven surface.

"Say, Kid," he said, "come over to Jersey and play with my club."

"Aw, I can't play with you big fellows," Heinie retorted.

"I'll take a chance on you," said Rodenbach. "Now, I'll tell you what I'll do. You come over with us and if you make good I'll slip you half a dollar." Wagner agreed.[2]

Believing there was no better way to "gather in easier money than in baseball," after graduating from high school in 1898 Wagner landed his first regular paying work on the New York semipro circuit, earning a dollar a game for the Murray Hills nine.[3] In the spring of 1902, after a brief jump to Waverly in the New York State League, Wagner signed on to play short with the Columbus Senators, the smallest by population of the six charter cities in the newly re-formed American Association.

Wagner's break into the big leagues came in Columbus at midseason of 1902. Desperate to fill the spikes of ailing Joe Bean at shortstop, in late June John McGraw offered Wagner a shot with the Giants in New York. Heinie accepted without batting an eye, and in his July 2 debut he brought the New York fans to their feet with a spectacular grab of a Fred Tenney line drive.[4] Wagner made 17 appearances over the next two weeks, hitting .214 in 56 at-bats, but McGraw—perhaps mistaking Wagner's mellow demeanor as a lack of competitive fire—was unimpressed. He handed Heinie his unconditional release on July 17.

Wagner was not out of the game for long. The following spring, Heinie signed on with Walt Burnham's Newark Sailors in the Eastern League (today's International League). He never hit better than .241 in his four years with the club, but his deft fielding and deadly accurate arm solidified his reputation as a premier middle infielder. Wagner also made a name for himself as one of the league's most gifted brawlers, even winning an arrest during a contest with Jersey City in September of 1906 for punching an umpire in the face for a call Wagner deemed off the mark. Big league eyes may well have been watching that afternoon, for not two weeks later his contract was picked up by the New York Americans. Almost overnight, and amid little fanfare, the Highlanders turned him over to owner John I. Taylor and the Boston Americans.

On September 26 in Chicago, Heinie Wagner appeared in the first of the 805 games he would eventually play in a Boston uniform. He committed an error to open the contest but went on to nail out two clean hits to win accolades from the press. "Wagner played a great game," the *Boston Globe* wrote the next day. "He has all the earmarks of a real find."[5] A "real find" was exactly what the beleaguered 1906 Boston team needed that summer. Only two years away from championship glory, Taylor's club had inexplicably sputtered and spiraled their way from first to dead last in the American League. Taylor, hoping to infuse his aging club with young guns, made Wagner and rugged Holy Cross catcher Bill Carrigan the first installments of a team Taylor vowed would be rebuilt on youth, power, and, above all else, speed.

Wagner's work in late 1906 was more than enough to earn him an invitation to train with Boston the following spring, and on March 1 he dutifully joined his teammates aboard the 9:50 A.M. train out of New York bound for Little Rock. It was a taxing summer from the outset. After enduring five weeks of camp as a rookie newcomer, on the eve of opening day Wagner and his teammates were rocked by the horrifying suicide of enormously popular manager, Chick Stahl. For Wagner, the season only went downhill from there. Playing under no fewer than four managers over the next five months, Wagner fought bitter battles with disgruntled Freddy Parent, who was none too pleased to be dumped from his regular position at short to make way for the upstart Wagner. "Naturally, the presence of Parent on the same team worried Wagner a great deal," the *Boston Post* later wrote. "[Wagner] did not do himself full justice and was at times moody and morose."[6] In October, John I. Taylor put an end to the conflict by sending Parent to Chicago as part of a three-team deal that brought infielder Frank LaPorte from New York to Boston.

Wagner playing catch, 1913.

With Parent now out of the picture, in the spring of 1908 Heinie Wagner found a home for himself in Boston; that was no less the case away from baseball, where the pieces of Wagner's personal life similarly fell into place. Back in '04, Wagner had wed fellow New Yorker Martha Hahn, whose sister, Augusta, had married Heinie's older brother, George, a year prior. Within a year of their wedding, Martha gave birth to the couple's first child—a girl, Elizabeth—and in 1906 Heinie and George moved their growing broods 45 minutes north of Harlem to the tiny hamlet of New Rochelle, where the duo purchased a sprawling duplex on Webster Avenue. In addition to serving with his brother as a volunteer firefighter, Wagner—famously at the time—began raising chickens in the back yard of the property. "He was something of a star in his hometown," daughter Eleanor Wagner recalled with great fondness in 2001. "Dad was always manager of the kids on the New Rochelle team. Even when my oldest brother was very little, he was the manager. And he always made it a point to make sure the black kids and the white kids all had the opportunity to play alongside one another—he was adamant about it, in fact."[7] Outside of coaching neighborhood youngsters during the offseason, however, rarely did baseball intervene in what was otherwise a quiet home life. During the regular season, Martha rarely traveled to New York or Boston to watch her husband play, and after spending weeks and months crisscrossing the American countryside by rail, Heinie had no interest in venturing anywhere outside New Rochelle when the season came to a close. "I regret to see Charley leaving home, as it seems so long each time before he returns," Martha lamented in a rare interview during the winter of 1910. "Some day, however, he will give up baseball and settle down to a quiet home life."[8]

That would be many years off. As Wagner etched steady work for himself with the newly christened Red Sox, club president Taylor followed up on his earlier promise and, one by one, assembled one of the youngest, swiftest squads in baseball: Eddie Cicotte, Harry Lord, and Tris Speaker; Joe Wood, Larry Gardner, and Ray Collins; Harry Hooper and Duffy Lewis. Off the field, they were cliquish and at times their own best enemies, divided—like most of America at the time—along the seemingly impenetrable lines of religion and ethnicity. But on the field it was a different matter. "I had heard there was a division on the team, but my dad never said much about it," recalled Eleanor Wagner. "They were divided at times, and possibly religion was a part of it. In spite of the differences, they got along, and when they were on the field they played baseball."[9]

Clubhouse tensions centered on ongoing ill-will between Catholics Lewis, Wagner, and Carrigan, and High Mason Tris Speaker, and flared into open warfare more than once. In early August of 1910 things came to a head once again, this time over disgruntled team captain Harry Lord. The merits of Taylor's decision to deal Lord and second baseman Amby McConnell to Chicago in August 11 would be debated for days, but no one at the time questioned manager Patsy Donovan's decision to appoint Heinie Wagner as Lord's replacement in the field. "Quiet and unassuming in his work, he has gradually worked his way to the front rank of ball players in this country," lauded one Hub scribe. "Although lacking grandstand playing and manners assumed by some players, he has rapidly made a place in the hearts of the fans all over the county by his wonderful stops and throws and knowledge of inside base ball."[10]

Just as Wagner found his permanent place on the Red Sox roster, a series of injuries began that would interfere with the rest of his professional career. The exhaustive schedule during the 1911 spring training trip to California left a number of men coming back from the coast in bandages. Wagner's injury happened right at the end of training, and caused him to be sidelined for much of the season.

On the heels of back-to-back disappointing seasons, in September 1911 the Taylor family sold their control of the American League franchise to Washington manager Jimmy McAleer and Robert McRoy, Ban Johnson's personal secretary. It was no secret to anyone that Johnson was behind the deal, but to Hub fans weary of nine years of John I. Taylor, it was welcome news regardless. Even better news came weeks later, when McAleer announced that he had enticed first baseman Jake Stahl out of retirement to manage the team for 1912. Under the firm hand of McAleer and with Stahl back in the fold, Boston looked to improve on its disappointing fourth-place finish in 1911. Still, few outside the Hub were ready to predict that Boston was in any position to challenge Connie Mack's powerful Athletics for supremacy in the American League.

After a series of maddening rain delays, on April 20, 1912, Heinie Wagner went 1-for-5 and stole a base in Boston's 7-6, 11-inning victory over New York to officially open Boston's new ball field, Fenway Park. The player-manager of any baseball team of the time also functioned as the captain of the team, but this was not the way the Red Sox were organized in 1912. Jake Stahl managed the team and also played first base, but Heinie Wagner was the Red Sox captain. What manager Stahl said before the game was law, but once the game started, and Jake covered the first base bag, Heinie Wagner took over control on the field, and the manager became just another player who took orders from Wagner over at shortstop. The system worked well, much to the astonishment of baseball purists of the time.[11]

Boston trailed Chicago for the first weeks of the summer, but a surge in early June put the Sox atop the American League to stay. Holding down shortstop "like a ballerina," as Joe Wood later put it, Wagner enjoyed the best season of his career, hitting a career best .272 in 144 games to help lead Boston to its first pennant in eight years and a World Series date with John McGraw and the Giants.[12]

Through the ghost pen of the *Boston Post's* Paul Shannon, Wagner provided the day-to-day "inside dope" of each of the hotly contested games, which culminated in Fenway Park on October 16, the eighth game of the Series (Game Two had ended in a 6-6 tie, stopped by darkness after 11 innings).

Only 17,034 fans turned out for the Series finale—many rooters boycotting the game after a ticket blunder the day before caused a full-blown riot in center field—but Boston's 3-2 defeat of Christy Mathewson in the bottom of the 10th remains one of the storied finishes in World Series play.

During the 1912 World Series, John McGraw realized what he had missed by passing over young Charley Wagner. "If I had you with me the series would be all over now," he said at one point. "I always knew you would make a great ball player."[13] Smoky Joe Wood offered his own evaluation: "The work of one

Shortstop Heinie Wagner at Fenway Park, 1915.

man stood out prominently all through the game. I never saw such playing at shortstop as that of Heinie Wagner."[14] The New York papers praised him as well, and lamented that Wagner, "one of the greatest shortstops that has represented Boston in the big leagues," had slipped through the otherwise astute grasp of John J. McGraw in 1902, only to extract a modicum of sweet revenge with a World Series win.[15]

Heinie returned to Hot Springs in March of 1913 carrying bold predictions of a second straight Red Sox championship. McAleer had the utmost confidence in his popular shortstop—he told James O'Leary, reporter for the *Boston Globe*, "I am not unreasonable enough to expect any improvement in 'Heinie' Wagner. No one could play a better game than he did last season, and if he does as well this year, that will be good enough. And he will be there, you may be sure."[16]

Wagner would not come close to his work at the plate the season before, hitting a disappointing .227, but in the field he turned out the finest defensive effort of his career. One of his specialties was covering second base on steals. He could take the catcher's throw on a run, often one-handed, and apply the tag just in the nick of time. Ty Cobb admitted that Wagner caught him far more often than did any other infielder in the American League.

Wagner was his reliable self at middle infield, but things were not nearly so memorable for the rest of his team. Dogged by injuries and persistent squabbles in the clubhouse and front office, the Sox never made it out of the starting gate. In the midst of a midsummer slump in July, Jake Stahl was shown the door; six months later, McAleer and McRoy were gone as well.

Injuries dogged the veteran players and ultimately doomed the team to fourth place. Wagner dealt with episodes of infection from spike injuries, blood poisoning, and shoulder and arm pain that relegated him to the sidelines on several occasions, allowing greater opportunities for Harold Janvrin to preside over the shortstop position.

And when spring training rolled around in March 1914, it looked as though Heinie Wagner's days in Boston might well be at an end.

Over the winter, fans in Boston read that Wagner would likely be bumped to second base to make room for the enormously promising Everett Scott, who was already drawing a hefty salary from the franchise. When he arrived in Hot Springs with Carrigan in March, Heinie appeared sickly and thin. He did not bother donning his uniform, limiting his workout to solo walks through the Hot Springs hills, and reporters looked on in disgust as he relied on teammates to cut his meat at the hotel dining room. Days later, accompanying sports scribes revealed that he had suffered an attack of rheumatism over the winter and was being shipped back north for treatment. Back in New Rochelle four weeks later, Heinie issued a statement saying he was suffering from "recurring weakness [and] rheumatism in the right arm," and had "given up all hope of ever playing big league ball again."[17]

Wagner's retirement was brief. Irked by his club's lax work and hungry for help from the coaching line, in late June Bill Carrigan called Wagner back to Boston to serve as his third base coach and "all around right eye." Wagner and Carrigan collaborated on strategy as well. They were inseparable friends and celebrated their accomplishments together. Wagner named one of his sons after Bill, and, as an ultimate tribute, Wagner, an amateur poultry raiser in the off-season, named his favorite rooster Rough.[18]

Heinie would not make a single plate appearance during the summer of '14, but his steady presence in the third base coaching box was a boost to the club and, in particular, to his friend Carrigan. The move clearly pleased new Sox owner Joe Lannin, too. In October he offered Heinie $4,000 to remain with the club for 1915.

Rumors about Wagner's future in Boston continued to percolate over the winter of 1914-15. One was that he was negotiating a jump to the Federal League; another had it that he was to take over as manager of the Eastern League Providence Grays. However, when the first day of training rolled around at Hot Springs in March, a surprisingly healthy Heinie Wagner was in uniform and ready to play. Now largely a utility infielder, he hit a modest .240 in 84 games in 1915 as the Red Sox won the pennant and spent his nonplaying time coaching at third. Wagner also found himself saddled with an additional, unforeseen duty on the road: overseeing the off-the-field shenanigans of a raw rookie from Baltimore, Babe Ruth. Heinie was included on the eligible players list, but he did not make an appearance during the Series, and instead collaborated with Bill Carrigan on strategy. Under the duo of Carrigan and Wagner and armed with a new generation of young guns on the mound, the Red Sox put their differences aside and again clawed their way to World Series victory, this time whipping Grover Cleveland Alexander and the Philadelphia Phillies, four games to one.

Fresh from victory, in January of 1916 the Red Sox released Wagner unconditionally, the franchise revealing only that he "might obtain a berth as a manager in one of the minor leagues."[19] For his part, Heinie had long been skeptical of the idea of managing anywhere outside of New Rochelle ("Managers, especially big league managers, have tough jobs," he said with a grimace six months earlier), but whatever his misgivings, in March he agreed to take the reins at Hartford in the Eastern League.[20] It was not a great fit. Wagner navigated the Senators to a 19-24 mark by midseason, but unable to "get big league players for nothing and develop a winning club," he was fired abruptly.[21] Wagner wasted no time in getting in touch with Carrigan, who on June 28 once again called him back to Boston.

The Red Sox were on their way to a second straight AL pennant by September, when Carrigan surprised Hub rooters by confirming his intention to retire when the season was out. Even the sweetness of a second straight World Series pin and promises of more money could not sway the resolute Carrigan, who over the winter affirmed that he was through. Wagner's name was mentioned prominently as a possible replacement for Carrigan, but in January Red Sox owner Harry Frazee announced captain and second baseman Jack Barry as the "logical choice" to manage the club in 1917. With Heinie again at third, Boston rolled up 90 wins to finish second in the AL, nine games back of pennant-winning Chicago.[22]

At the close of 1917, Harry Frazee assured Wagner that he would be back with Boston in 1918, and over the winter Wagner received a copy of his contract in the mail as usual. When Frazee hired Ed Barrow to replace Jack Barry at the helm of the team, however, the Red Sox owner did an about-face, announcing that he was dumping Wagner at third in favor of former Chicago Cub Johnny Evers. "Good, old Heinie…will not shout out 'stay up' from the third base lines this year," the Globe said with a hint of regret. "The Red Sox owner figures that…Evers will be more valuable to his club."[23]

A youthful-looking Wagner on a cigarette card.

As for Heinie Wagner, Frazee thought there might be a place for him somewhere. His loyalty and years of service to the Red Sox deserved something in return. The Globe's Ed Martin recalled that Wagner's loyalty also cost him financially. In 1914, Federal League agents offered him $25,000 to sign a three-year contract, Martin wrote, but Heinie remained loyal to the Red Sox and to his friend Bill Carrigan, although his salary with Boston was less than half of what the Federal League would have paid him.

When the players arrived at Hot Springs in March 1918 for spring training, they soon found out that this year's session would be different when manager Barrow and coach Evers announced some changes. Gone was the annual hike over the mountains, not a favorite of coach Wagner, either—he approved of the walk but deplored the snakes he often encountered. Manager Barrow complained, "You will understand we are not training to win a mountain climbing championship."[24]

The Evers experiment was doomed almost from the start. On the return trip from Hot Springs, weeks of tension between the sharp-tongued Evers and the explosive Barrow collapsed into all-out war.

Midway through spring training, a Hugh Fullerton dispatch carried in the Boston American weighed in on the 1918 Red Sox team. Frazee was throwing money around the league looking for players, but Fullerton asked, "Can money build a ball club?" He was skeptical of Barrow's ability to pull the team together, and considered Johnny Evers a smart man but incapable of coaching himself, let alone a team of notoriously fragile egos. He theorized that Frazee had hired Barrow and Evers as a "happy medium," but concluded that the result of the partnership would do practically nothing positive for team management. Fullerton said the Red Sox once had a great manager—Heinie Wagner—and called him one of the greatest of ball players who possessed every quality required of a manager, but he also conceded that Evers and Wagner never would have seen eye to eye. For their part, veteran players were incensed at losing Heinie, and the hiring of Evers provided no consolation.[25]

On opening day, April 15, Barrow issued a terse statement that Evers had been released and Wagner called back to Boston. With Evers awkwardly looking on from the Fenway Park grandstand, that afternoon Heinie was again in uniform and standing at his old post at third. Once again, it seems, the Red Sox needed Heinie Wagner far more than he needed them.

Under the dark cloud of war, the growing menace of the Spanish influenza, dwindling fan turnout, and staggering losses at the box office, the summer of 1918 was anything but ordinary. Still, as he had done for a dozen years now, Heinie Wagner served his team with loyalty and dedication. He did his level best to keep an eye on an increasingly cantankerous Babe Ruth, and it was Wagner who was ordered to Baltimore to retrieve the slugging pitcher when he bolted the club in early July. "The veteran has seen the last of his playing days but is one of the cagiest coaches in the business," lauded one observer.[26] Indeed, Heinie rarely took the field, having appeared in only six games in the past two years. However, in Washington on July 3, he made his third appearance of 1918. Heinie committed an error and was robbed of a hit by a brilliant stab by first baseman George Burns, but in the bottom of the ninth he ripped a clean single to left off Vean Gregg for his 845th career hit. It would be his last at-bat.

His playing days were over, but at 37, Heinie Wagner had lost none of his competitive fire. "He was quiet but when something was important he'd speak right up and fight for what he wanted," Eleanor Wagner remembered. "My dad was a fighter."[27] That fact was never more in evidence than during Game Two of the 1918 World Series, when Wagner got into a bench-clearing brawl with Chicago third base coach Otto Knabe on the floor of the Cubs dugout. Whoever was responsible for starting the fight was never fully sorted out (by all appearances, it was mutual), but in the end it was Wagner who got the short end of the fight. After being pulled from the melee with a broken finger and uniform that "looked like he had been working on a flivver," Heinie wrapped the injury and resumed work at third. However, Garry Hermann, president of baseball's governing body, the National Commission, was not about to let the event go unpunished. Two days later both men were called in front of the Commission and told in no uncertain terms that if either had any further desire to pick up where they left off, there was "lots of opportunity 'over there.' "[28]

In February 1919, Wagner was out again as part of the Red Sox club. There was a player limit imposed on teams, and non-essential personnel were cut. Wagner got his release once again. In April, he and Bill Carrigan teamed up again and looked into purchasing the rights to the Portland club of the New England League. They at first found Portland's Bayside Park management

Though he didn't live far outside New York City, Wagner raised chickens in the backyard of his home in New Rochelle. *Boston Post*

holding to an agreement they made with Hugh Duffy, and the two were required to wait Duffy out until he moved aside. Hugh finally did, and the Carrigan-Wagner team was back in business on the baseball diamond. But by the middle of July the league crumbled as two of the six teams collapsed, and they sold out to John Donnelly of the Lowell franchise. Carrigan looked into movie house investments in Lewiston, and Heinie was once again footloose until Ed Barrow approached him to return to Boston in order to clear up the atmosphere of dissension that clouded the Red Sox as they dropped deeper in the American League standings. Despite his infusion of "pep" as the newspapers welcomed him back, it was too late for a comeback for the champions. In January 1920, just days before trading Babe Ruth to New York, owner Harry Frazee announced that he had released Heinie Wagner.

Wagner would return to the Red Sox in 1927, brought out retirement by his old pal Carrigan to resume work at third base, but manager Carrigan had been handed little material to work with, and neither he nor Wagner was able to rekindle the magic of the previous decade. When Carrigan had seen enough at the close of the 1929 campaign, Heinie took up duties as manager but with no more luck. After piloting the woeful 1930 Sox (52-102) to a last place finish in the American League (a whopping 50 games back of pennant-winning Philadelphia) to no one's surprise Heinie resigned the day after the season ended and returned to New Rochelle, this time for good. There Wagner spent his final years working as a supervisor at a local lumberyard, as a volunteer firefighter, and as manager of the New Rochelle police and fire department baseball teams.

Heinie Wagner suffered from numerous health problems in his later years, and on March 20, 1943, at the age of 62, he suffered a massive heart attack and died instantly at his home on Van Guilder Avenue. Although he had been employed at the lumberyard for twelve years, on his death certificate his family noted "baseball" as his "usual occupation" and "player and manager" his business.

Endnotes

1. *Atlanta Constitution*, January 21, 1914, 8.

2. "The Sporting Parade," Reviewed by a Veteran, October 1912. Wagner file in the Baseball Hall of Fame.

3. *Boston Daily Globe*, December 25, 1910, SM3.

4. *Boston Globe*, July 2, 1902, 5; *New York Times*, July 2, 1902, 7. Reports of Wagner's whereabouts when John McGraw brought him to the Giants vary. Three days after his debut, the *Washington Post* reported that Wagner had been playing for Providence; the *New York Times*, conversely, indicated that Wagner had been picked up from the Murray Hills club (a version of Wagner's story that was reiterated by the *Boston Post* eight years later when Wagner was made captain of the Red Sox). However, Wagner's obituary and Eleanor Wagner (as confirmed in Columbus papers) state clearly that he was in fact with Columbus when he was contacted by telephone by McGraw.

5. *Boston Globe*, September 27, 1906, 8.

6. *Boston Post*, August 7, 1910, 22.

7. Michael Foster telephone interview with Eleanor Wagner, October 10, 2001.

8. *Boston Daily Globe*, December 25, 1910, SM3. *Boston Post*, August 7, 1910, 22.

9. Michael Foster telephone interview with Eleanor Wagner, October 10, 2001.

10. *Boston Post*, August 7, 1910, 22.

11. *Baseball Magazine*, "A Curious Situation" that it probably didn't happen in Fenway's first season—November 1916.

12. Frank Williams. "The 1912 Boston Red Sox." Unpublished article courtesy of Frank Williams.

13. Paul H. Shannon. "Journeys to the Homes of New England's Ball Players that it probably didn't happen in Fenway's first season—Heinie Wagner," *Boston Post*, February 22, 1913, 6.

14. Joe Wood. "Wood Takes Off His Hat To Captain Wagner", *Boston Globe*, October 12, 1912, 7.

15. "Heinie Did It, Says McGraw", *Boston Globe*, November 5, 1912, 7.

16. "Credit to Wagner", August 3, 1912. Hall of Fame file.

17. *Washington Post*, April 28, 1914, 8.

18. Paul H. Shannon. "Journeys to the Homes of New England's Ball Players that it probably didn't happen in Fenway's first season—Heinie Wagner," *Boston Globe*, February 23, 1913, 6.

19. *Washington Post*, January 11, 1916, 8.

20. *Washington Post*, July 18, 1915, SP2.

21. *Boston Daily Globe*, June 29, 1916, 9.

22. *Boston Daily Globe*, January 6, 1917, 1.

23. *Boston Daily Globe*, February 21, 1918, 11.

24. Edward F. Martin. "Schang Looked Good at the Hot Corner," *Boston Daily Globe*, March 14, 1918, 4.

25. Hugh S. Fullerton. "Fullerton Is Not Strong For Frazee," *Boston American*, March 19, 1918.

26. *Washington Post*, May 1, 1918, 8.

27. Michael Foster telephone interview with Eleanor Wagner, October 10, 2001.

28. *Washington Post*, September 8, 1918, 17.

Smoky Joe Wood
by Michael Foster

G	ERA	W	L	SV	GS	GF	CG	SHO	IP	H	R	ER	BB	SO	HR	HBP	WP	BFP
43	1.91	34	5	1	38	5	35	10	344	267	104	73	82	258	2	12	7	1328

G	AB	R	H	2B	3B	HR	RBI	BB	SO	BA	OBP	SLG	SB	HBP
43	124	16	36	13	1	1	13	11	28	.290	.348	.435	0	0

Joe Wood's reign as one of the most dominating pitchers in baseball history lasted a brief two seasons, but it left an indelible impression on those who witnessed his greatness first-hand. "Without a doubt," Ty Cobb later recalled, "Joe Wood was one of the best pitchers I ever faced throughout my entire career." In 1911 and 1912, Smoky Joe Wood won 57 games for the Boston Red Sox, including a no-hitter against the St. Louis Browns on July 29, 1911, and an American League record-tying 16 straight wins in the second half of the 1912 campaign. He was by no means large or overpowering, standing 5'11 3/4" and weighing in at 180 pounds, but concealed in his lanky frame was one of the most overpowering fastballs of the Deadball Era. "I have seen a lot of speedy pitchers in my time," Red Sox catcher Tubby Spencer quipped in the spring of 1909, "but Joe Wood can make sparks fly better than anyone else I ever saw throw a ball." Three years later, Walter Johnson could only agree. "Can I throw harder than Joe Wood?" he asked a waiting reporter. "Listen, mister, no man alive can throw harder than Smoky Joe Wood."

Howard Ellsworth Wood was born in Kansas City, Missouri, on October 25, 1889, the second son of John and Rebecca Stevens Wood. The nickname by which he would be known for the rest of his life came to Howard by way of two circus clowns named Petey and Joey. "My folks thought it was all pretty funny, and after they came back home they started calling me and my brother Joey and Petey," Wood later explained. "My brother and I answered to 'Pete' and 'Joe' Wood from then on."

Joe Wood was not exaggerating when he once told an interviewer that, as a boy, his family was "always on the go." Generations of Joe's family had been content to farm the Pennsylvania lands colonial militia Private Jonathan Wood had secured from the Public Domain after the close of the American Revolution, but for Joe's restless father, the prospect of remaining on the family farm for life was unthinkable. After completing his education at the University of Pennsylvania, John Wood moved to Ness City, Kansas, started his family, then moved again to Kansas City, where Joe was born. But no sooner had Joe entered the world before his father uprooted the family again in 1890, drawn north to Chicago by the promise of work and a safe haven with his wife's uncle.

In Chicago, John Wood became a successful attorney, amassing an estate approaching a quarter of a million dollars. But for Joe's father, an ample income and a successful legal career were simply not enough. Driven by a pair of itchy feet and the scent of Alaskan gold, in March of 1898 he sent his family back to Pennsylvania and ventured off into the Klondike. After eight months of prospecting he returned, half frozen and suffering from collywobbles, but his dream of striking it rich was undimmed. During the summer of 1900, he loaded his family and belongings

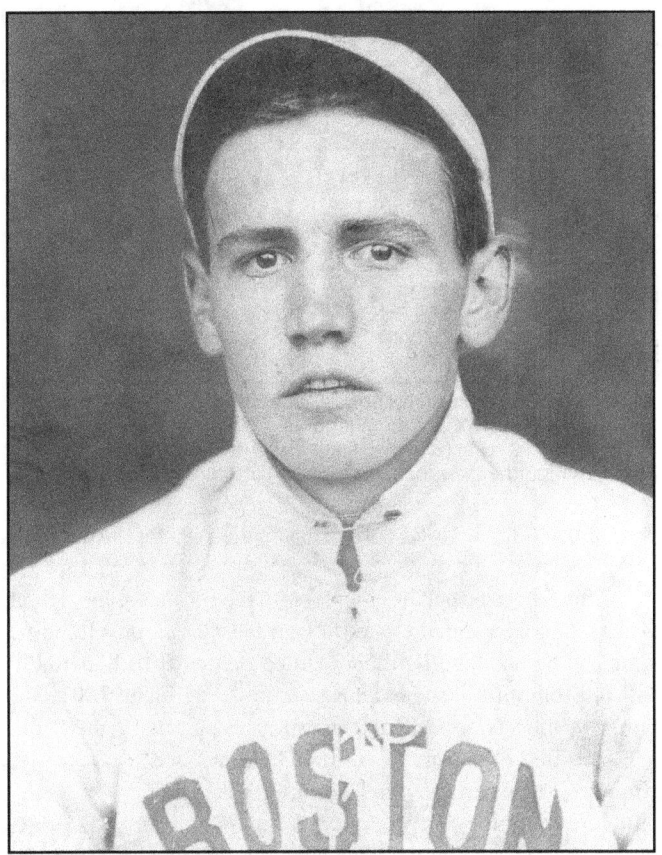

Smoky Joe led the league in earned run average again in 1915 with a 1.49 ERA.

aboard a covered wagon and headed west to Colorado, eventually settling in the tiny mining town of Ouray. Working out of the family's 5th Street home, he renewed his legal practice and began publishing a weekly newspaper, the Ouray Times.

Drawn back to Ness City, Kansas in 1905, the family fell on hard times when John Wood lost his substantial fortune on dubious land deals in Western Kansas. With Pete Wood preparing to enroll at the University of Kansas that fall, Joe—schooling now a thing of the past—passed the time working odd jobs and playing ball with the local Ness City club.

As the close of the 1906 season approached, baseball fans in Ness City learned from posters pasted on storefronts across town that the Ness City Nine was slated to take on an unusual opponent, the National Bloomer Girls out of Kansas City. Though they advertised themselves as an all-girls team, the popular bloomers outfit routinely augmented their strength by adding young boys, "toppers" as they were known, to the roster. Joe sparkled in a 23-2 trouncing of the visitors that afternoon, and at the close of the contest Bloomer owner Logan

Joe Wood famously began his professional career in the latter part of the summer of 1906 as a member of the "Bloomer Girls"—a female touring baseball team (which often had a couple of male players on board, though the males had to dress the part). *Boston Post*

Galbraith offered him $21 a week to join the team for the duration of the summer.

After he closed out the summer with the Bloomers, Joe signed on as an infielder with the Three-I League Cedar Rapids Rabbits, managed by one time Baltimore Oriole Belden Hill. Reportedly "all full up" with infielders, however, in the spring of 1907 Hill unceremoniously scratched Joe from his roster and handed his contract, free of charge, to his friend Jason "Doc" Andrews, manager of the Western Association Hutchinson White Sox. Joe started the season at infield, but weeks into the campaign, the pitching-starved White Sox dispatched Joe to the mound. By late September his uncanny speed caught the attention of numerous scouts, among them George Tebeau, owner of the American Association Kansas City Blues. Tebeau purchased Joe's contract for $3,500 and ordered him to Association Park in Kansas City in March of 1908.

Joe's 7-12 record in 24 appearances with the mediocre Blues was nothing to gloat over, but his strong exhibition work against Joe Cantillon's Washington Senators back at spring training and a near perfect no-hitter in Milwaukee on the 21st of May were more than enough to attract big league interest. After a fair bit of contractual wrangling, Joe's contract was purchased by the Boston Red Sox, and on August 24th, 1908, the 18-year-old made his big league debut at the Huntington Avenue Grounds. Joe was bested by Doc White and the Chicago White Sox, 6-4.

In the first instance of a pattern that would dog him for much of his career, in the spring of 1909 Joe suffered a foot injury during a hotel room wrestling match with his best friend, Tris Speaker, which knocked him out of action until mid-June. Joe pitched well on his return, notching 11 wins against 7 defeats, and his strong work continued through the first half of 1910. But, once again, injury intervened, this time courtesy of a Harry Hooper line drive to the ankle during batting practice. Surgery to remove a blood clot would sideline Joe for better than a month.

On a club rife with cliques and infighting, Joe Wood was as rugged as they came. "He talked out of the corner of his mouth and used language that would have made a steeple horse jockey blush," Hugh Fullerton would recall years later. "He challenged all opponents and dilated upon their pedigrees." But for the underachieving 1910 Red Sox, Joe's rough demeanor off the field (not to mention his disappointing 12-13 finish) won him no praise among Red Sox brass. Exasperated by his club's disappointing 4th place finish, at the close of the summer Boston owner John I. Taylor announced he had drawn up a list of so-called "malcontents" among his players, and Joe Wood's name, word had it, stood unceremoniously at the top of his list. Weeks later, rumors swirled out of Boston that Taylor was on the verge of shipping Joe, along with battery mate Bill Carrigan, out of Boston permanently.

Had Taylor traded Joe—and given the Red Sox owner's dubious track record, there is no evidence to suggest he was not serious—he would have single-handedly deprived Boston of one of the most electrifying summers of baseball on record. After nailing down 23 victories in 1911, in 1912 Wood rose to the very top of his game. Pitching in newly opened Fenway Park, he got off to a modest 3-2 start (twice defeated by Clark Griffith's Senators), but by the close of June his 16-3 mark placed him second in the AL to Philadelphia's Eddie Plank. Joe came up short, 4-3, against Plank on July 4th, but from there he was literally

Yale University coach Joe Wood at Fenway Park in 1946 with Cy Young, Lefty Grove, and Walter Johnson.

unbeatable. On August 28, he tied down his 12th straight win, bringing him to within four of Walter Johnson's record of 16. "Gee," remarked *Boston Post* sportswriter Paul Shannon, as he watched Joe from foul territory one afternoon, "that boy throws smoke." A baseball sobriquet was born.

With the Red Sox bearing down on the pennant in early September, the stage was set for one of the most storied moments of the Deadball Era. "Up until that time Johnson had his sixteenth [straight win] and lost his seventeenth. I had about eleven [actually thirteen]," remembered Joe. "Well, old Foxy Clark Griffith comes in and says, 'Walter Johnson should have the right to defend his record of 16 straight', so he challenged Joe Wood to meet Walter Johnson." On September 6 a circus-like crowd estimated at 35,000 packed every crevice of Fenway Park—filling the stands, outfield and even foul territory along the right- and left-field foul lines—and cheered wildly with every strike Joe burned across. One boy, hit by a foul ball behind home plate, had to be carried from the field; another reportedly "fainted from excitement" and had to be escorted from the stands. In the end, Joe prevailed 1-0, a victory made possible when back-to-back fly balls by Tris Speaker and Duffy Lewis (that would have been playable under ordinary circumstances) fell harmlessly into the crowd and were ruled as doubles. Nine days later, Joe tied Johnson's record with a 2-1 victory over St. Louis.

On September 20 in Detroit, an error by Red Sox shortstop Marty Krug (in addition to Wood's own mediocre pitching) deprived Joe of a 17th consecutive win, but he bounced back to win his final two starts of the summer to bring his record to 34-5, to go along with a 1.91 ERA and career-bests in innings (344), and strikeouts (258). He went on to win three more games against John McGraw's New York Giants in the World Series, capping his extraordinary summer with a 4-3 win in relief of Hugh Bedient in Game Eight on October 16.

Married to Kansas City, Missouri, native Laura O'Shea in the offseason, in the spring of 1913 Smoky Joe Wood stood atop the Majors. "I was the king of the hill," he recalled, "top of the heap, right along with the very best." But, once again, he was vexed by injury. The first mishap occurred in Detroit on July 18, 1913, when Joe slipped on the wet grass fielding a Bobby Veach infield grounder along the third base line, breaking his thumb and (with exception of one inning of relief in September) ending his season. Joe was confident about a healthy return to the majors in 1914, but days before he was scheduled to depart for spring training, he was struck by an appendicitis which sidelined him another two months.

Wood went on to close out 1914 at a respectable 9-3, and in 1915 he led the AL with a career best 1.49 ERA, in just 157 ⅓ innings of work. To onlookers it was obvious that something was wrong with the erstwhile phenom. "Joe Wood has not been right since he was operated on for appendicitis," wrote the Washington Post. "At times…he has shown flashes of his former smoke, but it is uncertain what he can do…" Those fears were confirmed in early October when Joe was seen clinging to his shoulder in pain in his final start of the summer, a 3-1 loss to Walter Johnson. He

Smoky Joe limbers up at Fenway Park.

did not factor into Boston's 4 games to 1 World Series victory over Philadelphia two weeks later.

Refusing to accept a cut in pay, in 1916 Joe remained at home in Twin Lakes, Pennsylvania, working out at a New York University gymnasium while tending to his ailing arm under the care of New York Chiropractor A.A. Crucius. In February of 1917, his contract was sold to Cleveland for $15,000. "My arm is just as good as it ever was," he announced at camp a month after the sale. "I don't expect any trouble at all, provided I don't work it too fast now." Wood could not have been more mistaken. At his debut in Cleveland on May 26th, he was shelled by the Yankees in eight innings of work, and three weeks later sportswriters revealed that, in all probability, he was through as a pitcher. "It is a wonder you have any arm left," Joe's physician, Dr. Robert Drury, scolded publicly. Wood refused Indian owner Jim Dunn's offer to keep him on in an advisory role and removed himself from the club payroll in early July.

The Deadball Era is replete with story upon story of pitchers whose careers were cut short by shoulders torn to shreds; rarely, if ever, did such men make or even contemplate a return to the diamond. Five months after leaving the Indians, however, Joe made the surprising announcement that he intended to attempt a return to the big leagues by converting himself from pitcher to outfielder. In the war-torn summer of 1918 he stepped into Cleveland's starting lineup, hitting a respectable .296 in 119 appearances. From 1919 to 1921 he was platooned with Elmer Smith (his best season coming in 1921 when he hit .366 in 66 games), and in 1920 he made his second and final World Series appearance, going 4-for-10 over four games in Cleveland's win over Brooklyn. He enjoyed another strong season with the Indians in 1922, hitting .296 in 142 games, but citing family obligations he opted not to return to baseball for 1923.

"Few players last ten years in the Big Leagues, [and] fewer still reach such heights in their profession as Joe Wood," eulogized F.C. Lane near the end of Joe's career. "Joe Wood faced the most difficult task a player can be called upon to face and against all seemingly insurmountable handicaps he made good." Those qualities would serve Wood long after he left the game.

Smoky Joe warming up for the Red Sox in 1913.

Through his lifelong friend Tris Speaker, in 1923 Joe was hired by Yale University to coach the freshman nine and, one year later, he was promoted to coach the varsity. There was speculation that Wood's career at Yale might be in jeopardy in late 1926, when, along with Cobb and Speaker, he was accused of being one of three central figures in an alleged game-fixing scandal dating back to the 1919 season. But after an all night session, the Yale Board of Control declared it had "no evidence [which] discredits the honesty and integrity of his past record." Joe would remain with the University for another 15 years, amassing a coaching record of 283-228-1. At the end of his coaching career, Wood coached his son, Joe Wood, Jr. who went on to a brief major league career, pitching three games for the Boston Red Sox during the 1944 season. Two other sons, Stephen and Robert, played collegiate ball at Colgate. Wood and his wife also had one daughter, Virginia.

Citing "economic exigencies occasioned by war conditions," in March of 1942 the University dismissed Joe and two other University coaches. Wood then left New England for California, where he opened a golfing range with his brother, Pete. "I made more money in that seven years than I did my entire time playing and coaching baseball," he later recalled with a chuckle. Wood then returned to New England, and, by 1960, he was settled into comfortable retirement at 90 Marvel Road in New Haven, Connecticut.

Over the next quarter century, Joe looked on as his former teammates and adversaries, one by one, won induction into the Baseball Hall of Fame in Cooperstown, NY. Probably due to his frequent injuries and the fact that his record did not meet the Hall of Fame's requirement that a player's career be "outstanding for a long period of time," the Hall of Fame passed over Wood time and again. In January of 1985 Yale University president A. Bartlett Giamatti presented Wood with an honorary doctorate in Human Letters. At the ceremony, Joe wept uncontrollably.

Two months later, on March 25, 1985, Smoky Joe Wood died at the age of 95 while residing at a convalescent home in New Haven. He was buried in the Wood family ancestral grounds, in Shohola, Pennsylvania.

Note: An earlier version of this biography originally appeared in David Jones, ed., *Deadball Stars of the American League* (Washington, D.C.: Potomac Books, Inc., 2006).

Sources:

Wood family archives, including family papers, news clipping scrapbooks and recordings.

Lawrence Ritter. *The Glory of Their Times: The Story of the Early Days of Baseball Told By the Men Who Played It*. (New York : W. Morrow, 1984)

Genealogical and archival records provided by the Pike County Historical Society, Pike County, PA, and Ness City Historical Society, Ness City, KS.

News accounts taken from the *Boston Globe*, *Boston Post*, *Boston American*, *Sporting Life* and *The Sporting News* obtained through the SABR lending library and at the Boston Public Library Microtext department.

Steve Yerkes
by Tony Bunting

G	AB	R	H	2B	3B	HR	RBI	BB	SO	BA	OBP	SLG	SB	HBP
131	523	73	132	22	6	0	42	41	39	.252	.312	.317	4	4

Quietly dependable though seldom spectacular for most of his five full major-league seasons as an infielder, Steve Yerkes grasped immortality when he played a central role in one of baseball's legendary episodes. In the bottom of the 10th inning of the deciding game of the epic 1912 World Series, Yerkes raced home with the winning run on a sacrifice fly to cap the Boston Red Sox' dramatic comeback over the New York Giants. Yerkes' sprint to glory came moments after he drew a walk from control artist Christy Mathewson. Tucked amid a sequence of shocking plays—and misplays—in the inning, Yerkes' base on balls and subsequent championship tally punctuated an outstanding Series for the 24-year-old second baseman. His key hits in Games One and Five led to Red Sox victories, and he was nearly perfect in the field against the Giants. Yerkes' heroics catapulted him to temporary celebrity and a permanent place in World Series lore.

The rest of Yerkes' career failed to approach the soaring heights of his October 1912 performance. He was hailed by the Red Sox brass as baseball's next great second baseman, but Yerkes' syrupy footwork caused him to swiftly fall out of favor on a Boston team christened the Speed Boys. He joined Pittsburgh in the Federal League in 1914 and thrived in the upstart circuit. When the league collapsed, he logged part of one season with the Chicago Cubs, gaining service in all three major leagues. Charismatic and intelligent, Yerkes spent his post-playing days as a successful manager in the minors, despite suffering personal tragedy.

Born on May 15, 1888, in Hatboro, Pennsylvania, a town about 15 miles north of Philadelphia, Stephen Douglas Yerkes seemed destined for a career on the diamond. (Yerkes himself cited nearby Willow Grove as his birthplace on both his World War I and World War II draft registration cards.) The youngest of eight surviving children of Joseph Ball and Rebecca Valentine (maiden name Yerkes) Yerkes, Steve became one of four brothers—Harman, Claude, and William were the others—to play professional baseball. Steve's father was an accomplished man, who did not dissuade his sons' ballfield aspirations. A farm owner, Joseph held jobs as a school director and teacher and a justice of the peace, and served three years in the Pennsylvania Legislature.

When Steve was a toddler, a terrible accident marked him for the rest of his life. He tumbled onto a scorching coal-and-wood-burning stove in the kitchen of the family home, searing both sides of his face and the area around his mouth. The mishap left him badly scarred and self-conscious about his appearance. But it did not impair his maturation. As an adolescent, Steve manned the infield for teams in Hatboro and nearby Jenkintown. A voracious reader growing up, he enrolled at the University of Pennsylvania in the fall of 1905 and secured the starting shortstop spot on the varsity team the following spring.

Second baseman Steve Yerkes stole four bases in 1912, but was caught 16 times.

That summer, Yerkes tested his ability in the small professional ranks at Millville, New Jersey, the hometown of his future wife, Mary Menz. He teamed with brother William, a pitcher, to help capture the South Jersey League championship. He then caught on with Altoona of the Tri-State League and assumed the name Williamson to protect his college eligibility. Fearing exposure, he abruptly quit the team. But pro baseball proved to be a greater pull than the academic life. Steve left Penn after only two years, and embarked on a vagabond existence during the summers of 1907 and 1908. Swinging a potent right-handed bat and possessing an abundance of on-field savvy, he made stops at Stroudsburg, Chester, and Altoona, Pennsylvania; Millville; and New Bern, North Carolina.

Yerkes launched his initial ascent to the major leagues in 1909. After beginning the year at Altoona, he landed with Wilson (North Carolina) of the Eastern Carolina League. He stayed long enough to encounter Jim Thorpe of Rocky Mount, during the world-class athlete's foray into minor-league baseball that ultimately cost him his amateur status and 1912 Olympic awards ("Steve Yerkes is one of the men who has admitted that he played against Jim Thorpe," the *Miami Herald Record* wrote in 1913, shortly after the news of Thorpe's professionalism broke. "He didn't put up any shout, however.")

Before Yerkes got accustomed to life on Tobacco Road, the Red Sox purchased him for $1,000 and transferred him to Worcester of the New England League. Starting at shortstop, Steve helped the Busters take the league title. Still challenging for the American League pennant, the Red Sox reclaimed Yerkes near the end of the season and inserted the 21-year-old against the Chicago White Sox on September 16. Playing short and batting cleanup at Boston's Huntington Avenue Grounds, he struck out on Doc White's sneaky slowball in his first big-league at-bat, then singled and scored a run off the colorful left-hander. Steve went 1-for-4 in the game and handled three chances cleanly. Unable to make the big-league grade in five games with the Red Sox, Yerkes spent all of 1910 with Chattanooga of the Southern Association. There, the Pennsylvanian flourished. In 141 games with the Lookouts, he batted .279—second-best on the team and 12th overall in the league behind batting champion Joe Jackson of New Orleans—and won a place on sportswriter Grantland Rice's All-Southern Association team.

The effort earned Yerkes a spring-training trip to California with the Red Sox in 1911. This time, he stuck. Projected as a backup infielder, the 5-foot-9, 165-pound rookie quickly undertook a prominent role for Boston. While shortstop Heinie Wagner recovered from a sore shoulder early in the season, Yerkes replaced him and hit and fielded so superbly that he remained in the lineup on a regular basis. "These members of (manager) Patsy Donovan's tribe can't figure out how it is possible to keep Yerkes out of the game when Capt. Wagner gets back in harness at short," one observer wrote. "They say the kid has played the position just as well as Wagner could have done. What's more he has been delivering hits when they were needed."[1] Upon Wagner's return, Donovan worked his rookie around the infield, with satisfactory results. Steve finally settled in at shortstop (Wagner was shifted to second) and completed an impressive first full season for the fourth-place Red Sox. In 502 at-bats, Yerkes became one of the American League's strongest-hitting middle infielders, batting .279, driving in 57 runs, and finishing third in the league with 31 sacrifice hits.

In 1912, Yerkes experienced one of the most extraordinary years of his life. Under Boston's new manager, Jake Stahl, he found his niche in both the Red Sox infield and batting order. Recognizing the sturdy 23-year-old's limitations in range, Stahl placed him at second base. Exuding irrepressible spirit, Steve roused his teammates with shouts of "All together, boys, work hard!" and mastered the Deadball Era art of blocking baserunners en route to second. In the batting order, the Boston leader slotted Yerkes second between future Hall of Fame outfielders Harry Hooper and Tris Speaker, maximizing his ability to sacrifice and pull off the hit and run. Although Yerkes' offensive numbers slipped, the Speed Boys enjoyed their greatest run production in team history.

Throughout the year, Yerkes performed his biggest feats when the glare was the brightest. At the grand opening of the sparkling new home of the Red Sox, Fenway Park, on April 20, he starred in Boston's 7-6 victory over the New York Highlanders (Yankees). Before 24,000 festive fans on a sun-splashed afternoon, Steve was the first Red Sox player to get a base hit and score a run at Fenway, when he doubled to left field and crossed the plate on Speaker's two-bagger in the bottom of the first inning. Yerkes rapped five hits in the game and scored the winning run in the 11th.

He soon developed a reputation for his uncanny poise in pressure situations. *The Sporting News* correspondent and *Boston Globe* baseball writer Tim Murnane deemed Yerkes "[as] cool as an iceberg." The *Boston Post* concurred: "His coolness and courage are the things which have endeared him most strongly to his teammates, and at the bat, whether he faces Big Ed Walsh or the merest rookie, he swings his war club with that same old confident air that has allowed him to bat many a winning run across for the Red Sox."

Yerkes became a favorite among his teammates off the field, too, thanks to his easygoing manner. "Steve is known as the 'Crab' on the Red Sox roster," remarked the *Post*, "but in reality he is the most good-natured man on the team. In fact, his good nature makes him the victim of many practical jokes, and when his teammates tire of poker or other diversions, they turn upon Steve and torment him unmercifully. Yet there is no player on the team to whose defense they would more quickly rally."

Behind the superior outfield play of Hooper, Speaker, and Duffy Lewis, and the sensational pitching of Smoky Joe Wood, the Red Sox breezed to the American League championship. In the World Series, they met John McGraw's perennial powerhouse, the New York Giants. The nine-day October battle for the world title would briefly transform Yerkes' life.

Analysts pegged the second baseman as a weakness in the Boston attack. Undeterred, Yerkes made an immediate impact. In the opener at the Polo Grounds, he blasted a two-out, two-run single to left field in the seventh inning off spitballer Jeff Tesreau, breaking a 2-2 tie. It turned out to be the decisive blow in a 4-3 Red Sox victory. The game-winning hit shocked the 35,730 in attendance and inspired a prescient forecast from the *Washington Post's* Joe S. Jackson. "It will occasion no surprise…if Steve Yerkes, ordinary fielder, fair hitter, and poor runner, should shine with some brilliancy," he wrote. "Already he has produced the hit that won a game. He is likely to butt in at any time with a blow that helps to tell the story. And he acts like a young man who is not impressed with the seriousness of the situation, and who will play a world series just as he would a championship [regular season] game."

In Game Five at Boston, another colossal smash by Yerkes threw 34,683 fans—the largest baseball crowd in the city's history— into near hysteria and placed his club on the brink of a world title. He followed Hooper's third-inning triple off Christy Mathewson with one of his own to deep left-center and tallied on Speaker's error-inducing smash to second. Mathewson didn't allow another baserunner the rest of the afternoon, and the Red Sox won, 2-1, giving them a three-games-to-one advantage (Game Two had ended in a tie).

A pair of easy Giants victories drew the Series even and set the stage for Game Eight at Fenway Park and the thrilling conclusion to the 1912 World Series. In the top of the 10th, with Wood and Mathewson locked in a 1-1 struggle, the Giants scored a run to take the lead. The Red Sox came to bat. At the home of Steve Yerkes' parents, outside Philadelphia, the second baseman's wife, Mary, who received inning-by-inning updates throughout the game, instructed her 2-year-old son, Steve Jr., to kneel and pray for a Boston triumph. After Giants center fielder

Fred Snodgrass's seismic two-base muff of Clyde Engle's fly ball and circus catch of Hooper's drive, Yerkes stepped in to face the masterful Matty. "What the pressure on Yerkes must have been, with $1300 [the approximate difference between the shares of the winner: $4,024.69—and loser—$2,566.47; it was actually more than $1,450, not $1,300] for himself and for each of his team mates hanging on the end of his bat, is hard to imagine," wrote the *Globe's* Frank P. Sibley. "How he managed to wait it out nobody can guess. But he did and Mathewson passed him." Yerkes' base on balls occurred after he got ahead in the count, 3-1, and ignored his manager's edict to swing away. "I looked over at the bench and saw Manager Stahl nodding to go after the next ball," he later told Murnane. "Stahl had a lot of confidence in my hitting, and all summer I had taken his tips, but now I was up against a serious proposition and determined to do my own figuring….I decided to take a chance and wait. I called the turn, as the ball was a poor one, and I drew a pass. That was the only time that I disobeyed orders last year, but Jake rather enjoyed the idea of my having the spunk to assume the responsibility with so much depending on the move."

The walk proved vital. After the Giants famously flubbed Speaker's pop foul, the Red Sox great singled home Engle, and Yerkes hurried to third. Mathewson intentionally walked Lewis. And when Larry Gardner's fly ball fell into the glove of right fielder Josh Devore, Steve tagged up and hustled home with the Series-winning—and -ending—run, triggering a wild celebration at Fenway.

Steve's outstanding World Series—he hit safely in all but one game and committed just one error in 38 chances—and his heroics in the clutch earned him instant fame. Yerkes pocketed his winner's share, which dwarfed his $2,400 salary, and returned to his adopted home of Millville—where his big-league windfall spurred the construction of a spacious new house—to receive a conquering hero's welcome. Greeting him at the railroad station, brass bands and automobiles escorted Yerkes through the streets of the city and deposited him at a local hotel. Hundreds swarmed the lobby to rub shoulders with the World Series star who, in proper fashion, mounted the street balcony and regally addressed the throng below. A week later, the residents of his native Hatboro and Jenkintown tossed him another celebration, attended by Philadelphia Athletics manager Connie Mack. Yerkes spent the offseason indulging his love of hunting and prepared for the 1913 campaign by hiking the terrain around Millville, sometimes more than 20 miles a day.

For his accomplishments, the Red Sox front office rewarded Yerkes with a $600 bonus and boosted his salary to $3,500 for 1913. Huge—and perhaps unrealistic—expectations accompanied the raise. "At second I have a coming star—a youngster yet, with only one full season's experience, but if I know ball players, Steve Yerkes will soon be rated in the [Larry] Doyle-[Eddie] Collins-[Johnny] Evers class," effused Boston team president James McAleer. "He has enough speed and more than enough courage. He will be better in 1913 than he was in 1912, for Steve is the type that improves—the type that waits to learn and watches with open eyes—and holds what he gains."

But Yerkes lacked the quickness of those elite second basemen and his pedestrian baserunning was soon judged a liability. In 1913, Steve got off to a wobbly start both in the field and at bat, and while he recuperated from an injury, Neal Ball replaced him. Gone were the halcyon days of 1912. Floundering beneath the .500 mark and 18½ games out of first place in mid-July, Boston fired Stahl and promoted catcher Bill Carrigan to the helm. Shortly after, the Red Sox put Yerkes on waivers. When Connie Mack of the eventual world champion Athletics claimed the one-time Philadelphia-area prospect for the stretch drive, Boston snatched him back, a scenario that repeated itself later that season. Despite the turmoil, Steve finished the year solidly at the plate for the Red Sox, pumping his average up to .267.

But his days in Boston were numbered. While hunting in North Carolina in the offseason, Yerkes became the last member of the Red Sox to sign a contract for 1914 (in 1913, he had been the first). Trade rumors flew in early February, and one erroneous report had him heading to New York to play for Frank Chance's Yankees. Perhaps disenchanted with the club and uncertain about his future, Yerkes listened to a Federal League representative at the Red Sox training camp in Hot Springs, Arkansas, and later agreed to play in the league in 1915. Back at second base for Boston and batting sixth at the beginning of 1914, Steve's production lagged, and his average plummeted to .182 in late May. When Red Sox president Joseph Lannin got wind of Yerkes' Federal League contract, he released him on August 21.

Steve instantly surfaced with the Pittsburgh Federal League club at shortstop and hammered the circuit's milquetoast pitching, batting .338, slugging .493, and driving in 25 runs in 142 at-bats. One of the better players in the short history of the league, Yerkes shifted to his familiar second-base spot for 1915 and teamed with former National League infielders Ed Konetchy, Mike Mowrey, and Marty Berghammer to lead the Rebels—so-

Yerkes, who fielded superbly throughout the 1912 World Series, loosens up before a game.

Yerkes in profile, 1912.

named for star player-manager Rebel Oakes—within a half-game of the pennant. For the year, the 27-year-old hit .288, 33 points higher than the league average.

After the Federal League dissolved, Yerkes, his big-league reputation rehabilitated, became a desirable commodity. In the winter of 1916, new Chicago Cubs manager Joe Tinker, who had regularly faced Yerkes as skipper of the Chicago Federals, targeted him to fill his vacancy at second base and urged Cubs owner Charles Weeghman to obtain him, which he did, forking over $6,500 for his rights to E.W. Gwinner, who owned the now-defunct Pittsburgh team.

"Yerkes is a much better ball player than the general public knows," said a pleased Tinker. "There isn't any department of the game he hasn't mastered. He is a sure and active fielder, a great hitter, especially for hit-and-run plays, can run the bases in fine style, and has a great head on him. With him to fill up that gap at second base, we will have a stone wall infield."

Earning the $5,000 annual salary stipulated in his Pittsburgh contact, Yerkes debuted for the Cubs at Cincinnati on April 12 and chalked up service in his third major league. Steve supplied "the brains of the outfit" for Chicago on defense, according to the *Chicago Tribune's* James Crusinberry, and furnished his typical pop at the plate; however, he struggled to stay in shape and his nagging deficiency in speed once again spelled his undoing. Tinker benched Yerkes a month into the season, then, in early June, shipped him to Atlanta of the Southern Association, apparently ending his major-league run. Syndicated sports columnist Grantland Rice, recalling the infielder he had covered at Chattanooga in 1910 and the World Series of 1912, penned a lengthy poetic tribute titled, simply, "Steve Yerkes."

If he felt despondent by the demotion, Yerkes didn't show it. Once again he prospered against lesser competition. As a member of the Crackers, he hit .329 (fourth-best in the league) and captured national press coverage for an impressive fielding streak of 127 errorless chances in 24 games. *The Sporting News* trumpeted his contributions on its cover. "Steve Yerkes has not only bolstered the team's offense," commented correspondent Al Weinfeld, "but his work around second has been sensational and, best of all, he has gingered up the entire team with his pep." Atlanta nixed a possible return to Boston for Yerkes, rebuffing the Braves' overtures for him in early September, and the Cubs got him back near the end of the campaign and thrust him into the annual postseason Chicago City Series.

Only 28, Yerkes had played his last major-league baseball. The Cubs trundled Steve to spring training in 1917, but jettisoned him after the club's projected second baseman, former New York Giant Larry Doyle, healed from an injury. Yerkes shuttled to Indianapolis of the American Association, where he did his usual thing: He paced the pennant-winners' regulars in hitting (.282) and outclassed the league's second basemen with a .979 fielding percentage. After rejecting an offer from Branch Rickey to suit up for the Cardinals in the war-torn year of 1918, he stuck close to his current home of Reading and played with Steelton of the Bethlehem Steel League, a haven for draft-spooked ballplayers. Yerkes reappeared with Indianapolis in 1919. Indians owner Jimmy McGill considered Steve for the team's managerial opening, but opted to recycle former pilot Jack Hendricks. Nonetheless, Yerkes captained the squad and enjoyed another superb season at second base. In 483 at-bats, he hammered 30 doubles and 11 triples, and registered a .321 batting average, good for eighth in the American Association.

Despite his success in the minors, Steve stayed in Pennsylvania for the next two years, emerged as a candidate to manage Reading of the International League—he missed out again—and played for the independent Franklin club. Back for one final stint with Indianapolis in the 1922 and '23 campaigns, he concluded his 18-year professional playing career by seeing limited action.

Yerkes finally secured a managerial post in 1924, directing Harrisburg of the New York-Pennsylvania League. But just as his new career in baseball got under way, tragedy struck. That year, Steve's teenage son died of spinal meningitis. Yerkes resigned at Harrisburg before the season ended and eventually concentrated his energies on owning and operating a bowling alley and billiards hall in Glenside, Pennsylvania, near his native Hatboro. Baseball never strayed far from his mind, though. His nephew Carroll Yerkes pitched for the Philadelphia Athletics and Chicago Cubs in the late 1920s and early '30s, and, in 1932 Steve resumed managing in the minors when he took the helm of Norristown/St. Clair (Pennsylvania) of the Class D Interstate League. For the last half of the 1930s, he guided clubs in the Class C Canadian-American League and won championships with Perth (Ontario) in 1936, and Cornwall (Ontario) in 1938. He then succeeded

Yerkes, glove in back pocket, seems to do an odd dance in the batter's box. The infielder's hits helped win Games One and Five of the 1912 World Series.

former Red Sox teammate Clyde Engle, who had died, as coach of the Yale freshman team in 1940 (Joe Wood coached the varsity).

Soon afterward, more trauma wracked Yerkes. His brother Harman, who had once pitched professionally and was Carroll's father, killed himself with a shotgun.

Heavy-hearted, Steve pressed on. He later scouted for the Philadelphia Blue Jays (Phillies) of the National League, then, at the age of 58, gave managing one final try, leading Ogdensburg, New York, of the Border League to a runner-up finish in 1947.

In the meantime, Yerkes maintained a vibrant personal life in the area where he grew up. "Uncle Steve had a wonderful sense of family and enjoyed being among his brothers, nephews, and nieces—he displayed his pleasure by a gentle laugh," said his great-grandnephew Wayne D. Mears of Hatboro. "Although he was a modest and humble person, he was also gregarious. It was good to be in his company. All of us adored him and we respected his privacy by not insisting he talk about his baseball career."

As he entered the waning years of his life, Yerkes saw the 1912 World Series grow in legend. Accounts of the climactic Game Eight and its incredible final inning sprang up in books, magazines, and newspapers. On April 21, 1962, Steve and eight of his Red Sox teammates returned to Fenway Park for a pregame ceremony to celebrate the 50th anniversary of the ballpark's opening, reacquainting fans with the 1912 world champions. In 1966, Lawrence Ritter's classic book *The Glory of Their Times*, a collection of player reminiscences of early 20th-century baseball, brought the 10th inning of Game Eight vividly to life through the words of Harry Hooper, Fred Snodgrass, and Giants catcher Chief Meyers. Once more, the unflappable young Boston infielder worked Christy Mathewson for a critical walk and made his historic run home to win the World Series.

Steve Yerkes died in Landsdale, Pennsylvania, on January 31, 1971, at the age of 82. He rests beside his wife, Mary, and son Stephen Jr. in Holy Sepulchre Cemetery in Cheltenham, Pennsylvania.

Sources:

Timothy M. Gay. *Tris Speaker: The Rough-and-Tumble Life of a Baseball Legend* (Lincoln and London: University of Nebraska Press, 2005).

Joe Hoppel. *The Series* (St. Louis: The Sporting News Publishing Co., 1988).

Josiah Granville Leach. *Chronicle of the Yerkes Family: With Notes on the Leech and Rutter Families*. (Whitefish, Montana: Kessinger Publishing, 2007).

Bill Nowlin and Jim Prime. *The Boston Red Sox World Series Encyclopedia [No Longer the World's Shortest Book]* (Burlington, Massachusetts: Rounder Books, 2008).

Joseph L. Reichler, ed. *The Baseball Encyclopedia* (New York: Macmillan Publishing Co., Inc., 1979).

Lawrence S. Ritter. *The Glory of Their Times: The Story of the Early Days of Baseball Told by the Men Who Played It* (New York: William Morrow and Company, Inc., 1984).

Glenn Stout and Richard A. Johnson. *Red Sox Century: One Hundred Years of Red Sox Baseball* (Boston and New York: Houghton Mifflin Company, 2000).

Robert W. Wheeler *Jim Thorpe, World's Greatest Athlete* (Norman, Oklahoma: University of Oklahoma Press, 1979).

Robert Peyton Wiggins. *The Federal League of Base Ball Clubs: The History of an Outlaw Major League, 1914-1915* (Jefferson, North Carolina, and London: McFarland & Company, Inc., 2008).

Marshall D. Wright. *The American Association: Year-by-Year Statistics for the Baseball Minor League, 1902-1952* (Jefferson, North Carolina, and London: McFarland & Company, Inc., 1997).

----------. *The Southern Association in Baseball, 1885-1961* (Jefferson, North Carolina, and London: McFarland & Company, Inc., 2002).

Paul J. Zingg. *Harry Hooper: An American Baseball Life* (Urbana and Chicago: University of Illinois Press, 1993).

Articles

T.H. Murnane. "Little Steve Yerkes Prayed for Success of Dad and Boston." *Boston Daily Globe*, March 2, 1913.

Wm. A. Phelon "Forecasts and Recollections." *Baseball Magazine*,

January 1917.

----------. "The Last Word From the Training Camps." *Baseball Magazine*, May 1916.

"Red Sox vs. Giants." *Baseball Magazine*, November 1912.

Jake Stahl. "Just Before the Final Struggle." *Baseball Magazine*, November 1912.

"Stars of the Federal League." *Baseball Magazine*, April 1916.

"Steve Yerkes, Called 'Crabb,' (sic) Really Best Natured Man on Team," *Boston Post*, September 9, 1912.

Al Weinfeld. "Yerkes Puts New Life in Cracker Club," *The Sporting News*, June 29, 1916.

"Who's Who." *Baseball Magazine*, September 1911.

"Who's Who in the Federal League." *Baseball Magazine*, July 1915.

Newspapers

Boston Globe

Boston Post

Chicago Tribune

Christian Science Monitor

Fort Worth Star-Telegram

Hartford Courant

Kansas City Star

Macon Weekly Telegraph

Miami Herald Record

New York Times

Philadelphia Evening Bulletin

Philadelphia Inquirer

San Jose Mercury News

Sporting Life

The Sporting News

Trenton Evening Times

Washington Post

Woodland (California) *Daily Democrat*

Web

access.newspaperarchive.com

ancestry.com

archives.upenn.edu/people/1800s/yerkes_stephen_douglas.html

baseballlibrary.com

baseballreference.com

chroniclingamerica.loc.gov

findagrave.com

heritagequestonline.com

hngraphical.proquest.com

infoweb.newsbank.com

la84foundation.org

mcpl.lib.mo.us

retrosheet.org

wikipedia.org/wiki/Jim_Thorpe

Archives

National Baseball Library, Cooperstown, New York. Steve Yerkes file.

University of Pennsylvania, University Archives and Records Center. Stephen Douglas Yerkes.

Correspondence

Wayne D. Mears (great-grandnephew of Steve Yerkes). Letter to author, December 28, 2009.

David T. Shannon Jr. (Millbrook Society, Hatboro, Pennsylvania). E-mails to author, September 15, 2009; November 1, 2009; November 8, 2009; November 11, 2009.

Betty Smith (Old York Road Historical Society, Jenkintown, Pennsylvania). E-mail to author, November 4, 2009.

Joseph Yerkes (grandnephew of Steve Yerkes). Letter to author, December 22, 2009.

Jimmy McAleer
By David L. Fleitz

Jimmy McAleer was not much of a hitter, but this brilliant defensive outfielder was a smart, clever, and ambitious man who helped create two of the original eight franchises of the American League. In 1900 he became the first manager of the Cleveland franchise now known as the Indians, and two years later league president Ban Johnson chose McAleer to assemble and manage a new team in St. Louis in direct competition with the established Cardinals of the rival National League. McAleer's new club, the Browns, nearly won the pennant in its first year of operation. Though the Browns soon fell to the second division, McAleer led the team for eight years, winning more games than any other manager in Browns team history. He then moved on to manage the Washington Senators, where he started Walter Johnson on the road to stardom, and ultimately became president and part owner of the Boston Red Sox in 1912. His Red Sox won the World Series that year, but a series of disputes both on and off the field drove him from the game and deprived the American League of one of its most talented leaders and organizers.

James Robert McAleer, the youngest of eight children, was born in Youngstown, Ohio, on July 10, 1864. His Irish-born father, Owen, and English-born mother, Mary Miller, had emigrated to Canada (where Jimmy's five older brothers were born), then moved to Ohio not long before Jimmy's birth Jimmy's father, who died before 1870, was a boilermaker, and all of his siblings found employment as factory laborers as soon as they were old enough to work. (Jimmy's older brother Owen later moved to California, founded an iron and steel company there, and became a wealthy industrialist and, from 1904 to 1909, mayor of Los Angeles.) Jimmy, however, loved baseball, and was not interested in spending his life in the steel mills of Youngstown. He was determined to earn a living in the game, and practiced diligently to that end.

Jimmy began his playing career with minor-league teams in his hometown during the early 1880s before advancing to Charleston (South Carolina) of the Southern Association in 1886. After a season and a half with Memphis in the same circuit, he moved to Milwaukee of the Western Association in 1888. His stellar fielding drew the attention of the Cleveland Spiders of the National League, which he joined in 1889. He switched to Cleveland's Players League entry in 1890, but returned to the Spiders at season's end, remaining with the team for eight more years.

McAleer, who stood 6 feet tall and weighed 180 pounds, was the prototypical good-field, no-hit outfielder. One of the weakest batters in the National League (in 1898, 84 of his 87 hits were singles), he more than compensated for his shortcomings at the plate with his brilliance in the field, in the eyes of many of his contemporaries. He was considered the best defensive outfielder of the 1890s, and veteran sportswriter Franklin Lewis, in his definitive history of Cleveland baseball published in 1949, called McAleer "perhaps the most graceful outfielder known to the game with the exception of Tris Speaker." McAleer covered vast expanses of ground and gave strong support to Cy Young, George "Nig" Cuppy, and other Cleveland pitchers.

Jimmy McAleer with the St. Louis Browns, 1902.

After the 1898 season, McAleer announced his retirement as a player and returned to Youngstown, where he purchased and managed the local Inter-State League team and waited for a chance to direct a team in the majors. He also opened a haberdashery, McAleer and Snodgrass, with a man named Charles H. Snodgrass at 18 West Federal Street in Youngstown. A managerial opportunity came in 1900, after the National League folded the Spiders and three other poorly performing franchises. Ban Johnson, president of the newly renamed American League, then placed a team in Cleveland and hired McAleer to manage it. His Cleveland ballclub finished sixth in 1900 and seventh in 1901, after the upstart circuit assumed major status and declared war against the National League.

The Cleveland manager played an important role in the battle between the leagues. He proved to be one of Ban Johnson's leading recruiters, persuading many National League stars to cast their lot with the new circuit. In late 1901, Johnson moved the struggling Milwaukee franchise to St. Louis and asked McAleer to manage the team, which was named the Browns, and recruit players for it. The new leader scored a coup when he induced seven members of the St. Louis Cardinals, including future Hall

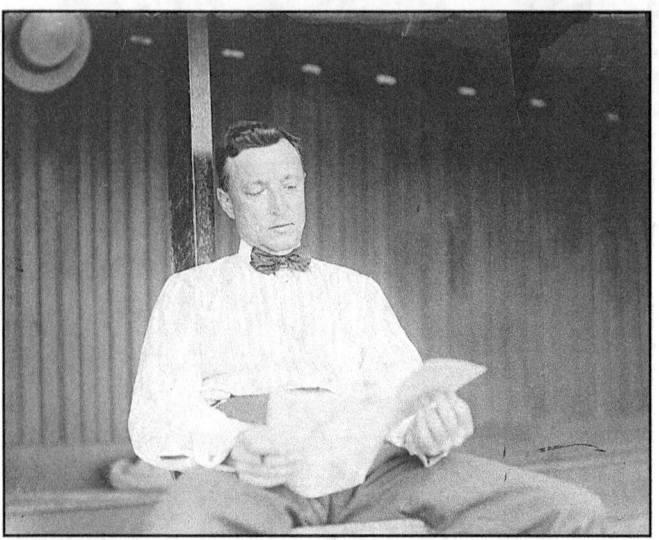
McAleer, 1912.

of Famers (and former Spiders teammates) Jesse Burkett and Bobby Wallace, to join his Browns. McAleer's raid devastated the Cardinals, who did not reach the first division again until 1914, and made the Browns the more popular team in St. Louis. Burkett batted .306 in 1902, while Jack Powell and Red Donahue won 22 games apiece as McAleer led the Browns to a strong second-place finish.

His playing career was virtually over by this time. McAleer played in only two games for the 1902 Browns, and (except for two pinch-running appearances in 1907) was a nonplaying manager from 1903 onward. Many teams in that era employed a bench manager and appointed a player as field captain, but McAleer directed the team from the coaching lines, assuming full responsibility for the club on the field and off. A captain, said McAleer, "is likely to feel that the duty of [arguing with the umpires] falls upon his shoulders. He may get too strenuous. Out of the game he will go, and the team will be without the services of a regular. But if I am chased the team will not be weakened."

Though McAleer managed the team for eight seasons, St. Louis never surpassed its 1902 performance under his leadership. The Browns dropped to sixth place in 1903, remained there in 1904, and fell to last place in 1905, though they drew more fans than the rival Cardinals. Several of the Browns, including outfielder Jesse Burkett, shortstop Bobby Wallace, pitcher Jack Powell, and catcher Jack O'Connor, were coming to the end of long careers, and the team fell in the standings as its key players aged.

McAleer tried to improve the Browns through trades. In December 1904, he sent the fading Burkett to the Boston Americans for cash and George Stone, an outfielder who had been the talk of the minors with Milwaukee in 1904. Stone blossomed in St. Louis, leading the league in hits in 1905 and winning the 1906 batting title. McAleer traded Jack Powell to the New York Highlanders for pitcher Harry Howell and cash in March 1904, then repurchased Powell the following year and restored him to the rotation. In 1908, McAleer purchased the erratic left-hander Rube Waddell, who had worn out his welcome with the Philadelphia Athletics. Though Waddell quit the team briefly that spring when McAleer refused him an advance on his salary, he won 19 games and teamed with Howell, Powell, and Bill Dinneen to form a formidable pitching corps. All four starters posted earned-run averages of 2.11 or better for McAleer that season.

The Browns battled the Tigers, Naps, and White Sox for the 1908 pennant, leading the league in July before fading to a fourth-place finish. McAleer expected the Browns to challenge again in 1909, but injuries and the protracted illness of George Stone knocked them out of contention. The team suffered through a 2-20 skid in May and June and fell to seventh place as the St. Louis newspapers produced a steady stream of condemnation. "There are things a manager should be held accountable for, and I am willing to get my share of criticism," said a defiant McAleer, "but unforeseen accidents and a steady run of ill luck are not among the causes for criticism." Owner Robert Hedges did not agree, so McAleer resigned in September 1909, accepting an offer of $10,000 per year to manage the Washington Senators. He had piloted the Browns to only two first-division finishes (in 1902 and 1908) in his eight years at the helm, but the team quickly fell to the bottom of the standings after his departure. The Browns did not finish as high as fourth place again until 1920.

Washington was a last-place team, but featured the most promising young pitcher in the major leagues. Walter Johnson, a 22-year-old fastballer, had compiled a 32-48 record in his first three seasons. His previous managers had used him irregularly, alternating flurries of activity (in 1908, Johnson pitched three complete-game shutouts in four days) with periods of inaction. McAleer gave Johnson a more regular workload, and the pitcher responded with a 25-win season. The Senators, led by Johnson, finished seventh in 1910 but won 24 more games than the previous year.

McAleer, who gained partial ownership of the Washington franchise, developed a reputation as an entrepreneur during this time. He put together all-star teams to play tune-up matches against the American League champion Philadelphia Athletics before the 1910 and 1911 World Series. The games helped the Athletics stay in shape for the Series, both of which they won. In July 1911, McAleer assembled one of the greatest all-star aggregations of all time to play a benefit game for the family of the late Cleveland pitcher Addie Joss. McAleer's team, which included Ty Cobb, Tris Speaker, Walter Johnson, and other stars, defeated Cleveland by a 5-3 score and raised almost $13,000 for the Joss family. McAleer also tried, unsuccessfully, to interest major-league players and executives in an exhibition tour of Japan that year.

Washington finished in seventh place again in 1911, and McAleer was ready to move on when the owners of the Boston Red Sox put half of their team up for sale. McAleer's longtime friend and hunting companion, Ban Johnson, arranged a deal in which McAleer and Robert McRoy, Johnson's personal secretary, bought 50 percent of the team. The deal was consummated in September 1911, and McAleer took over as president of the club. McAleer personally owned only 10 percent of the Red Sox, with the rest of the money coming from a syndicate of investors assembled by Johnson. One key shareholder was H.W. Mahan, a Chicago banker who was the father-in-law of Garland "Jake" Stahl, a former Boston infielder who had left the game to enter the banking world. McAleer, most likely at the insistence of his investors (and of Johnson, who was a close friend of Stahl's family), hired Stahl to manage the Red Sox.

The 1912 season, McAleer's first as club president, was an unqualified success. The team opened its new stadium, Fenway Park, on April 20, coasted to the pennant by 14 games over the second-place Senators, and defeated the New York Giants in the World Series. However, McAleer and Stahl, who was not McAleer's choice to manage the team, clashed often. The team was also divided by friction between Irish Catholic players, led by catcher Bill Carrigan, and the Protestant contingent headed by stars Tris Speaker and Joe Wood. McAleer was an Irish Catholic, while Stahl, a Protestant, was a close friend of Speaker and Wood. The two factions engaged in petty bickering and the occasional physical altercation, while Stahl and McAleer battled openly. The feuding on the Boston club provided much fodder for local newspaper columns and marred an otherwise successful season.

The differences between Stahl and McAleer came to a head during the World Series. With the Red Sox leading the Series three games to one (with one tie), Stahl chose Joe Wood to pitch Game Six at Fenway Park. McAleer, however, ordered his manager to send Buck O'Brien, an Irish Catholic, to the mound instead. McAleer had his way, and the Red Sox lost 5-2, with all five runs scored off O'Brien in the first inning. Wood was so angry with the outcome that he reportedly attacked O'Brien with a bat before the seventh game. Teammates broke up the ugly fight, but Wood pitched so poorly afterward that many believe to this day that he lost the game on purpose. He faced only nine batters in Game Seven, allowing six runs and seven hits before giving way to a reliever. He appeared to be merely lobbing the ball across the plate, perhaps to show his disgust with McAleer, or possibly because he was exhausted from the pregame fight with O'Brien. Though the Red Sox eventually prevailed in the eight-game Series, questions about the integrity of the seventh game of the 1912 World Series have lingered ever since.

McAleer's popularity in Boston was further damaged by a ticket fiasco before Game Seven. The Royal Rooters, Boston's boisterous, mostly Irish fan club headed by Mayor John "Honey Fitz" Fitzgerald, paraded on the field at Fenway Park before the game and proceeded to their usual block of seats in the left-field stands, only to find that club management had sold the seats out from under them. A near-riot ensued that delayed the game for nearly an hour before the police could gain control of the situation. McAleer blamed a "clerical error" for the mix-up, but the outraged Rooters called for a fan boycott of the eighth game the next day. As a result, only about 17,000 people, half of Fenway Park's capacity, saw the Red Sox win the world championship.

The Red Sox, with Wood suffering from injuries that eventually derailed his promising career, struggled to stay in the pennant race during the early part of the 1913 season. The Philadelphia Athletics built a sizable lead, and by mid-July the dissension-ridden Red Sox were mired in fifth place, 18 games behind the Athletics and two games under the .500 mark. The tension between the Catholics and Protestants had to be resolved, one way or another, and on July 15 McAleer came down firmly on the side of the Irish Catholics. He fired Jake Stahl as manager and replaced him with Bill Carrigan.

Carrigan's appointment as manager steadied the Red Sox, who played better ball during the last half of the 1913 season and finished in fourth place. However, McAleer's dismissal of Stahl spelled the end of his tenure as president of the team. The moneymen behind the club were angry at McAleer for dumping Stahl only nine months after winning the world championship. The fans were upset by the team's poor performance, and the Royal Rooters were still seething over the World Series ticket debacle of the previous fall. Ban Johnson was distressed by the turmoil in Boston and the imminent threat posed by the new Federal League, and secretly began looking for a man with deeper pockets to replace McAleer. A few months later, he found one in the person of a Canadian-born businessman, Joseph Lannin.

While McAleer was out of the country in late 1913, accompanying the Giants and White Sox on a round-the-world tour, Johnson met with members of McAleer's investment group and persuaded them to sell their stock in the Red Sox to Lannin. Before long, Lannin controlled enough shares to depose McAleer as head of the ballclub. A tersely-worded telegram from Johnson, sent to a surprised McAleer in early 1914, brusquely informed the Boston team president of his ouster. McAleer, stripped of power, had no choice but to sell out to Lannin as well, ending his association with the Red Sox and, as it turned out, with baseball itself. He never returned to the game, and never spoke to Johnson again.

McAleer married at least twice, the first time by 1900; the 1920 federal census shows McAleer

New owner James McAleer at the American League meetings, December 1911 at the Waldorf Astoria Hotel, New York.

with a wife six years his junior, Hannah (or Anna) McAleer. He pursued business interests in Youngstown until becoming ill with cancer in the early 1930s. On April 29, 1931, four months after his wife passed away, and two months after marrying singer Georgianna Rudge, Jimmy McAleer took his own life. He was 66 years old, and was buried at Oak Hill Cemetery in Youngstown.

Note: An earlier version of this biography originally appeared in David Jones, ed., *Deadball Stars of the American League* (Washington, D.C.: Potomac Books, Inc., 2006).

Sources:

For this biography, the author used a number of contemporary sources, especially those found in the subject's file at the National Baseball Hall of Fame Library.

Washington Post, August 22, 1909; December 21, 1909; September 18, 1911; April 30, 1931.

New York Times, September 16, 1911.

Peter Golenbock. *The Spirit of St. Louis: A History of the St. Louis Cardinals and Browns* (New York: William Morrow, 2000).

Franklin Lewis. *The Cleveland Indians*. (New York: G.P. Putnam's Sons, 1949).

State of Ohio Certificate of Death

Henry Thomas. *Walter Johnson: Baseball's Big Train.* (Phenom Press, 1995).

Robert L. Tiemann and Mark Rucker (editors). *Nineteenth Century Stars*. Society for American Baseball Research, 1989.

John I. Taylor
by John Stahl

John I. Taylor is one of the most controversial figures in Boston Red Sox history. After Boston won the first 20th-century World Series in 1903, American League president Ban Johnson faced a dilemma. The Boston championship team was owned and operated by Midwestern interests. Johnson wisely decided that the team should be sold to a local group. Gen. Charles Henry Taylor, publisher of the *Boston Globe*, bought the team. He immediately made the youngest of his three sons the team president. John I., as he was called, ran the team from 1904 through 1911.

Subsequently assessing Taylor's time as Boston's president, Red Sox historians were not impressed. Donald Hubbard in *The Red Sox Before the Babe* unfavorably characterized Taylor as a "spoiled" rich kid, a "screw-up," and an "incompetent." Frederick Lieb in *The Boston Red Sox* called Taylor the "worst enemy" of his own teams. Peter Golenbock in *Fenway–An Unexpurgated History of the Boston Red Sox* asserted that Charles Taylor bought the team only to give the "wild" John I. "something to do." Glenn Stout in *Red Sox Century* characterized Taylor's tenure as "easily the most unsuccessful of any Boston owner."

Nevertheless, after Boston won the 1904 American League pennant, Taylor's organization went through the unpleasant but necessary task of overhauling an aging team. After seven acrimonious years during which the team was incrementally disassembled and rebuilt with younger players, the franchise emerged with a highly competitive team that featured arguably the greatest set of outfielders in the history of baseball.

Tris Speaker, Duffy Lewis, and Harry Hooper were all excellent hitters and outstanding defensive outfielders. Hooper and Speaker were subsequently elected to the Baseball Hall of Fame. The three outfielders, along with the other young players assembled by the Taylor organization, won the 1912 World Series over the New York Giants. The 1912 team established the best regular season won-lost record in Boston baseball history. The same outfield trio won another world championship in 1915

John Irving Taylor was born on January 14, 1875, in Somerville, Massachusetts, outside Boston. He was the third and youngest son of Charles Henry Taylor and Georgiana Olivia Davis. He had two brothers (William and Charles) and two sisters (Elizabeth and Grace). His father was a Civil War veteran and joined the *Boston Globe* as a temporary business manager in 1873 at the age of 27. Taylor eventually became the paper's publisher and ultimately created a profitable, large-circulation newspaper. His descendants were publishers or presidents of the *Globe* until the paper was sold in 1999.

John Taylor, owner of the Boston Red Sox before the 1912 season.

After graduating from high school, John went to work for the *Globe*. For several years, he worked in both the *Globe's* advertising and editorial departments. Although John had journalism "in his blood," he discovered that he did not like the newspaper business. Being a good amateur athlete, he found himself increasingly drawn to baseball. He attended as many games as he could. Taylor's grandson later remembered, "My granddad was an absolute nut about baseball."

In 1903, Boston beat Pittsburgh in the World Series, the first ever held. With the new American League's foothold in Boston secure, Ban Johnson sought local buyers. Two bidders quickly emerged. Boston Mayor John F. "Honey Fitz" Fitzgerald headed one group. Charles Taylor led the second.

Eager to strongly sustain the team's success in Boston, Johnson accepted the Taylor bid. Taylor's ownership of the *Globe* was probably the deciding factor. The *Globe* would assure strong, sustained media coverage of the team's activities. Within that framework, Johnson's American League would receive plenty of ink. The selling price was reported to be about $145,000.

Charles Taylor immediately turned over the operation of the team to his son. John I. had been advertising manager of the *Globe* but left the position a few months before the April transaction, [*Boston Globe*, April 19, 1904] and was no longer employed at the *Globe* when the family purchased the club in his name. Charles's decision to entrust his new acquisition to the now unemployed John I. drew guffaws from the sports press, which saw the move as a thinly veiled attempt by a busy father to keep his playboy son out of trouble.

At 29, John I. became the Boston team president. The *Globe* subsequently described him as a "man of fine physique, tall and well-built, with large, piercing eyes." While thoroughly enjoying social occasions that included good drinks and lively women, Taylor was also both analytical and outspoken. He had great admiration for those who knew and measured up to their jobs. He also detested bluff and bluffers and had little time for what he called "bunk." Like most people, John I. was better fitted to ride with winning teams than to deal with the bumps of losing. Sportswriter Lieb noted that when the team lost, Taylor became a hot-tempered, sarcastic taskmaster to many of his players and managers.

Upon the announcement of the ownership change, Lieb wrote, John I. gave manager Jimmy Collins a strong public endorsement. "I have the utmost confidence in Jim Collins," he announced, "and consider him as good a manager as there is in the country and shall co-operate with him so far as it lies within my power to give Boston as good a ball (team) as it has had in the past, and will spare neither money nor effort in that direction."

The 1904 Boston team went on to win a thrilling pennant race, which went down to the final series of the season. According to author Donald Hubbard, one disastrous trade nearly cost Boston the pennant.

On June 17, 1904, the club sent hard-hitting and highly popular outfielder Patsy Dougherty to the New York Highlanders for utilityman Bob Unglaub. It was easily one of the most one-sided trades in Boston baseball history. Boston baseball fans were irate and blamed Taylor and his new organization. Taylor became a laughingstock in Boston and within professional baseball. Only the subsequent Boston pennant saved Taylor from a groundswell in Boston calling for his immediate removal. League president Ban Johnson may have had a hand in orchestrating the trade, the better to make the New York team more competitive, thus creating more of a draw and stronger ticket sales.

After Boston won the 1904 pennant, beating New York on the final day of the season, Taylor immediately issued a public challenge to the New York Giants to play a world championship series. (The World Series was not yet a fixed, permanent event.) Giants owner John T. Brush, who hated Ban Johnson and did not want to further elevate the American League to equal standing with the National League, refused, even though each team's players were looking forward to an additional postseason paycheck.

In 1905, Boston compiled a 78-74 record and dropped to fourth place, 16 games behind the pennant-winning Philadelphia Athletics. The team's pitching suffered a significant decline; the staff earned-run average was 2.84, fifth in the league. Except for Jesse Tannehill (22-9), no starting pitcher finished with a record above .500. The team simply didn't score many runs; Cy Young had a 1.82 ERA and was 18-19. In 1904, the staff had had a 2.12 ERA with three 20-game winners.

The effects of increasing age combined with complacency were beginning to weaken the team. The players who jumped from the National League to help establish both the Boston franchise and the American League were getting into their late 30s.

After the season, without consulting Jimmy Collins, Taylor sent new contracts to the players calling for a general cut in salaries. The players began grumbling immediately. In January 1906, *Sporting Life* reported that a syndicate that included Collins made an offer to Taylor to buy the team for $125,000.

According to Peter Golenbock, the working relationship between Collins and Taylor began to deteriorate rapidly. Collins began publicly attacking Taylor. Both men desperately wanted to win. They strongly disagreed on how to make that happen. Essentially, both wanted to have the power of a modern-day general manager to run the team. Ban Johnson backed Collins. Charles Taylor backed his son.

Hubbard writes that Collins considered many of his 1905 players his friends. Many won two pennants and a championship with him. Collins unwisely trusted them to do the right thing. As a result, he gave his team a lot of leeway in 1905 spring training and remained loyal to the group even as they faded from contention. At the start of the 1906 season, Hubbard writes, Charles Taylor dispatched John to Europe to ease the awkward situation.

One positive result emerging from his time in Europe was his marriage to Cornelia R. Van Ness, from a distinguished San Francisco family. Cornelia provided a much-needed stability to Taylor's social activities. They subsequently had four children. One of the streets bordering Fenway Park eventually was named Van Ness Street.

Fred Lieb called Boston's 1906 season "the great debacle" and a "season-long nightmare for Boston fans." The 1903-04 champions "plunged through the cellar door into a bottomless pit." The team finished in last place with a miserable 49-105 record, the worst in major-league baseball that season. The Boston Beaneaters of the National League were 49-102, which contributed to the "nightmare" of '06. As a team, the Americans' hitting and pitching both dropped significantly. Boston scored only 463 runs in 155 games, compared to 579 runs in 153 games in 1905. The 1906 pitching staff compiled a 3.42 ERA, worst in the majors.

One of the most symbolic events of this horrible season was the team's 20-game losing streak, which set a major league record at the time. The streak started on May 1 and ended on May 25, when Tannehill hurled a shutout. While attendance dropped initially, the fans returned to see when the Americans would end the string of losses.

The Taylor vs. Collins struggle for team control continued. In the clubhouse, particularly after a losing game, Taylor would sarcastically berate each player he thought should have performed better. Collins then strongly discouraged Taylor from going into the clubhouse. John I. countered by setting up a chair in the passageway leading to the clubhouse and verbally blasting each passing player who he believed needed it.

With a bad knee, Collins began not playing regularly anymore; he played in only 37 games in 1906. At the end of June, citing nerve problems, Collins began not wearing his uniform on the bench. Again citing nerve issues, he subsequently made outfielder Chick Stahl the temporary manager and took off to a nearby beach. He did not inform John I. of his beach trip and Taylor suspended him. In late August, Collins was again suspended, this time by Ban Johnson. Stahl took over as acting manager for the rest of the season.

The *1907 Reach Guide* summarized Boston's woeful 1906 effort: "The poor tail enders of 1906 presented the most melancholy spectacle ever witnessed in major league ball. The cause of this awful slump was the decadence of the team's veterans, which had set in the year before." However, a hint of a brighter future emerged with Taylor's signing of catcher Bill Carrigan out of Holy Cross College. In 1907, Taylor had a hectic season, as the club had four managers and one acting manager. In order of appearance they were Chick Stahl, Cy Young, George Huff, Bob Unglaub, and Jim McGuire.

The manager shuffle began after Chick Stahl committed suicide during spring training. It was a particularly tragic event. He had served as the club's acting manager at the end of 1906 and was well-liked in the Boston clubhouse. He swallowed carbolic acid after writing a suicide note. Boston scheduled a special exhibition game with the nearby Providence Grays as a tribute to Chick and to raise funds for his widow. Taylor canceled another potentially lucrative exhibition game scheduled to be played on that day. Each of the other major-league teams contributed $50 and the Cleveland players contributed $165. Taylor topped the other contributions by giving $500.

After Stahl's death, Cy Young took over as interim manager. Despite strong urging by Taylor to become the full-time manager, Young declined. Taylor then entered into negotiations with Hugh Duffy of the Grays, a former Boston idol, to manage the club. These fell apart over the length of the contract.

A frustrated Taylor turned to George Huff, who was director of athletics at the University of Illinois. Huff lasted only eight games, posting a 2-6 record. By May 1, finding the contentious Boston situation too much, Huff resigned and returned to his position at Illinois. Taylor, however, appreciated Huff's ability as an evaluator of baseball talent, and he hired Huff as a scout. It turned out to be a good move by Taylor. While Huff's stint as a manager was an embarrassment, he made an enormous contribution to the franchise by scouting and signing Tris Speaker.

To succeed Huff as manager, Taylor selected first baseman Bob Unglaub. Although his short tenure (9-20) has been generally dismissed, one key development happened while he was in charge. Taylor traded the 38-year-old Jimmy Collins to Philadelphia. Collins's erratic behavior in 1906 had lost him a great deal of public support in Boston. He was now a "poison" in the Boston clubhouse.

Taylor's choice for his fourth manager in 1907 was Fred "Deacon" McGuire. One day after Boston hired McGuire, Taylor traded another of the remaining members of the 1903-04 champions, pitcher Bill Dinneen, to St. Louis's American League club, the Browns. In return, Boston got $1,000 and Beany Jacobson, who, after pitching two innings, never pitched major-league baseball again. Boston finished 1907 with a 59-90 record in seventh place. The Americans ended 32½ games behind the first-place Detroit Tigers.

Although 1907 was another dismal season for Taylor, he did arrange for the first-ever night baseball game to be played at the Huntington Avenue Grounds. It was an exhibition game between a Cherokee Indian team and the local semipro Dorchesters. The Indians brought their own lights and placed them around the field. Their collective light was estimated at more than 50,000 candlepower.

In December 1907, Taylor announced that he was going to change the name of the Boston team from the Americans to the Red Sox for the coming year. Boston's National League team had dropped their characteristic red stockings after the 1907 season, and Taylor quickly adopted them for his team. Part of his rationale was to take advantage of a Boston tradition: The city's first professional baseball team (1876) had been the Red Stockings.

The newly renamed Red Sox compiled a 1908 record of 75-79 and finished in fifth place. Boston's old-to-new transition continued. The Red Sox sold or traded three 1903-04 holdovers, Hobe Ferris (to the Highlanders), Freddy Parent (to the Chicago White Sox), and Bob Unglaub (to Washington). Taylor paid off and released manager McGuire. He subsequently chose Fred Lake, a longtime manager in the New England League, as the new Red Sox manager. The *Globe*'s announcement of Lake's selection mentioned that Lake and Taylor were planning a "sliding salary scale for each position." Apparently the plan was never implemented, although the concept did reflect Taylor's predisposition toward a pay-for-performance salary structure.

Taylor was a key figure in overseeing the birth of Fenway Park. Construction was underway as he attended the league meetings in December 1911.

According to Fred Lieb, Taylor was investing in his team, "spending money right and left." Taylor's intensive scouting effort began to pay dividends. Tris Speaker, Smoky Joe Wood, and Harry Hooper were all signed by Boston in 1908. Harry Lord replaced Collins at third base. At midseason, Taylor traded for Garland (Jake) Stahl who played a solid first base for the remainder of the season. As a former player-manager for Washington, Stahl provided a much-needed stabilizing influence in the clubhouse.

Although the 1908 Red Sox experienced significant transition, two of the biggest moves were made in the 1908-09 offseason. On December 11, Taylor traded Boston's longtime catcher and Cy Young favorite Lou Criger to the St. Louis Browns for $5,000 and catcher Tubby Spencer.

Although illness and injuries had significantly cut into Criger's playing time, Red Sox fans were still surprised to see him go. An upset Cy Young lavishly praised Criger's catching ability, saying, "He was one of the greatest catchers that ever donned a mask. … So confident am I of his judgment that I never shake my head."

If the fans were surprised to see Criger being packed off, they were bewildered when Taylor traded Cy Young to Cleveland in February 1909. Taylor had repeatedly said that Young would spend the rest of his career in Boston. According to Lieb, some fans thought Taylor had lost his mind, while others thought he was drunk when he made the trade. As for Young, he was publicly very gracious about Taylor's decision. He expressed his thanks to Boston fans and also thanked Taylor for trading him back to Cleveland, where he had started his big-league career. *The Sporting News* took a more positive view of the Young trade. It lauded Taylor for his "exceptional wisdom" in making his decision. The trade ultimately yielded little for the Red Sox (Charley Chech, Jack Ryan, and $12,500).

With the departure of longtime favorites Criger and Young, Boston fans started 1909 with low expectations. They were pleasantly surprised when their team posted an 88-63 record and finished in third place. As the season progressed, Boston's young, athletic players began making a larger impact. Tris Speaker, Harry Lord, and Harry Hooper all had good seasons. Perhaps Taylor had a bit more baseball acumen than the fans credited him with.

The Boston scouts signed two more college players from Vermont who would be future stars for the Red Sox: left-handed pitcher Ray Collins and infielder Larry Gardner, a key figure in three Red Sox world championships.

Once again, there was a managerial change in November 1909. When Lake discussed salary with Taylor, he named a figure and Taylor disagreed. The two men could not resolve their differences. As a result, Taylor released Lake and signed Patsy Donovan, a major-league outfielder for 17 years, as the new Red Sox manager.

According to Lieb, John I. Taylor later confessed: "I believe my 1910 season was my biggest disappointment." After surging in 1909, the Red Sox fell back a bit in 1910. They compiled an 81-72 record and finished fourth. The big story of 1910 was the Philadelphia Athletics, who simply pitched their way to the pennant. Their staff posted an outstanding 1.79 ERA for the regular season and subsequently won the 1910 World Series.

The 1910 season also marked the debut of the Lewis-Speaker-Hooper outfield combination. Lieb wrote, "Many fans and critics rank this outfield as the greatest of all time. Other outfields may have had more slugging power (Meusel, Combs, Ruth) but the Red Sox trio had better defensive skills." One baseball writer characterized the trio as covering the field "like a carpet."

Taylor enjoyed personally scouting on the West Coast, and Duffy Lewis was one of his discoveries. Taylor liked Lewis, a fancy dresser who became known as "John I.'s boy." Lewis later recalled, "John I. was a good boss. Maybe he was sharp at times, but he always bought the boys suits of clothes whenever they had big days."

After the season, Taylor also resolved a festering Boston team issue: Harry Lord, the team's third baseman. Several newspaper articles reported that Lord wanted Patsy Donovan's job. Lord was Boston's captain but was benched in August 1910. Taylor made infielder Heinie Wagner the new team captain. When Lord angrily demanded to be traded, Taylor quickly sent him to the Chicago White Sox. The Taylor-Lord problem reportedly originated over the funding of a postseason Red Sox exhibition game played in October 1909 against a team of Maine all-stars. Lord, who arranged the game, claimed he lost money on the game. When Lord wanted to play another exhibition game in Portland in 1910, Taylor refused. Lord emerged with a label of being "money crazy."

After the trade, Lord challenged the Red Sox to an exhibition game against a team of traded Red Sox assembled by him. The winners would get $2,000. Lord said, "(We) just wanted to show Boston that it has traded off a better team than it has now." Once again, Taylor refused.

Because of Taylor's fondness for the West Coast, he decided to have the team hold spring training at Redondo Beach, California, near Los Angeles, in 1911. A large number of players were brought into camp, enough to furnish two touring teams, and after a full schedule of games along the California coast, they broke into two teams and played games as they traveled east, in Arizona, Nevada, Utah, Colorado, Kansas, Texas, Nebraska, and Missouri—63 games in all.

As the 1911 season started, the Taylor family decided to leave the Huntington Avenue Grounds, which had been leased since the franchise began in 1901. The Taylors decided to use land they owned and build a ballpark to be called Fenway Park.

The Fenway Park project was probably a part of a bigger deal in which two key Taylor family objectives could be accomplished: By selling a share of the team after the new park was under way, the family would recoup a huge financial reward from its original investment; and John I. Taylor could shed the headaches of operating the team while still being associated with it.

The deal was also very attractive to the American League hierarchy. American League president Ban Johnson tolerated John I. Taylor, but it is debatable if he ever recognized Taylor as a true "baseball man." Perhaps Johnson was simply tired of regularly being called to Boston to settle issues he thought should be handled by club ownership. A group chosen by Johnson would operate the new club. John I. Taylor would become a Red Sox vice president and his father would sit on the board of directors.

Opening Fenway Park with Style: The World Champion 1912 Boston Red Sox

Hat in hand in 1914, Taylor had more time on his hands after selling the family's controlling share in the Red Sox.

As soon as the new stadium construction started, the Taylors sold half of their interest in the Red Sox for $150,000. The sale price recouped their original investment. They needed the money to complete the construction of Fenway Park. When finished, the stadium reportedly cost $350,000. A key part of the deal was that the family would remain the owners of Fenway Park and the land on which it was built, the park serving as a magnet to help develop the value of their adjoining real estate holdings. The subsequent team owners would rent the park for $30,000 a year. The Taylors rented Fenway for eight seasons (1912-1919). On January 4, 1912, Jimmy McAleer was named president of the Boston Red Sox. He and Robert McRoy had become owners of a 50% share of the ballclub in a sale on September 14, 1911. It was later revealed that Ban Johnson was involved as well, behind the scenes.

The last Red Sox game at the Huntington Avenue Grounds was a win over Washington. Taylor bade goodbye to the ballpark by allowing free access to all Boston boys under 12 years old to attend the game. A *Boston Globe* picture captures thousands of youthful fans enthusiastically watching their hometown heroes. It was good publicity for the newspaper as well. After the game, the sod was removed and taken to the new facility.

Fenway Park opened on April 20, 1912, to general acclaim, and the official "Dedication Day" took place on May 17. The Red Sox went on to win the 1912 pennant, compiling a 105-47 record. They won the World Series over the New York Giants. Every player on the 1912 Red Sox roster had either been signed by or acquired via trade by John I. Taylor and his organization. The *Globe* later estimated that over the span of Taylor ownership (1904-1911), John I. had acquired more than 110 players in his efforts to improve the team. In his obituary, in 1938, the *Globe* concluded, "While he was in the game, there was no closer student of the game than John I. Taylor. It was mainly on his own judgment of players themselves that he finally brought to Boston so many 'naturals' who came flying up to the big league grade."

In 1914, Joseph Lannin became principal owner of the Red Sox, after paying the Taylor family a reported $300,000 for their remaining common stock interest in the Red Sox. However, Gen. Charles Taylor retained "quite an interest" in the preferred stock of the club. He also was a trustee in Fenway Realty Trust, which financed Fenway Park.

Upon completion of the sale of the Red Sox to Lannin in 1914, Ban Johnson, who clashed repeatedly with John I. Taylor over the years, publicly praised him. "John I. Taylor was president of the club for eight years and his work in building up was one of the greatest value and paved the way for the great success of 1912," Johnson said.

In October 1916, immediately after the team won its third world championship in five years, Lannin cashed in and sold his common stock Red Sox holdings to Harry Frazee and a partner for a reported $675,000. As Red Sox owner, Frazee also bought Fenway Park in May 1920 from the Taylor family. Part of the money was provided by a $300,000 mortgage held by the New York Yankees as part of the package Frazee arranged when he sold Babe Ruth to the New York owners.

As for Charles I. Taylor, he enjoyed an active life during retirement. Peter Golenbock quoted his grandson William as remembering Charles I. as a "favorite with the next generation of Taylors because he would always take them to Fenway Park." He remained a close follower of the Red Sox, but his interests focused primarily on his family. He also liked tennis, golf, and polo. Extensive gardening occupied much of his time and he spent long hours caring for the flower beds and rock gardens at his home in Dedham, outside Boston. He died on January 26, 1938, at Massachusetts General Hospital after a brief illness. He was 63 years old.

In its obituary, the *Boston Globe* noted two innovations that Taylor had helped introduce, Ladies Day and the press box, writing: "He was one of the first magnates in the country to assign a day on which women were admitted free to the baseball park. He was the first president to assign private quarters away from the paying spectators for the baseball writers."

In a separate article, *Globe* columnist Melville Webb Jr. wrote, "It always has been a compliment to be considered 'a good baseball man.' John I. Taylor was that."

Sources:

Timothy Gay. *Tris Speaker, The Rough and Tumble Life of a Baseball Legend* (Lincoln, Nebraska: University of Nebraska Press, 2005)

Peter Golenbock. *Fenway: An Unexpurgated History of the Boston Red Sox* (New York: G.P. Putnam's and Sons, 1992)

Donald Hubbard. *The Red Sox Before the Babe* (Jefferson, North Carolina: McFarland, 2009)

Frederick G. Lieb. *The Boston Red Sox* (New York: G.P. Putnam's Sons, 1947)

James Morgan. *Charles H. Taylor, Builder of the Boston Globe* (Boston: Boston Globe, 1923)

Bill Nowlin. *Day by Day With the Boston Red Sox* (Cambridge, Massachusetts: Rounder Books, 2006)

Bill Nowlin. *Red Sox Threads—Odds & Ends from Red Sox History* (Burlington, Massachusetts: Rounder Books, 2008)

Bill Nowlin, ed. *When Boston Still Had the Babe, The 1918 World Champion Red Sox* (Burlington, Massachusetts: Rounder Books, 2008)

Glenn Stout and Richard A. Johnson. *Red Sox Century, The Definitive History of Baseball's Most Storied Franchise* (Boston: Houghton Mifflin, 2005)

John Thorn, Pete Palmer, and Michael Gershman. *Total Baseball Seventh Edition* (Kingston, New York: Total Sports Publishing, 2001)

Paul J. Zingg. *Harry Hooper, An American Baseball Life* (Champaign, Illinois: University of Illinois Press, 1995)

John I. Taylor obituary, *The Sporting News*, Necrology, February 3, 1938

"Death Takes John I. Taylor," *Boston Globe*, January 27, 1938

Boston Globe, Sporting Life, The Sporting News, Lowell (Massachusetts) *Sun, New York Times*

National Baseball Hall of Fame—John I. Taylor File

The Baseball Index, SABR, accessed November 20, 2009

Wikipedia.org, Charles H. Taylor, accessed December 9, 2009

baseball_reference.com

Ban Johnson
by Joe Santry and Cindy Thomson

The most powerful figure of the Deadball Era, Ban Johnson's rise to prominence in the national pastime was as improbable as it was meteoric. Relying neither on athletic renown (his amateur catching career was abruptly cut short by a thumb injury) nor inherited wealth (he dropped out of law school to become a journalist), the talented Johnson maneuvered his way into becoming president of the Western League in 1893, then skillfully transformed the fledgling circuit into one of the most formidable minor leagues of the late 19th century. At the turn of the 20th century, Johnson renamed the Western League the American League, declared major-league status, and then succeeded in challenging the one-league supremacy of the National League. Johnson's triumph marked a turning point in baseball history, cementing the modern two-league system and setting the stage for the unparalleled financial successes of the coming years.

The catalyst for these momentous changes was a jowly, arrogant man whose outward demeanor was as cold and unsympathetic as if he had been weaned on an icicle. Autocratic and humorless, Johnson almost single-handedly administered the American League during his tenure, drafting schedules, signing players and shifting franchises as he saw fit. Following the peace agreement with the National League in 1903, Johnson also became the most powerful force on the three-man National Commission that oversaw the sport, in the process making more than his share of enemies among the ownership ranks in both leagues. To writer Bob Considine, Johnson was "a ruthless dreamer who lived and died believing that baseball was perfected in order to serve him as a gigantic chess board on which to move his living pieces."[1] Yet there could be no denying his enduring impact on the sport. "His contribution to the game," Branch Rickey once observed, "is not closely equaled by any other single person or group of persons."[2]

Byron Bancroft Johnson was born in Norwalk, Ohio, on January 5, 1864, the fifth of six children of Alexander Byron and Eunice C. Fox Johnson. Shortly after Ban's birth, the Johnsons moved to Avondale, Ohio--then a Cincinnati suburb, though today it is part of the city--where A.B. Johnson served as a prominent school administrator. The elder Johnson, who hoped his son would continue the family lineage of educators and ministers, was irritated when Ban ignored his studies to run off to play baseball as a youth. After graduating from preparatory school, Ban showed a lack of focus in his studies, bouncing from Oberlin College to Marietta College to the University of Cincinnati Law School, where he would remain for less than two years. At Marietta, the big, sturdy Johnson gained a reputation as a fearless catcher on the school team, manning his position without a glove, mask, or chest protector. Not surprisingly, a thumb injury ended his baseball career. At the time of the injury, his experience consisted of a handful of games with the semipro Ironton, Ohio team while on vacation from school.

When Johnson dropped out of law school midway through his sophomore year in 1886 to take a job as sportswriter at the

Ban Johnson, founder and architect of the American League, ca. 1910.

Cincinnati Commercial Gazette at $25 a week, his father hit the roof. The paper's legendary editor, Murat Halstead, was finally able to convince Ban's father that journalism was an honorable profession. When sports editor O. P. Caylor left the Cincinnati paper to take a similar position in New York, Halstead named Johnson to the job.

Johnson soon earned a reputation for his knowledge of sports and willingness to speak his mind. From the beginning, he didn't back down from volatile topics of the day. For example, he was a champion of the Players League in 1890, which alienated, among others, Indianapolis Hoosiers owner John Brush. However, his strong opinions won him the friendship of others, such as star first baseman Charles Comiskey, who had joined the Players League.

When the Players League folded after 1890 and the American Association dissolved into the National League the following year, a new circuit, the Western League was created in 1892. The progressive new league was the brainchild of Jimmy Williams, a Columbus, Ohio, attorney. Williams was one of the founding fathers of the American Association and the minor league International Association and was named president-secretary-treasurer of the new league.

The circuit got off to a shaky financial start, however, and Williams was forced to close down the league in July, 1892. In the fall of 1893, members of the disbanded league sought to rekindle the circuit, but Williams begged off, claiming he could no longer take charge of keeping the league afloat financially. Comiskey, remembering his old friend, suggested Johnson to committee members Denny Long of Toledo and James Manning of Kansas City. That November, Ban Johnson was named President-Secretary-Treasurer of the Western League and given a salary of $2,500 a year.

In order to boost league attendance, Johnson crusaded against rowdiness in the league, supporting his umpires with better pay and backing up their rulings on the field with stiff penalties for bad behavior. Under Johnson's able stewardship, the league became more profitable over the rest of the 19th century. In 1897 the circuit drew nearly one million fans, with the top clubs in Kansas City, Milwaukee, and St. Paul drawing better than some National League franchises.

When the National League voted to scale down from 12 to eight teams prior to the 1900 season, Johnson saw his big opportunity. With the primary financial backing of millionaire Charles Somers, whose money would continue to fund Johnson's plans for the league, and others like Charles Comiskey, the Columbus franchise moved to Cleveland and the St. Paul club moved to Chicago.[3] Johnson changed the league's name to the American League. The following year, Johnson declared his organization a major league and abandoned the circuit's western roots, moving franchises into National League territories in Boston and Philadelphia, as well as Baltimore and Washington, cities the National League had abandoned the year before.

The newly named American League waived the National League's $2,400 salary cap and enticed 111 players from the National League to jump to the new venture, including top stars Cy Young, Napoleon Lajoie, and John McGraw. Before the 1902 season, Johnson transferred the Milwaukee club to St. Louis to compete head-to-head with the Cardinals, and continued his raid on National League rosters, coming away with more big name players, including sluggers Ed Delahanty, Jesse Burkett, and Elmer Flick. The results were impressive: in 1902 the American League outdrew the National League by more than 500,000 fans. In the four cities home to franchises in both leagues, the upstart American League outdrew the National League in all of them by wide margins.

Clearly outmatched, the hapless National League owners finally sued for peace following the 1902 season, and the resulting truce between the two leagues reaffirmed the principle of the reserve clause and the sanctity of contracts. A three-man National Commission was appointed to settle disputes, with Johnson, the National League president, and Cincinnati Reds executive Garry Herrmann, a friend of Johnson's, picked to chair the new governing body. While Herrmann was hardly Johnson's puppet, as he is often portrayed, his close relationship with the American League president did help Johnson to cement his power.

As chief executive of the American League, Johnson extended his efforts to stamp "rowdyism" out of the game. Supporting his umpires with a firm hand, Johnson swiftly punished players and managers who crossed the line. Johnson's tactics were not always successful. When Johnson and Baltimore manager John McGraw clashed over the skipper's unsportsmanlike behavior on the diamond during the 1902 season, McGraw jumped to the New York Giants and took many Orioles with him. Baltimore was able to complete the season only because owners from the other AL teams contributed players from their rosters. After the 1902 season, Johnson moved the Orioles to New York, where they would in time become the most successful franchise in the history of the sport.

Johnson also worked to try and help build the league by strengthening teams that needed a boost. Without question, he wanted to make the New York Highlanders a contender. As has been asked, "Why else would the World Champion Boston Americans trade one of their most popular players—Patsy Dougherty (.331 in 1903, he led the league with 195 hits and 103 runs)—for New York's untested infielder Bob Unglaub? Unglaub had only appeared in six games and was hitting .211; when he joined the Bostons, he hit .154…. If parity was Johnson's goal, he succeeded: the pennant was decided between Boston and New York on the final day of the season, and Dougherty played a role."[4]

The American League grew and prospered under Johnson. He dealt with each problem with a firm hand. Whether it was the Tigers striking over Ty Cobb's suspension in 1912 or floating loans to teams to strengthen the league, the obstinate Johnson usually got his way. He became so powerful he even changed the outcome of the 1910 batting race when the results did not suit him.

Ban Johnson in 1910.

But it was Johnson's arrogant manner and dictatorial inclinations, which eventually led to his downfall. During the last five years of the Deadball Era, four controversial rulings paved the way for the demise of the National Commission and fractured the ownership ranks of the American League into pro-Johnson and anti-Johnson camps.

In 1915, the National Commission ruled that George Sisler was the property of the American League's St. Louis Browns. As a 17-year-old, Sisler had signed a contract with the Akron club of the Ohio-Pennsylvania League. Akron was part of the vast farm system of Bobby Quinn and the Columbus Senators of the American Association. Sisler decided instead to attend the University of Michigan.

While in college, Sisler's contract was transferred to the parent club and Quinn sold it to the Pittsburgh Pirates. Sisler's coach at Michigan was Branch Rickey. Rickey became the manager of the Browns in 1913, and when Sisler was ready to turn pro, Branch represented the youngster in a legal battle to sign a contract with St. Louis. Rickey's argument was that because Sisler was a minor when he signed the Akron contract, his father's signature was required to make the contract binding. Johnson and Herrmann agreed, and Sisler became a Brown.

Barney Dreyfuss, owner of the Pirates, cried foul and vowed to destroy the National Commission. Cubs owner Charles Murphy, disgruntled after a Commission decision, was quoted by I.E. Sanborn in *The Sporting News* as saying he wanted the entire commission disbanded. His suggestion would later be partially fulfilled. Sanborn claimed that Murphy wanted, "...a non partisan, none [sic] baseball body of three or five men, among them an ex judge or two, appointed for life to adjudicate all the disputes now coming before the commission."[5] It was the first nail in the coffin.

On November 30, 1913, when New Yorker Joseph Lannin bought the half of the Red Sox shares owned by James McAleer and associates, the sale was more or less dictated by AL architect Ban Johnson. An indication of Johnson's involvement was how McAleer learned of the sale. Joe Cashman told Peter Golenbock that McAleer received a telegram reading, "You have just sold the Red Sox to Joseph Lannin. Ban Johnson."[6]

In 1917, another nail was driven when Atlanta of the Southern Association sold pitcher Scott Perry's contract to the Braves. Perry jumped the team to play semipro ball. The National Commission ruled that Atlanta could resign Perry for $2,000. The Crackers then sold the journeyman pitcher to the A's. When Boston objected, the National Commission awarded Perry's contract to Philadelphia. Once again, the American League had won a contract dispute, leaving some to wonder if the National League could ever win a case brought before the Commission.

Contract dispute number three came before Johnson in 1919, when the American League president awarded pitcher Jack Quinn to the Yankees instead of the Chicago White Sox. Johnson's action effectively ended the life-long friendship with his drinking buddy Comiskey. Gradually over the years, the men who had shared the same Chicago office for nearly two decades became bitter enemies.

A 1915 photograph shows Johnson with Red Sox owner Joseph Lannin at Fenway Park. L to R: Paul and Dorothy Lannin, Johnson, Mr. and Mrs. J. J. Lannin.

Later that season, star pitcher Carl Mays of the Boston Red Sox jumped the team and refused to return. The Red Sox traded Mays to the Yankees after Johnson ruled that Mays first had to return to Boston and serve a suspension before he could be traded. The Yankees owners Jacob Ruppert and Tillinghast Huston got a temporary restraining order allowing Mays to pitch for New York. Divided over the issue, the league split into the "Loyal 5" (St. Louis, Philadelphia, Cleveland, Detroit, and Washington) versus the "Insurrectionists" (New York, Boston, and Chicago). The Insurrectionists controlled the five-man Board of Directors and stripped Johnson of much of his power.

The owners met, voted in a new board, and reinstated Johnson. The New York owners then bombarded Johnson with lawsuits. Late that year things got so ugly that the Insurrectionists gave the league a one-week ultimatum. If an agreement could not be reached, the Yankees, Red Sox and White Sox would join a 12-team National League. The 12th team would be the first of the Loyal Five to jump. If no team moved, the National League planned to place a team in Detroit. Finally, Frank Navin, the Detroit owner, brokered a peace agreement, albeit a tenuous one. Johnson now was required to answer to the owners.

A few months later a story broke centering on suspicion that Comiskey's Chicago White Sox had thrown the 1919 World Series to gamblers. Johnson took some pleasure over his former friend's embarrassment. But when he tried to ride in and save the situation, the owners balked. To restore integrity to the game, baseball's magnates decided to replace the National Commission with an all-powerful commissioner.

Judge Kenesaw Mountain Landis was chosen for the position. Landis had limited baseball experience, but he was every bit as stubborn as Johnson, who opposed Landis's appointment. Over the next several seasons, Johnson had little interaction with Landis, concerning himself solely with league matters.

But in 1927, enraged that his authority had been undermined by Landis in the Ty Cobb-Tris Speaker gambling scandal, Johnson locked horned with the commissioner. In response, the judge gave an ultimatum to the owners, Johnson or Landis. The American League owners voted 7-1 to strip Ban of his powers, but allowed him to retain his title. Phil Ball of the Browns was the lone dissenting vote.

After three meetings on July 8, 1927 at the Belmont Hotel in New York, a sick and sullen Johnson passed his scribbled resignation through his hotel door to Ruppert. His resignation would take effect at the end of the season.

Johnson was still owed $320,000 for the balance of his contract running eight more years, but he refused to take any money for work not performed. As Branch Rickey once said, "The making or amassing of money was not part of Ban Johnson's life. He lived for the American League and the game of baseball."[7]

Ban and his wife of over 30 years, Jane Laymon, retired to Spencer, Indiana. Their marriage had not produced any children. His retirement years were spent fund raising for Marietta College and promoting baseball in Mexico. In his final interview, Johnson stated that major league baseball should extend coast-to-coast. Even near the end of his life, he was still 25 years ahead of his time.

Johnson died of diabetes on March 28, 1931 in St. Louis. He was buried in Riverside Cemetery, in Spencer.

Note: An earlier version of this biography appeared in David Jones, ed., *Deadball Stars of the American League* (Washington, D.C.: Potomac Books, Inc., 2006).

Sources:

Martin Appel and Bert Goldblatt. *Baseball's Best: The Hall of Fame Gallery* (New York: McGraw-Hill Book Company, 1974).

Edward Grant Barrow with James M. Kuhn. *My Fifty Years in Baseball* (New York: Coward-McCann, Inc., 1951).

Donald Hubbard. *The Red Sox Before The Babe* (Jefferson NC: McFarland and Company, Inc., Publishers, 2009).

Franklin Lewis. *The Cleveland Indians* (New York: G.P. Putnam's Sons, 1949).

Fredrick G. Lieb. *The Boston Red Sox* (New York: G.P. Putnam's Sons, 1947).

Eugene C. Murdock. *Ban Johnson Czar of Baseball* (Westport CT: Greenwood Press, 1982).

Branch Rickey with Robert Riger, *The American Diamond: A Documentary of the Game of Baseball* (New York: Simon and Schuster, 1965).

Joseph M. Santry. *Grazing Through Columbus Baseball* (2004).

Harold Seymour. *Baseball: The Early Years* (New York: Oxford University Press, 1960).

Harold Seymour. *Baseball: The Golden Age* (New York: Oxford University Press, 1971).

J. G. Spink. *Judge Landis and Twenty-Five Years of Baseball* (New York: Thomas Y. Crowell Company, 1947).

Glenn Stout and Richard Johnson. *The Red Sox Century* (Boston: Houghton Mifflin Company, 2000).

For this biography, a number of contemporary sources, especially those found in the subject's file at the National Baseball Hall of Fame Library were used.

Endnotes

1. *Life*, August 9, 1948, "Mr. Mack", p. 95

2. Branch Rickey with Robert Riger, *The American Diamond: A Documentary of the Game of Baseball* (New York: Simon and Schuster, 1965), 23.

3. Charles Somers was active in shipping on the Great Lakes, in coal, and in lumber. The willing magnate was of invaluable assistance to Johnson, not only providing initial funding for the Cleveland Indians but for the Boston Americans as well. Frederick Lieb writes that Somers also advanced $10,000 to Charles Comiskey to help him finance the Chicago White Sox and "was Connie Mack's original backer" in the Philadelphia Athletics. Somers thus had his financial fingers in half of the league's teams—four of the eight original American League clubs. See Bill Nowlin, *Red Sox Threads* (Burlington MA: Rounder Books, 2008) and Frederick Leib, *The Boston Red Sox* (Carbondale, IL: Southern Illinois University Press, 2003 reprint of original 1947 G. P. Putnam's Sons book.)

4. Bill Nowlin. *Day by Day with the Red Sox*. (Burlington MA: Rounder Books, 2006)

5. *The Sporting News*, January 18, 1912

6. Peter Golenbock, *Red Sox Nation*. (Chicago IL: Triumph Books, 2005), 42, 43

7. Branch Rickey with Robert Riger, op. cit.

A Question of Ownership
By Michael T. Lynch, Jr.

From 1933 to 1988 there was one constant in the Boston Red Sox organization—the Yawkey family. For 55 years, the team was owned by either Tom or his wife Jean, and three generations of my family lived, breathed, cried, and bled Boston Red Sox baseball under Yawkey's watch. And the Yawkey Trust owned the team for another 14 years after that, until 2002. But prior to Yawkey's purchase of the team, seven men acted as team president and a handful more owned stock in the franchise. From its inception in 1901 until 1932, the Red Sox were seemingly in a constant state of flux, presenting autocratic American League president Ban Johnson with one of his biggest challenges. But during the 1912-1913 seasons, a cloud of mystery hung over the franchise, most of it created by Johnson himself.

The Boston American League franchise was originally owned by Charles W. Somers, a native of Ohio, who was extremely wealthy, having earned a fortune in the coal mining and shipping industries, and who helped Johnson put teams in Cleveland, Chicago, Philadelphia, and Boston. He wasn't averse to spreading his wealth around and he provided the capital the junior circuit desperately needed to get off the ground while holding stock in half of the league's eight franchises.[1] The story has been told elsewhere how Ban Johnson orchestrated the founding of the league, the placement of teams in the initial eight cities, and the not-infrequent transfers of players from one pliant franchise to another in order to suit Johnson's sense of how to strengthen the league in its earliest days, but Somers was the willing financier of Johnson's ambitions. "Somers' faith in Ban Johnson and his open checkbook were the legs upon which the American League learned to walk," wrote Franklin Lewis.[2]

Somers ran the Red Sox, then known as the Americans or Somersets in his honor, for two years before selling his shares to Milwaukee lawyer Henry Killilea. Killilea saw Boston win its first World Series title in 1903 before selling the team in the spring of 1904 to *Boston Globe* founder Charles Henry Taylor, who bought the team for his son, John I. Taylor. John I. was a perfect fit for Johnson's league. Unlike local politician John "Honey Fitz" Fitzgerald, who was also attempting to buy the team, Taylor was less than ambitious and content to live off his family's wealth while spending his free time at the ballpark. He would also be easier for Johnson to control. Taylor offered $5,000 more than Fitzgerald and the club was his for the taking, with Johnson's blessing, of course.

Although Taylor's reign as owner of the Red Sox was marked by poor trades that, according to Glenn Stout, "precipitated a decline on the field far worse than that which was later blamed on the sale of Babe Ruth sixteen years later," poor relationships with his players and managers, and poor sportsmanship, the Taylor family provided stable ownership to a franchise that had little to that point.[3] But they had little success. After winning the American League pennant in 1904, Boston finished no higher than third place over the next seven seasons, and finished in last place in 1906, seventh place in 1907, and fifth place in 1908. The team continued to climb the standings, finishing third in 1909, and won 54% of its games from 1909-1911, but fell again, earning back-to-back fourth-place finishes in 1910-1911. To Taylor's credit, he began building a roster that would eventually set an American League record for wins in 1912, led by an outfield of Duffy Lewis, Tris Speaker, and Harry Hooper that is considered one of the greatest of all time.

Before 1911 came to a close the team underwent some dramatic changes that would have an immediate impact on its fortunes, while also indirectly leading to an eventual slide into what sportswriter Fred Lieb called "the subterranean caverns of the American League."[4] According to Lieb, the Taylors had decided in 1910 to allow the lease on the Huntington Avenue Grounds to expire so they could build a new ballpark. According to Red Sox outfielder and Hall of Famer Harry Hooper, John I. Taylor had started considering the idea as far back as 1908 when he mentioned during their first contract negotiation that he might need an engineer to help him build a new park. Hooper had a degree in civil engineering and thought he was going to be an engineer who played baseball on the side. But he ended up being a full-time ballplayer instead.[5]

When Ban Johnson decided to overhaul the Western League at the turn of the century and form

A perfect fit. Left to right: Ban Johnson, President of the American League, with cigar, Massachusetts Lieutenant Governor Curtis Guild and General Charles Taylor, publisher and owner of the *Boston Globe* at the Huntington Avenue Grounds on Opening Day, April 18, 1904. Guild threw out the first pitch during pregame ceremonies which included manager Jimmy Collins hoisting a 35-foot long blue flag on the flagpole, with white letters reading: BOSTON AMERICANS 1903 WORLD'S CHAMPIONS.

a new major league to compete with the senior circuit, he had sent Connie Mack to his home state of Massachusetts to secure a location for a new ballpark in Boston.[6] In time for the Boston franchise's inaugural season in 1901, Mack was able to lease the Huntington Avenue Grounds for five years, thanks in part to a $100,000 donation from Somers. The site for the new park was leased by the Boston Elevated Railway company and served as a water park known as "the Chutes," as well as a spot for traveling carnivals, circuses, and Buffalo Bill's Wild West Show.[7] In the summer, patrons would slide down a wooden slide into an artificial pond; in the winter, the pond became a skating rink.

Except for having to fill in the pond at the base of the chutes, the plot was idyllic for a ballpark and was 100,000 square feet larger than the plot of land on which the South End Grounds, home of the National League's Boston Beaneaters, stood. "There is no doubt that the Huntington Avenue Grounds are a splendid site for a ball park," reported sportswriter Peter Kelley.[8] D.L. Prendergast, Boston Elevated's real estate agent, agreed. "It strikes me the American League people have secured an ideal location for their business."[9]

Although the Huntington Avenue Grounds had been in use only since 1901, in less than 10 years, it was already antiquated. Fires had destroyed or damaged many stadiums built with wood, including the one on the South End Grounds, which burned down in 1894 when a group of boys set fire to a pile of rubbish under the right-field bleachers, and the Polo Grounds in New York, which was effectively destroyed on April 14, 1911.[10] Newer venues made of concrete and steel began to dot baseball's landscape, beginning with Shibe Park in Philadelphia, which opened its doors on April 12, 1909 and Forbes Field in Pittsburgh, which opened two-and-a-half months later on June 30.

In 1911, the Taylors finally decided to pull the trigger on a new concrete and steel stadium, prompted in part by Boston Elevated Railway's threat to cut two streets through the Huntington Avenue Grounds "by right of eminent domain."[11] In February, General Taylor attended a meeting held by Fenway area landowners, whose purpose was to "develop along broad lines of Fenway land," and "secure the best kind of buildings for this vicinity."[12]

"Attention of the landowners was called to the necessity of their consulting the executive committee before making any sales to undesirable persons, who might erect buildings out of harmony with the neighborhood," reported the *Boston Globe*. Out of this meeting emerged a new organization called the Fenway Improvement Association led by John H. Storer, who was elected president. That same day, the *Baltimore Sun* reported that Taylor had purchased a parcel of land in the Fenway neighborhood of Boston called the Dana Lands at public auction for $120,000. The 363,308 square foot plot, assessed at $219,200, was a half-mile from the Charles River and on the other side of the Muddy River, about a half-mile from the Huntington Avenue Grounds.[13]

According to the *Sun*, plans for the new park had already been drawn up and construction was to begin before the end of summer in 1911. With an expected seating capacity of 40,000, Fenway Park was to hold more than twice as many spectators as the team's old park, which held only 17,000.[14] But it wasn't until September 29 that the land was transferred over to Taylor and his partners, who were all trustees in the Fenway Realty trust, "created with a capital of $300,000, divided into 3000 shares of $100, practically all held by the owners of the club, this form being advised as the most convenient way to carry out the new development." [15] The firm of Millet, Roe & Hagen purchased $275,000 worth of nontaxable bonds to finance the building of the stadium.[16]

The building of Fenway Park was part of a grander plan hatched by the Taylors, who were looking to sell the team while holding on to Fenway with the intent of renting it out to future owners. The Taylors figured they would attract more bidders willing to pay a higher price for the team if they had new facilities in which to play. Two weeks before they broke ground on Fenway Park, the Taylors found buyers in the form of Washington Senators manager James McAleer and American League secretary Robert McRoy.

McAleer was a long-time baseball veteran from Youngstown, Ohio, who began his major-league career in 1889 as an outfielder with the National League's Cleveland Spiders. In 1890, he played with the Cleveland Infants of the short-lived Players League, then rejoined the Spiders, with whom he played until 1898. During his career, he earned a reputation for defensive prowess—Bill James named him the best outfielder of the 1890s, Franklin Lewis called him "perhaps the most graceful outfielder known to the game with the exception of Tris Speaker," and F.C. Lane called him "undoubtedly one of the greatest outfielders the game ever knew."[17]

American League baseball executives meeting in New York, December, 1911. Front row seated: Ben Shibe (Philadelphia Athletics), Charles Comiskey (Chicago White Sox), AL president Ban Johnson, Robert Hedges (St. Louis Browns), and Frank Farrell (New York Yankees). Back row standing: Jimmy McAleer (Boston Red Sox), John E. Bruce (St. Louis Browns attorney and Commission secretary), Charles Somers (Cleveland Indians), unknown, John I. Taylor (Boston Red Sox), Clark Griffith (Washington Senators), Frank Navin (Detroit Tigers), and Harry Grabiner (Chicago White Sox, secretary).

In 1899, McAleer moved back to Youngstown and purchased and managed the Youngstown Little Giants, a Class B minor league team in the Interstate League. The next year, he was named manager of the Cleveland Lake Shores of the newly formed, but still minor-league American League, and led his squad to a sixth-place finish. In 1901, the American League, led by president Ban Johnson, officially declared itself a major league. McAleer led the Cleveland franchise, now known as the Blues, to a seventh-place finish, 29 games behind the pennant-winning White Sox, but proved to be invaluable in the junior circuit's war against the snobbish National League, whose owners effectively told Johnson to "go to hell" when he expressed a desire to explain his league's demand for equality.

Johnson's response was to send recruiters to National League cities in an effort to convince N.L. players to jump ship and join the American League. With money in hand, and the promise of better working conditions such as the abolition of the reserve clause, Johnson's men found easy pickings. Of the 46 players approached, only one, Honus Wagner of the Pittsburgh Pirates, remained loyal to his team. Then, prior to the 1902 season, Johnson decided to move the floundering Milwaukee Brewers into St. Louis to compete directly with the senior circuit's most popular team, the Cardinals. The Cards drew almost 380,000 fans in 1901, 25,638 more than the next closest team, the Chicago White Sox, and 82,338 more than the New York Giants.

Johnson hired McAleer to manage the St. Louis Browns and enlisted him to talk to the Cardinals players personally in an effort to convince them to jump ship. McAleer had played with many of them and not only did he succeed in convincing them to jump leagues, but he gutted the Cardinals roster of most of its better players—future Hall of Famers Jesse Burkett and Bobby Wallace, second baseman Dick Padden, outfielder Emmet Heidrick, and pitchers Jack Powell, Jack Harper, and Willie Sudhoff. The Cardinals' winning percentage dropped from .543 in 1901 to .418 in 1902 and they fell from fourth to sixth place. Meanwhile the Browns went 78-58 and finished in second place, five games behind the pennant-winning Philadelphia Athletics. More importantly, the Browns captured the city's affection, drawing 45,866 more fans to their games than the Cardinals, partly because of their success and partly due to strategically-lower ticket prices than those of the National League.

Despite little success as a manager—from 1901-1911, McAleer's teams won only 45% of their games and only once finished out of the second division—the former flycatcher was well-liked and, according to William A. Phelon, "a suave, entertaining character, and a fine type of the men who have come up from the ranks of the players."[18]

Robert McRoy was from Chicago, the son of George G. McRoy, vice-president of Edson Keith & Co., a successful dry-goods wholesaler whose annual sales stood at $4.5 million in 1884, two years after Robert's birth.[19] After graduating from business college, McRoy went to work for Moore & Evans, a wholesale jewelry firm that eventually went bankrupt, before becoming Ban Johnson's secretary in 1900. "In this confidential capacity, McRoy, who was an amateur player of considerable skill, also secured a working knowledge of the business end of the game," wrote the Chicago Tribune. "He was business representative of the national commission in five world's series."[20]

Ban Johnson and August "Garry" Herrmann, at the World Series in New York on October 7, 1911.

He so admired Johnson that he named his son Burton Bancroft McRoy, paying tribute to his employer by bestowing Johnson's middle name on his boy.

"He knows the game from A to Z, and is a bright, capable, quick-thinking little fellow," wrote Phelon.[21] And Jacob C. Morse wrote, commenting on his new position with the Red Sox, "Robert McRoy will be business manager. This is a role of vital importance to the prosperity of the club and Mr. McRoy is eminently fitted to fill his difficult and responsible position."[22]

Before the deal was final, newspapers began to report the details—McAleer and McRoy would own 50 percent of the Red Sox for a price of $150,000—but the Washington Post wondered aloud how the two were going to come up with the money and insisted that Johnson must be involved. "As is usually the case in such deals, an air of mystery is being thrown over everything," reported the Post on September 14, 1911. "McAleer, in Youngstown, is quoted by the Associated Press as saying: 'There will be no one in this deal except myself. I do not expect to see Ban Johnson, and have no reason for seeing him.' This is idle, if correctly quoted. McAleer has made good money, and saved some of it. But he has not the money with which to swing a $150,000 deal, and he cannot swing it without advice and consent from President Johnson."[23]

The Post also speculated that Johnson would be the "dominant factor" because McRoy was the Red Sox's new financial man. Joe S. Jackson continued to beat the Post's drum when he reported the next day, "It will also raise some embarrassing and possibly wholly uncalled for queries as to how far President Johnson himself is concerned in the deal now completed. One thing can be said for the league executive—he looks out for his friends… McRoy has been a faithful and a not overpaid employee, and gets a chance to share in some of the fruits of his industry. A majority interest was not necessary, for, with an equal ownership, President Johnson's peculiar measure of authority assures the stockholders with whom he stands the balance of power in the case of any disputes."24

In fact, Johnson had already wielded his power by effectively ignoring John I. Taylor during negotiations. According to the *Washington Post*, "John I. Taylor… will sit in one corner of a room today and listen to what President Ban Johnson, who is engineering the sale, has to say about it."25 On September 16, newspapers reported that the deal was official and a press release was issued:

"Negotiations connected with the sale of an interest in the Boston American League baseball club have resulted in the purchase of a half interest by James R. McAleer, of Washington, and Robert B. McRoy, of Chicago. As both of these gentlemen have been actively engaged elsewhere, they will not be able to come to Boston until the beginning of the year 1912.

"At that time they will come to Boston to live and join in the active management of the Red Sox. Both are versed in baseball and have marked ability and they ought to greatly strengthen the organization. Plans for a new ball park which will be a credit to Boston will now be formulated and the work pushed ahead at a rapid rate."26

Based on the press release, the *Washington Post* inferred that John I. Taylor "will not be heard from after this season." That was the plan all along. Differing reports had General Taylor tired of seeing his son's name in his newspaper and John I. himself tired of the pressures of running a ball club. Either way, it looked like John I. was going to fade into the background. The *New York Times* went one step further and reported that former Red Sox first baseman Jake Stahl would be coming out of his brief retirement to play first base and manage the team. Stahl began his career with the Red Sox in 1903 before moving on to the Washington Senators, whom he managed to back-to-back seventh-place finishes in 1905-1906.

Stahl spent the 1907 season playing semipro ball in Chicago after Washington refused his request to be traded back to Boston, then played left field for the New York Highlanders during the first half of the 1908 season before being sold back to Boston on July 10, where he resumed first base duties. He enjoyed his two best seasons in 1909-1910, batting .282 and slugging .429, and paced the American League in homers in 1910 with a career-high 10 round-trippers, but left baseball in 1911 to become an officer and stockholder in Chicago's Washington Park National Bank, owned by his father-in-law H. W. Mahan.27

According to the papers, Stahl had hoped to become part owner of the Red Sox with McAleer and his good friend McRoy, but negotiations had dragged on too long and he dropped out.28 But according to other accounts, Stahl did, in fact, become part owner, as did his father-in-law, both of whom owned five percent of the team.29

News of the deal brought excitement to the New England area. *The Hartford Courant* practically handed John I. his hat and slammed the door behind him on his way out. "The greatest handicap which the Boston team has had to contend with in the past few years has been its owner, John I. Taylor," wrote the paper. "While he has been as anxious as any enthusiastic fan to bring a winning team to the Hub, his tendency to stick his hand into the management of the team and interfere with the work of the man whom he had put over the players, has done more than anything else to keep the Red Sox down in the list."30

But that same day, the *Washington Post* reported again that Ban Johnson was the actual buyer of half of Boston's stock and that McAleer only contributed $25,000. The deal was said to be for $125,000 and not the $150,000 previously reported and that Johnson wrote the Taylors a check for the entire amount.

Red Sox Treasurer Robert McRoy's 75 shares of Preferred Stock in the Boston American League Base-Ball Club (incorporated 1901 in New Jersey), issued on November 21, 1911 and signed by him and President James McAleer.

"McAleer is interested to the extent of probably not more than $25,000, and perhaps less," reported the *Post*. "McRoy's actual holdings were not estimated, but it may be surmised that he is in the deal largely as a personal representative of the Johnson interests. McAleer, under this arrangement, may be president of the club, but if he is, it will not be as one of the really big stockholders." A source close to the Taylors estimated that McAleer's actual investment was $15,000, which he raised by selling property he owned in Youngstown.[31]

The *Coshocton Daily Times* out of Ohio chimed in as well. "In baseball circles Ban Johnson is looked upon as the owner of the Boston American League franchise. The sale of the club recently to Jim McAleer and Rob McRoy made the knowing ones smile. Neither McAleer nor McRoy has been credited with being a wealthy man…those on the inside of baseball are confident that it was Johnson who put up the money."[32]

McAleer immediately issued denials that his investment was anything less than that initially reported and that he had contributed more than $50,000 towards the purchase. "So big a share of my savings have been taken by me from the banks in which they were deposited, or out of investments, and put into this deal, that if baseball were to die tomorrow I would have to start life anew," he told reporters. McAleer was allegedly worth approximately $75,000 and, had he invested all of it, would have owned 25% of the team's stock.[33] Since McRoy's contribution was never established, Johnson's name continued to come up as a major stockholder in the Red Sox, owning at least 25% of the team and possibly more if McAleer's investment was indeed closer to $15,000-$25,000 than the $50,000-$75,000 he insisted was his actual share.

Gossip about the sale and its details finally died down for a while and focus shifted to Stahl as autumn inched closer to winter. McAleer and McRoy announced on November 6 that Stahl had agreed to come back to baseball and manage the Red Sox, but Stahl denied the report and insisted he'd yet to make a decision, and intimated there was little chance he'd return.[34] Later it was reported that McAleer made at least a dozen trips to Chicago to convince Stahl to come back, telling him that he was the "missing link" the team needed to win a championship and with a new ballpark in place, they could make a lot of money. He also relayed to Stahl how much respect and admiration the players had for him. "Jim had felt out the players during the 1911 campaign," wrote the *Mansfield News*, "and he says that in all his experience he never found a player so universally popular with his teammates as Stahl. The Red Sox players admire Jake as much for his excellent qualities as a man as for his ability as a player."[35]

As is sometimes the case following such a terse denial Stahl signed a two-year contract five days later to play first base and manage the Red Sox from 1912-1913. On the day Stahl's agreement to return was reported, a list of investors was also made public, verifying that Stahl and his father-in-law were stockholders, as were McAleer, McRoy, and a Chicago investor named C.H. Randall, all of whom allegedly owned half the team.[36]

Before the ink was dry on Stahl's new contract, newspapers began trumpeting reports about McRoy's return to Chicago from Boston and his meetings with Johnson, in which the two discussed Boston's spring training plans. "Just how President Johnson figured in Boston club affairs was not stated specifically," Joe S. Jackson wrote in the *Washington Post* on November 14. "It is not customary for club owners to get instructions from league officials or outsiders as to their training plans."[37] In an effort to maintain some kind of authority, John I. Taylor announced that the Red Sox would return to Hot Springs, Arkansas to train in 1912, after abandoning Hot Springs in 1911 for Redondo Beach, California. McRoy conferred with Taylor about the decision, but McAleer did not.

Apparently Hot Springs enticed the Red Sox to come back by agreeing to build new baseball grounds that would satisfy two teams instead of one. Previously, the Red Sox and Cincinnati Reds would battle for time on the lone diamond and both teams' managers would complain about the fact that they only had half-a-day to train. But now each team would have its own diamond, assuming that McRoy and Reds president Garry Herrmann approved of the cost of construction.[38]

Prior to the start of the season, Red Sox brass still had to deal with red tape, but most of it was just a formality. McRoy resigned his post as American League secretary and was replaced by William Harridge.[39] Stahl was reinstated to good standing by the National Commission, which declared him eligible to play again on the grounds that he played ball only with the Woodlawn Business Men's Association in 1911 and only for charity, and that he didn't play with or against ineligible players, which would have drawn a fine at the very least.[40] Then McAleer was officially named president of the team, with John I. Taylor acting as vice-president, McRoy as treasurer, and General Taylor and his attorney, J.H. Turner, being named directors.[41]

McAleer's first order of business was to reduce his work force to 35 men by letting go of some of the team's scouts, although he hired Joseph Quirk, his former trainer in St. Louis and Washington. Of course, controversy continued to dog the franchise, as it was reported in late December that Johnson, McRoy, and Harridge left Chicago quietly for a "secluded spot" in which they were to meet National League president Thomas Lynch, Pirates owner Barney Dreyfuss, and N.L. secretary John Heydler for the purpose of discussing the playing schedule.[42] Those who might have wondered why McRoy accompanied the A.L. contingent need look no further than his commitment to stay on as acting secretary until the end of the year when Harridge would take over on a full-time basis. But conspiracy theorists relished the idea of McRoy and Johnson holding clandestine meetings about the Red Sox.

Approximately three weeks later, McAleer went on the defensive again, insisting to *Sporting Life* that Johnson had no financial interest in the Red Sox and that those who continued to crow about his involvement, especially Chicago Cubs owner Charles Murphy, were talking through their hats. Murphy told reporters that it wouldn't be long before baseball would see "Johnson's robust form nestling closely in the bosom of the Presidential chair of the Red Sox," and that by placing McAleer and McRoy in Boston's front office, "Johnson got in a 'wedge.'"

But McAleer refuted that in a statement he made to *Sporting Life* in its January 27, 1912 issue:

"You can take it from me and tell it to the public and any one that wants to hear it, that Ban Johnson doesn't own one penny's worth of this club. I'm telling you straight. It's my money and

McRoy's money that we have put into this club. I'm the president of the new club since the recent change in owners, and I'm going to be president until I get out of baseball or until I quit breathing. These people who are chirping about Johnson backing us give me a pain. They don't know what they're talking about, and for that reason they should be looked after and kept quiet. This goes for that Murphy person from Chicago. Ban Johnson is my friend, and, of course, he is McRoy's friend, too, for we worked for him for a good many years. He knows McRoy as he would his own son, and for that reason wants him to make good. The only thing Ban Johnson has in this club is his heart. That's here because McRoy is connected with it, and because he and I have always been warm friends. Take it straight from headquarters that it's heart and hope, not money and power, that Bancroft Byron Johnson [sic] has in this base ball club."[43]

Only two weeks passed before more controversy cropped up. On February 10, 1912, *Sporting Life* reported that Hugh McBreen, who acted as treasurer of the Red Sox from 1906-1909, invested his life savings in the Jersey City Skeeters of the Class AA International League and speculated that Jersey City would serve as a Red Sox farm team, which was illegal at the time.[44] The Red Sox acquired pitcher Hugh Bedient from Jersey City for a handful of players, including pitcher Jack Killilay, but of the 28 players on the Jersey City roster in 1912, only five ended up in Boston and only Bedient enjoyed any kind of success. Killilay pitched for the Sox in 1911, going 4-2 with a 3.54 ERA in 14 appearances, then spent the next five seasons in the minors, with his best season coming in 1912 when he went 15-4 with a 2.55 ERA with Oakland of the Pacific Coast League. Bedient went 20-9 for the Sox as a 22-year-old rookie in 1912, then pitched to a 0.50 ERA in four World Series appearances before a sore arm ended his major league career in 1915. Needless to say, both McBreen and McAleer denied any relationship between the Skeeters and the Red Sox.

While the team trained in Arkansas, Fenway Park was nearing completion. The Red Sox christened their new grounds on April 9 with a 2-0 exhibition win over Harvard University, then officially opened it on April 20 with a hard-fought 7-6, 11-inning victory over the New York Highlanders. The victory gave them a 5-1 record on the young season, but their play fell off and they went 11-9 in their next 20 games, putting them in second place at 16-10, five-and-a-half games behind the Chicago White Sox, on May 18. From there, though, the team took off and won at a .706 clip the rest of the way to finish with an American League record 105 wins.

Center fielder Tris Speaker was named the league's most valuable player after hitting .383 and leading the league in homers (10), doubles (53), and on-base percentage (.464). Smoky Joe Wood fashioned one of the greatest seasons of all time, going 34-5 with a 1.91 ERA and 258 strikeouts, and winning 16 consecutive games from July 8 to September 20. And while Stahl the manager was leading his team to 105 victories, Stahl the first baseman was hitting .301 with 60 RBIs in only 95 games.

Attendance across the A.L. dipped slightly from 1911 to 1912, dropping by two percent, but attendance in Boston was up 18% as nearly 600,000 fans watched the Sox play at Fenway Park. Braves attendance also climbed a modest four percent, but they drew only 121,000 patrons.

On June 8, with the Sox sitting in second place at 28-18 only one game behind the White Sox, Henry P. Edwards reported that all was rosy with Red Sox management. McAleer was more than happy to sit in his owner's box and let Jake Stahl do all the worrying. "I am genuinely happy to be where I am at the head of a club after all these years and just stick in a word of advice now and then—but never during the progress of the game. Not on your life."[45] But at least one writer gave all the credit to Stahl, calling McAleer "an autocratic sort of fellow when his interests are at stake." "The fact that McAleer is content to sit back quietly as an American League magnate is certainly a tribute to the diplomacy of Stahl," wrote W.J. MacBeth.[46]

The Red Sox tied the White Sox on June 10, then took over first place for good on the 11th and never looked back. In August, *Sporting Life* reported that Paul Powers, the majority owner of the Youngstown (OH) Steelmen of the Class B Central League was considering selling a half interest to McAleer.[47] Five days later, McAleer signed 19-year-old shortstop Everett Scott off the Youngstown roster.

As the season progressed, more details about McAleer's interest in the Red Sox emerged. In late September, it was reported that McAleer owned $200,000 worth of Red Sox stock and paid for it with $130,000 of his own money and (introducing yet another element into the confusing mix) $70,000 borrowed from White Sox owner Charles Comiskey.[48] *Sporting Life* corroborated that report in mid-October, adding that McAleer had made $20,000 a year for the last eight years of his managerial and scouting career and that he saved all of it.[49] At first blush, it would seem odd that another American League magnate would lend such a substantial sum of money to a rival, but Comiskey and McAleer were more than just mere acquaintances. They played against each other in the Players League in 1890 and in the National League from 1892-1894, and Comiskey always considered McAleer to be the best outfielder he'd ever seen. And Comiskey had his ties to Ban Johnson.

Later on McAleer and Comiskey became hunting buddies. During the offseason, Comiskey and his good friend Johnson would head to Minnesota and Wisconsin every fall to hunt and fish, taking other baseball executives, players, and writers with them on their excursions, the group rarely numbering less than 60. In 1907, Comiskey purchased the Jerome Hunting and Fishing Club on Trude Lake, 12 miles south of Mercer, Wisconsin and renamed it Camp Jerome. It became home to the "Woodland Bards," a group of Comiskey's friends that initially numbered 35, eventually grew to 250, and included McAleer, McRoy, and Stahl.[50] Later, McAleer and his wife would accompany Comiskey on his world tour in 1913.[51]

Towards the end of the season, some congratulated McAleer on his long-awaited success, while others gave him little credit for the team's fortunes. One newspaper pointed out that it was Taylor who'd acquired all of the players upon which the team was built, and that the McAleer/McRoy contingency contributed "no playing material and are reaping the profits resulting from Taylor's judgment."[52]

Either way, the team was a runaway success and headed into the World Series to take on the John McGraw-led New York Giants, who famously refused to meet Boston eight years earlier to determine a "world champion" at the conclusion of the

1904 season. The Red Sox took Games One, Four, and Five and went into Game Six with a three-games-to-one lead (Game Two ended in a 6-6 tie) and a clear path to their second World Series title. Everyone expected Joe Wood to start Game Six at the Polo Grounds and Red Sox players were so confident of victory behind "Smoky Joe" that they were already calculating their winning shares on the train trip to New York. McGraw was expected to counter with Rube Marquard, who began the season with a 19-game winning streak, en route to a league-leading 26 wins, and pitched brilliantly in the Giants' only win in the first five contests, allowing only one run on seven scattered hits in a 2-1 Game Three victory.

But an odd thing happened on the way to the championship. Needing only one more win to bring home the championship, Stahl tabbed Buck O'Brien, a 30-year-old journeyman hurler, who enjoyed a very good season, going 20-13 with a 2.58 ERA, then suffered a heartbreaking loss to Marquard in Game Three. But as good as he'd been that year, he was no Joe Wood. Stahl half-jokingly told reporters after Game Five that he was planning on starting O'Brien in Game Six. Many newspapers reported that Ray Collins would most likely get the start. O'Brien was an interesting selection for Stahl, who, according to Mike Vaccaro, "pushed every proper button" to that point in the Series. "He'd shown faith in Hugh Bedient," wrote Vaccaro. "He'd eschewed small ball in favor of big innings, a gamble that had paid off. Refusing to be intimidated by McGraw, he'd told his team to play the way they were accustomed to playing, not be sucked in by anything the Giants tried."[53]

But it wasn't Stahl's decision at all; it was McAleer's. It was an odd time for McAleer to go back on his earlier statement that he wouldn't interfere with Stahl's handling of the lineup, and his intentions were more Machiavellian than he was letting on, although no one was fooled. On the train to New York, McAleer sidled up next to Stahl and more or less demanded that O'Brien start Game Six so he could avenge his loss at the hands of Marquard in Game Three. Besides, he argued, Wood would get two extra days off instead of one and would be fresher for Game Seven at Fenway Park.

But everyone knew McAleer was hoping for an extra home game, which would bring in more revenue, especially with Wood on the mound. Stahl tried to convince McAleer that his strategy was risky, that O'Brien may have won 20 games but he also lost 13 during the regular season and his only World Series start, despite pitching well. But McAleer would have none of it. The move either backfired or worked perfectly, depending on the perspective. O'Brien lasted only eight batters and allowed five runs on six hits and an error before coming out of the game after only one inning. To add insult to injury, he balked the first run home that it probably didn't happen in Fenway's first season— the first balk in World Series history. Ray Collins took over in the second and was masterful, shutting out the Giants for the rest of the game on only five hits. But Marquard was brilliant again, going the distance and allowing only two unearned runs on seven hits in the 5-2 Giants victory.

Most were furious when they learned that O'Brien and not Wood was getting the nod. Wood's brother Paul, especially, who wagered $100 on his sibling, figuring it was money in the bank. Because it was a last-minute decision, O'Brien had allegedly been out drinking the night before and was in no shape to pitch. But Stahl sent him out there anyway, under McAleer's orders. After the game tensions were high, and according to Glenn Stout, Paul accosted O'Brien on the train back to Boston and punched him in the face, giving the hurler a black eye.[54] A separate report in the *Washington Post* claimed that O'Brien retaliated by punching Joe Wood in the face while the two argued about Game Six in the dugout prior to Game Seven. According to the article, Red Sox catchers Bill Carrigan and Hick Cady were also involved at one point or another.[55]

Meanwhile, just as McAleer had hoped, both teams' coffers continued to swell. Joe S. Jackson reported that the gate receipts for Game Six came to $66,654, that total receipts for the Series climbed to $403,133 and, that after the leagues got their cut, each team would easily clear over $100,000.[56]

Not to be outdone, however, McRoy blundered next by inexplicably selling the Royal Rooters' seats in the makeshift left-field bleachers to the general public prior to Game Seven. The Rooters were a band of Red Sox fans made up of Boston luminaries such as Boston mayor John Fitzgerald, Johnny Keenan, and Michael "Nuf Ced" McGreevey, owner of the Third Base Saloon and arbiter of all things baseball. They'd been vociferously rooting for the Red Sox since the team's inception, after abandoning the National League because of its syndicate practices, and had been instrumental in helping the Sox win games by incessantly singing "Tessie" from the Broadway musical *The Glass Slipper* to inspire their boys while distracting the opponent.

Three hundred Rooters arrived in New York for Game One, accompanied by a brass band, and received a round of applause from Giants fans who enjoyed the revelers' renditions of "Tessie," "Sweet Adeline," and a bastardized version of "Tammany," which boasted customized lyrics celebrating the Boston nine.[57] Then after Boston's 4-3 Game One

Charles Comiskey and Ban Johnson, 1912.

victory, the Rooters marched out of the Polo Grounds singing a tailored version of "In the Good Old Summertime."[58] And so it went—the Rooters would parade around the ballpark, singing, making noise, and carrying on; take their seats, sing, and make more noise; then parade out of the ballpark at contest's end.

By Game Six their numbers had doubled, and despite a disappointing 5-2 defeat at the hands of the Giants, the Rooters marched out of the Polo Grounds with the same fervor and swagger they always had. They marched into Fenway Park amid the same pomp and circumstance prior to Game Seven, paraded around the field to the strains of "Tessie," and then headed for their customary left field seats that it probably didn't happen in Fenway's first season—only to find them already occupied. After holding up the game with a near-riot eventually quelled by Keenan and Boston police, the dejected revelers were forced to take up residence wherever they could find room to stand. Needless to say, they were not happy, especially Fitzgerald, who promised he'd deal with McAleer and McRoy after the game.[59]

Once the game got underway, Smoky Joe Wood was obliterated by the Giants, who plated six first-inning runs on seven hits, a double steal, and a sacrifice, en route to a resounding 11-4 win that evened the Series at three wins apiece, and was deemed "a slaughter" by the *Boston Globe*'s Tim Murnane.[60] Wood lasted only one inning and faced all of nine batters before coming out in favor of Charley Hall, who surrendered five more runs in eight innings. The Rooters, who'd been silent throughout the contest, took the shellacking as expected and used the opportunity to voice their displeasure at the "utmost discourtesy" with which they were treated. After the game, they marched around the park and booed McRoy unmercifully, while cheering loudly for the Giants' management. Then they marched out of the park and towards the team's offices, insisting that McRoy make an appearance and explain himself.

McRoy explained that he had not been contacted by a member of the Rooters until 12:45, three hours later than was usual for them, and was afraid he'd be stuck with unsold tickets, so he ordered the reserved section be opened to the public. "The situation was the result of a misunderstanding," McRoy explained. "There was absolutely no intention on my part to be discourteous to the rooters. I have tried my best to please everyone, and if the Royal Rooters don't like it, they should take their medicine like the rest of us."[61] Keenan refuted McRoy's version of the events and insisted there was no way their block of tickets was still sitting on McRoy's desk at 12:45 because Keenan already received and distributed approximately half of them at 12:20. Timothy Mooney, chief of the bureau of information of the Mayor's office, corroborated Keenan's version of the story, claiming he'd signed for and picked up the tickets at noon.

The Rooters were incensed and weren't about to "take their medicine." In fact, Fitzgerald called for McRoy's head. "Secy McRoy of Chicago should be retired from all connection with the Boston Baseball Club, and a Boston man who understands conditions here given the place. Boston money supports the club, and there is certainly enough baseball brains in Boston to furnish a secretary."[62] The Rooters abandoned the Red Sox and refused to attend the final game of the Series, won by Boston, 2-1, in dramatic fashion. In fact, attendance was only 17,034, half of what it had been in previous games at Fenway Park. Some even claimed the days of the Royal Rooters were past and that they'd disband forever.

McAleer refused to comment until he knew more, but issued a public apology at the team's victory celebration held at Faneuil Hall the next day. Then he and McRoy headed to Camp Jerome with Charles Comiskey, Ban Johnson, Garry Herrmann, White Sox skipper Nixie Callahan, and more than 30 others for their annual hunting and fishing expedition. Despite the apology, Keenan swore he'd never set foot in Fenway Park as long as McRoy was still in the front office. While the Red Sox magnates were in Wisconsin, *Sporting Life* weighed in on the controversy. "That one or two of the new club officials are unpopular with Boston fans and the newspaper reporters is a fact that would be useless to try to conceal. Rank errors of judgment have been made…It is a pity that the new management has made itself unpopular with this best and fair-minded base ball community in the country. It would not be surprising if there was some kind of a change in officials here before another season rolls around."[63]

Upon arriving home from his trip to Camp Jerome, Ban Johnson also issued a statement, in which he expressed regret over the incident and promised to take steps to ensure the Rooters would be better taken care of in the future. But he also took Fitzgerald to task for not going to Johnson or McAleer directly, for "unjustly censuring" McRoy, and for being ungrateful for all that Johnson had done to ensure the Rooters had tickets for Game One in New York. "When Mayor Fitzgerald was turned down after requesting 300 seats for the rooters for the first game of the World's Series at the Polo Grounds it was through my personal efforts that he was finally accommodated…I also sent [National League Secretary John] Heydler to Boston to offer an apology when he delivered the reservation."[64]

Once the dust settled, it was time to get back to business and prepare for the 1913 campaign. *Sporting Life* reported in early November that the Red Sox made $450,000 during the 1912 season and that Stahl had cleared $35,000 thanks to his $10,000 salary as manager, his $4,024.69 World Series share, and dividends on his five percent ownership in the team.[65] The offseason was mostly uneventful—McAleer mailed out contracts to his players and then insisted that despite the mayor's call for a new secretary, McRoy was going nowhere and would not retire under outside threats or demands; he announced that 8,000 seats would go for 25 cents, more than any other park in major league baseball (this was something Fitzgerald practically demanded during the Game Seven ticket fiasco); and Jake Stahl announced he'd be coming back as Red Sox manager but would no longer play.[66]

Not long after ringing in the new year, McAleer predicted the upcoming pennant race would come down to the Red Sox, Philadelphia Athletics, and Washington Senators. But after hearing in March that the writers had pegged the A's to cop the pennant, McAleer became a bit indignant. "The team that will win the American League pennant this season…will be exactly the same club that won the flag and championship last Fall. There's nothing else to it."[67] The rest of the team felt the same way and broke camp with confidence. McAleer swore it was the best training camp with which he'd ever been involved, which was saying a lot considering he'd been associated with the game for 27 years.⁶⁸

But perhaps the team's confidence and McAleer's hubris was misplaced. During camp, Joe Wood sprained his ankle while reaching for a throw at third base, then severely injured his right thumb when he slipped on wet grass while fielding a grounder. "I don't know whether I tried to pitch too soon after that," Wood told Lawrence Ritter, "or whether maybe something happened to my shoulder at the same time. But whatever it was, I never pitched again without a terrific amount of pain in my right shoulder. Never again."⁶⁹ Wood battled through the pain into July and compiled a record of 11-5 and an ERA of 2.29 that ranked 10th in the American League. And despite the injury, he fanned more batters per nine innings (7.6) than ever before. But in mid-July he slipped during a rundown and broke his already wounded digit, putting him out of action until late September when he made a handful of relief appearances.

Even before Wood fractured his thumb, the team was in turmoil. The Sox started out 16-22 and found themselves in fifth place, already 12 games behind the front-running Athletics. They were much better in June, going 18-8 to get over the .500 mark, but still managed to lose ground to the surging A's, who extended their lead over Cleveland from only a half-game at the end of May to eight-and-a-half games by June's end, and were on pace to win 114 games. After Wood's last start of the year on July 18, a 5-1 loss to Hooks Dauss and the Detroit Tigers, the Red Sox were already hopelessly out of the race, 18 ½ games out of first.

Fissures in management began to form and by mid-July, newspapers were reporting that McAleer and Stahl were engaged in a battle for control of the team and one or the other would have to go. The *New York Times* reported that McAleer blamed Stahl for the team's poor performance and that Stahl was trying to undermine McAleer.⁷⁰ The *Washington Post* claimed that Stahl had been trying to unseat McAleer as president of the club since before the season started.⁷¹ *Sporting Life* took it a step further and reported that the fissure began almost from the beginning of the partnership, that Stahl and McRoy, already good friends, couldn't understand why McAleer was named president, and that McAleer was jealous of Stahl and McRoy's friendship. McAleer, of course, denied having a rift with Stahl, even though he was on his way to Chicago to meet with Ban Johnson about that very thing. Johnson also denied knowing about dissension among the Red Sox and was unaware why McAleer had scheduled a meeting with him.⁷²

When McAleer arrived in Chicago, he issued a statement to the press. "Early in the season I was told by a New York man that Jake Stahl was planning to get the presidency of the club. I spoke to Stahl about the matter. He denied the story and the matter was dropped. I am certain there is nothing to it, for Mr. Stahl is well aware that it would be utterly impossible to beat me out for the presidency I hold. You can say that Manager Stahl and I are in perfect accord and the best of friends."⁷³

Two days later, Stahl was released from his managerial duties. According to both men, Stahl had asked where he stood with the club and McAleer told him that if he wasn't playing and only managing he was "of little use to the club" and that he wouldn't be retained as manager after the season. McAleer wasn't fond of Stahl's managerial abilities and ignored the fact that his manager had a seriously injured foot that required surgery which

Ban Johnson, President of the American League sees off Frank Farrell, owner of the New York Yankees; Jimmy Callahan, manager of the Chicago White Sox; John McGraw, manager of the New York Giants; and Charles Comiskey, owner of the Chicago White Sox, on an extensive round-the-world tour after the World Series in 1913. Jimmy McAleer joined the group on the world tour. While McAleer was away, Johnson initiated action which led to the sale of the Red Sox to Joseph Lannin.

made him unable to play. McAleer felt that Stahl, the non-playing skipper, was too expensive to keep around, so he told the press that he released Stahl "for the good of the club." Other reports stated that the shareholders wanted a playing manager and not one who called the shots from the bench.

Stahl was incensed, although he insisted he was satisfied with the decision, especially since he was going to be paid through the end of the season. "McAleer didn't want me, and I don't propose to stay with any man that is not in full sympathy with me. That is about all there is to it." Seven-year veteran catcher Bill Carrigan was named as Stahl's successor.⁷⁴

It didn't take long for the backlash to hit the papers. Johnson issued a statement in which he called McAleer's decision "hasty, ill-advised, and unsportsmanlike" and wondered why the Sox magnate couldn't wait until the end of the season to change managers. "As it is, Stahl has been humiliated in his home city, and the American League has been placed in the unenviable position of dropping in mid-season a manager who won the World's Championship last Fall. Stahl was an honorable and competent manager and was highly esteemed in our league." McAleer immediately issued a rebuttal stating that Stahl "practically insisted on quitting then and there" when he was told a managerial change would be made during the offseason. "When Pres Johnson sees me and gets the story straight he will change his opinion," McAleer told the *Boston Globe*'s Tim Murnane.⁷⁵

A day later, Johnson was still waiting for an explanation, but McAleer claimed there was none to give. Then he quashed rumors about a deal that would have sent Tris Speaker to Detroit for Ty Cobb. Apparently McAleer was worried that Speaker would react unfavorably to Stahl's removal and thought he might have to trade him, but Speaker insisted that Stahl's release was none of his business and that he was playing for his salary and was satisfied with Boston.⁷⁶ Less than a week later, the *Los Angeles Times* reported that John I. and Charles Taylor were "after" McAleer and that they wanted to take full control of the team again.⁷⁷

Carrigan proved to be a success at the helm of the club, leading the Red Sox to a 40-30 finish, but criticism continued to land on McAleer. *Baseball Magazine* called Stahl's removal, "a stain of ingratitude and selfishness cast on organized baseball," and a "blunder," and William Phelon called Stahl "a good fellow, a splendid character, and an honor to the game."⁷⁸

In November, rumors began circulating that the Taylors were looking to sell their shares of stock, although *Sporting Life* wasn't buying it and thought the Taylors would sell only if they received $500,000, which was unlikely.⁷⁹ Then the same magazine reported two weeks later that the Taylors reversed course and offered McAleer and McRoy $220,000 for *their* shares in order to regain complete control of the team. A statement by Ban Johnson seemingly corroborated the report although the Taylors refused to confirm or deny the pending purchase.

Finally, the *Boston Globe* reported on December 1 that the shares owned by the "Chicago interests" led by McAleer, McRoy, and Stahl were to be sold to Joseph J. Lannin of the Lannin Realty Company, severing all ties McAleer, McRoy, and Stahl had with the Red Sox. It's also interesting to note that the *Globe* reported, "The change in ownership has the sanction of Pres Johnson of the American League, who had a prominent part in the negotiations…"⁸⁰ Not only did Johnson have a "prominent part," but he instigated them. According to various sources, McAleer told Johnson to sell his shares while he was touring the world with Comiskey, but evidence to the contrary suggests otherwise. According to Red Sox historian Bill Nowlin, "Joe Cashman told Peter Golenbock that McAleer received a telegram reading, 'You have just sold the Red Sox to Joseph Lannin. Ban Johnson.'"⁸¹ And both McRoy and Stahl were surprised at the news and claimed they knew nothing about the sale.⁸²

A Canadian, Lannin was a self-made man who worked as a bellhop at the St. Louis Hotel in Quebec, Canada in the 1880s before immigrating to Boston at only 15 and securing a similar position. He worked his way up to head bellboy, head of a watch, assistant head waiter, then steward of the Ocean View Hotel on Block Island, before becoming a real estate magnate after investing in property in a suburb of Boston known as Forest Hills. From there, he began leasing hotels in New Jersey and New York and formed the Lannin Real Estate Company.

His first love was lacrosse, but Lannin eventually fell in love with baseball and figured there was money to be made in America's Pastime. He bought stock in the Boston Braves before selling it to become part-owner of the Red Sox. "Warned by pessimists that baseball has reached or past its zenith as a money making proposition, the ex-Canadian…thinks enough of baseball's future to invest wealth he has earned in other business in a half interest of a baseball property conservatively estimated at $700,000," wrote Harvey T. Woodruff of the *Chicago Tribune*.⁸³

As for the sale of the shares held by the Chicago group, the *New York Tribune* put it most succinctly when it wrote, "As if to show that [Ban Johnson] is the complete master of the organization and that the individual owners are mere puppets in his hands, the banishment of Bob McRoy, James McAleer and Jake Stahl from the councils of the Boston Red Sox has been accomplished. So great is the power of Johnson that he can blacklist an owner as easily as he can suspend a player." Later the same paper reported again what the baseball establishment already knew, that Johnson was the real owner of the stock. "The remarkably peaceable way in which Johnson lopped off the heads of those he had marked, and the fact that neither Stahl not McRoy knew that negotiations were going on, leads to the belief that they were nothing but figureheads, lending their name to the real owner of the stock."⁸⁴

But McRoy wasn't about to go quietly and refused to sell his 62 shares of stock. It wasn't until Lannin, John I. Taylor, Charles Somers, Johnson, and Yankees president Frank Farrell dispensed advice to McRoy at the Hotel Wolcott in New York that he finally agreed to sign the transfer papers.

With that, Lannin was the Red Sox's new president and the triumvirate of McAleer, McRoy, and Stahl were stripped of their power just as quickly as it had been bestowed upon them.⁸⁵

Epilogue

Under Lannin's watch and the leadership of Bill Carrigan, who was retained as manager, the Sox rebounded from their pedestrian 1913 showing and won nearly 62% of their games and two World Series titles from 1914-1916 before Lannin sold the team to Harry Frazee in November 1916. At the time of the sale, Lannin stated that he was getting out of major league baseball because of a heart condition, but evidence suggests that he was simply tired of Ban Johnson meddling in his affairs. "The disgust that rankled in Lannin's mind after several clashes with Johnson, was the potent factor that drove Lannin to look for a way out of the national game," reported the *Atlanta Constitution*.⁸⁶

Lannin had bought the Taylors out in 1914 and took full control of the team. One of his first orders of business was to lock

Before Game Two of the 1916 World Series, which the Red Sox played at Braves Field, L to R: Red Sox owner Joseph Lannin, A. L. President Ban Johnson, N. L. President John K. Tener, and President of the National Baseball Commission August Herrmann. October 9, 1916.

up superstar center fielder Tris Speaker, who spurned the upstart Federal League to sign with Boston for two more years at $18,000 per annum. Lannin wasn't thrilled with the deal—he once accused his players of being "unreasonable" and "grasping" during contract negotiations—but he didn't have much choice. The presence of the Feds and their willingness to entice contract jumpers artificially raised salaries to unprecedented levels, forcing owners to pay more to keep their star players. But when the Federal League collapsed following an unsuccessful anti-trust lawsuit against the American and National Leagues in 1915, major-league owners couldn't wait to restore salaries back to their pre-Federal League levels.

Lannin offered Speaker a salary of $9,000 for the 1916 season, citing his declining batting average as the reason he was trying to cut Speaker's salary in half. Speaker, of course, declined the offer and held out, although he told the press that he was merely negotiating with Lannin and didn't want to be referred to as a "holdout." Then, without warning, Lannin dealt Speaker to the Cleveland Indians on April 8, 1916 for $55,000, pitcher "Sad Sam" Jones and infielder Fred Thomas. "The proverbial pin could have dropped a million times in the hotel corridor and it would have made a noise like the sudden bursting of an automobile," wrote the *Boston Globe*'s Mel Webb, Jr. upon hearing of the deal. "Everyone was speechless."[87]

Lannin claimed that he couldn't afford Speaker's $15,000 asking price, which on the face of it was ridiculous considering the man once bought an entire minor-league franchise just to acquire the rights to pitcher Carl Mays, and that the $55,000 "was so large…that he was obliged in fairness to all concerned to accept it."[88]

Those familiar with the situation smelled a rat, and his name was Ban Johnson. Johnson brokered the deal between Boston and Cleveland and speculation has it that he coerced Lannin into pulling the trigger on the trade, a transaction described by Fred Lieb as "one of those inside affairs put over by the astute Ban Johnson."[89] But Johnson wasn't the only one trying to steer Speaker towards the Indians. Cleveland's primary negotiator was none other than former American League secretary and Red Sox co-owner, Bob McRoy, who now owned shares in the Indians and was acting as the Tribe's vice-president.

Less than two months before the Speaker deal, Charles Somers was forced out as Indians owner by creditors to whom he owed almost $2 million. Johnson purchased the team and held title for four owners, alleged to be James C. Dunn and P.S. McCarthy, with McRoy also named, although not confirmed.[90] Whether or not McRoy was an actual owner, he was definitely placed in charge of the Indians by Johnson and Dunn, who was named team president, but relinquished control to McRoy. According to Harold Seymour, Dunn eventually paid Johnson back in order to take control of the team, but Johnson continued to hold $50,000 worth of stock in the club.[91]

Lannin kept the Sox for one more season, then sold it to Frazee and his business partner Hugh Ward. The deal marked the first time in the history of the American League that a team had been sold without Johnson's knowledge or blessing, perhaps lending further evidence to Lannin's dislike of the A.L. czar, and Frazee instantly became Johnson's chief nemesis. After two years of battling back and forth in the board room and the papers, things finally came to a head in 1919 when Frazee sold Carl Mays to the New York Yankees for $40,000 and pitchers Allen Russell and Bob McGraw. Mays, tired of pitching in front of teammates who couldn't stand him and played poorly with him on the mound, left the Red Sox in the middle of a game and swore he'd never pitch for them again. Johnson waited for Frazee to discipline Mays, but the Red Sox magnate took advantage of the multitude of offers he was receiving for the recalcitrant hurler, and sent him to the Yankees instead.

Johnson was furious and vetoed the trade, then suspended Mays himself. But Yankee owners Jacob Ruppert and Cap Huston filed an injunction against Johnson, claiming that his ruling was injurious to their team, and that his stockholdings in the Indians created a conflict of interest and motivated him to block the Yankees' acquisition of Mays. A judge ruled in the Yankees' (and indirectly Frazee's) favor on August 6 and Mays made his Yankees debut the next day and beat the St. Louis Browns, 8-2.

Eventually the Mays case went to court. During testimony, Johnson admitted that he owned $58,500 worth of stock in the Indians, the original $50,000 and an additional $8,500 that he had recently loaned Dunn. Then on September 11, 1919, Johnson confessed what everyone already knew despite multiple denials to the contrary, that he did, in fact, provide the money McAleer and McRoy needed to buy half interest in the Red Sox in 1911. According to W.O. McGeehan of the *New York Tribune*, New York Yankees attorney Charles Tuttle was about to conclude questioning when he turned his attention toward Johnson's alleged ownership of Red Sox stock in 1912.

> "Did you own the Boston [American League] club in 1912?" Tuttle asked Johnson.
> "I owned stock in the Boston club," Johnson admitted.
> "How much stock," demanded council.
> "I owned a considerable amount of the stock," replied Johnson.

"This admission, coming on top of the confession made by Johnson that he still is a part owner of the Cleveland Baseball Club, gives a new insight into the stout gentlemen whose bitterest allegation against the defunct Federal League was that it was a syndicated league," wrote McGeehan. "And all the time Johnson himself has been manipulating, buying and selling clubs."[92]

After his dismissal from the Red Sox, Jake Stahl went back to banking and became vice-president of Washington Park National Bank in Chicago. In 1917, he went off to fight in World War I, serving as a second lieutenant in the Army before returning to Washington Park to serve as president. He died of tuberculosis in 1922 at the age of 43.[93]

As for James McAleer, Johnson's unwillingness to support him in the wake of Stahl's firing caused a rift between the men that was never repaired. According to Frank B. Ward, a sports reporter with the *Youngstown Daily Vindicator*, McAleer felt Johnson's actions constituted a betrayal of trust and friendship, and that Johnson confided in McAleer that he owed Jake Stahl's father-in-law money and felt obligated to side with Stahl.[94]

McAleer left baseball for good after he was forced out by Johnson and went back to his hometown of Youngstown, Ohio. He was diagnosed with cancer in 1930 or '31, and on April 28, 1931 he shot himself in the head and died the next day. At the time of his death, it was reported that he'd died from his illness following an operation, but the *New York Times* reported on May 20, 1931 that Coroner M.E. Hayes concluded that McAleer died of a self-inflicted gunshot wound to the head.[95] He was 66 years old and, ironically, followed Ban Johnson's death by only a month.

Endnotes

1. Fred Schuld, "Charles W. Somers," *Deadball Stars of the American League*, ed. David Jones (Dulles, Virginia: Potomac Books, Inc., 2006), 390.

2. Ibid.; John E. Wray and J. Roy Stockton, "Ban Johnson's Own Story," *St. Louis Post-Dispatch*, February 10-March 3, 1929.

3. Glenn Stout and Richard A. Johnson. *Red Sox Century* (Boston: Houghton Mifflin, 2000), 57.

4. Frederick G. Lieb. *The Boston Red Sox* (New York: G.P. Putnam's Sons, 1947), 195-196.

5. Lawrence Ritter. *The Glory of Their Times* (New York: Macmillan, 1966), 131-133.

6. *Washington Post*, January 23, 1901.

7. Stout and Johnson. *Red Sox Century*, 9; Philip J. Lowry, *Green Cathedrals: The Ultimate Celebration of Major League and Negro League Ballparks* (New York: Walker & Company, 2006), 26-27.

8. Lieb, *Red Sox*, 11.

9. *Chicago Tribune*, January 18, 1901. Bill Nowlin covers this extensively in his *Red Sox Threads* (Burlington MA: Rounder Books, 2008).

10. Lowry, *Green Cathedrals*, 24, 150-151.

11. *Los Angeles Times*, February 26, 1911.

12. *Boston Globe*, February 15, 1911.

13. *Baltimore Sun*, February 15, 1911.

14. *Baltimore Sun*, February 15, 1911; Lowry, *Green Cathedrals*, 26-27.

15. *Ibid.*

16. *Boston Globe*, September 30, 1911.

17. Bill James. *The New Bill James Historical Baseball Abstract* (New York: Free Press, 2001), 764; David Fleitz, Jimmy McAleer biography at BioProj.SABR.org; F.C. Lane, *Baseball Magazine*, September 1913.

18. *Baseball Magazine*, January 1913.

19. http://www.encyclopedia.chicagohistory.org/pages/2734.html

20. *Chicago Tribune*, September 15, 1911; *New York Times*, May 1, 1902.

21. William A. Phelon, *Baseball Magazine*, January 1913.

22. Jacob C. Morse, *Baseball Magazine*, September 1912.

23. *Washington Post*, September 14, 1911.

24. *Washington Post*, September 15, 1911.

25. *Washington Post*, September 14, 1911.

26. *Washington Post*, September 16, 1911.

27. *Boston Globe*, September 17, 1911.

28. *Ibid.*

29. John Stahl, "Garland 'Jake' Stahl," in *Deadball Stars of the American League*, 429; Bill Nowlin e-mail; *Sporting Life*, November 2, 1912.

30. *Hartford Courant*, September 18, 1911.

31. *Washington Post*, September 18, 1911.

32. *Coshocton Daily Times*, February 7, 1912.

33. *Washington Post*, September 20, 1911.

34. *Washington Post*, November 7, 1911.

35. *Mansfield News*, October 7, 1912.

36. *Washington Post*, November 11, 1911; *New York Tribune*, November 11, 1911.

37. *Washington Post*, November 14, 1911.

38. *Boston Globe*, November 24, 1911.

39. *Christian Science Monitor*, December 19, 1911.

40. *New York Tribune*, December 21, 1911.

41. *San Francisco Chronicle*, January 5, 1912.

42. *New York Tribune*, December 29, 1911.

43. *Sporting Life*, January 27, 1912; It is interesting to note that McAleer was "warm friends" with Johnson, yet didn't know his name was Byron Bancroft Johnson and not Bancroft Byron Johnson.

44. *Sporting Life*, February 10, 1912.

45. *Sporting Life*, June 15, 1912.

46. *Lima News*, July 21, 1912.

47. *Sporting Life*, August 17, 1912.

48. *Mansfield News*, September 21, 1912.

49. *Sporting Life*, October 12, 1912.

50. G. W. Axelson. *"Commy:" The Life Story of Charles A. Comiskey* (Jefferson, North Carolina: McFarland & Company, Inc., 2003), 191-194.

51. *Ibid.*, 167.

52. *Mansfield News*, September 26, 1912.

53. Mike Vaccaro. *The First Fall Classic: The Red Sox, The Giants, and the Cast of Players, Pugs, and Politicos Who Reinvented the World Series in 1912* (New York: Doubleday, 2009), 174.

54. Stout and Johnson, *Red Sox Century*, 87.

55. *Washington Post*, October 16, 1912.

56. *Washington Post*, October 15, 1912.

57. Vaccaro, *The First Fall Classic*, 58-59. Vaccaro mis-states the song title as "Sweet Adelaide".

58. *Ibid.*, 73-74.

59. *Ibid.*, 209-211; Stout and Johnson, *Red Sox Century*, 88.

60. *Boston Globe*, October 16, 1912.

61. *Ibid.*

62. *Ibid.*

63. *Sporting Life*, October 26, 1912.

64. *Sporting Life*, November 2, 1912.

65. *Ibid.*

66. *Sporting Life*, December 14, 1912; *Sporting Life*, January 25, 1912; *Sporting Life*, February 1, 1913.

67. *Sporting Life*, March 22, 1913.

68. *Sporting Life*, April 12, 1913.

69. Ritter, *The Glory of Their Times*, 158.

70. *New York Times*, July 10, 1913.

71. *Washington Post*, July 10, 1913.

72. *Sporting Life*, July 19, 1913.

73. *Boston Globe*, July 14, 1913.

74. *Boston Globe*, July 16, 1913.

75. *Boston Globe*, July 17, 1913.

76. *Boston Globe*, July 19, 1913.

77. *Los Angeles Times*, July 24, 1913.

78. *Baseball Magazine*, September 1913.

79. *Sporting Life*, November 8, 1913.

80. *Boston Globe*, December 1, 1913.

81. Bill Nowlin. *Day by Day with the Boston Red Sox* (Cambridge MA: Rounder Books, 2006), 550.

82. *Boston Globe*, December 1, 1913.

83. *Chicago Tribune*, January 11, 1914; It was later reported that Lannin actually paid only $200,000 for half interest in the Red Sox.

84. *New York Tribune*, December 2, 1913.

85. *Boston Globe*, December 9, 1913.

86. *Atlanta Constitution*, August 16, 1919.

87. *Boston Globe*, April 9, 1916.

88. *Ibid.*

89. Lieb, *Red Sox*, 140.

90. *Boston Globe*, February 21, 1916.

91. Harold Seymour, *Baseball: The Golden Age* (New York: Oxford University Press, 1971), 267.

92. *New York Tribune*, September 12, 1919.

93. John Stahl, "Garland Stahl," *Deadball Stars of the American League*, 429.

94. *Youngstown Daily Vindicator*, April 29, 1931.

95. *New York Times*, May 20, 1931.

Opening Fenway Park with Style: The World Champion 1912 Boston Red Sox

This composite photograph showcases the 1912 Red Sox, with oversized images of Bill Carrigan and Jake Stahl. Oddly, the Boston player images are set against a background of Chicago's ballpark.

This 1912 Boston Red Sox silk pictorial display piece captures the team's panoramic image as its center point: "Opening Game American League - Fenway Park—April 20, 1912—Boston vs. New York." team, with "Red Sox—Champions—1912." The portrait images are centered by manager Jake Stahl, with the remaining four star players, "Smoky" Joe Wood, Tris Speaker, Heinie Wagner, and Bill Carrigan.

1912 Day by Day – A Season Timeline

The Boston Red Sox finished the 1911 season 24 games out of first place, pulling themselves over .500 only by winning the final six games of the season. The final record was 78-75.

Many thought the reason the Sox had floundered in 1911 was the loss of first baseman Jake Stahl, who had led the team in RBIs in 1910 but decided to leave baseball to take a position as president of his father-in-law's Chicago-based bank. Efforts to bring Stahl aboard in early 1911 went on until the 11th hour—even as the team train passed through Chicago on its way to spring training, but Stahl was resolute and did not play in 1911.

Even with a change in the ownership structure late in the season, the Red Sox still wanted to secure Stahl for 1912. With three games remaining on the 1911 schedule, incoming team president James McAleer announced that he was determined to entice Jake Stahl back to manage the team. He told the *Washington Post*, "I will offer Stahl inducements that I do not think he can afford to overlook. He is still a young man, with a long baseball life before him, and I believe that he will return to the game."

It had been a fallow period for Boston baseball, an unaccustomed one. There was nothing at all happening for Boston's National League team since the 20th century began. They had never once finished as close as 20 games to first place, and had often been 40 or more games back—up to 66 games behind in 1906, the year both Boston teams finished dead last in their leagues. The Boston Nationals had finished in last place in 1909, 1910, and 1911—and did so again in 1912.

The only hope rested with the Americans. They'd played well in the first few years of American League ball, winning the first World Series between the American and National Leagues in 1903 and presenting such a strong team in 1904 that the National League champion New York Giants—not wanting to "lower themselves" to play the winner of the upstart AL (but also perhaps fearful of losing) declined to play a postseason series for a world title. Beginning in 1905, though, Boston went into a doldrums. In the seven seasons 1905 through 1911, the Red Sox (their name beginning with the 1908 campaign) had won 508 games but lost 558. They had three winning seasons in a row from 1909 through 1911, but after the hopeful third-place finish in 1909 they lost ground both in wins percentage and in the standings in 1910 and again in 1911. The league was dominated by Detroit and Philadelphia, which had won six of the preceding seven pennants. The Red Sox needed something to turn them around, and so did Boston baseball in general.

Boston was one of the best cities for baseball, but the poor performance of the two teams was discouraging. Something had to change. Ban Johnson, the president (and architect) of the American League, held such control over the league as a whole that he could orchestrate changes which would boggle the mind today. He could move players from one team to another to boost the prospects of one team and improve the competitive balance that could energize a fan base. There seems little doubt that he engineered a change in the ownership of the Red Sox. The biggest change in 1911 was bringing McAleer into the ballclub; the first news of the change broke in July. Jimmy McAleer was a former player who had managed Cleveland in 1901 and the St. Louis American League team from 1902 through 1909. In 1910 and 1911, he moved to Washington and was the skipper of the Senators. There was talk even in the early summer of 1911 that Red Sox owner John I. Taylor might be selling the team, and that McAleer was the head of a group looking to buy it. Rumors along these lines had built to the point that McAleer entered a denial on July 18, saying that he hadn't even contemplated the matter. Before he was signed by the Senators, he had attempted to buy the St. Louis Browns but that was in the past. Taylor spoke up, too, and said, "I have not been approached in regard to the sale of the club." He did add that if he was offered enough money he'd sell the Red Sox or anything else he had. [1]

If negotiations hadn't started by then, they soon did. Just two months later, an announcement was made on September 12: McAleer and Robert McRoy would buy a 50 percent interest in the Boston Red Sox. The *Chicago Tribune* added, foreshadowing the construction of Fenway Park: "As soon as the papers are signed, actual work will begin on the construction of a new steel and concrete grandstand to cost $200,000. The work of grading the new site already has begun and the completed park will be ready for the opening of the 1912 season. The financing of the project already has been accomplished." The paper estimated that the total value of the franchise with the grounds and grandstand was about $750,000.[2] McRoy was, not coincidentally, the former secretary to American League founder Ban Johnson. There were still 21 games left on the Washington Senators' schedule, including four against the Red Sox—presenting a situation where the manager of one team was playing against another team he now owned. The Senators won the game on September 13, but lost the last four games of the year to Boston—though Washington was so solidly ensconced in seventh place that neither wins nor losses could affect their place in the standings at that point. McAleer was named president of the Boston Red Sox, and was determined to bring back Jake Stahl as manager. He stated forthrightly, "I will offer Stahl inducements that I do not think he can afford to overlook."[3]

Within less than two months, Mac had his man: Stahl was on board. He told McAleer this on October 24, the *Boston Globe* reported. The three men—McAleer, McRoy, and Stahl—were close friends. The *New York Times* reported it as a done deal in its November 7 edition. On November 10, John I. Taylor—who still held 50 percent of the stock in the club—received a formal telegram from Stahl announcing his decision to return. The inducements included a two-year contract and also a share in the ownership of the ballclub.[4] Since Stahl intended to play first base as well as manage the team, he would hold the unique position of being a player, manager, and owner all at the same time.

McRoy headed to Hot Springs in mid-November to make arrangements for spring training.

All the information in the timeline that follows is obtained from the Boston Post *unless otherwise indicated, as are otherwise unattributed quotations. The game story headlines often preceding the day's entry are similarly from the* Post.

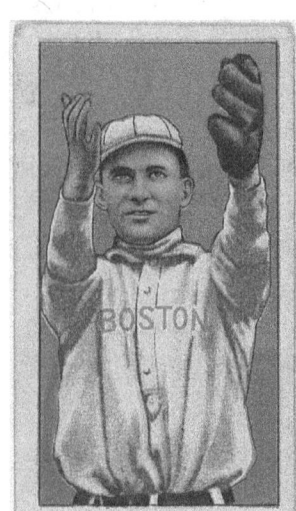

Jake Stahl was secured as manager for the 1912 Boston Red Sox.

1912—January

January 2—Incoming business manager Robert McRoy arrived in town with his family. Asked to comment on the coming season, he told the *Globe* that he was "not inclined to win pennants in the winter" but that he believed the Red Sox would prove a "real, fighting baseball team."

January 3—McRoy and Sox President James McAleer, in from Youngstown, Ohio, were ready to meet, the accounts were placed in order, and President John I. Taylor was prepared to turn over control of the club, taking a back seat to McAleer as had been determined the previous September. The two incoming executives had purchased the 50 percent of the stock sold by Taylor. Both secured rooms at the Copley Square Hotel and planned to make Boston their residence. Sportswriter Paul H. Shannon of the *Boston Post* reported that baseball observers were starting to see the Red Sox "as a formidable aggregation," adding, "The fact that Jake Stahl is to be manager has evidently impressed some of the writers with the idea that Jake may be able to get work out of his men that other managers have never succeeded in getting."

McAleer met with newspapermen and declared that they planned to give Boston a "first class club" and that he did not "desire or look for trouble with any one," by which he meant to indicate that if there was any trouble with Boston's National League club "it will be no fault of ours if relations are not thoroughly congenial." It was clear that the Red Sox were competing not only with their American League rivals on the field of play but also with the Boston Braves for the support of fans in the Hub.

The trainer would be Joe Quirk, who had worked with McAleer in St. Louis and Washington for six years running. The team had four scouts—P. J. Donovan, Arthur Cooper, Tom Dowd, "and one other" not mentioned in the *Post*. Unlike the previous spring, when the Red Sox placed their spring-training headquarters in Redondo Beach, California, the Sox planned to return to Hot Springs, Arkansas. And stay put (in 1911, they played as they traveled across the country, some 10 states in all in addition to California).[5] McAleer told reporters that he expected both Hick Cady and Marty Krug to be among the promising prospects who would make some of the veterans hustle a little more.

January 4—The mention of Cady the day before may have let the cat out of the bag, as news broke that President Taylor had quietly sold as many as seven of the Red Sox to Jersey City's International League team as far back as September. Apparently none of the players had been informed, either. They included Hal Janvrin, Walter Lonergan, Jack Thoney, Marty McHale, and Billy Purtell.

The *Globe* headline on January 4 had already perhaps startled a few people: "McAleer Plans to Stand Pat"—not the sort of proclamation one expects from the incoming owner of a team that finished in fifth place, 24 games out of first place, the year before. He would always be open to hearing about a proposed trade, but "I don't expect to go looking for any, as I believe we have the material on hand to play winning ball."

Forrest Leroy "Hick" Cady, enjoyed his first big-league season in 1912. He played for Boston in the World Series of 1912, 1915, and 1916.

January 6—McAleer spoke at length about his views of the team for 1912. He may well have known his baseball

A backup backstop, rookie Thomas appeared in 13 games for the Red Sox.

better than most owners. He had played major-league ball as an outfielder for 13 seasons, described by Cy Young as the best fielder he had ever seen. McAleer said the Red Sox were completely set with the superb outfield of Lewis, Speaker, and Hooper, and with Olaf Henriksen ("one of the fastest men in the country") as a reserve and to be called on in a pinch situation. Despite Stahl's having taken 1911 off, he was still just 32 years old and in good shape to play first base. Ready to step in and help out would be Hugh Bradley. If needed, Bradley could even catch—though with Carrigan, Nunamaker, Alva Williams, and Pinch Thomas, he thought there was no cause for concern. Williams was sold to New York the following month, and Cady made the team.

Larry Gardner was seen as solid at third base. It was the middle infielders who gave McAleer pause. He was hoping that Heinie Wagner's arm was back in shape and could play shortstop. He'd missed much of 1911. Depending on Wagner's arm, he said, "there is Steve Yerkes to be considered" and then named 1911's Jack Lewis and Marty Krug, and Jimmy Shinn from Sacramento.

"I don't think I shall make any changes in the pitching staff," he wound up. "We have a bunch of fine twirlers in Wood, O'Brien, Collins, Pape, Hall, Cicotte, and Killilay." Killilay was 4-2 with the Sox in 1911. Herb Byram was a promising pitcher from Princeton who had won 15 games for Sacramento in 1911. The team president was highest of all on Joe Wood. "Rightly managed, he ought to top them all this coming season and you can make up your mind that I will bring out the best there is in him." Who deserves the credit for Wood's spectacular season might be debated, but that he had one of the greatest seasons a pitcher will ever have is without doubt.

January 7—The *Post* gave big play to a rumor that the Red Sox were going to trade Tris Speaker to reacquire Harry Lord, "peerless third baseman of the American League" and current captain of the Chicago White Sox. Speaker liked Chicago and had relatives there; Lord's home was in Maine and he preferred the East. The unsigned story said, "It is a well known fact that Boston would never have let Lord go had it not been for a personal quarrel with Manager Patsy Donovan which assumed such serious proportions that one or the other had to go, President Taylor finally sticking by his manager." Stahl was in charge in place of Donovan now, and Lord very much liked Stahl. It was not to be. A couple of days later, Arthur Duffey wrote in his column that there was nothing to the rumor. The *Globe*'s Tim Murnane, looking ahead to the season, wrote, "With Stahl, Carrigan, and Wagner back in their best form, there is not a club in the American League any stronger."

January 9—It was a quiet day at the office, largely consumed with correspondence with players. No holdouts were expected. McAleer had originally thought of having a spring training without exhibition games outside Hot Springs other than three in Cincinnati and one against Harvard at the new ballpark under construction (Fenway Park), but agreed to games in Nashville and Dayton and was talking with Columbus. In the end it was Cincy for two and then one game against Harvard, and that was all.

It was an era of unconventional ideas regarding spring training. The 1911 Red Sox had given up their habitual Hot Springs venue and traveled all the way to Redondo Beach, California, then split into two squads and traveled east playing 63 games in places like Reno, Yuma, El Paso, Pueblo, Lincoln, and St. Joseph. As if that transcontinental trip wasn't enough, owner John I. Taylor had declared, "RED SOX MAY GO TO ORIENT NEXT YEAR," according to a headline in the *Boston American*. Taylor had talked about sending the team around the world for training in 1912 with club secretary Hugh McBreen proclaiming, "Honolulu, Philippines, and Japan for me next year."[6] With new ownership in place in 1912, they returned to Hot Springs instead.

January 10—The *Post* ran a letter from Joe Wood, from his father's poultry farm in Parker's Glen, Pennsylvania. He said he'd spent some of the fall hunting for pheasant and squirrels, unlike the jackrabbits he'd hunted on the Kansas prairies. He wrote, "I have been doing real work for a large part of the time, and, believe me, I feel as hard as nails. Believe me, I never felt better in my life." He debunked the notion that he'd gotten married and spoke of some hard-work logging yet to come.

Bill Carrigan was a wise choice to succeed Stahl as manager of the Red Sox in mid-1913, winning World Series titles in 1915 and 1916.

Opening Fenway Park with Style: The World Champion 1912 Boston Red Sox

January 13—The Sox would bring only a fairly minimal 31 players to Hot Springs, planning to reduce the number to 25 by Opening Day and then cut to 21 once they hit their stride. Shortstop Marty Krug was mentioned again as one of the most promising prospects. He had played winter ball in Cuba, so would be in playing condition when he hit Hot Springs.

January 16—Scratch Byram. He contacted McAleer and said that his health would not permit him to travel east. This left the team reliant on Ray Collins as the only left-hander on the pitching corps. Contracts were beginning to arrive, one by one. Larry Gardner wrote that he was in fine condition in Vermont: "I think snow shoeing cannot be beaten as an exercise." The *Globe* reported that workers were hard at work on the pavilion at the new ballpark under construction.

January 17—Eddie Cicotte "is one of the best pitchers in either of the two big leagues," McAleer stated. The pitcher had purchased a hotel in Michigan during the offseason but had kept in shape and was already below weight. Former pitcher Fred Burchell (1907-09) joined the ranks of businessmen himself, it was reported in the next day's paper, when he bought the Syracuse baseball franchise.

January 18—Jake Stahl asked Bill Carrigan to come to Hot Springs a little early, planning to huddle with him as an adviser for the season to come, Stahl having been out of the game for all of 1911. Carrigan was in business, too— the cigar business—and purchased a four-story brick building in Lewiston, Maine, this week. His leg, he wrote, was fully healed (he'd broken it in September). Hugh Bradley and the Red Sox Quartet had just played an engagement in Lewiston and expected to continue their vaudeville tour until March 4.

January 21—The Red Sox party would leave Boston for Hot Springs on March 8, it was announced during a very quiet week.

January 23—Hugh Bedient's contract was received. The Red Sox had sent seven players to the Jersey City Skeeters to obtain him.

January 25—The presidents of the Braves and Red Sox went bowling with a number of sportswriters and other team executives, Hugh Duffy, umpire Tommy Connolly, and Royal Rooter extraordinaire Jack Dooley.

January 28—The day's *Boston Globe* ran a lengthy article on the construction of Fenway Park, the new facility growing up around the infield sod that head groundskeeper Jerome Kelley had brought over in the autumn from the Huntington Avenue Grounds. Kelley had served as groundskeeper since at least 1906 at the old park and continued to do so through the end of the decade at Fenway Park.

January 29—Jack Killilay was "let out"–part of McAleer's overall housecleaning. It was a bit of an unpleasant parting; apparently another Red Sox pitcher—unnamed in the *Post* story—had written a letter to the Spokane newspaper (where Killilay had pitched for four seasons) saying that Killilay was to be sent to the minors because he was unwilling to accept advice and that his vanity caused him to be known as "Handsome Jack" to the other players.

January 30—Jersey City was not a farm club for the Red Sox, asserted co-owner Hugh McBreen (former secretary of the Red Sox). The seven players sent to the Skeeters were indeed in trade for Bedient, taken to build the ballclub instead of cash offers for $6,000 or more from other clubs.

A stern-looking Stahl led the ballclub to the pennant and World Series win as first baseman/manager.

February

February 4—Jimmy McAleer had not been to Hot Springs for 10 years, but planned to get down in time to see the two exhibition games planned against the Philadelphia Nationals. His memories of the resort town dated back to another era when it had been a wilder and woollier place. One morning, he told the *Globe*, he walked down Main Street and saw seven dead bodies "laid out on the sidewalk as a result of a shooting contest between State and local officers." The team had secured rooms at the Eastman Hotel, and would have Majestic Park for its exclusive use.

February 5—The *Post* rana letter from Jake Stahl saying he admitted he was "a little soft yet" but that he was working out two hours a day and would be ready soon. He added that he was looking forward to seeing Boston's new ballpark and hoped it would be ready on time. "I hope also that the fences will not be so far away but that a fellow will get a chance to put the ball over now and then, especially when he gets one right in the groove." He may have been surprised when he first saw Fenway Park's looming left-field wall and the distant one in right. He did hit one out, over the wall, on July 20. It was the only home run he ever hit at Fenway Park.

February 15—The Red Sox announced that they would open at home on April 19 with a doubleheader against the New York Highlanders. Joe Wood's contract arrived in the mail, along with a note from the pitcher reading, in part, "I am in great shape and I know that I will be better than ever this coming season."

February 17—Ray Collins's contract arrived with a note explaining that he'd be a married man when he turned up at Hot Springs, due to be wed to Lillian Lovely on February 28.

February 22—Catcher/first baseman Alva "Rip" Williams was sold to the Washington Senators. Actually, the *Washington Post* reported that he was purchased by the Highlanders, who released him to Washington in conjunction with a trade between the New York and Washington clubs.

February 25—Jake Stahl arrived at Hot Springs and checked into the Eastman, "only" 15 pounds overweight but two weeks early and with plenty of time to shed the weight. Aside from Bill Carrigan, the only other player who had already arrived was pitcher Fred Anderson, wanting another go after two years out of baseball. He'd taken part in a game on the 23rd between the "All-Americans" (led by Sam Crawford) and the "All-Nationals" (Germany Schaefer, skipper) and given up one scratch hit in five innings. Carrigan played first base for the Nationals team, but went hitless. Anderson hit a double. A *Washington Post* headline ran, "Hot Springs Is Once More Country's Baseball Capital."

February 27—The Red Sox purchased a large canvas cover (what we would today call the tarp) for the infield at Majestic Park; it came in nine sections, not just one large tarpaulin, and was large enough to cover the entire infield. The contract of Hubert "Dutch" Leonard arrived, giving the Sox another southpaw to join Collins.

February 28—Stahl said the only position not already settled was second base. He did plan to carry four catchers all season long—Carrigan, Nunamaker, Cady, and Thomas. Cy Young was back in town, though retired, and took Stahl and Carrigan on a 10-mile hike through the Ozarks. Also in town, arriving on the 28th, was fan extraordinaire Nuf Ced McGreevey. Fred Anderson pitched another game, this time for the Nationals, and was hit for three runs.

March

March 1—The weather kept the Sox off the field of play, but not from cross-country hikes to keep fit. On the first of March, the sheriff took steps to close the clandestine gambling halls in the area; he had shut down the big houses in earlier weeks. Paul Shannon wrote, "Raids are made by the county authorities and the gambling paraphernalia taken down to the sidewalk directly in front of the door and burned." That night, after the roulette wheels and card tables had been piled up in front of one of the establishments, the officers went back upstairs for a final look—and some locals made off with all the gear before they came back down. Shannon reckoned that the closing of the houses would help ballplayers both in training and the pocketbook.

March 2—Adding yet another blow to the local economy, and this time to the teams that had chosen to train at Hot Springs, the same reform-minded sheriff announced that there would be no Sunday baseball in the resort community. Several clubs said they'd not return in 1913 if Sheriff James Wood or his ilk were still in office. That the Catholic priests and business community in town were opposed to the Lord's Day prohibition was of no concern to the sheriff, who proclaimed that anyone practicing ball on Sundays would be arrested and prosecuted. The raids of the gambling halls were understood to be a bit of a sham, and Shannon wrote, "The players cannot understand how a town that stands for back door entrances to gambling resorts and winks at fake raids can see any harm in the playing of Sunday games." He added that the town's churches and philanthropies, and businesses, relied on income from all the ballclubs in town. Wood even went so far as to threaten arrest of players who turned up in uniform, simply on entering the grounds. Father Fanahy approved of the closing of the picture shows, billiards halls, and bowling alleys, but tried to prevail on the sheriff to permit baseball—to no avail. Wood was turned out in the November election, and apparently swarms of gamblers poured into town shortly afterward. As early as April 1913, the new sheriff and the former mayor were among those subject to new indictments.

March 5—There would be no series between Brooklyn and the Red Sox, because the Pirates had booked into Hot Springs and Brooklyn had to vacate to make room for them. The Red Sox weren't scheduled to begin real games until the 11th. The waiters at the Eastman couldn't wait for Brooklyn to leave, though, since the Boston players were considered better tippers and a hard-to-grasp confusion regarding a weekly "tipping club" resulted in enmity against Brooklyn. Back in Boston, part-owner McRoy placed the order for 12 flagpoles for Fenway Park. There were to be two for American flags, one for a Fenway flag, one for a special Red Sox flag, and one for each of the eight American League teams. Each team would have its own color, and its name on the flag. The Red Sox flag was red and the White Sox one was white. The Highlanders were Scotch plaid.

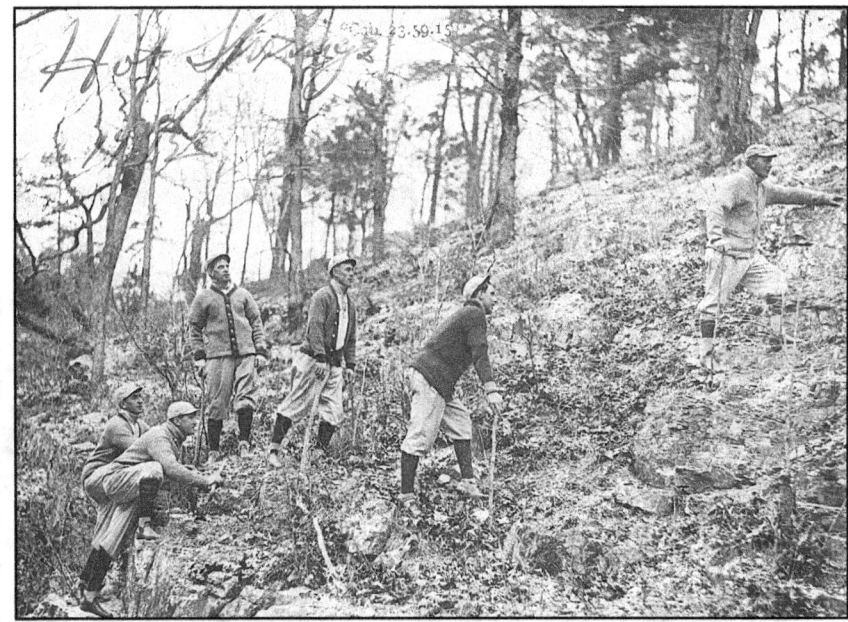

A walk in the Ozarks wasn't always just a simple stroll. Some of the Sox party are shown here taking a mountain hike in the spring of 1912.

March 6—Steve Yerkes signed on the 4th, and Buck O'Brien was the last to sign, on March 6. Buck was one of the four players who would travel all the way from Boston to Hot Springs, joined by Larry Gardner, Hugh Bradley, and Olaf Henriksen. Others would join the train in New York and in Cincinnati following the 1:00 A.M. New York, New Haven & Hartford Railroad train departing from track 15 at Boston's South Station on March 8 and due to arrive in Hot Springs at 3:55 P.M. on March 10. Because the grounds were too wet to play, Stahl planned to take those who were in camp on a 24-mile round-trip hike to Ozark Lithia Springs in the 44-degree weather.

March 11—Due to delays and a missed connection in Cincinnati after the wreck of a freight train, the Red Sox party arrived a little after midnight of the 10th, about nine hours late. The weather remained miserable. It may have been just as well—the uniforms for the players didn't get delivered until nearly noon. The players were housed three to a room, in some cases four. Different players were assigned different routes for mountain hikes, with Cicotte and Heinie Wagner given the hardest path.

March 12—Stahl swung at the very first pitch he saw in spring training and put a dent in the center-field fence.

March 13—The first real game of the spring was an interleague affair, the Regulars against the Yannigans. It was 8-6 Regulars, with a six-run rally helping them come from behind, homers courtesy of Hugh Bradley, Stahl, and pitchers O'Brien and Hall.

March 15—On the eve of the first game against an opponent (the Phillies), the Red Sox planned to test some of the rookies to see how they would perform. Meanwhile, Jake Stahl banned bowling, arguing that "bowling raised havoc with more than one pitcher's arm last season." Hooper advanced over Hall for the club's shooting championship, breaking the most clay pigeons.

March 16—The Phillies dominated the Red Sox, 12-2, in the first game of the springtime. Fred Anderson was "simply lobbing the ball over" and probably should have retired after four innings. Eight straight hits in the fifth plated six runs and put the game out of sight. Former Sox pitcher Benjamin Franklin "Highpockets" Hunt started for the Phils. After the game, more than a dozen of the Red Sox, clad in tuxedos, enjoyed a ball at the hotel.

March 18—The Sox started something more like their regular lineup in the next game, and this time they were the team to score 12 runs. They lost again, though, since the Phillies scored 15. Bedient, Bushelman, and Leonard were the victims on the mound, unable to capitalize on the 6-0 lead the Red Sox established in the first inning. There had been concern that Duffy Lewis would be subpar due to a hip injury but he was reported faster than ever. He was 2-for-4 in the game, playing despite technically an "outlaw" waiting to be reinstated by the National Commission. Lewis, Gardner, Speaker, and Stahl all hit home runs. Speaker signed his contract on the 19th.

March 19—In intrasquad competition, the Yannigans beat the Regulars, 8-6, on Hugh Bradley's home run over the left-field fence. He "had the most ginger of anybody on the team" and lacked only a triple to complete a cycle.

March 20—Stahl hit his third homer. Heinie Wagner played in his first game. Oddly, the game was delayed at one point when "Walter, the darkey attendant at the grounds" threw a fit in left field until the trainer arrived with a pail of water (to douse him?).

March 21—On the 20th, it was said to be as warm as August, on the 21st it rained, and then on the 22nd it was close to freezing.

March 22—In a *Boston Globe* story datelined March 22, it was reported that a Philadelphia newspaper had abbreviated the names of the Red Sox in the lineup about as briefly as you'll ever see (Hoo'r for Hooper, for instance). The full list; Hoo'r, Yer's, Spea'r, Stahl, Gar'r, Lewis, Krug, Nuna'r, Tho's, Hall, Bed't, Bush'n, Leo'd, Cady, Brad'y.

March 23—Joe Wood was a grizzled veteran, 23 years old. It was 18-year-old Dutch Leonard who was the youngster on the pitching staff, a former student at St. Mary's College of Oakland, which had graduated both Duffy Lewis and Harry Hooper. The Red Sox thought about testing the prohibition on Sunday baseball on the 24th (the Phillies had been permitted to play the week before), but the day was yet another washout, the third in a row.

March 27—There were three more Regulars/Yannigans games on the 25th, 26th, and 27th, the Regulars taking two of them while the middle game was a 6-6 tie. Leonard hit a foul ball over the right-field fence and it went through a window. Walter, now described as "the colored runner," was sent to retrieve it but was told he could have it back only if he paid 10 cents to replace the window.

Red Sox players and the leader of the Boston Royal Rooters rest after a hike during spring training in Hot Springs, Arkansas, 1912. Left to right: Bill Carrigan, Fred Anderson, Clyde Engle, Royal Rooter Michael T. McGreevey, Jake Stahl, and Charley Hall.

Opening Fenway Park with Style: The World Champion 1912 Boston Red Sox

March 28—The rains came again, so heavy that the Majestic Park outfield was deemed a "quagmire…nothing but a frog-ridden swamp"– so the team worked on base stealing. After midnight, Anderson was sold to Hugh Duffy's Milwaukee ballclub and he declared that he'd rather quit and return to dentistry than take the pay cut unless the Red Sox made up the difference. Krug's work had seemed so strong that Jack Lewis, Goodman, and Shinn were less likely to make the team. On the 30th, the first two were sold to St. Paul.

March 30—Stahl and McRoy, "wearied of the exorbitant demands by hotel managers and tired as well of the tipping system which drains the pockets of players and officials," conceived of a plan to join with three other teams and construct a large clubhouse at Hot Springs where the players could sleep and bathe, additionally avoiding any conflict with hotel guests. The tipping system was said to be costing players as much as an "unbearable" $3 per week.

March 31—In a month's-end feature, the Boston Sunday American presented some yarns about Red Sox players at the training camp. Bill Carrigan bemoaned that New England was no longer producing the number of ballplayers it used to. The reason, he said, was the lack of available space. The police would chase young players off city fields, and if the boys went out to the country, a farmer would come along with a pitchfork. Over the winter, Carrigan's business in Lewiston, Maine, had manufactured between 80,000 and 90,000 cigars. Joe Wood, in the poultry business, visited an ostrich farm near Hot Springs. He preferred his chickens to the big birds that produced only a dozen or so eggs a year. The paper also noted the big demand for tickets for the Opening Day game and the two scheduled for the April 19 holiday. The Red Sox office at 245 Washington Street was taking orders; ticket prices weren't cheap: First-tier box seats running $1.50 and upper boxes at $1.25 apiece. Four men were reported to have purchased boxes for the entire season.

April

April 1—Thanks to three weeks of rain, the Mississippi River was two inches from the danger point and the Red Sox, unable to make their planned getaway, called and canceled the games in Nashville and Dayton. On April 2 the Pirates let the Red Sox work out at their park since Majestic was fit only for boating. Photographs in the Boston Traveler showed Joe Wood riding a horse at a gallop past a shanty, and Charley Hall doing a circus stunt off the side of a horse; Hall was said to be an "expert equestrian."

Speaker led the league in doubles, home runs, and on-base percentage in 1912.

April 3—The final Yannigans/Regulars game saw the Yans finally win one, 7-6, with Bradley hitting one far over the center-field fence.

April 4—The team got in a final, spirited workout and was said to be in top condition, despite the many rainouts. They were lucky to get out of town when they did, traveling on a special that was the last train to cross the Mississippi at Memphis before the bridge was closed to wait for the waters to subside. Unfortunately, the baggage and the bats didn't make it so the trainer had to go buy 12 bats in Memphis. Seats were still being installed at Fenway Park, but it was expected that enough would be in place to accommodate the sizable crowd expected for the Harvard/Red Sox game on April 9. Groundskeeper Jerome Kelley was readying the field for baseball. The Harvard players had been working out in the cage.

April 6—"We fear no club," Stahl stated in a brief piece he wrote for the Post. "Wagner's arm is getting stronger every day. His condition was the one thing that worried us." It seemed he was in good shape. "The Red Sox will be in the fight from the very start, and we will be in there to stay." Stahl himself was hitting .514, Speaker .441, and Bradley .406, the team overall hitting .297. Boston crushed the Reds in Cincinnati, 13-1.

April 7—The Reds turned the tables on the Red Sox with a 6-2 win. Three of the runs scored on Boston errors and Cicotte's wildness. After the game, the Red Sox boarded the train for Boston.

April 9—Players and fans alike got their first look at brand-new Fenway Park. Several hundred seats weren't yet installed, and some of the runways weren't complete, but the accommodations were fine for the 3,000 who fans who turned out. The team had arrived by train at 9 P.M. on the evening of the 8th. When they arrived at the station, they were met by an "eager, jostling crowd.…Cheer after cheer went up as the bronzed athletes alighted." Most of them settled into the Copley Square Hotel for a night's rest in anticipation of the planned 3:30 P.M. game against Harvard College. The weather was far from the best, with "whirling flurries of snow" and a "wet and soggy field"; the Red Sox took care to avoid injury but still beat the Crimson nine, 2-0, in a game distinguished by very few base hits—four for the Red Sox and only one by Harvard, hit by the team captain, Bob Potter, off Boston's Casey Hageman. Harvard pitcher Sam Felton was "erratic," walking 10, and understandably few of the Red Sox players wanted to dig in against him. Hageman had two of Boston's four hits, and drove in both runs The closest Harvard came to scoring was snuffed out in the sixth inning when an attempted double steal saw Wigglesworth out at home plate. After Harvard batted in the top of the seventh, and given the frigid conditions, Jake Stahl signaled the umpire and the game was concluded. The 3,000 fans came out early and, having checked

Both Carrigan and O'Brien may have been fortunate that neither was hurt during a mock scrap during workouts.

out the new park, many left early, too. The weather was simply too discouraging.

April 11—On Wednesday the 10th, the Red Sox took the 1:00 P.M. train to New York for the first three games of the season. They'd originally planned to play an exhibition game in Worcester that day, but it was just too cold. On the 11th, at Hilltop Park, Smoky Joe Wood got the game ball for the Red Sox and held the Highlanders through eight innings to just two runs. The score was 2-1 New York at the end of eight, but the Boston batters broke out in the top of the ninth, scoring four times. It started with a walk and a sacrifice, followed by four straight hits. Wood allowed one run in the bottom of the ninth; the final was Boston 5-3.

As Lyle Spatz has written, "Like the Yankees, the Sox had also adopted pinstripes, but, unlike the New Yorkers, had them on both their home and road uniforms. In a change of more lasting significance to their home and road attire, they replaced the block-lettered 'BOSTON' on their shirt-fronts with the block-lettered 'RED SOX,' the first time that name had ever appeared on their uniform." [7]

April 12—"Red Sox Outclass Highlanders in Every Department and Win Again 5 to 2" read the game story subhead in the *Boston Post*. Buck O'Brien held the New Yorkers to six hits. Bill Carrigan was fortunate to escape serious injury when hit in the head so hard with a pitch that the carom bounded nearly to third base.

April 13—After the first inning it was 4-2 in favor of New York, Hageman replaced after securing just one out. Charley Hall pitched the rest of the game and didn't give up another run, benefiting big-time

Smoky Joe Wood only lost five games in all of 1912. The April 23 game was his first loss of the year.

from six Boston runs scored in the top of the fifth. The final score was 8-4. Carrigan suffered a split finger and missed the next week. Hageman missed most of the rest of the year. He only ever appeared in one more game, on April 29, and that only long enough to record three more outs. (Also see October 21.)

April 15—After a Sunday respite, veteran Philadelphia pitcher Eddie Plank held Boston to one run, while Red Sox starter Eddie Cicotte suffered from poor play in the very first inning. Gardner made two errors and Duffy Lewis displayed some "neglect" in allowing a short fly ball to drop in front of him in left field. Positioning paid off for the Athletics; three long drives by Stahl would have gone for extra bases but for how deeply the fielders were defending him. 4-1, Philly. It is worthy of note that in the Atlantic Ocean, the cruise liner *RMS Titanic* struck an iceberg and sank with a loss of 1,517 lives.

April 16—For the fifth game in a row, Sox starters were scored on in the first inning, but this time Boston had already put four runs across before Philadelphia came up to bat. Wood gave up 12 hits, but walked only one and pitched his way out of trouble when he needed to. He also doubled twice, part of an offense that saw the Sox win, 9-2. For the next week, news of sinking of the *Titanic* dominated the news in Boston and around the country.

April 17—The final game was rained out, and they took the train back to Boston. Stahl and the Sox were looking forward to the first-ever regular-season game at Fenway Park and the opportunity to take further advantage of the badly struggling Highlanders.

April 18—The scheduled grand opening of Fenway Park was deferred for a day due to rain. Consequently, two games were scheduled for Patriots Day, the 19th (a holiday in Massachusetts)—a 10:30 morning game and a 3:15 afternoon game.

April 19—Both games were rained out—though just 30 minutes after the second game was called off, the sun broke through and around 5,000 fans turned up at Fenway, anticipating the game. The grounds were drenched and unsuitable for play. Rather than plan a tripleheader

Steve Yerkes committed three errors but had five hits and scored three of Boston's seven runs on Opening Day.

for the 20th, and with that day no holiday, they went with just one game.

April 20—At last, Fenway had its regular-season opener—though with the postponements it became an understated one: There was no parade, no flag raising, and the "far-famed" Letter Carriers Band was unable to make it. Mayor John "Honey Fitz" Fitzgerald threw out the first pitch "but Boston's modest chief executive pulled off this feat so quietly that few, excepting those

Sheet music from 1912.

within closest proximity knew that this important duty had been transacted." There was no possibility of a home run being hit in the park's first game. So many fans turned out that there was standing room in the outfield (a common-enough practice of the day) and any hit that reached the crowd was agreed to be deemed a double.

There was an ominous start to the game as Buck O'Brien let New York score three times in the top of the first, and the Highlanders held a 5-1 lead after three. The Sox loaded the bases in the top of the fourth. Pinch-hitting for O'Brien, Olaf Henriksen drew a walk to force in a run. A fielder's choice scored another run, and a hit by Yerkes a third (one of his five hits, atoning for the three errors he made on the still-soggy field). By the end of six it was 5-5 and after eight it was 6-6. Hall pitched seven innings in relief, allowing only three hits. The game went into extra innings, and with darkness coming in, the 11th was sure to be the last inning. The first game at Fenway might have ended a tie. It was 6:25 when Yerkes reached first as New York third baseman Dolan committed two errors on the same play, one while fielding and the other on his throw. Another gift—a passed ball—moved him to third base, and then Speaker scorched one between short and third to win the game, 7-6. Yerkes had scored three of the seven runs. Writing in the next day's *Globe*, Tim Murnane said that the ground rules had made doubles of three Red Sox hits which might otherwise have become Fenway Park's first home run, or at least a triple. The overflow crowd of perhaps 27,000 (the *Globe* put the figure at 24,000) was the largest to ever see baseball in Boston.

April 21—No game scheduled. It was Sunday. In a bylined article that appeared in the *Post*, Philadelphia second baseman Eddie Collins predicted that Boston would "give us the hardest battle."

April 22—Heavy mist. With the season still less than two weeks old, the Red Sox suffered their fifth postponement. Both the Sox and the Senators got in some batting practice, though.

April 23—With the teams playing on a field still so wet the ball deadened the minute it hit the ground, two three-run innings did in Joe Wood. There were nine errors, attributable to the "numbing cold" weather, and the Senators won, 6-2.

April 24—Walter Johnson held the Sox to two runs, while Eddie Cicotte was not at his best. A 5-2 loss dropped Boston into second place.

April 25—CHARLEY HALL THE BOY TO STOP THEM. Hall was the story, holding the Senators to four hits and one run, while scoring two of Boston's four runs himself. Hall was now 3-0 in the young season. Left-fielder Duffy Lewis began to lay his claim to the earthen incline in left field above which the wall rose. In the eighth inning Washington's catcher John Henry hit a line drive to left. "Lewis went like a deer for the high and dangerous bank, turned up [when] he reached the bottom and, while tripping over the obstruction, put up his gloved hand. The ball stuck there." Lewis recorded seven putouts and one assist.

April 26—HUGH BRADLEY THE HERO OF RED SOX WIN OVER CHAMPS. Stahl had missed a few games with a sprained wrist, and Hugh Bradley subbed at first base. In the first inning, he slammed a "screaming drive" high off the left-field wall, striking perhaps about 10 feet from the top. It went for a two-run double, but was one of those balls that—for the last 100 years—left fans saying it would have been a home run anywhere else but in Fenway Park. No one expected a batter to ever hit one over the new park's left-field wall, but when Bradley came to bat again in the seventh inning (the Sox down 6-4), he did just that, and it was a three-run game-winner. The *Post* noted that it had been "wafted by the friendly breeze high over the taxicab sign on the wooden obstruction," and said in a sidebar that his wind-aided drive "will probably not be duplicated this season." It was Boston 7, Philadelphia 6.

April 27—Bradley starred again, driving in three more runs and then unexpectedly laying down a bunt, sacrificing to set up the winning runs in the bottom of the eighth for another 7-6 defeat of the Athletics. The reigning world champions had lost but two games, both due in part to Bradley's batting.

April 28—No game scheduled

April 29—Eddie Plank allowed just one run, and his fellow Philadelphians scored seven to support him for a rainy day 7-1 win over the Red Sox. It was only the fourth loss of the young season, and Plank had dealt two of them.

April 30—Turning the tables, Hall and Bedient combined

to hold the Athletics to one run on just three hits, none after the fourth inning. It was Bradley's first-inning double that drove in the first of the three runs the Red Sox scored then; they added three more as the game went on. Reading newspaper accounts of games of this era, it's still disorienting to see the Red Sox described as "the Speed Boys." Bedient had come in to replace Hall, after Fenway Park saw its first ejection, Hall

Half of the "kid battery," Pinch Thomas was a veteran by the time of this 1916 photo, the year in which he played on his third World Championship team with the Red Sox.

tossed by umpire Silk O'Loughlin. Hall was so exercised by a pitch the umpire called a strike that he slammed his glove to the ground. Any player would be routinely tossed today, but Murnane fulminated that it was "one of the most arbitrary moves ever made on a ball field."

May

May 1—WOOD'S WILD PITCH DEFEATS RED SOX. Playing in Washington's Griffith Stadium, the Sox tied it 1-1 in the eighth, then things fell apart in the bottom of the ninth. First, a two-base error, then—with two outs—an intentional walk to get to the Senators' pitcher, Dixie Walker—who walked to load the bases. Wood struck out the final batter, Moeller, but the ball struck the corner of home plate and went "bounding off into the grandstand" as the winning run scored.

May 2—Neither Bob Groom nor Charley Hall had lost a game yet. The *Washington Post* characterized it as a "freaky game" since an evenly-divided six of the 11 runs in Boston's 6-5 win were "gifts one to the other" in a series of "freaks and flukes and foozles." Hall was the one to maintain his undefeated streak.

May 3—WALTER JOHNSON RED SOX MASTER. "It was a case of too much Johnson," wrote Paul Shannon in the *Boston Post*. The Big Train allowed three hits and no more, while Buck O'Brien let the Senators score four of their five runs.

May 4—CICOTTE WEAKENS AND SENATORS WIN. Bedient had begun, but lasted just two innings. Speaker was 4-for-4 with a homer and a double. The Sox scored seven runs. But Washington scored eight. Speaker had nine hits in his last 15 at-bats. He and Gardner had combined for 13 hits over the four games in Washington; the rest of the team collectively hit 11.

May 5—BALTIMORE DOWNED BY BUSHELMAN. It was an exhibition game, and the "kid battery" of Bushelman and Thomas won the game, 4-2. Red Sox veterans Parent and Unglaub played for the Orioles.

May 6—The game in New York was postponed, despite the grounds being dry and the sun starting to come out. Shannon suggested that the New Yorkers didn't want to have to face Joe Wood on a somewhat dark day. The Red Sox returned home to wait for the Tigers (pitchers Hall and O'Brien had come home earlier, to be better rested for pitching duties. The columnist writing as "Sportsman" in the *Boston Globe* opined, "Fenway Park will be the fans' Mecca for some time to come." Indeed.

May 7—The brief 1-3 road trip was done, and the team was back in Boston all the way until June 1. Wood pitched against Detroit, but lacked his usual stuff. He gave up four runs, and only the ninth-inning rally falling short prevented the Tigers from matching the five runs the Red Sox had accumulated. Strong defense helped support the Sox pitcher.

May 8—Spongy grounds resulted in a postponement, and both teams went to enjoy a boxing match.

May 9—For the second game in a row, the Sox scored four times in the bottom of the sixth. Bedient bailed out Hall, and the Red Sox downed Detroit, 7-4, despite drenching rains and a Ty Cobb home run.

May 10—A little seesaw action saw the score tied 2-2 after four, then both teams scoring once in the seventh. Detroit's Sam Crawford hit a three-run homer over Hooper's head in the top of the ninth, and Gardner's two-run double got two runs back for Boston, but Lewis tapped one to second and the game was over. A 6-5 loss.

May 11—JOE WOOD IS STILL BROWNS' MASTER. Smoky Joe threw a three-hitter, striking out 11, and the Red Sox

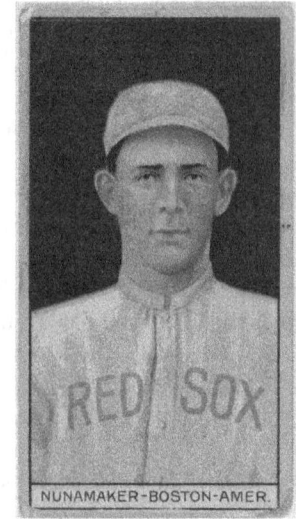

Les Nunamaker.

Cicotte baseball card, with his name misspelled.

beat St. Louis, 8-1. In 1911, Wood had faced the Browns twice, throwing a no-hitter and a one-hitter. The Sox scored all of their runs in the first three frames. Catcher Les Nunamaker was caught off base by the hidden ball trick, one of only 11 times in Red Sox history that a Sox player was victimized. It was the third out of the inning and the *Boston Globe* wrote that probably not one in a thousand fans could understand why the Boston players all started taking their positions in the field.

May 12—No game scheduled on the Sunday

May 13—RED SOX BEAT THE BROWNS IN COMEDY. The score of the "weirdest game" of the season was 14-9, said to have offered "all the elements of a ham night programme at an amateur show." Taking 2 hours and 15 minutes to play, it was said to be "exceptionally long." Among the features were a four-run first for St. Louis, a seven-run second by the Red Sox, and five Browns bobbles.

May 14—RED SOX WIN IN 8TH INNING RALLY. The Sox were trailing 5-1 with one out in the bottom of the eighth and things looked grim. They scored one run, then Heinie Wagner cleared the bases with a game-tying triple, and scored himself on Pinch Thomas's sacrifice fly. "Knuckles" Cicotte went the distance and wound up with an unexpected W.

May 15—WOOD BEATS PELTY IN PITCHING DUEL. Boston scored twice, in the bottom of the first and the bottom of the ninth. The sole Browns run came in the sixth, and Wood won his second game from St. Louis during the four-game set.

With two outs and nobody on base, Hugh Bradley shot one "like a bullet from a gun" that banged off the left-field wall just above the scoreboard. Wagner lined one over the leftfielder's head and it rolled to the scoreboard as Heinie jogged toward first while Brad ran home.

May 16—The 16th was meant to be the "grand opening" of Fenway Park, with bunting and band in place, but—once again—heavy rains drenched the place and prompted postponement. With more than a little hyperbole, the *Boston American* reported "thousands of disconsolate fans…wailing and gnashing of teeth and weeping."

May 17—The formal opening of Fenway Park. Boston had a 2-1 lead over the first-place White Sox, and Larry Pape retired the first two Chicago batters in the top of the ninth. Up came pitcher Ed Walsh, a good-hitting pitcher who already had two hits, and he hit a "puny grounder" that took three bounces back to Pape and then glanced off his heel. A single was followed by an intentional walk to Harry Lord. Frank Lange came up—the second pitcher to bat in the inning (he was playing left field in place of Callahan, who'd been ejected in the bottom of the eighth). Pape hit him. The game was tied. Ping Bodie hit a "measly grounder" to Engle at second, but it scored the go-ahead run. Shano Collins drove in a couple of insurance runs. Fans faulted Stahl for not having put in the well-warmed-up Buck O'Brien to throw the ninth.

May 18—WHITE SOX AGAIN RED SOX PUZZLE. Bedient pitched well, but the White Sox put on a classic, "outguessing and outthinking" the Red Sox as they worked three runs across, in the fourth, sixth, and eighth. Stahl tried three consecutive pinch-hitters in the bottom of the ninth—Henriksen, himself, and Thomas—but all three were retired in order.

Speaker starting to loosen up his fabled arm along the third-base side before the game.

May 19—Sunday; no game. The White Sox held a 5 1/2-game lead over the second-place Red Sox.

May 20—JOE WOOD HUMBLES BIG ED WALSH 2-0. Future Hall of Famer Walsh was Chicago's ace, a 40-game winner (that's not a typo) in 1908. He won 27 games in 1911 and 27 again in 1912, but you're not going to win a game if your team is shut out. This was Smoky Joe Wood's ninth start of the season, the 27th game of the year for the Red Sox. Chicago got five hits off Wood, and one base on balls. The Red Sox committed three errors, one of them Wood's, but the White Sox never scored off the "Kansas Cyclone."

May 21—Buck O'Brien had a no-hitter going into the seventh and, in the end, let the Naps get only three hits and one run. Cleveland complained that O'Brien or first baseman Bradley were using sandpaper, or slippery elm, or licorice, but umpire Silk O'Loughlin searched both men's pockets and found nothing at all. The *Globe*'s Tim Murnane suggested that the only real problem was with the eyes of the Cleveland ballplayers. The Red Sox won, 3-1.

May 22—RED SOX SHUT OUT CLEVELAND, 9 TO 0. Tris Speaker was 3-for-4 and stole three bases. Pitcher Charley Hall was 3-for-3 himself, and shut out Cleveland on six hits. Credit him for some fine fielding as well; he racked up seven assists with nary an error.

May 23—WILD THROW KILLS NAPS' ONLY CHANCE. Eddie Cicotte started, but "wobbled in the ninth" and three runs scored, tying the game 5-5. Joe Wood came in to stabilize the situation. In the bottom of the 10th, Speaker singled to kick things off. Lewis sacrificed to third, and, seeing the third baseman come in to make the play, Speaker streaked around second, running pell-mell for third base. Cleveland first baseman Eddie Hohnhorst fired the ball toward third but uncorked a "lurid throw over into left field" that allowed Speaker to come home with the winning run. In separate news, McAleer denied there was anything to the rumor that he was talking trade with the New York Highlanders, Henriksen and Bradley for Hal Chase.

May 24—CHAMPIONS TAMED BY HUGH BEDIENT. The Red Sox beat the Athletics, 4-3, in what was dubbed one of the most exciting games of the season. Not only did Bedient hold Philadelphia to six hits, but he drove in Wagner with the tying run and then scored the go-ahead run on Speaker's hit in the bottom of the seventh.

May 25—JOE WOOD'S WILDNESS GIVES ATHLETICS AN 8 TO 2 WIN. Three walks and nine hits, including a four-run top of the ninth, led to one of Smoky Joe's five losses of the year. Philadelphia's Jack Coombs, a farmer from the state of Maine, held the Sox to just three hits, and it's a rare game that can be won with just three safeties and Wood clearly off his form.

May 26—It was Sunday, and a day of rest.

May 27—RED SOX PITCHERS MEAT FOR MACKMEN. The Athletics were, after all, the reigning world champions, and the offense kicked into high gear with 17 hits off Buck O'Brien, Ray Collins, and Hugh Bedient. The Sox scored six runs off a trio of A's pitchers, and had even pulled within a run with a four-run fifth, driving Eddie Plank out of the box in mid-frame, but the final was a lopsided 12-6.

May 28—CONNIE'S COLTS A PIPE FOR RED SOX. Connie Mack used four young pitchers, saving his bigger guns for the coming visit to New York. The Red Sox took advantage and Charley Hall pitched well enough for a 7-3 win.

May 29—TWO WEIRD WINS FOR THE RED SOX. Washington came to town, and a doubleheader saw a total of 52 runners cross the plate. The *Globe* headline read "Speed Boys 33, Washington 19." An anomaly in the Deadball Era, Boston won the first game 21-8 (not a game that Wood would be proud of) and then "the fearfully bad twirling" of Cicotte and Pape spotted the Senators six runs in the top of the first in the second game, but the Sox were more efficient at scoring baserunners—though a total of 24 men were left on base. The 12-11 final saw the Senators score six times in the top of the first, but Boston wore them down as the innings wore on. Boston left four men on base, but the Senators stranded 11. There were—boxscores vary—something like 60 hits, 14 errors, and 19 bases on balls, and darkness fell so they didn't even get a chance to play the ninth inning in the second game.

May 30—The Sox were shut out for the first time in 1912. They'd be blanked just three more times, including two 1-0 home losses in mid-July. This time it was Walter Johnson, striking out 13 Red Sox and holding them to five hits for a 5-0 defeat. But Bedient had won the morning game, 3-2.

May 31—The train from Boston arrived in Cleveland just before 5 o'clock, glad for the day off after the back-to-back twinbills in the Hub. The train was busy with baseball men; the Senators were on their way to St. Louis, and the New York team was on board part of the way as they traveled to play the Tigers in Detroit. Even a couple of umpires were on board. In the standings, the Red Sox had made considerable progress and were just two games behind the White Sox, while enjoying a 5 ½-game lead over third-place Philadelphia.

June

June 1—CLEVELAND ENJOYS A REAL SWATFEST. Charley Hall had his first loss of the year hung on him, the first two runs due to his own first-inning throwing error. Collins didn't help, either, and

An upright Charley Hall plays catch before a game.

Boston lost, 9-2, in what the *Globe* dubbed a "bingle picnic" as Naps batters struck six doubles and eight singles. Hall was now 7-1.

June 2—It was OK to play baseball in Cleveland on Sundays, so they did and it was quite a game. Stahl was able to play once more and he tripled and doubled; even though the Red Sox outhit their hosts by a good margin, and outplayed them in the field, only a ninth-inning run tied it for the Red Sox, 4-4. Boston won it for Wood in the 10th, 5-4.

June 3—RED SOX PRESENT A GAME TO NAPS. "Buck O'Brien Might Have Won His Game but for Scratch Hits and a Bad Error." Boston scored three times in the top of the first, but never again, and the Naps notched one run in each of four innings. 4-3 loss. McAleer put Cicotte on waivers as a feeler to see what clubs might have interest.

June 4—A four-run fourth at Bedient's expense was the margin in a 5-1 defeat at the hands of Vean Gregg (11 strikeouts) and the Naps. Cicotte took over for Bedient in the fourth and held Cleveland scoreless from that point. It was Lajoie Day at League Park, and the Cleveland star was presented with 1,000 silver dollars "set in a huge floral horseshoe" that took four men to carry.

June 5—RED SOX PITCHING GIVES TIGERS GAME. A six-run sixth sank the Sox, wiping out the four runs Boston had scored in the top of the first and the run they'd added in the second. Charley Hall, however, was left on the mound too long, and Stahl seemingly panicked, bringing in Wood, who had not warmed up, instead of Collins, who had. The final four runs resulted, and with the 8-6 loss the Sox had now lost four of their last five games. Boston was three games behind Chicago in the standings.

June 6—RED SOX FIELDING GIVES BUCK A WIN. Buck O'Brien held the Tigers to two runs on seven hits, while the Red Sox scored five off Mullin (starting with three in the top of the first), but Buck was "a mighty lucky individual" due to "sensational fielding" by outfielders Hooper and Speaker.

June 7—Detroit pitcher Jean Dubuc (3-for-4 at the plate) had a 4-0 lead going into the ninth, but the Red Sox rallied to score three and had men on first and second when Speaker flied out to left field and the Sox fell just short.

June 8—SOX CINCH GAME IN FIRST INNING. Winning 8-3, the Sox scored early and late. Smoky Joe Wood was handed a 4-0 lead in the top of the first, and the three runs the Tigers scored all came as a result of Red Sox errors. Wood, the *Globe* wrote, "never worked more earnestly for a game." With Ty Cobb in a position to wreak havoc a few times, the "Kansas Cyclone cut the Georgia Peach off without the semblance of a hit."

June 9—SPEAKER AND KRUG THE WHOLE THING. In St. Louis, Tris Speaker hit for the cycle and drove in a pair, while Marty Krug drove in four with a three-hit day—but hurt himself sliding into second and after the game found he could hardly

After leading the league again in 1915 with a 1.49 ERA, Wood was hurt and no longer effective as a pitcher and was sold to the Cleveland Indians in January 1917. He became an outfielder and hit .297 over six seasons with Cleveland.

walk. Bedient held the Browns to two runs in the 9-2 game, despite walking five and allowing 10 hits. Speaker's hitting was a hit with the fans at Sportsman's Park, who repeatedly cheered him despite his working for the opposition.

June 10—RED SOX NOW LEAD IN AMERICAN RACE. The White Sox fell to New York, while Buck O'Brien saw his teammates score three times in the late innings (sixth, eighth, and ninth) to beat the Browns, 3-2. The Sox squandered several opportunities and left 12 men on base, scoring the go-ahead run on a St. Louis error as Yerkes motored all the way around from first base. The win put them in first place.

June 11—HALL SHUTS OUT ST. LOUIS BROWNS. Charley Hall distributed five hits, the Sea Lion serving up a "variety of benders and shoots." Steve Yerkes had a 4-for-5 day for the Red Sox. Another injury struck the Red Sox, Nunamaker hit by a ball that split open the catcher's unprotected right hand and required a hospital visit and several stitches. Fortunately, the Sox had three other catchers on the squad.

June 12—RED SOX CLEAN UP WITH THE BROWNS. Joe Wood secured a sweep for the Red Sox, 5-3 over Jack Powell, both with his pitching and his bat. He hit one of Powell's pitches "a mile in the air and over the right-field screen" for a two-run homer in the top of the fifth. The Red Sox headed for Chicago with a one-game lead over the White Sox.

June 13—WALSH, NOT DATE, THE REAL HOODOO. It was the 13th day of August and the 13th game of the road trip, but the real problem for the Red Sox was Chicago's Big Ed Walsh, who held Boston to three hits. Ray Collins pitched well, too, on a very rainy day complete with a one-hour delay, and the score was tied, 2-2, heading into the bottom of the ninth. With two out and a man on second, Walsh swung at the first pitch he saw and drove in the winning run. The entire Boston bench—eight players—was

Opening Fenway Park with Style: The World Champion 1912 Boston Red Sox

Do Not Throw Bottles—The South Side Park (Chicago) message above Carrigan at the White Sox home field in 1909 is reflective of the Deadball Era (1901-1920). White Sox shortstop Freddy Parent who had played with Rough on the Red Sox reflected in his retirement years, "People [today] get real excited when someone throws a paper cup or something at a player. They didn't throw those kinds of things in my days. They threw beer bottles. And they aimed at your head!"

banished to the right-field bullpen after an argument in the fourth on a play that killed a Red Sox rally. The win pulled the White Sox nearly even with Boston in the standings, just percentage points behind.

June 14—Rain caused the day's game to be postponed, a shame because there was a large crowd, it being both Ladies Day and Jake Stahl Day, with a number of Chicago bank presidents among those planning to come to the game. Meanwhile, the Senators had crept closer to both teams, winning 15 games in a row, and were now lurking just one game behind.

June 15—RED SOX HUMBLE WALSH'S CONCEIT. Manager Jimmy Callahan asked Walsh to pitch again on one day's rest, somewhat of a reprise of his May 17 and 20 starts in Boston. He was pounded in the top of the first for three runs. The 4-3 win resulted from the Red Sox run scored in the seventh; Walsh was gone by the third. The *Post*'s Paul Shannon wrote snidely, "It seems a pity that the egotistical flinger does not get the credit for the defeat." Shannon further griped about the umpires and the behavior of 20,000 loud White Sox fans. Buck O'Brien got the win. The Senators won, too.

Wagner's only other homer of the year had come on May 29. Wagner played for the Red Sox from 1906 through 1918 and contributed to four World Series titles.

June 16—RED SOX SHATTER WHITE SOX HOPES. Jake Stahl, who'd received a chest of silverware the day before, singled in the eighth to produce the tie-breaking run on the way to a 6-4 Boston win for Wood, who had allowed only five hits and recovered from his one bad inning that saw three Chicago runs in the bottom of the first. The *Boston American* ran a profile on Boston's center fielder declaring that Tris Speaker had now been "crowned king of all baseball players."

June 17— RED SOX HAMMER ED WALSH AGAIN. Back for his third start against Boston in five days, Walsh threw a complete game but allowed four runs while Charley Hall should have had a shutout but for the one run he allowed right after coming off the field winded from trying to stretch his RBI triple into an inside-the-park home run. Boston battered Big Ed for four triples and two doubles, and 13 hits in all. Wagner was suspended for three games; he'd almost come to blows with Umpire Sheridan after the game on the 16th. Despite this rough patch, Walsh still won 27 games for the White Sox in 1912.

Tigers manager Hugh Jennings declared that the pennant race looked like a tight one, but that Boston had the best chance. "I never saw an outfield play better ball in my life than Hooper, Speaker, and Lewis showed against us," he said.

June 18—A travel day from Chicago saw the Red Sox train pull into New York at 9 P.M. The Senators won their 17th game in a row and hung close.

June 19—Bedient and his teammates were "easy victors" over the "disorganized outfit that represents New York" with a 5-2 win. Hugh might have had a five-hit shutout but for a couple of Red Sox errors. Washington dropped a pair to Philadelphia, starting a brief four-game losing streak that removed them as an immediate threat.

Collins was on his way to a good 13-8 campaign.

June 20—RED SOX HAMMER A WIN OFF FORD. Buck O'Brien Bad, but Russell Is a Lot Worse, and Boston Wins 15 to 8. Building on an early 7-0 lead, the Sox never faltered and the hits kept coming, Boston collecting 18 hits to New York's 16. Heinie Wagner had a couple of doubles, and a home run, and a single, too.

June 21—SEVENTH STRAIGHT FROM HIGHLANDERS. Another 16 hits and another 11 runs were more than sufficient to handle hapless Highlander hurler Jack Quinn by a score of 11-3, built off a 6-0 lead (one run less than the lead they'd enjoyed on the 20th). Joe Wood racked up another win.

June 22—A double drubbing, 13-2 and 10-3, completed a five-game sweep in New York by combined run totals of 54-18. Hall and Collins collected the two Ws. The wins marked the 14th and 15th consecutive complete games for Red Sox pitchers. The streak reached 18 games before being broken. Both Wagner and Lewis elevated their batting averages over .300.

Opening Fenway Park with Style: The World Champion 1912 Boston Red Sox

June 23—On a scheduled day off, the Red Sox went to Baltimore and gave both Bushelman and Cicotte a chance to pitch; the Baltimores pounded the pair for 14 runs and took the exhibition game, 14-8, revenge for their defeat on May 5. The crowd was apparently rather small: Boston "didn't play a game worthy of the name. It was a case of get a little money, and they got little."

June 24—WASHINGTON FALLS TO HUGH BEDIENT. The 3-1 win was the ninth in a row by the streaking Red Sox (and 14th of their last 15.) A "big delegation of Boston rooters comprising delegates to the Democratic convention at Baltimore, came down to Washington by special train to see the contest." The 75 or so in the group were vocal in their support of the Red Sox and were not disappointed. Hugh held the Senators to four hits, and Hooper's triple in the sixth pushed Bedient across with the tying run; he scored a few moments later with the winning run.

The 1912 Red Sox starting pitchers, from left to right: Larry Pape, Hugh Bedient, Buck O'Brien, Charley Hall, Ray Collins, and Joe Wood.

June 25—The day's game was rained out, prompting a doubleheader on the 26th. The *Post* alleged that Washington called the game off much earlier than usual, the better to give Walter Johnson an extra day of rest. The Red Sox purchased infielder Neal Ball from Cleveland, since Krug (see June 9) was still unable to play.

June 26—Bob Groom beat Buck O'Brien, 3-2, in the first game, but Wood shut out the Senators, 3-0, in the second, giving Walter Johnson a loss. The first game was an extra-inning affair. Buck walked the first batter in the bottom of the 10th, and a long hit to left on the hit-and-run brought him all the way around to score. Johnson retired the first 13 men he faced, and held the Red Sox to just four hits in the second game, but Wood allowed only three. Wood's were well-scattered, but in the end, all it took was one trip around the bases by Larry Gardner in the fifth. He singled, then ran all the way to third base when Senators right-fielder Tilly Walker let the ball get by him. Gardner tried for home, and would have been out since Eddie Ainsmith had the plate well-blocked—but when Ainsmith took the throw, he couldn't hold onto it. The two-run triple Tris Speaker struck in the sixth sealed the defeat of the Big Train.

Fresh from Cleveland, Cornelius Ball's contract was purchased for $2,500.

June 27—The Sox wound up one of the more successful road trips in team history with a 17-8 record, despite losing the final game to Washington, 8-4. Hall lasted only three innings, and Pape succeeded him. The winner was Tom Hughes, who had been a 20-game winner for Boston back in 1903. Both teams had 11 hits, but the Senators reaped twice as many runs. The game was called after 7½ innings to enable the Red Sox to catch the train to Boston.

June 28—RED SOX ADD 2 TO WINNING LIST. Home at last, the Red Sox reeled off five wins in a row, the first two being their 10th and 11th wins in a row against New York. Bedient and Hall pitched in the 5-4 first game, and Collins and Bedient pitched in the 6-4 second game, making up an earlier rainout. Hall saved Bedient in game one, and the offense rallied in the seventh and eighth to overcome a 4-2 deficit. Bedient bailed out Collins in game two, holding the lead. Speaker became the league's first "centurion," registering his 100th hit of the season.

June 29—SOX ADD TWO TO LIST OF WINS. The *Post*'s headline writer must have forgotten the headline from the day before, or enjoyed presenting a sense of déjà-vu to the paper's readers. The 15,000 fans from the day before were outdone by 20,000 this day, and the two games were quite different from each other. First up was a 13-6 victory, O'Brien (and Pape) over Quinn, who surrendered every one of Boston's 21 hits, all singles but for one two-bagger by Wagner. Quinn didn't walk a batter. In the second game, Wood gave up all of one hit in a 10-1 triumph, not one New Yorker reaching second base; the game was called after seven innings due to darkness.

June 30—Sunday was a day of rest for a tired team. As of the end of June, Speaker was batting .387 to lead the team. Carrigan was hitting .317 and Gardner .316. Stahl and Wagner were both batting .302. And Wagner was close to the .300 mark at .299. The team's overall average was .285; opponents were hitting .250 against Red Sox pitching. The Red Sox had gone 21-8 in June. They held a six-game lead over the second-place Athletics. Chicago was 7 ½ games back.

July

July 1—RED SOX LUCKY TO BEAT HIGHLANDERS. The outfielders—Hooper, Speaker, Lewis—each had one hit, the only three the Sox got, but they beat New York, 4-1. Lewis's sixth-inning double was the only hit of the inning, but drove in two. Hall was glad to take the win. A saying of the day lost to history: "Cady lost his cap while chasing a foul and revealed one of the nicest '999' haircuts imaginable." [8]

July 2—Bedient lasted only two innings, and it was 6-5 for New York after eight. Might marriage have interfered with Bedient's focus or stamina? He'd married Miss Imogene P. Palmer of Buffalo the day before, in Brookline. Pape pitched the rest of the game and he had been pitching OK, but was tagged for three in the top of the ninth and the Sox scored just twice. New York won a 26-hit, high-scoring 9-7 ballgame. Three of the hits were Gardner's—two homers and a double. Duffy Lewis hit one over the wall in left, only the second one socked by the Sox to go out. Remarkably, of the 10 homers the Red Sox hit at home in all of 1912, three of them came in this one game.

The Red Sox had beaten New York in every one of their last 14 meetings before this day's defeat. Before they left town for Philadelphia, the Red Sox let out the word that the distant center-field bleachers would be moved 60 feet closer to home plate and that a new sidewalk was going to be installed outside the park.

July 3—RED SOX BAT OUT WIN, 7-2. It was the day that Philadelphia chose to raise its 1911 pennant, complete with fireworks, two brass bands, and a 100-person chorus. But the mighty Jack Coombs couldn't hold back Boston. Connie Mack had five starters warming up before the game in a bit of gamesmanship to psych out the opposition. Stahl warmed up both Joe Wood and Ray Collins; when he learned that Mack was going with Coombs, he countered with Collins, the better to save Wood for the morrow. Collins held the Athletics to five hits, walked only one (intentionally), and wasn't far from a shutout. It was a close enough 3-2 game, though, until the Sox scored four times in the top of the ninth. After the game, one of the bands played "O What Can the Matter Be?"

It wasn't only during World Series time that crowds gathered to watch the progress of road games shown on bulletin boards on Newspaper Row or on Tremont Street, and 500 had gathered to follow the game in the latter location—thoroughly entertained

Smoky Joe was well on his way to a spectacular 34-5 season, and becoming a big draw.

by an inebriated fan who was "shouting and yelling" every time information was posted. "His every sally was greeted with cheers and roars of laughter." When a policeman tried to arrest him, the crowd resented the interference and began to bump up against the policeman and jeer at him. A mounted policeman arrived, and "Mr. Rooter" was taken into custody, though not before delivering a kick to one policeman and tangling with another.

July 4—RED SOX WIN ONE LOSE ONE. The Athletics delivered a rare defeat (4-3) to Smoky Joe in the morning, thanks to a couple of base-running gaffes and Wood's own wild pitch; the *Globe* wrote that they "fooled away" the game. They then overcame an early 4-0 deficit in the afternoon game to split, with a 6-5 win. In the early game, Wood himself was 2-for-3 with a double; Charley Hall drove in the sixth run in the late game. 28,000 Philly fans went to the first game, and 27,000 to the second, both times spilling out onto the field itself. As was the custom of the day—thoroughly bizarre by today's standards—many patrons brought loaded revolvers to the park and fired them off to help celebrate Independence Day.

July 5—Another doubleheader in Philly and another split with both games close ones. The Sox lost the first game in the bottom of the ninth, 3-2, when Stuffy McInnis drove home Eddie Collins on a two-out single. They won the second, 5-3, the final run coming in the top of the ninth after Cy Morgan had walked the bases loaded and gone 2-0 on Speaker, whereupon Herb Pennock was called on in relief, and his first two pitches walked Speaker, to force in the fifth run. A spectacular one-handed catch by McInnis then robbed Duffy Lewis of what looked like a sure triple. This was the fourth doubleheader in seven days,

July 6—RED SOX WIN LAST FROM THE MACKMEN. Stahl's Men Victors in an Uphill Battle, With the Final Score 11 to 5. Uncharacteristically, both clubs used three pitchers. Cicotte "fell over a grounder, hit a man in the back at second, and floundered about for four innings" (*Globe*), allowing five runs in the process, giving Philadelphia a 5-2 lead. Henriksen hit for Cicotte in the top of the fifth and tripled, starting a four-run rally. Hall relieved but developed cramps, and Bedient had to finish. The exact same scenario repeated itself as in the July 5 game—in this case, it was Jack Coombs who walked the bases full of Red Sox in the seventh (on 12 pitches), and got to 2-0 on Lewis. Pennock was brought in from the pen, and again walked in a run. And then another run, too. After the game, Jake Stahl staked a claim to the American League pennant, straightforwardly telling the *Washington Post*, "We expect to win the pennant."

Wagner's freak hit won the July 13 game.

July 7—It was a day off and the Sox traveled by train back to Boston. Second baseman Eddie Collins of the Athletics wrote a bylined column in the *Boston Post* which credited Boston's manager for the team's success: "Stahl appears to have done wonders with this club, practically the same collection of men which was easy to beat last year." The Red Sox settled into Boston for a scheduled 20-game homestand.

July 8—NOT A CHANCE FOR BROWNS WITH WOOD. What might have been a sparsely attended game drew a solid 3,500 fans, as a little pennant fever began to grip the Hub. That Wood was pitching surely helped fill some seats, too. It was becoming more evident that this was a special season for Smoky Joe. Boston took the first game from St. Louis, 5-1, with the Browns' only run coming in the top of the first inning but Boston immediately tripling that tally before the inning was out.

July 9—BUCK O'BRIEN HAS HIS WINNING TURN. In another déjà-vu experience, the July 5 game was, in a way, mirror-imaged. Again, it was Buck O'Brien on the mound. Again the score was 3-2, with the winning run coming in the bottom of the ninth. This time, though, the Sox were at home. And it was O'Brien who scored the winning run, after singling. Yerkes then singled, and Speaker got his third hit of the game, plating O'Brien. Burt Shotton's leadoff homer had perhaps dismayed the Fenway faithful just settling into their seats, but all's well that ends well and it was a thrilling finale. On this day, Eddie Cicotte was sold to the White Sox.

July 10—Had the Red Sox not already had disappointing performances from Bedient, Pape, and Collins, Doug Smith may never had the opportunity to pitch in a major-league ballgame. He entered a game the Sox were losing to St. Louis, 8-2, threw three innings, and saw the game end with the score not materially worse: 9-2. It was the only big-league appearance of his career. And he neither fielded a ball nor had a chance to bat. Was he denied later opportunities because of African American ancestry? See Mike Foster's biography for discussion of that possibility.

July 11—The game scheduled against the Browns was rained out, and the Tigers arrived in town.

July 12—SOX GET TWO TIGER PELTS—*Globe*. The lengthy *Post* subhead told much of the story: "Collins Holds Detroit Tigers to Four Hits in the First Game, Winning 4 to 1—In Second Game Red Sox Score Only and Winning Run in 11th on Speaker's Hit, an Error, and Lewis' Single." In 20 innings, Ray Collins held Detroit to four hits in the first game and Joe Wood held them to five in the longer second game. Paul Shannon wrote, "Never did a Boston team display more splendid balance and strength than did the Red Sox yesterday. Wood's 11-inning 1-0 shutout over Ed Willett was dubbed "one of the greatest pitching feats that a Red Sox twirler has achieved for many a day." In the bottom of the 11th, Tris Speaker tripled and Lewis singled him home. Wood's season record was now 18-4.

July 13—21,000 SEE RED SOX DEFEAT DETROIT AGAIN. O'Brien's "brilliant" 4-0 shutout was satisfying to all the Sox fans in the stands. There were a couple of "hair-raising catches" by the Detroit defense and "two of the greatest plays of the year" made by Heinie Wagner, who drove in the winning run when his sharply-struck ball took a freak hop over Sam Crawford's head and went for three bases, scoring Duffy Lewis.

July 14—No baseball in Boston on Sunday. Not until 1929. Ty Cobb led the AL with a .398 average, but Speaker was close behind with .396.

July 15—SOME REVENGE FOR SNARLING TIGERS. The headline gave it away—the Red Sox went down to defeat. Sea Lion Hall was not in his best form, and lost 6-4, leaving after three innings with the score 5-0. Hall would have been better off sitting out a few more days after hurting his side in Philadelphia, but he offered to pitch and unfortunately Stahl took him up on it. Cobb was 3-for-4, with seven

Eddie Cicotte, late of the Red Sox, was hit hard in the July 18 game.

total bases; Speaker was 3-for-5 with six TB: a home run and two singles.

July 16—SOX MADE IT FOUR OUT OF FIVE. Detroit was put down, 7-2, as Ray Collins came through again, his fifth win in a row, holding the Tigers to six hits and riding an early 4-0 lead to victory. Hooper was 3-for-3 with a triple.

July 17—"White Sox Spitball Artist Downs Red Sox 1-0, but Joe Wood Wins Second Game, 7 to 3." So read the *Post*'s subhead. Big Ed Walsh—on his way to his second consecutive 27-win season—shut out the Red Sox on two hits, spoiling another exceptional effort by Buck O'Brien, who spun a six-hitter but gave up one run in the top of the ninth on a single and a triple. Had Gardner reached home on a double steal attempt, it would have tied the game—but he was erased. Wood wasn't as sharp, but seven runs were more than enough; Speaker shone, singling three times and stealing twice.

July 18—TEN RED SOX RUNS ALL GO TO WASTE. You can't throw a spitball effectively when it's drizzling out. Nine days after they sold him to Chicago, Eddie Cicotte was hammered for six runs by the Red Sox in the very first inning, and reliever Bell gave up four more—but none of the 10 runs counted and the inning never came to a close because the game was rained out before Chicago could record the third out. The Red Sox purchased the contract of Worcester's best pitcher, Ben Van Dyke, calling for him to report in September.

Joe Wood had become a 20-game winner, and there was still a week left in the month of July.

July 19—Ray Collins shut out Chicago in the first game, 8-0, all those runs coming across without the Red Sox making an extra-base hit. Cicotte decided to take the mound again in this day's second game, seeking better fortune than all those rained-out runs he'd been spared the day before. He held the Red Sox to one run through 11 innings (as did Bedient hold the White Sox for Boston.) In the bottom of the 12th, Bedient singled, then scored on a ball Hooper hit so deep that it would have been an inside-the-park home run had the Sox pitcher not scored the winning run ahead of him.

July 20—RED SOX WIN FROM WALSH IN 9TH INNING. It was another walkoff win. Hall and Walsh each kept their respective opponents to two runs. In the bottom of the ninth White Sox manager Nixey Callahan pretty much cost his team the game; with one out and Lewis on third after a single, passed ball, and sacrifice, Callahan ordered back-to-back intentional walks to Stahl and Wagner, to get to Bill Carrigan. Stahl had homered in the second inning (over the left-field wall, the third one Boston batted out in Fenway's first season) and Wagner had tripled, but—still—hadn't Callahan yet learned that "those walks'll get you every time"? Then he had the infield play in, rather than take their normal positions and perhaps go for the double play. Carrigan whacked the ball past the shortstop to score Lewis with the tie-breaking run.

July 21—The Red Sox were already seven games ahead of the second-place Senators, with a spectacular 61-27 record, so much so that the *Post* suggested they were dropping a game now and then as a "rester" for the next series on the schedule. The sports page cartoon suggested five ways in which the Sox could be stopped: dumping barrels of soft soap on Duffy's Cliff in left field, chaining Tris Speaker to a chain in center, kidnapping Harry Hooper, seeing Smoky Joe's right arm simply drop off his body, and driving home runners in a motorcar so that Bill Carrigan couldn't tag them out at the plate.

Stahl standing in front of the grandstands at Comiskey Park.

July 22—RED SOX START IN ON CLEVELANDERS. The game got underway at 3:15 P.M. and almost seemed over by 3:30, after the Red Sox scored three runs in the bottom of the first starting with Harry Hooper's leadoff triple. It would probably have rolled to the wall for an inside-the-park home run, but the Red Sox had readjusted the outfield fence by bringing it closer in. The series with the White Sox had featured a number of triples, many of which reportedly might have been home runs had not the confines been made more confining. When Cleveland scored two in the top of the fourth, the Red Sox scored three more times to extend their lead. O'Brien secured the 8-3 win over the Naps.

July 23—Both teams had nine hits. Boston scored six times and Cleveland scored thrice. Wood got the win (and also tripled). The game was closer than the score might indicate, the Red Sox holding only a slim 2-1 lead through 5½. Wood was now a 20-game winner, only bearing four losses.

July 24—RED SOX PUT TWO NINES ON THE FIELD. Cleveland won, 11-6, but it wasn't for want of trying just about everything—seeing 18 players in the game, only three of them moundsmen. Cleveland pitchers did try to help even things out, issuing nine bases on balls, but Boston bungled seven balls for errors. The game seemed so hopeless that after 6½, down 10-2, Stahl sent in seven new men, keeping only Hooper and Lewis of those who'd started.

July 25—NAPS' LONE RUN IN SECOND WINS GAME. The 1-0 Cleveland victory came when Collins coughed up three hits in a row. He allowed only four other safeties in the game. Vean Gregg shut out the Sox with just four hits. And the one hour, 32-minute game gave both teams time to spare to catch their train. It was a 12-5 homestand, following their 19-9 road trip. Despite dropping the last two games, the Sox still held a seven-game lead over the Senators. The back-to-back losses were the only two games in succession the Sox dropped between June 5 and September 17.

July 26—The special baseball train to Chicago arrived so early that the Red Sox were able to spend the night in a hotel instead of two in a row on the rails. Both the Naps and Red Sox took the same train out of Boston. At Albany, the cars carrying the White Sox from New York were coupled on. The Naps got off in Cleveland, prepared to host the Senators. Both sets of Sox players carried on to Chicago.

July 27—HOMER BY SPEAKER WINS FOR RED SOX. The Red Sox scored once in the ninth to make it 3-3, then in the top of the 10th, Speaker hit a two-out, two-run homer over White Sox Park's left-field fence and into the crowd for a 5-3 lead ("Walsh looked as though his best friend had suddenly passed away.") O'Brien retired the side with a 1-2-3 ending. It was the third time in the last four games he'd faced them that Boston had beaten Big Ed.

Back home at Fenway Park, the field hosted its first non-Red Sox event, a baseball game between a team from the *Christian Science Monitor* newspaper and the Somerville Independents. The game ended in an 8-8 tie in 12 innings. One week later, on August 3, the two teams played a do-over and the Monitor team beat Somerville, 4-1. On August 8, the religious newspaper nine beat the *Boston Transcript* team in a newspaper league game, 2-1.

July 28—BEDIENT RESCUES RED SOX. It wasn't one of Joe Wood's better games, but he received credit for the win thanks to Bedient holding off the White Sox for the final 4 innings, arriving in the nick of time after Wood had nearly wasted his team's 5-0 lead by seeing it drop to 5-4 and two men still on base. Under today's rules, requiring five full innings to earn a win, Wood would have fallen one-third of an inning short. Bedient put out the fire. Stahl tripled, homered, and singled, all off Cicotte.

July 29—LORD 'BOOTS' BALL; RED SOX WIN 7-5. Former Red Sox third baseman Harry Lord had been with Chicago since August 1910; of his three errors in this game, the one that helped Boston the most was a bad throw with two outs in the third, after which four runs crossed the plate.

July 30—HALL'S GENEROSITY DISHES RED SOX. It wasn't just Hall, but the three walks he handed out in the very first inning led to two runs, enough for the White Sox to win it, 6-5, despite a Red Sox rally in the late innings—two in the seventh and three in the eighth; and had Stahl put down a sacrifice, he could have tied the score, but he hit into an out instead.

July 31—STAHL'S MEN BAG ST. LOUIS OPENER. Bedient had thrown the final two innings in Chicago just the day before, but now tacked on a complete game five-hitter. Had the Browns not made three errors, though, they might have won the game, 1-0. Instead, it went into the books as a 4-1 Red Sox win. The Boston defense was stellar.

Hooper walked to load the bases in the top of the 11th, and then Yerkes drove in two.

August

August 1—RED SOX COULD GET ON, BUT THEY COULDN'T GET ACROSS. An unusual though descriptive headline. The *Globe* headline read: BROWNIES NEVER GOT ONE CHEAPER. The Browns put together only three hits off O'Brien but won the game, 2-1. Boston's lone run came on Gardner's second-inning homer to center field. In the eighth inning Speaker led off with a double, but Boston couldn't even lay down a successful sacrifice.

August 2—JOE WOOD HANDS OUT HIS OLD MEDICINE TO BROWNS. For the second day in a row, St. Louis was limited to three hits. This time, though, they were blanked, 9-0. Stahl and Hooper homered, Stahl's a grand slam into the right-field bleachers—part of a six-run fourth inning. Wood himself was 2-for-4 with three total bases. There was a scare in the bottom of the fourth when Pratt's liner back to the box hit Wood's hand so sharply that it sounded as though every bone was broken. He pitched even better from that point forward.

August 3—BIG JAKE PAVES THE WAY FOR DOWNFALL OF RED SOX. Only four Browns runs scored (in the 4-2 loss) but Boston employed three pitchers. Big Jake Stahl, Boston's own manager/first baseman, was charged with one error, but blundered at least twice—and the *Globe*'s Tim Murnane directly ascribed every one of St. Louis's runs to his poor play. Hooper was picked off base, and "Yerkes was asleep all the afternoon." Suffice it to say the *Post*'s Paul Shannon was not impressed with the day's effort. It was the first time St. Louis had beaten the Sox in 1912, after 10 losses in a row. The game was Hall's last start until September 15. He was needed more out of the pen, to be able to spell the starters as both Bedient and now Wood (see July 28 and August 2) were showing some signs of wear, though one might hardly know it in Wood's case.

August 4—RED SOX PITCHERS FAIL, BUT HEAVY ARTILLERY SAVES DAY. Collins Canned and O'Brien Bad, but Cleveland Boxmen Worse. The five runs the Red Sox scored in the top of the third, driving Vean Gregg from the game, helped with the 8-6 win. Cleveland collected 13 hits; Boston got 14. There were eight extra-base hits, all doubles.

August 5—RED SOX NARROWLY ESCAPE A SHUTOUT. Some solace that; they still lost, 3-1. The Sox collected 10 hits and a walk, but could bring only one runner home against Gregg—the same Cleveland starter they'd bombed out of the game the day before. Hugh Bedient only allowed five hits. Again, the Red Sox didn't likely feel any better to know that. Nor was it much comfort that they'd held an early 1-0 lead. It still went down as a loss. Two of the five Naps hits were off the bat of right-fielder Joe Jackson, a triple and a double driving in all three Cleveland runs.

August 6—SWAT BY YERKES IN 11TH LANDS BACON FOR RED SOX. Joe Wood and Cleveland's Fred Blanding were locked in a 3-3 tie after 10 innings. Leading off the 11th, as darkness began to gather, the Red Sox put two on but Blanding struck out the next two. The runners moved up on a passed ball, and Blanding didn't want to pitch to Harry Hooper, so he walked him on purpose. Steve Yerkes—whom Murnane dubbed "the king of timely batsmen"– slashed a single to center and drove in two; Wood let up a bit and let one run score in the bottom of the 11th. There was a runner on third, the potential tying run. Boldly, he streaked for home and might have stolen the base, but pinch-hitter Bill Hunter swung and fouled off the pitch for strike two. On the next pitch, Hunter struck out and ended the game.

August 7—FANS FEAR RED SOX PITCHERS ARE ON VERGE OF CRACKING. So headlined a *Boston Traveler* story. The Red Sox had lost four of their last eight games, all on the road, and only three of the preceding games were complete games. They had a record of 70-33, and a six-game lead over the second-place Senators. And this induced panic? The day's game

Hack Engle drove in 18 runs for the Red Sox in 1912.

was a 4-4 tie, the first tie of the year. Speaker was 2-for-2 with a single and a double, and was batting .396 at this point in the year, through 414 at-bats. Boston was down 4-0 after five innings, and the game was delayed because of rain. The Red Sox were lucky that play resumed, and that they scored twice in the sixth (after which the game was delayed again) and then twice in the eighth, which tied it. After nine, the score still tied. Umpire Egan called the game "in spite of the protests of everyone."

President McAleer was reportedly trying to buy the Youngstown, Ohio, ballclub to convert it into an "out-and-out farm" for the Red Sox.

August 8—RED SOX TOUCH UP TIGERS' STRIPES WITH WHITEWASH. Ray Collins shut out Detroit on nine hits; the Red Sox won, 5-0; Hooper tripled and homered. Speaker scrambled back to deep center field and caught a Sam Crawford drive that would have been a sure home run had he not reached out and snagged it. Lewis topped that, reeling in Ty Cobb's deep drive, albeit using his glove to do so; he caught it leaping in midair just before crashing into the center-field scoreboard and hitting the ground. Each catch saved two runs.

August 9—The Tigers barely escaped being shut out again, losing 6-1. Bedient let one run across in the first, but Cobb was caught trying to steal home, and that was it for Detroit. The Red Sox responded with one, added another in the fourth, and poured four across in the fifth. It was another good game for the Boston defense: "The Boston infield worked smoothly, while the classiest outfield in the business covered ground like shadows."—T.H. Murnane.

Red Sox team in front of the dugout. Note trainer Joe Quirk on the far left of the photograph.

August 10—The combination of three bases on balls and a double steal gave the Tigers one run in the bottom of the first inning, but it was the only one they scored, while Boston put up five zeroes. The Sox scored twice in the sixth and added single runs in the seventh and eighth. Every one of the five sacrifice hits in the game was by Boston. Smoky Joe, author of one of the sacrifices, settled down after the first and dealt out goose eggs the rest of the way. 4-1. The Sox' lead over the Senators grew to 8½ games.

At Fenway Park, during a Boston Lodge of Elks field day, it was Winthrop Knights of Columbus 3, Lynn Elks 1 in seven innings.

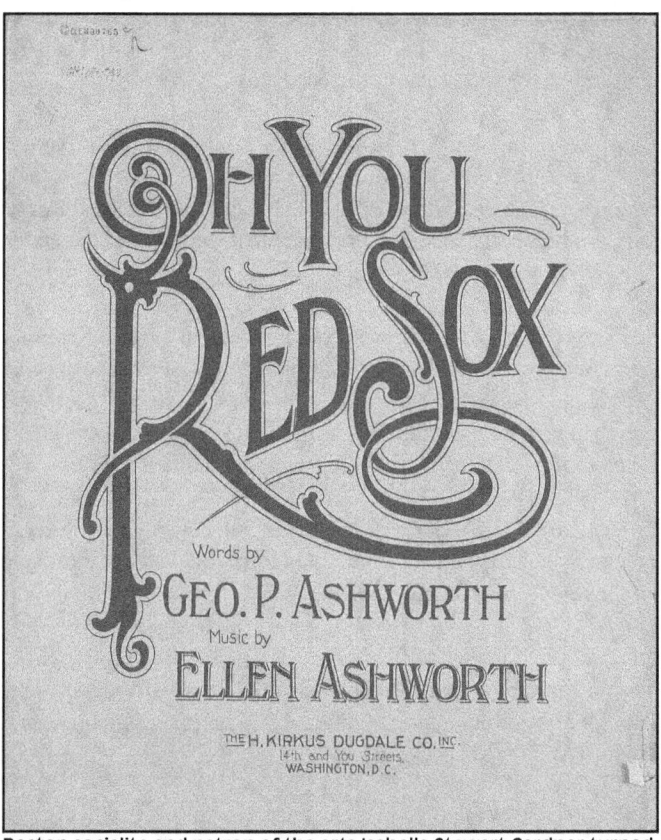

Boston socialite and patron of the arts Isabella Stewart Gardner turned up at her box at the Boston Symphony sporting a head scarf reading, "Oh, You Red Sox!" The unconventional garb left some aghast in what was still a staid City of Boston.

August 11—COLLINS' WILDNESS COST RED SOX GAME. The Tigers managed to win one, 4-2, with the Red Sox scoring once in the first and once in the ninth, but Detroit plating four in the innings in between. Speaker was hitting .399—but Cobb was hitting .419. For Detroit's Jean Dubuc, it was his 11th consecutive win. The Red Sox were satisfied with a 10-5 road trip.

August 12—It was a travel day and the Red Sox pulled into Back Bay Station at 3 P.M., with a "big crowd" waiting to welcome them. After playing 16 days in a row, the team was grateful for a day off on the following day.

August 13—The pure day off was indeed most welcome. The Red Sox were looking forward to hosting the St. Louis Browns in a scheduled doubleheader on the 14th. Arthur Duffey wrote in the *Post* that if the Sox could take both games, a World Series berth was all but secure. Many of the Red Sox went to the South End Grounds and watched the Cubs take the fourth game of a series sweep from the Boston Braves. The team let it be known that fans should start holding onto their rain checks; if the Sox won the pennant, a collection of stubs would prove them to be regular fans and they would be given extra consideration when it came to World Series ticket distribution.

August 14—The Red Sox found the Browns "easy prey" and took two, 8-2 and 8-0. St. Louis got 10 hits total, six off O'Brien and Hall in the first game and four off Smoky Joe in the shutout. For Wood, it was his 25th win—and it was only mid-August. One oddity in the first game: Browns pitcher George Washington Baumgardner became so incensed at a pitch called a ball by the umpire that he threw his glove down and walked off the field, and it took nearly 10 minutes to persuade him to return. When he resumed pitching, he struck Stahl out. It was the first day the Sox sported their new home uniforms, with "swell crimson coats that made a big hit with the crowd." (*Globe*)

August 15—Scoring seven runs in the second inning put the Sox in good stead, and even though Bedient was far from his sharpest, the "spasm of savage hitting" saw the BoSox prevail over Jack Powell and the Browns, 13-6. Stahl took the day off and gave Clyde Engle a day to play in his stead. Engle starred on offense, with a triple, a double, and two singles, scoring three times and driving in the first two of seven Red Sox runs in the second inning.

In 10 days, the Sox had nearly doubled their lead in the standings from five games to 9½. Jimmy McAleer crowed, "No ballclub in the world can spot my team 10 games and catch it in 40." [9]

Like Heinie Wagner, Hooper (inducted into the National Baseball Hall of Fame in 1971) was part of four Red Sox world championship teams.

August 16—BROWNS BEAT RED SOX 3 TO 2; CARRIGAN MAKES FATAL SLIP. The *Post*'s Paul Shannon prefaced his remarks on catcher Carrigan by noting that he'd previously prevented two runs from scoring by "wonderful blocking of the plate." The slip the headline referred to was when he "missed his man" when he "should have been out by 15 feet." The tying run scored and the next batter doubled in the go-ahead run off starter Buck O'Brien. The Browns added one more in the sixth. Joe Wood was used, perhaps unwisely (given that he was said to have a sore arm), to pitch the eighth and ninth.

August 17—25,000 SEE THE RED SOX WIN. It was "one of the most thrilling contests of the year" as they entered the bottom of the seventh losing 3-0, but scored five runs that inning to take the lead, and ultimately win, 6-4, over Detroit. It was a large crowd, and an enthusiastic one. "Grey-haired enthusiasts, women and children waved their hands and the din was deafening. Over in the left field corner, where the overflow pranced wildly, and back in the innermost recesses of the right field bleachers the temporary fit of insanity held sway." It was the largest crowd of the season, well beyond Fenway's capacity in its first year, and even the players were called upon to help drive in fence posts in the left-field corner to help keep the crowd from encroaching too far onto the field of play. Again Wood was used in relief.

Cleveland was playing in Washington and after that game, almost every one of the 8,000 or so fans stayed in the park to watch the progress of the Detroit-Boston game. When the Sox scored those five runs to take the lead in the bottom of the seventh, "a chorus of groans arose" as Washington fans realized their pennants hopes were pretty much kaput.

August 18—No game. The next day's *Post* had a front-page article headlined TY COBB SURE SOX WILL WIN. He predicted that Boston would beat the New York Giants in the World Series. He had no doubt that the Red Sox were the better team. Somewhat-biased Eddie Collins of the still-contending Philadelphia Athletics wrote that the "Boston club is slowly fading." The papers of these days were often filled with bylined columns purportedly written by the players in question. Former manager Patsy Donovan came back to Boston after a lengthy scouting trip around the country.

August 19—RED SOX WIN OUT BY 1 RUN. "Boston got all the breaks," allowed the *Post*. Taking advantage of a bad seventh-inning throwing error by Detroit's catcher that allowed Speaker to run all the way from home to third base, the Sox snapped a 3-3 tie when he scored on a sacrifice fly to left field. Earlier, Cobb's attempt at a clever move, pretending to bobble his fielding of Speaker's single to induce Spoke to try for second base, backfired—Speaker beat his throw. The *Globe* credited the "gilt-edged work" of the Red Sox infield with keeping the Tigers sufficiently in check.

Leader of the "Speed Boys," Speaker hit .383 on the year and stole 52 bases, a team record for 61 seasons.

August 20—RED SOX TAKE LAST GAME FROM DETROIT. Neal Ball continued to draw plaudits for his play, and Wood resumed a starting role again—and beat Dubuc, 6-2, for his 12th win in a row and 26th of the season. Dubuc himself had only recently come off a 12-in-a-row win streak. Gardner made three errors at third; otherwise, Wood might well have whitewashed the Tigers.

The Sox let it be known that they were drawing up plans to expand the seating at Fenway Park, both temporary seating for the World Series and some permanent seating that would be built in time for the Series.

August 21—NAPS TAKE IT OUT ON BOSTON BOYS. Coming off a seven-game losing streak against Washington and Philadelphia, Cleveland cruised to an easy 9-4 win. With three in the first (Buck O'Brien lasted only the one inning) and three more in the second, it was pretty much all over early. Shoeless Joe Jackson was 4-for-4 and scored twice on squeeze plays—in the fifth and in the ninth. The Naps struck for 15 base hits to Boston's eight. Four Red Sox errors were costly, too.

August 22—RED SOX WAKE UP AND PLAY. "All that the Red Sox didn't do on Wednesday they did yesterday" as they handled the Clevelanders, 9-0. Credit Ray Collins with allowing only two hits in the game, the first one not coming until the sixth. The Indians committed five errors.

August 23—On a wet and muddy field, both teams played quite well, but one run in the first inning and four in the second gave Hugh Bedient and his Boston mates more than enough to put down Cleveland in another one-sided game, 5-1. Bedient seemed relaxed throughout. He struck out six and recorded four assists.

August 24—JOE WOOD BESTS SOUTHPAW GREGG. A pitcher's duel was expected and 23,000 packed Fenway Park, but Gregg didn't bring his best game, coughing up three runs in the first and four more in the fourth, after which he called it a day. Two Hooper doubles were the only extra-base hits of the game; five Boston errors made Wood look worse than he was in the 8-4 finale, but he struck out eight and benefited from some fine work by Steve Yerkes at second base.

August 25—On the Sunday off, Philadelphia's Eddie Collins turned in "his" column to the *Post* and admitted, "As a prophet, I feel that I have sort of faded. …Nothing can stop the Red Sox from winning." He added, "I don't figure how the Giants are ever going to beat 'Joe' Wood." Wood was now 27-4. Speaker was batting .401

August 26—WALSH NEEDED NO ALIBI YESTERDAY. Even though the Red Sox scored one early run, Chicago's Big Ed Walsh beat Collins and Pape, 4-2. Four infield errors undercut the Boston pitchers.

August 27—DARKNESS ENDS LONG STRUGGLE. Red and White Sox Play 12 Innings to Tie. There were 30 hits, seven Red Sox errors (and four by Chicago), and 16 runs scored—but the runs were split evenly, 8-8, after seven innings. Neither team scored from that point on, though a 20-minute argument during which the entire White Sox team swarmed the umpire killed a lot of valuable time, and darkness fell. Hitters couldn't see the ball, and "even the pitcher could not see his catcher's signal." Time to call the game.

With two major-league teams in Boston, the September 6 matchup of Wood and Walter Johnson drew the largest crowd in Boston baseball history to that time.

August 28—RED SOX WIN TWO AND GAIN. The "two sharply and well contested contests sent the White Sox away with a double defeat." Another huge crowd enjoyed the day, seeing the hometown team win 5-3 behind Buck O'Brien in the first game and 3-0 (a six-hitter) by Smoky Joe Wood in the second. The Red Sox held a 10-game lead over the second-place Senators.

August 29—ATHLETICS LOSE TO RED SOX. World's Champs Are Outplayed at Every Point. Far from fading, Stahl's Sox took on the reigning champs and trounced them, 8-1. Ray Collins was the beneficiary—and allowed only five scattered hits—and Eddie Plank and company the losers.

August 30—RED SOX SWAMPED FADING CHAMPIONS. Stahl and Hall were the stars as the Red Sox overcame a 4-0 deficit. As soon as Hall replaced Bedient, the scoring stopped and the Sox started scoring—seven times. Coombs gave up two runs each in the third and fourth, and the game was tied. Connie Mack called on Chief Bender, but he gave up the three runs that made the difference, the first two on a two-run single up the middle by Jake Stahl.

August 31—33,000 SEE RED SOX WIN FROM ATHLETICS 2 to 1. "One of the greatest crowds in baseball history," declared the *Post*. The crowd was "banked in solid masses in front of the grand stand, encircling the entire playing field"—in other words, on the field in front of the stands, where some 6,000 were roped off. They saw the Sox take the third game in a row from the 1911 world champions. Each pitcher (O'Brien for Boston and Jack Coombs for Philadelphia) held the other team to six hits. Philadelphia's only run came in the ninth inning. The second Red Sox run came in the eighth inning when Speaker walked, advanced on a sacrifice, then stole third base and scored on the catcher's wild throw to third. It was one of Speaker's 52 stolen bases of the season, a team record which held until Tommy Harper's 54 in 1973.

The Red Sox finished August at 87-37, able to luxuriate in an 11-game lead over the second-place Senators.

September

September 1—No game scheduled. Any number of articles lionized the Sox for playing their best ball of the season. The real battle in the league was for second place.

September 2—RED SOX WIN A DOUBLE HEADER. Boston extended its lead to 13 games by taking two tight games from New York on a drizzly day at the Polo Grounds. It was Labor Day and both games were as close as could be, 2-1 (behind Bedient, who threw a two-hitter) and 1-0 (behind Joe Wood). The Sox overcame a 1-0 lead in the eighth inning of the first game, the go-ahead run scoring on a balk by Russ Ford. The only run in the second game arrived in the top of the first courtesy of a single over the second-base bag by Harry Hooper, an errant pickoff throw, a sacrifice hit, and a sacrifice fly. In the second game, the Red Sox outfield had mostly just stood around—the "golden outfield" didn't record even one putout or assist. The Red Sox had won every one of their 1912 road games against New York.

September 3—A rainout, and the Red Sox rode the train right back to Boston. They had nevertheless won every one of the 10 games they'd played in New York. Jimmy McAleer was quoted as saying the Red Sox hoped the Giants would win, for the bigger gate and for the ease in travel, allowing the players to sleep in hotels rather than aboard trains.

September 4—RED SOX FIND SENATORS EASY VICTIMS, 6 TO 2. Four runs in the top of the second were enough to win. Ray Collins limited the visitors to six hits, improving his record to 12-4. The Red Sox lead increased to 13½ games.

September 5—RED SOX WIN ON CASHION'S PASSES. The speedy Speaker was caught stealing three times, and rubbed out another time trying to stretch a triple into an inside-the-park home run. But Washington's Carl Cashion was generous, issuing seven bases on balls, helping Boston build up to a 4-3 victory, their ninth win in a row.

September 6—WOOD WINS PITCHING DUEL WITH JOHNSON. Thousands Storm the Park Unable to Gain Admission. A crowd estimated by the *Post* at between 35,000 and 40,000—the biggest crowd in Boston baseball history—saw a game for the ages. The *Globe* said there were 29,000. There were many thousands who simply could not get in. So many fans were on the field that the players couldn't even get into the dugouts! As the *Globe* put it, "the players' pits were abandoned, the contestants bringing their war clubs almost out to the base lines, and not seeing the confining walls of their dugouts from one end of the battle to another." Smoky Joe Wood was going for his 30th win of the season and Walter Johnson was going for his 29th. Mounted police had to help push the crowds back so the two teams could play.

It was Wood's 14th consecutive win. Johnson held the Red Sox hitless through the first five, and the only run of the game scored in the bottom of the sixth. Johnson got the first two batters and had Speaker in a hole—but Spoke hit a double down the left-field foul line. Then Lewis, a pull-hitter, was late to get around on a Johnson fastball and hit one that dropped about 100 feet down the right-field foul line, fair by about 20 feet, for another double. It was one of those lucky balls that fell in just out of reach, and Speaker scored. 1-0, Red Sox. A single and a sacrifice in the top of the ninth set up the possibility of Washington tying up the game, but Wood bore down and struck out the final two batters.

September 7—Washington won, 5-1, and the *Post* pinned the blame on the "inexperience of young Krug"—Wagner had taken ill and Marty Krug filled in for him at shortstop. He didn't make an error, but Paul Shannon felt that a Texas Leaguer that dropped in behind him would have been caught by Wagner while Krug "turned dizzily about in an effort to locate the ball." There was another play where Wagner would have fielded a bunt and tried to cut down the lead runner at third base, but Krug held his ground, figuring Gardner would go for it. To be fair, the writer admitted that "the Red Sox could not hit Groom with much success." Krug, in fact, had Boston's best hit—a triple.

September 8—No game; the Red Sox had a day off for travel to Chicago. Work began at Fenway Park on the expanded seating announced on August 20.

Wagner, age 31, was one of the older players on the team. He and the battered Bill Carrigan were both given a week off, to get ready for the postseason.

September 9—No game—rain.

September 10—JOE WOOD WINS HIS FIFTEENTH. Not his 15th of the season—he'd already doubled that total—but rather his 15th consecutive win. It was a good thing that Wood singled in the seventh and came around to score the fifth Red Sox run, because he tired in sweltering Chicago and let a 5-1 lead tighten to 5-3 after eight-plus innings. Hall came on in relief, allowed one inherited runner to score but then shut the barn door.

September 11—COLLINS BLANKS CHICAGO. Ray Collins, the sole Sox southpaw, held the ChiSox to six hits, without a run, while his Red Sox teammates put

Boston Globe cartoonist Wallace Goldsmith showed the Sox sprinting to the finish, leaving the other American League clubs in the dust.

six runs across. Collins was perhaps no Joe Wood, but had won 15 of his last 17 games. Olaf Henriksen came into the game to spell Speaker, and impressed with his fielding as well as collecting two hits in his two at-bats.

September 12— JAKE STAHL'S BIG SWAT WINS RED SOX GAME, 3-1. It was a 0-0 ballgame after seven innings, Lange against O'Brien and Lange permitting only two base hits to Boston. With two outs and the bases loaded, Stahl slammed a double over the left-fielder's head. Chicago got one back in the bottom of the eighth, but neither team scored in the ninth. The Chicago banking community was well represented in the person of Stahl's father-in-law and several other bankers as well. The ball he clouted was hit hard; in the words of *Globe* writer Murnane, "The report that followed was like that of a mule kicking a hole through a plate glass window." One foot higher and it would have cleared the low wall.

September 13—BROWNS FAIL TO DISTURB RED SOX. Bedient held St. Louis to two runs and five hits; the confident Red Sox team scored six times, with the three first-inning runs all they truly needed. By beating the Browns, the Sox had posted a 23-4-1 record since August 14. Grantland Rice commented in the *Boston Traveler*: "It doesn't seem to make much difference whom the Red Sox pitch. That bunch has now developed the habit to such a degree that it can't lose for winning."

September 14—There was no game, due to rain in St. Louis. Joe Wood was suffering from a minor case of tonsillitis.

September 15—It was Sunday, but the Red Sox were in St. Louis and there was no prohibition there against Sunday baseball. There was good news and bad news. The bad news was that the Sox lost the first game of the day's doubleheader, 5-4. Charley Hall hadn't made it through the second inning, allowing all five runs; Ben Van Dyke mopped up in style, allowing only three hits in 6 innings. "He was cool at all times," approved the *Post*. He walked three, but struck out seven. It was his first major-league appearance since working two games for the Phillies back in 1909. The good news was the 2-1 nightcap, which ended after eight, the Sox taking the lead in the top of the eighth—and thereby giving Smoky Joe Wood his 16th win in a row and his 32nd victory of the season. It was, in fact, Wood who scored the winning run, scampering home from third base on a bases-loaded wild pitch.

September 16—RED SOX NEED BUT ONE GAME. There was no game scheduled for the Red Sox, so after they arrived in Cleveland at the Colonial Hotel, the whole team went out to the park to see the Naps play the Athletics. A Philly loss would have clinched the pennant for the Red Sox. It didn't work out that way. Nevertheless, numerous players began to issue predictions regarding the World Series. Eddie Collins of the Athletics wrote a column saying the Sox were certain to win, mainly on the strength of the two teams' sets of outfielders. Christy Mathewson declared himself fit, thought his Giants teammate Jeff Tesreau would be unbeatable, and said that Joe Wood's streak would be his undoing because he'd be bound to deplete himself chasing the record and not keeping himself in sufficient shape for the Series.

In this era, there was a very strong rivalry between leagues. The Athletics finished up a visit to Cleveland on this date, winning the final game of a four-game series, 8-0. Both teams stayed at the Colonial, and the *Boston Globe* let readers know that the Philadelphia players "spent considerable time this afternoon advising the Red Sox how to play the New York Giants"—the team they had beaten in the 1911 World Series—despite being mathematically still in contention.

September 17—HISTORY GETS AWFUL JOLT WHEN RED SOX LOSE TWO. The Naps were playing good baseball. They had taken three of four from Philadelphia and now won both games of a doubleheader against the Red Sox. A Boston win would have given them the AL flag, but Cleveland took the first game in 11 innings, 4-3, on Lajoie's drive to the right-field fence. Cleveland was ahead 3-2 when the second game was called due to darkness right after it became official when the Red Sox completed batting in the top of the fifth. Buck O'Brien had pitched well, allowing just three hits, but Cleveland's Blanding had granted only two. Philadelphia had the day off, so they couldn't be eliminated. On the 18th the Sox had another shot against the Naps, and the Athletics had two opportunities to get eliminated facing the White Sox in Chicago.

Bill Carrigan and Heinie Wagner were given a full week off, planning to rest up and meet the club in New York on Tuesday the 24th. Stahl said the rest would do them good, and he'd give Gardner and a few other veterans some time off too once the Red Sox truly clinched.

September 18—RED SOX WIN THE PENNANT. The Red Sox game was rained out by a heavy downpour, but the White Sox beat Philadelphia 9-1 in the first of two in Chicago, thus handing the pennant to Boston. Jimmy McAleer crowed, "I'm the happiest man in baseball. We have known, of course, for a long time that we were sure to win the flag, but now that it is ours beyond a possibility of doubt, I pay tribute to what I think is the greatest baseball team the game has ever known." He credited Jake Stahl, who himself declared, "I can only say that all my efforts to bring the pennant to Boston would have been unavailing unless every man on the team had given me his best efforts. No man ever had such loyal followers." He went on to note that the team had never slumped and never had a big winning streak, but just won consistently throughout the season. He was reported to be "almost too happy to speak at all." The Red Sox could lose every one of their remaining 15 games and still not be overtaken. Philadelphia's Connie Mack predicted that the Red Sox would win the World Series. Carpenters had already begun installing temporary seating at Fenway Park to add 10,000 to its capacity of 22,000. As for the rest of the Red Sox, the news of the White Sox win left them "like a bunch of schoolboys on a lark." Once Washington had been eliminated, President Taft had begun to root for the Red Sox and planned to be "down among the fans" at Fenway Park.

There was one mathematical situation that presented itself. Should the Red Sox lose every single game remaining on their schedule, and should both the Athletics and Senators win every single game they had left, all three teams would be tied 97-57. This wasn't possible, however, in that the Athletics and Senators had to play each other. If one of the two swept the other, however, the prevailing team would be in a position to tie Boston. Was the Red Sox celebration premature? Not really. There was a postponed game against New York which still had not been played. By league rule, the managers of the teams determined the dates on which to play postponed games, but it took the consent of both teams to make the arrangement and there would be no benefit to Boston to risk losing such a game. The worst the Sox could end up would be 97-56. The best either of the other two teams could end up would be 97-57. McAleer notified New York that the Red Sox would not play that postponed game.

Gardner played one more game before his planned week off. For a while, it seemed a disastrous game.

A comparison of the rosters of the 1911 and 1912 teams shows that the position players were almost exactly the same, with the exception of Jake Stahl as the primary first baseman. Some hit better, and some hadn't hit as well in 1912 as they had in 1911. It more or less balanced out. The team batting averages and on-base percentages were nearly identical; the differences

Those quarters added up and Boston Mayor Fitzgerald presented manager Stahl with the automobile during the ceremonies on October 17.

rested in the pitching.

September 19—The Sox were swept for the second doubleheader in a row, losing to Cleveland 9-3 in a five-inning first game and 6-0 in a six-inning second game. Hall was bombed in game one, called after five due to rain. First Stahl and then Speaker was ejected in the first game, Stahl for protesting the Naps runner being called safe on a play at home plate. The *Globe's* Murnane called it "absolutely the worst decision that I ever saw." Speaker was thrown out for coming in to argue and then taking too long to get back to his position in center. After the first game was called, both teams stuck around for an hour as sawdust was put down on the baselines. They began to play the second game but the field was a mire, and they gave up two-thirds of the way through (it was officially called due to darkness). The Red Sox had their eyes on the 102-win season that the Athletics had put up in 1910, hoping to set a new mark for league games won in a season, although by giving so many of the veterans some time off, they weren't truly going all out just to rack up win totals. The second game featured catcher Forrest Cady playing first base in a lineup that "looked like a Hot Springs Yanigans outfit" per Murnane, who cautioned, "The work of the day did the Red Sox much harm, as dumb and bad ball playing will."

After the games, the team traveled to Detroit by boat. It was a rough crossing, as it happened, leaving a few players discomfited. They arrived not long before game time on the 20th.

Back in Boston, Nuf Ced McGreevey let it be known that the Royal Rooters would be reconvened and estimated they'd be 1,000 strong. The *Boston Journal* reported that the Winter League group of fans were prime movers in reviving the organized rooting tradition and that a committee had been formed by McGreevey, Jack Dooley, Charlie Lavis, and the usual crowd. They planned to hire a 30-piece band and were already arranging parodies on the hit songs of the day. Each rooter would be provided a megaphone, and the song *Tessie* was certain to be featured once more.

September 20—TIGERS PUT END TO JOE'S RECORD. What hope Wood had of winning 17 in a row foundered when Detroit dealt him a 6-4 defeat. "Two men are responsible for Wood's Waterloo," wrote Charles E. Young in the *Post*. "Joe himself and Martin Krug who is wobbling around in Heinie Wagner's shoes at shortstop. Joe paved the way for the toboggan in the third when, with two men down, he passed four men in succession." That blame could hardly be shifted to anyone else, unless it was to Cady behind the plate instead of Wood's accustomed Bill Carrigan. Murnane acknowledged the possibility that having the second-stringers behind him weighed on Wood: "He well knew that the Red Sox players were not on edge, and that the chances for good support were slight." Stahl sat out the game in civilian clothes and later murmured that he hadn't realized the record had been so important to Smoky Joe, who hadn't lost a game for 78 days. He was tense, barking at the umpire, and even firing off remarks at a couple of his teammates about "bonehead plays." Wood was battling a cold and had wobbled in both of his last couple of starts. He'd also been aboard the steamer that crossed Lake Erie. But losing the game was still a true disappointment to him.

"With one run in and the bases choked, Krug muffed a puny fly raised by Cobb and two more runs came across." It wasn't Joe's day. Young said that you could see the strain the streak had placed on young Wood; Mathewson may have been right that the streak could do him in. With an eye on postseason play,

Fans crowded around the train at Boston's South Station.

Hick Cady outsprints Buck O'Brien and trainer Joe Quirk.

perhaps it was fortunate to get it out of the way this early. The *Globe* quoted Stahl: "Defeat was the very best thing that could come to Wood. Another week of thinking about his pitching record and he would be fit for a nurse." After the game on Saturday, Gardner was scheduled to take off a week at his home in Enosburg Falls, Vermont.

September 21—LARRY GARDNER BREAKS FINGER. That was front-page news in the next day's *Boston Sunday Post*. The Red Sox beat the Tigers, 11-4, but the big news was Gardner diving for a ball in the eighth inning of the meaningless and already-resolved game and reportedly snapping the little finger on his right hand in the process—just hours before he was due for a breather. The *Globe* reporting was more accurate: It was actually more of a dislocation than a true break, and Gardner played in every game of the World Series.

The same paper told readers the team would hardly recognize Fenway when they returned from the road. On Duffy's Cliff in left, there were now rows and rows of bleachers to seat 1,200 patrons. The space to the left of the wall, in foul territory, had been left vacant before the season when construction had to wrap up early, but had now filled in with a "substantial addition" to the grandstand that added 4,700 more seats. There were additional bleachers set up in right-center field sufficient to accommodate 4,500 fans, with a probable price of $1.00 for the Series games. Boxes to seat 1,000 had been added in front of the grandstand, just past the dugouts on both sides.

September 22—Sunday. No game. The *Boston Sunday American* ran a front-page story asking readers to each contribute 25 cents to buy an automobile for Jake Stahl. The paper also announced that, during World Series games in New York, some 8,000 seats at the Boston Arena would be available for those wishing to get the latest results by telegraph wire direct from the Polo Grounds. (The Giants hadn't clinched yet, but were widely expected to.) "The *Boston American*'s baseball experts will be on both ends and reproduce every play and happening the instant it occurs through the medium of a gigantic board showing the diamond and the players. Another feature will be the complete running account of the games through specially built megaphones."

September 23—No game, but the team was feted on its return from Detroit. Several thousand fans surrounded South Station and flocked around Track 13 so tightly that it was difficult for the players to get from the train to vehicles that paraded them to Boston Common through dense streets clogged with so many people that there was barely enough room for the automobiles to get through. The *Globe* estimated that some 220,000 people in all flocked the streets, including a notable number of women. This would be almost precisely one-third of the city's population. Mayor Fitzgerald and thousands of fans awaited them on the Common. The mayor was able to say a few words, but the singers who had hoped for an "opportunity to warble" were denied the chance. No one wanted anyone but the ballplayers. Their remarks were quite brief.

September 24—SPLIT BILL AT FENWAY. The Highlanders won the first one, 5-2, after scoring four times in the top of the first; the second game saw some of the second-stringers play for the Sox, and they won it behind O'Brien, 3-1, when Lewis tripled in two in the bottom of the eighth and (as it turned out) final inning, gaining the Red Sox win number 99. Construction of the new seating in the park was well underway, but not fully complete, but the work paused long enough to get in the games.

September 25—Though the Giants didn't clinch until the following day, the 26th, it seemed a foregone enough conclusion that the National Commission held a coin toss anyhow. The Giants called "tails" and won the toss. New York wanted to start the Series on Tuesday, but the

> ## "Pitching for Red Sox"
>
> A brief story datelined September 25 in Cleveland appeared in the September 26 *Boston Globe*. It ran in full, as follows: "Peter Polivia, who walks in his sleep, aroused his neighbors on West 7th Street last night by crashing bricks against the houses. A patrolman summoned from the West 25th Street police station found Peter on top of his house tearing bricks from the chimney and hurling them to the street. A yell finally told the policeman that the game was over, and he yanked Peter from the roof. 'Well, we won anyway,' said Peter as he was hustled to the station. Then he woke up. He said he had been reading of the World's Series games and dreamed that he was pitching for [the] Boston Red Sox."

Red Sox preferred Monday. Again the Giants called tails and prevailed. The plan was to alternate cities and games, back and forth until the Series was resolved. Prices in Boston were to range from 50 cents to $5.00. Meanwhile, back in Boston, Smoky Joe Wood showed he was in fine form and held New York's American League team to two hits, and won a 6-0 game that ended with a spectacular catch by Hooper, who then fired the ball in to nip a baserunner who had never thought Hooper had a prayer of catching the ball. It was win 100 for the Red Sox.

In a series of sprints before the game, some of the Speed Boys competed against each other (and even against trainer Joe Quirk) to see who was the fastest on the team. Cady beat O'Brien and Quirk, and Henriksen beat out Nunamaker.

September 26—BASEBALL FARCE AT FENWAY PARK. "It was virtually impossible to tell how the game would have resulted if properly played," sniffed the *Post*. Van Dyke let up seven runs on eight hits, three walks, and a hit batsman. Pape wasn't much better, letting in five runs in the sixth before settling down. Twelve runs on 17 hits might have seemed sufficient for the visitors to win, but New York pitchers managed to allow three runs in the fifth, four in the sixth, and eight in the eighth in part thanks to six consecutive walks (four of them with the bases loaded) followed by a hit batsman. It was getting dark enough that there was no point prolonging New York's agony so Speaker deliberately swung wildly at three pitches to bring it to an end. It's in the books as a 15-12 win for the Red Sox.

September 27—No game. The Sox had finished their home games and headed out for a final six, three apiece in Washington and Philadelphia. The National Commission announced the 23 Giants and 22 Red Sox who would be eligible for World Series play.

September 28—Washington pitcher Carl Cashion walked 10 batters and threw two wild pitches, but allowed only four hits and the Red Sox lost, 3-2. Paul Shannon guessed that he was simply so wild that hitters feared digging in against him in the batter's box. Ray Collins could well have had a shutout, but for the lackluster infield play behind him. Carrigan, back in a game after his week off, split a fingernail on his throwing hand and was expected to be out for at least three more games. In a bylined column, Ty Cobb picked Boston to win the World Series.

September 29—Sunday. No game. The National Commission announced full details for the Series games, showing

Rough Carrigan back in the game.

Tris Speaker is seen here at Fenway, as workers in the background are seen getting the park into readiness for its first postseason.

considerable concern to try to frustrate scalpers. The rosters of eligible players were posted. They also ruled that neither team nor individual players would be allowed to play postseason exhibition games. Eddie Collins wrote a column asserting that Jake Stahl was the managerial peer of the great John McGraw. The day's *Boston Globe* featured almost a full page on the spitball, under the headline "Spitball Will Be Big Factor in World's Championship Series."

September 30—SENATORS PROVE EASY FOR CHAMPS. Washington wasn't really giving the Red Sox the sort of stiff competition that would keep them in fighting form and primed to face the Giants. More than one Boston paper said it expected Philadelphia to help the Sox by playing tough, experienced ball. In part due to their loyalty to the league, "the Athletics will as far as possible play the New York style of ball and will try hard to win." As the Sox tied the AL record with their 102nd win, Buck O'Brien threw no-hit ball through the first six innings, the game more one-sided than the final 7-5 score suggests.

October

October 1—SOX RIGHT THERE WITH THE WALLOP. Hoping to assess the Red Sox, Giants manager John McGraw sat in the stands and watched as Boston recorded win number 103 by a decisive 12-3 score, while in New York, the Giants' Tesreau and Marquard lost a doubleheader to the second-division Phillies. Five Senators errors helped the Red Sox pile up the runs. Duffy Lewis was 4-for-6 with a pair of doubles. McGraw thought the experience of having played in the 1911 World Series would help his club. "Go back over the records," he said. "I think you will find that in every case where the same team has played in the world series in consecutive years it was a stronger aggregation the second time than it was the first." [10]

October 2—ATHLETICS ADOPT GIANTS' TACTICS. No game, but the Athletics and Red Sox worked out behind closed gates, the Athletics helping the Sox prepare for the World Series by allowing Boston to "practice some new plays and new signals." This loyalty to the league would seem remarkable today, but was reciprocity for the similar assistance that Jimmy McAleer had accorded the Athletics in 1910 and 1911 when he'd managed the Senators. Connie Mack was "in a very genial mood" and prepared to help however he could. "All that the Athletics learned from their series with the Giants last fall [Philadelphia beat the Giants four games to two in the 1911 World Series] they are eager and willing to impart to the Boston team. This noon Connie Mack called Manager Stahl, Captain Wagner and Bill Carrigan into consultation and for half an hour this quartet sat together on the Philadelphia bench while Connie told the Boston players a few of the many points he has gleaned concerning the McGraw outfit."*Globe* sports cartoonist Wallace Goldsmith conjured up some scenes from the workout.

October 3—CHAMPIONS BURY ATHLETICS, 17-5. After four innings it was 3-0 in Philadelphia's favor, but then came the fifth. Carl Brown walked Jake Stahl, who was doubled home by Hick Cady. Then Brown walked four batters in a row and surrendered a grand slam to Duffy Lewis. It wasn't exactly the hard-fought contest the Sox were looking for to put them in tip-top shape. Neither team played all that well, "the worst-looking game played in Philadelphia this season." The Sox scored in every inning after the fifth, though, so they got some hitting in. Tris Speaker learned he had won the Chalmers award (a complimentary automobile) as the most valuable player in the American League. Second-baseman Larry Doyle of the Giants won the Chalmers for the NL. Mathewson and Marquard of the Giants sat in the stands and took mental notes on the Red Sox batters.

October 4—CHAMPIONS LOSE PRACTICE GAME. A loss can be as good as a win, when preparing in the springtime or getting ready for the fall classic. Losing brings about a bit of humility, and offers other lessons of its own. A close 4-3 loss can be salutary. Happily, Larry Gardner was back with the team, working out before the game. He was ready to play and so was Bill Carrigan, who'd also been hurt and missed considerable time, and who proved he could throw from behind the plate, cutting down four of the five Philadelphia runners who tried to steal second (and give Carrigan the practice).

The Royal Rooters were prepared to trot out *Tessie* once again, as they planned to parade from 44th Street to the Polo Grounds for Game One of the World Series. Of the song, one

YES, THE RED SOX ARE GOING TO SCHOOL AGAIN AT PHILADELPHIA
Wallace Goldsmith *Boston Globe* October 2, 1912

Philadelphia Athletics manager Connie "The Teacher" Mack provides advice to Boston's Jake Stahl, Heinie Wagner, and Bill Carrigan in preparation for the 1912 World Series against the New York Giants.

Rooter said, "It has won one world's championship for us and it is going to win another." The *Boston American* announced that demand for the 8,000 seats at the Boston Arena was so strong that the facility would be "taxed to the utmost." There was a special "ladies' section" set aside, the Naval Brigade Band had been hired, and "five baseball song leaders will help entertain the crowds." White Sox captain Harry Lord picked the Red Sox to win in a column he authored for the *American*.

October 5—SHOW REAL CLASS IN SEASON WINDUP. Mack had both Bender and Coombs pitch, to give the Sox some work against two experienced aces. The score was 3-0, Buck O'Brien holding Philly to six hits while Boston scored one run each in the sixth, eighth, and ninth. It was "one of the grandest fielding contests of the year" with error-free ball from both teams. Gardner played in the game, 2-for-4 with a double, and went all out in the field, even somersaulting over the concrete wall to haul in a foul fly in left field. The Red Sox had finished the season 105-47. Washington wound up 14 games behind, in second place, and Philadelphia was 15 games behind, in third. Joe Wood led the majors with his 34 wins and 10 shutouts, but Walter Johnson's 1.39 ERA easily beat Wood's 1.91 mark. On offense, Speaker's .464 on-base percentage and his 53 doubles led all AL batters. His 10 homers tied him with Home Run Baker for the league lead. In no other key pitching or offensive category did Red Sox players rank first. It could well be said that winning 105 games was a true team effort.

October 6—In the competition to secure name columnists to comment on the games, the *Boston Post* announced it had signed exclusives with Cy Young, Ty Cobb, Giants manager John McGraw, and Boston team captain Heinie Wagner. Each would contribute his thoughts daily throughout the World Series. The October 6 *Post* offered profiles of each key player on both teams.

October 7—The team traveled through New York and back to Boston for a workout at Fenway Park by way of a final tuneup before heading to Manhattan to take on McGraw, Mathewson, and the Giants. Connie Mack proclaimed, "The Boston club is the greatest team I have ever seen, and I do not except my own club of last year or the great Chicago team either. It is the best balanced outfit I have ever seen work and their gameness and class have made them the undisputed champions of the American League. I do not believe that the Giants will give them much trouble." Christy Mathewson felt otherwise, as one would expect. Acknowledging that all the dope favored the Red Sox, he pointed out that past performance doesn't count for too much when it comes to baseball. Many of Boston's ballplayers had never appeared in a World Series before. Any team anointed the favorite is at a bit of a psychological disadvantage. The Giants were the underdogs, he said, and they were determined to win. Of the Sox, Eddie Collins countered, "There never was a team so well prepared for a world's series or so confident of victory."

Despite the Giants' refusal to meet the Red Sox after the 1904 season, 1912 wasn't the first time the two teams had met in postseason competition. They had squared off three Octobers earlier, in 1909, in five exhibition games. The Giants won the first one, then the Red Sox took four in a row. The 1909 scores:

October 8 at New York: Giants 4, Red Sox 2
October 9 at New York: Red Sox 9, Giants 5
October 12 at Boston: Red Sox 5, Giants 4
October 13 at Boston: Red Sox 2, Giants 0
October 14 at Boston: Red Sox 5, Giants 4

There was a considerable overlap between the 1909 and 1912 teams in both camps. A majority of the 1912 Giants had also been on the 1909 team. A third of the Red Sox played for both teams, too. Hooper hit .500 (10-for-20) in the 1909 exhibition series while Speaker topped even that, going 12-for-20 (.600, with his ninth-inning home run winning the only game—the October 12 contest—in which he had just one hit).

Opening Fenway Park with Style: The World Champion 1912 Boston Red Sox

The 1912 team was as different as night and day from the fifth-place 1911 Red Sox, who finished 24 games behind Philadelphia.

Now Smoky Joe Wood was pretty good in 1911—who's going to complain about a 23-17 (2.02 ERA) pitcher on a break-even (78-75) ballclub? But in 1912, he put up colossal numbers: 34-5 with a 1.19 earned-run average. In 1911, Eddie Cicotte (11), Ray Collins (11), and Larry Pape (10) each reached double digits in the wins column, but both Cicotte and Collins had more losses than wins. The 1911 outfield had three .300 hitters in Duffy Lewis (.307 with 86 RBIs), Tris Speaker (.334 with 70 RBIs), and Harry Hooper (.311 with 45 RBIs). Not one starting position player hit below .257. The Red Sox scored 680 runs while allowing only 643, but still won only 51 percent of their games.

In 1912 Speaker batted .383. Lewis drove in 109 runs. Third baseman Larry Gardner jumped from 44 runs batted in to 86. Jake Stahl came back to baseball after a year off running a bank in Chicago to deposit a .301 average and cash in 60 RBIs. Heinie Wagner went from 38 RBIs to 68. Almost everyone blossomed on offense.

The real change was on the mound. In 1912 the team boasted two 20-game winners (as well as the 34-game-winning Wood), both of them rookies: Buck O'Brien (20-13, 2.58 ERA), who'd gotten his feet wet in 1911, and the 22-year-old Hugh Bedient (20-9, 2.92 ERA). Collins was 13-8 and Charlie Hall was 15-8. The pitching and defense allowed 544 runs while the offense scored 799, and they won what still remains a franchise-high 105 games against just 47 losses.

The Red Sox were also playing in a new home ballpark, Fenway Park, and apparently felt right at home; they won 74 percent of their decisions at Fenway. The Sox were under new ownership—former player and manager James McAleer—and he'd installed Jake Stahl as manager (and first baseman) of the 1912 team. Stahl was, interestingly, a player on the 1903 championship team—the only man to play for both the 1903 and 1912 world champions.

Needless to say, it all made a big difference. The Red Sox finished 14 games ahead of second-place Washington, a 27-game swing for the Sox from the year before. They were ready to take on the New York Giants, at the Polo Grounds, on October 8. The Giants had won handily, too, 10 games ahead of the Pirates.

On September 25, McAleer called "heads" and lost the coin toss to determine where the Series would open. The Red Sox wanted to begin the very day after the regular season ended, which would be October 7. New York wanted to start on October 8. McAleer called "heads" again, but tails came up a second time. The two clubs agreed on a system used in both 1906 and 1911, under which they would alternate home fields until the Series was won. This meant that after the game on October 8, both teams had to travel to Boston for Game Two, then would board trains back to New York for Game Three, and so forth. The same shifting from city to city was used again in 1913, between New York and Philadelphia.

1912 World Series
Boston Red Sox 4, New York Giants 3
(with one tie game)

The Polo Grounds—The Polo Grounds is actually the story of several stadiums. The final three were located beneath Coogan's Bluff in upper Manhattan, including the one in this 1912 image taken just prior to the Series opener.

The 1912 World Series opened in New York with the first game played at the famed Polo Grounds. Fans from both New York and Boston packed the park, excited for the games to get underway. The two teams came onto the field, a number of dignitaries did as well, the two starting pitchers posed shaking hands before the game, and then the umpires and managers gathered at home plate. The Series was about to get underway.

Rooters Road Trip—Boston's Rooters left Beantown by train the afternoon of October 7, destined for Game One of the 1912 World Series at the Polo Grounds in New York the following day. They announced their presence upon their arrival in New York, parading in the street with their band and displaying their Boston Rooter banners. The Rooter fandom captured in the image above seemed anxious, excited, and ready to cheer the Sox in the first game in a section dedicated to the guest "Boston Delegation."

Opening Fenway Park with Style: The World Champion 1912 Boston Red Sox

The A.L. champion Red Sox coming onto the field before Game One of the World Series.

The N. L. champion Giants on the field prior to the first game of the 1912 World Series.

Boston Mayor (and Royal Rooter) John Francis Fitzgerald tips his derby acknowledging the fans at the Polo Grounds in New York during the 1912 World Series. Being escorted towards the infield are: Captain Hill; Eugene Noble Foss, Governor of Massachusetts; New York City Mayor William Jay Gaynor; and Fitzgerald.

John McGraw of the New York Giants greets visiting manager Jake Stahl. A Hall of Fame member, McGraw managed in the majors for 33 years, winning ten pennants and three World Series titles.

New York Giants manager John McGraw (back to camera) and Boston's skipper Jake Stahl meet with the umpiring crew before Game One of the 1912 World Series. The umpires for the Series opener were Bill Klem behind the plate, Billy Evans at first, Cy Rigler at second, and Silk O'Loughlin at third base.

The Games

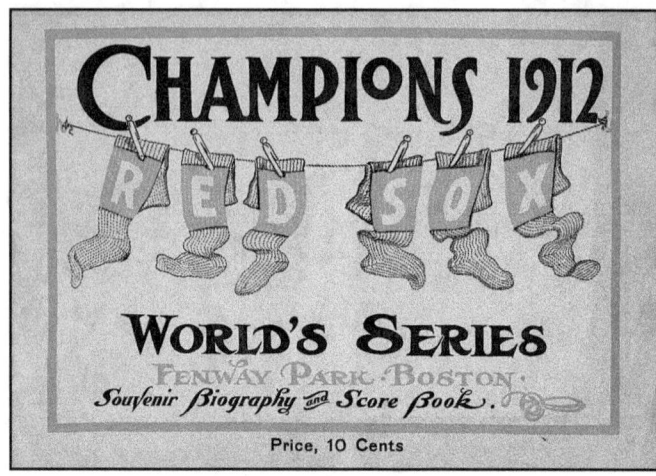

Game One: Polo Grounds, New York / October 8, 1912

Boston 4, New York 3

Boston	000 001 300—4 6 1
New York	002 000 001—3 8 1

WP: Wood (1-0)
LP: Tesreau (0-1)

The Polo Grounds was home to several baseball teams, most notably the New York Giants until the team moved to San Francisco following the 1957 season. Its horseshoe-shaped grandstand and elongated playing area provided for ridiculously short distances down the foul lines and equally ridiculous long distances to the power alleys and center field. So short were its foul-line distances that inches were sometimes included in the measurements—279 feet, 8 inches to left and 257 feet, 8 inches to right. As for the distance to center (nearly 500 feet), the figure almost could have been rounded to the nearest hundred. The facility was rebuilt in 1911 after a fire, and described by Allan Sangree of *Baseball Magazine* as "the mightiest temple ever erected to the goddess of sport and the crowning achievement among notable structures devoted to baseball."

Though the Red Sox had won 105 games, the Giants weren't going to be pushovers. They'd won 103 themselves. They had driven in more runs, hit for a higher average, scored more runs, and in Christy Mathewson and Rube Marquard had a couple of 20-game winners of their own. McGraw was still the manager for the New Yorkers, as he had been back in 1904. Joshua Pahigian writes, "Red Sox fans still remembered how McGraw had dodged the Boston Americans in 1904 and they believed the Giants manager had deprived them of a world championship that had been rightfully theirs." At least among the fans, there was a bit of a reckoning at stake.

Game One featured the Giants' stingiest pitcher, Jeff Tesreau—his 1.96 earned-run average led the National

Smoky Joe Wood and Giants rookie spitballer Jeff Tesreau meet before their World Series opener matchup.

Opening Fenway Park with Style: The World Champion 1912 Boston Red Sox

New York fans arrived early and enthused, but left disappointed as the Giants lost the opener, 4-3.

League and helped him post a 17-7 record, though the rookie spitballer was "the algebraic X" in the words of the *Los Angeles Times*, an unknown quantity. The Red Sox started Smoky Joe. If Tesreau was stingy, Wood was equally miserly with his ERA of 1.91 and an astonishing 34 victories in 38 starts with—perhaps not surprisingly, in light of the ERA—10 shutouts among them.

Facing the best the National League had to offer, Wood didn't shut down the Giants' offense for long. They put the first two runs on the board after two outs in the bottom of the third, when right fielder Red Murray, New York's leading RBI man (92 for the season) singled in Josh Devore and Larry Doyle with a shot into center field. Murray was cut down trying to make it to second base on the play. Tesreau, who had been a trifle shaky the first three frames, seemed to settle down after going up 2-0.

For 5 innings, the Red Sox hit only two balls out of the infield—both easy fly balls. Tesreau had a no-hitter going until Speaker tripled in the top of the sixth. The ball "shot through the racing [Fred] Snodgrass's outstretched hands and rolled to the fence." (*New York Times*) Duffy Lewis grounded out to second base; Doyle's only play was to first base and Speaker scored.

In the top of the seventh, the Red Sox struck—and maybe got a break. After Jake Stahl grounded out, Heinie Wagner singled to center, and so did Hick Cady. With runners on first and second, Wood grounded to second base but only the middle runner was retired. And therein lay the break. Christy Mathewson, in a ghostwritten syndicated column, said it was a ready-made double-play ball to Doyle at second, but "it took a jump away from him and to his right. He was lucky to knock it down and very lucky to get Cady." The Giants narrowly missed getting out of the inning without a run coming across. Behind in the count 0-2, Harry Hooper hit a "fierce smash" (Hugh Fullerton, writing in the *New York Times*) of a double over the first-base bag and easily drove in Wagner; Wood held up at third base. With two men in scoring position, Sox second baseman Steve Yerkes brought them both home with a single to left field. Speaker struck out, but the Sox had added three runs and taken a 4-2 lead.

The *New York Times* termed Snodgrass's sixth-inning play a "blunder" in that Devore was closer to the ball but Snodgrass called him off. Giants manager McGraw agreed, ripping Snodgrass in print in his own newspaper column. He wrote that Snodgrass "turned what should have been a sure out into a three-base hit." McGraw couldn't have been angling for friends among his men. McGraw also took Meyers to task for failing to catch a foul popup and giving Hooper fresh life in the seventh.

With one on and two outs in the bottom of the seventh, Tesreau was taken out for pinch-hitter Moose McCormick, who got hold of one but flied out to left field. Doc Crandall relieved Tesreau and retired the Red Sox in the eighth and ninth, giving up only a double to Wagner.

Wood kept the ball in the infield in the eighth with two grounders to shortstop and a popup to Gardner at third, but faltered in the ninth. Fred Merkle swung at the first pitch and hit a one-out single to left, and Buck Herzog singled the other way—to right. Hooper may have failed to fully track it in the late-afternoon shadows. The third single in a row, by catcher Chief Meyers, scored Merkle. Herzog took third and Meyers took second on the futile throw to Cady at home plate. Herzog might well have scored save for Hooper's fielding the ball barehanded and firing it home in time to hold Herzog on third base. With runners on second and third and just one out, the game hung in the balance. Joe Wood had been smoked for three consecutive singles, but now Wood buckled down and struck out both shortstop Art Fletcher and the pitcher Crandall (a good-hitting pitcher, he'd batted .313 during the 1912 regular season and had 19 runs batted in).

Like McGraw and Mathewson, Wood, Speaker, and Tesreau all had bylined newspaper columns. Wood admitted he'd feared Fletcher would try to squeeze home Herzog from third in the ninth. He called Crandall a "hitting pitcher" and said, "No one can safely take chances with him." Crandall worked the count to 3 and 2. Then, Wood wrote, "I saw that Crandall was standing well away from the plate, and so I put one over the outside corner, which he missed." Strike three. Game over. Red Sox 4, Giants 3. Wood had struck out 11, eight of them looking.

Wood, Mathewson wrote, showed he was under considerable strain in the ninth and "pitching on nerve alone." Mathewson said the Giants were not discouraged. He felt the Sox had showed a certain lack of aggressiveness and "I don't think that we will have so much to fear from now on." He didn't anticipate that this best-of-seven Series was going to go eight games.

Opening Fenway Park with Style: The World Champion 1912 Boston Red Sox

A Red Sox team photo taken in front of the Fenway Park dugout just prior to the 1912 World Series. Top row (left to right): Joseph Quirk (trainer), Tris Speaker, Zoe Wood (Joe's six-year old sister), Joe Wood, Hick Cady, Pinch Thomas, Buck O'Brien, Hugh Bradley, Duffy Lewis. Middle row: Harry Hooper, Bill Carrigan, Steve Yerkes, Olaf Henriksen, Clyde Engle, Les Nunamaker, Charley Hall, Larry Gardner, Ray Collins, Jake Stahl. Front row: Heinie Wagner, Hugh Bedient, Jerry McCarthy (mascot/bat-boy), Larry Pape, Marty Krug.

STOOD IN LINE ALL NIGHT—
Fenway Park before Game Two

There were no lotteries for tickets to World Series games, no virtual waiting rooms for the opportunity to buy a ticket to the games. As was true through the 1980s, if you wanted to be sure to gain a ticket to the game, your best chance was to get in line outside the ticket office. The earlier you got there, the better your shot at tickets. Even 100 years later, this is still the way to try and secure a day-of-game ticket to a game. The last time Fenway offered large numbers of tickets to the general public in this fashion was the first year that Green Monster Seats went on sale. In 2003, fans lined up beginning around 4:00 to get the standing room tickets.

In 1912, the *Boston Globe* offered a glimpse at the scene:

ABOUT THOSE TICKETS.
By WALLACE GOLDSMITH.

When dawn broke today an unusual spectacle was disclosed at the corner of Ipswich st and Auto rd in the Back Bay Fens, where 1000 to 1500 men waited in orderly lines leading to the bleacher gates of Fenway Baseball Park, all eager to purchase seats for the second great battle in the World Series between the Red Sox and the Giants, to determine the National baseball championship.

It was a spectacle such as is rarely seen in this city. Hundreds of men and boys were there, who had shivered throughout the dark, cold night, solely that they might retain places in the lines which assured them of the coveted privilege of purchasing tickets at the opening of the box offices today for seats in the unreserved stands for the great game.

Then there were the inevitable ticket speculators, who are always on hand at such occasions, seeking a change to make a few dollars. They had places in the lines as early as 9 last night, and every man who approached them today was asked by these eager fellows if he wanted to buy a place in the line. Very few bought them when they heard the prices. These fellows were asking as high as $15 for their places this morning which would make the cost of a place on the bleachers as high as $16 for the one game of today.

Some came prepared for their long wait. They had devised ingenious methods of passing their time comfortably. They had camp stools, soap boxes, wooden horses and other things to seat themselves upon during the long wait. Some had nailed pieces of small board across the top of a short stick and were utilizing these as seats. Many had attendants with them who did their bidding, such as running errors to procure cigars, eatables and wraps when the night air was biting.

From midnight to daybreak it was very cold and some of the fans who were against the fence built fires with newspapers and old boxes. They greatly enjoyed the heat from the flames and were moved to song and laughter. While they seemed mad over baseball and the World Series, they were very rational about everything else, and were orderly and happy. They sang "Tenting Tonight on the Old Camp Ground," "Tessie," and "Sweet Adeline". When Kelly, a well-known young business man arrived on the scene, they sang the song "Kelly".

At 7 this morning there were eight lines reaching from the doors leading to the eight ticket booths back of them far out into the streets and around the fence enclosing the grounds. Nestling against the great doors to the entrance to the ticket selling room were lads who had been there since 9 last night, when they came and secured the first places in the lines. They were the only subdued and quiet ones of the great host of baseball fans. This was because they were hoarse from shouting during the early hours of the waiting, and because they were chilled through and hungry and sleepy.

Some of the youngsters played harmonicas, others sang and danced to the music, and the policemen laughed and were happy. The policemen were evidently there for appearances sake and to keep the throng company, for there was no occasion for them to act officially at any time in the long night.

Opening Fenway Park with Style: The World Champion 1912 Boston Red Sox

NOT A PANIC IN STATE STREET JUST MR AVERAGE FAN TRYING TO GET NEXT TO A COUPLE OF TICKETS

Sergt Mason and patrolmen John Smith and Lindsey Morrison were about during the first hours of the long vigil, and shortly after 1 this morning Sergt Kneeland and a big squad of patrolmen came and stood about, chatting with the fans.

About 4 this morning Capt Thomas Good, with two sergeants and a big squad of patrolmen arrived. By then the host of waiting fans had become so great that it was necessary to line them up strictly and closely and in a manner not calculated to block traffic on the streets leading to the park.

Lunches were being served all through the morning, but the fashionable breakfast hour was between 7 and 8 a.m. when the fellows who had remained away from their own breakfast tables began to feel the pangs of hunger. One enterprising lad carried about a basket filled with home-made sandwiches, which he quickly disposed of. The purchasers devoured them ravenously. He also carried a 10-quart can filled with milk and a basket filled with individual drinking mugs. He peddled the milk and sold out quickly and then went and got more.

Some of the youngsters in the lines, even, had seen the game in New York yesterday, and had come to Boston, arriving at 2 this morning, and had gone straight to the waiting lines, taken places and remained there without sleep or rest, so that they might see the game today.

There were four business men from a far away city in Maine, who arrived in Boston late last night and went straight to the baseball park and took their places in the line, where they remained until the gates opened. They ate sandwiches, drank coffee and smoked strong cigars constantly, and were wide awak and full of enthusiasm at 8 o'clock this morning. They were so loyal that they could not refrain from leading the cheering every time the name of "Smoky Joe" Wood or any other of the Red Sox aggregation was mentioned.

The first to arrive last night were two lads from Roxbury—James Lehan and Frank Riley. Lehan lives at 44 Field st and Riley at 117 Cabot st. They huddled in the doorway at the bleacher entrance at 8 p.m. At 9 p.m. an automobile rolled up to the door and out jumped a man of evidently easy circumstances, followed by three messenger boys. The messengers were Joseph Camp, Joseph Barrett, and James Mede., and they took their places at the head of the second line opposite to the Lehan and Riley lads. They were not long alone, for soon others came straggling along and took places behind them in the two lines.

October 9, 1912 *Boston Globe*

Ticket prices

How much did World Series tickets at Fenway cost in 1912? They ranged from 50 cents apiece in the center-field bleachers to $5.00 per ticket in the box seats. Regular patrons could purchase three-day reserved-seat tickets for $9.00 or $6.00 each—these bought you a ticket for three games (money refunded if only two were played) at $3.00 for seats in the steel and concrete grandstand or $2.00 for seats in the new covered seating constructed along the third-base line.

Game Two: Fenway Park, Boston / October 9, 1912

Boston 6, New York 6 (tie, 11 innings)

New York   010 100 030 10—6 11 5
Boston   300 010 010 10—6 10 1

No winning pitcher and no losing pitcher.

There was strong suspicion that by starting Tesreau against Boston's best pitcher, Wood, Giants manager John McGraw may have partially conceded Game One so that he could throw his two big guns (Christy Mathewson and Rube Marquard) against two supposedly lesser Red Sox pitchers (Ray Collins and Buck O'Brien) and thus gain a two-games-to-one edge. The Series had, after just one game, reverted to Boston without a day off in accord with the questionable plan of alternating cities until the Series was completed.

Collins, in the fourth of seven seasons he pitched for the Red Sox, was ready to go. He was the only left-hander on the staff. It was his only Series start, despite a good 13-8 (2.53 ERA) regular season record.

Though Snodgrass doubled into the temporary stands in left to lead off the game, Collins retired the next three men, leaving Snodgrass on third. Boston benefited from three quick runs in the bottom of the first. Hooper singled, the ball glancing off Mathewson's glove, then stole second off him. Shortstop Fletcher's error let Hooper reach third with Yerkes on first. Speaker bunted for a base hit and loaded the bases, as Hooper held. Duffy Lewis hit the ball to Herzog at third, who threw home to cut down Hooper; the two other runners moved up. Gardner grounded out back to the mound, but again the ball ticked off Matty's outstretched glove. It caromed to Doyle at second, whose only play was at first, and Yerkes came in the back door with the first run. Jake Stahl singled past third base and drove in two more before Wagner popped out to end the inning. 3-0, Red Sox.

Herzog tripled to the right-field barrier and Meyers singled when the ball bounced up freakishly and glanced off Gardner's face, and the Giants put a run on the board in the top of the second. They added another in the fourth on Red Murray's leadoff triple and, two batters later, Herzog's sacrifice fly to Speaker in center. The Red Sox scored once more in the bottom of the fifth. After Collins struck out,

Ray Collins on the mound for the Sox in Game Two at Fenway Park. This photograph was taken by Genevieve Collins Finney, who frequently traveled to Boston with her husband Dr. Frank Finney from their home in upper New York to watch her brother Ray pitch.

Hooper singled to center field (his third hit of the game). The sun was giving Murray trouble in right field so McGraw had Murray and left-fielder Snodgrass switch defensive positions. Meyers threw out Hooper stealing second—but Fletcher dropped the ball, and Harry was safe. Yerkes tripled to center field, scoring Hooper, but Speaker failed to cash in, lining into a shortstop-to-third base double play.

In the top of the eighth, the Giants took a 5-4 lead. Duffy Lewis made the only error of the game for Boston, and Snodgrass reached first. When Doyle singled to Speaker, Snodgrass moved up one base. He took third when center fielder Beals Becker's grounder forced Doyle at second. With runners on first and third, Murray doubled and drove in Snodgrass. Manager Stahl reacted

Parading along the outfield fencing at Fenway Park to their seats in left field are Boston's Royal Rooters led by Michael T. "Nuf Ced" McGreevey. The Boston Lodge of Elks Band leads the tunes with chants with the likes of "Tessie" and the 1912 "Oh, You Red Sox".

Ray Collins pitched effectively through seven frames but was responsible for three runs in the eighth. He pitched 7 1/3 innings, giving up three earned runs with five strikeouts and no walks. Ray later pitched seven shutout innings of relief in Game Six, finishing the 1912 World Series with a 1.88 ERA. This Harris & Ewing, Inc. photograph shows Ray warming up on the sidelines the following season.

After the first inning, the Fenway Park scoreboard shows Boston with 3-0 lead.

quickly and brought in Sea Lion Hall to pitch to Merkle. Merkle fouled out to catcher Carrigan. Herzog doubled and drove in Becker and Murray, before Hall got Meyers to ground out.

The slim New York lead didn't last long, though at first it looked as though Mathewson would escape without trouble as he retired both Yerkes and Speaker. Lewis hit one off the right-field bleacher fence for two bases, though, and scored from second when Fletcher fumbled Gardner's ball. Then Stahl reached on Doyle's error and stole second, but Wagner whiffed. The errors were the third and fourth miscues committed by Giants fielders. Fletcher had three all by himself. The game was tied, 5-5.

Though Hall walked the bases loaded with two outs in the top of the ninth, Murray hit into a force play. Mathewson set down the Red Sox 1-2-3 without letting the ball leave the infield.

Leadoff triples are never good for the team in the field, and when Merkle hit a three-bagger to start the 10th, Boston fans held their breath. Herzog grounded out, Wagner looking Merkle back to third base before throwing to first for the initial out. Meyers was walked intentionally, and McGraw inserted the speedier Tillie Shafer to run for the Chief. He then brought in Moose McCormick to bat for Fletcher. As in the first game, Moose flied out to left—but this time it was a successful sacrifice fly that scored Merkle. Mathewson, still in the game, popped up to second.

Yerkes grounded out in the bottom of the 10th. But Tris Speaker tripled to the fence in center field and scored on the play as the relay was fumbled momentarily by substitute shortstop Shafer. As Speaker ran for the plate, Shafer recovered and threw in time to catcher Art Wilson, who had just entered the game. But Wilson dropped the ball. The score was tied again, on yet another New York error. Mathewson hadn't walked a batter; he had given up six runs, but not one of them was an earned run. Nonetheless, it was a whole new ballgame. Though Duffy Lewis doubled, Mathewson bore down and got two groundballs to close out the 10th. Had Speaker not scored, as Hugh Fullerton pointed out, it might well have led to scandal since he was interfered with

Boston Globe

three times while running the bases—incredibly, not one of them called by an umpire.

Hugh Bedient came on in relief of Hall—and hit the first batter, Snodgrass. But Carrigan promptly cut him down on an attempted steal. After Doyle was called out on strikes, Becker walked, and Carrigan did it once again—threw out the man trying to steal. Carrigan had thrown out three men in the game, a tight contest the *Globe* described as "desperately fought."

Matty induced three groundballs, fielding the third of them himself. It was 6-6 after 11, but at that juncture the game was called on account of darkness. The Giants had used their marquee moundsman, but the five Giants errors had deprived him of a win. Mathewson's loss and the poor fielding by the Giants encouraged the Red Sox.

This was one of only three World Series games to end in a tie (the others were Game One of the 1907 Series and Game Two in 1922, Giants against the Yankees.) Because the game ended in a tie and the hour was late, both teams stayed in Boston to play Game Three before resuming the back-and-forth travel between cities.

Fans approaching Fenway Park on Jersey Street (now Yawkey Way) for Game Three of the World Series.

Game Three: Fenway Park, Boston / October 10, 1912

New York 2, Boston 1

```
New York    010 010 000—2 7 1
Boston      000 000 001—1 7 0
```

WP: Marquard (1-0)
LP: O'Brien (0-1)

Rube Marquard (26-11) faced Buck O'Brien (20-13) in Game Three. Both pitched exceptionally well. Marquard had started off the 1912 season like gangbusters. He won every one of his first 19 decisions from Opening Day on April 11 through July 3. And he truly should have been credited with a 20th win, on April 20. He entered the game in relief and, after he put out the fire in the top of the ninth, the Giants scored twice to win the game in the bottom of the ninth, but the scorer did not credit Rube with the victory. Joe Wood had run off a string of 16 straight victories in 1912, too, but today Rube would be matched against O'Brien for Boston.

Josh Devore hit a leadoff single just over O'Brien's glove, was almost picked off first, and was shortly cut down stealing. Marquard kept the ball in the infield and retired the first three Boston batters.

O'Brien was touched for another leadoff hit in the second, this time a double to center by Red Murray. Merkle sacrificed Murray to third, and Herzog hit a fly ball to Hooper that got him home. Meyers grounded out to third and it was one run for the Giants.

Duffy Lewis singled in the second and Tris Speaker managed another base hit in the fourth, but that was all the Sox could get off Marquard through the first four. The Giants added one more run in the top of the fifth. It was another leadoff hit, another double, that set up the run when Buck Herzog hit the ball over the third-base bag. Meyers tried to hit away, but produced an inadvertent sacrifice, bouncing back to O'Brien—who had to throw to first as Herzog took third. Art Fletcher slammed a single—his first hit of the Series—and Herzog came home. There was considerably more action, but just the one run came in. O'Brien was fortunate to have given up only two runs in the game, though the three walks and seven hits don't look that bad in the boxscore.

Stahl singled in the fifth, Yerkes singled in the sixth, and Stahl doubled in the seventh—only the second Red Sox runner to reach second base—but the Red Sox were held scoreless through eight. Stahl's ball had nearly gone out; it hit off the top of the wall and bounced back into play.

Hugh Bedient pitched the top of the ninth for Boston, O'Brien having been pinch-hit for by Neal Ball in the eighth (Ball struck out). Bedient hit the first batter, Herzog, but he was thrown out trying to steal second a minute or two later. Meyers singled, but Fletcher flied into a double play, Meyers being doubled off the first-base bag. The score still stood 2-0, Giants.

Speaker popped out in the bottom of the ninth, but Lewis singled to Merkle at first base (Marquard failed to cover the bag in time) and Larry Gardner doubled down the first-base line, scoring Lewis. On the play, a coaching mixup hurt the Sox. Heinie Wagner was coaching third, but since he was due up after Stahl, Speaker had moved over to third base to relieve him. Unfortunately, Gardner saw both Wagner and Speaker first hold up Lewis and then yell at him to score; Gardner had to hold up at second when he could well have taken third. Stahl hit back to the mound, and Marquard threw to third to cut down Gardner for the second out. Speaker wrote that he thought Gardner was nonetheless safe,

In a pregame ceremony, around 2 PM, "a pretty automobile came rolling in at the gate between the stands, with Hugh Chalmers and Ren Mulford Jr in it, for the presentation without which no World's Series game thus far has been complete. Larry Doyle got his on Tuesday;... this one was for Speaker, as the player who has done the most individually for his team in the whole American League this season. Speaker jumped into his car, and taking Larry Doyle as a passenger drove the car himself all the way round the field. A great roar of cheering ran along the crowd ahead of him as he went, its crest showing in the wildly vibrating hats and flags." (*Boston Globe*)

believing that Herzog had dropped the ball. Olaf Henriksen came in to pinch-run for Stahl at first base. Wagner hit a ball that Merkle misplayed, dropping the ball, and sending Henriksen to third—and it was first and third, two outs. Wagner stole second, putting both the tying and winning runs in scoring position. Then came the play of the game. Forrest "Hick" Cady was at the plate. It was his first time up. Carrigan had been the starting catcher but Hack Engle had batted for Carrigan in the eighth.

Cady hit a long, uncatchable drive to deep right-center field and hundreds of Red Sox fans went home happy, glad that the Sox had won the game. But it was a case of premature exuberance. "The Boston crowd was already celebrating a second victory. … The bands were blaring, the bass drums were rumbling, and the cymbals were crashing. The grandstands were afire with waving red flags," wrote the *New York Times*. The first rush of fans harbored a false confidence and hoped to beat the masses out of the park. Right fielder Josh Devore had sprung into action with one of the greatest catches in World Series history. Tim Murnane wrote of Devore that "while under a full head of steam he leaped in the air, and, with hands extended over his head and his back to the infield, he came out of the air with the ball." There truly were fans who believed the Red Sox had won, only to learn later that the 5-foot-6 "midget outfielder" (*Hartford Courant*) Devore had saved the day for the Giants and evened the Series at one win apiece. Chalk one up for the little guys.

The *Times* suggested that if the remaining games in the Series were anything like the first three, every one a game that went down to the wire, "New York and Boston will fill all the nerve sanitariums with their citizens."

AN EXTRA NOTE: The Red Sox likely benefited from an unusual scouting report. It came from Connie Mack, manager of the Philadelphia Athletics, who had won the pennant the two prior years (and would win it the following two). Jake Stahl asked Mack to brief the Boston players on the Giants, whom the A's had beaten in the 1911 Series. Norman Macht quotes Heinie Wagner as saying, "He told us more in ten minutes than all our scouts discovered watching them for several weeks, or what we could have learned about them in a year. I doubt we would have beaten New York without the knowledge that Mack put into us." [11]

Buck O'Brien gets out of a jam, when Giant centerfielder Fred Snodgrass flied out to left field with the bases loaded and two outs in the 5th inning.

Game Four: Polo Grounds, New York / October 11, 1912

Boston 3, New York 1

Boston   010 100 001—3 8 1
New York   000 000 100—1 9 1

WP: Wood (2-0)
LP: Tesreau (0-2)

It was Wood vs. Tesreau once more, and once more Wood came out on top. Tesreau got off to a shaky start when Hooper singled through the box and Meyers pounced on Yerkes' bunt but threw wildly to second. The threat ended when Speaker hit into a double play and Lewis grounded out. The Giants got a one-out single from Doyle. He was forced at second by Snodgrass's grounder, and then Snodgrass was picked off first to end the inning.

Tesreau started off shakily again in the second frame, surrendering a first-pitch triple to Larry Gardner that went into deep right-center—and then threw a wild pitch by Meyers, allowing Gardner to grab a quick run for the Red Sox. Another hit and a stolen base—but also another missed opportunity—followed for the Giants in the second.

Boston got the first two men aboard in the third (Wood with a single) but three groundballs ended that threat. A routine grounder and two strikeouts made for a quick bottom of the third for New York.

For the fourth inning in a row, the Red Sox got their leadoff man on board, this time Gardner via the base on balls. He was forced when Tesreau handled Stahl's bunt well, but Stahl stole second and then moved to third base when Wagner grounded to Merkle at first base. Cady—the man who had hit the long ball to Devore to end Game Three, squeaked a single past Fletcher into left field to score Jake Stahl. It was the hit that proved the winning run, but there was drama yet to come in Game Four.

The Red Sox bats were pretty much silenced but for a single by Steve Yerkes (a great one-handed catch by Murray robbed Hooper of what looked like a triple), but Tesreau started a threat in the Giants' sixth, lining a single to left field. Devore followed with a single of his own—off Wood's shin—and New York had runners on first and second with nobody out. Doyle, though, swung at the first pitch and popped up to third. Snodgrass grounded to second base and the middle runner was erased, and Red Murray, too, hit into a near carbon copy second-to-short forceout.

Wood was reasonably effective, though the Giants did collect nine hits, six of them after the fifth. He proved best in the pinches and may have had the Giants batters off in their timing; contemporary reports say that as the game progressed he relied much less on his smoking fastball and instead used his curve and change of pace most effectively. More than once in the Series, sportswriters commented on Heinie Wagner's defensive prowess at shortstop. Hugh Fullerton wrote that in this game alone, Wagner "made two of the greatest stops of the season." It was not until the seventh that the Giants put up a run of their own. Herzog singled and Art Fletcher doubled down the right-field line and drove in Herzog. McGraw had McCormick bat for Jeff Tesreau and it looked as though it had paid off when McCormick

Tris Speaker had a solid Series, hitting an even .300.

singled—but Yerkes knocked the ball down, gathered it in, and threw a bullet from second base to Cady at the plate, getting the speedy Fletcher (thrown out by as much as 15 feet) and keeping the Giants from knotting the score. Sending Fletcher home was probably McGraw's biggest mistake of the game, though in his column on October 15 he said he'd do it again in a two-out situation like that.

Red Ames took over pitching for New York and Speaker doubled off the top of the bleacher fence in the top of the eighth, but nothing came of it. The Giants got runners on first and third in the bottom of the inning after Wagner's error and Murray's single through the hole (vacated at short when Wagner moved to cover on the hit-and-run), but Smoky Joe struck out Fred Merkle on three curveballs. The *Globe*'s Tim Murnane observed that though the game was played in New York, the "majority of those present seemed to favor the Boston men."

It was another 2-1 game and Wood was looking for an insurance run in the top of the ninth to give him a little breathing room. Larry Gardner singled sharply to center field, and Stahl sacrificed perfectly to push Gardner to second. Wagner walked, though, setting up a force play, and Cady obliged, grounding out to shortstop to get Wagner at second. Gardner took third, and then Wood took matters into his own hands with a single to the wall in the Polo Grounds' exceptionally short right field. Hooper flied out but it was 3-1 in favor of the visitors.

Wood settled down again on the mound. Herzog flied out to Speaker in center field, but that was the only solidly-hit ball in the bottom of the ninth. Meyers lifted a foul popup to Cady and Fletcher popped up to Stahl at first base. The Red Sox took a 2-1 lead in the Series, and both

teams hopped back on the train to head north to Massachusetts. Neither team had yet won a game at home.

As had happened after Game One, some New York fans showed their displeasure at the defeat. After Game One, the automobiles of the Royal Rooters were "stoned and deluged with dirt by the urchins lined up along the streets and avenues." After Game Four, "it was the automobiles occupied by the players that were bombarded and many of the occupants suffered from dirt being thrown." Fortunately, there were no serious injuries despite "some of the oldest of the hoodlums being particularly good marksmen." Buck O'Brien was hit in the face by a sharp stone that cut the skin. (O'Brien had a rough Series; he would be struck by one of his teammates in the aftermath of Game Six.) The Red Sox complained that New York's finest stood by without intervening.

A close play at second during Game Four action at the Polo Grounds.

Dignitaries and fans alike enjoying the World Series, with a friendly vendor in the background providing sandwiches for 10 cents.

Game Five: Fenway Park, Boston / October 12, 1912

Boston 2, New York 1

```
New York   000 000 100—1 3 1
Boston     002 000 00x—2 5 1
```

WP: Bedient (1-0)
LP: Mathewson (0-1)

It was a dark, damp, foggy, gloomy day and up until noontime, the playing of the game was still in question. Down two games to one, McGraw had his ace Mathewson up his sleeve, if not a sure bet at least even money to tie the Series. There had been only two days off since the 11-inning tie game in which Matty had gone the distance, and there could have been questions raised as to whether the 12-year veteran's career had peaked. Whatever worries might have obtained, Mathewson pitched a great game. It seemed to take him just a while to settle in; he gave up two singles in the first and one in the second, but pitched his way through to two scoreless innings.

The rookie Hugh Bedient was Stahl's selection. Winner of 20 games, the "modest youth" was the fourth starter for Stahl and pitched an even better game than Christy Mathewson. Bedient,

One of the first five players of the inaugural group of inductees into the National Baseball Hall of Fame, New York's Christy Mathewson was 3-0 in the 1905 World Series, and put up a superb 0.94 ERA in 1912, but was charged with eight unearned runs and failed to win a game.

Boston Globe

too, faced a little trouble in the cold weather, walking the leadoff batter in both the first and second innings, each time on four pitches. Bedient issued free passes to three batters in all, and served up a single to Mathewson in the first three frames. Yet no Giant got past second base and Bedient didn't walk a man in the final six innings; he was fairly consistently ahead in the count, throwing a lot of first-pitch strikes. Oddly for the era, never once did either team try to lay down a bunt, nor was there an attempted steal—even though the Red Sox of the day were sometimes known as the "Speed Boys."

Harry Hooper tripled to the left-field corner to lead off the Red Sox third. The ball rolled between the stands of the temporary bleachers and Josh Devore disappeared from sight before coming up with the ball fast enough to hold Hooper to three bases. Steve Yerkes swung at the first pitch and tripled to center field, the ball rolling to the fence to drive in Hooper. Second baseman Larry Doyle went to field Speaker's grounder but, glancing up to assess his chances of holding Yerkes at third, he lost track of the ball just long enough that it ended up in right field. It was the lone error of the game for New York. Yerkes scored the second run, of course, but Speaker was too aggressive in trying to reach second. He was thrown out, Red Murray to shortstop Art Fletcher. Both Lewis and Gardner subsequently grounded out. It was 2-0 for the Red Sox.

Mathewson retired every Red Sox batter he faced for the remainder of the game, setting down 17 in a row. He'd held Boston to but five hits, but the two runs proved one too many.

In the fourth, fifth, and sixth, Bedient was almost as dominant, allowing just one baserunner, Meyers on a leadoff single in the fifth, after he had fouled off six pitches. Fred Merkle hit a ground-rule double to

start the seventh, the ball bouncing into the bleachers. It was only the third hit off Bedient in the game, and it was to be the last. Herzog struck out. Meyers flied deep enough to Speaker in center that Tris had to go back to reel in the ball (Speaker traditionally played a shallow center field, and set a record for unassisted double plays by an outfielder, but fortunately for the Red Sox this time was playing deeper than usual). Merkle was able to tag up and take third. McCormick batted for Fletcher, his fourth pinch-hit appearance of the Series. For the third time, it looked as if he might have made something happen. He reached base on Gardner's error, and Merkle scored. Mathewson, though, grounded out to end the inning. It was now a one-run game.

And was to remain so. Bedient pitched a perfect eighth and ninth, only Merkle's deep fly ball in the ninth escaping the infield. Speaker had to run to haul that one in. The Red Sox starter had thrown a three-hitter, with just one unearned run allowed. Finally, the loyal hometown fans were rewarded by seeing their team win and it was a jubilant throng that left Fenway Park after the one hour, 43 minute game with the Red Sox up three games to one.

After the game, in a column under Doyle's byline, Larry took responsibility for the error that brought in Boston's second run, but blamed Snodgrass for not cutting off Yerkes' ball to center. "He could have at least stopped the ball if he had not fielded it cleanly," Doyle charged. He said he felt badly for Matty, who was pitching with a sore arm but threw a masterful game. Jeff Tesreau in his column echoed something else Doyle confessed: "We had expected to encounter a nervous youngster in Bedient, erratic and inclined to be wild on the slightest provocation, and instead we met a pitcher as cool as ice." Indeed, the Giants tried to provoke the Boston pitcher, with aggressive bench jockeying, but to no avail.

Wood put pen to paper after the game, too, praising Mathewson for not letting a Boston player reach base after the third, but reserving his greater praise for Hugh Bedient, who would have pitched a shutout had not Gardner taken his eye off the ball for a split second in the seventh. Of Bedient, after the first couple of innings, Wood said, "He showed fine nerve all the way through and tightened like a steel trap on the one or two occasions that men got on bases."

It had seemed that Mathewson was the last hope the New Yorkers had and that the Series was now a lead-pipe cinch to be won by Boston.

Red Sox President Jimmy McAleer, who comes across as a crafty businessman in Game Six, was formerly a brilliant defensive outfielder.

Rookie Hugh Bedient relieved in Games Two and Three, threw a three-hitter in Game Five, and the first seven innings of the deciding Game Eight, some 18 innings of work with an 0.50 ERA, more than a run below anyone else on the Red Sox. Others got more accolades, but Bedient delivered the goods.

Pete Brandom, Pete Wood, and Joe Wood in Ness City, Kansas prior to the 1909 season.

Opening Fenway Park with Style: The World Champion 1912 Boston Red Sox

Game Six: Polo Grounds, New York / October 14, 1912

New York 5, Boston 2

Boston   020 001 000—2   7   2
New York   500 000 00x—5   11   2

WP: Marquard (2-0)
LP: O'Brien (0-2)

The sixth game of the Series was the one that produced the most controversy. Fans wanted Stahl to go for the throat by starting Smoky Joe, but word was that owner Jimmy McAleer had ordered Stahl to start Buck O'Brien and save Wood to pitch, if necessary, in Game Seven at Fenway. [Troy Soos, *Before the Curse*, p. 139] It wasn't bad strategy, but with Sunday the 13th as a day off, Wood had had a couple of days' rest and the Sox players smelled blood. They wanted a win, and even though Buck had pitched well enough in Game Two, he'd still lost. And even though he'd won 20 games in the regular season, Wood had won 34.

Glenn Stout and Dick Johnson contend in *Red Sox Century* that McAleer "was a shrewd businessman who knew the value of the gate he and his partners would collect if Wood were to start an additional game at Fenway Park." And victory did seem assured, which may have left the Sox owner "both confident enough and greedy enough to gamble near-certain victory and a world championship for a chance at another lucrative Fenway payday." Stahl argued, but lost the debate, and when the players heard the news their dreams of a quick wrapup to the Series were deflated. Perhaps with a little hyperbole, Stout and Johnson suggest that "by the time they reached the Polo Grounds the Red Sox were already a beaten ballclub." It shouldn't have seemed like such a surprise, though. Murnane predicted in the *Globe* the

Opposing backstops in the 1912 World Series, Bill Carrigan and "Chief" Meyers of the New York Giants spend time together before a game at the Polo Grounds. John Tortes Meyers, a Cahuilla Indian, could not avoid being saddled with the nickname "Chief" playing in this era. He was recognized as one of the best offensive catcher of the Deadball Era, retiring with a .291 average for his nine-year career.

Buck O'Brien, Game Three starter for the Red Sox.

morning of the 13th that "Joe Wood might have gone in tomorrow had the Red Sox lost out yesterday but now the chances are that they will have O'Brien for a starter…keeping a face card back in Joe Wood for the game here on Tuesday, if necessary." Hugh Fullerton's syndicated column also foresaw Wood held in reserve with O'Brien and Collins ready to go. The Associated Press predicted that Collins would start, but agreed that Wood would be held. Several of the players writing columns expected O'Brien or perhaps Collins.

The Red Sox did little in the first and, initially, it looked as though O'Brien would escape unscathed as well. Devore grounded out. Doyle singled, a slow hit to Yerkes, and then stole second, but O'Brien struck out Snodgrass. Murray singled to deep shortstop—another infield hit—but Doyle held at third base. Then O'Brien balked. Doyle was waved home and Murray was sent to second. Did the balk unnerve O'Brien? Stout and Johnson suggest he might have drunk too much the night before, not expecting to be given the ball, though the consensus in the press that he was one of the two likely starters appears to belie that notion. Nevertheless, and all of a sudden, the dike broke. Mathewson in his post-game column talked about how the two coaches were riding O'Brien from the lines. He revealed that McGraw had signaled for a double steal, but the balk rendered that academic. "The balk beat O'Brien," Matty wrote. "He could not come back. He just caved in, and right there our luck changed; we got all of the 'breaks' and, with two out, we gave O'Brien a harder whaling than any other pitcher had received in the Series."

Merkle doubled against the wall in right. Herzog doubled down the third-base line. Meyers singled, yet another infield hit. With runners on first and third, a double steal saw Herzog

Boston field general Jake Stahl approaching third base.

pilfer home with the fourth Giants run while Meyers not only stole second but took third on Yerkes' error. Fletcher bunted, squeezing in Meyers from third base. The inning was finally brought to conclusion when O'Brien picked off Fletcher—but five runs were in.

The Giants never scored again, but they didn't have to, though the Red Sox immediately struck back for two runs in the top of the second.

Marquard fumbled Gardner's grounder. Stahl singled on a shot to center, Gardner taking second. Wagner and Cady both made outs, a strikeout and a foul to the catcher. With O'Brien due up, Stahl took him out and put in Hack Engle, who doubled off the wall in left to drive in both Gardner and Stahl. Hooper popped up. Those were all the runs the Red Sox were to score on this day. The final was 5-2.

Ray Collins took over pitching duties for the Red Sox and pitched very well. He scattered five hits over seven innings; there were two singles in the Giants' third but both hitters erased themselves—Murray by trying to stretch his single to a double, and Merkle, who unsuccessfully tried to steal second.

The Red Sox hit two long drives in the top of the third, but both were caught. Wagner was robbed of a homer by Snodgrass in the fourth; the Sox got a couple of singles, but Collins hit into an inning-ending double play. There were more long balls hit, and a few hard-hit grounders, but the Red Sox got only one hit in the final five innings.

Red Sox Century says Joe Wood's brother Pete, "enraged at losing one hundred dollars on the game, sought out O'Brien and blackened one of the pitcher's eyes in a wild fistfight. Although the incident was widely reported and later denied, the team was clearly in trouble."

With an extra day of rest, though, Smoky Joe had the opportunity to close it out before the home crowd. Tim Murnane reported that the Red Sox left New York "confident that they will win the game tomorrow." The Boston rooters at the game didn't seem the least discouraged; they staged an animated snake dance around the Boston bench and then paraded left to right, back and forth, making for the exits with the band blaring and shouts of "tomorrow we'll show them!"

Tesreau, in his column, said the Sox "had none of the ginger that had characterized them in the other games, and if I am not mistaken, they have shot their bolt." He thought they'd been too eager to wrap it up, and were now "beginning to stagger." That was the theme of McGraw's piece: his article about his Giants in the *New York Times* was headlined "Team Has Struck Its Stride."

Game Seven: Fenway Park, Boston / October 15, 1912

New York 11, Boston 4

New York   610 002 101—11 16 4
Boston   010 000 210— 4 9 3

WP: Tesreau (1-2)
LP: Wood (2-1)
HR: Doyle (1), Gardner (1)

If McAleer had made a bundle betting against his own team in Game Six, he may have lost it all in Game Seven when Smoky Joe failed to deliver. New York had scored five runs in the first inning the day before. Now, facing Boston's best pitcher, they scored six runs before the Red Sox even got up to bat.

Wood may have still been ticked off, or worse, from the events of the day before, and Stout and Johnson claim he even beat O'Brien with a baseball bat before the game. The game was delayed by a bad mistake in seatting. Red Sox management had let others take the seats routinely held for the team's booster club, the Royal Rooters, and the 300-strong troupe paraded into the park only to find their seats filled. This did not set well, and there was a lot of pushing and shoving on the field with five mounted policemen having to push back the team's most loyal fans and causing a delay in the start of the game. The Rooters felt aggrieved and many joined in booing Red Sox management in a demonstration after the game that even featured loud cheers for the New York owners who had reserved a special section for them while at the Polo Grounds. Most boycotted the ballclub the following day. It was no coincidence that about 40 percent of the park was devoid of fans on the 16th, even though it was the final game of the championship.

Wood had to pitch with a number of circumstances stacked against him, not to mention a "high cold wind" that repeatedly sent "clouds of dust over the field" and an arm he said was subpar. But he was 2-0 and Jeff Tesreau was 0-2 against the Red Sox.

The Giants came out hitting. Every one of the first seven New York batters achieved a level of success, and even the eighth and ninth batters contributed in a way. Josh Devore singled on the first pitch, fumbled a bit by Wagner but not enough for an error to be charged. Doyle hit the first pitch he saw for a single to center. Wood inexplicably took a big windup and the two baserunners executed such a clean double steal that Cady didn't even throw. Snodgrass plated them both with a double to right field. Murray bunted Snodgrass from second to third. Merkle singled, scoring Snodgrass and taking second on Lewis's errant throw to the plate. Herzog hit the ball back to Wood, who whirled and got Merkle in a rundown—but Herzog took second while Murray was being chased down. And he scored when Meyers singled. Fletcher got in the act, singling to the right side. Meyers ran to third. The pitcher, Tesreau, hit the ball off his counterpart's hand and reached safely. Meyers scored on the play and Fletcher took third. Tesreau was caught stealing second, in a rundown, but not until Fletcher had scored on the delayed double steal. The Giants had hit aggressively, all this happening on 15 or fewer pitches. New York 6, Boston coming to bat.

Boston batted but didn't succeed at it. Jake Stahl had allowed Wood to complete the first inning but wasn't about to send him out for the second. Charley Hall came in, and some adventures on the basepaths ensued. Hall set the stage by walking Devore who then stole second. He walked Doyle, too, and it was getting interesting again, but Hall picked off Devore. Snodgrass singled and Doyle stopped at second. He was apparently picked off second, too—but Hall committed an error and Doyle rounded third and scored. Finally, Hall got the last two batters. 7-0, Giants.

The *New York Times* concluded after the game that Wood had needed at least one more day's rest "after his nerve-wracking games of last week. He is not tireless like Walter Johnson or 'Ed' Walsh. He needed a good rest, he didn't get it, and he cracked."

Larry Gardner bounced a home run over the center-field fence in the bottom of the second (such bounces into the stands in fair territory counted for home runs in those days) to help make the Red Sox feel just a little bit better. The next three batters were put down easily, though.

The Giants extended their lead with two more runs in the top of the sixth when Devore walked and Doyle added a bounce home run.

Tesreau drove in another run in the seventh, singling in Meyers.

Speaker singled after the seventh-inning stretch, and Lewis doubled. Speaker scored on Gardner's grounder to short. Larry Doyle misplayed Stahl's ball and Lewis scored. All told,

Upset Rooters. When the Boston Royal Rooters parade arrived at Fenway Park just prior to the Game Seven, they were astounded to see their destined regular bleacher seats along Duffy's Cliff in left field already occupied. A tussle resulted in mounted police called to defuse the disturbance. The Rooters eventually settled in an alternate and very crowded standing room section. The Rooters' frustration and organized protest carried over into a bit of a boycott the next day, resulting in only 17,034 in attendance for the deciding game.

BOSTON "RED SOX," Champions of the American League																
	1	2	3	4	5	6	7	8	9	10	11	R	H	O	A	E
1. HOOPER, R. F.																
2. YERKES, 2nd B.																
3. SPEAKER, C. F.																
4. LEWIS, L. F.																
5. GARDNER, 3rd B.																
6. STAHL, 1st B.																
7. WAGNER, S. S.																
8. CADY, C.; 9. CARRIGAN, C.; 11. THOMAS, C.; 12. NUNAMAKER, C.																
14. WOOD, P.; 15. HALL, P.; 16. O'BRIEN, P.; 17. COLLINS, P.; 18. BEDIENT, P.; 22. PAPE, P.																
Total	0/0	1/1	0/1	0/1	0/1	0/1	0/2	2/3	1/4							

(Look for number on score board for pitcher and catcher)

23. BALL, Inf.; 31. ENGLE, Inf.; 49. KRUG, Inf. 51. BRADLEY, Inf.; 61. HENRIKSEN, O. F.
UMPIRES—(1) RIGLER and (2) KLEM, National League. (3) EVANS and (4) O'LOUGHLIN, American League.

BATTING FOR FOUR HUNDRED FOR THIRTY YEARS

CUSHING PROCESS

TWO STORES

166 CANAL STREET, NEAR NORTH STATION   AND   WASHINGTON STREET, CORNER HAYWARD PLACE

A scored program from Game Seven.

the Red Sox put at least one man on in every inning. In all, 19 Red Sox reached base. Several were erased, but 12 men were left on, and the Sox failed to take advantage of the vulnerable Tesreau. Hugh Fullerton decried Boston's baserunning as "the most wretched exhibition of base running ever given a championship team. They ran bases like a bunch of farmers." Hall put more than his share of Giants on base, too, walking five—three of whom came in to score. It wasn't the prettiest of games.

In the bottom of the eighth, after Cady reached on Doyle's second error (the Giants made four in the game), the Red Sox scraped together another run on Hall's single (Cady took third on Devore's error), and a sacrifice fly to center.

The Giants made it 11-4, the final score, after Herzog walked and Wilson singled to center field. Speaker made an uncharacteristic error and Herzog was able to round the bases and score. The only lopsided game of the Series left Boston fans discouraged and presented Hugh Bedient with the responsibility of salvaging what days before had seemed a predestined World Series win for the Red Sox.

One of the disputed tickets to Game Seven of the World Series, the fourth game played at Fenway Park.

Game Eight: Fenway Park, Boston / October 16, 1912

Boston 3, New York 2 (10 innings)

New York   001 000 000 1—2 9 2
Boston   000 000 100 2—3 8 4

WP: Wood (3-1)
LP: Mathewson (0-2)

Breaking the pattern of alternation again, because there had been no firm decision where to play an eighth game, another coin toss was held and Boston won. With the Rooters genuinely and fervently upset, and with fans discouraged by the dismal play of the Red Sox in losing the last two games, attendance dropped precipitously from an average of 32,000 to barely over 17,000.

The deciding game of the 1912 World Series was one of the great games of all time. It began with a matchup of the rookie Hugh Bedient against the veteran Christy Mathewson. The first couple of innings were a little shaky: The Red Sox committed three errors behind Bedient, who walked one and gave up a single. No New Yorkers scored. Mathewson gave up two singles and a walk, but no Red Sox scored.

The Giants got one run in the top of the third. Devore walked, and stood on second after Doyle's grounder to third base. Snodgrass grounded to first base, and Devore took third. Red Murray doubled, scoring Devore.

Herzog doubled in the top of the fourth and Gardner doubled in the bottom. Neither team took advantage. Two Giants singles in the top of the fifth resulted in no further scoring; the lead man was cut down stealing. But Harry Hooper made a great catch, robbing Larry Doyle of a possible home run, catching the ball in his bare hand and falling into the seats.

Bedient wasn't at his best, but all he really did was walk Meyers in the sixth and give up a single to Mathewson in the seventh. The score remained 1-0, Giants.

In the bottom of the seventh, with time running out, Gardner flied out to center field. Then Stahl singled, a Texas Leaguer that frustratingly fell in between three New York fielders, and Heinie Wagner walked. Cady just missed getting good wood on the ball, and popped up to Fletcher at short. Hugh Bedient was due up, but Stahl knew he could get a couple of innings out of Joe Wood, so he asked the Red Sox' Danish-born pinch-hitting specialist, Olaf Henriksen (.321 for the season), to see what he could do against Mathewson. Henriksen doubled to left field and tied the game, pushing Stahl across home plate while Wagner took third. It wasn't the most classic of doubles—the ball actually hit the third-base bag—but it did the trick. Hooper flied out. The score was tied heading into the eighth inning. And Wood toed the rubber.

Smoky Joe, looking to make up for his previous performance, kept the ball down, and induced three groundouts (around a single by Herzog). Mathewson, too, got three groundouts in succession.

It was the ninth inning of the final game of the World Series. Wood got McCormick to fly out, then struck out Mathewson. Devore worked a walk, but Doyle grounded out. Bottom of the ninth: Stahl doubled, but his hit was bracketed by three fly balls that all went for outs.

The game extended into extra innings. Some observers doubtless must have wondered if the classic battle would end in another unsatisfying tie.

In the top of the 10th, Snodgrass grounded out to Wood. But Red Murray hit the ball into the left-center-field stands—it counted only as a ground-rule double, since it landed in temporary seating set up for the Series. Murray scored when Fred Merkle singled to center field. Speaker tried a short-hop grab of the ball down near his shoestrings to fire to home plate, but instead fumbled it as the go-ahead run came in. (The Red Sox made four errors in Game Eight.) Merkle took second base on the misplay—but Wood struck out Herzog and got Meyers to hit a hard grounder that glanced off his pitching hand. Wood grabbed the ball and threw to first to record the third out. The Giants held a 2-1 lead, and only three outs stood between them and the world championship.

In the bottom of the inning Hack Engle pinch-hit for Wood. He was a mere .234 hitter but he'd doubled and driven in both Red Sox runs in Game Six. Wood hit .290 during the year, but his hand was hurting. Engle hit the ball to center field but Fred Snodgrass let the ball pop right out of his glove. Engle was safe—reaching second base on the play—and "the Snodgrass muff" went down in history, after the rest of the 10th unfolded. After flubbing a couple of sacrifice bunt attempts, Hooper flied out to center, and Snodgrass snared that one—not an easy catch—but it was deep enough that Engle could tag up and take third base. Mathewson walked Steve Yerkes. Tris Speaker hit an easy foul—but it fell in between Merkle and Meyers, and Spoke had new life. He took advantage and boosted his Series batting average to an even .300 with a single to right field, easily scoring Engle with the tying run. Each team had committed a 10th-inning error in center field and each time a run resulted.

Speaker took second on the late throw to the plate, and Yerkes was on third. To set up a play at any base, or perhaps a double play, McGraw had Mathewson intentionally walk Duffy Lewis (0-for-4 in the game). In the on-deck circle was Larry Gardner. He had hit .315 for the season, with a third-best 86 RBIs, but only .179 in the Series. Gardner was, however, tied for the lead in World Series RBIs. He hit a fly ball to right field, to the same Josh Devore who had made such a spectacular catch to end Game Three. Devore caught this one much more easily, but it was deep enough to serve as a sacrifice fly, and it won the game when Yerkes tagged up and scored. Red Sox 3, Giants 2.

MANHATTAN VS. SMOKY JOE

Of all sad words from tongue or pen
The saddest are "Wood pitched again";
Sadder than any throbbing note
That old Doc Chopin ever wrote;
Aye, sadder in its somber skit
Than life's worse message—"Please remit."

Wood Pitched Again—tell me no more
The ultimate—the final score;
Waste no vain words in praise or blame,
Explaining which side copped the game;
Who blew the works—who had the stuff—
Wood Pitched—that's bally well enough.

Wood pitched Again—O bitter phrase—

O blighting echo of the days;
Sadder than any New York cop,
Or "could you slip me five, old top?"
Aye, in each dreary Harlem flat
Sadder than "Baker at the bat."

O Death, where is thy sting like this?
O Grave, where is thy serpent's kiss?
O Baker, Bender, Coombs and Plank,
You look like money in the bank,
Compared to this last scratch of pen—
"Wood pitched again."

Probable author—Grantland Rice
Boston Traveler and Evening Herald, October 12, 1912.

Smoky Joe Wood shown with opposing Game Eight starter Christy Mathewson just prior to the finale. Wood was the victor in relief, following a stellar performance by Hugh Bedient. This notched Wood's third Series win. When one adds his 34-5 regular season record, it was one of the best seasons any pitcher has ever enjoyed.

Harry Hooper played for the Red Sox in the 1912, 1915, 1916, and 1918 World Series, and Larry Gardner in the first three. Though he hit just .179, Gardner was productive in the 1912 Series, leading the Sox with five RBIs and tied for the lead in runs scored with four.

Game Eight, 1912—Christy Mathewson was, oddly enough, a cousin to Jack Billingham who posted a 1-3 record (11.10 ERA) for the 1980 Red Sox. Billingham threw nine innings against the Red Sox for the Reds in the 1975 World Series, allowing just one earned run. Mathewson himself pitched brilliantly in the 1912 Series. It was his third World Series. He'd won three games for the Giants in 1905, with a 0.00 ERA (all three games were shutouts of the Philadelphia Athletics). He was a hard-luck loser of a couple of games in the 1911 Series, also against the Athletics, one of which was lost on an unearned run in the 11th inning. He had won the first game that year, 2-1.

In 1912, the veteran right-hander pitched with excellence—an earned run average of 1.26. He was 0-2, but both losses came on unearned runs. And there was the tie game, too, Game Two. Had Art Wilson not committed an error in the 10th inning, Matty and the Giants would have won that one. He lost Game Five by a 2-1 score; the second run came in on Larry Doyle's error. He lost Game Eight, 3-2, after Fred Snodgrass's error in the bottom of the 10th.

A subhead in a *Sporting News* column read: "Error By Snodgrass Beats Masterly Pitching of Mathewson." A neighboring column that was not bylined was less forgiving: "To Snodgrass alone must the blame be given, and he is entitled to every bit of condemnation that may be heaped on his youthful shoulders. When a player tries to spike a man in one World's Series, as has been charged this player for his attempt to disable Frank Baker last year, and when that same player deliberately throws a ball with all his power at a boy over-eager to capture a souvenir baseball which he would prize many times more than Rockefeller his money, there is no excuse for any misplay he may make, or sympathy he may

Fred Snodgrass in 1911, before "the Snodgrass Muff" in Game Eight.

desire. Snodgrass deserves everything that he may receive from press, public, and members of the New York base ball team." Think the writer might have been a little bitter? Mathewson, deservedly, was one of the first five inductees into the National Baseball Hall of Fame.

The Giants outhit the Red Sox .270 to .220, outscored the Red Sox by six runs, and pitched dramatically better (an earned run average of 1.59 to Boston's 2.92). The Giants committed 18 errors, including some key ones, to Boston's 15. But so much of it is in the timing. New York won one game by seven runs and another by three. The Red Sox won three one-run games and the other by two runs.

The Red Sox ride in convertibles through the downtown crowd celebrating the World Series.

Opening Fenway Park with Style: The World Champion 1912 Boston Red Sox

Offered as a premium by a tobacco company of the day, this rare item was handled by Robert Edward Auctions in 2011. It was 31 inches long and 1 ½ inches wide. The REA catalog description ran in part: During the early 1900s a straw hat was the norm for any gentleman attending a ball game. Since most straw hats looked alike, it was only natural that someone would come up with a way for a fan to distinguishing himself from the crowd and, at the same time, to declare his allegiance to the home club. The answer was a silk band to be worn around the top. The ornate tricolor design features a Red Sox pennant that is flanked on either side by an identical Boston Red Sox motif displaying the date, "1912," above it, and the words "World's Champions" below. The design is embroidered (as opposed to printed). When worn on a hat, the pennant would be featured in the front, and the two Red Sox motifs would be seen on the sides.

This large crowd followed the game outside the offices of the *Boston Globe*.

The Rest of 1912

October 17—A "seething whirlpool of humanity" packed the streets of Boston all the way from Park Square to Faneuil Hall, which was "literally packed with a yelling, singing and ear-splitting mob." Some even climbed on provision wagons, onto the awnings over the sidewalk, and from there in through the second-floor windows. The crush of the crowd entering the hall was so great that "a man could actually take and keep his feet off the ground and still be carried along." Hub fans were, in a word, delirious about the triumph of the Red Sox. Mayor John F. Fitzgerald paid tribute to the team, the trainer, even the mascot. He also proclaimed, "There will be excuse next season for the managers to charge $1 for the majority of the seats, for they have had a most prosperous season, and should do justice to the baseball public."

October 18—Herb Bradley and Buck O'Brien and the Red Sox Quartet announced that they would open their second season of vaudeville with performances at the National Theater on the 21st. Bill Carrigan returned home to a hero's welcome in Lewiston, Maine, complete with red fire and the booming of cannon. He was presented a new automobile.

October 19—The *Boston Globe* printed an image of the $88,543.44 check from the National Commission to the Red Sox, which would be divided into shares. Each player received $4,024.68.

Team mascot Jerry McCarthy addresses the Rooters.

October 20—Tim Murnane, who had attended every World Series game ever played, wrote in the *Globe* that the 1912 Series was no "put-up job," and he decried numerous rumors to that effect which had circulated during the games, suggesting they were planted by interested parties hoping to influence the wagering. He specifically denied stories that Buck O'Brien and Joe Wood had come to blows, or that Buck had been "unfit" before his last start. Murnane and others had been with him all day.

A large crowd and a brass band welcomed Ray Collins home to Burlington, Vermont. Meanwhile, in Boston, 40-year-old Eugene O'Connor was arrested on the Common for violating the law against playing baseball on Sunday. It was a deliberate act of civil disobedience, intended to challenge the Lord's Day law that prohibited Sunday ball. O'Connor, sports editor of the *Boston American*, was the brother-in-law of John Dooley, one of the more active Royal Rooters and loyal Red Sox fans (see his story in the book *Red Sox Threads*).

October 21—Casey Hageman had appeared in two early-season games, throwing 1 innings for the Red Sox and giving up five runs. His troubles with the Red Sox had begun in June. "He had been farmed to Jersey City for a while, then was recalled and ordered to report to Denver, with a later announcement telling him that his salary would be cut $150 a month. He objected, and appealed to the National Commission, as there were other clubs willing to guarantee his regular salary for his services." As of June 23, Hageman began the practice of reporting for practice at Fenway Park every day, claiming that he was still a member of the Red Sox. A first ruling went against him, but now he appealed to the National Commission that he should receive a share of the World Series proceeds.

October 22—Tris Speaker and Joe Wood were offered $1,000 a week to do vaudeville (exactly what it was thought they might do is not mentioned); Wood had no interest, but Speaker was reportedly thinking about it. The Red Sox Quartet (Bradley, O'Brien, Marty McHale, and Bill Lyons) sold out two packed houses at the National Theatre. They all wore Red Sox uniforms while singing. The entire audience joined in boisterously when *Tessie* was sung.

October 25—Mascot Jerry McCarthy received a Red Sox check for $200 accompanied by a letter "expressing appreciation for the part his singing did to keep the players cheered up and help them win the world's series." John I. Taylor also gave Jerry a present (later reported by the *Los Angeles Times* as $1,000; the *Times* also wrote in its November 6 edition that each player had given Jerry $50). Sox second baseman Steve Yerkes was honored at a banquet at Moore's Inn in Hatboro, Pennsylvania. Connie Mack and a number of the Philadelphia Athletics joined 100 local fans at the dinner. Yerkes gave credit to Mack for helping inspire the Red Sox.

October 26—The *New York Times* quoted Heinie Wagner as saying of the assistance Connie Mack had provided the Red Sox when he'd briefed them on the Giants: "I doubt if we could have beaten the Giants without the knowledge that Mack gave us."

October 29—Honoring a local boy, Canton, Massachusetts, held "Henriksen Night" and thousands of spectators from Canton and neighboring towns turned out to see the red fire, fireworks, a torchlight parade, and a band. John I. Taylor was among numerous speakers.

About 450 (two-thirds of them students) turned out in Burlington at the Hotel Vermont to honor Ray Collins and Larry Gardner, with a parade led by the University of Vermont band.

Tim Murnane was among the speakers.

Further cashing in on his modest fame, mascot Jerry McCarthy "in a special act, is the feature on an excellent bill at Scenic Theatre. Other acts included a comedienne, some piano playing, singing, dancing, and whistling."

October 30—A reception for Jake Stahl was held in Bloomington, Illinois.

October 31—Fans were turned away from Hartford's Empire Theatre after all seats were sold for two showings of a 20-minute film on the 1912 World Series.

November

November 2—National columnist Hugh S. Fullerton wrote that mascot McCarthy had retired, but that his 9-year-old younger brother was hoping to secure the position.

In other news, team president James McAleer cut short any Hot Stove discussions regarding the Red Sox by announcing that he was already set for 1913. "We have shut up shop. We're out of the baseball market. We have all the players we want for 1913. We're satisfied with what we have. No more purchases or trades."[12] McAleer had bought one outfielder (George Walsh) and two shortstops (Everett Scott and Swede Carlstrom), and exercised the option the Sox held on Hal Janvrin. And now he felt he was set.

Goldsmith of the *Boston Globe* showed what some of the Red Sox planned to do in the offseason.

November 3—The *Washington Post* printed a column detailing the travails of an American stuck in London, trying to follow the World Series from across the ocean (despite being assured, "You can get anything you want in London"). When he finally was able to learn the result of the first game, it was well after midnight and the answer he got from a sports writer on a morning newspaper was "Red Sox won." When he asked the score, the writer replied, "Don't know. Didn't bother asking."

In Los Angeles, Charley Hall played in a game at Washington Park, on the same side as Fred Snodgrass, the captain of the Oxnard team. Hall was very active in the game—though not on the mound. He played second base and ranged far and wide making plays—including an unassisted putout at first base. He walked, doubled twice, and drove in two runs.

November 4—Speaking at a Boston Athletic Association reception, Giants manager John McGraw said that Heinie Wagner made the difference in the World Series "That's the fellow that beat us. With him off your Boston team, we should have won the championship....He played such a marvelous fielding game that it was a big block to us." In terms of one spectacular play, McGraw praised Boston's right fielder: "Hooper made the greatest catch I ever saw on a ball field."

November 10—The *Chicago Tribune* carried the full story of how Smoky Joe Wood had started his professional baseball career as a Bloomer Girl.

November 12—Treasurer Robert McRoy arrived by train in Hot Springs to spend a few days making plans for spring training. The Sox had a four-year lease on Majestic Park, but hoped to make the community their permanent home.

November 14—The Red Sox closed down their offices at Fenway Park and moved to a downtown location in the Tremont Building, the reason suggested being "Fenway Park is a rather cheerless place to spend the winter."

November 17—The Red Sox Quartet headed the week's show at the Orpheum.

November 18—McRoy contracted for a bathing pool to be built in Hot Springs for the world champion Red Sox and was trying to induce the street railway company to construct a railroad spur to Majestic Park.

November 21—Marty Krug was released to Indianapolis.

November 26—Readers of the *Globe* learned that Hugh Bradley's contract had been sold outright to Jersey City. In Capitola, California, Harry Hooper married Miss Esther Henchey of Santa Cruz.

November 28—Fenway Park hosted its first non-baseball event as the Boston Latin School football team beat rival Boston English, 7-6.

November 30—The National High School Football Championship was held at Fenway Park, and coach Robert Zuppke's Oak Park High School from the Chicago suburb toppled Everett High School, 32-12, drawing a crowd of over 10,000 people filling the bleachers. Zuppke's team won its third title in a row (the first three years of the competition) and later became coach at the University of Illinois, where he led the Illini to four national titles between 1914 and 1927 and seven Big Ten titles.

December

December 1—The Red Sox Quartet (still including Bradley) moved to a week's engagement at the Old Howard, where they would share the bill with the Bohemian Burlesquers starting at 7:00 PM this evening.

December 4—McAleer reiterated that he thought the Sox were set for 1913, but he left the door open a bit more than he had on November 2, saying that he was always ready to trade or purchase a contract but he didn't see anything likely to change: "We have a great team as it stands, and if anybody has better men than we have, you may safely bet that he is going to hang on to them."

December 5—All of the contracts for the 1913 season were mailed out from the Red Sox office.

December 7—Manager Fred Clarke of the Pittsburgh Pirates accepted McAleer's challenge to play a series of games at Hot Springs.

December 8—An amusing article in the *Washington Post* calculated that Neal Ball had been paid at the rate of $804,600 per day to play in the 1912 World Series. Ball's sole contribution in the Series had been to swing three times at a pitch and miss each time, during his pinch-hitting appearance in Game Three. The author allowed one minute per swing and then cited the $4,024 World Series pay Ball had collected. That was more work than Marty Krug did, though. Krug sat on the bench. The pitchers who weren't used at least helped out throwing batting practice, the catchers warmed up pitchers or helped with the coaching, the other utility players pinch-hit (e.g., Ball) or pinch-ran. but Krug's "labors consisted solely in doing much heavy thinking."

December 9—The chairman of the National Commission, August Herrmann, proposed the adoption of interleague play, suggesting that teams play a 112-game season within their league and then embark on a 64-game interleague championship series. "Inter-league schedule is bound to be adopted in due time," he said. [*Boston Globe*, December 10, 1912] Eighty-five years later, interleague play was introduced in Major League Baseball.

December 16—Jake Stahl said the Red Sox would be in the race all the way in 1913. He was counting on Hal Janvrin to play the games at first base that he did not.

December 17—Both leagues announced that Opening Day 1913 would fall on April 10. In Bangor, Maine, the Pine Cone Council of the Knights of Columbus presented Bill Carrigan with a silver loving cup. Clyde Engle's contract for the coming year arrived, making him the fifth player to come to terms. Umpire Tommy Connolly dropped by the team's headquarters and spoke highly of Hugh Bedient, among other things saying, "I believe he will have a brilliant career."

December 18—Much was expected of Hubert Leonard for 1913, reported a piece in the *Washington Post*; all in all the Red Sox felt very good about their pitching staff for the campaign to come.

December 19—Hugh Bradley was released to Jersey City.

December 20—The *Los Angeles Times* reported that Jake Stahl might decide to live in L.A. He was there, the paper wrote, "in the role of Garland Stahl, the banker." In Boston, the contract of Rutland, Vermont, native George Walsh arrived at the Red Sox offices. Walsh was an outfielder who had played well for Fall River in 1912.

December 23—North Easton 30, Boston Red Sox 19. At least for a while, there was a basketball team also named the Boston Red Sox. They didn't fare as well as the world champions in the game played at Ames Gymnasium in North Easton.

December 27—The contract of right-handed pitcher Joe Martina arrived at the Red Sox offices.

December 28—SOX' PRESTIGE NOT IN PERIL. The *Globe* reassured readers in all seriousness that even if the Pirates should outplay the Red Sox during the spring series at Hot Springs, they would not thereby become world champions.

In separate news from California, Frank Arellanes announced that to please his wife he was retiring from baseball to become a businessman.

1913 and 1914

The Red Sox won back-to-back world championships in 1915 and 1916, then won another in 1918. This was indeed the golden era of Red Sox baseball. But there were two years between the 1912 and 1915 World Series and for those two years—1913 and 1914—the Red Sox were bereft of a title.

Many of the Royal Rooters remained alienated because of the ticket problem at Game Seven of the 1912 Series, but there were still over 20,000 who flocked to Fenway for 1913's Opening Day. Attendance dropped nearly 27 percent by year's end, but significantly the number of Red Sox home wins also dropped, from 57 to 41, a decline of 39 percent. Overall, the Sox won 25 percent fewer games in 1913—from 105 to 79. Some have argued that the small turnout of 6,500 for the June 25 raising of the pennant demonstrated an ongoing boycott of sorts, but the Boston newspapers reported that the "weather was threatening and all day it looked as if it might rain." Furthermore, it was a "raw" day of "extreme cold."

Wins were down because the club just wasn't clicking. Joe Wood hurt his ankle early in spring training and then injured his thumb in mid-May, breaking it entirely later in the season.

The 1913 Red Sox program honoring the world champions.

The star pitcher with the 34-5 record in 1912 posted a mark of 11-5 in 1913. The pitcher with the best record was Collins, with a 19-8 mark. Bedient slipped from 20-9 to 15-14. Rookie Dutch Leonard won 14 games but lost 16. The team ERA increased from 2.76 to 2.94. The team batting average dipped from .277 to .268. The Athletics won 96 games and Boston was 15½ games behind, in fourth place.

Before the 1914 season began, the Red Sox had a new owner in Joseph Lannin. Ban Johnson was still pulling the strings and, after ensuring that Bill Carrigan had replaced Jake Stahl as manager during the season, further orchestrated Lannin replacing McAleer as principal owner.

The Red Sox finished in second place in 1914, their 91 wins still leaving them 8½ games behind Philadelphia. This was the year of the "Miracle Braves"—so at least one of Boston's teams captured the World Series, sweeping the Athletics. In fact, the two 1914 World Series home games played in Boston were both played in the newer and larger Fenway Park, which had now hosted Series play in two of its three years of existence.

The additional 17 Sox wins were reflected in the records of their best pitchers. Leonard set a single-season earned-run average mark that has never been beaten—0.96, helping him to a 19-5 record. Collins was 20-13. Rube Foster (14-8, 1.70 ERA) and Ernie Shore (10-5, 2.00 ERA) contributed. Team batting dropped to .250, but the team ERA also dropped, dramatically, to 2.36.

In 1915 the Red Sox led the league for the second half of the season. They had five 15-game winners: Joe Wood contributed again (15-5, 1.79 ERA), as did Leonard (15-7). Rube Foster and Ernie Shore each had identical 19-8 records, and the new kid—Babe Ruth—was 18-8. Team ERA was more or less the same as the prior year, 2.39. Team batting improved to .260. The rookie pitcher, Ruth, even hit four home runs, double anyone else on the team. There were four tie games, but the Red Sox won 101 while losing 50. They finished 2½ games ahead of the second-place Detroit Tigers. Boston had beaten Detroit in 14 of their 22 encounters.

In the National League, the Phillies (90-62) finished 7½ games ahead of the second-place Boston Braves. This year the Braves accorded the Red Sox the use of their brand-new and significantly larger Braves Field. Whereas in 1914 the Braves had played their home Series games at Fenway, now the Red Sox played at the home of the Braves.

The portion of the timeline which presents the day-by-day story of the 1912 World Series is only slightly adapted, and comes with permission, from *The Red Sox World Series Encyclopedia* by Bill Nowlin and Jim Prime (Rounder Books). The image of the 1912 pennant which is at the beginning of the article is courtesy of Robert Edward Auctions. The pennant itself is 18 inches in length.

Endnotes

1. *Washington Post*, July 19, 1911

2. *Chicago Tribune*, September 13, 1911

3. *Washington Post*, October 6, 1911

4. *Washington Post*, November 11, 1911

5. The 1911 spring season was a bizarre one. See Bill Nowlin, *The Great Red Sox Spring Training Tour of 1911*. Jefferson, N.C.: McFarland, 2011.

6. *Boston American*, March 24, 1911

7. Lyle Spatz. *New York Yankee Openers: An Opening Day History of Baseball's Most Famous Team, 1903-1996*. Jefferson, N.C.: McFarland, 1997, 41.

8. *Boston Globe*, July 2, 1912

9. *Boston Traveler*, August 18, 1912

10. *Washington Post*, October 2, 1912

11. Norman Macht, *Connie Mack and the Early Years of Baseball*, Lincoln: University of Nebraksa Press, 2007, 563.

12. *Washington Post*, November 3, 1912

Smoky Joe at Fenway Park.

The World Champion medal presented to each member of the triumphant Red Sox team of 1912.

Fenway Park – The First Renovation

Fenway Park was built so quickly that it wasn't 100% ready when the season began, but it was built so well that it has lasted a full century. Construction was still underway and seats along the first-base line were still being installed even at the time of the first game against Harvard on April 9. Nor were the clubhouses completed. For the Harvard game, the Red Sox changed into their uniforms across the street at the Park Riding School on Ipswich Street. Neither in left field nor in right did the grandstand seats extend as far as the foul poles. Along the first-base side, the grandstand seating went just a bit past first base but perhaps not even as far as where today's Canvas Alley is, and on the third-base side to about today's Section 27 (look at any map of Fenway and it's easy to see the little wedge of Section 28, which represents the dividing point on that side).

When it became clear that the Red Sox were bound to win the pennant and draw much larger crowds for the World Series, plans were drawn up – hastily – to expand seating while the Red Sox were on the road for much of mid to late September and through October 5.

Some before and after shots give us an idea of the work done during the first renovation of Fenway.

The right-field side

This initial photograph from the first part of 1912 shows how far out the grandstand seating went along the first-base side, with the bleachers shown in center field. Some of the area in between (behind the fans shown on a roped-off section of right field) was used for parking, for those who had motor vehicles.

The Red Sox broke their road trip for two days, on September 24 and 25. This section of a photograph used elsewhere in the book shows the construction of the right-field bleachers in the background.

Work is much further advanced just about 10 days later, as the first game of the World Series drew nearer.

The right-field bleachers were completed in time for the World Series. This photograph taken in 1914 displays the new seating section.

Opening Fenway Park with Style: The World Champion 1912 Boston Red Sox

Down the left-field line

The new left-field pavilion seats to the left of the partially-displayed "The Georgian" sign are largely in place down the left-field line.

Here we see the seating in place and populated and jutting out toward the field in the now-familiar configuration. Note the bleacher-style seating in front of the left-field wall in the background.

Workers putting final touches on the wall at the far end of the new left-field seating, with the bleacher seats in front of the wall shown on the right side of the photograph.

The left field corner completed and occupied by fans as displayed in this isolated version of a 1912 World Series image shown in another section of the book.

Duffy's Cliff and the left-field wall

In the background of this post-1912 image, after the temporary World Series seating was removed, one can see the earthen berm which became known as Duffy's Cliff. It served as a retaining wall for the higher level of Lansdowne Street behind it (the field at Fenway is below street level) and during sold-out games fans were allowed to sit on the grass.

The Fenway Park scoreboard

Fans visiting Fenway Park today are rightly fascinated by the old manual scoreboard on the left-field wall, and newer parks such as Denver's Coors Field have installed similar manually-run scoreboard sections. It was, of course, the norm at the time. There are references to it as one of the first "electronic" scoreboards, but there in fact was no electronic feature to the scoreboard itself, no lights that illuminated on command. In his masterful book on the construction of Fenway Park, Glenn Stout explains, "The 'electronic' designation meant that the press box keyboard operator could communicate some information to the scoreboard operators electronically. Operators stationed on the scoreboard's backside scrambled up and down a network of ladders and steps and benches, out of view of the fans inside the park. While some information may have been conveyed through some kind of electronic device, most was communicated by hand." (*Fenway 1912*)

After the 1912 season was over, additional work was done to complete the park over the next year or two, such as pouring concrete atop the previously earthen concourses and making more permanent some of the additional seating provided in late 1912. In 1914, the park hosted its second World Series.

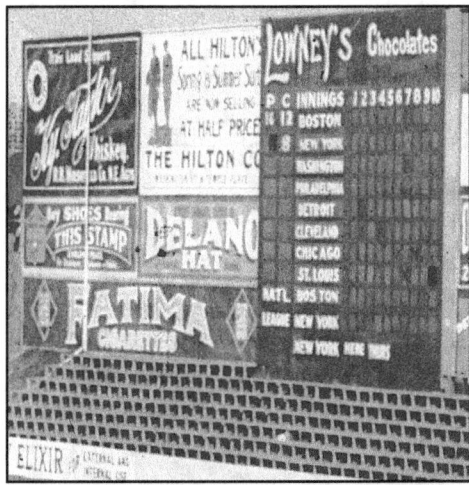

This closeup shot of the left-field wall shows the original scoreboard, with Boston hosting New York for the games of September 24 and 25. The scoreboard displayed the scores of out-of-town American League games as well and reflected fan interest in the Boston Braves with a spot at the bottom to show the score of Braves games.

With the regular season over, and no other game scores to report, the Lawson ad was placed on the wall covering most of the scoreboard—and providing a little more revenue for the Red Sox. This photograph taken after the first inning of Game Two shows Boston with a 3-0 lead.

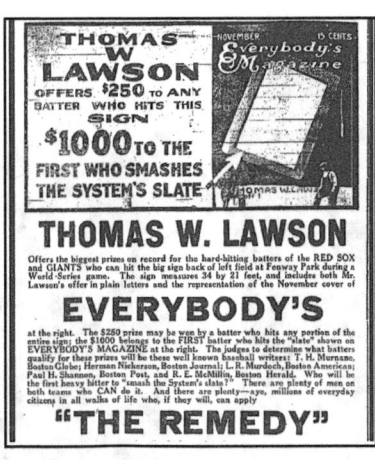

In its October 12 issue, the *Boston Globe* carried an advertisement placed by Thomas W. Lawson promoting the Boston publication *Everybody's Magazine*. As the text explains, a larger 34 x 21 foot ad was placed on the left-field wall at Fenway and the first player who might hit the sign during a World Series game would win at least $250, and $1,000 if he hit the drawing of the slate which was on the cover of the magazine. No one did. The July 25, 1911 *Boston Globe* described Lawson as "financier, author, patron of the arts, student of the classics, model of fashion and distinguished in ever so many lines"—a man whose "principal fun in life in collecting statuettes of elephants."

A longer shot of the wall in left, taken after 8 ½ innings of Game Two, also shows (between the Pureoxia Ginger Ale and Haffenreffer Lager Beer ads) the other portion of the scoreboard, which displayed the number of strikes and balls on the batter and the number of outs.

The Press Box

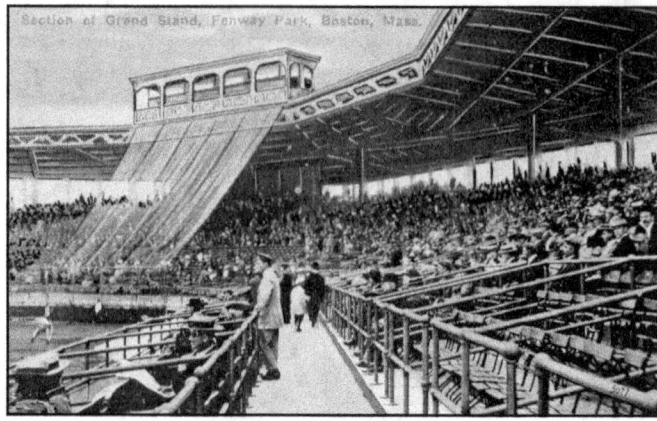

The images above show the Fenway Park press box before it was replaced prior to the 1912 World Series. The photograph on the left was taken from the right-centerfield stands by the Bain News Service on September 28, 1912. Glenn Stout reports that the enclosure could house up to 16 telegraphers and at least the seven reporters he names. The postcard image shows the press box from the third-base side. Both show the screen or net to protect patrons from foul balls.

The newly installed press box is displayed in these images. The photograph to the left, taken by the Pictorial News Agency of New York during the first inning of the Game Two, shows the expanded press box. The second image with two Red Sox and a Giants player in the infield prior to a Series game, shows the new press box extended along the third-base side.

Keeping Up With the Red Sox: Getting the News in 1912

By Donna L. Halper

Today most of us take for granted that as soon as a trade is made or a manager is fired, the news will be readily available, whether from the newer media (Internet blogs, sports websites, Twitter) or the traditional media (newspapers, TV, radio). But when the Red Sox won the pennant in 1912, the public did not have an expectation of instant information. There was no radio yet, nor would there be until 1920; and by most accounts, the first efforts to broadcast baseball occurred in 1921. In October of that year, the first World's Series broadcasts took place (during the 1910s and into the 1920s, most newspapers referred to it as the "World's Series," rather than the World Series). The games were carried by KDKA in Pittsburgh and WJZ in Newark; and a number of experimental and amateur stations, including greater Boston's pioneering station, 1XE, relayed scores and updates. But such things could only be dreamed of in 1912. The most popular new technology was the telephone, but it was mainly available in big cities; many parts of the country were not yet wired.

Loyal fans who wanted to know what was happening with the team tended to rely on the press (nobody called it "the media" yet). Fortunately for fans in New England, Boston had many newspapers to choose from. They included the *Boston Globe*, the *Boston Post*, the *Boston Herald*, the *Boston Traveler*, the *Boston Telegram*, the *Boston American*, the *Boston Evening Record*, and several others that did not offer thorough coverage of professional sports, such as the *Boston Evening Transcript* and the *Christian Science Monitor*. The *Transcript* was the newspaper favored by the so-called "Boston Brahmins," and other members of upper-class Boston society. Its sports coverage tended to focus mainly on athletics at private schools and at colleges like Harvard. As for the *Monitor*, it too covered sports at the major colleges, and sometimes reported on amateur athletics. However, when the Red Sox won the Series, the *Monitor* published a very thorough article about the victory, and then sang the team's praises in an editorial. But at other times during the year, coverage of the Red Sox had been either brief or nonexistent. In addition to the Boston papers, sports fans could read about baseball in newspapers from other cities in Eastern Massachusetts: the *Lowell Sun*, the *Quincy Patriot and Daily Ledger*, and the *Fitchburg Sentinel* reported on baseball; even Cape Cod newspapers like the *Barnstable Patriot* carried the occasional baseball story, especially if a local resident was making the long journey to Boston to attend a game.

In 1912 the average newspaper cost one cent, although a few cost 2 cents; the *Boston Evening Transcript* cost 3 cents. A typical newspaper like the *Boston Globe* published multiple editions through the day—there was a morning *Globe*, a midday *Globe*, and an afternoon *Globe*; if there was a major story, what we today would call "breaking news," newspapers would put out an "extra" edition, sending the newsboys (and a few newsgirls) out to sell the paper all over the city, announcing this special edition with the famous shout, "Extra! Extra! Read all about it!"

The largest newspapers had their own sports reporters, who went out to cover the various games; in many instances, these reporters got stories as a result of their close relationship with the team. In that era before air travel, players and sportswriters were usually on the same trains together, and during long road trips, or on days when there was a rainout, there were many opportunities to come up with interesting stories to share with the fans. Then, as now, fans wanted to know a little more about the players, but detailed personal profiles were rare. Reporters typically kept private indiscretions as private, managing to cater to the curiosity of the fans without betraying any confidences. And while there were some fans who cared only about the latest statistics, many others liked to learn about what the manager was purportedly

Newspaper Row: A majority of Boston's daily newspapers during this era were crammed together in a section in Downtown Boston called "Newspaper Row," with five papers located on Washington Street and some others on adjacent streets. This circa-1915 postcard image of "Newspaper Row" displays the Red Sox Championship banner for that year, overhanging the sidewalk to the left.

thinking, or get some reactions from the players about yesterday's game. Like most major-league cities, Boston had a dedicated group of baseball writers; in addition to the *Globe*'s Tim Murnane, they included the *Post*'s Paul "Herbie" Shannon, the *Journal*'s Herman Nickerson, and the *Herald*'s Ralph McMillin.

In the smaller cities, where there was no professional team and often no local reporters to cover the pros, several well-known syndicated sportswriters like Hugh S. Fullerton and Grantland Rice filled the bill; their insights were greatly appreciated, and even the Boston papers sometimes carried their columns. It was an era when bylines were not commonly used, and only the best-known local reporters (such as Tim Murnane and Herman Nickerson) had their name on the story they had written. In fact, if you read the newspaper in 1912, you would have seen many sports stories (and an equal number of news stories) that were written anonymously.

And while modern fans think of reading the paper as a solitary activity, in Boston, the newspapers often brought people together. Five of the most widely read publications (the *Globe*, the *Post*, the *Transcript*, the *Evening Record*, and the *Journal*) were located on lower Washington Street in downtown Boston, and several other newspapers were one or two streets over. As a result of their proximity, this part of Boston was called Newspaper Row. Whenever there was a major news event (such as a presidential election) or a major sporting event (such as the Harvard-Yale game or the World Series), lower Washington Street was transformed into a gathering place, as people stood in front of the office of their favorite paper and waited for bulletins to arrive.

The Role of Wireless Telegraphy

What made all of this possible was an invention that most people knew about but few were able to use: the telegraph. For newspapers, the development of telegraphy was a major improvement in how news was gathered. The telegraph could send Morse code messages over long distances, and it accelerated the speed with which news could be disseminated. One of the first examples of using the telegraph to cover a sporting event occurred in 1849, when a description of a championship boxing match between Tom Hyer and Yankee Sullivan was sent from Baltimore to the *New York Herald*, which was able to publish the accounts on page one the next day. This was a major breakthrough: Prior to the telegraph, a typical news story could take as long as three days to reach the newspaper, and now it was there in a matter of hours. As the technology improved and more telegraph offices opened, newspapers would soon be able to receive messages from distant locations in a matter of minutes. Then, in the late 1800s, veteran newsman Walter P. Phillips developed a unique version of Morse code, which came to be called the Phillips code; it made the telegrapher's job easier by providing special abbreviations for frequently used words. (A few of these abbreviations still survive: the term POTUS, president of the United States, for example, originated with telegraphy, but is a popular abbreviation that reporters use even now.)

Telegraphy affected all aspects of the newspaper: The president could give a speech in Washington and the story would arrive in time for the next edition. Reviewers could attend a play or a concert and submit a report as soon as the show ended. And for sports fans, the telegraph meant that sports could now be a national (rather than a regional or local) passion. Fans were not only able to read about the home team, but they could also find out about some of the other teams, especially those that might be coming to town. If there was an exciting pennant race, people all over the country could keep up with it. In 1912, news about the Red Sox' drive toward the pennant was not only available in the Boston papers; thanks to the telegraph (as well as the telephone), reporters were able to keep fans up to date no matter where they lived. Readers of the *Chicago Tribune*, the *Baltimore Sun*, the *Detroit Free Press*, the *Los Angeles Times*, and many others were able to follow the latest exploits of the "Speed Boys" (the popular nickname for the Sox, first used in 1909 by veteran *Boston Globe* reporter and former major-league player Tim Murnane). A good example of the reach of news about the Red Sox could be seen in the *Portland Oregonian*: A local sportswriter surveyed fans in Portland, nearly all of whom picked the Red Sox to win it all.

Whether at a game or on a train, reporters depended on a telegrapher, who usually worked for the Western Union Company. Few reporters knew how to send Morse code, so finding a reliable telegrapher was a very important part of news coverage. As for the smaller newspapers, many of which lacked the budget to send reporters to a distant city to cover a game, they could join an organization like the Associated Press (AP), a cooperative; for a weekly fee, AP would send out reporters and then transmit the stories back to the member newspaper. So important was the telegraph to the functioning of a newsroom that a number of papers had a telegraph

Telegraphers waiting for the next pitch at a World Series game.

editor, whose job it was to receive all the wired messages each day and decide which stories were right for that paper. Telegraphers were expected to be fast yet accurate, able to transmit information from the site of the story back to the newspaper. In fact, the telegraph had become so central to journalism that some newspapers hired their own telegraphers; these men (most were men, although there were a small number of women in this profession) sat in the newsroom, ready to receive or send at a moment's notice. Some of these telegraphers fell in love with the newspaper profession and decided to become reporters; interestingly, one of the *Boston Globe*'s best sportswriters in the 1910s was Jim O'Leary, who joined the *Globe* as a telegrapher and then moved up to copy editor before finally becoming a baseball writer.

The telegraph was not just an essential device for journalists: the teams also used this technology. Managers sent telegrams when they wanted to bid on a player's contract; managers also sent telegrams to the newspapers when there was a rumor about a trade and they wanted to deny it. Players used the telephone to call home, but in the absence of a telephone, telegrams had to suffice. And just like today, when people get upset because their Internet connection isn't working, the players back then would get frustrated if they could not get their messages out— sometimes bad weather caused the telegraph lines to go down, and the only alternative was driving to a neighboring town and hoping there was service available. And as might be expected, the telegraph was used by politicians prior to the World Series: In October 1912, Mayor John Fitzgerald of Boston and Mayor

Outsiders Keep Informed: Boston fans unable to attend games at Fenway Park were eager to get game updates. This cartoon displays some of the daring and adventurous methods they may have used to follow the games. Many fans also ventured downtown to Newspaper Row, getting continuous updates throughout the game as provided by the newspapers. *Boston Globe*

William Gaynor of New York exchanged telegrams in which they jokingly taunted each other's teams and predicted a positive outcome for their own.

Being a Fan in 1912

If you were a Red Sox fan in 1912, you would have seen some newspapers still referring to "base ball," and you would also have seen headlines about the Boston Americans—to people who did not follow sports, that may have been confusing, since there was a newspaper called the *Boston American*, but the fans understood that the headlines referred to the American League team (the Red Sox); the newspapers also talked about the Boston Nationals, referring to the National League team that was now known as the Braves. For Red Sox fans, 1912 was a banner year with the opening of Fenway Park. Sports reporters made sure their stories included directions to the new venue, and publicized the ticket prices. Filing their stories after the opening game was rained out and a stretch of bad weather prompted two more postponements among the first four scheduled games, the sportswriters remained optimistic about how the Red Sox would do this year. Having spent spring training covering them, the *Boston Journal*'s sports editor, Herman Nickerson, wrote on April 18, "With a new leader on the field, new owners, and a new park, the Speed Boys have certainly played the game so far like a new team."

But if you were living in Boston in April 1912, your mind was probably not completely on sports. Several days earlier, the *Titanic* had sunk, and page one of every newspaper was still covering the story, especially since a number of famous people were now presumed dead. On the other hand, if you were frustrated by the rainouts at Fenway Park and wanted some escapist entertainment, professional wrestling was in town: promoter George Tuohey was putting on a card that featured local favorite Cyclone Burns, and in that era, wrestling was actually covered on the sports page. There were also some vaudeville stars in town, and you may have seen Lew Dockstader and his Minstrels at the Majestic Theater, or perhaps you went to see a play at the Hollis Street Theatre, where Billie Burke was starring in *The Runaway*.

Despite the lack of such technologies as radio, the newspapers found a way to bring the game to the fans. Each day, the papers on Newspaper Row would put the headlines on a blackboard outside their building so that people on their lunch hour could come by and find out what was happening in the world. When a big event occurred, like an election, the newspapers would use a stereopticon (sometimes called a magic lantern) to flash headlines onto a screen; and especially during sporting events, a sort of camaraderie would develop.

Unlike the daily headlines and bulletins, which people saw while they were passing by, sporting events brought out

Fans who couldn't fit into Fenway following telegraphed reports of 1912 World Series games in front of the *Boston Globe*.

Enjoying the World Series

Telegraphing Day of Game Information

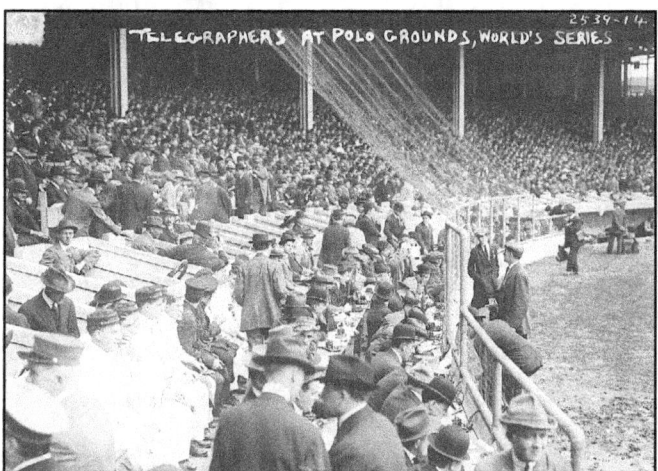

Telegraphers at their designated ground-level seats behind home plate at the Polo Grounds during a 1912 World Series game in New York.

Press, telegraphers, and photographers prepare for another day at the park in New York. Visiting telegraphers described activities on the field to their newspaper offices back home.

Prepare Articles for Newspaper Distribution

The telegraphed game accounts are sent to the offices located in Boston's Newspaper Row on Washington Street, displayed in this image.

Opening Fenway Park with Style: The World Champion 1912 Boston Red Sox

A chipper looking group of "newsies" in this Sunday 5:00 a.m. photo taken in front of the *Boston Globe* office.

Newsboys ready for delivering their *Boston Journal* newspapers.

Baseball Game Reproducer: A large crowd gathers in Washington, DC, following the progress of Game Seven of the 1912 World Series as provided by the *Washington Post*. The scoreboard operator provides pitch-by-pitch telegraph updates.

The scoreboard included a bell and lights to capture and emphasize game activities for the Washington Nationals away games, and was also used during the World Series while accommodating large crowds such as those demonstrated above.

Some may view this as an early version of today's MLB.com's Gameday on the internet.

Fans wait in line along a fence outside the Polo Grounds in New York at 7:00 a.m. hoping to purchase World Series tickets. Many who were unlucky ventured to alternate locations such as the *New York Journal* building to watch reproductions of the games.

Fans in New York tracking Game Three outside the office of the *New York Journal*.

large numbers of fans who came to Newspaper Row to spend the afternoon: They would get the latest scores and enjoy being with other fans. The *Globe* and the *Post* were in competition for the largest crowds, and each newspaper showed photographs of the throngs gathered outside its office; the stories often praised the attendance, saying there had never been a larger or more boisterous gathering.

The baseball games were covered for Newspaper Row spectators this way: A telegrapher and a reporter were at the game, and the description of each at-bat was wired back to the newspaper. Telegraphers were known for being able to transcribe quickly, and as soon as the sports reporter told his telegrapher what to send, the result was received by the newspaper within seconds. (To expedite the process, telegraphers had developed special abbreviations for the plays, such as FB for "foul ball," or PTF for "pitcher throws to first.") Once the information was received and transcribed by the newspaper's telegrapher, an employee with a megaphone and a loud voice would call out the plays to the crowd. Sometimes, the newspaper would use a replica of a scoreboard and miniature figurines to act out the plays as they occurred. And although there was no way to see the game, the audiences that stood along Washington Street seemed to have a great time, cheering and booing as if they were listening to the game directly, rather than relying on telegraph messages and megaphones.

When the Red Sox got into the World's Series, hundreds of newspapers wanted to cover it, and telegraphers were very much in demand. The *Washington Post* estimated as many as 10,000 telegraphers might be needed nationwide. The *Post* compared the excitement to a political convention, with hundreds of people working behind the scenes to make sure everything went smoothly. In cities all over the United States, editors scrambled to make arrangements for coverage. The Associated Press provided some of it, but its main competition, United Press (a paid service rather than a cooperative like the AP), picked up a great deal of business by announcing that star sportswriter Grantland Rice would be doing the reporting. This was such big news that one newspaper in Lima, Ohio, placed the

Fans follow the 1912 Series game updates in front of the *Boston Globe* in downtown Boston. To the left is a *Globe* staffer on top of a storefront scaffold capturing the score on a chalkboard.

Cameramen on the field during a World Series game anxiously prepare for photograph opportunities.

While reporters and telegraphers were obviously important in providing news in 1912, we should not underscore the photographer's increasing impact in "getting the news" to fans. Their images enriched baseball articles during this era. Their baseball photographs in newspapers and publications also provided most New England fans their only visualizations of Fenway Park and the Red Sox team in 1912, and for many the only images they ever saw in their lifetime.

announcement on the front page, promising more up-to-the-minute and detailed coverage than any other newspaper in the state. As the Boston papers did on Newspaper Row, out-of-town newspapers also promised readers an experience to remember. In Worcester, as local movie theaters advertised that they had leased Western Union wires to provide the scores, fans also gathered in front of the *Worcester Evening Gazette*; crowd estimates reached as high as 4,000. The *Hartford Courant* invited fans to come to the Courant building, where the score would be displayed on a scoreboard, while the "Megaphone Man" with his "leather lungs" would provide the play-by-play, as soon as it was received via the wires. And as far away as San Francisco, fans gathered at the office of the *San Francisco Chronicle*, enthusiastically following the game as if they were listening to two local teams. Interest was so strong that even the Supreme Court asked to receive bulletins; updates were sent during lunch and when the court was in recess, allowing the justices to keep up with the Series.

On Newspaper Row, the fans who could not get tickets (and even some who seemed to prefer listening to the game on a crowded street, along with thousands of their fellow fans) turned out in large numbers, blocking traffic and making plenty of noise; as they had done in years past, the *Globe* and the *Post* did their part to make the experience fun for all. While the crowd was mostly men, there were a number of women and even some children, all enjoying the game. Interestingly, the crowd seemed to be very egalitarian, with people from every walk of life, rich people and working-class people, all standing in the street together, eagerly cheering their team on to victory. When the Red Sox triumphed and won the Series, pandemonium reigned in the streets. Reporting on the reaction from the fans on Newspaper Row, an anonymous *Globe* reporter noted that they were "good-natured" and not too rowdy; but during the final game, the crowd kept getting larger, as workers left their offices early, to join the throngs in the street and listen to the play-by-play. When the winning run was scored, the fans shouted so loudly that they could be heard all over Washington Street. "Men danced and yelled and shook hands and patted each other on the back." For Red Sox fans, this was "the greatest year in the history of the game."[1] And it was thanks to the telegraph, as well as to the ingenuity of the newspapers, that the fans were able to keep up with the Red Sox and feel connected, even when the team was hundreds of miles away.

Bibliography:

"Boston Fans Celebrate By Blocking Traffic in the Street." *Chicago Tribune*, October 9, 1912, 23.

"Boston Is Picked By Portland Fans." *Portland Oregonian*, October 6, 1912, 4.

"Come to the Game!" *Hartford Courant*, October 8, 1912, 1.

"Frenzied Yell at End of Game." *Boston Globe*, October 17, 1912, 5.

"Hundreds Leaving Boston." *Galveston* (Texas) *Daily News*, October 8, 1912, 4.

"Last Tribute Paid to 'Tim' Murnane." *Boston Globe*, February 11, 1917, 24.

Jerry Nason. "A Century of Globe Sports." *Boston Globe*, March 13, 1972, 26.

Herman Nickerson. "Red Sox Home, Open the New Park Today." *Boston Journal*, April 18, 1912, 8.

Herman Nickerson. "Red Sox Opening Stopped By Rain, Carded for Today." *Boston Journal*, April 19, 1912, 8.

"Red Sox Still the Favorites." *Washington Post*, October 6, 1912, S2.

Mike Sowell. "The Birth of National Sports Coverage." *Journal of Sports Media*, (vol. 3 #1), Spring 2008, 51-75.

"Supreme Court Gets News From Fenway Park." *Boston Globe*, October 17, 1912, 1.

"The News Will Handle World's Series Right Up-to-the-Minute." *Lima* (Ohio) *News*, October 7, 1912, 1.

"The National Game." *San Francisco Chronicle*, October 10, 1912, 6.

"World Series Opens Oct. 8 in New York." *Boston Globe*, September 26, 1912, 1.

"World Series To Be Played In This City." *New Brunswick* (New Jersey) *Times*, October 7, 1912, 1.

Endnotes

1. Boston Globe, October 17, 1912, 5

Writing About the Red Sox in 1912
By Donna L. Halper

In October 1912 syndicated sports reporter Hugh S. Fullerton had baseball fans talking. Hughie, as he was known to his colleagues, made his annual World Series predictions, and asserted that the Red Sox were the superior team. While Boston's supporters were understandably pleased that a well-respected baseball expert like Fullerton believed the Red Sox would win it all, New York Giants fans reacted with outrage: they accused him of bias (he evidently had friends among the Boston sportswriters), and they said he had no credibility.[1] For several days, newspaper reporters across the country weighed in on whether Fullerton was right; and much as we see with today's call-in sports-talk shows, fans back then expressed their point of view by writing angry letters to their local newspaper. In that era before radio, it was through the newspapers that you kept up with your favorite sports.

For Red Sox fans in 1912, there were many publications that reported on the team. Most of the reporting emanated from Boston, a city with fierce competition among the nine newspapers that covered baseball. Newspapers in cities outside greater Boston tended to focus on their own local sporting scene, and they relied on the Associated Press or syndicated columnists when they needed a story about the Red Sox. In the city of Quincy, for example, one of the local newspapers, the *Quincy Daily Ledger*, rarely mentioned sports at all. The *Quincy Telegram* had a sports editor (Pete Morrison), but he followed only the schoolboy and amateur athletic contests. The paper published brief Red Sox articles during the season, but it used unsigned stories, probably from the Associated Press. (Quincy was actually adjacent to Boston.) And even when the Red Sox were in the World Series, the *Telegram* put the daily stories on either page 3 or page 4. That policy did not change when the Red Sox won the Series. "Red Sox Take Championship" was longer than many of the previous Red Sox stories, but it was still found on page 3, next to a lengthy report about how the Quincy High School football team had just defeated South Boston High, 12–0.

However, not every newspaper outside Boston ignored what the Red Sox were doing. The *Worcester Evening Gazette* provided thorough coverage of baseball; in fact, it was far more involved with the Boston sports scene than its main competitor, the *Worcester Daily Telegram*. While the *Daily Telegram* focused mainly on high-school and college sports, the *Evening Gazette* offered Red Sox coverage written by sports editor James H. Power; Power, a Worcester native, was a big sports fan, and his coverage of the Red Sox was as passionate as that of the Boston baseball writers. And even though Worcester was about 45 miles from Boston (a long trip in that era before superhighways), there was so much interest in the Red Sox that the *Evening Gazette* printed the inning-by-inning World Series results on page 1, with

Boston Baseball Writers. Former 19th Century player John Irwin hosted some of Boston's baseball community at his Sweet Summer Dream Hotel on Peddocks Island in Boston Harbor in the summer of 1908. Attendees included the Boston diehard Red Sox fans Royal Rooters, former players, and members of the sporting press. Pictured here in front of the hotel are Boston's most prominent sportswriters.

Top, left to right: O.W. Brown (*Boston Traveler*), Mose Chandler and Samuel Carrick (*Boston Journal*), Charles Leary (*Fall River Daily Globe*), Timothy Murnane (*Boston Globe*), Sam Crane (*New York Journal*), and O.J. Burke (*Boston Journal*).

Bottom: Wallace Goldsmith (*Boston Globe* sports cartoonist), Arthur Cooper (*Boston Post*), Herman Nickerson (*Boston Journal*), Ralph McKenna (*Boston Herald*), J.C. Morse (*Baseball Magazine*), and Paul Shannon (*Boston Post*).

the final score sent out as an Extra; the paper also announced bulletins and regular updates by megaphone to eager fans who gathered outside the newspaper's office.

In 1912 it was still the custom for most newspaper articles to be anonymous, whether the newspaper was in a big city like Boston or a small city like Fitchburg. But a few high-profile reporters had earned the right to have their own byline. On the news side, these men (and several women) tended to be international correspondents or reporters with a particular expertise, such as politics or the latest news of upper-class society. There were also some popular sportswriters with a byline: In addition to syndicated baseball writers like Hugh S. Fullerton, a number of cities had at least one or two local writers with bylines. Among Boston's best-known sportswriters of 1912 were Timothy Hayes "Tim" Murnane and James C. "Uncle Jim" O'Leary of the *Boston Globe*, Paul H. "Herbie" Shannon and Samuel P. "Sam" Carrick of the *Post*, Ralph E. McMillin of the *Herald*, L.R. "Riley" Murdoch of the *American*, Earl C. Deland of the *Evening Record*, and Herman Nickerson of the *Boston Journal*. Today only the most diehard sports fans know their names, but in 1912 readers who followed the Red Sox couldn't wait to find out what they had to say.

An early illustration of Tim Murnane from the November 27, 1886 *National Police Gazette*. A legendary publication that ran for over 130 years and presumably devoted to police matters, the *Police Gazette* was a tabloid-like publication which included a bi-monthly baseball column. Note their alternate spelling of "Murnan" in this image.

The most famous Boston baseball writer was Tim Murnane. (In the custom of that era, reporters used their first two initials, so many of his articles had T.H. Murnane as the byline.) A former major-league player now considered the dean of Boston's sports reporters, he was so well-respected that newspapers nationwide frequently quoted him.[2] Murnane was born on June 4, 1851, and most sources say that he grew up in Naugatuck, Connecticut, not far from Waterbury, a fact Murnane mentioned in several of his own columns (for example, in a 1904 *Globe* article about former Boston first baseman George Lachance, who now lived near Waterbury, Murnane remarked that he too had been born and raised nearby.[3] But interestingly, the *Hartford Courant* and the *Naugatuck Evening News*, when writing Murnane's obituary, both stated that he had actually been born in Tipperary, Ireland, and that his family had emigrated to the United States, settling in Naugatuck, when he was 6 years old.

Whether Murnane was born in the US (as he said in several of his articles, and as he asserted on his passport application in 1874), or whether he came over as a boy, we know few details about his childhood; we do know that he attended a country school in Naugatuck, and we also know from his writings that he loved baseball from the first time he learned the game. By 1869, when he was 18 years old, he had begun playing semipro ball for clubs in Stratford and Norwalk, Connecticut, and at that time newspapers spelled his last name "Murnan." While he would later be known as a first baseman, early in his career he was a catcher. As with many aspiring ballplayers, he supported himself by doing factory work, and then played baseball for the local town team; while playing for Middletown, for example, he was employed by the Douglas Pump Works.[4] He left Connecticut in late 1870 to play in Savannah, Georgia. The Savannah team, which one old-timer later recalled was known as the Savannah Seniors, toured the Eastern United States in 1871, and in one of his first efforts as a writer, Murnane kept a journal about the cities he went to and the way the game was played.[5] These reflections would stand him in good stead later on, when he became a reporter for the *Boston Globe* and wrote columns in which he looked back on baseball in the 1870s.[6]

By 1872 Murnane had made the leap to the major leagues, joining the Middletown Mansfields and then the 1873 Philadelphia Athletics; he was part of the Athletics when they visited England in 1874 to demonstrate American baseball to a British audience that much preferred cricket but was very polite and appreciative towards the American players.[7] Murnane, who now played first base and sometimes center field, next played a year for the Philadelphia Whites, before coming to Boston in 1876 to play for the team sometimes called the Boston Nationals and at other times the Boston Red Stockings. He played for the Providence Grays in 1878, and in 1879 and 1880 he seems to have played part-time in Albany, New York, for the Hop Bitters (named for a patent medicine and beer whose maker sponsored the team), the former Albany team known in the press as the Capitol City Base-Ball Club, before retiring from the game to open a saloon and billiard parlor.[8] His love of baseball drew him back to it: He became the player-manager of the Boston Reds of the Union Association in 1884, appeared in 14 games for the Jersey City Skeeters in 1885, and managed the Boston Blues in the New England League in 1886.

While a thorough examination of his baseball career is outside the scope of this essay, he was described by his contemporaries as a reliable fielder and a speedy runner.[9] And his statistics during eight years in the majors showed that he was a good (but not great) hitter, posting a .261 batting average and driving in 130 runs. But for some unexplained reason, he became the subject of an urban legend, involving his allegedly light hitting. In 1923, six years after he died, a syndicated column appeared in the *Los Angeles Times*, *Cleveland Plain Dealer*, and several other papers. Claiming that Murnane was "weak at the bat," the anonymous article asserted that one day "his bat gave a weak tap, half-hearted, unplanned" and when the pitcher could not field it, Tim ended up on first base. He then decided to use this technique more often so that he could get on base.[10]

The problem with the story was that it was demonstrably false. Murnane himself acknowledged that the inventor of the bunt had been Dick Pearce, a fact he stated in a 1905 profile of Pearce for the *Boston Globe*. The headline read "Baseball 'Bunt' Inventor," and in the article Pearce recalled how he had first begun working on it in 1867, before Murnane ever played professional baseball. By the time he became a sportswriter, Murnane had already developed a

Murnane played professional baseball for five teams from 1872-78 and 1884, including as a charter member of Boston Red Stockings. He also served as president of the New England Baseball League for 23 years. It's probably safe to assume that his experience as a player helped him achieve success as a reporter and writer, both in knowledge of the game and the respect of the players on whom he reported.

reputation as a historian of the game, and in his columns for the *Globe*, he often interviewed the "old timers," with whom he clearly enjoyed reminiscing. But in this case, he especially wanted to make sure the story was told correctly, because he had a specific memory of watching Pearce play. As Murnane explained in his story about Pearce, "The first professional ball game I ever witnessed was at Brooklyn, June 14, 1870. Mr. Pearce was one of the star players of that memorable event. ..."[11] Yet, despite Murnane's best efforts, the erroneous story of the bunt's inception was repeated in other newspapers for years, including in the *Boston Globe*, which ran a version of it on March 23, 1930.

In addition to his years as a player, Murnane also served as president of the New England League from 1892 to 1915.[12] His writing career seems to have begun in 1885, when he founded a weekly sports journal called the *Boston Referee*, and it led him to pursue a position as a full-time sportswriter; he was hired by the *Boston Globe* in 1888, and remained there for nearly 30 years.[13] In addition to sportswriting for the *Globe*, he published a 50-page guide called *How to Play Baseball* in 1903, which was described in a brief *New York Times* book review as "about the best work of its kind ever published"; the book was reissued and updated in 1907.[14] And in October 1908 Murnane joined with a group of other sports reporters to form the Baseball Writers Association of America; he was on the board, serving as the organization's first treasurer.

Murnane was such a well-respected expert that in the summer of 1888, there were some fans who wanted him named manager of the Boston Beaneaters, according to the *Boston Globe*. The paper held a fan poll, and while the current manager, John Morrill, got most of the votes—200 of them, Murnane got 45, a respectable showing for a sportswriter.[15] Fans enjoyed reading Tim Murnane's daily reports. Not only did he write about the current Red Sox team and what was happening around the league; he seemed to know all of the players and managers, and provided an inside look at the game. Murnane could explain rule changes, analyze the manager's strategy, or get a quote from the league's president, Byron Bancroft "Ban" Johnson. He could take current fans on a trip down memory lane, sharing his recollections of how the game used to be played, as he did in an article about catcher John E. Clapp, whom Murnane first saw as a teammate playing for Middletown, Connecticut, in 1872, and who was also a teammate on the Philadelphia Athletics team that toured England in 1874.[16] He was not afraid to be critical of the umpires, or take the players to task, although when he did so, his tone was never rude or irate. In his obituary, tributes from some of the players he had covered and the journalists who had worked with him mentioned how much he respected the game and how courteous he was.[17]

When the Red Sox opened the 1912 season in their new ballpark, it was Tim Murnane who did the page 1 story in the *Boston Globe*, and throughout the season it was he who wrote the majority of the articles about the "Speed Boys," the name he had first applied to them in 1909. But while Murnane was certainly the best-known of the Boston sportswriters, and a dominant figure in the world of baseball, there were other influential writers in town as well. One of them was the *Boston Journal*'s Herman Nickerson, another Boston writer who was frequently quoted by out-of-town newspapers. Born in Boston on May 20, 1870, Nickerson came from a notable family: Three of his ancestors had fought in the Revolutionary War. Unlike Murnane, Nickerson had not played professional baseball, nor had he been a sportswriter until a few years before the 1912 season; he had covered business and finance at the *Boston Post*, and was a news reporter when he joined the *Journal*. But around 1909, he began reporting on baseball and soon was focusing on the game exclusively, moving up to sports editor. He too joined the Baseball Writers Association, and in 1911 he served as the official scorer for Boston's National

Boston Braves Secretary Herman Nickerson (back row, far right) at a February 11, 1913 meeting of National League owners and representatives that included Garry Herrmann, Charles Ebbets, and Mrs. Helene Robison Britton. Nickerson left the Boston Journal shortly after the Red Sox won the 1912 World Series, becoming secretary of the Boston Braves of the National League. During his tenure, he participated in the remarkable midseason last-to-first transformation of the 1914 "Miracle" Braves World Championship team.

League team, that season called the Rustlers. (They became the Braves the next season.) Nickerson was so well regarded that he was one of a small contingent of reporters (usually led by Murnane) who traveled by train with the Red Sox on road trips.[18] This contributed to the insights he was able to provide to his readers. Nickerson's reports were sometimes syndicated, which meant that fans in cities as far away as Galveston, Texas, and Ogden, Utah, could keep up with the Red Sox.

In 1912 Nickerson predicted that the Red Sox would win the pennant and the World Series, but perhaps because he was a local sportswriter rather than a nationally known figure like Hugh S. Fullerton, his prediction did not cause the controversy that Fullerton's did.[19] Nickerson also was given a very influential position in September 1912: It was he who was in charge of the press box during the World Series. This meant that any out-of-town reporter who wanted to get one of the limited number of seats in the press box had to apply to him and make a good case. Evidently many were able to do so. Despite initially saying that access would be restricted to working journalists from major newspapers, Nickerson and his colleagues were able to make room for more than 260 journalists and a large number of telegraphers; an expanded press area was created to accommodate all the interest.[20]

The month after the Red Sox won the World Series, Nickerson left the *Boston Journal* to become secretary to the Boston Braves, a position he held until 1915. His timing was excellent: while the team of perpetual underachievers continued to struggle in 1913, the next season Nickerson was there to witness an amazing transformation, as the Braves went from league doormats to the Miracle Braves, who not only won the pennant but then completed a four-game sweep of the heavily favored Philadelphia Athletics in the World Series. Nickerson had now seen both Boston teams become World Series champions.

Another important local journalist in 1912 was Paul H. "Herbie" Shannon of the *Boston Post*; he too was in the group of Boston writers who often traveled with the Red Sox. Like his colleagues Tim Murnane and Herman Nickerson, Shannon was an early member of the Baseball Writers Association. Born in September 1875 and raised in greater Boston, he attended Boston College before becoming a journalist. Shannon spent nearly all of his career at the *Boston Post*, with the exception of September 1906 to April 1907; due to poor health, he needed to work in a warmer climate for a while, so he accepted an offer from the *San Antonio Times* and once he had recovered, he returned to Boston, where the *Post* welcomed him back.[21] Shannon was one of the most popular local sportswriters, praised for his eloquence with the pen; out-of-town newspapers that did not have the personnel to focus on Boston sports found him an excellent resource for inside information on what the managers and team executives were doing, and his reporting was often quoted in such papers as the *Lowell Sun*. He also developed some lasting friendships at newspapers in New Hampshire. Early in his career, before he became a full-time sportswriter, he was a news reporter for the *Post* and went to Portsmouth, New Hampshire, in 1905 to cover the negotiation of a peace treaty to end the Russo-Japanese war. While there he became friendly with members of the *Portsmouth Herald*; years later, that newspaper continued to follow his career. When he married in July 1911, the *Herald* put the story of the

Paul Shannon of the *Boston Post* (in vest), one of the best-known baseball writers in Boston in this era, also served as the President of the Baseball Writers Association of America. Depicted as well are "Nuf Ced" McGreevey in the Boston shirt and Amby McConnell, with cap in hand on March 2, 1909 during Spring Training in Hot Springs, Arkansas.

wedding on page 1, remarking that Shannon's activities were still of interest to local newsmen, who remembered him from his work in the region in 1905.[22]

It is fair to say, based on the number of times they were quoted in other newspapers, that Murnane, Nickerson, and Shannon were considered the best-known Boston baseball writers of 1912. But there was another writer who had a unique distinction: He was also a poet. Ralph Edward McMillin (his byline often read R.E. McMillin) was a sportswriter for the *Boston Herald*. Born in Amsterdam, New York, in June 1882, he was raised in North Adams, Massachusetts. He attended Williams College in Williamstown, Massachusetts, before beginning his career as a reporter with the *Boston Evening Record*. He joined the *Herald* in 1905 and worked his way up from reporter to sports editor, the position he held in 1912. At first, he covered college sports, but it did not take long before he became one of the regular Red Sox reporters. McMillin would later report for the *Boston Journal*, covering college sports as well as baseball; in 1914, it was he who had the job formerly done by Herman Nickerson, deciding which reporters would have press-box access during that year's World Series.

But while professional baseball was his first love, McMillin often wanted to express his observations about what he saw around him, and he began writing poetry as a hobby. Some of the local newspapers published his verses, many of which were patriotic. One particularly touching poem was written in tribute to his colleague Tim Murnane, when the veteran sportswriter died suddenly in February 1917.[23] Sadly, McMillin himself would die young, at the age of 35, in 1918, a victim of pneumonia during the devastating flu epidemic that year. A colleague at the *Hartford Courant* who knew his work commented that he undoubtedly could have had a successful career in literature once his career as a sportswriter had ended.[24] McMillin's father, Edward, published a book of his son's verses not long after his death.

Also popular in 1912 was the columnist regularly referred to as L.R. Murdoch. His real name (which he seems to have rarely used) was Louis Rae Murdoch. His friends and colleagues called him Riley. He was born in Washington, D.C., in March 1876, and was raised in Syracuse, New York. After attending Cornell, he began a long career in journalism, first in Syracuse and then in Boston, Chicago, and other cities; at various periods in his career, he was a war correspondent and a news reporter, but during his years in Boston, he was mainly known as a sportswriter. In 1912 you would have read him in the *Boston American*, where he wrote "Riley's Column" and covered both the Red Sox and the Braves.

And if you were a sports fan in 1912, there is one other group of men (and they were all men at that time) whose work you enjoyed: cartoonists. Nearly every newspaper had at least one artist whose specialty was providing clever illustrations to go along with the reporter's story. Some cartoonists used humor to examine changing customs and attitudes in society, as Gene Carr, a syndicated illustrator on the *New York World*, often did; while others focused mainly on sports, providing caricatures of the players or amusing scenes from the previous day's game.

Two of Boston's best known sports cartoonists in 1912 were the *Globe*'s Wallace Goldsmith and the *Journal*'s Sid Greene. Both men created illustrations to accompany a story: Greene frequently illustrated Herman Nickerson's columns, while Goldsmith was so valued as an illustrator that he sometimes accompanied Tim Murnane on road trips, cartooning about the Red Sox from a number of different cities.[25] But while both men were very talented, some modern researchers might find their work problematic, since they sometimes utilized racist or sexist stereotypes. In fairness, Greene and Goldsmith reflected the views of their era and undoubtedly were seen by readers as trying to be funny. Still, it might be difficult for modern fans to feel comfortable while reading Goldsmith's black-themed comic strip, "Asa Spades." It ran in the *Globe* from 1910 through 1912, and featured a lead character who spoke the kind of error-filled English later associated with Amos 'n' Andy, and who exemplified every stereotype of what were then called "negroes." Modern criticisms aside, in an era before photography had taken full command, when it was easier to illustrate an article using pen and ink, Boston's sports cartoonists were widely read and greatly appreciated. Their work enhanced the reader's understanding of what was being reported.

One other interesting fact about the 1912 Boston sportswriters is that in 1913 some of them were involved in a controversy over what we would today call ghost-writing. During the World Series, numerous newspapers (the *Globe* and the *Denver Post* among them) trumpeted that their sports pages would feature commentary about the Series from such important players as Walter Johnson, Tris Speaker, Honus Wagner, and Cy Young. While the fans were undoubtedly impressed to hear from such experts, it was later revealed that these players had not written the "behind the scenes" articles attributed to them. In fact, it was sportswriters from New York and Boston who assumed the persona of the players. Reacting to the news, American League President Ban Johnson decreed that ballplayers would be barred from writing articles for newspapers. There were two problems, as he saw it: One was that the practice was deceptive, leading readers to believe they were actually hearing from the players when in fact, the words on the page were written by someone else; and the statements written in the newspapers, while usually bland and benign, occasionally made critical comments or even seemed to taunt other players.[26]

One ballplayer whose name was on some of the 1912 World Series articles was pitcher Christy Mathewson, and he felt unfairly accused. He insisted that he had in fact written his own articles, although he did acknowledge that at times, when under a deadline, he had dictated his thoughts to a newspaper reporter who compiled them;

Tim Murnane Benefit Day–September 27, 1917. Dipping back into time to re-utilize an old team name, the Boston Americans played an exhibition game organized as a benefit for the family of Murnane, who had passed away early in 1917. The Murnane Day game was the second of the two most important charity fundraisers of the decade, a reflection the impact Murnane had on Boston and the baseball world, the first being an event for Addie Joss' family following his untimely passing in 1911.

Opposing the Americans were a group of All-Stars, including Rabbit Maranville, Ty Cobb, Tris Speaker, Joe Jackson, Ray Chapman, Buck Weaver, and Stuffy McInnis. The Americans won, 2-0, behind the shutout pitching of Babe Ruth and Rube Foster who out-performed the likes of Walter Johnson. Retired championship boxer John L. Sullivan coached at third base for the Americans, and actress Fanny Brice helped hawk programs. Shoeless Joe Jackson won a pre-game throwing contest with a 396-foot heave. Ruth won in fungo hitting. Will Rogers performed lariat tricks from horseback, and both Speaker and Cobb took turns on the steed.

but he said he always looked over the final story before it went to press, to make sure it reflected what he actually had said. And he also insisted that all of his teammates had written their own stories, too. But two syndicated columnists, William Peet and Tommy Clark, persisted in reporting on the controversy; both men seemed unpersuaded by Mathewson's defense of himself and his teammates. Peet, a columnist for the *Washington Herald*, even published a list of the players who had falsely claimed to write their own stories, and next to them, he listed the journalists who were their ghost-writers: he entitled it "Some of the Fakers." (In his story, he insisted that Mathewson did in fact have a ghost-writer, *New York Herald* sportswriter Jack Wheeler. Mathewson immediately denied it.) Peet also noted that the players had good reason to favor (and defend) this practice, since they were paid extra money by the newspapers for the use of their name.[27]

As for which reporters were included in the list of fakers, there were some surprises. As Clark reported, "Walter Johnson's screeds came from the pen of Ralph McMillin, a Boston sporting editor. Cy Young's pieces were turned out by Samuel Carrick [of the *Boston Post*]. Paul Shannon was the author of Charley Wagner's effusions….[and] Tim Murnane wrote for Tris Speaker." And noting Ban Johnson's later edict that forbade players to act as sportswriters, Clark observed that enforcing such an ultimatum would be difficult. The newspapers liked it because having big-name players as "reporters" sold papers, and the players liked it because they could make extra money just for letting their name be put on an article.[28] But while the story ran in a number of out-of-town newspapers, most of which appeared ambivalent about whether this was really a problem, the Boston newspapers seemed to downplay it. The *Globe* issued an opinion piece lamenting the passing of the "Player-Author" and managed to report the story without once mentioning that anyone from the paper had been accused. And perhaps wanting to show the public they recognized an ethical issue, in mid-March, 1913, the New York and Brooklyn chapters of the Baseball Writers Association issued a joint resolution condemning the practice of attributing articles to players who did not write them.[29]

But in 1912, the average baseball fan was probably not outraged by the idea that players might be getting some help writing the stories that appeared under their byline in the newspaper. There were other things to think about, and an exciting pennant race to follow. Boston had loyal and passionate fans, and they wanted to be informed about their favorite team. And every day Boston's baseball writers did just that: They kept the fans informed and entertained, providing solid writing, interesting stories and opinions, topics for debate, and a chronicle of a season to remember.

A tip of the cap to a student of mine at Lesley University, Paul-Michael Russo, a devoted baseball fan who helped gather some of the research in this article. And eternal appreciation to the Microfilm Department of the Boston Public Library and the Worcester Public Library.

Sources:

"A Game's Grand Old Man." *Kansas City Star*, February 15, 1917, 15.

"Ban Johnson's Edict Will Bar Trouble." *Hartford Courant*, March 15, 1913, 18.

"Base-Ball in Boston," *Baltimore Sun*, April 24, 1884, 5.

"Baseball Panorama." *Cleveland Plain Dealer*, November 28, 1923, 18.

"Baseball Writers are Organized." *Detroit Free Press*, October 15, 1908, 7.

"Before and After." *Hartford Courant*, February 12, 1918, 14.

Charlie Bevis. *The New England League: A Baseball History, 1885-1949*. (Jefferson, North Carolina: McFarland, 2008).

"Book Review: How to Play Baseball." *New York Times*, April 11, 1903, 11.

Tommy Clark. "Bomb Hurled at Player-Authors." *Sheboygan* (Wisconsin) *Press*, March 22, 1913, 8.

Wallace Goldsmith. "Mr. Asa Spades and The Pup Do Their Best to Hunch in Another Red Sox Run." *Boston Globe*, July 29, 1910, 7.

Wallace Goldsmith. "They're On Their Way." *Boston Globe*, February 25, 1909, 1.

"Great Baseball Experts Will Write for the Post." *Denver Post*, September 20, 1912, 14.

Charles A. Lamar. "The Old Time Fan Delves Into Mutuals V. Savannah Baseball of Early Seventies." *Atlanta Constitution*, August 10, 1913, 11.

Christy Mathewson. "Defends Players Writing Articles for Newspapers." *Indianapolis Star*, February 27, 1913, 11.

Ralph E. McMillin with Edward A. McMillin. *The Poems of Ralph McMillin*. (Self-published, Boston, 1919).

Gerry Moore. "Paul H. Shannon is Victim of Accidental Drowning." *Boston Globe*, January 21, 1938, 13.

"Loving Tributes To T.H. Murnane: Murnane as a Player." *Boston Globe*, February 8, 1917, 7.

"Morrill the Favorite." *Boston Globe*, August 12, 1888, 6.

"Murnane Drops Dead in Theatre: Baseball Editor of the *Globe* For 30 Years." *Boston Globe*, February 8, 1917, 1, 7.

Tim Murnane. "Ball Heroes: Some of Those at the Chicago Meeting." *Boston Globe*, November 30, 1896, 9.

Tim Murnane. "Baseball Bunt Inventor: Dick Pearce, the Oldest Living Professional Ball Player." *Boston Globe*, December 17, 1905, SM5.

Tim Murnane. "King of Naugatuck Valley." *Boston Globe*, December

25, 1904, SM3.

Tim Murnane. "Merely a Romp for the Red Sox." *Boston Globe*, April 18, 1909, 10.

Tim Murnane. "Murnane President of Eastern League." *Boston Globe*, February 25, 1916, 7.

Tim Murnane. "Old Reliable Got There: Tim Murnane on Base Ball in 1871." *Boston Globe*, December 31, 1888, 8.

Tim Murnane. "Wonder in His Time." *Boston Globe*, January 21, 1889, 6.

Herman Nickerson. "Boston Expert Picks the Red Sox to Win in Not Over Five Games." *Chicago Tribune*, October 6, 1912, C2.

Herman Nickerson. "Five Games Should End the Series." *Boston Journal*, October 7, 1912, 8.

"Nickerson to be Club Secretary." *Christian Science Monitor*, November 7, 1912, 3.

"Passing of the Player-Author." *Boston Globe*, March 23, 1913, 11.

William Peet. "Do You Know Who Writes the Dope You Read?" *Denver Post*, February 28, 1913, 13.

"Red Sox in Town for Game Today." *Abilene* (Texas) *Daily Reporter*, March 29, 1911, 1.

"Riley Murdoch, News Editor, Dies Here." *Boston Evening American*, March 3, 1938, 12.

"Shannon-Magner." *Portsmouth* (New Hampshire) *Herald*, July 6, 1911, 1.

"Skilled Writers Will Report Games." *Reno Evening Gazette*, September 23, 1912, 6.

"Sudden Death of Tim Murnane." *Naugatuck* (Connecticut) *Daily News*, February 8, 1917, 3.

"Watch-Tower Observations." *Portland Oregonian*, October 13, 1912, 4.

"Will Locate in Texas." *Portsmouth* (New Hampshire) *Herald*, February 12, 1906, 8.

"World Series Writers Plans." *Washington Post*, September 23, 1912, 8.

Endnotes

1. "Watch Tower Observations," 4

2. Examples include the *St. Louis Post-Dispatch*, the *Chicago Tribune*, and the *Cleveland Plain Dealer*

3. Murnane, "King of Naugatuck," SM3

4. "Murnane as a Player," 7

5. Lamar, "The Old Time Fan," 11

6. Murnane, "Old Reliable," 8. Murnane bylines were often rendered as T.H. Murnane, and at least once as Timothy Murnane, but we have listed them all as a more familiar Tim Murnane here.

7. "A Game's Grand Old Man," 15

8. After he returned to baseball, while some stories stressed how much he missed the game and wanted to get back into it, which may certainly have been true, the *Baltimore Sun* reported that Murnane returned to the game "after a failure in business." "Base-Ball in Boston," *Baltimore Sun*, April 24, 1884, 5

9. "A Game's Grand Old Man," 15

10. "Baseball Panorama," 4

11. Murnane, "Baseball Bunt Inventor," December 17, 1905, SM5

12. Bevis, 146

13. "A Game's Grand Old Man," 15

14. "Book Review," 11

15. "Morrill the Favorite," August 12, 1888, 6

16. Murnane, "Wonder in His Time," 6

17. "Murnane Drops Dead in Theatre," 1

18. "Red Sox in Town," 1

19. Nickerson, "Boston Expert," C2

20. "Skilled Writers" 6

21. "Will Locate in Texas," 8

22. "Shannon-Magner," 1

23. McMillin and McMillin, 61

24. "Before and After," 14

25. Goldsmith, "They're On Their Way," 1

26. "Ban Johnson's Edict," 18

27. Peet, 13

28. Clark, 8

29. "Passing of the Player-Author,"11

A Brief Note on Boston's "Other Big-League Team"
By Bill Nowlin

There was another big-league team in town—the Boston Braves. SABR has in the works something of a companion volume to this one looking at the 1914 World Champion "Miracle Braves," and that will be an opportunity to delve more deeply into a look at the Braves.

One would think the Red Sox might have been "the other team" in town. After all, the Red Sox were the upstart in Boston, with only 11 years under their belts at the beginning of the 1912 campaign. The Braves were one of the charter franchises in the National League, playing since 1876. They had been a successful team over the years, winning the pennant eight times between 1877 and 1898 as the Boston Red Stockings and the Boston Beaneaters.

After the American League launched in 1901, however, the team (first named the Braves in 1912) had not fared well in head-to-head competition for fans in Boston. Yet another publication in this series—devoted to the 1901 Boston Americans—tells the story of how the American League entered Boston and instantly drew support away from Boston's NL team. Signing several of their bigger stars, including the man they made manager—Jimmy Collins—was a start. Undercutting them on ticket prices was another technique which worked to perfection. It didn't hurt that the new team had a new ballpark, where the Beaneaters were playing in a somewhat substandard all-wooden South End Grounds. By contrast, the Huntington Avenue Grounds home of the new club looked "impressive in comparison to the modest all-wood park Soden had built for his NL club after the fire of '94 had wiped out their castle-like home."[1]

Ban Johnson's new American League was offering salaries that may have averaged more than 20% higher than the National League, and promised not to bind players with a reserve clause which would restrict their ability to sell their services as free agents in future years. The Royal Rooters booster group of fans followed some of the players with whom they had become friendly, such as Collins, and transferred more of their loyalties to the upstart Americans.[2] In their first season the new AL team outdrew the more established Braves (they were known as the Beaneaters in 1901), 289,448 to 146,502 paying patrons, the lowest attendance of any of the NL teams.

For the first four years of the century, 1901 through 1904, the two teams sometimes played home games at the same time, but beginning in 1905 the two league schedules were coordinated so that when one team was in town, the other would be on the road.

In the first 11 years of head-to-head competition, the Red Sox outdrew the Braves in attendance 5,187,055 to 1,757,780—basically three to one. In 1912, the Sox drew 597,096 while the last-place Braves only drew 121,000—almost five times as many fans heading to Fenway than to see the Braves.

In 1912, the Boston Braves finished in last place in the National League. Although there wasn't as much fuss as one might have expected regarding the opening of a new ballpark, Fenway Park, the Red Sox were really the team which drew the lion's share of fan attention. The newspapers were generally even-handed in matters such as placement of game stories in the sports pages, giving something approaching equal space to both teams. But the Red Sox had the more compelling story—a very successful season—and so won more front-page attention as the season progressed.

Even when the Braves won the National League pennant just two years later, in 1914, while the Red Sox finished 8½ games out of first place, the Braves still couldn't catch up with the Red Sox in attendance, attracting 382,913 patrons to the Red Sox total of 481,359. It was an ongoing struggle which was valiantly waged for more than half a century but ultimately resulted in the Braves leaving Boston in 1953.

Two years after the Red Sox won the World Series, the 1914 "Miracle Braves" did the same, playing in the larger Boston ballpark: Fenway Park. Shown here before Game Three at Fenway on October 12, 1914, are Boston Mayor Fitzgerald, catcher Hank Gowdy (whose home run in the bottom of the tenth helped the Braves overcome a 4-2 deficit, and who doubled to set up the winning run in the bottom of the 12th), and Braves owner James E. Gaffney.

Endnotes

1. Saul Wisnia, *From Yawkey to Milwaukee*, forthcoming manuscript. Thanks to Bob Brady and Saul Wisnia of the Boston Braves Historical Association for commenting on a draft of this brief article. In an e-mail communication, Bob mentioned that the cheapness of the Beaneaters owners was reflected both in their under-insuring the first South End Grounds ballpark and in their penuriousness as to player salaries, which rendered their roster ripe for plucking. He added, "Viewing club president Arthur Soden as a 'cheapskate' may be too simplistic a conclusion. He was said to be a man of unquestioned integrity (during a period in baseball history when such a trait was scarce) and a reflection of (and a captive of) his Yankee heritage—conservative and frugal. While much negativity is associated with his birthing of the reserve clause, it was a stabilizing factor at a time when the National League was battling the Union Association, Players League and American Association for supremacy. While the club was successful on the field during his reign, its financial footings didn't fully match its performance. Soden's creation of a reserve clause was a reaction to players jumping teams (e.g., the National's loss of George Wright and Jim O'Rourke to Providence in 1879) and its effect on fan loyalty and financial stability. He was once quoted as saying, 'What man in his right mind will invest money in this kind of business? Today he has some assets. Tomorrow he may have none.' However, his (and the National League's) inability to alter their rigid business strategy to address the challenges posed by Ban Johnson and the American League, greatly aided the establishment of the Junior Circuit and the evolution of Boston into an American League town."

2. As Glenn Stout wrote in *Red Sox Century*, "The Rooters were sympathetic. A spirit of reform was in the air and trade unionism was on the rise. They shared the players' immigrant, working-class roots, and the National League's refusal to recognize the Ballplayers' Protective Association or even listen to their complaints touched a nerve. The boys at McGreevey's were such staunch unionists they even sponsored benefit ballgames to help striking steelworkers."

After the conclusion of Fenway's 100th season, the Red Sox staged an event in December 2011 to announce plans for the 100th anniversary celebrations in 2012. Outside the park were some vintage automobiles while inside there was a dramatic rendering of the auction at which the land on which the park was built first changed hands.

Contributors

Marc Z Aaron is a Certified Public Accountant and Certified Valuation Analyst with a tax practice in Randolph, Vermont. He is also an adjunct professor of economics at Vermont Technical College and the Anglo American University in Prague and an adjunct professor of accounting at Norwich University and the University of New York in Prague. A born and bred Yankees fan, Marc has four sons, coached little league for six seasons, and like Tony La Russa, retired after his team (sadly named Red Sox) won the league championship. Marc, a tournament tennis player, has been a ranked singles player by the New England United States Tennis Association (USTA) and has captained several USTA league teams.

Ron Anderson grew up in the Boston area, first and foremost a Braves fan, but morphed permanently to the vicissitudes of a Red Sox team upon the Braves departure in 1953. He has contributed to several SABR as well as other baseball publications, and is the author of *Long Taters: A Baseball Biography of George "Boomer" Scott*, McFarland Publishing, released in December 2011. He lives with his wife, Gail, in North Sutton, NH.

Mark Armour is the director of SABR's Baseball Biography Project and the author of three books, including *Joe Cronin—A Life In Baseball* (Nebraska, 2010). He lives in Oregon's Willamette Valley with Jane, Maya and Drew.

Maurice Bouchard, a SABR member since 1999, spends more time in front of his computer trying to find the maiden names of obscure players' mothers than he should admit. He has worked as an author, editor, or fact-checker on nine SABR team books, starting in 2005 with *'75: The Red Sox Team that Saved Baseball*. An academic cicada, Bouchard recently completed a second masters degree (this one from Simmons College Graduate School of Library and Information Science) fourteen years after his first one, which in turn was fourteen years after his undergraduate degree. The discipline for the 2025 degree is anyone's guess. At the time of publication, Bouchard and his painfully beautiful wife Kim are living with their two pooches in Westford, New York, just ten minutes drive from 25 Main Street, Cooperstown.

Tony Bunting writes about baseball in the early decades of the 20th century. His article on the Cubs' and White Sox' electrifying dash to the 1906 World Series appeared in *108* magazine, and he's contributed biographies to two books: *Deadball Stars of the American League* and *When Boston Still Had the Babe: the 1918 World Champion Red Sox*. An employee at the Art Institute of Chicago, Bunting lives on the Windy City's northwest side, a 45-minute walk from Wrigley Field.

Dan Desrochers' ventures to Fenway Park began in 1967 as a 12 year-old who had a passionate desire to attend a Red Sox game. Unbeknownst to his parents, he schemed and plotted his "Impossible Dream" Maine-to-Boston venture that combined bicycling, hiking, and bus and train rides to catch his first Red Sox game. He completed the 200-mile trip and managed to get home before dark. He now lives in Portsmouth, New Hampshire though he still considers himself to be a Mainer—and continues to organize Red Sox trips without his mom's permission. He was behind the Red Sox dugout in St. Louis when the Red Sox won it all in 2004.

Doug Dowell is a Professor of Sociology and Social Work at Heartland Community College in Normal, Illinois. A life-long Cubs fan he has passed this obsession onto his sons, Will and Christian. He is a native of Bishop Hill, Illinois and now makes his home in Bloomington, Illinois with his two sons and wife, Stacia.

David Fleitz, a computer systems analyst from Pleasant Ridge, Michigan, has written seven books on baseball history, including biographies of Shoeless Joe Jackson, Louis Sockalexis, and Cap Anson. David's latest work, *Silver Bats and Automobiles: The Hotly Competitive, Sometimes Ignoble Pursuit of the Major League Batting Championship*, was published by McFarland in 2011. He is currently working on a biography of Napoleon Lajoie. David is also a trivia expert, having won the individual trivia competition at three consecutive SABR conventions beginning in 2006.

David Forrester is a technology executive and lifelong Red Sox fan now living in exile with the Seattle Mariners. After spending his first 36 years in and around Boston, he is the proud owner of a New England temperament. He joined SABR ten years ago when his research uncovered Allie Moulton, the first person of African American ancestry known to have played in the segregated major leagues.

Michael Foster is a Senior Lecturer at Curry College in Milton, Massachusetts and Librarian and Social Studies teacher at Saint Raphael Academy in Pawtucket, Rhode Island. He has been a member of SABR since 2001 and has published numerous deadball era player biographies and research articles in that time. He is a native of Middlebury, Vermont, who now makes his home in Hopkinton, Massachusetts, with Sarah, Maggie and Griffin.

ReBecca Glidewell-Hall was born at Madigan Army Hospital, Tacoma Pierce County, Washington. Married to the grandson of Charley Hall, Charles Louis Hall III, she discovered a family bible that began its line of descent in 1804. This began the love of genealogy. Charley's granddaughters have heard many of the family stories and hope to share them with their descendants.

Donna L. Halper is an Assistant Professor of Communication at Lesley University, Cambridge MA. A media historian who specializes in the history of broadcasting, Dr. Halper is the author of five books and many articles. She is also a former broadcaster and print journalist.

Tom Hawthorn is a columnist for the *Globe and Mail* newspaper who lives in Victoria, British Columbia. He saw his first big-league game from the Jonesville bleachers at Jarry Park in Montreal.

Joanne Hulbert, co-chair of the Boston Chapter and SABR's Baseball Arts Committee, spends long hours obsessively gathering baseball poetry when not at Fenway Park. A resident of Mudville, a village of Holliston, MA she occasionally leaves her poetic pursuit to indulge in something completely different. She has found that there's always something poetic about the life of an obscure and often forgotten player who has a story just as important and valuable to baseball history as any hall of fame inductee.

Don Jensen is a Senior Fellow at the Center for Transatlantic Relations, Nitze School of Advanced International Studies, Johns Hopkins University, He is the author of *Timeline History of Baseball* and has written widely on the game in the Nineteenth Century and Deadball Era. He is currently working on a book devoted to lives and times of John Montgomery Ward and Helen Dauvray. Jensen lives in Alexandria, Virginia, but, as a native San Franciscan, remains a devoted fan of the Giants and Seals.

Craig Lammers is both a SABR member and Country/Bluegrass Music Director at WBGU radio in Bowling Green Ohio. He's currently working on a Deadball era history of minor league baseball in Ohio. Craig is a member of the Wood County Infirmary Inmates Vintage Base Ball team. A catcher, his speed has been compared to an ice wagon going backward.

Len Levin was taken to his first Red Sox game at a very early age and was told later in life that Jimmie Foxx hit a home run in the game. One of his research quests is to find out which game that was. A resident of Providence, Rhode Island, and a retired newspaper editor, he now spends much of his time editing for SABR-sponsored publications.

Mike Lynch was born in the heart of Red Sox nation in the year of Yastrzemski and has been a diehard Red Sox fan ever since. He lives in Portland, Oregon and has been a member of SABR since 2004. Lynch founded the popular website Seamheads.com in 2007 to promote his first book, *Harry Frazee, Ban Johnson and the Feud That Nearly Destroyed the American League*, published by McFarland Publishing in 2008 and named a finalist for the 2009 Larry Ritter Award in addition to being nominated for the Seymour Medal. His second book, *It Ain't So: A Might-Have-Been History of the White Sox in 1919 and Beyond*, was released by McFarland in December 2009.

John McMurray is Chair of the Society for American Baseball Research's Deadball Era Committee. He contributed to SABR's 2006 book *Deadball Stars of the American League* and is a past chair of SABR's Ritter Award subcommittee, which annually presents an award to the best book on Deadball Era baseball published during the year prior. He has contributed many interview-based player profiles to *Baseball Digest* in recent years.

Bill Nowlin is co-founder of Rounder Records, and author or editor of somewhere around 30 books on baseball, most of them about the Boston Red Sox. He has been vice president of SABR for quite a few years now and is an active contributor to BioProject, as well as co-editor of *Can He Play? A Look at Baseball Scouts and their Profession* and *Red Sox Baseball in the Days of Ike and Elvis*.

Elizabeth A. (Betsy) Reed came by her devotion to the Red Sox honestly. A product of New England, she learned to keep a perfect scorebook listening the '75 Sox, and also learned the emotional investment required to be a true member of the Red Sox Nation. Currently living in Henderson, Nevada, she is also first cousin to Doug Pappas, founder of SABR's Business of Baseball Committee, and the namesake for the award that recognizes the best oral research presentation at SABR's annual convention.

Jim Sandoval is a history teacher, baseball writer, and associate scout for the Minnesota Twins who collects ballparks and baseball scout sightings. He contributed to SABR's National League and American League Deadball Stars books and *The Fenway Project*, along with biographies for SABR's BioProject. He is the co-editor of *Can He Play? A Look at Baseball Scouts and their Profession*. A former small-college baseball player, he realized he was more of a prospect writing baseball than playing it. He currently is cochairman of SABR's Scouts committee.

Joe Santry has been the Historian for the Columbus Clippers of the International League since 1987. He is also the Clippers Media Director and the Director of Communications. Joe was only the second Historian in professional baseball history; Joe Overfield of Buffalo was the first. Joe's father was born and raised in South Boston.

Tom Simon has founded the Gardner-Waterman (Vermont) Chapter of SABR, the Deadball Era Committee, and, most recently, the Buster Olney (Vermont Kids) Meet-Up, with a dozen members between the ages of 7 and 12 who gather in his renovated attic every other week for SABR-style meetings.

John Stahl grew up in St. Louis rooting for Stan "the Man" Musial. He still has his Cardinal scorecard from the 1964 World Series. Later, he added the Red Sox, Orioles, and Nats to his baseball passions. He is a retired CPA and lives with his wife Pamela in suburban Maryland. They have two grown children and two young grandsons, whom they hope will be running the bases soon. As a member of SABR's Biography Project, he's researched and written a number of SABR biographies.

Saul Wisnia is author of *Fenway Park: The Centennial* and *For the Love of the Boston Red Sox*, and has co-authored or contributed to numerous other books on Boston's baseball history. His articles have appeared in *The Washington Post*, *Sports Illustrated*, *The Boston Herald*, and *The Boston Globe*, and he is the longtime senior publications editor at Dana-Farber Cancer Institute. He blogs about all things Fenway at http://saulwisnia.blogspot.com/, and can be reached at saulwizz@gmail.com or @saulwizz.

Cindy Thomson co-authored the only full-length biography on Cubs hall of famer Mordecai Brown: *Three Finger, The Mordecai Brown Story*. Brown is her relative. She has also written fiction and non-fiction books and articles and is currently at work on a three-book historical fiction series. She lives with her husband Tom in central Ohio where she writes full time. You can find her on the web at www.cindyswriting.com.

Paul Zingg came to the Red Sox through Harry Hooper and a lifelong loathing of the Yankees. He even forgives Harry and his teammates for defeating his beloved National League Giants in the 1912 World Series. His baseball books include a biography of Hooper (*Harry Hooper: An American Baseball Life*) and a history of the old Pacific Coast League (*Runs, Hits, and an Era: The Pacific Coast League, 1903-1958*). He is the president of California State University, Chico, home of a perennial participant in the NCAA Division-II World Series.

Image Credits

Boston Public Library:
26, 30 (top), 30 (bottom)

Courtesy of the Boston Public Library, Print Department:
6, 64, 76, 85, 113, 157, 169, 249 (center), 274 (top, r)

Edmunds E. Bond Collection (Boston Public Library):
271 (bottom)

Components of this panorama are from three of the Boston Public Library Print Department's Edmunds E. Bond collection original 1914 glass negatives, with the digital composite created by Panopticon Gallery.

Leslie Jones Collection (Boston Public Library):
114, 124 (bottom), 151 (top), 174 (bottom), 250 (top, r), 265 (center), 273 (top, r), 278

Michael T. McGreevey Collection (Boston Public Library):
4, 14, 15, 18, 49, 52, 82, 183, 187, 194, 197, 205, 215, 216, 260, 266, 272 (center, r), 283, 286

Boston Red Sox:
101, 134, 149, 153, 173, 222

Courtesy of the Bostonian Society:
7, 275

Courtesy of David Brule:
144, 145, 147

Chautauqua Sports Hall of Fame and the Hugh Imus and Greg Peterson Collections:
45, 46, 244 (top, r), 257 (bottom, r)

Chicago History Museum / Chicago Daily News negatives collection:
42, 71, 84, 140, 177, 218 (bottom, l), 224 (top, l), 224 (bottom, l), 228 (top)

Collins Family Archive:
73, 75, 224 (r), 249 (top)

Dan Desrochers Collection:
272 (bottom)

Michael Foster Collection:
257 (bottom, r)

Norman Furrow Collection:
25, 59, 67 (bottom)

Photos courtesy of Heritage Auctions, www.ha.com:
248 (bottom), 252 (r)

Courtesy of Hunt Auctions, www.huntauctions.com:
27, 210 (top), 244 (bottom), 251, 252 (bottom, l), 253, 254 (bottom), 256 (bottom, r)

274 (bottom, r), 287

John F. Kennedy Presidential Library:
243 (center)

Courtesy of Marie (Henriksen) Leary:
110, 111

Legendary Auctions:
69

Lelands Auctions
200 (top), 200 (bottom), 261 (bottom), 265 (bottom)

The Library of Congress
Library of Congress Prints and Photographs Division:
5, 117, 167, 193, 280 (top, l), 280 (top, r)

Benjamin K. Edwards Collection (Library of Congress):
50, 56, 72, 83 (top), 96, 106, 156 (top), 156 (bottom), 170, 212 (l), 212 (r), 213 (top), 213 (bottom), 214, 217, 218 (r), 220 (bottom), 221 (top), 225 (bottom), 227 (bottom), 228 (l), 230 (top), 232, 234 (bottom), 235, 238 (top), 285 (top)

George Grantham Bain Collection (Library of Congress):
2 (top)*, 3(top)*, 11, 37, 47, 63, 65, 67 (top), 70, 77, 90, 95, 98, 107, 116, 120, 121, 124 (top), 125 (top), 126, 129, 132, 136, 138, 154 (top), 159, 162, 175, 180, 185, 189, 191, 195, 198, 199, 206, 218 (top), 220, 221 (bottom), 223, 226, 227 (top), 229, 237, 238 (bottom), 242 (top), 242 (bottom), 243 (top-l), 243 (top-r), 243 (bottom-l), 243 (bottom-r), 244, 245, 246, 254 (top), 255 (top), 255 (bottom), 258 (bottom), 259, 263 (bottom), 264 (top), 270 (top), 271 (center, l), 271 (center, r), 272 (top, l), 272 (center, l), 273 (top, l), 274 (top ,l), 276, 279 (top, l), 279 (top, r), 280 (bottom, l), 281 (bottom), 285 (bottom), 290

*Components of this panorama are from the Library of Congress, Prints and Photographs Division, George Grantham Bain Collection, digitally sewn together and retouched by i-concepts, LLC (www.i-concepts.org).

Detroit Publishing Company Collection (Library of Congress):
12, 13, 279 (bottom)

Harris & Ewing Collection (Library of Congress):
38, 40, 62, 66, 68 (top), 86, 88, 115 (bottom), 123, 127, 135, 155, 158, 168, 176, 181, 184, 203, 231 (r), 250 (top, r), 256 (bottom, l), 257 (top, r), 258 (top), 280 (center, l), 280 (center, r)

Library of Congress, Music Division:
219, 231 (l)

Courtesy of the Logue Family:
8 (top)

Courtesy of the Massachusetts Historical Society:
270 (bottom)

Archive of Bette Clark Mott:
79

Peter Nash Collection:
3 (bottom), 230 (bottom), 236 (top), 264 (bottom), 272 (top, r), 280 (bottom, r)

National Baseball Hall of Fame Library /Cooperstown, NY:
2 (bottom), 44, 55, 102, 108, 109, 118, 119, 150, 151 (bottom), 179, 225 (top), 249 (bottom), 263 (top), 274 (bottom, l)

Courtesy of Bill Nowlin:
5 (bottom), (292, top), 292 (center), 292 (bottom)

Robert Edward Auctions, LLC:
1, 32 (bottom, l), 32 (bottom, c), 32 (bottom, r), 33 (bottom, l), 33 (bottom, c), 33 (bottom, r), 210 (bottom), 211, 233, 236 (bottom), 244 (top, l), 261 (top), 265 (top), 269, 271 (top), 273 (bottom)

Courtesy of Paul J. Zingg:
28

SABR BioProject Books

In 2002, the Society for American Baseball Research launched an effort to write and publish biographies of every player, manager, and individual who has made a contribution to baseball. Over the past decade, the BioProject Committee has produced over 2,200 biographical articles. Many have been part of efforts to create theme- or team-oriented books, spearheaded by chapters or other committees of SABR.

THE YEAR OF BLUE SNOW:
THE 1964 PHILADELPHIA PHILLIES
Catcher Gus Triandos dubbed the Philadelphia Phillies' 1964 season "the year of the blue snow," a rare thing that happens once in a great while. This book sheds light on lingering questions about the 1964 season—but any book about a team is really about the players. This work offers life stories of all the players and others (managers, coaches, owners, and broadcasters) associated with this star-crossed team, as well as essays of analysis and history.
Edited by Mel Marmer and Bill Nowlin
$19.95 paperback (ISBN 978-1-933599-51-9)
$9.99 ebook (ISBN 978-1-933599-52-6)
8.5"X11", 356 PAGES, over 70 photos

DETROIT TIGERS 1984:
WHAT A START! WHAT A FINISH!
The 1984 Detroit tigers roared out of the gate, winning their first nine games of the season and compiling an eye-popping 35-5 record after the campaign's first 40 games—still the best start ever for any team in major league history. This book brings together biographical profiles of every Tiger from that magical season, plus those of field management, top executives, the broadcasters—even venerable Tiger Stadium and the city itself.
Mark Pattison and David Raglin, editors
$19.95 paperback (ISBN 978-1-933599-44-1)
$9.99 ebook (ISBN 978-1-933599-45-8)
8.5"x11", 250 pages (Over 230,000 words!)

SWEET '60: THE 1960 PITTSBURGH PIRATES
A portrait of the 1960 team which pulled off one of the biggest upsets of the last 60 years. When Bill Mazeroski's home run left the park to win in Game Seven of the World Series, beating the New York Yankees, David had toppled Goliath. It was a blow that awakened a generation, one that millions of people saw on television, one of TV's first iconic World Series moments.
Edited by Clifton Blue Parker and Bill Nowlin
$19.95 paperback (ISBN 978-1-933599-48-9)
$9.99 ebook (ISBN 978-1-933599-49-6)
8.5"X11", 340 pages, 75 photos

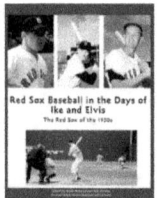

RED SOX BASEBALL IN THE DAYS OF IKE AND ELVIS: THE RED SOX OF THE 1950S
Although the Red Sox spent most of the 1950s far out of contention, the team was filled fascinating players that captured the heart of their fanbase. In *Red Sox Baseball*, members of SABR present 46 biographies on players such as Ted Williams and Pumpsie Green as well as season-by-season recaps.
Edited by Mark Armour and Bill Nowlin
$19.95 paperback (ISBN 978-1-933599-24-3)
$9.99 ebook (ISBN 978-1-933599-34-2)
8.5"X11", 372 PAGES, over 100 photos

The SABR Digital Library

The Society for American Baseball Research, the top baseball research organization in the world, disseminates some of the best in baseball history, analysis, and biography through our publishing programs. The SABR Digital Library contains a mix of books old and new, and focuses on a tandem program of paperback and ebook publication, making these materials widely available for both on digital devices and as traditional printed books.

MEMORIES OF A BALLPLAYER
by Bill Werber and C. Paul Rogers III
Bill Werber's claim to fame is unique: he was the last living person to have a direct connection to the 1927 Yankees, "Murderers' Row," a team hailed by many as the best of all time. Rich in anecdotes and humor, Memories of a Ballplayer is a clear-eyed memoir of the world of big-league baseball in the 1930s. Werber played with or against some of the most productive hitters of all time, including Babe Ruth, Ted Williams, Lou Gehrig, and Joe DiMaggio.
$14.95 paperback (ISNB 978-0-910137-84-3)
$6.99 ebook (ISBN 978-1-933599-47-2)
250 PAGES, 6"X9"

BATTING **by F. C. Lane**
First published in 1925, *Batting* collects the wisdom and insights of over 250 hitters and baseball figures. Lane interviewed extensively and compiled tips and advice on everything from batting stances to beanballs. Legendary baseball figures such as Ty Cobb, Casey Stengel, Cy Young, Walter Johnson, Rogers Hornsby, and Babe Ruth reveal the secrets of such integral and interesting parts of the game as how to choose a bat, the ways to beat a slump, and how to outguess the pitcher.
$14.95 paperback (ISBN 978-0-910137-86-7)
$7.99 ebook (ISBN 978-1-933599-46-5)
240 PAGES, 5"X7"

NINETEENTH CENTURY STARS: 2012 EDITION
First published in 1989, *Nineteenth Century Stars* was SABR's initial attempt to capture the stories of baseball players from before 1900. With a collection of 136 fascinating biographies, SABR has re-released *Nineteenth Century Stars* for 2012 with revised statistics and new form. The 2012 version also includes a preface by **John Thorn**.
Edited by Robert L. Tiemann and Mark Rucker
$19.95 paperback (ISBN 978-1-933599-28-1)
$9.99 ebook (ISBN 978-1-933599-29-8)
300 PAGES, 6"X9"

GREAT HITTING PITCHERS
Published in 1979, *Great Hitting Pitchers* was one of SABR's early publications. Edited by SABR founder Bob Davids, the book compiles stories and records about pitchers excelling in the batter's box. Newly updated in 2012 by Mike Cook, *Great Hitting Pitchers* contain tables including data from 1979-2011, corrections to reflect recent records, and a new chapter on recent new members in the club of "great hitting pitchers" like Tom Glavine and Mike Hampton.
Edited by L. Robert Davids
$9.95 paperback (ISBN 978-1-933599-30-4)
$5.99 ebook (ISBN 978-1-933599-31-1)
102 PAGES, 5.5"x8.5"

SABR Members can purchase each book at a significant discount (often 50% off) and receive the ebook edtions free as a member benefit. Each book is available in a trade paperback edition as well as ebooks suitable for reading on a home computer or Nook, Kindle, or iPad/tablet.

Join SABR today!

If you're interested in baseball—writing about it, reading about it, talking about it—there's a place for you in the Society for American Baseball Research.

SABR was formed in 1971 in Cooperstown, New York, with the mission of fostering the research and dissemination of the history and record of the game. Our members include everyone from academics to professional sportswriters to amateur historians and statisticians to students and casual fans who merely enjoy reading about baseball history and occasionally gathering with other members to talk baseball.

SABR members have a variety of interests, and this is reflected in the diversity of its research committees. There are more than two dozen groups devoted to the study of a specific area related to the game—from Baseball and the Arts to Statistical Analysis to the Deadball Era to Women in Baseball. In addition, many SABR members meet formally and informally in regional chapters throughout the year and hundreds come together for the annual national convention, the organization's premier event. These meetings often include panel discussions with former major league players and research presentations by members. Most of all, SABR members love talking baseball with like-minded friends. What unites them all is an interest in the game and joy in learning more about it.

Why join SABR? Here are some benefits of membership:

- Two issues annually of the *Baseball Research Journal*, which includes articles on history, biography, statistics, personalities, book reviews, and other aspects of the game.
- One issue annually of *The National Pastime*, which focuses on baseball in the region where that year's national convention is held (in 2013, it's Philadelphia)
- Regional chapter meetings, which can include guest speakers, presentations and trips to ballgames
- "This Week in SABR" e-newsletters every Friday, with the latest news in SABR and highlighting SABR research
- Online access to back issues of *The Sporting News* and other periodicals through *Paper of Record*
- Access to SABR's lending library and other research resources
- Online member directory to connect you with an international network of passionate baseball experts and fans
- Discount on registration for our annual conferences
- Access to SABR-L, an e-mail discussion list of baseball questions and answers that many feel is worth the cost of membership itself
- The opportunity to be part of a passionate international community of baseball fans

SABR membership is on a "rolling" calendar system; that means your membership lasts 365 days no matter when you sign up! Enjoy all the benefits of SABR membership by signing up today at SABR.org/join or by clipping out the form below and mailing it to: **SABR, 4455 E. Camelback Rd., Ste. D-140, Phoenix, AZ 85018.**

SABR 2013 MEMBERSHIP FORM

2013 dues payable by check, money order, Visa, MasterCard or Discover Card;
online at: http://store.sabr.org; or by phone at (602) 343-6455

	Annual	3-year	Senior	3-yr Sr.	Under 30
US	❏ $65	❏ $175	❏ $45	❏ $129	❏ $45
Canada/Mexico	❏ $75	❏ $205	❏ $55	❏ $159	❏ $55
Overseas	❏ $84	❏ $232	❏ $64	❏ $186	❏ $55

Add a Family Member: $15 each family member at same address (list on back)
Senior: 65 or older before 12/31/2013
All dues amounts in US dollars or equivalent

Participate in Our Donor Program!
I'd like to designate my gift to be used toward:
❏ General Fund ❏ Endowment Fund ❏ Research Resources ❏ _____
❏ I want to maximize the impact of my gift; do not send any donor premiums
❏ I would like this gift to remain anonymous.
Note: Any donation not designated will be placed in the General Fund. SABR is a 501(c)(3) not-for-profit organization & donations are tax-deductible to the extent allowed by law.

NAME _____
ADDRESS _____
CITY _____ STATE ____ ZIP _____
HOME PHONE _____ BIRTHDAY _____
E-MAIL: _____
(Your e-mail address on file ensures you will receive the most recent SABR news.)

Dues $ _____
Donation $ _____
Amount Enclosed $ _____
Do you work for a matching grant corporation? Call (602) 343-6455 for details.
❏ check/money order enclosed   ❏ VISA, Master Card, Discover Card
CARD # _____
EXP DATE _____ SIGNATURE _____

Mail to: SABR, 4455 E. Camelback Rd., Ste. D-140, Phoenix, AZ 85018

www.ingramcontent.com/pod-product-compliance
Lightning Source LLC
Chambersburg PA
CBHW051401070526
44584CB00023B/3240